MAN
PAST AND PRESENT

MAN
PAST AND PRESENT

BY

A. H. KEANE

REVISED, AND LARGELY RE-WRITTEN, BY

A. HINGSTON QUIGGIN

AND

A. C. HADDON

READER IN ETHNOLOGY, CAMBRIDGE

CAMBRIDGE
AT THE UNIVERSITY PRESS
1920

CAMBRIDGE UNIVERSITY PRESS
Cambridge, New York, Melbourne, Madrid, Cape Town,
Singapore, São Paulo, Delhi, Tokyo, Mexico City

Cambridge University Press
The Edinburgh Building, Cambridge CB2 8RU, UK

Published in the United States of America by Cambridge University Press, New York

www.cambridge.org
Information on this title: www.cambridge.org/9780521234108

First published 1920
First paperback edition 2011

A catalogue record for this publication is available from the British Library

ISBN 978-0-521-23410-8 Paperback

PREFACE TO NEW EDITION

THOSE who are familiar with the vast amount of ethnological literature published since the close of last century will realize that to revise and bring up to date a work whose range in space and time covers the whole world from prehistoric ages down to the present day, is a task impossible of accomplishment within the compass of a single volume. Recent discoveries have revolutionised our conception of primeval man, while still providing abundant material for controversy, and the rapidly increasing pile of ethnographical matter, although a vast amount of spade work remains to be done, is but one sign of the remarkable interest in ethnology which is so conspicuous a feature of the present decade. Even to keep abreast of the periodical literature devoted to his subject provides ample occupation for the ethnologist, and few are those who can now lay claim to such an omniscient title.

Under such circumstances the faults of omission and compression could not be avoided in revising Professor Keane's work, but it is hoped that the copious references which form a prominent feature of the present edition will compensate in some measure for these obvious defects. The main object of the revisers has been to retain as much as possible of the original text wherever it fairly represents current opinion at the present time, but so different is our outlook from that of 1899 that certain sections have had to be entirely rewritten and in many places pages have been suppressed to make room for more important formation. In every case where new matter has been inserted references are given to the responsible authorities and the fullest use has been made of direct quotation from the authors cited.

Mrs Hingston Quiggin is responsible for the whole work of revision with the exception of Chapter XI, revised by Miss Lilian Whitehouse, while Dr A. C. Haddon has criticised, corrected and supervised the work throughout.

A. H. Q.
A. C. H.

10th October 1919

CONTENTS

LIST OF ILLUSTRATIONS

(at the end of the volume)

PLATE I.
1. Hausa slave of Tunis (Western Sudanese Negro).
2. Zulu girl, South Africa (Bantu Negroid).
3, 4. Abraham Lucas, age 32, South Africa (Koranna Hottentot).
5, 6. Swaartbooi, age 20, South Africa (Bushman).

PLATE II.
1. Andamanese (Negrito).
2. Semang, Malay Peninsula (Negrito).
3. Aeta, Philippines (Negrito).
4. Central African Pygmy (Negrillo).
5-7. Tapiro, Netherlands New Guinea (Negrito).

PLATE III.
1, 2. Jemmy, native of Hampshire Hills, Tasmania (Tasmanian).
3, 4. Native of Oromosapua, Kiwai, British New Guinea (Papuan).
5, 6. Native of Hula, British New Guinea (Papuo-Melanesian).

PLATE IV.
1. Chinese man (mixed Southern Mongol).
2. Chinese woman of Kulja (mixed Southern Mongol).
3, 4. Kara-Kirghiz of Semirechinsk.
5. Kara-Kirghiz woman of Semirechinsk.
6. Solon of Kulja (Manchu-Tungus).

PLATE V.
1. Jelai, an Iban (Sea-Dayak) of the Rejang river, Sarawak, Borneo (mixed Proto-Malay).
2. Buginese, Celebes (Malayan).
3. Bontoc Igorot, Luzon, Philippines (Malayan).
4. Bagobo, Mindanao, Philippines (Malayan).
5, 6. Kenyah girls, Sarawak, Borneo (mixed Proto-Malay).

PLATE VI.
1. Samoyed, Tavji.
2. Tungus.
3. Ostiak of the Yenesei (Palaeo-Siberian).
4. Kalmuk woman (Western Mongol).
5. Gold of Amur river (Tungus).
6. Gilyak woman (N.E. Mongol).

ix

We offer our sincere thanks for the use of the following photographs :

A. H. Keane, *Ethnology* (1896), IV. 2, 3, 4, 5, 6 ; IX. 3, 4 ; XII. 6 ; XIV. 5, 6.

A. H. Keane, *Man, Past and Present* (1899), I. 2 ; II. 3 ; V. 2 ; VI. 4, 5, 6 ; VII. 5 ; IX. 1, 2 ; X. 4, 6 ; XII. 5.

A. R. Brown, II. 1.

Prof. R. B. Yapp, II. 2.

Field Museum of Natural History, Chicago, II. 4 ; V. 4 ; VII. 1, 2 ; VIII. 1, 2, 3, 4 ; IX. 5, 6 ; XV. 1, 2.

Dr Wollaston, cf. *Pygmies and Papuans*, p. 212 ; II. 5, 6, 7.

Dr G. Landtman, III. 3, 4.

Anthony Wilkin, III. 5, 6.

Prof. C. G. Seligman, V. 1 ; (*The Veddas*, pl. v) X. 1 ; XII. 3, 4 ; XIII. 1, 2, 3, 5, 6.

L. F. Taylor, v. 3.

A. C. Haddon, I. 3, 4, 5, 6 ; III. 1, 2 ; IV. 1 ; V. 5, 6 ; VII. 6 ; XI. 1, 2, 3 ; XII. 1, 2 ; XIII. 4 ; XVI. 1, 2, 3, 4.

Miss M. A. Czaplicka, VI. 1, 2, 3.

Dr W. Crooke (cf. *Northern India*, pl. III), XV. 3.

Baelz, VII. 3, 4.

Bureau of American Ethnology, VIII. 5, 6.

E. Thurston (*Castes and Tribes of Southern India*, II. p. 387), X. 3 ; (*ibid.* IV. pp. 236, 240), XV. 5 ; XV. 6.

Sir Baldwin Spencer and F. J. Gillen and Messrs Macmillan & Co. (*Across Australia*, II. fig. 169), X. 5.

Prof. J. Kollmann, XI. 5, 6.

P. W. Luton, XII. 2.

Prof. F. von Luschan and the Council of the Royal Anthropological Institute (*Journ. Roy. Anth. Inst.*, XLI., pl. XXIV, 1, 2, pl. XXX, 1, 2), XIV. 1, 2, 3, 4.

Dr W. H. Furness, XVI. 5, 6.

CHAPTER I

GENERAL CONSIDERATIONS

The World peopled by Migration from one Centre by Pleistocene Man—The Primary Groups evolved each in its special Habitat—Pleistocene Man : *Pithecanthropus erectus* ; The Mauer jaw, *Homo Heidelbergensis* ; The Piltdown skull, *Eoanthropus Dawsoni*—General View of Pleistocene Man—The first Migrations—Early Man and his Works—Classification of Human Types : *H. primigenius*, Neanderthal or Mousterian Man ; *H. recens*, Galley Hill or Aurignacian Man—Physical Types—Human Culture : Reutelian, Mafflian, Mesvinian, Strepyan, Chellean, Acheulean, Mousterian, Aurignacian, Solutrian, Magdalenian, Azilian—Chronology—The early History of Man a Geological Problem—The Human Varieties the Outcome of their several Environments—Correspondence of Geographical with Racial and Cultural Zones.

In order to a clear understanding of the many difficult questions connected with the natural history of the human family, two cardinal points have to be steadily borne in mind—the specific unity of all existing varieties, and the dispersal of their generalised precursors over the whole world in pleistocene times. As both points have elsewhere been dealt with by me somewhat fully,[1] it will here suffice to show their direct bearing on the general evolution of the human species from that remote epoch to the present day.

The World peopled by Migration from one Centre by Pleistocene Man.

It must be obvious that, if man is specifically one, though not necessarily sprung of a single pair, he must have had, in homely language, a single cradle-land, from which the peopling of the earth was brought about by migration, not by independent developments from different species in so many independent geographical areas.

It follows further, and this point is all-important, that, since the world was peopled by pleistocene man, it was

[1] *Ethnology*, Chaps. V. and VII.

peopled by a generalised proto-human form, prior to all later racial differences. The existing groups, according to this hypothesis, have developed in different areas independently and divergently by continuous adaptation to their

The Primary Groups evolved each in its special Habitat. several environments. If they still constitute mere varieties, and not distinct species, the reason is because all come of like pleistocene ancestry, while the divergences have been confined to relatively narrow limits, that is, not wide enough to be regarded zoologically as specific differences.

The battle between monogenists and polygenists cannot be decided until more facts are at our disposal, and much will doubtless be said on both sides for some time to come.[1] Among the views of human origins brought forward in recent years should be mentioned the daring theory of Klaatsch.[2] Recognising two distinct human types, Neanderthal and Aurignac (see pp. 8, 9 below), and two distinct anthropoid types, gorilla and orang-utan, he derives Neanderthal man and African gorilla from one common ancestor, and Aurignac man and Asiatic orang-utan from another. Though anatomists, especially those conversant with anthropoid structure,[3] are not able to accept this view, they admit that many difficulties may be solved by the recognition of more than one primordial stock of human ancestors.[4] The questions of adaptation to climate and environment,[5] the possibilities of degeneracy, the varying degrees of physiological activity, of successful mutations, the effects of crossing and all the complicated problems of heredity are involved in the discussion, and it must be acknowledged that our information concerning all of these is entirely inadequate.

Nevertheless all speculations on the subject are not based merely on hypotheses, and three discoveries of late years have provided solid facts for the working out of the problem.

These discoveries were the remains of *Pithecanthropus*

---

[1] See A. H. Keane, *Ethnology*, 1909, Chap. VII.

[2] H. Klaatsch, "Die Aurignac-Rasse und ihre Stellung im Stammbaum des Menschen," *Ztschr. f. Eth.* LII. 1910. See also *Prähistorische Zeitschrift*, Vol. I. 1909.

[3] Cf. A. Keith's criticisms in *Nature*, Vol. LXXXV. 1911, p. 508.

[4] W. L. H. Duckworth, *Prehistoric Man*, 1912, p. 146.

[5] W. Ridgeway, "The Influence of Environment on Man," *Journ. Roy. Anthr. Inst.*, Vol. XL. 1910, p. 10.

erectus [1] in Java, in 1892, of the Mauer jaw,[2] near Heidelberg, in 1907, and of the Piltdown skull [3] in Sussex in 1912. Although the Mauer jaw was accepted **Pleistocene Man.** without hesitation, the controversy concerning the correct interpretation of the Javan fossils has been raging for more than twenty years and shows no sign of abating, while *Eoanthropus Dawsoni* is too recent an intruder into the arena to be fairly dealt with at present. Certain facts however stand out clearly. In late pliocene or early pleistocene times certain early ancestral forms were already in existence which can scarcely be excluded from the *Hominidae*. In range they were as widely distributed as Java in the east to Heidelberg and Sussex in the west, and in spite of divergence in type a certain correlation is not impossible, even if the Piltdown specimen should finally be regarded as representing a distinct genus.[4] Each contributes facts of the utmost importance for the tracing out of the history of human evolution. *Pithecanthropus* raises the vexed question as to whether the erect attitude or brain development **Pithecanthropus erectus.** came first in the story. The conjunction of prehuman braincase with human thighbone appeared to favour the popular view that the erect attitude was the earlier, but the evidence of embryology suggests a reverse order. And although at first the thighbone was recognised as distinctly human, it seems that of late doubts have been cast on this interpretation,[5] and even the claim to the title *erectus* is called in question. The characters of straightness and slenderness on which much stress was laid are found in exaggerated form in gibbons and lemurs. The intermediate position in respect of mental endowment (in so far as brain can be estimated by cranial capacity) is shown in the accompanying diagram, in which the cranial measurements of *Pithecanthropus* are compared with those of a chimpanzee and prehistoric man. The

---

[1] E. Dubois, " *Pithecanthropus erectus*, transitional form between Man and the Apes," *Sci. Trans. R. Dublin Soc.* 1898.

[2] O. Schoetensack, *Der Unterkiefer des Homo Heidelbergensis*, etc., 1908.

[3] C. Dawson and A. Smith Woodward, " On the Discovery of a Palaeolithic Skull and Mandible," etc., *Quart. Journ. Geol. Soc.* 1913.

[4] This was the view of A. Smith Woodward when the skull was first exhibited (*loc. cit.*), but in his paper, "Missing Links among Extinct Animals," *Brit. Ass.*, Birmingham, 1913, he is inclined to regard " Piltdown man, or some close relative," as " on the direct line of descent with ourselves." For A. Keith's criticism see *The Antiquity of Man*, 1915, p. 503.

[5] W. L. H. Duckworth, *Prehistoric Man*, 1912, p. 8.

teeth strengthen the evidence, for they are described as too large for a man and too small for an ape. Thus *Pithecan-thropus* has been confidently assigned to a place in a branch of the human family tree.

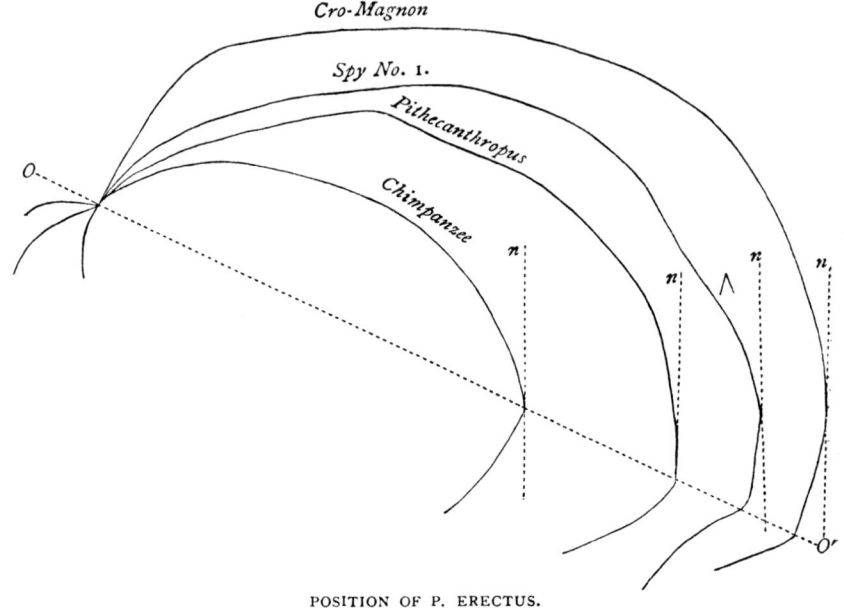

Cro-Magnon

Spy No. 1.

Pithecanthropus

Chimpanzee

O

POSITION OF P. ERECTUS.

(Manouvrier, *Bul. Soc. d'Anthrop.* 1896, p. 438.)

The Mauer jaw, the geological age of which is undisputed, also represents intermediate characters. The extraordinary strength and thickness of bone, the wide as-cending ramus with shallow sigmoid notch (distinctly simian features) and the total absence of chin[1] would deny it a place among human jaws, but the teeth, which are all fortunately preserved in their sockets, are not only definitely human, but show in certain peculiarities less simian features than are to be found in the dentition of modern man.[2]

Mauer jaw.
Homo Heidel-bergensis.

[1] For the relation between chin formation and power of speech, see E. Walkhoff, " Der Unterkiefer der Anthropomorphen und des Menschen in seiner funktion-ellen Entwicklung und Gestalt," E. Selenka, *Menschenaffen*, 1902 ; H. Obermaier, *Der Mensch der Vorzeit*, 1912, p. 362 ; and W. Wright, " The Mandible of Man from the Morphological and Anthropological points of view," *Essays and Studies presented to W. Ridgeway*, 1913.

[2] Cf. W. L. H. Duckworth, *Prehistoric Man*, 1912, p. 10, and A. Keith, *The Antiquity of Man*, 1915, p. 237.

The cranial capacity of the Piltdown skull, though variously estimated,[1] is certainly greater than that of Piltdown skull. *Pithecanthropus*, the general outlines with steeply Eoanthropus rounded forehead resemble that of modern Dawsoni. man, and the bones are almost without exception typically

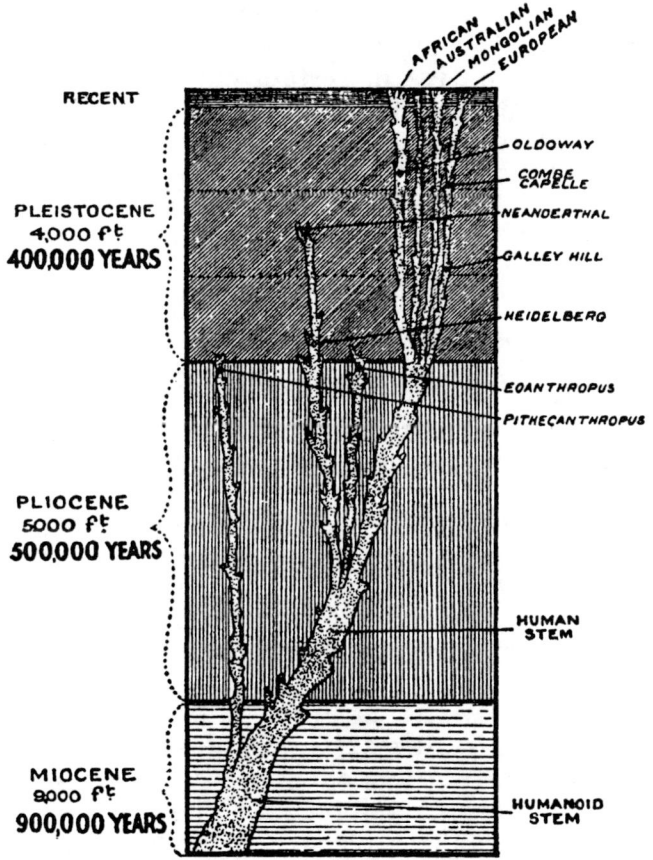

GENEALOGICAL TREE OF MAN'S ANCESTRY.
(A. Keith, *The Antiquity of Man*, 1915; fig. 187, p. 501.)

human. The jaw, however, though usually attributed to the same individual,[2] recalls the primitive features of the

---

[1] A. Smith Woodward, 1070 c.c.; A. Keith, 1400 c.c.

[2] G. G. MacCurdy, following G. S. Miller, *Smithsonian Misc. Colls.* Vol. 65, No. 12 (1915), is convinced that " in place of *Eoanthropus Dawsoni* we have two individuals belonging to different genera," a human cranium and the jaw of a chimpanzee. *Science*, N.S. Vol. XLIII. 1916, p. 231. See also Appendix A.

Mauer specimen in its thick ascending portion and shallow notch, while in certain characters it differs from any known jaw, ancient or modern.[1]   The evidence afforded by the teeth is even more striking.   The teeth of *Pithecanthropus* and of *Homo Heidelbergensis* were recognised as remarkably human, and although primitive in type, are far more advanced in the line of human evolution than the lowly features with which they are associated would lead one to expect.   The Piltdown teeth are more primitive in certain characters than those of either the Javan or the Heidelberg remains.   The first molar has been compared to that of Taubach, the most ape-like of human or pre-human teeth hitherto recorded, but the canine tooth (found by P. Teilhard in the same stratum in 1913 [2]) finds no parallel in any known human jaw ; it resembles the milk canine of the chimpanzee more than that of the adult dentition.

It cannot be said that any clear view of pleistocene man can be obtained from these imperfect scraps of evidence, valuable though they are.   Rather may we agree with Keith that the problem grows more instead of less complex.   " In our first youthful burst of Darwinianism we pictured our evolution as a simple procession of forms leading from ape to man.   Each age, as it passed, transformed the men of the time one stage nearer to us—one more distant from the ape.   The true picture is very different.   We have to conceive an ancient world in which the family of mankind was broken up into narrow groups or genera, each genus again divided into a number of species— much as we see in the monkey or ape world of to-day.   Then out of that great welter of forms one species became the dominant form, and ultimately the sole surviving one—the species represented by the modern races of mankind." [3]

General View of Pleistocene Man.

We may assume therefore that the earth was mainly peopled by the generalised pleistocene precursors, who moved about, like the other migrating faunas, unconsciously, everywhere following the lines of least resistance, advancing or receding, and acting generally on blind impulse rather than of any set purpose.

The first Migrations.

[1] For a full description see *Quart. Journ. Geol. Soc.* March, 1913.   Also A. Keith, *The Antiquity of Man*, 1915, p. 320, and pp. 430–452.

[2] C. Dawson and A. Smith Woodward, "Supplementary Note on the Discovery of a Palaeolithic Human Skull and Mandible at Piltdown (Sussex),'' *Quart. Journ. Geol. Soc.* April, 1914.

[3] *The Antiquity of Man*, 1915, p. 209.

That such must have been the nature of the first migratory movements will appear evident when we consider that they were carried on by rude hordes, all very much alike, and differing not greatly from other zoological groups, and further that these migrations took place prior to the development of all cultural appliances beyond the ability to wield a broken branch or a sapling, or else chip or flake primitive stone implements.[1]

Herein lies the explanation of the curious phenomenon, which was a stumbling-block to premature systematists, that all the works of early man everywhere present the most startling resemblances, affording abso- Early Man and lutely no elements for classification, for instance, his Works. during the times corresponding with the Chellean or first period of the Old Stone Age. The implements of palaeolithic type so common in parts of South India, South Africa, the Sudan, Egypt, etc., present a remarkable resemblance to one another. This, while affording a *prima facies* case for, is not conclusive of, the migrations of a definite type of humanity.

After referring to the identity of certain objects from the Hastings kitchen-middens and a barrow near Sevenoaks, W. J. L. Abbot proceeds : " The first thing that would strike one in looking over a few trays of these implements is the remarkable likeness which they bear to those of Dordogne. Indeed many of the figures in the magnificent ' Reliquiae Aquitanicae ' might almost have been produced from these specimens."[2]   And Sir J. Evans, extending his glance over a wider horizon, discovers implements in other distant lands " so identical in form and character with British specimens that they might have been manufactured by the same hands. . . . On the banks of the Nile, many hundreds of feet above its present level, implements of the European types have been discovered, while in Somaliland, in an ancient river valley, at a great elevation above the sea, Seton-Karr has collected a large number of implements formed of flint and quartzite, which, judging from their form and character, might have been dug out of the drift-deposits of the Somme and the Seine, the Thames or the ancient Solent."[3]

[1] Thus Lucretius :
       " Arma antiqua manus, ungues, dentesque fuerunt,
         Et lapides, et item silvarum fragmina rami."
[2] *Jour. Anthrop. Inst.* 1896, p. 133.
[3] *Inaugural Address*, Brit. Ass. Meeting, Toronto, 1897.

It was formerly held that man himself showed a similar uniformity, and all palaeolithic skulls were referred to one long-headed type, called, from the most famous example, the Neanderthal, which was regarded as having close affinities with the present Australians.   But this resemblance is shown by Boule [1] and others to be purely superficial, and recent archaeological finds indicate that more than one racial type was in existence in the Palaeolithic Age.

Classification of Human Types.   W. L. H. Duckworth on anatomical evidence constructs the following table [2]:

Group I. Early ancestral forms.
          Ex. gr. H. Heidelbergensis.
Group II. *Subdivision A.   H. primigenius.*
          Ex. gr. La Chapelle.
          Subdivision B.   H. recens; with varieties
          { *H. fossilis.   Ex. gr. Galley Hill.*
          { *H. sapiens.*

H. Obermaier [3] argues as follows : *Homo primigenius* is neither the representative of an intermediate species between ape and man, nor a lower or distinct type than *Homo sapiens*, but an older primitive variety (race) of the latter, which survives in exceptional cases down to the present day.[4] Clearly then, according to the rules of zoological classification, we must term the two, *Homo sapiens var. primigenius*, as compared with *Homo sapiens var. recens.*

Whatever classification or nomenclature may be adopted the dual division in palaeolithic times is now generally recognised.   The more primitive type is com-

H. primigenius, Neanderthal or Mousterian Man.   monly called Neanderthal man, from the famous cranium found in the Neanderthal cave in 1857, or Mousterian man, from the culture associations.   To this group belong the Gibraltar skull,[5] and the skeletons from Spy,[6] and Krapina, Croatia,[7] together with

---

[1] M. Boule, "L'homme fossile de la Chapelle-aux-Saints," *Annales de Paléontologie*, 1911 (1913).   Cf. also H. Obermaier, *Der Mensch der Vorzeit*, 1912, p. 364.
[2] *Prehistoric Man*, 1912, p. 60.
[3] *Der Mensch der Vorzeit*, 1912, p. 365.
[4] This is not generally accepted.   See A. Keith's diagram, p. 5 and pp. 9–10.
[5] W. J. Sollas, "On the Cranial and Facial Characters of the Neanderthal Race," *Phil. Trans.* 1907, CXCIV.
[6] J. Fraipont and M. Lohest, "Recherches Ethnographiques sur les Ossements Humains," etc., *Arch. de Biologie*, 1887.
[7] Gorjanovič-Kramberger, *Der diluviale Mensch von Krapina in Kroatia*, 1906.

the later discoveries (1908–11) at La Chapelle[1] (Corrèze),
Le Moustier,[2] La Ferassie[3] (Dordogne) and many others.

Palaeolithic examples of the modern human type have
been found at Brüx (Bohemia),[4] Brünn (Moravia)[5] and Galley
Hill in Kent,[6] but the most complete find was *H. recens, Galley*
that at Combe Capelle in 1909.[7] The numerous *Hill or Aurig-*
skeletons found at Cro-Magnon[8] and at the *nacian Man.*
Grottes de Grimaldi at Mentone,[9] though showing certain
skeletal differences, may be included in this group, the earliest
examples of which are associated with Aurignacian culture.[10]

From the evidence contributed by these examples the
main characteristics of the two groups may be indicated,
although, owing to the imperfection of the *Physical Types.*
records, any generalisations must necessarily be
tentative and subject to criticism.

The La Chapelle skull recalls many of the primitive
features of the " ancestral types." The low receding forehead, the overhanging brow-ridges, forming *Homo primi-*
continuous horizontal bars of bone overshadow- *genius.*
ing the orbits, the inflated circumnasal region,
the enormous jaws, with massive ascending ramus, shallow
sigmoid notch, " negative " chin and other " simian " characters
seem reminiscent of *Pithecanthropus* and *Homo Heidelbergensis.* The cranial capacity however is estimated at
over 1600 c.c., thus exceeding that of the average modern
European, and this development, even though associated, as
M. Boule has pointed out, with a comparatively lowly brain,
is of striking significance. The low stature, probably about
1600 mm. (under 5½ feet), makes the size of the skull and
cranial capacity all the more remarkable. " A survey of the

[1] M. Boule, " L'homme fossile de la Chapelle-aux-Saints," *L' Anthr.* xix.
1908, and *Annales de Paléontologie*, 1911 (1913).

[2] H. Klaatsch, *Prähistorische Zeitschrift*, Vol. I. 1909.

[3] Peyrony and Capitan, *Rev. de l'École d'Anthrop.* 1909 ; *Bull. Soc. d'Anthr.
de Paris*, 1910.

[4] G. Schwalbe, " Der Schädel von Brüx," *Zeitschr. f. Morph. u. Anthr.* 1906.

[5] Makowsky, " Der diluviale Mensch in Löss von Brünn," *Mitt. Anthrop.
Gesell. in Wien*, 1892.

[6] See A. Keith, *The Antiquity of Man*, 1915, Chap. X.

[7] H. Klaatsch, " Die Aurignac-Rasse," etc., *Zeitschr. f. Ethn.* lii. 1910.

[8] L. Lartet, " Une sépulture des troglodytes du Périgord," and Broca, " Sur
les crânes et ossements des Eyzies," *Bull. Soc. d'Anthr. de Paris*, 1868.

[9] R. Verneau, *Les Grottes de Grimaldi*, 1906–11.

[10] For a complete list with bibliographical references, see H. Obermaier,
" Les restes humains Quaternaires dans l'Europe centrale," *Anthr.* 1905,
p. 385, 1906, p. 55.

characters of Neanderthal man—as manifested by his skeleton, brain cast, and teeth—have convinced anthropologists of two things: first, that we are dealing with a form of man totally different from any form now living ; and secondly, that the kind of difference far exceeds that which separates the most divergent of modern human races." [1]

The earliest complete and authentic example of "Aurignacian man" was the skeleton discovered near Combe Capelle (Dordogne) in 1909.[2] The stature is low, not exceeding that of the Neanderthal type, but the limb bones are slighter and the build is altogether lighter and more slender. The greatest contrast lies in the skull. The forehead is vertical instead of receding, and the strongly projecting brow-ridges are diminished, the jaw is less massive and less simian with regard to all the features mentioned above. Especially is this difference noticeable in the projection of the chin, which now for the first time shows the modern human outline. In short there are no salient features which cannot be matched among the living races of the present day.

Homo recens.

On the cultural side no less than on the physical, the thousands of years which the lowest estimate attributes to the Early Stone Age were marked by slow but continuous changes.

Human Culture.

The Reutelian (at the junction of the Pliocene and Pleistocene), Mafflian and Mesvinian industries, recognised by M. Rutot in Belgium, belong to the doubtful Eolithic Period, not yet generally accepted.[3]

Reutelian, Maf-flian, Mesvinian.

The lowest palaeolithic deposit is the Strepyan, so called from Strépy, near Charleroi, typically represented at St Acheul, Amiens, and recognised also in the Thames Valley.[4] The tools exhibit deliberate flaking, and mark the transition between eolithic and palaeolithic work. The associated fauna includes two species of elephant,

Strepyan.

[1] A. Keith, *The Antiquity of Man*, 1915, p. 158. See also W. J. Sollas, *Ancient Hunters*, 1915, p. 186 ff.

[2] H. Klaatsch, "Die Aurignac-Rasse," *Zeitschr. f. Eth.* 1910, LII. p. 513.

[3] The Mesvinian implements are now accepted as artefacts and placed by H. Obermaier immediately below the Chellean, though M. Commont interprets them as Acheulean or even later. See W. J. Sollas, *Ancient Hunters*, 1915, p. 132 ff.

[4] R. Smith and H. Dewey, "Stratification at Swanscombe," *Archaeologia*, LXIV. 1912.

E. meridionalis and *E. antiquus*, two species of rhinoceros, *R. Etruscus* and *R. Merckii*, and the hippopotamus. It is possible that the Mauer jaw and the Piltdown skull belong to this stage.

The Chellean industry,[1] with the typical coarsely flaked almond-shaped implements, occurs abundantly in the South of England and in France, less commonly in Belgium, Germany, Austria-Hungary and Russia, Chellean. while examples have been recognised in Palestine, Egypt, Somaliland, Cape Colony, Madras and other localities, though outside Europe the date is not always ascertainable and the form is not an absolute criterion.[2]

Acheulean types succeed apparently in direct descent but the implements are altogether lighter, sharper, more efficient, and are characterised by finer workmanship and carefully retouched edges. A small finely Acheulean. finished lanceolate implement is typical of the sub-industry or local development at La Micoque (Dordogne).

The Chellean industry is associated with a warm climate and the remains of *Elephas antiquus*, *Rhinoceros Merckii* and hippopotamus. Lower Acheulean shows little variation, but with Upper Acheulean certain animals indicating a colder climate make their appearance, including the mammoth, *Elephas primigenius*, and the woolly rhinoceros, *R. tichorhinus*, but no reindeer.

The Mousterian industry is entirely distinct from its predecessors. The warm fauna has disappeared, the reindeer first occurs together with the musk ox, arctic fox, the marmot and other cold-loving animals. Mousterian. Man appears to have sought refuge in the caves, and from complete skeletons found in cave deposits of this stage we gain the first clear ideas concerning the physical type of man of the early palaeolithic period. Typical Mousterian implements consist of leaf-like or triangular points made from flakes struck from the nodule instead of from the dressed nodule itself, as in the earlier stages. The Levallois flakes, occurring at the base of the Mousterian (sometimes included in the Acheulean stage), initiate this new style of workmanship, but the Mousterian point shows an improvement in

---

[1] So called from Chelles-sur-Marne, near Paris.
[2] Cf. J. Déchelette, *Manuel d'Archéologie préhistorique*, I. 1908, p. 89.

shape and a greater mastery in technique, producing a more efficient tool for piercing and cutting. Scrapers, carefully retouched, with a curved edge, are also characteristic, besides many other forms. The complete skeletons from Le Moustier itself, La Chapelle, La Ferassie, and Krapina all belong to this stage, which marks the end of the lower palaeolithic period, the Age of the Mammoth.

The upper palaeolithic or Reindeer Age is divided into Aurignacian, Solutrian, and Magdalenian [1] culture stages, with

Aurignacian.   the Azilian [2] separating the Magdalenian from the neolithic period. Each stage is distinguished by its implements and its art. The Aurignacian fauna, though closely resembling the Mousterian, indicates an amelioration of climate, the most abundant animals being the bison, horse, cave lion, and cave hyena, and human settlements are again found in the open. Among the typical implements are finely worked knife-like blades (Châtelperron point, Gravette point), keeled scrapers (Tarté type), *burins* or gravers, and various tools and ornaments of bone. Art is represented by engravings and wall paintings, and to this stage belong statuettes representing nude female figures such as those of Brassempouy, Mentone, Pont-à-Lesse (Belgium), Predmost and Willendorf, near Krems. The Neanderthal type appears to have died out and Aurignacian man belongs to the modern type represented at Combe Capelle. If the evidence of the figurines is to be accepted, a steatopygous race was at this time in existence, which Sollas is inclined to connect with the Bushmen. [3]

The Solutrian stage is characterised by the abundance of the horse, replaced in the succeeding period by the reindeer.

Solutrian.   The Solutrians seem to have been a warlike steppe people who came from the east into western Europe. Their subsequent fate has not been elucidated. The culture appears to have had a limited range, centring in the Dordogne region, and extending to southern France and northern Spain, only a few stations being found outside Dordogne and the neighbouring departments. The technique, as shown in the laurel-leaf and willow-leaf points, exhibits a perfection of workmanship unequalled in the

---

[1] From Aurignac (Haute-Garonne), Solutré (Saône-et-Loire), and La Madeleine (Dordogne).
[2] Mas-d'Azil, Ariège.   [3] W. J. Sollas, *Ancient Hunters*, 1915, pp. 378–9.

Palaeolithic Age, and only excelled by late prehistoric knives of Egypt.

The rock shelter at La Madeleine has given its name to the closing epoch of the Palaeolithic Age. The flint industry shows distinct decadence, but the working in bone and horn was at its zenith; indeed, so marked is the contrast between this and the preceding stage that Breuil is convinced that " the first Magdalenians were not evolved from the Solutrians; they were new-comers in our region."[1] The typical implements are barbed harpoons in reindeer antler (later that of the stag), often decorated with engravings. Sculpture and engravings of animals in life-like attitudes are among the most remarkable records of the age, and the polychrome pictures in the caves of Altamira, " the Sistine chapel of Quaternary Art," are the admiration of the world.[2]

Magdalenian.

In the cave of Mas-d'Azil, between the Magdalenian and Neolithic deposits occurs a stratum, termed Azilian, which, to some extent, bridges over the obscure transition between the Palaeolithic and Neolithic Ages. The reindeer has disappeared, and its place is taken by the stag. The realistic art of the Magdalenians is succeeded by a more geometric style. In flint working a return is made to Aurignacian methods, and a particular development of pygmy flints has received the name *Tardenoisian*.[3]

Azilian.

The characteristic implement is still the harpoon, but it differs in shape from the Magdalenian implement, owing to the different structure of the material. Painted pebbles, marked with red and black lines, in some cases suggesting a script, have given rise to such controversy. Their meaning at present remains obscure.[4]

The question of prehistoric chronology is a difficult one, and the more cautious authorities do not commit themselves to dates. Of late years, however, such researches as those of A. Penck and E. Brückner

Chronology.

[1] " Les Subdivisions de paléolithique supérieur," *Congrès Internat. d'Anth.* 1912, XIV. pp. 190–3.

[2] H. Breuil and E. Cartailhac, *La Caverne d'Altamira*, 1906. For a list of decorated caves, with the names of their discoverers, see J. Déchelette, *Manuel d'Archéologie préhistorique*, I. 1908, p. 241. A complete *Répertoire de l'Art Quaternaire* is given by S. Reinach, 1913; and for chronology see E. Piette, " Classifications des Sédiments formés dans les cavernes pendant l'Age du Renne," *Anthr.* 1904.

[3] From La Fère-en-Tardenois, Aisne.

[4] Cf. W. J. Sollas, *Ancient Hunters*, 1915, pp. 95, 534 f.

in the Alps[1] and of Baron de Geer and W. C. Brøgger in Sweden,[2] have provided a sound basis for calculations. Penck recognises four periods of glaciation during the pleistocene period, which he has named after typical areas, the Günz, Mindel, Riss and Würm. He dates the Würm maximum at between 30,000 and 50,000 years ago and estimates the duration of the Riss-Würm interglacial period at about 100,000 years. According to his calculations the Chellean industry occurs in the Mindel-Riss, or even in the Günz-Mindel interval, but it is more commonly placed in the mild phase intervening before the last (Würm) glaciation, this latter corresponding with the cold Mousterian stage. At least four subsequent oscillations of climate have been recognised by Penck, the Achen, Bühl, Gschnitz and Daun, and the correspondence of these with palaeolithic culture stages may be seen in the following table[3]:

Penck and Brückner.			Obermaier and others.	Rutot.
Post-glacial with oscillations	Daun, Gschnitz } Azilian; Bühl, Achen } Magdalenian		Proto-Neolithic; Azilian; Magdalenian; Solutrian and Aurignacian	} Neolithic
IV. Würm. 4th Glacial			Mousterian; Lower Mousterian and Acheulean	Lower Magdalenian
Riss-Würm. 3rd Interglacial	Solutrian and Aurignacian; Warm Mousterian		Chellean	Upper Mousterian
III. Riss. 3rd Glacial	Cold Mousterian			Lower Acheulean; Chellean
Mindel-Riss. 2nd Interglacial	Acheulean; Chellean		Mauer jaw; Pre-Palaeolithic	Strepyan; Mesvinian; Mafflian
II. Mindel. 2nd Glacial				
Günz-Mindel. 1st Interglacial	} No artefacts		} No artefacts	
I. Günz. 1st Glacial				

James Geikie,[4] under the heading, "Reliable and Unreliable estimates of geological time," points out that the absolute duration of the Pleistocene cannot be determined, but such investigations as those of Penck "enable us to form

[1] *Die Alpen in Eiszeitalter*, 1901–9. See also "Alter des Menschengeschlechts," *Zeit. f. Eth.* XL. 1908.
[2] See W. J. Sollas, *Ancient Hunters*, 1915, p. 561.
[3] H. Obermaier, *Der Mensch der Vorzeit*, 1911–2, p. 332.
[4] *The Antiquity of Man in Europe*, 1914, p. 301.

some conception of the time involved." He accepts as a
rough approximation Penck's opinion that " the Glacial period
with all its climatic changes may have extended over half
a million years, and as the Chellean stage dates back to
at least the middle of the period, this would give somewhere between 250,000 and 500,000 years for the antiquity
of man in Europe. But if, as recent discoveries would
seem to indicate, man was an occupant of our Continent
during the First Interglacial epoch, if not in still earlier
times, we may be compelled greatly to increase our estimate
of his antiquity " (p. 303).

W. J. Sollas, on the other hand, is content with a far more
contracted measure. Basing his calculations mainly on the
investigations of de Geer, he concludes that the interval that
separates our time from the beginning of the end of the last
glacial episode is 17,000 years. He places the Azilian age at
5500 B.C., the middle of the Magdalenian age somewhere
about 8000 B.C., Mousterian 15,000 B.C., and the close of the
Chellean 25,000 B.C.[1]

But when all the changes in climate are taken into consideration, the periods of elevation and depression of the
land, the transformations of the animals, the evolution of
man, the gradual stages of advance in human culture, the development of the races of mankind, and their distribution over
the surface of the globe, this estimate is regarded by many
as insufficient. Allen Sturge claims " scores of thousands of
years " for the neolithic period alone,[2] and Sir W. Turner
points out the very remote times to which the appearance of
neolithic man must be assigned in Scotland. After showing
that there is undoubted evidence of the presence of man in
North Britain during the formation of the Carse clays, this
careful observer explains that the Carse cliffs, now in places
45 to 50 feet above the present sea-level, formed the bed of
an estuary or arm of the sea, which in post-glacial times
extended almost, if not quite, across the land from east to
west, thus separating the region south of the Forth from
North Britain. He even suggests, after the separation of
Britain from the Continent in earlier times, another land
connection, a " Neolithic land-bridge " by which the men of
the New Stone Age may have reached Scotland when the

[1] *Ancient Hunters*, 1915, p. 567.
[2] *Proc. Prehist. Soc. E. Anglia*, I. 1911, p. 60.

upheaved 100-feet terrace was still clothed with the great forest growths that have since disappeared.[1]

One begins to ask, Are even 100,000 years sufficient for such oscillations of the surface, upheaval of marine beds, appearance of great estuaries, renewed connection of Britain with the Continent by a "Neolithic land-bridge"? In the Falkirk district neolithic kitchen-middens occur on, or at the base of, the bluffs which overlook the Carse lands, that is, the old sea-coast. In the Carse of Gowrie also a dug-out canoe was found at the very base of the deposits, and immediately above the buried forest-bed of the Tay Valley.[2]

That the neolithic period was also of long duration even in Scandinavia has been made evident by Carl Wibling, who calculates that the geological changes on the south-east coast of Sweden (Province of Bleking), since its first occupation by the men of the New Stone Age, must have required a period of " at least 10,000 years." [3]

Still more startling are the results of the protracted researches carried on by J. Nüesch at the now famous station of Schweizersbild, near Schaffhausen in Switzerland.[4] This station was apparently in the continuous occupation of man during both Stone Ages, and here have been collected as many as 14,000 objects belonging to the first, and over 6000 referred to the second period. Although the early settlement was only post-glacial, a point about which there is no room for doubt, L. Laloy [5] has estimated " the absolute duration of both epochs together at from 24,000 to 29,000 years." We may, therefore, ask, If a comparatively recent post-glacial station in Switzerland is about 29,000 years old, how old may a pre- or inter-glacial station be in Gaul or Britain ?

From all this we see how fully justified is J. W. Powell's remark that the natural history of early man becomes more and more a geological, and not merely an ethnological problem.[6] We also begin to understand how it is that, after an existence of some five score millenniums, the first specialised human

The early History of Man a Geological Problem.

[1] Discourse at the R. Institute, London, *Nature*, Jan. 6 and 13, 1898.
[2] *Nature*, 1898, p. 235.
[3] *Tiden för Blekings första bebyggande*, Karlskrona, 1895, p. 5.
[4] " Das Schweizersbild, eine Niederlassung aus palaeolithischer und neolithischer Zeit," in *Nouveaux Mémoires Soc. Helvétique des Sciences Naturelles*, Vol. xxxv. Zurich, 1896. This is described by James Geikie, *The Antiquity of Man in Europe*, 1914, pp. 85–99.
[5] *L'Anthropologie*, 1897, p. 350.   [6] *Forum*, Feb. 1898.

varieties have diverged greatly from the original types, which have thus become almost "ideal quantities," the subjects rather of palaeontological than of strictly anthropological studies.

And here another consideration of great moment presents itself. During these long ages some of the groups—most African negroes south of the equator, most Oceanic negroes (Negritoes and Papuans), and Australian and American aborigines—have remained in their original habitats ever since what may be called the first settlement of the earth by man. Others again, the more restless or enterprising peoples, such as the Mongols, Manchus, Turks, Ugro-Finns, Arabs, and most Europeans, have no doubt moved about somewhat freely ; but these later migrations, whether hostile or peaceable, have for the most part been confined to regions presenting the same or like physical and climatic conditions. Wherever different climatic zones have been invaded, the intruders have failed to secure a permanent footing, either perishing outright, or disappearing by absorption or more or less complete assimilation to the aboriginal elements. Such are some "black Arabs" in Egyptian Sudan, other Semites and Hamites in Abyssinia and West Sudan (Himyarites, Fulahs and others), Finns and Turks in Hungary and the Balkan Peninsula (Magyars, Bulgars, Osmanli), Portuguese and Netherlanders in Malaysia, English in tropical or sub-tropical lands, such as India, where Eurasian half-breeds alone are capable of founding family groups.

The Human Varieties the Outcome of their several Environments.

The human varieties are thus seen to be, like all other zoological species, the outcome of their several environments. They are what climate, soil, diet, pursuits and inherited characters have made them, so that all sudden transitions are usually followed by disastrous results.[1] "To urge the emigration of women and children, or of any save those of the most robust health, to the tropics, may not be to murder in the first degree, but it should be classed, to put it mildly, as incitement to it."[2] Acclimatisation may not be impossible

---

[1] The party of Eskimo men and women brought back by Lieut. Peary from his Arctic expedition in 1897 were unable to endure our temperate climate. Many died of pneumonia, and the survivors were so enfeebled that all had to be restored to their icy homes to save their lives. Even for the Algonquians of Labrador a journey to the coast is a journey to the grave.

[2] W. Z. Ripley, *The Races of Europe*, 1900, p. 586.

but in all extreme cases it can be effected only at great sacrifice of life, and by slow processes, the most effective of which is perhaps Natural Selection. By this means we may indeed suppose the world to have been first peopled.

At the same time it should be remembered that we know little of the climatic conditions at the time of the first migrations, though it has been assumed that it was everywhere much milder than at present. Consequently the different zones of temperature were less marked, and the passage from one region to another more easily effected than in later times. In a word, the pleistocene precursors had far less difficulty in adapting themselves to their new surroundings than modern peoples have when they emigrate, for instance, from Southern Europe to Brazil and Paraguay, or from the British Isles to Rhodesia and Nyassaland.

What is true of man must be no less true of his works ; from which it follows that racial and cultural zones correspond
Correspondence of Geographical with Racial and Cultural Zones. in the main with zones of temperature, except so far as the latter may be modified by altitude, marine influences, or other local conditions. A glance at past and existing relations the world over will show that such harmonies have at all times prevailed. No doubt the overflow of the leading European peoples during the last 400 years has brought about divers dislocations, blurrings, and in places even total effacements of the old landmarks.

But, putting aside these disturbances, it will be found that in the Eastern hemisphere the inter-tropical regions, hot, moist and more favourable to vegetable than to animal vitality, are usually occupied by savage, cultureless populations. Within the same sphere are also comprised most of the extra-tropical southern lands, all tapering towards the antarctic waters, isolated, and otherwise unsuitable for areas of higher specialisation.

Similarly the sub-tropical Asiatic peninsulas, the bleak Tibetan tableland, the Pamir, and arid Mongolian steppes are found mainly in possession of somewhat stationary communities, which present every stage between sheer savagery and civilisation.

In the same way the higher races and cultures are confined to the more favoured north temperate zone, so that between the parallels of 24° and 50° (but owing to local conditions falling in the far East to 40° and under, and in the extreme West rising to 55°) are situated nearly all the great centres, past and present, of human activities—the Egyptian, Babylonian, Minoan (Aegean), Hellenic, Etruscan, Roman, and modern European. Almost the only exceptions are the early civilisations (Himyaritic) of Yemen (Arabia Felix) and Abyssinia, where the low latitude is neutralised by altitude and a copious rainfall.

Thanks also to altitude, to marine influences, and the contraction of the equatorial lands, the relations are almost completely reversed in the New World. Here all the higher developments took place, not in the temperate but in the tropical zone, within which lay the seats of the Peruvian, Chimu, Chibcha and Maya-Quiché cultures; the Aztec sphere alone ranged northwards a little beyond the Tropic of Cancer.

Thus in both hemispheres the iso-cultural bands follow the isothermal lines in all their deflections, and the human varieties everywhere faithfully reflect the conditions of their several environments.

CHAPTER II

THE METAL AGES—HISTORIC TIMES AND PEOPLES

Progress of Archaeological Studies—Sequence of the Metal Ages—The Copper Age—Egypt, Elam, Babylonia, Europe—The Bronze Age—Egypt and Babylonia, Western Europe, the Aegean, Ireland—Chronology of the Copper and Bronze Ages—The Iron Age—Hallstatt, La Tène—Man and his Works in the Metal Ages—The Prehistoric Age in the West, and in China—Historic Times—Evolution of Writing Systems—Hieroglyphs and Cuneiforms—The Alphabet—The Persian and other Cuneiform Scripts—The Mas-d'Azil Markings—Alphabetiform Signs on Neolithic Monuments—Character and Consequences of the later historic Migrations—The Race merges in the People—The distinguishing Characters of Peoples—Scheme of Classification.

IF, as above seen, the study of human origins is largely a geological problem, the investigation of the later developments, during the Metal Ages and prehistoric **Progress of Archaeological Studies.** times, belongs mainly to the field of Archaeology. Hence it is that for the light which has in recent years been thrown upon the obscure interval between the Stone Ages and the strictly historic epoch, that is to say, the period when in his continuous upward development man gradually exchanged stone for the more serviceable metals, we are indebted chiefly to the pioneer labours of such men as Worsaae, Steenstrup, Forchhammer, Schliemann, Sayce, Layard, Lepsius, Mariette, Maspero, Montelius, Brugsch, Petrie, Peters, Haynes, Sir J. Evans, Sir A. J. Evans and many others, all archaeologists first, and anthropologists only in the second instance.

From the researches of these investigators it is now clear that copper, bronze, and iron were successively in use in **Sequence of the Metal Ages.** Europe in the order named, so that the current expressions, " Copper," " Bronze," and " Iron " Ages remain still justified. But it also appears that overlappings, already beginning in late Neolithic times, were everywhere so frequent that in many localities it is quite impossible to draw any well-marked dividing lines between the successive metal periods.

That iron came last, a fact already known by vague tradition to the ancients,[1] is beyond doubt, and it is no less certain that bronze of various types intervened between copper and iron. But much obscurity still surrounds the question of copper, which occurs in so many graves of Neolithic and Bronze times, that this metal has even been denied an independent position in the sequence.

But we shall not be surprised that confusion should prevail on this point, if we reflect that the metals, unlike stone, came to remain. Once introduced, they were soon found to be indispensable to civilised man, so that in a sense the " Metal Ages " still survive, and must last to the end of time. Hence it was natural that copper should be found in prehistoric graves associated, first with polished stone implements, and then with bronze and iron, just as, since the arrival of the English in Australia, spoons, clay pipes, penknives, pannikins, and the like, are now found mingled with stone objects in the graves of the aborigines.

But that there was a true Copper Age[2] prior to that of Bronze, though possibly of not very long duration, except of course in the New World,[3] has been placed beyond reasonable doubt by recent investiga- The Copper tions. Considerable attention was devoted to the Age. subject by J. H. Gladstone, who finds that copper was worked by the Egyptians in the Sinaitic Peninsula, that is, in the famous mines of the Wadi Maghára, from the fourth to the eighteenth dynasty, perhaps from 3000 to 1580 B.C.[4] During that epoch tools were made of pure copper in Egypt and Syria, and by the Amorites in Palestine, often on the model of their stone prototypes.[5]

Elliot Smith[6] claims that " the full story of the coming of

---

[1] Thus Lucretius :
		" Posterius ferri vis est aerisque reperta,
			Sed prior aeris erat quam ferri cognitus usus."
[2] J. Déchelette points out that the term Copper " Age " is not justified for the greater part of Europe, as it suggests a demarcation which does not exist and also a more thorough chemical analysis of early metals than we possess. He prefers the term aeneolithic (*aeneus*, copper, λίθος, stone), coined by the Italians, to denote the period of transition, dating, according to Montelius, from about 2500 B.C. to 1900 B.C. *Manuel d'Archéologie préhistorique*, II. I, *Age du Bronze*, 1910, pp. 99–100, 105.		[3] *Eth.*, Chap. XIII.
[4] See G. Elliot Smith, *The Ancient Egyptians*, 1911, pp. 97–8.
[5] Paper on " The Transition from Pure Copper to Bronze," etc., read at the Meeting of the Brit. Assoc. Liverpool, 1896.
[6] *Loc. cit.* p. 3. But cf. H. R. Hall, *The Ancient History of the Near East*, 1912, pp. 33 and 90 *n.* 2.

copper, complete in every detail and circumstance, written in
Egypt. a simple and convincing fashion that he who runs
may read," has been displayed in Egypt ever
since the year 1894, though the full significance of the evidence is not recognised until Reisner called attention to
the record of pre-dynastic graves in Upper Egypt when
superintending the excavations at Naga-ed-dêr in 1908.[1]
These excavations revealed the indigenous civilisation of the
ancient Egyptians and, according to Elliot Smith, dispose of
the idea hitherto held by most archaeologists that Egypt
owed her knowledge of metals to Babylonia or some other
Asiatic source, where copper, and possibly also bronze, may
be traced back to the fourth millennium B.C. There was
doubtless intercourse between the civilisations of Egypt and
Babylonia, but " Reisner has revealed the complete absence
of any evidence to show or even to suggest that the language,
the mode of writing, the knowledge of copper . . . were imported " (p. 34). Elliot Smith justly claims (p. 6) that in no
other country has a similarly complete history of the discovery
and the evolution of the working of copper been revealed, but
until equally exhaustive excavations have been undertaken on
contemporary or earlier sites in Sumer and Elam, the question
cannot be regarded as settled.

The work of J. de Morgan at Susa[2] (1907–8) shows the
extreme antiquity of the Copper Age in ancient Elam, even if
Elam. his estimate of 5000 B.C. is regarded as a millennium too early.[3] At the base of the mound on
the natural soil, beneath 24 metres of archaeological layers,
were the remains of a town and a necropolis consisting
of about 1000 tombs. Those of the men contained copper
axes of primitive type ; those of the women little vases of
paint, together with discs of polished copper to serve as
mirrors. At Fara, excavations by Koldewey in 1902, and by
Andrae and Nöldeke in 1903 on the site of Shuruppak (the
Babylonia. home of the Babylonian Noah) in the valley of
the Lower Euphrates, revealed graves attributed

---

[1] G. A. Reisner, *The Early Cemeteries of Naga-ed-dêr* (University of California Publications), 1908, and *Report of the Archaeological Survey of Nubia,* 1907–8.

[2] " Campagnes de 1907–8," *Comptes Rendus de l'Académie des Inscriptions et Belles-Lettres*, 1908, p. 373.

[3] Cf. J. Déchelette, *Manuel d'Archéologie préhistorique*, II. 1, *Age du Bronze,* 1910, pp. 53–4.

to the prehistoric Sumerians, containing copper spear heads, axes and drinking vessels.[1]

In Europe, North Italy, Hungary and Ireland [2] may lay claim to a Copper Age, but there is very little evidence of such a stage in Britain. To this period also may be attributed the nest or *cache* of pure copper ingots found at Tourc'h, west of the Aven Valley, Finisterre, described by M. de Villiers du Terrage, and comprising 23 pieces, with a total weight of nearly 50 lbs.[3]   These objects, which belong to " the transitional period when copper was used at first concurrently with polished stone, and then disappeared as bronze came into more general use," [4] came probably from Hungary, at that time apparently the chief source of this metal for most parts of Europe.   Of over 200 copper objects described by Mathaeus Much [5] nearly all were of Hungarian or South German *provenance*, five only being accredited to Britain and eight to France.

The study of this subject has been greatly advanced by J. Hampel, who holds on solid grounds that in some regions, especially Hungary, copper played a dominant part for many centuries, and is undoubtedly the characteristic metal of a distinct culture.   His conclusions are based on the study of about 500 copper objects found in Hungary and preserved in the Buda Pesth collections.   Reviewing all the facts attesting a Copper Age in Central Europe, Egypt, Italy, Cyprus, Troy, Scandinavia, North Asia, and other lands, he concludes that a Copper Age may have sprung up independently wherever the ore was found, as in the Ural and Altai Mountains, Italy, Spain, Britain, Cyprus, Sinai, such culture being generally indigenous, and giving evidence of more or less characteristic local features.[6]   It was formerly assumed that such an independent Copper Age was developed not only in the region of the Great Lakes of North America, but also among certain Bantu peoples of Africa, but Elliot Smith and Perry attribute these industries to immigrants already acquainted with metalworking.   Copper is not an alloy like bronze, but a soft,

Europe.

---

[1] Cf. L. W. King, *A History of Sumer and Akkad*, 1910, p. 26.
[2] G. Coffey, *The Bronze Age in Ireland*, 1913, p. 6.
[3] *L' Anthropologie*, 1896, p. 526 sq.   This antiquary aptly remarks that " l'expression âge de cuivre a une signification bien précise comme s'appliquant à la partie de la période de la pierre polie où les métaux font leur apparition."
[4] *L'Anthropologie*, 1896, p. 526 sq.
[5] In *Die Kupferzeit in Europa*, 1886.
[6] " Neuere Studien über die Kupferzeit," in *Zeitschr. f. Eth.* 1896, No. 2.

easily-worked metal occurring in large quantities and in a tolerably pure state near the surface in many parts of the world.   The wonder is, not that it should have been found and worked at a somewhat remote epoch in several different centres, but that its use should have been so soon superseded in so many places by the bronze alloys.

From copper to bronze, however, the passage was slow and progressive, the proper proportion of tin, which was probably preceded in some places by an alloy of antimony, having been apparently arrived at by repeated experiments often carried out with no little skill by those prehistoric metallurgists.

The Bronze Age.

As suggested by Bibra in 1869, the ores of different metals would appear to have been at first smelted together empirically, and the process continued until satisfactory results were obtained.   Hence the extraordinary number of metals, of which percentages are found in some of the earlier specimens, such as those of the Elbing Museum, which on analysis yielded tin, lead, silver, iron, antimony, arsenic, sulphur, nickel, cobalt, and zinc in varying quantities.[1]

Some bronzes from the pyramid of Medum analysed by J. H. Gladstone[2] yielded the high percentage of 9.1 of tin, from which we must infer, not only that bronze, but bronze of the finest quality, was already known to the Egyptians of the fourth dynasty, *i.e.* 2840 B.C.   The statuette of Gudea of Lagash (2500 B.C.) claimed as the earliest example of bronze in Babylonia is now known to be pure copper, and though objects from Tello (Lagash) of earlier date contain a mixture of tin, zinc, arsenic and other alloys, the proportion is insignificant.   The question of priority must, however, be left open until the relative chronology of Egypt and Babylonia is finally settled, and this is still a much disputed point.[3]   Neither would all the difficulties with regard to the origin of bronze be cleared up should Egypt or Babylonia establish her claim to possess the earliest example of metal, for neither country appears

Egypt and Babylonia.

---

[1] Otto Helm, " Chemische Untersuchungen vorgeschichtlicher Bronzen," in *Zeitschr. f. Eth.* 1897, No. 2.   This authority agrees with Hampel's view that further research will confirm the suggestion that in Transylvania (Hungary) "eine Kupfer-Antimonmischung vorangegangen, welche zugleich die Bronzekultur vorbereitete " (*ib.* p. 128).

[2] *Proc. Soc. Bib. Archaeol.* 1892, pp. 223–6.

[3] For the chronology of the Copper and Bronze Ages, see p. 27.

to possess any tin. The nearest deposit known in ancient times would seem to be that of Drangiana, mentioned by Strabo, identified with modern Khorassan.[1]

Strabo and other classical writers also mention the occurrence of tin in the west, in Spain, Portugal and the Cassiterides or tin islands, whose identity has given rise to so much speculation,[2] but " though in after times   **Western Europe.** Egypt drew her tin from Europe, it would be bold indeed to suppose that she did so [in 3000 B.C.] and still bolder to maintain that she learned from northern people how to make the alloy called bronze." [3]   Apart from the indigenous Egyptian origin maintained by Elliot Smith (above), the hypothesis offering fewest difficulties is that the earliest bronze is to be traced to the region of Elam, and that the knowledge spread from S. Chaldaea (Elam-Sumer) to S. Egypt in the third millennium B.C.[4]

There seems to be little doubt that the Aegean was the centre for dispersal for the new metals throughout the Mediterranean area, and copper ingots have been   **The Aegean.** found at various points of the Mediterranean, marked with Cretan signs.[5] Bronze was known in Crete before 2000 B.C., for a bronze dagger and spear-head were found at Hagios Onuphrios, near Phaistos, with seals resembling those of the sixth to eleventh dynasties.[6]

From the eastern Mediterranean the knowledge spread during the second millennium along the ordinary trade routes which had long been in use. The mineral ores of Spain were exploited in pre-Mycenean times and probably contributed in no small measure to the industrial development of southern Europe. From tribe to tribe along the Atlantic coasts the traffic in minerals reached the British Isles, where the rich ores were discovered which, in their turn, supplied the markets of the north, the west and the south.

Even Ireland was not left untouched by Aegean influence,

---

[1] Copper and tin are found together in abundance in Southern China, but this is archaeologically speaking an unknown land ; " to search for the birthplace of bronze in China is therefore barren of positive results," *British Museum Guide to the Antiquities of the Bronze Age*, 1904, p. 10.

[2] T. Rice Holmes, *Ancient Britain*, 1907, pp. 483–498.

[3] *British Museum Guide to the Antiquities of the Bronze Age*, 1904, p. 10.

[4] J. de Morgan, *Les Premières Civilisations*, 1909, pp. 169, 337 ff.

[5] J. Déchelette, *Manuel d'Archéologie préhistorique*, II. 1, *Age du Bonze*, 1910, pp. 98 and 397 ff.

[6] J. Déchelette, *loc. cit.* p. 63 *n.*

which reached it, according to G. Coffey,[1] by way of the
Danube and the Elbe, and thence by way of
Ireland. Scandinavia, though this is a matter on which
there is much difference of opinion. Ireland's richness in
gold during the Bronze Age made her a " kind of El Dorado
of the western world," and the discovery of a gold torc found
by Schliemann in the royal treasury in the second city of
Troy raises the question as to whether the model of the torc
was imported into Ireland from the south,[1] or whether (which
J. Déchelette [2] regards as less probable) there was already an
exportation of Irish gold to the eastern Mediterranean in pre-
Mycenean times.

Of recent years great strides have been made towards
the establishment of a definite chronology linking the historic
Chronology of with the prehistoric periods in the Aegean, in
the Copper and Egypt and in Babylonia, and as the estimates
Bronze Ages. of various authorities differ sometimes by a
thousand years or so, the subjoined table will be of use to
indicate the chronological schemes most commonly followed ;
the dates are in all cases merely approximate.

It has often been pointed out that there is no reason why
iron should not have been the earliest metal to be used by
man. Its ores are more abundant and more
The Iron Age. easily reduced than any others, and are worked
by peoples in a low grade of culture at the present day.[3]
Iron may have been known in Egypt almost as early as
bronze, for a piece in the British Museum is attributed to the
fourth dynasty, and some beads of manufactured iron were
found in a pre-dynastic grave at El Gerzeh.[4] But these and
other less well authenticated occurrences of iron are rare, and
the metal was not common in Egypt before the middle of the
second millennium. By the end of the second millennium the
knowledge had spread throughout the eastern Mediterranean,[5]
and towards 900 at latest iron was in common use in Italy
and Central Europe.

[1] G. Coffey, *The Bronze Age in Ireland*, 1913, pp. v, 78.
[2] J. Déchelette, *Manuel d'Archéologie préhistorique*, ii. 1, *Age du Bronze*, 1910,
p. 355 *n.*
[3] *Guide to the Antiquities of the Early Iron Age* (British Museum), 1905, p. 2.
[4] Wainwright, " Pre-dynastic iron beads in Egypt," *Man*, 1911, p. 177.   See
also H. R. Hall, " Note on the early use of iron in Egypt," *Man*, 1903, p. 147.
[5] W. Belck attributes the introduction of iron into Crete in 1500 B.C. to the
Phoenicians, whom he derives from the neighbourhood of the Persian Gulf.   He
suggests that these traders were already acquainted with the metal in S. Arabia in

CHRONOLOGICAL TABLE.

	Egypt [1]	Babylonia [2]	Aegean [3]	Greece [4]	Bronze Age in Europe [5]
3300	Dynasty I				
3200					
3100					
3000		Dynasty of Opis	?Early Minoan I	?Pre-Mycenean	
2900		Dyn. of Kish			
2800	Dyn. III, IV	Dyn. of Erech			
		Dyn. of Akkad [6]			
2700					
2600	Dyn. V	2nd Dyn. of Erech			
2500	Dyn. VI	Gutian Domination	Early Minoan II		Period I. Eneolithic (implements of stone, copper and bronze, poor in tin)
2400		Dyn. of Ur			
2300	Dyn. IX				
2200		Dyn. of Isin	Middle Minoan I		
2100	Dyn. XI		Mid. Minoan II		
2000	Dyn. XII	1st Dyn. Babylon		Mycenean I	
1900		2nd Dyn.	Mid. Minoan III		Period II
1800					
1700	Dyn. XIII	3rd Dyn.	Late Minoan I		
1600	Dyn. XV				Period III
1500	Dyn. XVIII		Late Minoan II	Mycenean II	
1400			Late Minoan III		
1300	Dyn. XIX				Period IV
1200	Dyn. XX			Homeric Age	
1100		4th Dyn.			
1000	Dyn. XXI	5th to 7th Dyn.		Close of Bronze Age [7]	
900	Dyn. XXII	8th Dyn.			Hallstatt

the fourth millennium, and that it was through them that a piece found its way into Egypt in the fourth dynasty. " Die Erfinder des Eisentechnik," *Zeitschrift f. Ethnologie*, 1910. See also F. Stuhlmann, *Handwerk und Industrie in Ostafrika*, 1910, p. 49 ff., who on cultural grounds derives the knowledge of iron in Africa from an Asiatic source.

[1] E. Meyer, " Aegyptische Chronologie," *Abh. Berl. Akad.* 1904, and " Nachträge," *ib.* 1907. This chronology has been adopted by the Berlin school and others, but is unsatisfactory in allowing insufficient time for Dynasties XII to XVIII, which are known to contain 100 to 200 rulers. Flinders Petrie therefore adds another Sothic period (1461 years, calculated from Sothis or Sirius), thus throwing the earlier dynasties a millennium or two further back. Dynasty I, according to this computation, starts in 5546 B.C. and Dynasty XII at 3779. H. R. Hall, *The Ancient History of the Near East*, 1912, p. 23.

[2] L. W. King, *The History of Sumer and Akkad*, 1910, and " Babylonia," Hutchinson's *History of the Nations*, 1914.

[3] C. H. Hawes and H. Boyd Hawes, *Crete the Forerunner of Greece*, 1909.

[4] J. Déchelette, *Manuel d'Archéologie préhistorique*, II. 1, *Age du Bronze*, 1910, p. 61.

[5] J. Déchelette, *loc. cit.* p. 105 ff., based on the work of O. Montelius and P. Reinecke.

[6] The Dynasty of Akkad is often dated a millennium earlier, relying on the statement of Nabonidus (556–540 B.C.) that Narâm-Sin (the traditional son of Sargon of Akkad) reigned 3200 years before him; but this statement is now known to be greatly exaggerated. See the section on chronology in the Art. " Babylonia," in *Ency. Brit.* 1910.

[7] *Guide to the Antiquities of the Early Iron Age* (British Museum), 1905, p. 1.

The introduction of iron into Italy has often been attributed to the Etruscans, who were thought to have brought
the knowledge from Lydia.   But the most abundant remains
of the Early Iron Age are found not in Tuscany, but along
the coasts of the Adriatic,[1] showing that iron followed the
well-known route of the amber trade, thus reaching Central
Europe and *Hallstatt* (which has given its name to the early
Iron Age), where alone in Europe the gradual transition
from the use of bronze to that of iron has been clearly traced.
W. Ridgeway [2] believes that the use of iron was first discovered in the Hallstatt area and that thence it spread to
Switzerland, France, Spain, Italy, Greece, the Aegean area,
and Egypt rather than that the culture drift was in the
opposite direction.   There is no difference of opinion however as to the importance of this Central European area
which contained the most famous iron mines of antiquity.
Hallstatt culture extended from the Iberian

Hallstatt.   peninsula in the west to Hungary in the east,
but scarcely reached Scandinavia, North Germany, Armorica
or the British Isles, where the Bronze Age may be said to
have lasted down to about 500 B.C.   Over such a vast domain
the culture was not everywhere of a uniform type, and
Hoernes [3] recognises four geographical divisions distinguished
mainly by pottery and fibulae, and provisionally classified as
Illyrian in the South-West or Adriatic region, in touch with
Greece and Italy ; Celtic in the Central or Danubian area ;
with an off-shoot in Western Germany, Northern Switzerland
and Eastern France ; and Germanic in parts of Germany,
Bohemia, Moravia, Silesia and Posen.

The Hallstatt period ends, roughly, at 500 B.C., and the
Later Iron Age takes its name from the settlement of *La*

La Tène.   *Tène,* in a bay of the Lake of Neuchâtel in
Switzerland.   This culture, while owing much
to that of Hallstatt, and much also to foreign sources, possesses a distinct individuality, and though soon overpowered
on the Continent by Roman influence, attained a remarkable
brilliance in the Late Celtic period in the British Isles.

---

[1] Cf. J. Déchelette, *Manuel d'Archéologie préhistorique,* II. 2, *Premier Age du
Fer,* 1913, pp. 546, 562–3.
[2] *The Early Age of Greece,* 1900, pp. 594–630.
[3] " Die Hallstattperiode," *Ass. française p. l'av. des sciences,* 1905, p. 278, and
Kultur der Urzeit, III. *Eisenzeit,* 1912, p. 54.

That the peoples of the Metal Ages were physically well developed and in a great part of Europe and Asia already of Aryan speech, there can be no reasonable doubt. **Man and his** A skull of the early Hallstatt period, from a **Works in the** grave near Wildenroth, Upper Bavaria, is de- **Metal Ages.** scribed by Virchow as long-headed, with a cranial capacity of no less than 1585 c.c., strongly developed occiput, very high and narrow face and nose, and in every respect a superb specimen of the regular-featured, long-headed North European.[1] But owing to the prevalence of cremation the evidence of race is inadequate. The Hallstatt population was undoubtedly mixed, and at Glasinatz in Bosnia, another site of Hallstatt civilisation, about a quarter of the skulls examined were brachycephalic.[2]

Their works, found in great abundance in the graves, especially of the Bronze and Iron periods, but a detailed account of which belongs to the period of archaeology, interest us in many ways. The painted earthenware vases and incised metal-ware of all kinds enable the student to follow the progress of the arts of design and ornamentation in their upward development from the first tentative efforts of the prehistoric artists at pleasing effects. Human and animal figures, though rarely depicted, occasionally afford a curious insight into the customs and fashions of the times. On a clay vessel, found in 1896 at Lahse in Posen, is figured a regular hunting scene, where we see men mounted on horseback, or else on foot, armed with bow and arrow, pursuing the quarry (nobly-antlered stags), and returning to the penthouse after the chase.[3] The drawing is extremely primitive, but on that account all the more instructive, showing in connection with analogous representations on contemporary objects how in prehistoric art such figures tend to become conventionalised and purely ornamental, as in similar designs on the vases and textiles from the Ancon Necropolis, Peru. "Most ornaments of primitive peoples, although to our eye they may seem merely geometrical and freely invented designs, are in reality nothing more than degraded animal and human figures."[4]

[1] "Ein Schädel aus der älteren Hallstattzeit," in *Verhandl. Berlin. Ges. f. Anthrop.* 1896, pp. 243–6.
[2] *Guide to the Antiquities of the Early Iron Age* (British Museum), 1905, p. 8.
[3] Hans Seger, "Figürliche Darstellungen auf schlesischen Gräbgefässen der Hallstattzeit," *Globus*, Nov. 20, 1897.				[4] *Ibid.* p. 297.

This may perhaps be the reason why so many of the drawings of the metal period appear so inferior to those of the cave-dwellers and of the present Bushman. They are often more conventionalised reductions of pictorial prototypes, comparable, for instance, to the characters of our alphabets, which are known to be degraded forms of earlier pictographs.

Of the so-called "Prehistoric Age" it is obvious that no strict definition can be given. It comprises in a general way *The Prehistoric* that vague period prior to all written records, *Age in the* dim memories of which—popular myths, folk- *West,* lore, demi-gods,[1] eponymous heroes,[2] traditions of real events[3]—lingered on far into historic times, and supplied ready to hand the copious materials afterwards worked up by the early poets, founders of new religions, and later legislators.

That letters themselves, although not brought into general use, had already been invented, is evident from the mere fact that all memory of their introduction beyond the vaguest traditions had died out before the dawn of history. The works of man, while in themselves necessarily continuous, stretched back to such an inconceivably remote past, that even the great landmarks in the evolution of human progress had long been forgotten by later generations.

And so it was everywhere, in the New World as in the Old, amongst Eastern as amongst Western peoples. In the *and in China.* Chinese records the "Age of the Five Em- perors"—five, though nine are named—answers somewhat to our prehistoric epoch. It had its eponymous hero, Fu Hi, reputed founder of the empire, who invented nets and snares for fishing and hunting, and taught his people how to rear domestic animals. To him also is ascribed the institution of marriage, and in his time Tsong Chi is supposed to have invented the Chinese characters, symbols, not of sounds, but of objects and ideas.

---

[1] Homer's ἡμιθέων γένος ἀνδρῶν, *Il.* XII. 23, if the passage is genuine.

[2] Such as the Greek *Andreas*, the "First Man," invented in comparatively recent times, as shown by the intrusive *d* in ἄνδρες for the earlier ἄνερες, "men." Andreas was of course a Greek, sprung in fact from the river Peneus and the first inhabitant of the Orchomenian plain (Pausanias, IX. 34, 5).

[3] For instance, the flooding of the Thessalian plain, afterwards drained by the Peneus and repeopled by the inhabitants of the surrounding mountains (rocks, stones), whence the myth of Deucalion and Pyrrha, who are told by the oracle to repeople the world by throwing behind them the "bones of their grandmother," that is, the "stones" of mother Earth.

Then came other benevolent rulers, who taught the people agriculture, established markets for the sale of farm produce, discovered the medicinal properties of plants, wrote treatises on diseases and their remedies, studied astrology and astronomy, and appointed " the Five Observers of the heavenly bodies."

But this epoch had been preceded by the " Age of the Three [six] Rulers," when people lived in caves, ate wild fruits and uncooked food, drank the blood of animals and wore the skins of wild beasts (our Old Stone Age). Later they grew less rude, learned to obtain fire by friction, and built themselves habitations of wood or foliage (our Early Neolithic Age). Thus is everywhere revealed the background of sheer savagery, which lies behind all human culture, while the " Golden Age " of the poet fades with the "Hesperides " and Plato's " Atlantis " into the region of the fabulous.

Little need here be said of strictly historic times, the most characteristic feature of which is perhaps the general use of letters. By means of this most fruitful of human inventions, everything worth preserving Historic Times. was perpetuated, and thus all useful knowledge tended to become accumulative. It is no longer possible to say when or where the miracle was wrought by which the apparently multifarious sounds of fully-developed languages were exhaustively analysed and effectively expressed by a score or so of arbitrary signs. But a comparative study of the various writing-systems in use in different parts of the world has revealed the process by which the transition was gradually brought about from rude pictorial representations of objects to purely phonetical symbols.

As is clearly shown by the " winter counts " of the North American aborigines, and by the prehistoric rock carvings in Upper Egypt, the first step was a *pictograph*, Evolution of the actual figure, say, of a man, standing for a Writing given man, and then for any man or human Systems. being. Then this figure, more or less reduced or conventionalised, served to indicate not only the term *man*, but the full sound *man*, as in the word *manifest*, and in the modern rebus. At this stage it becomes a *phonogram*, or *phonoglyph*, which, when further reduced beyond all recognition of its original form, may stand for the syllable *ma* as in *ma-ny*, without any further reference either to the idea or the sound *man*. The phonogram has now become the symbol of a monosyllable, which is normally made up of two elements, a consonant and a vowel, as in the Devanágari, and other syllabic systems.

Lastly, by dropping the second or vowel element the same symbol, further modified or not, becomes a *letter* representing the sound *m*, that is, one of the few ultimate elements of articulate speech. A more or less complete set of such characters, thus worn down in form and meaning, will then be available for indicating more or less completely all the phonetic elements of any given language. It will be a true *alphabet*, the wonderful nature of which may be inferred from the fact that only two, or possibly three, such alphabetic systems are known with absolute certainty to have ever been independently evolved by human ingenuity.[1] From the above exposition we see how inevitably the Phoenician parent of nearly all late alphabets expressed at first the consonantal sounds only, so that the vowels or vowel marks are in all cases later developments, as in Hebrew, Syriac, Arabic, Greek, the Italic group and the Runes.

In primitive systems, such as the Egyptian, Sumerian, Chinese, Maya-Quiché and Mexican, one or more of the various transitional steps may be developed and used simultaneously, with a constant tendency to advance on the lines above indicated, by gradual substitution of the later for the earlier stages. A comparison of the Sumerian cuneiform and Egyptian hieroglyphic systems brings out some curious results. Thus at an extremely remote epoch, some millenniums ago, the Sumerians had already got rid of the pictorial, and to a great extent of the ideographic, but had barely reached the alphabetic phase. Consequently their cuneiform groups, although possessing phonetic value, mainly express full syllables, scarcely ever letters, and rarely complete words. Ideographs had given place first to phonograms and then to mere syllables,

Hieroglyphs and Cunei-forms.

---

[1] Such instances as George Guest's Cherokee system, and the crude attempt of a Vei (West Sudanese) Negro, if genuine, are not here in question, as both had the English alphabet to work upon. A like remark applies to the old Irish and Welsh Ogham, which are more curious than instructive, the characters, mostly mere groups of straight strokes, being obvious substitutes for the corresponding letters of the Roman alphabet, hence comparable to the cryptographic systems of Wheatstone and others.

"complex syllables in which several consonants may be distinguished, or simple syllables composed of only one consonant and one vowel or *vice versa.*"[1]

The Egyptians, on the other hand, carried the system right through the whole gamut from pictures to letters, but retained all the intermediate phases, the initial tending to fall away, the final to expand, while the bulk of the hieroglyphs represented in various degrees the several transitional states. In many cases they "had kept only one part of the syllable, namely a mute consonant; they detached, for instance, the final *u* from *bu* and *pu*, and gave only the values *b* and *p* to the human leg ⌡ and to the mat ▦. The peoples of the Euphrates stopped half way, and admitted actual letters for the vowel sounds *a, i* and *u* only."[2]

In the process of evolution, metaphor and analogy of course played a large part, as in the evolution of language itself. Thus a lion might stand both for the animal and for courage, and so on. The first essays in phonetics took somewhat the form of a modern rebus, thus: ○ = *khau* = sieve, ▦ = *pu* = mat; ◯ = *ru* = mouth, whence ○▦ = *kho-pi-ru* = to be, where the sounds and not the meaning of the several components are alone attended to.[3]

By analogous processes was formed a true alphabet, in which, however, each of the phonetic elements was represented at first by several different characters **The Alphabet.** derived from several different words having the same initial syllable. Here was, therefore, an *embarras de richesses*, which could be got rid of only by a judicious process of elimination, that is, by discarding all like-sounding symbols but one for the same sound. When this final process of reduction was completed by the scribes, in other words, when all the phonetic signs were rejected except 23, *i.e.* one for each of the 23 phonetic elements, the Phoenician alphabet as we now have it was completed. Such may be taken as the real origin of this system, whether the scribes in question were Babylonians, Egyptians, Minaeans, or Europeans, that is, whether the Phoenician alphabet had a cuneiform, a hieroglyphic, a South Arabian, a Cretan (Aegean), Ligurian or Iberian origin, for all these and perhaps other peoples have

---

[1] Maspero, *The Dawn of Civilisation*, 1898, p. 728.
[2] *Ibid.*   [3] *Ibid.* p. 233.

been credited with the invention. The time is not yet ripe for deciding between these rival claimants.[1]

But whatever be the source of the Phoenician, that of the Persian system current under the Achaemenides is clear

The Persian and other Cuneiform Scripts.

enough. It is a true alphabet of 37 characters, derived by some selective process directly from the Babylonian cuneiforms, without any attempt at a modification of their shapes. Hence although simple compared with its prototype, it is clumsy enough compared with the Phoenician script, several of the letters requiring groups of as many as four or even five " wedges " for their expression. None of the other cuneiform systems also derived from the Sumerian (the Assyrian, Elamite, Vannic, Medic) appear to have reached the pure alphabetic state, all being still encumbered with numerous complex syllabic characters. The subjoined table, for which I have to thank T. G. Pinches, will help to show the genesis of the cuneiform combinations from the earliest known pictographs. These pictographs themselves are already reduced to the merest outlines of the original pictorial representations. But no earlier forms, showing the gradual transition from the primitive picture writing to the degraded pictographs here given, have yet come to light.[2]

Here it may be asked, What is to be thought of the already-mentioned pebble-markings from the Mas-d'Azil

The Mas-d'Azil Markings.

Cave at the close of the Old Stone Age ? If they are truly phonetic, then we must suppose that palaeolithic man not only invented an alphabetic writing system, but did this right off by intuition, as it were, without any previous knowledge of letters. At least no one will suggest that the Dordogne cave-dwellers were already in possession of pictographic or other crude systems, from which the Mas-d'Azil " script " might have been slowly evolved. Yet E. Piette, who groups these pebbles, painted with peroxide of iron, in the four categories of numerals, symbols, pictographs, and alphabetical characters, states, in reference to these last, that 13 out of 23 Phoenician characters were equally Azilian graphic signs. He even suggests that there may be an approach to an inscription in

---

[1] See P. Giles, Art. "Alphabet," *Ency. Brit.* 1910.
[2] See A. J. Booth, *The Discovery and Decipherment of the Trilingual Cuneiform Inscriptions*, 1902.

one group, where, however, the mark indicating a stop implies a script running Semitic-fashion from right to left, whereas the letters themselves seem to face the other way.[1] G. G. MacCurdy,[2] who accepts the evidence for the existence

EVOLUTION OF THE SUMERIAN CUNEIFORMS.

1000 B.C. and later.	About 2500 to 1500 B.C.	Oldest known line forms, 3000 B.C. and earlier.		
				"bird."
			—	"sheep" (probably a sheepfold).
				"ox."
				"to go," "to stand."
			—	"hand."
				"man."
			—	"dagger."
			—	"fish."
	—			"reed."
	—			"reed."
			—	"corn" ("ear of corn").
			—	"god," "heaven."
			—	"constellation," "star."

of writing in Azilian, if not in Magdalenian times, notes the close similarity between palaeolithic signs and Phoenician, ancient Greek and Cypriote letters. But J. Déchelette,[3]

[1] *L'Anthr.* xv. 1904, p. 164.
[2] *Recent Discoveries bearing on the Antiquity of Man in Europe* (Smithsonian Report for 1909), 1910, p. 566 ff.
[3] *Manuel d'Archéologie préhistorique*, I. 1908.

reviewing (pp. 234, 236) the arguments against Piette's claims, points out in conclusion (p. 320) the impossibility of admitting that the population of Gaul could suddenly lose so beneficial a discovery as that of writing. Yet thousands of years elapse before the earliest appearance of epigraphic monuments.

A possible connection has been suggested by Sergi between the Mas-d'Azil signs and the markings that have

Alphabeti-
form Signs on
Neolithic
Monuments.

been discovered on the megalithic monuments of North Africa, Brittany, and the British Isles. These are all so rudimentary that resemblances are inevitable, and of themselves afford little ground for necessary connections. Primitive man is but a child, and all children bawl and scrawl much in the same way. Nevertheless C. Letourneau [1] has taken the trouble to compare five such scrawls from " Libyan inscriptions " now in the Bardo Museum, Tunis, with similar or identical signs on Brittany and Irish dolmens. There is the familiar circle plain and dotted O $\odot$, the cross in its simplest form +, the pothook and segmented square $\cap$ $\sqcap$, all of which recur in the Phoenician, Keltiberian, Etruscan, Libyan or Tuareg systems. Letourneau, however, who does not call them letters but only " signes alphabétiformes," merely suggests that, if not phonetic marks when first carved on the neolithic monuments, they may have become so in later times. Against this it need only be urged that in later times all these peoples were supplied with complete alphabetic systems from the East as soon as they required them. By that time all the peoples of the culture-zone were well-advanced into the historic period, and had long forgotten the rude carvings of their neolithic forefathers.

Armed with a nearly perfect writing system, and the correlated cultural appliances, the higher races soon took a foremost place in the general progress of mankind, and gradually acquired a marked ascendancy, not only over the

Character and
Consequences
of the later
(historical)
Migrations.

less cultured populations of the globe, but in large measure over the forces of nature herself. With the development of navigation and improved methods of locomotion, inland seas, barren wastes, and mountain ranges ceased to be insurmountable obstacles to their movements, which within

[1] " Les signes libyques des dolmens," *Bul. Soc. d'Anthrop.* 1896, p. 319.

certain limits have never been arrested throughout all recorded time.

Thus, during the long ages following the first peopling of the earth by pleistocene man, fresh settlements and readjustments have been continually in progress, although wholesale displacements must be regarded as rare events. With few exceptions, the later migrations, whether hostile or peaceful, were, for reasons already stated,[1] generally of a partial character, while certain insular regions, such as America and Australia, remained little affected by such movements till quite recent times. But for the inhabitants of the eastern hemisphere the results were none the less far-reaching. Continuous infiltrations could not fail ultimately to bring about great modifications of early types, while the ever-active principle of convergence tended to produce a general uniformity amongst the new amalgams. Thus the great varietal divisions, though undergoing slow changes from age to age, continued, like all other zoological groups, to maintain a distinct regional character.

Flinders Petrie has acutely observed that the only meaning the term "race" now can have is that of a group of human beings, whose type has become unified by their rate of assimilation exceeding the rate of change produced by foreign elements.[2] We are also reminded by Gustavo Tosti that "in the actual state of science the word 'race' is a vague formula, to which nothing definite may be found to correspond. On the one hand, the original races can only be said to belong to palaeontology, while the more limited groups, now called races, are nothing but peoples, or societies of peoples, brethren by civilisation more than by blood. The race thus conceived ends by identifying itself with nationality."[3] Hence it has been asked why, on the principle of convergence, a fusion of various races, if isolated long enough in a given area, may not eventually lead to a new racial type, without leaving any trace of its manifold origin.[4]

The "Race" merges in the "People."

Such new racial types would be normal for the later varietal groups, just as the old types were normal for the

[1] *Eth.* Chap. XIII.
[2] *Address*, Meeting British Assoc. Ipswich, 1895.
[3] *Amer. F. of Sociology*, Jan. 1898, pp. 467–8.
[4] A. Vierkandt, *Globus*, 72, p. 134.

earlier groups, and a general application might be given to Topinard's famous dictum that *les peuples seuls sont des réalités*,[1] that is, peoples alone—groups occupying definite geographical areas—have an objective existence. Thus, the notion of race, as a zoological expression in the sense of a pure breed or strain, falls still more into the background, and, as Virchow aptly remarks, " this term, which always implied something vague, has in recent times become in the highest degree uncertain." [2]

The distinguishing Characters of Peoples. Hence Ehrenreich treats the present populations of the earth rather as zoological groups which have been developed in their several geographical domains, and are to be distinguished not so much by their bony structure as by their external characters, such as hair, colour, and expression, and by their habitats and languages. None of these factors can be overlooked, but it would seem that the character of the hair forms the most satisfactory basis for a classification of mankind, and this has therefore been adopted for the new edition of the present work. It has the advantage of simplicity, without involving, or even implying, any particular theory of racial or geographical origins. It has stood the test of time, being proposed by Bory de Saint Vincent in 1827, and adopted by Huxley, Haeckel, Broca, Topinard and many others.

The three main varieties of hair are the *straight*, the *wavy* and the so-called *woolly*, termed respectively *Leiotrichous, Cymotrichous* and *Ulotrichous*.[3] Straight hair usually falls straight down, though it may curl at the ends, it is generally coarse and stiff, and is circular in section. Wavy hair is undulating, forming long curves or imperfect spirals, or closer rings or curls, and the section is more or less elliptical. Woolly hair is characterised by numerous, close, often interlocking spirals, 1–9 mm. in diameter, the section giving the form of a lengthened ellipse. Straight hair is usually the longest, and woolly hair the shortest, wavy hair occupying an intermediate position.

---

[1] *Éléments d'Anthropologie Générale*, p. 207.
[2] *Rassenbildung u. Erblichkeit; Bastian-Festschrift*, 1896, p. 1.
[3] From Gk. λεῖος, smooth, κῦμα, wave, οὖλος, fleecy, and θρίξ, τριχός, hair. J. Deniker (*The Races of Man*, 1900, p. 38) distinguishes four classes, the Australians, Nubians etc. being grouped as *frizzy*. He gives the corresponding terms in French and German :—straight, Fr. *droit, lisse*, Germ. *straff, schlicht* ; wavy, Fr. *ondé*, Germ. *wellig* ; frizzy, Fr. *frisé*, Germ. *lochig* ; woolly, Fr. *crépu*, Germ. *kraus*.

SCHEME OF CLASSIFICATION.

I. ULOTRICHI (Woolly-haired).

  1. The African Negroes, Negrilloes, Bushmen.
  2. The Oceanic Negroes : Papuans, Melanesians in part, Tasmanians, Negritoes.

II. LEIOTRICHI (Straight-haired).

  1. The Southern Mongols.
  2. The Oceanic Mongols, Polynesians in part.
  3. The Northern Mongols.
  4. The American Aborigines.

III. CYMOTRICHI (Curly or Wavy-haired).

  1. The Pre-Dravidians : Vedda, Sakai, etc., Australians.
  2. The " Caucasic " peoples :

    A. Southern Dolichocephals : Mediterraneans, Hamites, Semites, Dravidians, Indonesians, Polynesians in part.

    B. Northern Dolichocephals : Nordics, Kurds, Afghans, some Hindus.

    C. Brachycephals : Alpines, including the short Cevenoles of Western and Central Europe, and tall Adriatics or Dinarics of Eastern Europe and the Armenians of Western Asia.

CHAPTER III

THE AFRICAN NEGRO : I. SUDANESE

Conspectus—The Negro-Caucasic " Great Divide "—The Negro Domain—Negro Origins—Persistence of the Negro Type—Two Main Sections : Sudanese and Bantus—Contrasts and Analogies—Sudanese and Bantu Linguistic Areas—The " Drum Language "—West Sudanese Groups—*The Wolofs* : Primitive Speech and Pottery ; Religious Notions—*The Mandingans* : Culture and Industries ; History ; the Guiné and Mali Empires—*The Felups* : Contrasts between the Inland and Coast Peoples ; Felup Type and Mental Characters —*Timni*—African Freemasonry—*The Sierra Leonese*—Social Relations—*The Liberians*—*The Krumen*—*The Upper Guinea Peoples*—Table of the Gold Coast and Slave Coast Tribes—Ashanti Folklore—Fetishism ; its true inwardness—Ancestry Worship and the " Customs "—The Benin Bronzes—*The Mossi*—African Agnostics—Central Sudanese—General Ethnical and Social Relations—*The Songhai*—Domain—Origins—Egyptian Theories—Songhai Records—*The Hausas*—Dominant Social Position—Speech and Mental Qualities—Origins—*Kanembu* ; *Kanuri* ; *Baghirmi* ; *Mosgu*—Ethnical and Political Relations in the Chad Basin—The Aborigines—Islám and Heathendom—Slave-Hunting—Arboreal Strongholds—Mosgu Types and Contrasts—The Cultured Peoples of Central Sudan—Kanem-Bornu Records—Eastern Sudanese—Range of the Negro in Eastern Sudan—*The Mabas*—Ethnical Relations in Wadai—*The Nubas*—The Nubian Problem—Nubian Origins and Affinities—The Negro Peoples of the Nile-Congo Watersheds—Political Relations—Two Physical Types—*The Dinka*—Linguistic Groups—Mental Qualities—Cannibalism—The African Cannibal Zone—Arts and Industries—High Appreciation of Pictorial Art—Sense of Humour.

CONSPECTUS OF SUDANESE NEGROES.

Present Range. *Africa south of the Sahara, less*
Distribution in *Abyssinia, Galla, Somali and Masai lands ;*
Past and *Tripolitana, Mauritania and Egypt sporadically ;*
Present Times. *several of the southern United States ; West Indies ; Guiana ; parts of Brazil and Peru.*

Hair, *always black, rather short, and crisp, frizzly or woolly, flat in transverse section ;* **skin-colour,** *very dark*
brown or chocolate and blackish, never quite
Physical *black ;* **skull,** *generally dolichocephalous (index*
Characters. *72) ;* **jaws,** *prognathous ;* **cheek-bone,** *rather small, moderately retreating, rarely prominent ;* **nose,** *very*

broad at base, flat, small, platyrrhine; **eyes,** *large, round, prominent, black with yellowish cornea;* **stature,** *usually tall, 1.78 m. (5 ft. 10 in.);* **lips,** *often tumid and everted;* **arms,** *disproportionately long;* **legs,** *slender with small calves;* **feet,** *broad, flat, with low instep and larkspur heel.*

Temperament, *sensous, indolent, improvident; fitful, passionate and cruel, though often affectionate and faithful; little sense of dignity, and slight* Mental self-consciousness, hence easy acceptance of yoke Characters. *of slavery; musical.*

Speech, *almost everywhere in the agglutinating state, generally with suffixes.*

Religion, *anthropomorphic; spirits endowed with human attributes, mostly evil and more powerful than man; ancestry-worship, fetishism, and witchcraft very prevalent; human sacrifices to the dead a common feature.*

Culture, *low; cannibalism formerly rife, perhaps universal, still general in some regions; no science or letters; arts and industries confined mainly to agriculture, pottery, woodcarving, weaving, and metallurgy; no perceptible progress anywhere except under the influence of higher races.*

West Sudanese : *Wolof; Mandingan; Felup; Timni; Kru; Sierra Leonese; Liberian; Tshi, Ewe,* Main [1] *and Yoruba; Ibo; Efik; Borgu; Mossi.* Divisions.

Central Sudanese : *Songhai; Hausa; Mosgu; Kanembu; Kanuri; Baghirmi; Yedina.*

East Sudanese : *Maba; Fúr; Nuba; Shilluk; Dinka; Bari; Abaka; Bongo; Mangbattu; Zandeh; Momfu: Basé; Barea.*

From the anthropological standpoint Africa falls into two distinct sections, where the highest (Caucasic) and the lowest (Negro) divisions of mankind have been con- The Negro-terminous throughout all known time. Mutual Caucasic encroachments and interpenetrations have prob- " Great Divide." ably been continuous, and indeed are still going on. Yet so marked is the difference between the two groups, and such is the tenacity with which each clings to its proper domain, that, without any very distinct geographical frontiers, the ethnological parting line may still be detected. Obliterated at one

[1] For a tentative classification of African tribes see T. A. Joyce, Art. " Africa : Ethnology," *Ency. Brit.* 1910, p. 329.

or two points, and at others set back always in favour of the higher division, it may be followed from the Atlantic coast along the coast of the Senegal river east by north to the great bend of the Niger at Timbuktu ; then east by south to Lake Chad, beyond which it runs nearly due east to Khartum, at the confluence of the White and Blue Niles.

From this point the now isolated Negro groups (Basé and Barea), on the northern slope of the Abyssinian plateau, show that the original boundary was at first continued still east to the Red Sea at or about Massowa. But for many ages the line appears to have been deflected from Khartum along the White Nile south to the Sobat confluence, then continuously south-eastwards round by the Sobat Valley to the Albert Nyanza, up the Somerset Nile to the Victoria Nyanza, and thence with a considerable southern bend round Masailand eastwards to the Indian Ocean at the equator.

All the land north of this irregular line belongs to the Hamito-Semitic section of the Caucasic division, all south of it **The Negro Domain.** to the western (African) section of the Ulotrichous division. Throughout this region—which comprises the whole of Sudan from the Atlantic to the White Nile, and all south of Sudan except Abyssinia, Galla, Somali and Masai lands—the African Negro, clearly distinguished from the other main groups by the above summarised physical [1] and mental qualities, largely predominates everywhere and in many places exclusively. The route by which he probably reached these intertropical lands, where he may be regarded as practically indigenous, has been indicated in *Ethnology*, Chs. X. and XI.

As regards the date of this occupation, nothing can be clearly proved. " The history of Africa reaches back but a **Negro Origins.** short distance, except, of course, as far as the lower Nile Valley and Roman Africa is concerned ; elsewhere no records exist, save tribal traditions, and these only relate to very recent events. Even archaeology, which can often sketch the main outlines of a people's history, is here practically powerless, owing to the insufficiency of

---

[1] Graphically summed up in the classical description of the Negress :
" Afra genus, totâ patriam testante figurâ,
Torta comam labroque tumens, et fusca colorem,
Pectore lata, jacens mammis, compressior alvo,
Cruribus exilis, spatiosâ prodiga plantâ."

data. It is true that stone implements of palaeolithic and neolithic types are found sporadically in the Nile Valley,[1] Somaliland, on the Zambesi, in Cape Colony and the northern portions of the Congo Free State, as well as in Algeria and Tunisia ; but the localities are far too few and too widely separated to warrant the inference that they are to be in any way connected. Moreover, where stone implements are found they are, as a rule, very near, even actually on, the surface of the earth," and they are rarely, if ever, found in association with bones of extinct animals. " Nothing occurs resembling the regular stratification of Europe, and consequently no argument based on geological grounds is possible." [2] The exceptions are the lower Nile and Zambesi where true palaeoliths have been found not only on the surface (which in this case is not inconsistent with great antiquity) but also in stratified gravel. Implements of palaeolithic *type* are doubtless common, and may be compared to Chellean, Mousterian and even Solutrian specimens,[3] but primitive culture is not necessarily pleistocene. Ancient forms persisted in Egypt down to the historic period, and even patination is no sure test of age, so until further evidence is found the antiquity of man in Africa must remain undecided.[4]

Yet since some remote if undated epoch the specialised Negro type, as depicted on the Egyptian monuments some thousands of years ago,[5] has everywhere been maintained with striking uniformity. " Within this wide domain of the black Negro there is a remarkably general similarity of type. . . . If you took a Negro from the Gold Coast of West Africa and passed him off amongst a number of Nyasa natives, and if he were not remarkably distinguished from them by dress or tribal marks, it would not be easy to pick him out." [6]

Persistence of the Negro Type.

Nevertheless considerable differences are perceptible to

---

[1] See H. R. Hall, papers and references in *Man*, 19, 1905.

[2] T. A. Joyce, " Africa : Ethnology," *Ency. Brit.* 1910, I. 327.

[3] J. P. Johnson, *The Prehistoric Period in South Africa*, 1912.

[4] See H. H. Johnston, " A Survey of the Ethnography of Africa," *Journ. Roy. Anthr. Inst.* XLIII. 1913.

[5] The skeleton found by Hans Reck at Oldoway in 1914 and claimed by him to be of Pleistocene age exhibits all the typical Negro features, including the filed teeth, characteristic of East African negroes at the present day, but the geological evidence is imperfect.

[6] H. H. Johnston, *British Central Africa*, 1897, p. 393.

the practised eye, and the contrasts are sufficiently marked
to justify ethnologists in treating the *Sudanese*

Two Main Sections : Su-danese and Bantus. and the *Bantu* as two distinct subdivisions of
the family. In both groups the relatively full-
blood natives are everywhere very much alike,
and the contrasts are presented chiefly amongst the mixed or
Negroid populations. In Sudan the disturbing elements are
both Hamitic (Berbers and Tuaregs) and Semitic (Arabs) ;
while in Bantuland they are mainly Hamitic (Galla) in all the
central and southern districts, and Arabs on the eastern seaboard from the equator to Sofala beyond the Zambesi. To
the varying proportions of these several ingredients may
perhaps be traced the often very marked differences observable
on the one hand between such Sudanese peoples as the Wolof,
Mandingans, Hausa, Nubians, Zandeh,[1] and Mangbattu, and
on the other between all these and the Swahili, Baganda,
Zulu-Xosa, Be-Chuana, Ova-Herero and some other Negroid
Bantu.

But the distinction is based on social, linguistic, and
cultural, as well as on physical grounds, so that, as at present
constituted, the Sudanese and Bantu really constitute two
tolerably well-defined branches of the Negro

Contrasts and Analogies. family. Thanks to Muhammadan influences,
the former have attained a much higher level of
culture. They cultivate not only the alimentary but also the
economic plants, such as cotton and indigo ; they build stone
dwellings, walled towns, substantial mosques and minarets ;
they have founded powerful states, such as those of the
Hausa and Songhai, of Ghana and Bornu, with written
records going back a thousand years, although these historical
peoples are all without exception half-breeds, often with more
Semitic and Hamitic than Negro blood in their veins.

No such cultured peoples are anywhere to be found in
Bantuland except on the east coast, where the " Moors "
founded great cities and flourishing marts centuries before the
appearance of the Portuguese in the eastern seas. Among
the results of the gold trade with these coastal settlements
may be classed the Zimbabwe monuments and other ruins
explored by Theodore Bent in the mining districts south of

[1] Zandeh is the name usually given to the groups of tribes akin to Nilotics,
but probably with Fulah element, which includes the *Azandeh* or Niam Niam,
Makaraka, Mangbattu and many others. Cf. T. A. Joyce, *loc. cit.* p. 329.

the Zambesi. But in all the Negro lands free from foreign influences no true culture has ever been developed, and here cannibalism, witchcraft, and sanguinary " customs " are often still rife, or have been but recently suppressed by the direct action of European administrations.

Numberless authorities have described the Negro as unprogressive, or, if left to himself, incapable of progress in his present physical environment. Sir H. H. Johnston, who knows him well, goes much further, and speaks of him as a fine animal who, "in his wild state, exhibits a stunted mind and a dull content with his surroundings, which induces mental stagnation, cessation of all upward progress, and even retrogression towards the brute. In some respects I think the tendency of the Negro for several centuries past has been an actual retrograde one." [1]

There is one point in which the Bantu somewhat unaccountably compare favourably with the Sudanese. In all other regions the spread of culture has tended to bring about linguistic unity, as we see in the Hellenic world, where all the old idioms were gradually absorbed in the " common dialect " of the Byzantine empire, again in the Roman empire, where Latin became the universal speech of the West, and lastly in the Muhammadan countries, where most of the local tongues have nearly everywhere, except in Sudan, disappeared before the Arabic, Persian, and Turkish languages.

Sudanese and Bantu Linguistic Areas.

But in Negroland the case is reversed, and here the less cultured Bantu populations all, without any known exception, speak dialects of a single mother-tongue, while the greatest linguistic confusion prevails amongst the semi-civilised as well as the savage peoples of Sudan.

Although the Bantu language may, as some suppose,[2] have originated in the north and spread southwards to the Congo, Zambesi, and Limpopo basins, it cannot now be even remotely affiliated to any one of the numerous distinct forms of speech current in the Sudanese domain. Hence to allow time for its

---

[1] *British Central Africa*, p. 472. But see R. E. Dennett, *At the Back of the Black Man's Mind*, 1906, and A. G. Leonard, *The Lower Niger and its Tribes*, 1906, for African mentality.

[2] For theories of Bantu migrations see H. H. Johnston, *George Grenfell and the Congo*, 1908, and " A Survey of the Ethnography of Africa," *Journ. Roy. Anthr. Soc.* XLIII. 1913, p. 391 ff. Also F. Stuhlmann, *Handwerk und Industrie in Ostafrika*, 1910, p. 138 f., 147, with map, Pl. I. B. For the date see p. 92.

diffusion over half the continent, the initial movement must be assigned to an extremely remote epoch, and a corresponding period of great duration must be postulated for the profound linguistic disintegration that is everywhere witnessed in the region between the Atlantic and Abyssinia. Here agglutination, both with prefixed and postfixed particles, is the prevailing morphological order, as in the Mandingan, Fulah, Nubian, Dinkan, and Mangbattu groups. But every shade of transition is also presented between true agglutination and inflection of the Hamito-Semitic types, as in Hausa, Kanuri, Kanem, Dasa or Southern and Teda or Northern Tibu.[1]

Elsewhere, and especially in Upper Guinea, the originally agglutinating tongues have developed on lines analogous to those followed by Tibetan, Burmese, Chinese, and Otomi in other continents, with corresponding results. Thus the Tshi, Ewe, and Yoruba, surviving members of a now extinct stock-language, formerly diffused over the whole region between Cape Palmas and the Niger Delta, have become so burdened with monosyllabic homophones (like-sounding monosyllables), that to indicate their different meanings several distinguishing tones have been evolved, exactly as in the Indo-Chinese group. In Ewe (Slave Coast) the root *do*, according as it is toned may mean to put, let go, tell, kick, be sad, join, change, grow big, sleep, prick, or grind. So great are the ravages of phonetic decay, that new expedients have been developed to express quite simple ideas, as in Tshi (Gold Coast) *addanmu*, room (*addan* house, *mu* interior) ; *akwancherifo*, a guide (*akwan* road, *cheri* to show, *fo* person) ; *ensahtsiabah*, finger (*ensah* hand, *tsia* small, *abbah* child = hand's-little-child) ; but middle-finger = " hand's-little-chief " (*ensahtsiahin*, where *ehin* chief takes the place of *abbah* child).[2]

Common both to Sudanese and Bantus, especially about the western borderlands (Upper Guinea, Cameruns, etc.) is the " drum-language," which affords a striking illustration of the Negro's musical faculty.

The " Drum Language."

" Two or three drums are usually used together, each producing a different note, and they are played either with the fingers or with two sticks. The lookers-on generally beat time by clapping the hands. To a European, whose

---

[1] Even a tendency to polysynthesis occurs, as in Vei, and in Yoruba, where the small-pox god *Shakpanna* is made up of the three elements *shan* to plaster, *kpa* to kill, and *enia* a person = one who kills a person by plastering him (with pustules).

[2] The Nilotic languages are to a considerable extent tonic.

ear and mind are untrained for this special faculty, the rhythm of a drum expresses nothing beyond a repetition of the same note at different intervals of time ; but to a native it expresses much more.   To him the drum can and does speak, the sounds produced from it forming words, and the whole measure or rhythm a sentence.   In this way, when company drums are being played at an *ehsádu* (palaver), they are made to express and convey to the bystanders a variety of meanings. In one measure they abuse the men of another company, stigmatising them as fools and cowards ; then the rhythm changes, and the gallant deeds of their own company are extolled.   All this, and much more, is conveyed by the beating of drums, and the native ear and mind, trained to select and interpret each beat, is never at fault.   The language of drums is as well understood as that which they use in their daily life.   Each chief has his own call or motto, sounded by a particular beat of his drums.   Those of Amankwa Tia, the Ashanti general who fought against us in the war of 1873–4, used to say *Pĭrĭhūh*, hasten.   Similar mottoes are also expressed by means of horns, and an entire stranger in the locality can at once translate the rhythm into words." [1]

Similar contrasts and analogies will receive due illustration in the detailed account here following of the several more representative Sudanese groups.

West Sudanese.

Wolofs. Throughout its middle and lower course the Senegal river, which takes its name from the Zenaga Berbers, forms the ethnical " divide " between the Hamites and the Sudanese Negroes.   The latter are here represented by the Wolofs, who with the kindred *Jolofs* and *Serers* occupy an extensive territory between the Senegal and the Gambia rivers.   Whether the term " Wolof " means " Talkers," as if they alone were gifted with the faculty of speech, or " Blacks " in contrast to the neighbouring " Red " Fulahs, both interpretations are fully justified by these Senegambians, at once the very blackest and amongst the most garrulous tribes in the

[1] A. B. Ellis, *The Tshi-speaking Peoples*, etc., 1887, pp. 327–8. Only one European, Herr R. Betz, long resident amongst the Dualas of the Cameruns district, has yet succeeded in mastering the drum language ; he claims to understand nearly all that is drummed and is also able to drum himself. (*Athenaeum,* May 7, 1898, p. 611.)

whole of Africa. The colour is called "ebony," and they are commonly spoken of as "Blacks of the Black." They are also very tall even for Negroes, and the Serers especially may claim to be "the Patagonians of the Old World," men six feet six inches high and proportionately muscular being far from rare in the coast districts about St Louis and Dakar.

Their language, which is widespread throughout Sene-gambia, may be taken as a typical Sudanese form of speech, unlike any other in its peculiar agglutinative **Primitive Wolof Speech.** structure, and unaffected even in its vocabulary by the Hamitic which has been current for ages on the opposite bank of the Senegal. A remarkable feature is the so-called "article," always postfixed and subject to a two-fold series of modifications, first in accordance with the initial consonant of the noun, for which there are six possible consonantal changes (*w, m, b, d, s, g*), and then according as the object is present, near, not near, and distant, for which there are again four possible vowel changes (*i, u, o, a*), or twenty-four altogether, a tremendous redundancy of useless variants as compared with the single English form *the*. Thus this Protean particle begins with *b, d* or *w* to agree with *báye*, father, *digene*, woman, or *fos*, horse, and then becomes *bi, bu, bo, ba* ; *di, du* etc. ; *wi, wu* etc. to express the presence and the varying distances of these objects : *báye-bi*=father-the-here ; *báye-bu*=father-the-there ; *báye-bo*=father-the-yonder ; *báye-bá*=father-the-away in the distance.

All this is curious enough ; but the important point is that it probably gives us the clue to the enigmatic alliterative system of the Bantu languages as explained in *Ethnology*, p. 273, the position of course being reversed. Thus as in Zulu *in-* kose requires *en-* kulu, so in Wolof *baye* requires *bi*, *dig*ene *di*, and so on. There are other indications that the now perfected Bantu grew out of analogous but less developed processes still prevalent in the Sudanese tongues.

Equally undeveloped is the Wolof process of making earthenware, as observed by M. F. Regnault amongst the natives brought to Paris for the Exhibition of **Primitive Wolof Pottery.** 1895. He noticed how one of the women utilised a somewhat deep bowl resting on the ground in such a way as to be easily spun round by the hand, thus illustrating the transition between hand-made and turned pottery. Kneading a lump of clay, and thrusting it into the bowl, after sprinkling the sides with some black dust to prevent sticking, she made a hollow in the mass, enlarging and pressing it against the bowl with the back of the fingers bent in, the hand being all the time kept in a vertical position. At the same time the bowl was spun round with the left palm, this movement combined with the pressure exerted by the right hand causing the sides of the vessel to rise and take shape. When high enough it was finished off by thickening the clay to make a rim. This was held in the right hand and made fast to the mouth of the vessel by the friction caused by again turning the bowl with the left hand. This transitional process is frequently met with in Africa.[1]

Most of the Wolofs profess themselves Muhammadans, the rest Catholics, while all alike are heathen at heart ; only the former have charms with texts from the Koran which they cannot read, and the latter medals and scapulars of the " Seven Dolours " or of the Trinity, which they cannot understand. Many old rites still flourish, the household gods are not forgotten, and for the lizard, most popular of tutelar deities, the customary milk-bowl is daily replenished. Glimpses are thus afforded of the totemic system which still survives in a modified form amongst the Be-Chuana, the Mandingans, and several other African peoples, but has elsewhere mostly died out in Negroland. The infantile ideas associated with plant and animal totem tokens have been left far behind, when a people like the Serers have arrived at such a lofty conception as Takhar, god of justice, or even the more materialistic Tiurakh, god of wealth, although the latter may still be appealed to for success in nefarious projects which he himself might scarcely be expected to countenance. But the harmony between religious and ethical thought has scarcely yet been reached even amongst some of the higher races.

Mandingans. In the whole of Sudan there is scarcely a more numerous or widespread people than the Mandingans, who—with their endless ramifications, *Kassonké, Jallonké, Soninké, Bambara, Vei* and many others—occupy most of the region between the Atlantic and the Joliba (Upper Niger) basin, as far south as about 9° N. latitude. Within these limits it is

Religious Notions.

Mandingan Groups, Culture and Industries.

[1] Cf. H. S. Harrison, *Handbook to the cases illustrating stages in the evolution of the Domestic Arts.* Part II. Horniman Museum and Library. Forest Hill, S.E.

often difficult to say who are, or who are not members of this great family, whose various branches present all the transitional shades of physical type and culture grades between the true pagan Negro and the Muhammadan Negroid Sudanese.

Even linguistic unity exists only to a limited extent, as the numerous dialects of the Mandé stock-language have often diverged so greatly as to constitute independent tongues quite unintelligible to the neighbouring tribes. The typical Mandingans, however—Faidherbe's Malinka-Soninké group —may be distinguished from the surrounding populations by their more softened features, broader forehead, larger nose, fuller beard, and lighter colour. They are also distinguished by their industrious habits and generally higher culture, being rivalled by few as skilled tillers of the soil, weavers, and workers in iron and copper. They thus hold much the same social position in the west that the Hausa do in the central region beyond the Niger, and the French authorities think that " they are destined to take a position of ever increasing importance in the pacified Sudan of the future." [1]

Thus history brings about its revenges, for the Mandingans proper of the Kong plateau may fairly claim, despite their late servitude to the Fulah conquerors and their present ready acceptance of French rule, to be a historical people with a not inglorious record of over 1000 years, as founders of the two great empires of Melle and Guiné, and of the more recent states of Moasina, Bambara, Kaarta, Kong, and others about the water-parting between the head-streams of the Niger, and the rivers flowing south to the Gulf of Guinea. Here is the district of Manding, which is the original home of the *Manding'ké*, *i.e.* " People of Manding," as they are generally called, although *Mandé* appears to be the form used by themselves.[2] Here also was the famous city of Mali

---

[1] E. T. Hamy, " Les Races Nègres," in *L'Anthropologie*, 1897, p. 257 sq.

[2] " Chaque fois que j'ai demandé avec intention à un Mandé, ' Es-tu Peul, Mossi, Dafina ? ' il me répondait invariablement, ' *Je suis Mandé.*' C'est pourquoi, dans le cours de ma relation, j'ai toujours désigné ce peuple par le nom de *Mandé*, qui est son vrai nom." (L. G. Binger, *Du Niger au Golfe de Guinée*, 1892, Vol. II. p. 373.) At p. 375 this authority gives the following subdivisions of the Mandé family, named from their respective *tenné* (idol, fetish, totem):

    1. *Bamba*, the crocodile : *Bammana*, not *Bambara*, which means kafir or infidel, and is applied only to the non-Moslem Mandé groups.

    2. *Mali*, the hippopotamus : *Mali'nké*, including the Kagoros and the Tagwas.

    3. *Sama*, the elephant : *Sama'nké*.

    4. *Sa*, the snake : *Sa-mokho*.

Of each there are several sub-groups, while the surrounding peoples call them

or Melle, from which the Upper Niger group take the name of *Mali'nké*, in contradistinction to the *Soni'nké* of the Senegal river, the *Jalo'nké* of Futa-Jallon, and the *Bamana* of Bambara, these being the more important historical and cultured groups.

According to native tradition and the annals of Ahmed Bábá, rescued from oblivion by Barth,[1] the first Mandingan state of Guiné (Ghána, Ghánata), a name still surviving in the vague geographical term "Guinea," goes back to pre-Muhammadan times. Wakaya-mangha, its legendary founder, is supposed to have flourished 300 years before the Hejira, at which date twenty-two kings had already reigned. Sixty years after that time the Moslem Arabs or Berbers are said to have already reached West Sudan, where they had twelve mosques in Ghána, first capital of the empire, and their chief stronghold till the foundation of Jinni on the Upper Niger (1043 A.D.).

History.

The Guiné and Mali Empires.

Two centuries later (1235–60) the centre of the Mandingan rule was transferred to Mali, which under the great king Mansa-Musa (1311–31) became the most powerful Sudanese state of which there is any authentic record. For a time it included nearly the whole of West Sudan, and a great part of the western Sahara, beside the Songhai State with its capital Gogo, and Timbuktu. Mansa-Musa, who, in the language of the chronicler, "wielded a power without measure or limits," entered into friendly relations with the emperor of Morocco, and made a famous pilgrimage to Mecca, the splendours of which still linger in the memory of the Mussulman populations throughout whose lands the interminable procession wound its way. He headed 60,000 men of arms, says Ahmed Bábá, and wherever he passed he was preceded by 500 slaves, each bearing a gold stick weighing 500 mitkals (14 lbs.), the whole representing a money value of about £4,000,000 (?). The people of Cairo and Mecca were dazzled by his wealth and munificence; but during the journey a great part of his followers were seized by a painful malady called in their language *tuat*, and this word still lives in the Oasis of Tuat, where most of them perished.

all collectively *Wakoré, Wangara, Sakhersi*, and especially *Diula*. Attention to this point will save the reader much confusion in consulting Barth, Caillié, and other early books of travel.

[1] *Travels*, Vol. IV. p. 579 sqq.

Even after the capture of Timbuktu by the Tuaregs (1433), Mali long continued to be the chief state in West Nigritia, and carried on a flourishing trade, especially in slaves and gold. But this gold was still supposed to come from the earlier kingdom of Guiné, which word consequently still remains associated with the precious metal in the popular belief. About the year 1500 Mali was captured by the Songhai king, Omar Askia, after which the empire fell to pieces, and its memory now survives only in the ethnical term *Mali'nké*.

Felups. From the semi-civilised Muhammadan negroid Mandingans to the utterly savage full-blood Negro Felups the transition is abrupt, but instructive. In other regions the heterogeneous ethnical groups crowded into upland valleys, as in the Caucasus, have been called the " sweepings of the plains." But in West Sudan there are no great ranges towering above the lowlands, and even the " Kong Mountains " of school geographies have now been wiped out by L. G. Binger.[1] Hence the rude aborigines of the inland plateau, retreating before the steady advance of Islám, found no place of refuge till they reached the indented fjord-like Atlantic seaboard, where many still hold their ground. This is the explanation of the striking contrasts now witnessed between the interior and so many parts of the West coast ; on the one hand powerful political organisations with numerous, more or less homogeneous, and semi-civilised negroid populations, on the other an infinite tangle of ethnical and linguistic groups, all alike weltering in the sheerest savagery, or in grades of barbarism even worse than the wild state.

Contrasts between the Inland and Coast Peoples.

Even the *Felups*, whose territory now stretches from the Gambia to the Cacheo, but formerly reached the Geba and the Bissagos Islands, do not form a single group. Originally the name of an obscure coast-tribe, the term Felup or Fulup has been extended by the Portuguese traders to all the surrounding peoples— *Ayamats, Jolas, Jigúshes, Vacas, Joats, Karons, Banyúns, Banjars, Fulúns, Bayots* and some others who amid much local diversity, presented a sufficiently general outward re- semblance to be regarded as a single people by the first

Felup Type and Mental Characters.

[1] " La chaîne des Montagnes de Kong n'a jamais existé que dans l'imagination de quelques voyageurs mal renseignés," *Du Niger au Golfe de Guinée*, 1892, I. p. 285.

European settlers. The Felups proper display the physical and mental characters of the typical Negro even in an exaggerated form—black colour, flat nose, wide nostrils, very thick and everted lips, red on the inner surface, stout muscular frame, correlated with coarse animal passions, crass ignorance, no arts, industry, or even tribal organisation, so that every little family group is independent and mostly in a state of constant feud with its neighbours. All go naked, armed with bow and arrow, and live in log huts which, though strongly built, are indescribably filthy.[1]

Mother-right frequently prevails, rank and property being transmitted in the female line. There is some notion of a superhuman being vaguely identified with the sky, the rain, wind or thunderstorm. But all live in extreme terror of the medicine-man, who is openly courted, but inwardly detested, so that whenever it can be safely done the tables are turned, the witch-doctor is seized and tortured to death.

Timni, Kru, Sierra-Leonese, Liberians. Somewhat similar conditions prevail all along the seaboard from Sierra Leone to, and beyond, Cape Palmas, disturbed or modified by the Liberian intruders from the North American plantations, and by the slaves rescued in the thirties and forties by the British cruisers and brought to Sierra Leone, where their descendants now live in settled communities under European influences. These " coloured " citizens of Sierra Leone and Liberia, who are so often the butt of cheap ridicule, and are themselves perhaps too apt to scorn the kindred " niggers " of the bush, have to be carefully distinguished from these true aborigines who have never been wrenched from their natural environment.

In Sierra Leone the chief aboriginal groups on the coastlands are the *Timni* of the Rokelle river, flanked north and south by two branches of the *Bulams*, and still further south the *Gallinas*, *Veys* and *Golas*; in the interior the *Lokkos*, *Limbas*, *Konos*, and *Kussas*, with *Kurankos*, *Mendis*, *Hubus*, and other Mandingans and Fulahs everywhere in the Hinterland.

Of all these the most powerful during the British occupation have always been the Timni (Timani, Temné), who sold to the English the Peninsula on which now stands Freetown, but afterwards crying off the bargain, repeatedly tried to drive the white and coloured

Timni Beliefs.

[1] Bertrand-Bocandé, " Sur les Floups ou Féloups," in *Bul. Soc. de Géogr.* 1849.

intruders into the sea. They are a robust people of softened Negro type, and more industrious farmers than most of the other natives. Like the Wolofs they believe in the virtue both of Christian and Moslem amulets, but have hitherto lent a deaf ear to the preachers of both these religions. Nevertheless the Protestant missionaries have carefully studied the Timni language, which possesses an oral literature rich in legends, proverbs, and folklore.[1]

The Timni district is a chief centre of the so-called *porro* fraternity,[2] a sort of secret society or freemasonry widely
West African Freemasonry. diffused throughout the coastlands, and possessing its own symbols, skin markings, passwords, and language. It presents curious points of analogy with the brotherhoods of the Micronesian islanders, but appears to be even more potent for good and evil, a veritable religious and political state within the state. " When their mandates are issued all wars and civil strife must cease, a general truce is established, and bloodshed stopped, offending communities being punished by bands of armed men in masks. Strangers cannot enter the country unless escorted by a member of the guild, who is recognised by passwords, symbolic gestures, and the like. Their secret rites are celebrated at night in the depths of the forest, all intruders being put to death or sold as slaves."[3]

In studying the social conditions prevalent amongst the Sierra Leonese proper, it should be remembered that they
The Sierra Leonese. are sprung, not only from representatives of almost every tribe along the seaboard, and even in the far interior, but also to a large extent from the freedmen and runaways of Nova Scotia and London, besides many maroons of Jamaica, who were settled here under the auspices of the Sierra Leone Company towards the close of the eighteenth and beginning of the nineteenth century. Others also have in recent years been attracted to the settlements from the Timni and other tribes of the neighbouring districts. The Sierra Leonese are consequently not

---

[1] A full account of this literature will be found in the Rev. C. F. Schlenker's valuable work, *A Collection of Temne Traditions, Fables and Proverbs*, London, 1861. Here is given the curious explanation of the tribal name, from *o-tem*, an old man, and *né*, himself, because, as they say, the Temné people will exist for ever.

[2] There is also a sisterhood—the *bondo*—and the two societies work so far in harmony that any person expelled from the one is also excluded from the other.

[3] Reclus, Keane's English ed., XII. p. 203.

themselves a tribe, nor yet a people, but rather a people in course of formation under the influence of a new environment and of a higher culture.   An immediate consequence of such a sudden aggregation of discordant elements was the loss of all the native tongues, and the substitution of English as the common medium of intercourse.   But English is the language of a people standing on the very highest plane of culture, and could not therefore be properly assimilated by the *disjecta membra* of tribes at the lowest rung of the social ladder. The resultant form of speech may be called ludicrous, so ludicrous that the Sierra Leonese version of the New Testament had to be withdrawn from circulation as verging almost on the blasphemous.[1]

It has also to be considered that all the old tribal relations were broken up, while an attempt was made to merge these waifs and strays in a single community based on social conditions to which each and all were utter strangers.   It is not therefore surprising that the experiment has not proved a complete success, and that the social relations in Sierra Leone leave something to be desired.   Although the freedmen and the rescued captives received free gifts of land, their dislike for the labours of the field induced many to abandon their holdings, and take to hucklestering and other more pleasant pursuits.   Hence their descendants almost monopolise the petty traffic and even the " professions " in Freetown and the other colonial settlements.   Although accused of laziness and dishonesty, they have displayed a considerable degree of industrial as well as commercial enterprise, and the Sierra Leone craftsmen— smiths, mechanics, carpenters, builders—enjoy a good reputation in all the coast towns.   All are Christians of various denominations, and even show a marked predilection for the " ministry."   Yet below the surface the old paganism still slumbers, and vodoo practices, as in the West Indies and some of the Southern States, are still heard of.

Morality also is admittedly at a low ebb, and it is curious to note that this has in part been attributed to the freedom

---

[1] " Da Njoe Testament, translated into the Negro-English Language by the Missionaries of the Unitas Fratum," Brit. and For. Bible Soc., London, 1829. Here is a specimen quoted by Ellis from *The Artisan* of Sierra Leone, Aug. 4, 1886, " Those who live in ceiled houses love to hear the pit-pat of the rain overhead whilst those whose houses leak are the subjects of restlessness and anxiety, not to mention the chances of catching cold *that is so frequent a source of leaky roofs.*"

enjoyed under the British administration. "They have passed from the sphere of native law to that of British law, which is brought to this young community like an article of ready-made clothing. Is it a wonder that the clothes do not fit? Is it a wonder that kings and chiefs around Sierra Leone, instead of wishing their people to come and see how well we do things, dread for them to come to this colony on account of the danger to their morals? In passing into this colony, they pass into a liberty which to them is license."[1]

An experiment of a somewhat different order, but with much the same negative results, has been tried by the well-
The Liberians. meaning founders of the Republic of Liberia. Here also the bulk of the "civilised aristocrats" are descended of emancipated plantation slaves, a first consignment of whom was brought over by a philanthropic American society in 1820-22. The idea was to start them well in life under the fostering care of their white guardians, and then leave them to work out their own redemption in their own way. All control was accordingly withdrawn in 1848, and since then the settlement has constituted an absolutely independent Negro state in the enjoyment of complete self-government. Progress of a certain material kind was undoubtedly made. The original "free citizens" increased from 8000 in 1850 to perhaps 20,000 in 1898,[2] and the central administration, modelled on that of the United States, maintained some degree of order among the surrounding aborigines, estimated at some two million within the limits of the Republic.

But these aborigines have not benefited perceptibly by contact with their "civilised" neighbours, who themselves stand at much the same level intellectually and morally as their repatriated forefathers. Instead of attending to the proper administration of the Republic, the "Weegee," as they are called, have constituted themselves into two factions, the "coloured" or half-breeds, and the full-blood Negroes who, like the "Blancos" and "Neros" of some South American States, spend most of their time in a perpetual struggle for

---

[1] Right Rev. E. G. Ingham (Bishop of Sierra Leone), *Sierra Leone after a Hundred Years*, London, 1894, p. 294. Cf. H. C. Lukach, *A Bibliography of Sierra Leone*, 1911, and T. J. Alldridge, *A Transformed Colony*, 1910.

[2] This increase, however, appears to be due to a steady immigration from the Southern States, but for which the Liberians proper would die out, or become absorbed in the surrounding native populations.

office. All are of course intensely patriotic, but their patriotism takes a wrong direction, being chiefly manifested in their insolence towards the English and other European traders on the coast, and in their supreme contempt for the " stinking bush-niggers," as they call the surrounding aborigines. In 1909 internal and external difficulties led to the appointment of a Commission by President Roosevelt with the result that the American Government took charge of the finances, military organisation, agriculture and boundary questions, besides arranging for a loan of £400,000. The able administration of President Barclay, a pure-blooded Negro, though not of Liberian ancestry, is perhaps the happiest augury for the future of the Republic.[1]

The *Krus* (Kroomen, Krooboys),[2] whose numerous hamlets are scattered along the coast from below Monrovia nearly to Cape Palmas, are assuredly one of the most interesting people in the whole of Africa. The Krumen. Originally from the interior, they have developed in their new homes a most un-African love of the sea, hence are regularly engaged as crews by the European skippers plying along those insalubrious coastlands.

In this service, in which they are known by such nicknames as " Bottle-of-Beer," " Mashed-Potatoes," " Bubble-and-Squeak," " Pipe-of-Tobacco," and the like, their word may always be depended upon. But it is to be feared that this loyalty, which with them is a strict matter of business, has earned for them a reputation for other virtues to which they have little claim. Despite the many years that they have been in the closest contact with the missionaries and traders, they are still at heart the same brutal savages as ever. After each voyage they return to the native village to spend all their gains and pilferings in drunken orgies, and relapse generally into sheer barbarism till the next steamer rounds the neighbouring headland. " It is not a comfortable reflection," writes Bishop Ingham, whose testimony will not be suspected of bias, " as we look at this mob on our decks, that, if the ship chance to strike on a sunken rock and become unmanageable, they would rise to a man, and seize all they could lay hands on, cut the very rings off our fingers if

[1] H. H. Johnston, *Liberia*, 1906.
[2] Possibly the English word " crew," but more probably an extension of *Kraoh*, the name of a tribe near Settra-kru, to the whole group.

they could get them in no other way, and generally loot the ship. Little has been done to Christianise these interesting, hard-working, cheerful, but ignorant and greedy people, who have so long hung on the skirts of civilisation." [1]

It is only fair to the Kru to say that this unflattering picture of them stands alone. "There is but one man of all of us who have visited West Africa who has not paid a tribute to the Kruboy's sterling qualities," says Miss Kingsley. Her opinion coincides with that of the old coasters based on life-long experience, and she waxes indignant at the ingratitude with which Kruboy loyalty is rewarded. "They have devoted themselves to us English, and they have suffered, laboured, fought, been massacred and so on with us generation after generation . . . Kruboys are, indeed, the backbone of white effort in West Africa." [2]

But the very worst "sweepings of the Sudanese plateau" seem to have gathered along the Upper Guinea Coast, occupied by the already mentioned *Tshi*, *Ewe*, and *Yoruba* groups. [3] They constitute three branches of one linguistic, and probably also of one ethnical family, of which, owing to their historic and ethnical importance, the reader may be glad to have here subjoined a somewhat complete tabulated scheme.

The Upper Guinea Peoples.

The *Ga* of the Volta delta are here bracketed with the Tshi because A. B. Ellis, our great authority on the Guinea peoples, [4] considers the two languages to be distantly connected. He also thinks there is a foundation of fact in the native traditions, which bring the dominant tribes—Ashanti, Fanti, Dahomi, Yoruba, Bini—from the interior to the coast districts at no very remote period. Thus it is recorded of

---

[1] *Sierra Leone after a Hundred Years*, p. 280.

[2] Mary H. Kingsley, *Travels in West Africa*, 1899, pp. 54–5.

[3] Since the establishment of British authority in Nigeria (1900 to 1907) much light has been thrown on ethnological problems. See among other works C. Partridge, *The Cross River Natives*, 1905 ; A. G. Leonard, *The Lower Niger and its Tribes*, 1906 ; A. J. N. Tremearne, *The Niger and the Western Sudan*, 1910, *The Tailed Head-Hunters of Nigeria*, 1912 ; R. E. Dennett, *Nigerian Studies*, 1910 ; E. D. Morel, *Nigeria, its People and its Problems*, 1911, besides the *Anthropological Reports* of N. W. Thomas, 1910, 1913, and papers by J. Parkinson in *Journ. Roy. Anthr. Inst.* xxxvi. 1906, xxxvii. 1907.

[4] The services rendered to African anthropology by this distinguished officer call for the fullest recognition, all the more that somewhat free and unacknowledged use has been made of the rich materials brought together in his classical works on *The Tshi-speaking Peoples* (1887), *The Ewe-speaking Peoples* (1890), and *The Yoruba-speaking Peoples* (1894).

the Ashanti and Fanti, now hereditary foes, that ages ago they formed one people who were reduced to the utmost distress during a long war with some inland power, perhaps the conquering Muhammadans of the Ghana or Mali empire. They were saved, however, some by eating of the *shan*, others of the *fan* plant, and of these words, with the verb di, " to eat," were made the tribal names *Shan-di*, *Fan-di*, now *Ashanti*, *Fanti*. The *seppiriba* plant, said to have been eaten by the Fanti, is still called *fan* when cooked.

Ashanti
Folklore.

TRIBES OF TSHI AND GA SPEECH *Gold Coast*	TRIBES OF EWE SPEECH *Slave Coast West*	TRIBES OF YORUBA SPEECH *Slave Coast East and Niger Delta*
Ashanti	Dahomi	Yoruba [1]
Safwhi	Eweawo	Ibadan
Denkera	Agotine	Ketu
Bekwai	Anfueh	Egba
Nkoranza	Krepe	Jebu
Adansi	Avenor	Remo
Assin	Awuna	Ode
Wassaw	Agbosomi	Ilorin
Ahanta	Aflao	Ijesa
Fanti	Ataklu	Ondo
Agona	Krikor	Mahin
Akwapim	Geng	Benin (Bini)
Akim	Attakpami	Kakanda
Akwamu	Aja	Wari
Kwao	Ewemi	Ibo [1]
Ga	Appa	Efik [1]

Other traditions refer to a time when all were of one speech, and lived in a far country beyond Salagha, open, flat, with little bush, and plenty of cattle and sheep, a tolerably accurate description of the inland Sudanese plateaux. But then came a red people, said to be the Fulahs, Muhammadans, who oppressed the blacks and drove them to take refuge in the forests. Here they thrived and multiplied, and after many vicissitudes they came down, down, until at last they reached the coast, with the waves rolling in, the white foam hissing and frothing on the beach, and thought it was all boiling water until some one touched it and found it was not hot, and so to this day they call the sea *Eh-huru den o nni*

---

[1] N. W. Thomas classifies Yoruba, Edo, Ibo, and Efik as four main stocks in the Western Sudanic language group. " In the Edo and Ibo stocks people only a few miles apart may not be able to communicate owing to diversity of language " (p. 141). *Anthropological Report of the Ibo-speaking Peoples of Nigeria*, Part I. 1913.

shew, " Boiling water not hot," but far inland the sea is still
" Boiling water." [1]

To A. B. Ellis we are indebted especially for the true
explanation of the much used and abused term *fetish*, as
applied to the native beliefs. It was of course
already known to be not an African but a Portuguese word,[2] meaning a charm, amulet, or even
witchcraft. But Ellis shows how it came to be wrongly
applied to all forms of animal and nature worship, and how
the confusion was increased by De Brosses' theory of a
primordial fetishism, and by his statement that it was impossible to conceive a lower form of religion than fetishism,
which might therefore be assumed to be the beginning of all
religion.[3]

Fetishism—its true inwardness.

On the contrary it represents rather an advanced stage, as
Ellis discovered after four or five years of careful observation
on the spot. A fetish, he tells us, is something tangible and
inanimate, which is believed to possess power in itself, and is
worshipped for itself alone. Nor can such an object be
picked up anywhere at random, as is commonly asserted, and
he adds that the belief " is arrived at only after considerable
progress has been made in religious ideas, when the older
form of religion becomes secondary and owes its existence to
the confusion of the tangible with the intangible, of the
material with the immaterial; to the belief in the indwelling
god being gradually lost sight of until the power originally
believed to belong to the god, is finally attributed to the
tangible and inanimate object itself."

But now comes a statement that may seem paradoxical to
most students of the evolution of religious ideas. We are
assured that fetishism thus understood is not specially or at
all characteristic of the religion of the Gold Coast natives,
who are in fact " remarkably free from it " and believe in
invisible intangible deities. Some of them may dwell in a
tangible inanimate object, popularly called a " fetish "; but
the idea of the indwelling god is never lost sight of, nor is

---

[1] *The Tshi-speaking Peoples*, p. 332 sq.
[2] *Feitiço*, whence also *feiticeira*, a witch, *feiticeria*, sorcery, etc., all from
feitiço, artificial, handmade, from Lat. *facio* and *factitius*.
[3] *Du Culte des Dieux Fétiches*, 1760. It is generally supposed that the word
was invented, or at least first introduced, by De Brosses; but Ellis shows that
this also is a mistake, as it had already been used by Bosman in his *Description
of Guinea*, London, 1705.

the object ever worshipped for its own sake.   True fetishism, the worship of such material objects and images, prevails, on the contrary, far more " amongst the Negroes of the West Indies, who have been christianised for more than half-a century, than amongst those of West Africa.   Hence the belief in Obeah, still prevalent in the West Indies, which formerly was a belief in indwelling spirits which inhabited certain objects, has now become a worship paid to tangible and inanimate objects, which of themselves are believed to possess the power to injure.   In Europe itself we find evidence amongst the Roman Catholic populations of the South, that fetishism is a corruption of a former *culte*, rather than a primordial faith.   The lower classes there have con- fused the intangible with the tangible, and believe that the images of the saints can both see, hear and feel.   Thus we find the Italian peasants and fishermen beat and ill-treat their images when their requests have not been complied with. . . . These appear to be instances of true fetishism." [1]

Another phase of religious belief in Upper Guinea is ancestry worship, which has here been developed to a degree unknown elsewhere.   As the departed have to Ancestry be maintained in the same social position beyond Worship and the grave that they enjoyed in this world, they the " Customs." must be supplied with slaves, wives, and attendants, each according to his rank.   Hence the institution of the so-called " customs," or anniversary feasts of the dead, accompanied by the sacrifice of human victims, regulated at first by the status and afterwards by the whim and caprice of chiefs and kings.   In the capitals of the more powerful states, Ashanti, Dahomey, Benin, the scenes witnessed at these sanguinary rites rivalled in horror those held in honour of the Aztec gods.   Details may here be dispensed with on a repulsive subject, ample accounts of which are accessible from many sources to the general reader.   In any case these atrocities teach no lesson, except that most religions have waded through blood to better things, unless arrested in mid-stream by the intervention of higher powers, as happily in Upper Guinea, where the human shambles of Kumassi, Abomeh, Benin and most other places have now been swept away.

[1] *The Tshi-speaking Peoples*, Ch. XII. p. 194 and *passim*.   See also R. H. Nassau, *Fetishism in West Africa*, 1904.

On the capture of Benin by the English in 1897 a rare and unexpected prize fell into the hands of ethnologists.

The Benin Bronzes.

Here was found a large assortment of carved ivories, woodwork, and especially a series of about 300 bronze and brass plates or panels with figures of natives and Europeans, armed and in armour, in full relief, all cast by the *cire perdue* process,[1] some barbaric, others, and especially a head in the round of a young negress, showing high artistic skill. Many of these remarkable objects are in the British Museum, where they have been studied by C. H. Read and O. M. Dalton,[2] who are evidently right in assigning the better class to the sixteenth century, and to the aid, if not the hand, of some Portuguese artificers in the service of the King of Benin. They add that " casting of an inferior kind continues down to the present time," and it may here be mentioned that armour has long been and is still worn by the cavalry, and even their horses, in the Muhammadan states of Central Sudan. " The chiefs (*Kashelláwa*) who serve as officers under the Sultan [of Bornu] and act as his bodyguard wear jackets of chain armour and cuirasses of coats of mail." [3] It is clear that metal casting in a large way has long been practised by the semi-civilised peoples of Sudan.

Within the great bend of the Niger the veil, first slightly raised by Barth in the middle of the nineteenth century,

The Mossi.

has now been drawn aside by L. G. Binger, F. D. Lugard and later explorers. Here the *Mossi, Borgu* and others have hitherto more or less successfully resisted the Moslem advance, and are consequently for the most part little removed from the savage state. Even the " Faithful " wear the cloak of Islám somewhat loosely, and the level of their culture may be judged from the case of the Imám of Diulasu, who pestered Binger for nostrums and charms against ailments, war, and misfortunes. What he wanted chiefly to know was the names of Abraham's two

---

[1] That is, from a wax mould destroyed in the casting. After the operation details were often filled in by chasing or executed in *repoussé* work.

[2] " Works of Art from Benin City," *Journ. Anthr. Inst.* February, 1898, p. 362 sq. See H. Ling Roth, *Great Benin, its Customs*, etc., 1903.

[3] A. Featherman, *Social History of Mankind*, The Nigritians, p. 281. See also Reclus, French ed., Vol. XII. p. 718 : " Les cavaliers portent encore la cuirasse comme au moyen âge. . . . Les chevaux sont recouverts de la même manière." In the mythical traditions of Buganda also there is reference to the fierce Wakedi warriors clad in " iron armour " (Ch. IV.). Cf. L. Frobenius, *The Voice of Africa*, II. 1913, pl. p. 608.

wives. "Tell me these," he would say, " and my fortune is made, for I dreamt it the other night ; you must tell me ; I really must have those names or I'm lost." [1]

In some districts the ethnical confusion is considerable, and when Binger arrived at the Court of the Mossi King, Baikary, he was addressed successively in Mossi, Hausa, Songhai, and Fulah, until at last it was discovered that Mandingan was the only native language he understood. Waghadugu, capital of the chief Mossi state, comprises several distinct quarters occupied respectively by Mandingans, Marengas (Songhai), Zang-wer'os (Hausas), Chilmigos (Fulahs), Mussulman and heathen Mossis, the whole population scarcely exceeding 5000. However, perfect harmony prevails, the Mossi themselves being extremely tolerant despite the long religious wars they have had to wage against the fanatical Fulahs and other Muhammadan aggressors.[2]

Religious indifference is indeed a marked characteristic of this people, and the case is mentioned of a nominal Mussulman prince who could even read and write, and say his prayers, but whose two sons "knew nothing at all," or, as we should say, were "Agnostics." One of them, however, it is fair to add, is claimed by both sides, the Moslems asserting that he says his prayers in secret, the heathens that he drinks *dolo* (palmwine), which of course no true believer is supposed ever to do.

African Agnostics.

CENTRAL SUDANESE

In Central Sudan, that is, the region stretching from the Niger to Wadai, a tolerably clean sweep has been made of the aborigines, except along the southern fringe and in parts of the Chad basin. For many centuries Islám has here been firmly established, and in Negroland Islám is synonymous with a greater or less degree of miscegenation. The native tribes who resisted the fiery Arab or Tuareg or Tibu proselytisers were for the most part either extirpated, or else driven to the

General Ethnical and Social Relations.

---

[1] *Du Niger au Golfe de Guinée*, 1892, I. p. 377.

[2] Early in the fourteenth century they were strong enough to carry the war into the enemy's camp and make more than one successful expedition against Timbuktu. At present the Mossi power is declining, and their territory has been parcelled out between the British and French Sudanese hinterlands.

southern uplands about the Congo-Chad water-parting. All who accepted the Koran became merged with the conquerors in a common negroid population, which supplied the new material for the development of large social communities and powerful political states.

Under these conditions the old tribal organisations were in great measure dissolved, and throughout its historic period of about a millennium Central Sudan is found mainly occupied by peoples gathered together in a small number of political systems, each with its own language and special institutions, but all alike accepting Islám as the State religion. Such are or were the Songhai empire, the Hausa States, and the kingdoms of Bornu with Kanem and Baghirmi, and these jointly cover the whole of Central Sudan as above defined.

Songhais.[1] How completely the tribe[2] has merged in the people[2] may be inferred from the mere statement that, although no longer an independent nation,[2] the negroid Songhais form a single ethnical group of about two million souls, all of one speech and one religion, and all distinguished by somewhat uniform physical and mental characters. This territory lies mainly about the borderlands between Sudan and the Sahara, stretching from Timbuktu east to the Asben oasis and along both banks of the Niger from Lake Debo round to the Sokoto confluence, and also at some points reaching as far as the Hombori hills within the great bend of the Niger.

Songhai Domain.

Here they are found in the closest connection with the Ireghenaten ("mixed") Tuaregs, and elsewhere with other Tuaregs, and with Arabs, Fulahs or Hausas,[3] so that exclusively Songhai communities are now somewhat rare. But the bulk of the race is still concentrated in Gurma and in the district between Gobo and Timbuktu, the two chief cities of the old Songhai empire.

They are a distinctly negroid people, presenting various

---

[1] Also *Sonrhay*, *gh* and *rh* being interchangeable throughout North Africa ; *Ghat* and *Rhat*, *Ghadames* and *Rhadames*, etc. In the mouth of an Arab the sound is that of the guttural ﻍ *ghain*, which is pronounced by the Berbers and Negroes somewhat like the Northumberland *burr*, hence usually transliterated by *rh* in non-Semitic words.

[2] It should be noticed that these terms are throughout used as strictly defined in *Eth.* Ch. I.

[3] Barth's account of Wulu (IV. p. 299), " inhabited by Tawárek slaves, who are *trilingues*, speaking Temáshight as well as Songhay and Fulfulde," is at present generally applicable, *mutatis mutandis*, to most of the Songhai settlements.

shades of intermixture with the surrounding Hamites and Semites, but generally of a very deep brown or Songhai Type and Temperament. blackish colour, with somewhat regular features and that peculiar long, black, and ringletty hair, which is so characteristic of Negro and Caucasic blends, as seen amongst the Trarsas and Braknas of the Senegal, the Bejas, Danakils, and many Abyssinians of the region between the Nile and the Red Sea. Barth, to whom we still owe the best account of this historical people, describes them as of a dull, morose temperament, the most unfriendly and churlish of all the peoples visited by him in Negroland.

This writer's suggestion that they may have formerly had relations with the Egyptians [1] has been revived in an exaggerated form by M. Félix Dubois, whose views Songhai Origins. have received currency in England through uncritical notices of his *Timbouctou la Mystérieuse* (Paris, 1897). But there is no "mystery" in the matter. The Songhai are a Sudanese people, whose exodus from Egypt is a myth, and whose Egyptian Theories. Kissur language, as it is called, has not the remotest connection with any form of speech known to have been at any time current in the Nile Valley.[2] Nor has it any evident affinities with any group of African tongues. H. H. Johnston regards the Songhai as the result of the mixing of "the Libyan section of the Hamitic peoples, reinforced by Berbers (Iberians) from Spain," with the pre-existing Fulah type and the Negroids ; as also from the far earlier intercourse between the Fulah and the Negro.[3]

The Songhai empire, like that of the rival Mandingans, claims a respectable antiquity, its reputed founder Za-el-Yemeni having flourished about 680 A.D. Za Songhai Records. Kasi, fifteenth in succession from the founder,

[1] As so much has been made of Barth's authority in this connection, it may be well to quote his exact words : " It would seem as if they (the Sonrhay) had received, in more ancient times, several institutions from the Egyptians, with whom, I have no doubt, they maintained an intercourse by means of the energetic inhabitants of Aujila from a relatively ancient period " (IV. p. 426). Barth, therefore, does not bring the people themselves, or their language, from Egypt, but only some of their institutions, and that indirectly through the Aujila Oasis in Cyrenaica, and it may be added that this intercourse with Aujila appears to date only from about 1150 A.D. (IV. p. 585).

[2] Hacquard et Dupuis, *Manuel de la langue Soñgay, parlée de Tombouctou à Say, dans la boucle du Niger*, 1897, *passim*.

[3] " A Survey of the Ethnography of Africa," *Journ. Roy. Anthr. Soc.* XLIII. 1913, p. 386.

K.	5

was the first Muhammadan ruler (1009) ; but about 1326 the country was reduced by the Mandingans, and remained throughout the fourteenth and the great part of the fifteenth century virtually subject to the Mali empire, although Ali Killun, founder of the new Sonni dynasty, had acquired a measure of independence about 1335-6. But the political supremacy of the Songhai people dates only from about 1464, when Sonni Ali, sixteenth of the Sonni dynasty, known in history as " the great tyrant and famous miscreant," threw off the Mandingan yoke, " and changed the whole face of this part of Africa by prostrating the kingdom of Melle." [1] Under his successor, Muhammad Askia,[2] " perhaps the greatest sovereign that ever ruled over Negroland," [3] the Songhai Empire acquired its greatest expansion, extending from the heart of Hausaland to the Atlantic seaboard, and from the Mossi country to the Tuat oasis, south of Morocco. Although unfavourably spoken of by Leo Africanus, Askia is described by Ahmed Bábá as governing the subject peoples " with justice and equity, causing well-being and comfort to spring up everywhere within the borders of his extensive dominions, and introducing such of the institutions of Muhammadan civilisation as he considered might be useful to his subjects." [4]

Askia also made the Mecca pilgrimage with a great show of splendour. But after his reign (1492-1529) the Songhai power gradually declined, and was at last overthrown by Mulay Hamed, Emperor of Morocco, in 1591-2. Ahmed Bábá, the native chronicler, was involved in the ruin of his people,[5] and since then the Songhai nation has been broken into fragments, subject here to Hausas, there to Fulahs, elsewhere to Tuaregs, and, since the French occupation of Timbuktu (1894), to the hated Giaur.

Hausas. In everything that constitutes the real greatness

---

[1] Barth, IV. pp. 593-4.

[2] The *Ischia* of Leo Africanus, who tells us that in his time the " linguaggio detto Sungai" was current even in the provinces of Walata and Jinni (VI. ch. 2). This statement, however, like others made by Leo at second hand, must be received with caution. In these districts Songhai may have been spoken by the officials and some of the upper classes, but scarcely by the people generally, who were of Mandingan speech.

[3] Barth, IV. p. 414.   [4] *Ib.* p. 415.

[5] Carried captive into Marakesh, although later restored to his beloved Timbuktu to end his days in perpetuating the past glories of the Songhai nation ; the one Negroid man of letters, whose name holds a worthy place beside those of Leo Africanus, Ibn Khaldún, El Tunsi, and other Hamitic writers.

of a nation, the Hausas may rightly claim pre-eminence amongst all the peoples of Negroland. No doubt early in the nineteenth century the historical Hausa States, occupying the whole region between the Niger and Bornu, were overrun and reduced by the fanatical Fulah bands under Othmán Dan Fodye. But the Hausas, in a truer sense than the Greeks, " have captured their rude conquerors," [1] for they have even largely assimilated them physically to their own type, and the Hausa nationality is under British auspices asserting its natural social, industrial and commercial predominance throughout Central and even parts of Western Sudan.

The Hausas— their dominant Social Position.

It could not well be otherwise, seeing that the Hausas form a compact body of some five million peaceful and industrious Sudanese, living partly in numerous farmsteads amid their well-tilled cotton, indigo, pulse, and corn fields, partly in large walled cities and great trading centres such as Kano,[2] Katsena, Yacoba, whose intelligent and law-abiding inhabitants are reckoned by many tens of thousands. Their melodious tongue, with a vocabulary containing perhaps 10,000 words,[3] has long been the great medium of intercourse throughout Sudan from

Hausa Speech and Mental Qualities.

---

[1]
      " Graecia capta ferum victorem cepit, et artes
        Intulit agresti Latio." Hor. *Epist.* II. 1, 156–7.
The epithet *agrestis* is peculiarly applicable to the rude Fulah shepherds, who were almost barbarians compared with the settled, industrious, and even cultured Hausa populations, and whose oppressive rule has at last been relaxed by the intervention of England in the Niger-Benue lands.

[2] " One of their towns, Kano, has probably the largest market-place in the world, with a daily attendance of from 25,000 to 30,000 people. This same town possesses, what in central Africa is still more surprising, some thirty or forty schools, in which the children are taught to read and write " (Rev. C. H. Robinson, *Specimens of Hausa Literature*, University Press, Cambridge, 1896, p. x).

[3] See C. H. Robinson, *Hausaland, or Fifteen Hundred Miles through the Central Soudan*, 1896 ; *Specimens of Hausa Literature*, 1896 ; *Hausa Grammar*, 1897 ; *Hausa Dictionary*, 1899. Authorities are undecided whether to class Hausa with the Semitic or the Hamitic family, or in an independent group by itself, and it must be admitted that some of its features are extremely puzzling. While Sudanese Negro in phonology and perhaps in most of its word roots, it is Hamitic in its grammatical features and pronouns. But the Hamitic element is thought by experts to be as much Kushite, or even Koptic, as Libyan. " On the whole, it seems probable," says H. H. Johnston, " that the Hausa speech was shaped by a double influence : from Egypt, and Hamiticized Nubia, as well as by Libyan immigrants from across the Sahara." " A Survey of the Ethnography of Africa," *Journ. Roy. Anthr. Soc.* XLIII. 1913, p. 385. Cf. also Julius Lippert, "Über die Stellung der Hausasprache," *Mitteilungen des Seminars für Orientalische Sprachen*, 1906. It is noteworthy that Hausa is the only language in tropical Africa which has been reduced to writing by the natives themselves.

Lake Chad to and beyond the Niger, and is daily acquiring even greater preponderance amongst all the settled and trading populations of these regions.

But though showing a marked preference for peaceful pursuits, the Hausas are by no means an effeminate people. Largely enlisted in the British service, they have at all times shown fighting qualities of a high order under their English officers, and a well-earned tribute has been paid to their military prowess amongst others by Sir George Goldie and Lieut. Vandeleur.[1] With the Hausas on her side England need assuredly fear no rivals to her beneficent sway over the teeming populations of the fertile plains and plateaux of Central Sudan, which is on the whole perhaps the most favoured land in Africa north of the equator.

According to the national traditions, which go back to no very remote period,[2] the seven historical Hausa States known

Hausa Origins.

as the " Hausa bokoy " (" the seven Hausas ") take their name from the eponymous heroes *Biram, Daura, Gober, Kano, Rano, Katsena* and *Zegzeg*, all said to be sprung from the Deggaras, a Berber tribe settled to the north of Munyo. From Biram, the original seat, the race and its language spread to seven other provinces— *Zanfara, Kebbi, Nupe (Nyffi), Gwari, Yauri, Yariba* and *Kororofa*, which in contempt are called the " Banza bokoy " (" the seven Upstarts "). All form collectively the Hausa domain in the widest sense.

Authentic history is quite recent, and even Komayo, reputed founder of Katsena, dates only from about the fourteenth century. Ibrahim Maji, who was the first Moslem ruler, is assigned to the latter part of the fifteenth century, and since then the chief events have been associated with the Fulah wars, ending in the absorption of all the Hausa States in the unstable Fulah empire of Sokoto at the beginning of the nineteenth century. With the fall of Kano and Sokoto

---

[1] *Campaigning on the Upper Nile and Niger*, by Lt. Seymour Vandeleur, with an Introduction by Sir George Goldie, 1898. " In camp," writes Lt. Vandeleur, " their conduct was exemplary, while pillaging and ill-treatment of the natives were unknown. As to their fighting qualities, it is enough to say that, little over 500 strong (on the Bida expedition of 1897), they withstood for two days 25,000 or 30,000 of the enemy ; that, former slaves of the Fulahs, they defeated their dreaded masters," etc.

[2] The Kano Chronicle, translated by H. R. Palmer, *Journ. Roy. Anthr. Inst.* XXXVIII. 1908, gives a list of Hausa kings (Sarkis) from 999 A.D.

in 1903 British supremacy was finally established throughout the Hausa States, now termed Northern Nigeria.[1]

Kanembu; Kanuri; [2] *Baghirmi, Mosgu.* Round about the shores of Lake Chad are grouped three other historical Muhammadan nations, the Kanembu ("People of Kanem") on the north, the Kanuri of Bornu on the west, and the Baghirmi on the south side. The last named was conquered by the Sultan of Wadai in 1871, and overrun by Rabah Zobeir, half Arab, half Negro adventurer, in 1890. But in 1897 Emile Gentil,[3] French commissioner for the district, placed the country under French protection, although French authority was not firmly established until the death of Rabah and the rout of his sons in 1901. At the same time Kanem was brought under French control, and shortly afterwards Bornu was divided between Great Britain, France and Germany.

Ethnical and Political Relations in the Chad Basin.

In this region the ethnical relations are considerably more complex than in the Hausa States. Here Islám has had greater obstacles to contend with than on the more open western plateaux, and many of the pagan aborigines have been able to hold their ground either in the archipelagos of Lake Chad (*Yedinas, Kuri, Buduma*),[4] or in the swampy tracts and uplands of the Logon-Shari basin (*Mosgu, Mandara, Makari*, etc.).

It is also the policy of the Muhammadans, whose system is based on slavery, not to push their religious zeal too far, for, if all the natives were converted, where could they procure a constant supply of slaves, those who accept the teachings of the Prophet being *ipso facto* entitled to their freedom? Hence the pagan districts

The Aborigines.

---

[1] For references to recent literature see note on p. 58. Also R. S. Rattray, *Hausa Folk-lore*, 1913 ; A. J. N. Tremearne, *Hausa Superstitions and Customs*, 1913, and *Hausa Folk-Tales*, 1914.

[2] By a popular etymology these are *Ka-Núri*, "People of Light." But, as they are somewhat lukewarm Muhammadans, the zealous Fulahs say it should be *Ka-Nari*, "People of Fire," *i.e.* foredoomed to Gehenna !

[3] E. Gentil, *La Chute de l' Empire de Rabah*, 1902.

[4] The Buduma, who derive their legendary origin from the Fulahs whom they resemble in physique, worship the *Karraka* tree (a kind of acacia). P. A. Talbot, "The Buduma of Lake Chad," *Journ. Roy. Anthr. Inst.* XLI. 1911. The anthropology of the region has lately been dealt with in *Documents Scientifiques de la Mission Tilho* (1906–9), *République Française, Ministère des Colonies*, Vol. III. 1914 ; R. Gaillard and L. Poutrin, *Étude anthropologique des Populations des Régions du Tchad et du Kanem*, 1914.

were, and still are, regarded as convenient preserves, happy hunting-grounds to be raided from time to time, but not utterly wasted ; to be visited by organised razzias just often enough to keep up the supply in the home and foreign markets. This system, controlled by the local governments themselves, has long prevailed about the border-lands between Islám and heathendom, as we know from Barth, Nachtigal, and one or two other travellers, who have had reluctantly to accompany the periodical slave-hunting expeditions from Bornu and Baghirmi to the territories of the pagan Mosgu people with their numerous branches (*Margi, Mandara, Makari, Logon, Gamergu, Keribina*) and the other aborigines (*Bede, Ngisem, So, Kerrikerri, Babir*) on the northern slopes of the Congo-Chad water-parting. As usual on such occasions, there is a great waste of life, many perishing in defence of their homes or even through sheer wantonness, besides those carried away captives. " A large number of slaves had been caught this day," writes Barth, " and in the evening a great many more were brought in ; altogether they were said to have taken one thousand, and there were certainly not less than five hundred. To our utmost horror, not less than 170 full-grown men were mercilessly slaughtered in cold blood, the greater part of them being allowed to bleed to death, a leg having been severed from the body."[1] There was probably just then a glut in the market.

Islám and Heathendom.

Slave-Hunting.

A curious result of these relations is that in the wooded districts some of the natives have reverted to arboreal habits, taking refuge during the raids in the branches of huge bombax-trees converted into temporary strongholds. Round the vertical stem of these forest giants is erected a breast-high look-out, while the higher horizontal branches, less exposed to the fire of the enemy, support strongly-built huts and store-houses, where the families of the fugitives take refuge with their effects, including, as Nachtigal assures us,[2] their domestic animals, such as goats, dogs, and poultry. During the siege of the aërial fortress, which is often successfully defended, long light ladders of withies are let down at night, when no attack need be feared, and the supply of water and provisions is

Arboreal Strongholds.

---

[1] III. p. 194.   [2] *Sahara and Sudan*, II. p. 628.

thus renewed from *caches* or hiding-places round about.   In
1872 Nachtigal accompanied a predatory excursion to the
pagan districts south of Baghirmi, when an attack was made
on one of these tree-fortresses.   Such citadels can be stormed
only at a heavy loss, and as the Gaberi (Baghirmi) warriors
had no tools capable of felling the great bombax-tree, they
were fain to rest satisfied with picking off a poor wretch now
and then, and barbarously mutilating the bodies as they fell
from the overhanging branches.

Some of these aborigines disfigure their faces by the disk-
like lip-ornament, which is also fashionable in Nyassaland,
and even amongst the South American Boto-
cudos.   The type often differs greatly, and while   Mosgu Types
some of the widespread Mosgu tribes are of a   and Contrasts.
dirty black hue, with disagreeable expression, wide open
nostrils, thick lips, high cheek-bones, coarse bushy hair, and
disproportionate knock-kneed legs, other members of the
same family astonished Barth " by the beauty and symmetry
of their forms, and by the regularity of their features, which
in some had nothing of what is called the Negro type.   But
I was still more astonished at their complexion, which was
very different in different individuals, being in some of a
glossy black, and in others of a light copper, or rather rhubarb
colour, the intermediate shades being almost entirely wanting.
I observed in one house a really beautiful female who, with
her son, about eight or nine years of age, formed a most
charming group, well worthy of the hand of an accomplished
artist.   The boy's form did not yield in any respect to the
beautiful symmetry of the most celebrated Grecian statues.
His hair, indeed, was very short and curled, but not woolly.
He, as well as his mother and the whole family, were of a
pale or yellowish-red complexion, like rhubarb." [1]

There is no suggestion of albinism, and the explanation
of such strange contrasts must await further exploration in
the whole of this borderland of Negroes and Bantus about
the divide between the Chad and the Congo basins.   The
country has until lately been traversed only at rare intervals
by pioneers, interested more in political than in anthropological matters.

Of the settled and more or less cultured peoples in the

---

[1] II. pp. 382–3.

Chad basin, the most important are the *Kanembu*,[1] who
The Cultured introduce a fresh element of confusion in this
Peoples of region, being more allied in type and speech
Central Sudan. to the Hamitic Tibus than to the Negro stock,
or at least taking a transitional position between the two ; the
Kanuri, the ruling people in Bornu, of somewhat coarse
Negroid appearance ;[2] and the southern *Baghirmi*, also
decidedly Negroid, originally supposed to have come from
the Upper Shari and White Nile districts.[3] Their civilisation,
such as it is, has been developed exclusively under Moslem
influences, but it has never penetrated much below the
surface. The people are everywhere extremely rude, and for
the most part unlettered, although the meagre and not altogether trustworthy Kanem-Bornu records date from the time
of Sef, reputed founder of the monarchy about 800 A.D.
Kanem-Bornu Duku, second in descent from Sef, is doubtfully
Records. referred to about 850 A.D. Hamé, founder of a
new dynasty, flourished towards the end of the
eleventh century (1086-97), and Dunama, one of his successors, is said to have extended his sway over a great part
of the Sahara, including the whole of Fezzan (1221-59).
Under Omar (1394-98) a divorce took place between Kanem
and Bornu, and henceforth the latter country has remained
the chief centre of political power in the Chad basin.

A long series of civil wars was closed by Ali (1472-1504),
who founded the present capital, Birni, and whose grandson,
Muhammad, brought the empire of Bornu to the highest
pitch of its greatness (1526-45). Under Ahmed (1793-

---

[1] That is " Kanem-men," the postfix *bu, be,* as in *Ti-bu, Ful-be,* answering to
the Bantu prefix *ba, wa,* as in *Ba-Suto, Wa-Swahili,* etc. Here may possibly be
discovered a link between the Sudanese, Teda-Daza, and Bantu linguistic groups.
The transposition of the agglutinated particles would present no difficulty ; cf.
Umbrian and Latin (*Eth.* p. 214). The Kanembu are described by Tilho, who
explored the Chad basin, 1906-9. His reports were published in 1914. *République
Française Ministère des Colonies, Documents Scientifiques de la Mission Tilho*
(1906-9), Vol. III. 1914.
[2] Barth draws a vivid picture of the contrasts, physical and mental, between
the Kanuri and the Hausa peoples ; " Here we took leave of Hausa with its fine
and beautiful country, and its cheerful and industrious population. It is remarkable what a difference there is between the character of the ba-Haushe and the
Kanuri—the former lively, spirited, and cheerful, the latter melancholic, dejected,
and brutal ; and the same difference is visible in their physiognomies—the former
having in general very pleasant and regular features, and more graceful forms,
while the Kanuri, with his broad face, his wide nostrils and his large bones, makes
a far less agreeable impression, especially the women, who are very plain and
certainly among the ugliest in all Negroland " (II. pp. 163-4).
[3] See Nachtigal, II. p. 690.

1810) began the wars with the Fulahs, who, after bringing the empire to the verge of ruin, were at last overthrown by the aid of the Kanem people, and since 1819 Bornu has been ruled by the present Kanemíyîn dynasty, which though temporarily conquered by Rabah in 1893, was restored under British administration in 1902.[1]

EASTERN SUDANESE.

As some confusion prevails regarding the expression "Eastern Sudan," I may here explain that it bears a very different meaning, according as it is used in a political or an ethnical sense. Politically it is practically synonymous with Eygptian Sudan, that is the whole region from Darfur to the Red Sea which was ruled or misruled by the Khedivial Government before the revolt of the Mahdi (1883–4), and was restored to Egypt by the British occupation of Khartum in 1898. Ethnically Eastern Sudan comprises all the lands east of the Chad basin, where the Negro or Negroid populations are predominant, that is to say, Wadai, Darfur, and Kordofan in the West, the Nile Valley from the frontier of Egypt proper south to Albert Nyanza, both slopes of the Nile-Congo divide (the western tributaries of the White Nile and the Welle-Makua affluent of the Congo), lastly the Sobat Valley with some Negro enclaves east of the White Nile, and even south of the equator (Kavirondo, Semliki Valley). *Range of the Negro in Eastern Sudan.*

Throughout this region the fusion of the aborigines with Hamites and Arabs, Tuareg, or Tibu Moslem intruders, wherever they have penetrated, has been far less complete than in Central and Western Sudan. Thus in Wadai the dominant Maba people, whence the country is often called Dar-Maba ("Mabaland"), are rather Negro than Negroid, with but a slight strain of foreign blood. In the northern districts the *Zoghâwa*, *Gura'an*, *Baele* and *Bulala* Tibus keep quite aloof from the blacks, as do elsewhere the *Aramkas*, as the Arabs are collectively called in Wadai. Yet the *Mahamid* and some other Bedouin tribes have here been *The Mabas.* *Ethnical Relations in Wadai.*

---

[1] For recent literature see Lady Lugard's *A Tropical Dependency*, 1905, and the references, note 3, p. 58.

settled for over 500 years, and it is through their assistance
that the Mabas acquired the political supremacy they have
enjoyed since the seventeenth century, when they reduced or
expelled the *Tynjurs*,[1] the former ruling race, said to be
Nubians originally from Dongola. It was Abd-el-Kerim,
founder of the new Moslem Maba state, who gave the country
its present name in honour of his grandfather, *Wadai*. His
successor Kharúb I removed the seat of government to
Wara, where Vogel was murdered in 1856. Abeshr, the
present capital, dates only from the year 1850. Except for
Nachtigal, who crossed the frontier in 1873, nothing was
known of the land or its people until the French occupation
at the end of the last century (1899). Since that date it has
been prominent as the scene of the attack on a French
column and the death of its leader, Colonel Moll, in 1910,
and the tragic murder of Lieutenant Boyd Alexander earlier
in the same year.[2]

Nubas. As in Wadai, the intruding and native populations have been either imperfectly or not at all assimilated in
The Nubian Problem. Darfur and Kordofan, where the Muhammadan
Semites still boast of their pure Arab descent,[3]
and form powerful confederacies. Chief among
these are the *Baggara* (Baqqara, " cow-herds "), cattle-keepers
and agriculturalists, of whom some are as dark as the blackest
negroes, though many are fine-looking, with regular, well-
shaped features. Their form of Arabic is notoriously corrupt.
Their rivals, the *Jaalan* (Jalin, Jahalin), are mostly riverain

---

[1] These are the same people as the *Tunjurs* (*Tunzers*) of Darfur, regarding
whose ethnical position so much doubt still prevails. Strange to say, they
themselves claim to be Arabs, and the claim is allowed by their neighbours,
although they are not Muhammadans. Lejean thinks they are Tibus from the
north-west, while Nachtigal, who met some as far west as Kanem, concluded from
their appearance and speech that they were really Arabs settled for hundreds of
years in the country (*op. cit.* II. p. 256).

[2] A. H. Keane, " Wadai," *Travel and Exploration*, July, 1910 ; and H. H.
Johnston, on Lieut. Boyd Alexander, *Geog. Journ.* same date.

[3] H. A. MacMichael has investigated the value of these racial claims in the
case of the Kababish and indicates the probable admixture of Negro, Mediterranean, Hamite and other strains in the Sudanese Arabs. He says, " Among the
more settled tribes any important sheikh or faki can produce a table of his
ancestors (*i.e.* a *nisba*) in support of his asseverations . . . I asked a village sheikh
if he could show me his pedigree, as I did not know from which of the exalted
sources his particular tribe claimed descent. He replied that he did not know
yet, but that his village had subscribed 60 piastres the month before to hire a faki
to compose a *nisba* for them, and that he would show me the result when it was
finished." " The Kababish : Some Remarks on the Ethnology of a Sudan Arab
Tribe," *Journ. Roy. Anthr. Inst.* XL. 1910, p. 216.

"Arabs," a learned tribe, containing many scribes, and their language is said to be closer to classical Arabic than the form current in Egypt. These are the principal slave-hunters of the Sudan, and the famous Zobeir belonged to their tribe. The *Yemanieh* are largely traders, and trace their origin from South Arabia. The *Kababish* are the wealthiest camel-owning tribe, perhaps less contaminated by negro blood than any other Arab tribe in the Sudan.[1] The *Nuba* and the *Nubians* have been a source of much confusion, but recent investigations in the field such as those of C. G. Seligman [2] and H. A. MacMichael,[3] and the publications of the Archaeological Survey of Nubia conducted by G. A. Reisner, help to elucidate the problem. We have first of all to get rid of the "Nuba-Fulah" family, which was introduced by Fr. Müller and accepted by some English writers, but has absolutely no existence. The two languages, although both of the agglutinative Sudanese type, are radically distinct in all their structural, lexical, and phonetic elements, and the two peoples are equally distinct. The Fulahs are of North African origin, although many have in recent times been largely assimilated to their black Sudanese subjects. The Nuba on the contrary belong originally to the Negro stock, with hair of the common negro type, and are amongst the blackest skinned tribes in the Sudan, their colour varying from a dark chocolate brown to the darkest shade of brown black.

But rightly to understand the question we have carefully to avoid confusion between the Nubians of the Nile Valley and the Negro *Nubas*, who gave their name to the Nuba Mountains, Kordofan, where most of the aborigines (*Kargo, Kulfan, Kolaji, Tumali, Lafofa, Eliri, Talodi*) still belong to this connection.[3] Kordofan is probably itself a Nuba word meaning "Land of the Kordo" (*fán*=Arab, *dár*, land, country). There is a certain amount of anthropological evidence to connect the Nuba with the *Fur* and the *Kara* of Darfur to the west.[4] But it is a different anthropological type that is represented in the three groups of *Matokki*

---

[1] See the Kababish types, Pl. xxxvii. in C. G. Seligman's "Some Aspects of the Hamitic Problem in the Anglo-Egyptian Sudan," *Journ. Roy. Anthr. Inst.* XLIII. 1913, but cf. also p. 626 and n. 2.

[2] "The Physical Characters of the Nuba of Kordofan," *Journ. Roy. Anthr. Inst.* XL. 1910, "Some Aspects of the Hamitic Problem," etc., *tom. cit.* XLIII. 1913.

[3] See H. A. MacMichael, *The Tribes of Northern and Central Kordofán*, 1912.

[4] Cf. A. W. Tucker and C. S. Myers, "A Contribution to the Anthropology of the Sudan," *Journ. Roy. Anthr. Inst.* XL. 1910, p. 149.

(*Kenus*) between the First Cataract and Wadi-el-Arab, the *Mahai* (*Marisi*) between Korosko and Wadi-Halfa, at the Second Cataract, and the *Dongolawi*, of the province of Dongola between Wadi-Halfa and Jebel Deja near Meroe.

These three groups, all now Muhammadans, but formerly Christians, constitute collectively the so-called " Nubians " of
Nubian Origins and Affinities. European writers, but call themselves *Barabra*, plural of *Berberi*, *i.e.* people of Berber, although they do not at present extend so far up the Nile as that town.[1] Possibly these are Strabo's "Noubai, who dwell on the left bank of the Nile in Libya [Africa], a great nation etc.";[2] and are also to be identified with the *Nobatae*, who in Diocletian's time were settled, some in the Kharga oasis, others in the Nile Valley about Meroe, to guard the frontiers of the empire against the incursions of the restless Blemmues. But after some time they appear to have entered into peaceful relations with these Hamites, the present Bejas, even making common cause with them against the Romans ; but the confederacy was crushed by Maximinus in 451, though perhaps not before crossings had taken place between the Nobatae and the Caucasic Bejas. Then these Bejas withdrew to their old homes, which they still occupy, between the Nile and the Red-Sea above Egypt, while the Nobatae, embracing Christianity, as is said, in 545, established the powerful kingdom of Dongola which lasted over 800 years, and was finally overthrown by the Arabs in the fourteenth century, since which time the Nile Nubians have been Muhammadans.

There still remains the problem of language which, as shown by Lepsius,[3] differs but slightly from that now current amongst the Kordofan Nubas. But this similarity only holds in the north, and is now shown to be due to Berberine

[1] This term, however, has by some authorities been identified with the *Barabarà*, one of the 113 tribes recorded in the inscription on a gateway of Thutmes, by whom they were reduced about 1700 B.C. In a later inscription of Rameses II at Karnak (1400 B.C.) occurs the form *Beraberata*, name of a southern people conquered by him. Hence Brugsch (*Reisebericht aus Ægypten*, pp. 127 and 155) is inclined to regard the modern *Barabra* as a true ethnical name confused in classical times with the Greek and Roman *Barbarus*, but revived in its proper sense since the Moslem conquest. See also the editorial note on the term *Berber*, in the new English ed. of Leo Africanus, Vol. I. p. 199.

[2] 'Εξ ἀριστερῶν δὲ ῥύσεως τοῦ Νείλου Νοῦβαι κατοικοῦσιν ἐν τῇ Λιβύῃ, μέγα ἔθνος, etc. (Book XVII. p. 1117, Oxford ed. 1807). Sayce, therefore, is quite wrong in stating that Strabo knew only of " Ethiopians," and not Nubians, " as dwelling northward along the banks of the Nile as far as Elephantiné " (*Academy*, April 14, 1894).

[3] *Nubische Grammatik*, 1881, *passim*.

immigration into Kordofan.[1] Recent investigations show
that the Nuba and the Barabra, in spite of this linguistic
similarity which has misled certain authors,[2] are not to be
regarded as belonging to the same race.[3] "The Nuba are a
tall, stoutly built muscular people, with a dark, almost black
skin. They are predominantly mesaticephalic, for although
cephalic indices under 70 and over 80 both occur, nearly
60 per cent. of the individuals measured are mesaticephals,
the remaining being dolichocephalic and brachycephalic in
about equal proportions." The hair is invariably woolly.
The Barabra, on the contrary, is of slight, or more commonly
medium build, not particularly muscular and in skin colour
varies from a yellowish to a chocolate brown. The hair is
commonly curly or wavy and may be almost straight, while
the features are not uncommonly absolutely non-Negroid.
"Thus there can be no doubt that the two peoples are
essentially different in physical characters and the same holds
good on the cultural side " (p. 611). Barabra were identified
by Lepsius with the Wawat, a people frequently mentioned
in Egyptian records, and recent excavations by the members
of the Archaeological Survey of Nubia show a close connection with the predynastic Egyptians, a connection supported
also on physical grounds. It seems strange, therefore, to
meet with repeated reference on Egyptian monuments to
Negroes in Nubia when, as proved by excavations, the inhabitants were by no means Negroes or even frankly Negroid.
Seligman's solution of the difficulty is as follows (p. 619).
It seems that only one explanation is tenable, namely that for
a period subsequent to the Middle Kingdom the country in
the neighbourhood of the Second Cataract became essentially
a Negro country and may have remained in this condition
for some little time. Then a movement in the opposite
direction set in ; the Negroes, diminished by war, were in
part driven back by the great conquerors of the New Empire ;
those that were left mixed with the Egyptian garrisons and
traders and once more a hybrid race arose which, however,

---

[1] B. Z. Seligman, " Note on the Languages of the Nubas of S. Kordofan,"
Zeitschr. f. Kol.-spr. I. 1910–11 ; C. G. Seligman, " Some Aspects of the Hamitic
Problem," etc., *Journ. Roy. Anthr. Inst.* XLIII. 1913, p. 621 ff.

[2] See A. H. Keane, *Man, Past and Present*, 1900, p. 74.

[3] C. G. Seligman, " The Physical Characters of the Nuba of Kordofan,"
Journ. Roy. Anthr. Inst. XL. 1910, p. 512, and " Some Aspects of the Hamitic
Problem," etc., *Journ. Roy. Anthr. Inst.* XLIII. 1913, *passim.*

preserved the language of its Negro ancestors. Although Seligman regards the conclusion that this race gave rise directly to the present-day inhabitants of Nubia as "premature," and suggests further mixture with the Beja of the eastern deserts, Elliot Smith recognises the essential similarity between the homogeneous blend of Egyptian and Negro traits which characterise the Middle Nubian people (contemporary with the Middle Empire, XII–XVII dynasties), a type which "seems to have remained dominant in Nubia ever since then, for the span of almost 4000 years."[1]

Before the incursions of the Nubian-Arab traders and raiders, who began to form settlements (*zeribas*, fenced stations) in the Upper Nile regions above Khartum about the middle of the nineteenth century, most of the Nile-Congo divide (White Nile tributaries and Welle-Makua basin) belonged in the strictest sense to the Negro domain. Sudanese tribes, and even great nations reckoned by millions, had been for ages in almost undisturbed possession, not only of the main stream from the equatorial lakes to and beyond the Sobat junction, but also of the Sobat Valley itself, and of the numerous south-western head-waters of the White Nile converging about Lake No above the Sobat junction. Nearly all the Nile peoples—the *Shilluks* and *Dinkas* about the Sobat confluence, the *Bari* and *Nuers* of the Bahr-el-Jebel, the *Bongos* (*Dors*), *Rols*, *Golos*, *Mittus*, *Madis*, *Makarakas*, *Abakas*, *Mundus*, and many others about the western affluents, as well as the *Funj* of Senaar—had been brought under the Khedivial rule before the revolt of the Mahdi.

The Negro Peoples of the Nile-Congo Watersheds.

The same fate had already overtaken or was threatening the formerly powerful *Mombuttu* (*Mangbattu*) and *Zandeh*[2] nations of the Welle lands, as well as the *Krej* and others about the low watersheds of the Nile-Congo and Chad basins. Since then the Welle groups have been subjected to the jurisdiction of the Congo Free State, while the political destinies of the Nilotic tribes must henceforth be controlled by the British masters of the Nile lands from the Great Lakes to the Mediterranean.

Political Relations.

Although grouped as Negroes proper, very few of the

---

[1] *Archaeological Survey of India*, Bull. III. p. 25.
[2] See note I, p. 44.

Nilotic peoples present the almost ideal type of the blacks, such as those of Upper Guinea and the Atlantic coast of West Sudan. The complexion is in general less black, the nose less broad at the base, the lips less everted (Shilluks and one or two others excepted), the hair rather less frizzly, the dolichocephaly and prognathism less marked.

Apart from the more delicate shades of transition, due to diverse interminglings with Hamites and Semites, two distinct types may be plainly distinguished—one black, often very tall, with long thin legs, and long-headed (*Shilluks, Dinkas, Bari, Nuers, Alur*), the other reddish or ruddy brown, more thick-set, and short-headed (*Bongos, Golos, Makarakas*, with the kindred *Zandehs* of the Welle region). No explanation has been offered of their brachycephaly, which is all the more difficult to account for, inasmuch as it is characteristic neither of the aboriginal Negro nor of the intruding Hamitic and Semitic elements. Have we here an indication of the transition suspected by many between the true long-headed Negro and the round-headed Negrillo, who is also brownish, and formerly ranged as far north as the Nile head-streams, as would appear from the early Egyptian records (Chap. IV.) ? Schweinfurth found that the Bongos were " hardly removed from the lowest grade of brachycephaly,"[1] and the same is largely true of the Zandehs and their Makaraka cousins, as noticed by Junker : " The skull also in many of these peoples approaches the round form, whereas the typical Negro is assumed to be long-headed."[2] But so great is the diversity of appearance throughout the whole of this region, including even " a striking Semitic type," that this observer was driven to the conclusion that " woolly hair, common to all, forms in fact the only sure characteristic of the Negro."[3]

Dinka is the name given to a congeries of independent tribes spread over a vast area, stretching from 300 miles south of Khartum to within 100 miles of Gondokoro, and reaching many miles to the west in the Bahr-el-Ghazal Province. All these tribes according to C. G. Seligman [4] call themselves *Jieng* or *Jenge*, corrupted

Two Physical Types.

The Dinka.

[1] *Op. cit.* I. p. 263.
[2] *Travels in Africa*, Keane's English ed., Vol. III. p. 247.
[3] *Ibid.*, p. 246.
[4] C. G. Seligman, Art. " Dinka," *Encyclopaedia of Religion and Ethics*.

by the Arabs into Dinka ; but no Dinka nation has arisen, for the tribes have never recognised a supreme chief, as do their neighbours, the Shilluk, nor have they even been united under a military despot, as the Zulu were united under Chaka. They differ in manners and customs and even in physique and are often at war with one another. One of the most obvious distinctions in habits is between the relatively powerful cattle-owning Dinka and the small and comparátively poor tribes who have no cattle and scarcely cultivate the ground, but live in the marshes in the neighbourhood of the Sudd, and depend largely for their sustenance on fishing and hippopotamus-hunting. Their villages, which are generally dirty and evil-smelling, are built on ground which rises but little above the reed-covered surface of the country. The Dinka community is largely autonomous under leadership of a chief or headman (*bain*) who is sometimes merely the local magician, but in one community in each tribe he is the hereditary rain-maker whose wish is law. " Cattle form the economic basis of Dinka society ; . . . they are the currency in which bride-price and blood-fines are paid ; and the desire to acquire a neighbour's herds is the common cause of those inter-tribal raids which constitute Dinka warfare."

Some uniformity appears to prevail amongst the languages of the Nile-Welle lands, and from the rather scanty materials

Linguistic Groups. collected by Junker, Fr. Müller was able to construct an " Equatorial Linguistic Family," including the Mangbattu, Zandeh, Barmbo, Madi, Bangba, Krej, Golo and others, on both sides of the water-parting. Leo Reinisch, however, was not convinced, and in a letter addressed to the author declared that " in the absence of sentences it is impossible to determine the grammatical structure of Mangbattu and the other languages. At the same time we may detect certain relations, not to the Nilotic, but the Bantu tongues. It may therefore be inferred that Mangbattu and the others have a tolerably close relationship to the Bantu, and may even be remotely akin to it,

See also the same author's " Cult of Nyakangano the Divine Kings of the Shilluk," *Fourth Report Wellcome Research Lab. Khartoum*, Vol. B, 1911, p. 216 ; S. L. Cummins, *Journ. Anthr. Inst.* XXXIV. 1904, and H. O'Sullivan, " Dinka Laws and Customs," *Journ Roy. Anthr. Inst.* XL. 1910. Measurements of Dinka, Shilluk etc. are given by A. W. Tucker and C. S. Myers, " A Contribution to the Anthropology of the Sudan," *Journ. Roy. Anthr. Inst.* XL. 1910. G. A. S. Northcote, " The Nilotic Kavirondo," *Journ. Roy. Anthr. Inst.* XXXVI. 1907, describes an allied people, the *Jaluo*.

judging from their tendency to prefix formations."[1]   Future research will show how far this conjecture is justified.

Although Islám has made considerable progress, throughout the greater part of the Sudanese region, though not among the Nilotic tribes, the bulk of the people are still practically pagan.   Witchcraft continues to flourish amongst the equatorial peoples, and important events are almost everywhere attended by sanguinary rites.   These are absent among the true Nilotics. The Dinka are totemic, with ancestor-worship.   The Shilluk have a cult of divine kings.

Mental Qualities.

Cannibalism however, in some of its most repulsive forms, prevails amongst the Zandehs, who barter in human fat as a universal staple of trade, and amongst the Mangbattu, who cure for future use the bodies of the slain in battle and " drive their prisoners before them, as butchers drive sheep to the shambles, and these are only reserved to fall victims on a later day to their horrible and sickly greediness."[2]

Cannibalism.

In fact here we enter the true " cannibal zone," which, as I have elsewhere shown, was in former ages diffused all over Central and South Africa, or, it would be more correct to say, over the whole continent,[3] but has in recent times been mainly confined to " the region stretching west and east from the Gulf of Guinea to the western head-streams of the White Nile, and from below the equator northwards in the direction of Adamáwa, Dar-Banda and Dar-Fertit.   Wherever explorers have penetrated into this least-known region of the continent they have found the practice fully established, not merely as a religious rite or a privilege reserved for priests, but as a recognised social institution."[4]

The Cannibal Zone.

---

[1] *Travels in Africa*, Keane's Eng. ed., III. p. 279.   Thus the Bantu *Ba, Wa, Ama*, etc., correspond to the *A* of the Welle lands, as in *A-Zandeh, A-Barmbo, A-Madi, A-Bangba, i.e.* Zandeh people, Barmbo people, etc.   Cf. also Kanem*bu*, Tib*u*, Fulb*e*, etc., where the personal particle (*bu, be*) is postfixed.   It would almost seem as if we had here a transition between the northern Sudanese and the southern Bantu groups in the very region where such transitions might be looked for.

[2] Schweinfurth *op. cit.* II. p. 93.

[3] G. Elliot Smith denies that cannibalism occurred in Ancient Egypt, *The Ancient Egyptians*, 1911, p. 48.

[4] *Africa*, 1895, Vol. II. p. 58.   In a carefully prepared monograph on " Endocannibalismus," Vienna, 1896, Dr Rudolf S. Steinmetz brings together a great body of evidence tending to show " dass eine hohe Wahrscheinlichkeit dafür spricht den Endocannibalismus (indigenous anthropophagy) als ständige Sitte

Yet many of these cannibal peoples, especially the Mangbattus and Zandehs, are skilled agriculturists, and cultivate
some of the useful industries, such as iron and
copper smelting and casting, weaving, pottery
and wood-carving, with great success. The
form and ornamental designs of their utensils display real
artistic taste, while the temper of their iron implements is
often superior to that of the imported European hardware.
Here again the observation has been made that the tribes
most addicted to cannibalism also excel in mental qualities
and physical energy. Nor are they strangers to the finer
feelings of human nature, and above all the surrounding
peoples the Zandeh anthropophagists are distinguished by
their regard and devotion for their women and children.

Arts and Industries.

In one respect all these peoples show a higher degree of
intelligence even than the Arabs and Hamites. "My later
experiences," writes Junker, "revealed the remarkable fact that certain negro peoples, such
as the Niam-Niams, the Mangbattus and the
Bantus of Uganda and Unyoro, display quite a surprising
understanding of figured illustrations or pictures of plastic
objects, which is not as a rule exhibited by the Arabs and
Arabised Hamites of North-east Africa. Thus the Unyoro
chief, Riongo, placed photographs in their proper position,
and was able to identify the negro portraits as belonging to
the Shuli, Lango, or other tribes, of which he had a personal
knowledge. This I have called a remarkable fact, because
it bespoke in the lower races a natural faculty for observation,
a power to recognise what for many Arabs or Egyptians of
high rank was a hopeless puzzle. An Egyptian pasha in
Khartum could never make out how a human face in profile
showed only one eye and one ear, and he took the portrait of
a fashionable Parisian lady in extremely low dress for that of the
bearded sun-burnt American naval officer who had shown him

High Appreciation of Pictorial Art.

der Urmenschen, sowie der niedrigen Wilden anzunehmen " (pp. 59, 60). It is
surprising to learn from the ill-starred Bôttego-Grixoni expedition of 1892–3 that
anthropophagy is still rife even in Gallaland, and amongst the white (" floridi ")
Cormoso Gallas. Like the Fans, these prefer the meat "high," and it would
appear that all the dead are eaten. Hence in their country Bôttego found no
graves, and one of his native guides explained that " questa gente seppellisce i
suoi cari nel ventre, invece che nella terra," *i.e.* these people bury their dear ones
in their stomach instead of in the ground. Vittorio Bôttego, *Viaggi di Scoperta*,
etc., Rome, 1895.

the photograph." [1]   From this one is almost tempted to infer
that, amongst Moslem peoples, all sense of plastic, figurative,
or pictorial art has been deadened by the Koranic precept
forbidding the representation of the human form in any way.

The Welle peoples show themselves true Negroes in the
possession of another and more precious quality, the sense of
humour, although this is probably a quality
which comes late in the life of a race. Any-   Sense of
how it is a distinct Negro characteristic, which   Humour.
Junker was able to turn to good account during the building
of his famous *Lacrima* station in Ndoruma's country. " In
all this I could again notice how like children the Negroes
are in many respects. Once at work they seemed animated
by a sort of childlike sense of honour. They delighted in
praise, though even a frown or a word of reproach could also
excite their hilarity. Thus a loud burst of laughter would,
for instance, follow the contrast between a piece of good and
bad workmanship. Like children, they would point the
finger of scorn at each other." [2]

One morning Ndoruma, hearing that they had again
struck work, had the great war-drum beaten, whereupon they
rushed to arms and mustered in great force from all quarters.
But on finding that there was no enemy to march against,
and that they had only been summoned to resume operations
at the station, they enjoyed the joke hugely, and after a
general explosion of laughter at the way they had been taken
in, laid aside their weapons and returned cheerfully to work.
Some English overseers have already discovered that this
characteristic may be utilised far more effectively than the
cruel kurbash. Ethnology has many such lessons to teach.

[1] I. p. 245.   [2] II. p. 140.

CHAPTER IV

THE AFRICAN NEGRO: II. BANTUS—NEGRILLOES—BUSHMEN—HOTTENTOTS

The Sudanese-Bantu Divide—Frontier Tribes—*The Bonjo Cannibals*—*The Baya Nation*—A " Red People "—The North-East Door to Bantuland—Semitic Elements of the Bantu Amalgam—Malay Elements in Madagascar only—Hamitic Element everywhere—*The Ba-Hima*—Pastoral and Agricultural Clans—The Bantus mainly a Negro-Hamitic Cross—Date of Bantu Migration—*The Lacustrians*—Their Traditions—The Kintu Legend—*The Ba-Ganda*, Past and Present—Political and Social Institutions—Totemic System—Bantu Peoples between Lake Victoria and the Coast—*The Wa-Giryama*—Primitive Ancestry-Worship—Mulungu—*The Wa-Swahili*—The Zang Empire—*The Zulu-Xosas*—Former and Present Domain—Patriarchal Institutions—Genealogies—Physical Type—Social Organisation—" Common Law "—*Ma-Shonas* and *Ma-Kalakas*—The mythical Monomotapa Empire—The Zimbabwe Ruins—*The Be-Chuanas*—*The Ba-Rotse* Empire—*The Ma-Kololo* Episode—Spread of Christianity amongst the Southern Bantus—King Khama—*The Ova-Herero*—Cattle and Hill Damaras—*The Kongo People*—Old Kongo Empire—The Kongo Language—The Kongo Aborigines—Perverted Christian Doctrines—*The Kabindas* and " *Black Jews* "—*The Ba-Shilange* Bhang-smokers—*The Ba-Lolo* " Men of Iron "—The West Equatorial Bantus—*Ba-Kalai*—*The Cannibal Fans*—Migrations, Type, Origin—*The Camerun Bantus*—Bantu-Sudanese Borderland—Early Bantu Migrations—Eastern Ancestry and Western Nature-worshippers—Conclusion—*Vaalpens*—*Strandloopers*—*Negrilloes*—Negrilloes at the Courts of the Pharaohs—Negrilloes and Pygmy Folklore—*The Dume* and *Doko* reputed Dwarfs—*The Wandorobbo* Hunters—*The Wochua* Mimics—*The Bushmen and Hottentots*—Former and Present Range—*The Wa-Sandawi*—Hottentot Geographical Names in Bantuland—Hottentots disappearing—Bushman Folklore Literature—Bushman-Hottentot Language and Clicks—Bushman Mental Characters—Bushman Race-Names.

CONSPECTUS.

Present Range. Bantu : *S. Africa from the Sudanese*
Distribution in   *frontier to the Cape ;* Negrillo : *West Equatorial*
Past and   *and Congo forest zones ;* Bush.-Hot. : *Namaqua-*
Present Times.   *lands ; Kalahari ; Lake Ngami and Orange*
basins.

Hair. Bantu : *same as Sudanese, but often rather longer ;*
Negrillo : *short, frizzly or crisp, rusty brown ;* Bush.-Hot. :

much the same as Sudanese, but tufty, simulating bald partings.
Colour. Bantu : *all shades of dark brown,*
sometimes almost black ; Negrillo *and* Bush.-   Physical
Hot. : *yellowish brown.* **Skull.** Bantu : *generally*   Characters.
dolicho, but variable ; Negrillo : *almost uniformly mesati ;*
Bush.-Hot. : *dolicho.* **Jaws.** Bantu : *moderately prognathous*
and even orthognathous ; Negrillo *and* Bush.-Hot. : *highly*
prognathous. **Cheek-bones.** Bantu : *moderately or not at*
all prominent ; Negrillo *and* Bush.-Hot. : *very prominent,*
often extremely so, forming a triangular face with apex at
chin. **Nose.** Bantu : *variable, ranging from platyrrhine to*
leptorrhine ; Negrillo *and* Bush.-Hot. : *short, broad at base,*
depressed at root, always platyrrhine. **Eyes.** Bantu : *generally*
large, black, and prominent, but also of regular Hamitic type ;
Negrillo *and* Bush.-Hot. : *rather small, deep brown and black.*
Stature. Bantu : *tall, from* 1.72 *m. to* 1.82 *m.* (5 *ft.* 8 *in.*
to 6 *ft.*) ; Negrillo : *always much under* 1.52 *m.* (5 *ft.*), *mean*
about 1.22 *m.* (4 *ft.*) ; Bushman : *short, with rather wide*
range, from 1.42 *m. to* 1.57 *m.* (4 *ft.* 8 *in. to* 5 *ft.* 2 *in.*) ;
Hot. : *undersized, mean* 1.65 *m.* (5 *ft.* 5 *in.*).

Temperament. Bantu : *mainly like the Negroid Su-*
danese, far more intelligent than the true Negro, equally
cruel, but less fitful and more trustworthy ;
Negrillo : *bright, active and quick-witted, but*   Mental
vindictive and treacherous, apparently not cruel   Characters.
to each other, but rather gentle and kindly ; Bushman : *in all*
these respects very like the Negrillo, but more intelligent ; Hot. :
rather dull and sluggish, but the full-blood (Nama) *much less*
so than the half-caste (Griqua) *tribes.*

Speech. Bantu : *as absolutely uniform as the physical*
type is variable, one stock language only, of the agglutinating
order, with both class prefixes, alliteration and postfixes ;[1]
Negrillo : *unknown ;* Hot. : *agglutinating with postfixes only,*
with grammatical gender and other remarkable features ; of
Hamitic origin.

Religion. Bantu : *ancestor-worship mainly in the east,*
spirit-worship mainly in the west, intermingling in the centre,
with witchcraft and gross superstitions everywhere ; Negrillo :
little known ; Bush.-Hot. : *animism, nature-worship, and*

---

[1] C. Meinhof holds that Proto-Bantu arose through the mixture of a Sudan language with one akin to Fulah. *An Introduction to the Study of African Languages,* 1915, p. 151 sqq.

reverence for ancestors; among Hottentots belief in supreme powers of good and evil.

Culture. Bantu: *much lower than the Negroid Sudanese, but higher than the true Negro; principally cattle rearers, practising simple agriculture;* Negrillo *and* Bush.: *lowest grade, hunters;* Hot.: *nomadic herdsmen.*

Bantus:[1] *Bonjo; Baya; Ba-Ganda; Ba-Nyoro; Wa-Pokomo; Wa-Giryama; Wa-Swahili; Zulu-Xosa; Ma-Shona; Be-Chuana; Ova-Herero; Eshi-Kongo; Ba-Shilange; Ba-Lolo; Ma-Nyema; Ba-Kalai; Fan; Mpongwe; Dwala; Ba-Tanga.*

Main Divisions.

Negrilloes: *Akka; Wochua; Dume (?); Wandorobbo (?); Doko (?); Obongo; Wambutte (Ba-Mbute); Ba-Twa.*

Bushmen: *Family groups; no known tribal names.*

Hottentots: *Wa-Sandawi (?); Namaqua; Griqua; Gonaqua; Koraqua; Hill Damaras.*

In ethnology the only intelligible definition of a Bantu is a full-blood or a half-brood Negro of Bantu speech;[2] and from the physical standpoint no very hard and fast line can be drawn between the northern Sudanese and southern Bantu groups, considered as two ethnical units.

Thanks to recent political developments in the interior, the linguistic divide may now be traced with some accuracy right across the continent. In the extreme west, Sir H. H. Johnston has shown that it coincides with the lower course of the Rio del Rey, while farther east the French expedition of 1891 under M. Dybowski found that it ran at about the same parallel (5° N.) along the elevated plateau which here forms the water-parting between the Congo and the Chad basin. From this point the line takes a south-easterly trend along the southern borders of the Zandeh and Mangbattu territories to

The Sudanese-Bantu Divide.

---

[1] Bantu, properly Aba-ntu, " people." *Aba* is one of the numerous personal prefixes, each with its corresponding singular form, which are the cause of so much confusion in Bantu nomenclature. To *aba, ab, ba* answers a sing. *umu, um, mu,* so that sing. *umu-ntu, um-ntu* or *mu-ntu,* a man, a person; plu. *aba-ntu, ab-ntu, ba-ntu.* But in some groups *mu* is also plural, the chief dialectic variants being, *Ama, Aba, Ma, Ba, Wa, Ova, Va, Vua, U, A, O, Eshi,* as in Ama-Zulu, Mu-Sarongo, Ma-Yomba, Wa-Swahili, Ova-Herero, Vua-Twa, Ba-Suto, Eshi-Kongo. For a tentative classification of African tribes see T. A. Joyce, Art. " Africa: Ethnology," *Ency. Brit.* 1910, p. 329. For the classification of Bantu tongues into 44 groups consult H. H. Johnston, Art. " Bantu Languages," *loc. cit.*

[2] *Eth.* Ch. XI.

the Semliki Valley between Lakes Albert Edward and Albert Nyanza, near the equator. Thence it pursues a somewhat irregular course, first north by the east side of the Albert Nyanza to the mouth of the Somerset Nile, then up that river to Mruli and round the east side of Usoga and the Victoria Nyanza to Kavirondo Bay, where it turns nearly east to the sources of the Tana, and down that river to its mouth in the Indian Ocean.

At some points the line traverses debatable territory, as in the Semliki Valley, where there are Sudanese and Negrillo overlappings, and again beyond Victoria Nyanza, where the frontiers are broken by the Hamitic Masai nomads and their Wandorobbo allies. But, speaking generally, everything south of the line here traced is Bantu, everything north of it Sudanese Negro in the western and central regions, and Hamitic in the eastern section between Victoria Nyanza and the Indian Ocean.

In some districts the demarcation is not quite distinct, as in the Tana basin, where some of the Galla and Somali Hamites from the north have encroached on the territory of the Wa-Pokomo Bantus on the south side of the river. But on the central plateau M. Dybowski passed abruptly from the **Frontier Tribes— The Bonjo Cannibals.** territory of the Bonjos, northernmost of the Bantu tribes, to that of the Sudanese Bandziri, a branch of the widespread Zandeh people. In this region, about the crest of the Congo-Chad water-parting, the contrasts appear to be all in favour of the Sudanese and against the Bantus, probably because here the former are Negroids, the latter full-blood Negroes. Thus Dybowski[1] found the Bonjos to be a distinctly Negro tribe with pronounced prognathism, and altogether a rude, savage people, trading chiefly in slaves, who are fattened for the meat market, and when in good condition will fetch about twelve shillings. On the other hand the Bandziri, despite their Niam-Niam connection, are not cannibals, but a peaceful, agricultural people, friendly to travellers, and of a coppery-brown complexion, with regular features, hence perhaps akin to the light-coloured people met by Barth in the Mosgu country.

Possibly the Bonjos may be a degraded branch of the

[1] *Le Naturaliste*, Jan. 1894.

Bayas or *Nderes*, a large nation, with many subdivisions
widely diffused throughout the Sangha basin,
where they occupy the whole space between the

The Baya Nation.

Kadei and the Mambere affluents of the main
stream (3° to 7° 30′ N. ; 14° to 17° E.). They are described
by M. F. J. Clozel [1] as of tall stature, muscular, well-proportioned, with flat nose, slightly tumid lips, and of black colour,
ut with a dash of copper-red in the upper classes. Although
cannibals, like the Bonjos, they are in other respects an
intelligent, friendly people, who, under the influence of the
Muhammadan Fulahs, have developed a complete political
administration, with a Royal Court, a Chancellor, Speaker,
Interpreter, and other officials, bearing sonorous titles taken
chiefly from the Hausa language. Their own Bantu tongue
is widespread and spoken with slight dialectic differences as
far as the Nana affluents.

M. Clozel, who regards them as mentally and morally
superior to most of the Middle and Lower Congo tribes, tells
us that the Bayas, that is, the " Red People,"
came at an unknown period from the east,

A " Red People."

" yielding to that great movement of migration
by which the African populations are continually impelled
westwards." The Yangere section were still on the move
some twelve years ago, but the general migration has since
been arrested by the Fulahs of Adamawa. Human flesh is
now interdicted to the women ; they have domesticated the
sheep, goat, and dog, and believe in a supreme being called
So, whose powers are manifested in the dense woodlands,
while minor deities preside over the village and the hut, that
is, the whole community and each separate family group.
Thus both their religious and political systems present a
certain completeness, which recalls those prevalent amongst
the semi-civilised peoples of the equatorial lake region, and is
evidently due to the same cause—long contact or association
with a race of higher culture and intelligence.

In order to understand all these relations, as well as
the general constitution of the Bantu populations, we have
to consider that the already-described Black
Zone, running from the Atlantic seaboard eastwards, has for countless generations been almost

**The North-
East Door to
Bantuland.**

---

[1] *Tour de Monde*, 1896, I. p. I sq. ; and *Les Bayas ; Notes Ethnographiques et Linguistiques*, Paris, 1896.

everywhere arrested north of the equator by the White Nile. Probably since the close of the Old Stone Age the whole of the region between the main stream and the Red Sea, and from the equator north to the Mediterranean, has formed an integral part of the Hamitic domain, encroached upon in prehistoric times by Semites and others in Egypt and Abyssinia, and in historic times chiefly by Semites (Arabs) in Egypt, Upper Nubia, Senaar, and Somaliland. Between this region and Africa south of the equator there are no serious physical obstructions of any kind, whereas farther west the Hamitic Saharan nomads were everywhere barred access to the south by the broad, thickly-peopled plateaux of the Sudanese Black Zone. All encroachments on this side necessarily resulted in absorption in the multitudinous Negro populations of Central Sudan, with the modifications of the physical and mental characters which are now presented by the Kanuri, Hausas, Songhai and other Negroid nations of that region, and are at present actually in progress amongst the conquering Fulah Hamites scattered in small dominant groups over a great part of Sudan from Senegambia to Wadai.

It follows that the leavening element, by which the southern Negro populations have been diversely modified throughout the Bantu lands, could have been drawn only from the Hamitic and Semitic peoples of the north-east. But in this connection the Semites themselves must be considered as almost *une quantité négligeable*, partly because of their relatively later arrival from Asia, and partly because, as they arrived, they became largely assimilated to the indigenous Hamitic inhabitants of Egypt, Abyssinia, and Somaliland. Belief in the presence of a Semitic people in the interior of S.E. Africa in early historic times was supported by the groups of ruins (especially those of Zimbabwe), found mainly in Southern Rhodesia, described in J. T. Bent's *Ruined Cities of Mashonaland*.[1] More recently Elliot Smith and Perry have been led by their investigations into the dissemination of culture to support the view that the mines, buildings, and aqueducts were due to the influence of early immigrants by sea, and that the fortified buildings probably served as dis-

Semitic Elements of the Bantu Amalgam.

---

[1] See below, p. 105.

tributing centres for the gold traffic carried on with the
Semitic traders of the coast. For certainly in Muhammadan
times Semites from Arabia formed permanent settlements
along the eastern seaboard as far south as Sofala, and these
intermingled more freely with the converted coast peoples
(*Wa-Swahili*, from *sahel*="coast"), but not with the *Kafirs*,
or "Unbelievers," farther south and in the interior. In our
own days these Swahili half-breeds, with a limited number of
full-blood Arabs,[1] have penetrated beyond the Great Lakes
to the Upper and Middle Congo basin, but rather as slave-
hunters and destroyers than as peaceful settlers, and contract-
ing few alliances, except perhaps amongst the Wa-Yao and
Ma-Gwangara tribes of Mozambique, and the cannibal Ma-
Nyemas farther inland.

To this extent Semitism may be recognised as a factor in
the constituent elements of the Bantu populations. Malays
have also been mentioned, and some ethnologists have even brought the Fulahs of Western
Sudan all the way from Malaysia. Certainly if
they reached and formed settlements in Madagascar, there is no intrinsic reason why they should not have
done the same on the mainland. But I have failed to find
any evidence of the fact, and if they ever at any time established themselves on the east coast they have long disappeared,
without leaving any clear trace of their presence either in
the physical appearance, speech, usages or industries of the
aborigines, such as are everywhere conspicuous in Madagascar. The small canoes with two booms and double outriggers which occur at least from Mombasa to Mozambique
are of Indonesian origin, as are the fish traps that occur at
Mombasa.

Malay Elements in Madagascar only.

There remain the north-eastern Hamites, and especially
the Galla branch, as the essential extraneous factor in this
obscure Bantu problem. To the stream of migration described by M. Clozel as setting east
and west, corresponds another and an older
stream, which ages ago took a southerly direction along the
eastern seaboard to the extremity of the continent, where
are now settled the Zulu-Xosa nations, almost more Hamites
than Negroes.

Hamitic Element everywhere.

[1] Even Tipu Tib, their chief leader and "Prince of Slavers," was a half-caste
with distinctly Negroid features.

The impulse to two such divergent movements could have come only from the north-east, where we still find the same tendencies in actual operation. During his exploration of the east equatorial lands, Capt. Speke had already observed that the rulers of the Bantu nations about the Great Lakes (Karagwe, Ba-Ganda, Ba-Nyoro, etc.) all be- **The Ba-Himas.** longed to the same race, known by the name of *Ba-Hima*, that is, " Northmen," a pastoral people of fine appearance, who were evidently of Galla stock, and had come originally from Gallaland. Since then Schuver found that the Negroes of the Afilo country are governed by a Galla aristocracy,[1] and we now know that several Ba-hima communities bearing different names live interspersed amongst the mixed Bantu nations of the lacustrian plateaux as far south as Lake Tanganyika and Unyamweziland.[2] Here the Wa-Tusi, Wa-Hha, and Wa-Ruanda are or were all of the same Hamitic type, and M. Lionel Dècle " was very much struck by the extraordinary difference that is to be found between them and their Bantu neighbours."[3] Then this observer adds : " Pure types are not common, and are only to be found amongst the aristocracy, if I may use such an expression for Africans. The mass of the people have lost their original type through intermixture with neighbouring tribes."

J. Roscoe[4] thus describes the inhabitants of Ankole. " The pastoral people are commonly called Bahima, though they prefer to be called Banyankole ; they are a tall fine race though physically not very strong. Many of them are over six feet in height, their young king being six feet six inches and broad in proportion to his height. . . . It is not only the men who are so tall, the women also being above the usual stature of their sex among other tribes, though they do injustice to their height by a fashionable stoop which makes them appear much shorter than they really are. The features

---

[1] " Afilo wurde mir vom Lega-König als ein Negerland bezeichnet, welches von einer Galla-Aristokratie beherrscht wird " (*Petermann's Mitt.* 1883, v. p. 194).

[2] The Ba-Hima are herdsmen in Buganda, a sort of aristocracy in Unyoro, a ruling caste in Toro, and the dominant race with dynasties in Ankole. The name varies in different areas.

[3] *Journ. Anthr. Inst.* 1895, p. 424. For details of the Ba-Hima type see *Eth.* p. 389.

[4] J. Roscoe, *The Northern Bantu*, 1915, p. 103. Herein are also described the *Bakene*, lake dwellers, the *Bagesu*, a cannibal tribe, the *Basoga* and the Nilotic tribes the *Bateso* and *Kavirondo*.

of these pastoral people are good : they have straight noses with a bridge, thin lips, finely chiselled faces, heads well set on fairly developed frames, and a good carriage ; there is in fact nothing but their colour and their short woolly hair to make you think of them as negroids."

The contrast and the relationship between the pastoral conquerors and the agricultural tribes is clearly seen among **Pastoral and** the Ba-Nyoro. "The pastoral people are a tall, **Agricultural** well-built race of men and women with finely **Clans.** cut features, many of them over six feet in height. The men are athletic with little spare flesh, but the women are frequently very fat and corpulent : indeed their ideal of beauty is obesity, and their milk diet together with their careful avoidance of exercise tends to increase their size. The agricultural clans, on the other hand, are short, ill-favoured looking men and women with broad noses of the negro type, lean and unkempt. Both classes are dark, varying in shade from a light brown to deep black, with short woolly hair. The pastoral people refrain, as far as possible, from all manual labour and expect the agricultural clans to do their menial work for them, such as building their houses, carrying firewood and water, and supplying them with grain and beer for their households." "Careful observation and enquiry lead to the opinion that the agricultural clans were the original inhabitants and that they were conquered by the pastoral people who have reduced them to their present servile condition." [1]

From these indications and many others that might easily be adduced, it may be concluded with some confidence that **The Bantus** the great mass of the Bantu populations are **mainly a Negro-** essentially Negroes, leavened in diverse pro- **Hamitic Cross.** portions for the most part by conquering Galla or Hamitic elements percolating for thousands of generations from the north-eastern section of the Hamitic domain into the heart of Bantuland.

The date of the Bantu migrations is much disputed. "As far as linguistic evidence goes," says H. H. Johnston,[2] "the ancestors of the Bantu dwelt in some region like the Bahr-al-Ghazal, not far from the Mountain Nile on the east, from

[1] J. Roscoe, *loc. cit.* pp. 4, 5.
[2] "A Survey of the Ethnography of Africa," *Journ. Roy. Anthr. Inst.* XLIII. 1913, p. 390.

Kordofan on the north, or the Benue and Chad basins on the west. Their first great movement of expansion seems to have been eastward, and to have established them (possibly with a guiding aristocracy of Hamitic origin) in the region between Mount Elgon, the Northern Victoria Nyanza, Tanganyika, and the Congo Forest. At some such period as about 300 B.C. their far-reaching invasion of Central and South Africa seems to have begun." The date is fixed by the date of the introduction of the fowl from Nile-land, since the root word for fowl is the same almost throughout Bantu Africa, " obviously related to the Persian words for fowl, yet quite unrelated to the Semitic terms, or to those used by the Kushites of Eastern Africa." F. Stuhlmann, on the contrary, places the migrations practically in geological times. After bringing the Sudan Negroes from South Asia at the end of the Tertiary or beginning of the Pleistocene (*Pluvial period*), and the Proto-Hamites from a region probably somewhat further to the north and west of the former, he continues : From the mingling of the Negroes and the Proto-Hamites were formed, probably in East Africa, the Bantu languages and the Bantu peoples, who wandered thence south and west. The wanderings began in the latter part of the Pleistocene period.[1] He quotes Th. Arldt, who with greater precision places the occupation of Africa by the Negroes in the Riss period (300,000 years ago) and that of the Hamites in the Mousterian period (30,000 to 50,000 years ago).[2]

All these peoples resulting from the crossings of Negroes with Hamites now speak various forms of the same organic Bantu mother-tongue. But this linguistic uniformity is strictly analogous to that now prevailing amongst the multifarious peoples of Aryan speech in Eurasia, and is due to analogous causes—the diffusion in extremely remote times of a mixed Hamito-Negro people of Bantu speech in Africa south of the equator. It might perhaps be objected that the present Ba-Hima pastors are of Hamitic speech, because we know from Stanley that the late king M'tesa of Buganda was proud of his Galla ancestors, whose language he still spoke as his mother-tongue. But he also spoke Luganda, and every echo

---

[1] *Handwerk und Industrie in Ostafrika*, 1910, p. 147.
[2] " Die erste Ausbreitung des Menschengeschlechts." *Pol. Anthropol. Revue*, 1909, p. 72. Cf. chronology on p. 14 above.

of Galla speech has already died out amongst most of the Ba-Hima communities in the equatorial regions. So it was with what I may call the " Proto-Ba-Himas," the first conquering Galla tribes, Schuver's and Dècle's " aristocracy," who were gradually blended with the aborigines in a new and superior nationality of Bantu speech, because " there are many mixed races, . . . but there are no mixed languages." [1]

These views are confirmed by the traditions and folklore still current amongst the " Lacustrians," as the great nations may be called, who are now grouped round about the shores of Lakes Victoria and Albert Nyanza. At present, or rather

The Lacus-trians. before the recent extension of the British administration to East Central Africa, these peoples were constituted in a number of separate kingdoms, the most powerful of which were Buganda (Uganda),[2] Bunyoro (Unyoro), and Karagwe. But they remember a time when all these now scattered fragments formed parts of a mighty monarchy, the vast Kitwara Empire, which comprised the whole of the lake-studded plateau between the Ruwenzori range and Kavirondoland.

The story is differently told in the different states, each nation being eager to twist it to its own glorification ; but all

Their Tradi-tions—The Kintu Legend. are agreed that the founder of the empire was Kintu, "The Blameless," at once priest, patriarch and ruler of the land, who came from the north hundreds of years ago, with one wife, one cow, one goat, one sheep, one chicken, one banana-root, and one sweet potato. Af first all was waste, an uninhabited wilderness, but it was soon miraculously peopled, stocked, and planted with what he had brought with him, the potato being apportioned to Bunyoro, the banana to Buganda, and these form the staple food of those lands to this day.

Then the people waxed wicked, and Kintu, weary of their evil ways and daily bloodshed, took the original wife, cow, and other things, and went away in the night and was seen no more. But nobody believed him dead, and a long line of his mythical successors appear to have spent the time they

---

[1] *Ethnology*, p. 199.

[2] Uganda is the name now applied to the whole Protectorate, Buganda is the small kingdom, Baganda, the people, Muganda, one person, Luganda, the language. H. H. Johnston, *The Uganda Protectorate*, 1902, and J. F. Cunningham, *Uganda and its Peoples*, 1905, cover much of the elementary anthropology of East Central Africa.

could spare from strife and war and evil deeds in looking for the lost Kintu. Kimera, one of these, was a mighty giant of such strength and weight that he left his footprints on the rocks where he trod, as may still be seen on a cliff not far from Ulagalla, the old capital of Buganda. There was also a magician, Kibaga, who could fly aloft and kill the Ba-Nyoro people (this is the Buganda version) by hurling stones down upon them, and for his services received in marriage a beautiful Ba-Nyoro captive, who, another Delilah, found out his secret, and betrayed him to her people.

At last came King Ma'anda, who pretended to be a great hunter, but it was only to roam the woodlands in search of Kintu, and thus have tidings of him. One day a peasant, obeying the directions of a thrice-dreamt dream, came to a place in the forest, where was an aged man on a throne between two rows of armed warriors, seated on mats, his long beard white with age, and all his men fair as white people and clothed in white robes. Then Kintu, for it was he, bid the peasant hasten to summon Ma'anda thither, but only with his mother and the messenger. At the Court Ma'anda recognised the stranger whom he had that very night seen in a dream, and so believed his words and at once set out with his mother and the peasant. But the Katikiro, or Prime Minister, through whom the message had been delivered to the king, fearing treachery, also started on their track, keeping them just in view till the trysting-place was reached. But Kintu, who knew everything, saw him all the time, and when he came forward on finding himself discovered the enraged Ma'anda pierced his faithful minister to the heart and he fell dead wth a shriek. Thereupon Kintu and his seated warriors instantly vanished, and the king with the others wept and cried upon Kintu till the deep woods echoed Kintu, Kintu-u, Kintu-u-u. But the blood-hating Kintu was gone, and to this day has never again been seen or heard of by any man in Buganda. The references to the north and to Kintu and his ghostly warriors " fair as white people " need no comment.[1] It is noteworthy that in some of the Nyassaland

---

[1] The legend is given with much detail by H. M. Stanley in *Through the Dark Continent*, Vol. I. p. 344 sq. Another and less mythical account of the migrations of " the people with a white skin from the far north-east " is quoted from Emin Pasha by the Rev. R. P. Ashe in *Two Kings of Uganda*, p. 336. Here the immigrant Ba-Hima are expressly stated to have " adopted the language of the aborigines " (p. 337).

dialects *Kintu* (*Caintu*) alternates with *Mulungu* as the name of the Supreme Being, the great ancestor of the tribe.[1]

Then follows more traditional or legendary matter, including an account of the wars with the fierce Wakedi, who

The Ba-Ganda, past and present. wore iron armour, until authentic history is reached with the atrocious Suna II (1836–60), father of the scarcely less atrocious M'tesa. After his death in 1884 Buganda and the neighbouring states passed rapidly through a series of astonishing political, religious, and social vicissitudes, resulting in the present *pax Britannica*, and the conversion of large numbers, some to Islám, others to one form or another of Christianity. At times it might have been difficult to see much religion in the ferocity of the contending factions ; but since the establishment of harmony by the secular arm, real progress has been made, and the Ba-Ganda especially have displayed a remarkable capacity as well as eagerness to acquire a knowledge of letters and of religious principles, both in the Protestant and the Roman Catholic communities. Printing-presses, busily worked by native hands, are needed to meet the steadily increasing demand for a vernacular literature, in a region where blood had flowed continually from the disappearance of " Kintu " till the British occupation.

To the admixture of the Hamitic and Negro-elements amongst the Lacustrians may perhaps be attributed the

Political and Social Institutions. curious blend of primitive and higher institutions in these communities. At the head of the State was a Kabaka, king or emperor, although the title was also borne by the queen-mother and the queen-sister. This autocrat had his *Lukiko*, or Council, of which the members were the *Katikiro*, Prime Minister and Chief Justice, the *Kimbugwe*, who had charge of the King's umbilical cord, and held rank next to the *Katikiro*, and ten District chiefs, for the administration of the ten large districts into which the country was divided, each rendering accounts to the *Katikiro* and through him to the King. Each District chief had to maintain in good order a road some four yards wide, reaching from the capital to his country seat, a distance possibly of nearly 100 miles. Each District chief had sub-chiefs under

---

[1] Sir H. H. Johnston, *op. cit.* p. 514.

him, independent of the chief in managing their own portion of land. These were responsible for keeping in repair the road between their own residence and that of the District chief. In each district was a supreme court, and every sub-chief, even with only a dozen followers, could hold a court and try cases among his own people. The people, however, could take their cases from one court to another until eventually they came before the *Katikiro* or the King.

Yet together with this highly advanced social and political development a totemic exogamous clan system was in force throughout Uganda, all the Ba-Ganda belonging to one of 29 *kika* or clans, each possessing two totems held sacred by the clan. Thus the Lion (*Mpologma*) clan had the Eagle (*Mpungu*) for its second totem; the Mushroom (*Butiko*) clan had the Snail (*Nsonko*); the Buffalo (*Mbogo*) clan had a New Cooking Pot (*Ntamu*). Each clan had its chief, or Father, who resided on the clan estate which was also the clan burial-ground, and was responsible for the conduct of the members of his branch. All the clans were exogamous,[1] and a man was expected to take a second wife from the clan of his paternal grandmother.[2]

Totemic System.

No direct relations appear to exist between the Lacustrians and the *Wa-Kikuyu, Wa-Kamba, Wa-Pokomo, Wa-Gweno, Wa-Chaga, Wa-Teita, Wa-Taveita*, and others,[3] who occupy the region east of Victoria Nyanza, between the Tana, north-east frontier of Bantu-land, and the southern slopes of Kilimanjaro. Their affinities seem to be rather with the *Wa-Nyika, Wa-Boni, Wa-Duruma, Wa-Giryama*, and the other coast tribes between the Tana and Mombasa. All of these tribes have more or less adopted the habits and customs of the Masai.

Bantu Peoples between L. Victoria and the Coast.

We learn from Sir A. Harding[4] that in the British East

---

[1] Except the Lung-fish clan.
[2] J. Roscoe, *The Baganda*, 1911.
[3] For the *Wa-Kikuyu* see W. S. and K. Routledge, *With a Prehistoric People*, 1910, and C. W. Hobley's papers in the *Journ. Roy. Anthr. Inst.* XL. 1910, and XLI. 1911. The *Atharaka* are described by A. M. Champion, *Journ. Roy. Anthr. Inst.* XLII. 1912, p. 68. Consult for this region C. Eliot, *The East Africa Protectorate*, 1905; K. Weule, *Native Life in East Africa*, 1909; C. W. Hobley, *Ethnology of the A-Kamba and other East African Tribes*, 1910; M. Weiss, *Die Völkerstämme im Norden Deutsch-Ostafrikas*, 1910; and A Werner, "The Bantu Coast Tribes of the East Africa Protectorate," *Journ. Roy. Anthr. Inst.* XLV. 1915.
[4] *Official Report on the East African Protectorate*, 1897.

African Protectorate there are altogether as many as twenty-five distinct tribes, generally at a low stage of culture, with a loose tribal organisation, a fully-developed totemic system, and a universal faith in magic ; but there are no priests, idols or temples, or even distinctly recognised hereditary chiefs or communal councils. The Gallas, who have crossed the Tana and here encroached on Bantu territory, have reminiscences of a higher civilisation and apparently of Christian traditions and observances, derived no doubt from Abyssinia. They tell you that they had once a sacred book, the observance of whose precepts made them the first of nations. But it was left lying about, and so got eaten by a cow, and since then when cows are killed their entrails are carefully searched for the lost volume.

Exceptional interest attaches to the Wa-Giryama, who are the chief people between Mombasa and Melindi, the first trustworthy accounts of whom were contributed by W. E. Taylor,[1] and W. W. A. Fitzgerald.[2] Here again Bantus and Gallas are found in close contact, and we learn that the Wa-Giryama, who came originally from the Mount Mangea district in the north-east, occupied their present homes only about a century ago "upon the withdrawal of the Gallas." The language, which is of a somewhat archaic type, appears to be the chief member of a widespread Bantu group, embracing the Ki-nyika, and Ki-pokomo in the extreme north, the Ki-swahili of the Zanzibar coast, and perhaps the Ki-kamba, the Ki-teita, and others of the interior between the coastlands and Victoria Nyanza. These inland tongues, however, have greatly diverged from the primitive Ki-giryama,[3] which stands in somewhat the same relation to them and to the still more degraded and Arabised Ki-swahili[4] that Latin stands to the Romance languages.

The Wa-Giryama.

But the chief interest presented by the Wa-Giryama is

---

[1] *Vocabulary of the Giryama Language*, S.P.C.K. 1897.
[2] *Travels in the Coastlands of British East Africa*, London, 1898, p. 103 sq.
[3] A. Werner, " Girijama Texts," *Zeitschr. f. Kol.-spr.* Oct. 1914.
[4] Having become the chief medium of intercourse throughout the southern Bantu regions, Ki-swahili has been diligently cultivated, especially by the English missionaries, who have wisely discarded the Arab for the Roman characters. There is already an extensive literature, including grammars, dictionaries, translations of the Bible and other works, and even *A History of Rome* issued by the S.P.C.K. in 1898.

centred in their religious ideas, which are mainly connected with ancestry-worship, and afford an unexpected insight into the origin and nature of that perhaps most primitive of all forms of belief. There is, of course, a vague entity called a " Supreme Being " in ethnographic writings, who, like the Algonquian Manitu, crops up under various names (here *Mulungu*) all over east Bantuland, but on analysis generally resolves itself into some dim notion growing out of ancestry-worship, a great or aged person, eponymous hero or the like, later deified in diverse ways as the Preserver, the Disposer, and especially the Creator. These Wa-Giryama suppose that from his union with the Earth all things have sprung, and that human beings are Mulungu's hens and chickens. But there is also an idea that he may be the manes of their fathers, and thus everything becomes merged in a kind of apotheosis of the departed. They think " the disembodied spirit is powerful for good and evil. Individuals worship the shades of their immediate ancestors or elder relatives ; and the *k'omas* [souls ?] of the whole nation are worshipped on public occasions."

[margin note: Primitive Ancestry-Worship.]

[margin note: Mulungu and the Shades.]

Although the European ghost or " revenant " is unknown, the spirits of near ancestors may appear in dreams, and express their wishes to the living. They ask for sacrifices at their graves to appease their hunger, and such sacrifices are often made with a little flour and water poured into a coconut shell let into the ground, the fowls and other victims being so killed that the blood shall trickle into the grave. At the offering the dead are called on by name to come and partake, and bring their friends with them, who are also mentioned by name. But whereas Christians pray to be remembered of heaven and the saints, the Wa-Giryama pray rather that the new-born babe be forgotten of Mulungu, and so live. " Well ! " they will say on the news of a birth, " may Mulungu forget him that he may become strong and well." This is an instructive trait, a reminiscence of the time when Mulungu, now almost harmless or indifferent to mundane things, was the embodiment of all evil, hence to be feared and appeased in accordance with the old dictum *Timor fecit deos.*

At present no distinction is drawn between good and bad spirits, but all are looked upon as, of course, often, though not always, more powerful than the living, but still human beings subject to the same feelings, passions, and fancies as they are. Some are even poor weaklings on whom offerings are wasted. " The Shade of So-and-so's father is of no use at all ; it has finished up his property, and yet he is no better," was a native's comment on the result of a series of sacrifices a man had vainly made to his father's shade to regain his health. They may also be duped and tricked, and when *pombe* (beer) is a-brewing, some is poured out on the graves of the dead, with the prayer that they may drink, and when drunk fall asleep, and so not disturb the living with their brawls and bickerings, just like the wrangling fairies in *A Midsummer Night's Dream.*[1]

Far removed from such crass anthropomorphism, but not morally much improved, are the kindred Wa-Swahili, who by long contact and interminglings have become largely Arabised in dress, religion, and general culture. They are graphically described by Taylor as " a seafaring, barter-loving race of slave-holders and slave-traders, strewn in a thin line along a thousand miles of creeks and islands ; inhabitants of a coast that has witnessed incessant political changes, and a succession of monarchical dynasties in various centres ; receiving into their midst for ages past a continuous stream of strange blood, consisting not only of serviles from the interior, but of immigrants from Persia, Arabia, and Western India ; men that have come to live, and often to die, as resident aliens, leaving in many cases a hybrid progeny. Of one section of these immigrants—the Arabs—the religion has become the master-religion of the land, overspreading, if not entirely supplanting, the old Bantu ancestor-worship, and profoundly affecting the whole family life."

The The Wa-Swahili.

The Wa-Swahili are in a sense a historical people, for they formed the chief constituent elements of the renowned Zang (Zeng) empire,[2] which in Edrisi's time (twelfth century) stretched along the seaboard from Somaliland to and beyond the Zambesi.

The Zang Empire.

---

[1] W. E. H. Barrett, " Notes on the Customs and Beliefs of the Wa-Giriama," etc., *Journ. Roy. Anthr. Inst.* XLI. 1911, gives further details.   For a full review of the religious beliefs of Bantu tribes see E. S. Hartland, Art. " Bantu and S. Africa," *Ency. of Religion and Ethics,* 1909.

[2] The name still survives in *Zangue-bar* (" Zang-land ") and the adjacent island of *Zanzibar* (an Indian corruption).   *Zang* is " black," and *bar* is the same Arabic word, meaning dry land, that we have in *Mala-bar* on the opposite side of the Indian Ocean.   Cf. also *barran wa bahran,* " by land and by sea."

When the Portuguese burst suddenly into the Indian Ocean it was a great and powerful state, or rather a vast confederacy of states, with many flourishing cities—Magdoshu, Brava, Mombasa, Melindi, Kilwa, Angosha, Sofala—and widespread commercial relations extending across the eastern waters to India and China, and up the Red Sea to Europe. How these great centres of trade and eastern culture were one after the other ruthlessly destroyed by the Portuguese corsairs *co' o ferro e fogo* ("with sword and fire," Camoens) is told by Duarte Barbosa, who was himself a Portuguese and an eye-witness of the havoc and the horrors that not infrequently followed in the trail of his barbarous fellow-countrymen.[1]

Beyond Sofala we enter the domain of the *Ama-Zula* the *Ama-Xosa*, and others whom I have collectively called *Zulu-Xosas*,[2] and who are in some respects the most remarkable ethnical group in all Bantuland. Indeed they are by common consent regarded as Bantus in a pre-eminent sense, and this conventional term *Bantu* itself is taken from their typical *Bantu* language.[3] There is clear evidence that they are comparatively recent arrivals, necessarily from the north, in their present territory, which was still occupied by Bushman and Hottentot tribes probably within the last thousand years or so. Before the Kafir wars with the English (1811–77) this territory extended much farther round the coast than at present, and for many years the Great Kei River has formed the frontier between the white settlements and the Xosas.

The Zulu-Xosas.

Former and Present Domain.

But what they have lost in this direction the Zulu-Xosas,

---

[1] *Viage por Malabar y Costas de Africa,* 1512, translated by the Hon. Henry E. J. Stanley, Hakluyt Society, 1868.

[2] In preference to the more popular form *Zulu-Kafir,* where *Kafir* is merely the Arabic " Infidel " applied indiscriminately to any people rejecting Islám ; hence the *Siah Posh Kafirs* (" Black-clad Infidels ") of Afghanistan ; the *Kufra* oasis in the Sahara, where *Kufra,* plural of *Kafir,* refers to the pagan Tibus of that district ; and the Kafirs generally of the East African seaboard. But according to English usage *Zulu* is applied to the northern part of the territory, mainly Zululand proper and Natal, while Kafirland or Kaffraria is restricted to the southern section between Natal and the Great Kei River. The bulk of these southern " Kafirs " belong to the Xosa connection ; hence this term takes the place of *Kafir,* in the compound expression *Zulu-Xosa.* *Ama* is explained on p. 86, and the *X* of *Xosa* represents an unpronounceable combination of a guttural and a lateral click, this with two other clicks (a dental and a palatal) having infected the speech of these Bantus during their long prehistoric wars with the Hottentots or Bushmen. See p. 129.

[3] See p. 86 above.

or at least the Zulus, have recovered a hundredfold by their expansion northwards during the nineteenth century. After the establishment of the Zulu military power under Dingiswayo and his successor Chaka (1793–1828), half the continent was overrun by organised Zulu hordes, who ranged as far north as Victoria Nyanza, and in many places founded more or less unstable kingdoms or chieftaincies on the model of the terrible despotism set up in Zululand. Such were, beyond the Limpopo, the states of Gazaland and Matabililand, the latter established about 1838 by Umsilikatzi, father of Lobengula, who perished in a hopeless struggle with the English in 1894. Gungunhana, last of the Swazi (Zulu) chiefs in Gazaland, where the A-Ngoni had overrun the Ba-Thonga (Ba-Ronga),[1] was similarly dispossessed by the Portuguese in 1896.

North of Zambesi the Zulu bands—Ma-Situ, Ma-Viti, Ma-Ngoni (A-Ngoni), and others—nowhere developed large political states except for a short time under the ubiquitous Mirambo in Unyamweziland. But some, especially the A-Ngoni,[2] were long troublesome in the Nyasa district, and others about the Lower Zambesi, where they are known to the Portuguese as "Landins." The A-Ngoni power was finally broken by the English early in 1898, and the reflux movement has now entirely subsided, and cannot be revived, the disturbing elements having been extinguished at the fountain-head by the absorption of Zululand itself in the British Colony of Natal (1895).

Nowhere have patriarchal institutions been more highly developed than among the Zulu-Xosas, all of whom, except perhaps the Ama-Fingus and some other broken groups, claim direct descent from some eponymous hero or mythical founder of the tribe. Thus

Zulu-Xosa Genealogies.

---

[1] See the admirable monograph on the Ba-Thonga, by H. A. Junod, *The Life of a South African Tribe*, 1912.

[2] Robert Codrington tells us that these A-Ngoni (Aba-Ngoni) spring from a Zulu tribe which crossed the Zambesi about 1825, and established themselves south-east of L. Tanganyika, but later migrated to the uplands west of L. Nyasa, where they founded three petty states. Others went east of the Livingstone range, and are here still known as Magwangwara. But all became gradually assimilated to the surrounding populations. Intermarrying with the women of the country they preserve their speech, dress, and usages for the first generation in a slightly modified form, although the language of daily intercourse is that of the mothers. Then this class becomes the aristocracy of the whole nation, which henceforth comprises a great part of the aborigines ruled by a privileged caste of Zulu origin, "perpetuated almost entirely among themselves" ("Central Angoniland," *Geograph. Jour.* May, 1898, p. 512). See A. Werner, *The Natives of British Central Africa*, 1906.

in the national traditions Chaka was seventh in descent from a legendary chief Zulu, from whom they take the name of *Abantu ba-Kwa-Zulu*, that is " People of Zulu's Land," although the true mother-tribe appear to have been the now extinct Ama-Ntombela. Once the supremacy and prestige of Chaka's tribe were established, all the others, as they were successively reduced, claimed also to be true Zulus, and as the same process went on in the far north, the term Zulu has now in many cases come to imply political rather than blood relationship. Here we have an object lesson, by which the ethnical value of such names as " Aryan," " Kelt," " Briton," " Slav," etc. may be gauged in other regions.

So also most of the southern section claim as their founder and ancestor a certain *Xosa*, sprung from Zuide, who may have flourished about 1500, and whom the Ama-Tembus and Ama-Mpondos also regard as their progenitor. Thus the whole section is connected, but not in the direct line, with the Xosas, who trace their lineage from Galeka and Khakhabe, sons of Palo, who is said to have died about 1780, and was himself tenth in direct descent from Xosa. We thus get a genealogical table as under, which gives his proper place in the Family Tree to nearly every historical " Kafir " chief in Cape Colony, where ignorance of these relations caused much bloodshed during the early Kafir wars :

```
                        Zuide (1500 ?)
    ┌───────────────────────┼───────────────────────┐
  Tembu                  Zosa (1530 ?)             Mpondo
    |                     Palo (1780 ?)               |
Ama-Tembus                   |                ┌───────┴───────┐
(Tembookies)                 |           Mpondumisi (Mpondos)
          ┌──────────────────┴──────────────────┐
       Galeka                              Khakhabe
          |                                    |
       Klanta              ┌──────────────┬─────┴─────────────┐
          |              Omlao          Mbalu            Ndhlambe
       Hinza               |              |             ┌────┴────┐
          |            Gika (ob. 1828)  Gwali      Ama-Ndhlambes
       Kreli              |              |              (Tslambies)
    └────┬────┘        Macomo          Velelo
   Ama-Galekas            |              |
                       Sandili          Baxa
                    └────┬────┘      └────┬────┘
                     Ama-Gaikas      Ama-Mbalus
```

But all, both northern Zulus and southern Xosas, are essentially one people in speech, physique, usages and social institutions. The hair is uniformly of a some- **Physical Type.** what frizzly texture, the colour of a light or clear brown amongst the Ama-Tembus, but elsewhere very dark, the Swazis being almost " blue-black " ; the head decidedly long (72.5) and high (195.8) ; nose variable, both Negroid and perfectly regular ; height above the mean 1.75 m. to 1.8 m. (5 ft. 9 in. to 5 ft. 11 in.) ; figure shapely and muscular, though Fritsch's measurements show that it is sometimes far from the almost ideal standard of beauty with which some early observers have credited them.

Mentally the Zulu-Xosas stand much higher than the true Negro, as shown especially in their political organisation, which, before the development of Dingiswayo's

Social Organisation. military system under European influences, was a kind of patriarchal monarchy controlled by a powerful aristocracy. The nation was grouped in tribes connected by the ties of blood and ruled by the hereditary *inkose*, or feudal chief, who was supreme, with power of life and death, within his own jurisdiction. Against his mandates, however, the nobles could protest in council, and it was in fact their decisions that established precedents and the traditional

" Common Law." code of common law. " This common law is well adapted to a people in a rude state of society. It holds everyone accused of crime guilty unless he can prove himself innocent ; it makes the head of the family responsible for the conduct of all its branches, the village collectively for all resident in it, and the clan for each of its villages. For the administration of the law there are courts of various grades, from any of which an appeal may be taken to the Supreme Council, presided over by the paramount chief, who is not only the ruler but also the father of the people." [1]

In the interior, between the southern coast ranges and the Zambesi, the Hottentot and Bushman aborigines were in

Ma-Shonas and Ma-Kalakas. prehistoric ages almost everywhere displaced or reduced to servitude by other Bantu peoples such as the Ma-Kalakas and Ma-Shonas, the Be-Chuanas and the kindred Ba-Sutos. Of these the first arrivals (from the north) appear to have been the Ma-Shonas and Ma-Kalakas, who were being slowly " eaten up " by the

---

[1] Rev. J. Macdonald, *Light in Africa*, p. 194. Among recent works on the Zulu-Xosa tribes may be mentioned Dudley Kidd, *The Essential Kafir*, 1904, *Savage Childhood*, 1905 ; H. A. Junod, *The Life of a South African Tribe* (Ba-Thonga), 1912–3 ; G. W. Stow and G. M. Theal, *The Native Races of South Africa*, 1905.

Ma-Tabili when the process was arrested by the timely intervention of the English in Rhodesia.

Both nations are industrious tillers of the soil, skilled in metal-work and in mining operations, being probably the direct descendants of the natives, whose great chief *Monomotapa*, *i.e.* " Lord of the Mines," as I interpret the word,[1] ruled over the Manica and surrounding auriferous districts when the Portuguese first reached Sofala early in the sixteenth century. Apparently for political reasons [2] this Monomotapa was later transformed by them from a monarch to a monarchy, the vast empire of Monomotapaland, which was supposed to comprise pretty well everything south of the Zambesi, but, having no existence, has for the last two hundred years eluded the diligent search of historical geographers.

The Mono-motapa Myth.

But some centuries before the arrival of the Portuguese the Ma-Kalakas with the kindred Ba-Nyai, Ba-Senga and others, may well have been at work in the mines of this auriferous region, in the service of the builders of the Zimbabwe ruins explored and described by the late Theodore Bent,[3] and by him and many others attributed to some ancient cultured people of South Arabia. This theory of prehistoric Oriental origin was supported by a calculation of the orientation of the Zimbabwe " temple," by reports of inscriptions and emblems suggesting " Phoenician rites," and by the discovery, during excavation, of foreign objects. Later investigation, however, showed that the orientation was based on inexact measurements ; no authentic inscriptions were found either at Zimbabwe or elsewhere in connection with the ruins ; none of the objects discovered in the course of the excavations could be recognised as more than a few centuries old, while those that were not demonstrably foreign imports were of African type. In 1905 a scientific exploration of the ruins placed these facts beyond

The Zimbabwe Ruins.

[1] From *Mwana*, lord, master, and *tapa*, to dig, both common Bantu words.

[2] The point was that Portugal had made treaties with this mythical State, in virtue of which she claimed in the " scramble for Africa " all the hinterlands behind her possessions on the east and west coasts (Mozambique and Angola), in fact all South Africa between the Orange and Zambesi rivers. Further details on the "Monomotapa Question" will be found in my monograph on " The Portuguese in South Africa " in Murray's *South Africa, from Arab Domination to British Rule*, 1891, p. 11 sq. Five years later Mr G. McCall Theal also discovered, no doubt independently, the mythical character of Monomotapaland in his book on *The Portuguese in South Africa*, 1896.

[3] *Proc. R. Geogr. Soc.* May, 1892, and *The Ruined Cities of Mashonaland*, 1892.

dispute. The medieval objects were found in such positions as to be necessarily contemporaneous with the foundation of the buildings, all of which could be attributed to the same period. Finally it was established that the plan and construction of Zimbabwe instead of being unique, as was formerly supposed, only differed from other Rhodesian ruins in dimensions and extent. The explorers felt confident that the buildings were not earlier than the fourteenth or fifteenth century A.D., and that the builders were the Bantu people, remains of whose stone-faced kraals are found at so many places between the Limpopo and the Zambesi. Their conclusions, however, have not met with universal acceptance.[1]

With the Be-Chuanas, whose territory extends from the Orange river to Lake Ngami and includes Basutoland with a great part of the Transvaal, we again meet a people at the totemic stage of culture. Here the eponymous heroes of the Zulu-Xosas are replaced by baboons, fishes, elephants, and other animals from which the various tribal groups claim descent. The animal in question is called the *siboko* of the tribe and is held in especial reverence, members (as a rule) refraining from killing or eating it. Many tribes take their name from their *siboko*, thus the Ba-Tlapin, " they of the fish," Ba-Kuena, " they of the crocodile." The *siboko* of the Ba-Rolong, who as a tribe are accomplished smiths, is not an animal, but the metal iron.[2]

The Be-Chuanas.

With a section of the great Be-Chuana family, the Ba-Suto, and the Ba-Rotse is connected one of the most remarkable episodes in the turbulent history of the South African peoples during the nineteenth century. Many years ago an offshoot of the Ba-Rotse migrated to the Middle Zambesi above the Victoria Falls, where they founded a powerful state, the " Barotse (Marotse) Empire," which despite a temporary eclipse still exists as a British protectorate. The eclipse was caused by another migration northwards of a great body of Ma-Kololo, a branch of the Ba-Suto,

The Ba-Rotse Empire.

The Ma-Kololo Episode.

---

[1] D. Randall-MacIver, *Mediaeval Rhodesia*, 1906. But R. N. Hall strongly combats his views, *Great Zimbabwe*, 1905, *Prehistoric Rhodesia*, 1909, and *South African Journal of Science*, May, 1912. H. H. Johnston says, " I see nothing inherently improbable in the finding of gold by proto-Arabs in the south-eastern part of Zambezia ; nor in the pre-Islamic Arab origin of Zimbabwe," p. 396, " A Survey of the Ethnography of Africa," *Journ. Roy. Anthr. Inst.* XLIII. 1913.

[2] G. W. Stow, *The Native Races of South Africa*, 1905.

who under the renowned chief Sebituane reached the Zambesi about 1835 and overthrew the Barotse dynasty, reducing the natives to a state of servitude.

But after the death of Sebituane's successor, Livingstone's Sekeletu, the Ba-Rotse, taking advantage of their oppressors' dynastic rivalries, suddenly revolted, and after exterminating the Ma-Kololo almost to the last man, reconstituted the empire on a stronger footing than ever. It now comprises an area of some 250,000 square miles between the Chobe and the Kafukwe affluents,[1] with a population vaguely estimated at over 1,000,000, including the savage Ba-Shukulumbwe tribes of the Kafukwe basin reduced in 1891.[2]

Yet, short as was the Ma-Kololo rule (1835–70), it was long enough to impose their language on the vanquished Ba-Rotse.[3] Hence the curious phenomenon now witnessed about the Middle Zambesi, where the Ma-Kololo have disappeared, while their Sesuto speech remains the common medium of intercourse throughout the Barotse empire. How often have analogous shiftings and dislocations taken place in the course of ages in other parts of the world! And in the light of such lessons how cautious ethnographists should be in arguing from speech to race, and drawing conclusions from these or similar surface relations!

Referring to these stirring events, Mackenzie writes: "Thus perished the Makololo from among the number of South African tribes. No one can put his finger on the map of Africa and say, 'Here dwell the Makololo.'"[4] This will puzzle many who since the middle of the nineteenth century have repeatedly heard of, and even been in unpleasantly close contact with, Ma-Kololo so called, not indeed in Barotseland, but lower down the Zambesi about its Shiré affluent.

The explanation of the seeming contradiction is given by another incident, which is also not without ethnical significance. From Livingstone's *Journals* we learn that in 1859 he was accompanied to the east coast by a small party of Ma-Kololo and others, sent by his friend Sekeletu in quest of a cure for leprosy, from which the emperor was suffering.

---

[1] The British Protectorate was limited in 1905 to about 182,000 square miles.
[2] Cf. A. St H. Gibbons, *Africa South to North through Marotseland*, 1904, and C. W. Mackintosh, *Coillard of the Zambesi*, 1907, with a bibliography.
[3] The Ma-Kololo gave the Ba-Rotse their present name. They were originally Aälui, but the conquerors called them Ma-Rotse, people of the plain.
[4] *Ten Years North of the Orange River.*

These Ma-Kololo, hearing of the Ba-Rotse revolt, wisely stopped on their return journey at the Shiré confluence, and through the prestige of their name have here succeeded in founding several so-called " Makololo States," which still exist, and have from time to time given considerable trouble to the administrators of British Central Africa. But how true are Mackenzie's words, if the political be separated from the ethnical relations, may be judged from the fact that of the original founders of these petty Shiré states only two were full-blood Ma-Kololo. All the others were, I believe, Ba-Rotse, Ba-Toka, or Ba-Tonga, these akin to the savage Ba-Shukulumbwe.

Thus the Ma-Kololo live on, in their speech above the Victoria Falls, in their name below the Victoria Falls, and it

Death without Extinction. is only from history we know that since about 1870 the whole nation has been completely wiped out everywhere in the Zambesi valley. But even amongst cultured peoples history goes back a very little way, 10,000 years at most anywhere. What changes and shiftings may, therefore, have elsewhere also taken place during prehistoric ages, all knowledge of which is now past recovery ! [1]

Few Bantu peoples have lent a readier ear to the teachings of Christian propagandists than the Xosa, Ba-Suto, and Be-Chuana natives. Several stations in the heart of Kafirland—Blythswood, Somerville, Lovedale, and others—have for some time·been self-supporting, and prejudice alone would

Spread of Christianity among the Southern Bantus. deny that they have worked for good amongst the surrounding Gaika, Galeka, and Fingo tribes. Sogo, a member of the Blythswood community, has produced a translation of the *Pilgrim's Progress*, described by J. Macdonald as " a marvel of accuracy and lucidity of expression ; " [2] numerous village schools are eagerly attended, and much land has been brought under intelligent cultivation.

The French and Swiss Protestant teachers have also achieved great things in Basutoland, where they were welcomed by Moshesh, the founder of the present Basuto nation. The tribal nation has yielded to a higher social

[1] Cf. G. M. Theal, *The History of South Africa* 1908–9, and *The Beginning of South African History*, 1902.
[2] *Op. cit.* p. 47.

organisation, and the Ba-Tau, Ba-Puti, and several other tribal groups have been merged in industrious pastoral and agricultural communities professing a somewhat strict form of Protestant Christianity, and entirely forgetful of the former heathen practices associated with witchcraft and ancestry-worship. Moshesh was one of the rare instances among the Kafirs of a leader endowed with intellectual gifts which placed him on a level with Europeans. He governed his people wisely and well for nearly fifty years, and his life-work has left a permanent mark on South African history.[1]

In Bechuanaland one great personality dominates the social horizon. Khama, king of the Ba-Mangwato nation, next to the Ba-Rotse the most powerful section of the Be-Chuana, may be described as a true father of his people, a Christian legislator in the better sense of the term, and an enlightened reformer even from the secular point of view. — Khama.

When these triumphs, analogous to those witnessed amongst the Lacustrians and in other parts of Bantuland, are contrasted with the dull weight of resistance everywhere opposed by the full-blood Negro populations to any progress beyond their present low level of culture, we are the better able to recognise the marked intellectual superiority of the negroid Bantu over the pure black element.

West of Bechuanaland the continuity of the Bantu domain is arrested in the south by the Hottentots, who still hold their ground in Namaqualand, and farther north by the few wandering Bushman groups of the Kalahari desert. Even in Damaraland, which is mainly — The Ova-Herero.
Bantu territory, there are interminglings of long standing that have given rise to much ethnical confusion. The *Ova-Herero*, who were here dominant, and the kindred *Ova-Mpo* of Ovampoland bordering on the Portuguese possessions, are undoubted Bantus of somewhat fine physique, though intellectually not specially distinguished. — Cattle and Hill Damaras.
Owing to the character of the country, a somewhat arid, level steppe between the hills and the coast, they are often collectively called " Cattle Damaras," or " Damaras of the Plains," in contradistinction to the " Hill Damaras " of the coast ranges. To this popular nomenclature is due the prevalent confusion regarding these aborigines. The term

[1] G. Lagden, *The Basutos*, 1909.

" Damara " is of Hottentot origin, and is not recognised by the local tribes, who all call themselves Ova-Herero, that is, " Merry People." But there is a marked difference between the lowlanders and the highlanders, the latter, that is, the " Hill Damaras," having a strong strain of Hottentot blood, and being now of Hottentot speech.

The whole region is a land of transition between the two races, where the struggle for supremacy was scarcely arrested by the temporary intervention of German administrators. Though annexed by Germany in 1884, fighting continued for ten years longer, and, breaking out again in 1903, was not subdued until 1908, after the loss to Germany of 5000 lives and £15,000,000, while 20,000 to 30,000 of the Herero are estimated to have perished. Under the rule of the Union of South Africa this maltreatment of the natives will never occur again. Clearness would be gained by substituting for Hill Damaras the expression *Ova-Zorotu*, or " Hillmen," as they are called by their neighbours of the plains, who should of course be called Hereros to the àbsolute exclusion of the expression " Cattle Damaras." These Hereros show a singular dislike for salt ; the peculiarity, however, can scarcely be racial, as it is shared in also by their cattle, and may be due to the heavy vapours, perhaps slightly charged with saline particles, which hang so frequently over the coastlands.

No very sharp ethnical line can be drawn between Portuguese West Africa and the contiguous portion of the Belgian Congo south and west of the main stream. In the coastlands between the Cunene and the Congo estuary a few groups, such as the historical *Eshi-Kongo*[1] and the *Kabindas*, have developed some marked characteristics under European influences, just as have the cannibal *Ma-Nyema* of the Upper Congo through association with the Nubian-Arab slave-raiders. But with the exception of the *Ba-Shilange*, the *Ba-Lolo* and one or two others, much the same physical and mental traits are everywhere presented by the numerous Bantu populations within the great bend of the Congo.

The people who give their name to this river present some points of special interest. It is commonly supposed that **The Old Kongo Empire.** the old " Kongo Empire " was a creation of the Portuguese. But Mbanza, afterwards re-christened " San Salvador," was already the

---

[1] Variously termed *Ba-Kongo, Bashi-Kongo* or *Ba-Fiot.*

capital of a powerful state when it was first visited by the expedition of 1491, from which time date its relations with Portugal. At first the Catholic missionaries had great success, thousands were at least baptised, and for a moment it seemed as if all the Congo lands were being swept into the fold. There were great rejoicings on the conversion of the *Mfumu* ("Emperor") himself, on whom were lavished honours and Portuguese titles still borne by his present degenerate descendant, the Portuguese state pensioner, "Dom Pedro V, Catholic King of Kongo and its Dependencies." But Christianity never struck very deep roots, and, except in the vicinity of the Imperial and vassal Courts, heathenish practices of the worst description were continued down to the middle of the nineteenth century. About 1870 fresh efforts were made both by Protestant and Catholic missionaries to re-convert the people, who had little to remind them of their former faith except the ruins of the cathedral of San Salvador, crucifixes, banners, and other religious emblems handed down as heirlooms and regarded as potent fetishes by their owners. A like fate, it may be incidentally mentioned, has overtaken the efforts of the Portuguese missionaries to evangelise the natives of the east coast, where little now survives of their teachings but snatches of unintelligible songs to the Blessed Virgin, such as that still chanted by the Lower Zambesi boatmen and recorded by Mrs Pringle :—

> Sina mama, sina mamai,
> Sina mama Maria, sina mamai . . .
>
> Mary, I'm alone, mother I have none,
> Mother I have none, she and father both are gone, etc.[1]

It is probable that at some remote period the ruling race reached the west coast from the north-east, and imposed their Bantu speech on the rude aborigines, by whom it is still spoken over a wide tract of country on both sides of the Lower Congo. It is an **The Kongo Language.** extremely pure and somewhat archaic member of the Bantu family, and W. Holman Bentley, our best authority on the subject, is enthusiastic in praise of its " richness, flexibility, exactness, subtlety of idea, and nicety of expression," a language superior to the people themselves, " illiterate folk with an elaborate and regular grammatical system of speech of

[1] *Towards the Mountains of the Moon*, 1884, p. 128.

such subtlety and exactness of idea that its daily use is in
itself an education."[1]   Kishi-Kongo has the distinction of
being the first Bantu tongue ever reduced to written form,
the oldest known work in the language being a treatise on
Christian Doctrine published in Lisbon in 1624.   Since that
time the speech of the " Mociconghi," as Pigafetta calls them,[2]
has undergone but slight phonetic or other change, which is

The Kongo   all the more surprising when we consider the
Aborigines. rudeness of the present Mushi-Kongos and
             others by whom it is still spoken with con-
siderable uniformity.   Some of these believe themselves
sprung from trees, as if they had still reminiscences of the
arboreal habits of a pithecoid ancestry.

Amongst the neighbouring *Ba-Mba*, whose sobas were
formerly *ex officio* Commanders-in-chief of the Empire, still
dwells a potent being, who is invisible to everybody, and
although mortal never dies, or at least after each dissolution
springs again into life from his remains gathered up by the

Perverted   priests.   All the young men of the tribe undergo
Christian   a similar transformation, being thrown into a
Doctrines.   death-like trance by the magic arts of the
medicine-man, and then resuscitated after three days.   The
power of causing the cataleptic sleep is said really to exist,
and these strange rites, unknown elsewhere, are probably to
be connected with the resurrection of Christ after three days
and of everybody on the last day as preached by the early
Portuguese evangelists.   A volume might be written on the
strange distortions of Christian doctrines amongst savage
peoples unable to grasp their true inwardness.

In Angola the Portuguese distinguish between the *Pretos*,
that is, the " civilised," and the *Negros*, or unreclaimed natives.

The-Kabindas Yet both terms mean the same thing, as
and " Black   also does *Ba-Fiot*,[3] " Black People," which is
Jews."   applied in an arbitrary way both to the Eshi-
Kongos and their near relations, the *Kabindas* of the Portuguese

---

[1] *Dictionary and Grammar of the Kongo Language,* 1887, p. xxiii.   F. Starr
has published a *Bibliography of the Congo Languages,* Bull. v., Dept. of Anthropology, University of Chicago, 1908.

[2] " Li Mociconghi cosi nomati nel suo proprio idioma gli abitanti del reame
di Congo " (*Relatione,* etc., Rome, 1591, p. 68).   This form is remarkable, being
singular (*Moci=Mushi*) instead of plural (*Eshi*) ; yet it is still currently applied
to the rude " Mushi-Kongos " on the south side of the estuary.   Their real name
however is Bashi-Kongo.   See *Brit. Mus. Ethnog. Handbook,* p. 219.

[3] Often written *Ba-Fiort* with an intrusive *r*.

enclave north of the Lower Congo. These Kabindas, so named from the seaport of that name on the Loango coast, are an extremely intelligent, energetic, and enterprising people, daring seafarers, and active traders. But they complain of the keen rivalry of another dark people, the *Judeos Pretos*, or "Black Jews," who call themselves *Ma-Vambu*, and whose hooked nose combined with their peculiarities has earned for them their Portuguese name. The Kabindas say that these "Semitic Negroes" were specially created for the punishment of other unscrupulous dealers by their ruinous competition in trade.

A great part of the vast region within the bend of the Congo is occupied by the *Ba-Luba* people, whose numerous branches—*Ba-Sange* and *Ba-Songe* about the sources of the Sankuru, *Ba-Shilange* (*Tushilange*) about the Lulua-Kassai confluence, and many others—extend all the way from the Kwango basin to Manyemaland. Most of these are Bantus of the average type, fairly intelligent, industrious and specially noted for their skill in iron and copper work. Iron ores are widely diffused, and the copper comes from the famous mines of the Katanga district, of which King Mzidi and his Wa-Nyamwezi followers were dispossessed by the Congo Free State in 1892.[1]

Special attention is claimed by the *Ba-Shilange* nation, for our knowledge of whom we are indebted chiefly to C. S. Latrobe Bateman.[2] These are the people whom Wissmann had already referred to as "a nation of thinkers with the interrogative 'why' constantly on their lips." Bateman also describes them as "thoroughly honest, brave to foolhardiness, and faithful to each other. They are prejudiced in favour of foreign customs and spontaneously copy the usages of civilisation. They are the only African tribe among whom I have observed anything

The Tushilange Bhang-Smokers.

---

[1] Under Belgian administration much ethnological work has been undertaken, and published in the *Annales du Musée du Congo*, notably the magnificent monograph on the *Bushongo* (*Bakuba*) by E. Torday and T. A. Joyce, 1911. See also H. H. Johnston, *George Grenfell and the Congo*, 1908; M. W. Hilton-Simpson, *Land and Peoples of the Kasai*, 1911; E. Torday, *Camp and Tramp in African Wilds*, 1913; J. H. Weeks, *Among Congo Cannibals*, 1913, and *Among the Primitive Bakongo*, 1914; and Adolf Friedrich, Duke of Mecklenburg, *From the Congo to the Niger and the Nile*, 1913.

[2] *The First Ascent of the Kassai*, 1889, p. 20 sq. See also my communication to the *Academy*, April 6, 1889, and *Africa* (Stanford's Compendium), 1895, Vol. II. p. 117 sq.

like a becoming conjugal affection and regard.   To say nothing
of such recommendations as their emancipation from fetishism,
their ancient abandonment of cannibalism, and their national
unity under the sway of a really princely prince (Kalemba),
I believe them to be the most open to the best influences of
civilisation of any African tribe whatsoever.[1]   Their territory
about the Lulua, affluent of the Kassai, is the so-called Lubuka,
or land of " Friendship," the theatre of a remarkable social
revolution, carried out independently of all European influences,
in fact before the arrival of any whites on the scene.   It was
initiated by the secret brotherhood of the *Bena-Riamba*, or
" Sons of Hemp," established about 1870, when the nation
became divided into two parties over the question
Bantu "Progressives." of throwing the country open to foreign trade.
The king having sided with the " Progressives,"
the " Conservatives " were worsted with much bloodshed,
whereupon the barriers of seclusion were swept away.   Trading
relations being at once established with the outer world, the
custom of *riamba* (bhang) smoking was unfortunately introduced through the Swahili traders from Zanzibar.   The
practice itself soon became associated with mystic rites, and
was followed by a general deterioration of morals throughout
Tushilangeland.

North of the Ba-Luba follows the great *Ba-Lolo* nation,
whose domain comprises nearly the whole of the region between
the equator and the left bank of the Congo, and
The Ba-Lolo "Men of Iron." whose Kilolo speech is still more widely diffused,
being spoken by perhaps 10,000,000 within the
horseshoe bend.   These " Men of Iron " in the sense of
Cromwell's " Ironsides," or " Workers in Iron," as the name
has been diversely interpreted (from *lolo*, iron), may not be
all that they have been depicted by the glowing pen of
Mrs H. Grattan Guinness ; [2] but nobody will deny their claim
to be regarded as physically, if not mentally, one of the finest
Bantu races.   But for the strain of Negro blood betrayed by
the tumid under lip, frizzly hair, and wide nostrils, many might
pass for average Hamites with high forehead, straight or
aquiline nose, bright eye, and intelligent expression.   They
appear to have migrated about a hundred years ago from the
east to their present homes, where they have cleared the land

---

[1] *Op. cit.* p. 20.
[2] *The New World of Central Africa*, 1890, p. 466 sq.

both of its forests and the aborigines, brought extensive tracts under cultivation, and laid out towns in the American chessboard fashion, but with the houses so wide apart that it takes hours to traverse them. They are skilled in many crafts, and understand the division-of-labour principle, "farmers, gardeners, smiths, boatbuilders, weavers, cabinet-makers, armourers, warriors, and speakers being already differentiated amongst them." [1]

From the east or north-east a great stream of migration has also for many years been setting right across the cannibal zone to the west coast between the Ogowai and Cameruns estuary. Some of these cannibal bands, collectively known as *Fans, Pahuins, Mpangwes,*[2] *Oshyebas* and by other names, have already swarmed into the Gabún and Lower Ogowai districts, where they have caused a considerable dislocation of the coast tribes. They are at present the dominant, or at least the most powerful and dreaded, people in West Equatorial Africa, where nothing but the intervention of the French administration has prevented them from sweeping the *Mpongwes, Mbengas, Okandas, Ashangos, Ishogos, Ba-Tekes,*[3] and the other maritime populations into the Atlantic. Even the great *Ba-Kalai* nation, who are also immigrants, but from the south-east, and who arrived some time before the Fans, have been hard pressed and driven forward by those fierce anthropophagists. They are still numerous, certainly over 100,000, but confined mainly to the left bank of the Ogowai, where their copper and iron workers have given up the hopeless struggle to compete with the imported European wares, and have consequently turned to trade. The Ba-Kalai are now the chief brokers and middlemen throughout the equatorial coastlands, and their pure Bantu language is encroaching on the Mpongwe in the Ogowai basin.

When first heard of by Bowdich in 1819, the Paämways, as he calls the Fans, were an inland people presenting such marked Hamitic or Caucasic features that he allied them

The West Equatorial Bantus.

Ba-Kalai.

---

[1] *Op. cit.* p. 471.

[2] These *Mpangwe* savages are constantly confused with the *Mpongwes* of the Gabún, a settled Bantu people who have been long in close contact, and on friendly terms, with the white traders and missionaries in this district.

[3] The scanty information about the Ba-Teke is given, with references, by E. Torday and T. A. Joyce, "Notes on the Ethnography of the Ba-Huana," *Journ. Roy. Anthr. Inst.* XXXVI. 1906.

with the West Sudanese Fulahs. Since then there have
been inevitable interminglings, by which the
type has no doubt been modified, though still
presenting distinct non-Bantu or non-Negro
characters. Burton, Winwood Reade, Oscar Lenz and most
other observers separate them altogether from the Negro
connection, describing them as " well-built, tall
and slim, with a light brown complexion, often
inclining to yellow, well-developed beard, and
very prominent frontal bone standing out in a semicircular
protuberance above the superciliary arches. Morally also,
they differ greatly from the Negro, being remarkably intelligent, truthful, and of a serious temperament, seldom laughing
or indulging in the wild orgies of the blacks." [1]

The Cannibal Fans.

Migrations, Type, Origin.

M. H. Kingsley adds that " the average height in mountain
districts is five feet six to five feet eight (1.67 m. to 1.72 m.), the
difference in stature between men and women not being great.
Their countenances are very bright and expressive, and if once
you have been among them, you can never mistake a Fan.
The Fan is full of fire, temper, intelligence and go ; very
teachable, rather difficult to manage, quick to take offence
and utterly indifferent to human life." The cannibalism of
the Fans, though a prevalent habit, is not, according to
Miss Kingsley, due to sacrificial motives. " He does it in his
common-sense way. He will eat his next door neighbour's
relations and sell his own deceased to his next door neighbour
in return ; but he does not buy slaves and fatten them up for
his table as some of the Middle Congo tribes do. . . . He has no
slaves, no prisoners of war, no cemeteries, so you must draw
your own conclusions." [2] The Fan language has been grouped
by Sir H. H. Johnston among Bantu tongues, but he describes
it as so corrupt as to be only just recognisable as Bantu.
In linguistic, physical and mental features they thus show
a remarkable divergence from the pure Negro, suggesting
Hamitic probably Fulah elements.

In the Camerún region, which still lies within Bantu
territory, Sir H. H. Johnston [3] divides the numerous local

[1] My *Africa*, II. p. 58. Oscar Lenz, who perhaps knew them best, says : " Gut
gebaut, schlank und kräftig gewachsen, Hautfarbe viel lichter, manchmal stark
ins Gelbe spielend, Haar und Bartwuchs auffallend stark, sehr grosse Kinn-
bärte " (*Skizzen aus West-Afrika*, 1878, p. 73).

[2] M. H. Kingsley, *Travels in West Africa*, 1897, pp. 331-2.

[3] *Official Report*, 1886.

tribes into two groups, the aborigines, such as the *Ba-Yong, Ba-Long, Ba-Sa, Abo* and *Wuri*; and the later intruders—*Ba-Kundu, Ba-Kwiri, Dwala,* " *Great Batanga* " and *Ibea* — chiefly from the east and south-east. Best known are the Dwalas of the Camerún estuary, physically typical Bantus with almost European features, and well-developed calves, a character which would alone suffice to separate them from the true Negro. Nor are these traits due to contact with the white settlers on the coast, because the Dwalas keep quite aloof, and are so proud of their " blue blood," that till lately all half-breeds were " weeded-out," being regarded as monsters who reflected discredit on the tribe.[1]

The Camerûn Bantus.

Socially the Camerún natives stand at nearly the same low level of culture as the neighbouring full-blood Negroes of the Calabar and Niger delta. Indeed the transition in customs and institutions, as well as in physical appearance, is scarcely perceptible between the peoples dwelling north and south of the Rio del Rey, here the dividing line between the Negro and Bantu lands. The *Ba-Kish* of the Meme river, almost last of the Bantus, differ little except in speech from the Negro *Efiks* of Old Calabar, while witchcraft and other gross superstitions were till lately as rife amongst the Ba-Kwiri and Ba-Kundu tribes of the western Camerún as anywhere in Negroland. It is not long since one of the Ba-Kwiri, found guilty of having eaten a chicken at a missionary's table, was himself eaten by his fellow clansmen. The law of blood for blood was pitilessly enforced, and charges of witchcraft were so frequent that whole villages were depopulated, or abandoned by their terror-stricken inhabitants. The island of Ambas in the inlet of like name remained thus for a time absolutely deserted, " most of the inhabitants having poisoned each other off with their everlasting ordeals, and the few survivors ending by dreading the very air they breathed." [2]

Bantu-Sudanese Borderland.

Having thus completed our survey of the Bantu populations from the central dividing line about the Congo-Chad water-parting round by the east, south, and west coastlands, and so back to the Sudanese zone, we may pause to ask,

[1] H. H. Johnston, *George Grenfell and the Congo . . . and Notes on the Cameroons,* 1908.
[2] Reclus, English ed., XII. p. 376.

What routes were followed by the Bantus themselves during
the long ages required to spread themselves
over an area estimated at nearly six million
square miles ? I have established, apparently
on solid grounds, a fixed point of initial dispersion in the extreme north-east, and allusion has frequently
been made to migratory movements, some even now going
on, generally from east to west, and, on the east side of the
continent, from north to south, with here an important but
still quite recent reflux from Zululand back nearly to Victoria
Nyanza. If a parallel current be postulated as setting on
the Atlantic side in prehistoric times from south to north,
from Hereroland to the Camerúns, or possibly the other
way, we shall have nearly all the factors needed to explain
the general dispersion of the Bantu peoples over their vast
domain.

Early Bantu Migrations— a Clue to their Direction.

Support is given to this view by the curious distribution
of the two chief Bantu names of the "Supreme Being," to
which incidental reference has already been made. As first
pointed out I think by Dr Bleek, *(M)unkulun-
kulu* with its numerous variants prevails along
the eastern seaboard, *Nzambi* along the western,
and both in many parts of the interior ; while
here and there the two meet, as if to indicate prehistoric
interminglings of two great primeval migratory movements.
From the subjoined table a clear idea may be had of the
general distribution :

Eastern Ancestry and Western Nature Worshippers.

MUNKULUNKULU	NZAMBI
Mpondo : Ukulukulu	Eshi-Kongo : Nzambi
Zulu : Unkulunkulu	Kabinda : Nzambi Pongo
Inhambane : Mulungulu	Lunda : Zambi
Sofala : Murungu	Ba-Teke : Nzam̃
Be-Chuana : Mulungulu	Ba-Rotse : Nyampe
Lake Moero : Mulungu	Bihé : Nzambi
Lake Tanganyika : Mulungu	Loango : Zambi, Nyambi
Makua : Moloko	Bunda : Onzambi
Quillimane : Mlugu	Ba-Ngala : Nsambi
Lake Bangweolo : Mungu	Ba-Kele : Nshambi
Tete, Zambesi : Muungu	Rungu : Anyambi
Nyasaland : Murungu	Ashira : Aniembie
Swahili : Muungu	Mpongwe : Njambi
Giryama : Mulungu	Benga : Anyambi
Pokomo : Mungo	Dwala : Nyambi
Nyika : Mulungu	Yanzi : Nyambi
Kamba : Mulungu	Herero : Ndyambi
Yanzi : Molongo	
Herero : Mukuru	

Eastern Seaboard and Parts of Interior

Western Seaboard and Parts of Interior

Of *Munkulunkulu* the primitive idea is clear enough from its best preserved form, the Zulu *Unkulunkulu*, which is a repetitive of the root *inkulu*, great, old, hence a deification of the great departed, a direct outcome of the ancestry-worship so universal amongst Negro and Bantu peoples.[1] Thus Un-kulunkulu becomes the direct progenitor of the Zulu-Xosas : *Unkulunkulu ukobu wetu.* But the fundamental meaning of *Nzambi* is unknown. The root does not occur in Kishi-Kongo, and Bentley rightly rejects Kolbe's far-fetched explanation from the Herero, adding that " the knowledge of God is most vague, scarcely more than nominal. There is no worship paid to God."[2]

More probable seems W. H. Tooke's suggestion that Nzambi is " a Nature spirit like Zeus or Indra," and that, while the eastern Bantus are ancestor-worshippers, "the western adherents of Nzambi are more or less Nature-worshippers. In this respect they appear to approach the Negroes of the Gold, Slave, and Oil Coasts."[3] No doubt the cult of the dead prevails also in this region, but here it is combined with naturalistic forms of belief, as on the Gold Coast, where *Bobowissi*, chief god of all the southern tribes, is the " Blower of Clouds," the " Rain-maker," and on the Slave Coast, where the Dahoman *Mawu* and the Yoruba *Olorun* are the Sky or Rain, and the " Owner of the Sky " (the deified Firmament), respectively.[4]

It would therefore seem probable that the Munkulunkulu peoples from the north-east gradually spread by the indicated routes over the whole of Bantuland, everywhere imposing their speech, general culture, and ancestor-worship on the pre-Bantu aborigines, except along the Atlantic coastlands and in parts of the interior. Here the primitive Nature-worship, embodied in Nzambi, held and still holds its ground, both meeting on equal terms—as shown in the above table —

---

[1] So also in Minahassa, Celebes, *Empung*, " Grandfather," is the generic name of the gods. " The fundamental ideas of primitive man are the same all the world over. Just as the little black baby of the Negro, the brown baby of the Malay, the yellow baby of the Chinaman are in face and form, in gestures and habits, as well as in the first articulate sounds they mutter, very much alike, so the mind of man, whether he be Aryan or Malay, Mongolian or Negrito, has in the course of its evolution passed through stages which are practically identical " (Sydney J. Hickson, *A Naturalist in North Celebes*, 1889, p. 240).

[2] *Op. cit.* p. 96.

[3] " The God of the Ethiopians," in *Nature*, May 26, 1892.

[4] A. B. Ellis, *Tshi*, p. 23 ; *Ewe*, p. 31 ; *Yoruba*, p. 36.

amongst the Ba-Yanzi, the Ova-Herero, and the Be-Chuanas (*Mulungulu* generally, but *Nyampe* in Barotseland), and no doubt in other inland regions. But the absolute supremacy

Conclusion.

of one on the east, and of the other on the west, side of the continent, seems conclusive as to the general streams of migration, while the amazing uniformity of nomenclature is but another illustration of the almost incredible persistence of Bantu speech amongst these multitudinous illiterate populations for an incalculable period of time.[1]

THE VAALPENS AND THE STRANDLOOPERS.

Among the ethnological problems of Africa may be reckoned the *Vaalpens* and the *Strandloopers*. Along the

The Kattea or Vaalpens.

banks of the Limpopo between the Transvaal and Southern Rhodesia there are scattered a few small groups of an extremely primitive people who are generally confounded with the Bushmen, but differ in some important respects from that race. They are the "Earthmen" of some writers, but their real name is *Kattea*, though called by their neighbours either *Ma Sarwa* ("Bad People") or *Vaalpens* ("Grey Paunches") from the khaki colour acquired by their bodies from creeping on all fours into their underground hovels. But the true colour is almost a pitch black, and as they are only about four feet high they are quite distinct both from the tall Bantus and the yellowish Hottentot-Bushmen. For the Zulus they are mere "dogs" or "vultures," and are certainly the most degraded of all the aborigines, being undoubtedly cannibals, eating their own aged and infirm like some of the Amazonian tribes. Their habitations are holes in the ground, rock-shelters, or caves, or lately a few hovels of mud and foliage at the foot of the hills. Of their speech nothing is known except that it is absolutely distinct both from the Bantu and the Bushman. There are no arts or industries of any kind, not even any weapons beyond those procured in exchange for ostrich feathers, skins or ivory. But they can make fire, and are thus able to cook the offal thrown to them by the Boers in

[1] Cf. E. S. Hartland, Art. "Bantu and S. Africa," *Ency. of Religion and Ethics*, 1909.

return for their help in skinning the captured game. Whether they have any religious ideas it is impossible to say, all intercourse with the surrounding peoples being restricted to barter carried on with gesture language for nobody has ever yet mastered their tongue. A " chief " is spoken of, but he is merely a headman who presides over the little family groups of from thirty to fifty (there are no tribes properly so called), and whose purely domestic functions are acquired, not by heredity, but by personal worth, that is, physical strength. Altogether the Kattea is perhaps the most perfect embodiment of the pure savage still anywhere surviving.[1]

When the Hottentots of South Africa were questioned by scientific men a hundred years ago and more regarding their traditions, they were wont to refer to their predecessors on the coast of South Africa as a savage race living on the seashore and subsisting on shellfish and the bodies of stranded whales. From their habits these were styled in Dutch the Strandloopers or " Shore-runners." [2] According to F. C. Shrubsall the Strandlooper of the Cape Colony caves preceded the Bushman in South Africa. They were a race of short but not dwarfish men with a much higher skull capacity than that of the average Bush race. The extreme of cranial capacity in the Strandloopers was a maximum of over 1600 c.c., while the extreme minimum among the Bush people descends as low as 955 c.c. The frontal region of the skull is much better developed than in the Bush race, and in that respect is more like the Negro. There is little or no brow prominence, and one at least of the skulls is as orthognathous in facial angle as that of a European. L. Peringuey remarks also that the type was less dolichocephalic than the Bushmen and Hottentots, under 80 in cephalic index. " He was artistically gifted, like the race which occupied and decorated the Altamira . . . and other caves of Spain and France. He painted ; he possibly carved on rocks ; he used bone tools ; he made pottery ; he perforated stones for either heading clubs or to be used as make-weights for digging tools ; his ornaments consisted of sea-shells ; and the ostrich egg-shell discs which he made may be said to be

The Strandloopers.

[1] This account of the Vaalpens is taken from A. H. Keane, *The World's Peoples*, 1908, p. 149.
[2] This summary of our information about the Strandloopers, with quotations from F. C. Shrubsall and L. Peringuey, is taken from H. H. Johnston, " A Survey of the Ethnography of Africa," *Journ. Roy. Anthr. Inst.* XLIII. 1913, p. 377.

a typical product of his industry.   And this culture is retained in South Africa by a kindred race, but more dolichocephalic—the Bushmen-Hottentots.   Analogous are most of his tools and his expressions of culture to those of Aurignacian man."

THE NEGRILLOES.

The proper domain of the African Negrilloes is the inter-tropical forest-land, although they appear to be at present **The Negrilloes.** confined to somewhat narrow limits, between about six degrees of latitude north and south of the equator, unless the Bushmen be included.   But formerly they probably ranged much farther north, and in historic times were certainly known in Egypt some 4000 or 5000 years ago.   This is evident from the frequent references to them in the " Book of the Dead " as far back as the sixth Dynasty. Like the dwarfs in medieval times, they were in high request **Negrilloes at** at the courts of the Pharaohs, who sent expedi-**the Courts of** tions to fetch these *Danga* (*Tank*) from the **the Pharaohs.** " Island of the Double," that is, the fabulous region of Shade Land beyond Punt, where they dwelt.   The first of whom there is authentic record was brought from this region, apparently the White Nile, to King Assa (3300 B.C.) by his officer, Baurtet.   Some seventy years later Heru-Khuf, another officer, was sent by Pepi II " to bring back a pygmy alive and in good health," from the land of great trees away to the south.[1]   That the Danga came from the south we know from a later inscription at Karnak, and that the word meant dwarf is clear from the accompanying determinative of a short person of stunted growth.

It is curious to note in this connection that the limestone statue of the dwarf Nem-hotep, found in his tomb at Sakkara and figured by Ernest Grosse, has a thick elongated head suggesting artificial deformation, unshapely mouth, dull ex-pression, strong full chest, and small deformed feet, on which he seems badly balanced.   It will be remembered that Schweinfurth's Akkas from Mangbattuland were also repre-sented as top-heavy, although the best observers, Junker and others, describe those of the Welle and Congo forests as shapely and by no means ill-proportioned.

[1] Schiaparelli, *Una Tomba Egiziana*, Rome, 1893.

Kollmann also, who has examined the remains of the Neolithic pygmies from the Schweizersbild Station, Switzerland, "is quite certain that the dwarf-like proportions of the latter have nothing in common with diseased conditions. This, from many points of view, is a highly interesting discovery. It is possible, as Nüesch suggests, that the widely-spread legend as to the former existence of little men, dwarfs and gnomes, who were supposed to haunt caves and retired places in the mountains, may be a reminiscence of these Neolithic pygmies."[1]

Negrilloes and Pygmy Folklore.

This is what may be called the picturesque aspect of the Negrillo question, which it seems almost a pity to spoil by too severe a criticism. But "ethnologic truth" obliges us to say that the identification of the African Negrillo with Kollmann's European dwarfs still lacks scientific proof. Even craniology fails us here, and although the Negrilloes are in great majority round-headed, R. Verneau has shown that there may be exceptions,[2] while the theory of the general uniformity of the physical type has broken down at some other points. Thus the *Dume*, south of Galla-land, discovered by Donaldson Smith[3] in the district where the *Doko* Negrilloes had long been heard of, and even seen by Antoine d'Abbadie in 1843, were found to average five feet, or more than one foot over the mean of the true Negrillo. D'Abbadie in fact declared that his "Dokos" were not pygmies at all,[4] while Donaldson Smith now tells us that "doko" is only a term of contempt applied by the local tribes to their "poor relations." "Their chief characteristics were a black skin, round features, woolly hair, small oval-shaped eyes, rather thick lips, high cheek-bones, a broad forehead, and very well formed bodies" (p. 273).

The Dume and Doko, reputed Dwarfs.

The expression of the eye was canine, "sometimes timid and suspicious-looking, sometimes very amiable and merry, and then again changing suddenly to a look of intense anger."

[1] James Geikie, *Scottish Geogr. Mag.* Sept. 1897.
[2] Thus he finds (*L'Anthropologie*, 1896, p. 153) a presumably Negrillo skull from the Babinga district, Middle Sangha river, to be distinctly long-headed (73.2) with, for this race, the enormous cranial capacity of about 1440 c.c. Cf. the Akka measured by Sir W. Flower (1372 c.c.), and his Andamanese (1128), the highest hitherto known being 1200 (Virchow).
[3] *Through Unknown African Countries*, etc., 1897.
[4] *Bul. Soc. Géogr.* XIX. p. 440.

Pygmies, he adds, "inhabited the whole of the country north of Lakes Stephanie and Rudolf long before any of the tribes now to be found in the neighbourhood ; but they have been gradually killed off in war, and have lost their characteristics by inter-marriage with people of large stature, so that only this one little remnant, the Dume, remains to prove the existence of a pygmy race. Formerly they lived principally by hunting, and they still kill a great many elephants with their poisoned arrows " (pp. 274–5).

Some of these remarks apply also to the *Wandorobbo*, another small people who range nearly as far north as the

The Wando-robbo Hunters. Dume, but are found chiefly farther south all over Masailand, and belong, I have little doubt, to the same connection. They are the henchmen of the Masai, whom they provide with big game in return for divers services.

Those met by W. Astor Chanler were also " armed with bows and arrows, and each carried an elephant-spear, which they called *bonati*. This spear is six feet in length, thick at either end, and narrowed where grasped by the hand. In one end is bored a hole, into which is fitted an arrow two feet long, as thick as one's thumb, and with a head two inches broad. Their method of killing elephants is to creep cautiously up to the beast, and drive a spear into its loin. A quick twist separates the spear from the arrow, and they make off as fast and silently as possible. In all cases the arrows are poisoned ; and if they are well introduced into the animal's body, the elephant does not go far." [1]

From some of the peculiarities of the Achua (Wochua) Negrilloes met by Junker south of the Welle one can under-

The Wochua Mimics. stand why these little people were such favourites with the old Egyptian kings. These were " distinguished by sharp powers of observation, amazing talent for mimicry, and a good memory. A striking proof of this was afforded by an Achua whom I had seen and measured four years previously in Rumbek, and now again met at Gambari's. His comic ways and quick nimble movements made this little fellow the clown of our society. He imitated with marvellous fidelity the peculiarities of persons whom he had once seen ; for instance, the gestures and facial

---

[1] *Through Jungle and Desert*, 1896, pp. 358–9.

expressions of Jussuf Pasha esh-Shelahis and of Haj Halil at their devotions, as well as the address and movements of Emin Pasha, ' with the four eyes ' (spectacles). His imitation of Hawash Effendi in a towering rage, storming and abusing everybody, was a great success ; and now he took me off to the life, rehearsing after four years, down to the minutest details, and with surprising accuracy, my anthropometric performance when measuring his body at Rumbek." [1]

A somewhat similar account is given by Ludwig Wolf of the Ba-Twa pygmies visited by him and Wissmann in the Kassai region. Here are whole villages in the forest-glades inhabited by little people with an average height of about 4 feet 3 inches. They are nomads, occupied exclusively with hunting and the preparation of palm-wine, and are regarded by their Ba-Kubu neighbours as benevolent little people, whose special mission is to provide the surrounding tribes with game and palm-wine in exchange for manioc, maize, and bananas. [2]

Despite the above-mentioned deviations, occurring chiefly about the borderlands, considerable uniformity both of physical and mental characters is found to prevail amongst the typical Negrillo groups scattered in small hunting communities all over the Welle, Semliki, Congo, and Ogowai woodlands. Their main characters are thus described. Their skin is of a reddish or yellowish brown in colour, sometimes very dark. Their height varies from 1.37 m. to 1.45 m. (4 ft. 4¼ in. to 4 ft. 9¼ in.). [3] Their hair is very short and woolly, usually of a dark rusty brown colour ; the face hair is variable, but the body is usually covered with a light downy hair. The cephalic index is 79. The nose is very broad and exceptionally flattened at the root ; the lips are usually thin, and the upper one long ; the eyes are protuberant ; the face is sometimes prognathic. Steatopygia occurs. They are a markedly intelligent people, innately musical, cunning, revengeful and suspicious in disposition, but they never steal.

They are nomadic hunters and collectors, never resorting to agriculture. They have no domestic animals. Only meat is cooked. They wear no clothing. They use bows and

---

[1] *Travels,* III. p. 86.

[2] *Im Innern Afrika's,* p. 259 sq. As stated in *Eth.* Ch. XI. Dr Wolf connects all these Negrillo peoples with the Bushmen south of the Zambesi.

[3] One of the Mambute brought to England by Col. Harrison in 1906 measured just over 3½ feet.

poisoned arrows. Their language is unknown. They live in small communities which centre round a cunning fighter or able hunter. Their dead are buried in the ground. They differ from surrounding Negroes in having no veneration for the departed, no amulets, no magicians or professional priests. They have charms for ensuring luck in hunting, but it is uncertain whether these charms derive their potency from the supreme being, though evidence of belief in a high-god is reported from various pygmy peoples.[1]

The Bushmen and Hottentots.

Towards the south the Negrillo domain was formerly conterminous with that of the Bushmen, of whom traces were

Bushmen and Hottentots. Former and Present Range.

discovered by Sir H. H. Johnston[2] as far north as Lakes Nyasa and Tanganyika, and who, it has been conjectured, belong to the same primitive stock. The differences mental and physical now separating the two sections of the family may perhaps be explained by the different environments—hot, moist and densely wooded in the north, and open steppes in the south—but until more is known of the African pygmies their affinities must remain undecided.

The relationship between the Bushmen and the Hottentots is another disputed question. Early authorities regarded the Hottentots as the parent family, and the Bushmen as the offspring, but the researches of Gustav Fritsch, E. T. Hamy, F. Shrubsall[3] and others show that the Hottentots are a cross between the Bushmen—the primitive race—and the Bantu, the Bushman element being seen in the leathery colour, prominent cheek-bones, pointed chin, steatopygia and other special characters.

[1] See A. C. Haddon, Art. " Negrillos and Negritos," *Ency. of Religion and Ethics*, 1917.

[2] " It would seem as if the earliest known race of man inhabiting what is now British Central Africa was akin to the Bushman-Hottentot type of Negro. Rounded stones with a hole through the centre, similar to those which are used by the Bushmen in the south for weighting their digging-sticks, have been found at the south end of Lake Tanganyika. I have heard that other examples of these ' Bushman ' stones have been found nearer to Lake Nyasa, etc." (*British Central Africa*, p. 52).

[3] G. Fritsch, *Die Ein-geborenen Süd-Afrikas*, 1872, " Schilderungen der Hottentotten," *Globus*, 1875, p. 374 ff. ; E. T. Hamy, " Les Races nègres," *L'Anthropologie*, 1897, p. 257 ff. ; F. Shrubsall, " Crania of African Bush Races," *Journ. Anthr. Inst.* 1897. See also G. McCall Theal, *The Yellow and Dark-skinned People South of the Zambesi*, 1910.

In prehistoric times the Hottentots ranged over a vast area. Evidence has now been produced of the presence of a belated Hottentot or Hottentot-Bushman group as far north as the Kwa-Kokue district, between Kilimanjaro and Victoria Nyanza. The *Wa-Sandawi* people here visited by Oskar Neumann are not Bantus, and speak a language radically distinct from that of the neighbouring Bantus, but full of clicks like that of the Bushmen.[1] Two Sandawi skulls examined by Virchow[2] showed distinct Hottentot characters, with a cranial capacity of 1250 and 1265 c.c., projecting upper jaw and orthodolicho head.[3] The geographical prefix *Kwa*, common in the district (Kwa-Kokue, Kwa-Mtoro, Kwa-Hindi), is pure Hottentot, meaning "people," like the postfix *qua* (*Kwa*) of Kora-*qua* Nama-*qua*, etc. in the present Hottentot domain. The transposition of prefixes and postfixes is a common linguistic phenomenon, as seen in the Sumero-Akkadian of Babylonia, in the Neo-Sanskritic tongues of India, and the Latin, Oscan, and other members of the Old Italic group.

The Wa-Sandawi.

Farther south a widely-diffused Hottentot-Bushman geographical terminology attests the former range of this primitive race all over South Africa, as far north as the Zambesi. Lichtenstein had already discovered such traces in the Zulu country,[4] and Vater points out that " for some districts the fact has been fully established ; mountains and rivers now occupied by the Koɔssa [Ama-Xosa] preserve in their Hottentot names the certain proof that they at one time formed a permanent possession of this people."[5]

Hottentot Geographical Names in Bantuland.

Thanks to the custom of raising heaps of stones or cairns over the graves of renowned chiefs, the migrations of the

---

[1] " I have not been able to trace much affinity in word roots between this language and either Bushman or Hottentot, though it is noteworthy that the word for four . . . is almost identical with the word for four in all the Hottentot dialects, while the phonology of the language is reminiscent of Bushmen in its nasals and gutturals " (H. H. Johnston, " Survey of the Ethnography of Africa," *Journ. Roy. Anthr. Inst.* XLIII. 1913, p. 380).

[2] *Verhandl. Berliner Gesellsch. f. Anthrop.* 1895, p. 59.

[3] Of another skull undoubtedly Hottentot, from a cave on the Transvaal and Orange Free State frontier, Dr Mies remarks that " seine Form ist orthodolicho-cephal wie bei den Wassandaui," although differing in some other characters (*Centralbl. f. Anthr.* 1896, p. 50).

[4] From which he adds that the Hottentots " schon lange vor der Portugiesischen Umschiffung Afrika's von Kaffer-Stämmen wieder zurückgedrängt wurden " (*Reisen*, I. p. 400).

[5] Adelung und Vater, Berlin, 1812, III. p. 290.

Hottentots may be followed in various directions to the very heart of South Zambesia. Here the memory of their former presence is perpetuated in the names of such water-courses as Nos-ob, Up, Mol-opo, Hyg-ap, Gar-ib, in which the syllables *ob, up, ap, ib* and others are variants of the Hottentot word *ib, ip*, water, river, as in *Gar-ib*, the " Great River," now better known as the Orange River. The same indications may be traced right across the continent to the Atlantic, where nearly all the coast streams—even in Hereroland, where the language has long been extinct—have the same ending.[1]

On the west side the Bushmen are still heard of as far north as the Cunene, and in the interior beyond Lake Ngami nearly to the right bank of the Zambesi. But the Hottentots are now confined mainly to Great and Little Namaqualand.

Hottentots disappearing. Elsewhere there appear to be no full-blood natives of this race, the Koraquas, Gonaquas, Griquas, etc. being all Hottentot-Boer or Hottentot-Bantu half-castes of Dutch speech. In Cape Colony the tribal organisation ceased to exist in 1810, when the last Hottentot chief was replaced by a European magistrate. Still the Koraquas keep themselves somewhat distinct about the Upper Orange and Vaal Rivers, and the Griquas in Griqualand East, while the Gonaquas, that is, " Borderers," are being gradually merged in the Bantu populations of the Eastern Provinces. There are at present scarcely 180,000 south of the Orange River, and of these the great majority are half-breeds.[2]

Despite their extremely low state of culture, or, one might say, the almost total lack of culture, the Bushmen are distinguished by two remarkable qualities, a fine sense of pictorial

Bushman Folklore Literature. or graphic art,[3] and a rich imagination displayed in a copious oral folklore, much of which, collected by Bleek, is preserved in manuscript form in Sir George Grey's library at Cape Town.[4] The materials here stored for future use, perhaps long after the race itself has vanished for ever, comprise no less than 84 thick volumes of

---

[1] Such are, going north from below Walvisch Bay, Chuntop, Kuisip, Swakop, Ugab, Huab, Uniab, Hoanib, Kaurasib, and Khomeb.

[2] The returns for 1904 showed a " Hottentot " population of 85,892, but very few were pure Hottentots. The official estimate of those in which Hottentot blood was strongly marked was 56,000.

[3] M. H. Tongue and E. D. Bleek, *Bushman Paintings*, 1909. Cf. W. J. Sollas, *Ancient Hunters*, 1915, p. 399, with bibliography.

[4] W. H. I. Bleek and L. C. Lloyd, *Bushman Folklore*, 1911.

3600 double-column pages, besides an unfinished Bushman dictionary with 11,000 entries. There are two great sections, (1) Myths, fables, legends and poetry, with tales about the sun and moon, the stars, the *Mantis* and other animals, legends of peoples who dwelt in the land before the Bushmen, songs, charms, and even prayers ; (2) Histories, adventures of men and animals, customs, superstitions, genealogies, and so on.

In the tales and myths the sun, moon, and animals speak either with their own proper clicks, or else use the ordinary clicks in some way peculiar to themselves. Bushman-Thus Bleek tells us that the tortoise changes Hottentot clicks in labials, the ichneumon in palatals, the Language and jackal substitutes linguo-palatals for labials, while Clicks. the moon, hare, and ant-eater use " a most unpronounceable click " of their own. How many there may be altogether, not one of which can be properly uttered by Europeans, nobody seems to know. But grammarians have enumerated nine, indicated each by a graphic sign as under :

Cerebral	...... !	Palatal	.... ¡
Dental	...... |	Lateral (Faucal) .	||
Guttural	...... ⌉	Labial	.... ▯
Spiro-dental	... 7	Linguo-palatal	... ▢

Undefined ×

From Bushman—a language in a state of flux, fragmentary as the small tribal or rather family groups that speak it [1]— these strange inarticulate sounds passed to the number of four into the remotely related Hottentot, and thence to the number of three into the wholly unconnected Zulu-Xosa. But they are heard nowhere else to my knowledge except amongst the newly-discovered Wa-Sandawi people of South Masailand. At the same time we know next to nothing of the Negrillo tongues, and should clicks be discovered to form an element in their phonetic system also,[2] it would support the assumption of a common origin of all these dwarfish races now somewhat discredited on anatomical grounds.

M. G. Bertin, to whom we are indebted for an excellent

[1] See W. Planert, " Über die Sprache der Hottentotten und Buschmänner," *Mitt. d. Seminars f. Oriental. Sprachen z. Berlin*, VIII. (1905), Abt. III. 104–176.
[2] " In the Pygmies of the north-eastern corner of the Congo basin and amongst the Bantu tribes of the Equatorial East African coast there is a tendency to faucal gasps or explosive consonants which suggests the vanishing influence of clicks." H. H. Johnston, " A Survey of the Ethnography of Africa," *Journ. Roy. Anthr. Inst.* XLIII. 1913.

monograph on the Bushman,[1] rightly remarks that he is not,
Bushman Mental Characters. at least mentally, so debased as he has been described by the early travellers and by the neighbouring Bantus and Boers, by whom he has always been despised and harried. "His greatest love is for freedom, he acknowledges no master, and possesses no slaves. It is this love of independence which made him prefer the wandering life of a hunter to that of a peaceful agriculturist or shepherd, as the Hottentot. He rarely builds a hut, but prefers for abode the natural caves he finds in the rocks. In other localities he forms a kind of nest in the bush—hence his name of Bushman—or digs with his nails subterranean caves, from which he has received the name of 'Earthman.' His garments consist only of a small skin. His weapons are still the spear, arrow and bow in their most rudimentary form. The spear is a mere branch of a tree, to which is tied a piece of bone or flint; the arrow is only a reed treated in the same way. The arrow and spear-heads are always poisoned, to render mortal the slight wounds they inflict. He gathers no flocks, which would impede his movements, and only accepts the help of dogs as wild as himself. The Bushmen have, however, one implement, a rounded stone perforated in the middle, in which is inserted a piece of wood; with this instrument, which carries us back to the first age of man, they dig up a few edible roots growing wild in the desert. To produce fire, he still retains the primitive system of rubbing two pieces of wood—another prehistoric survival."

Touching their name, it is obvious that these scattered groups, without hereditary chiefs or social organisation of any kind, could have no collective designation. The
Bushman Race-names. term *Khuai*, of uncertain meaning, but probably to be equated with the Hottentot *Khoi*, "Men," is the name only of a single group, though often applied to the whole race. *Saan*, their Hottentot name, is the plural of *Sa*, a term also of uncertain origin; *Ba-roa*, current amongst the Be-Chuanas, has not been explained, while the Zulu *Abatwa* would seem to connect them even by name with Wolf's and Stanley's *Ba-Twa* of the Congo forest region. Other so-called tribal names (there are no "tribes" in the strict sense of the word) are either nicknames imposed upon them by their

---

[1] "The Bushmen and their Language," in *Journ. R. Asiatic Soc.* XVIII. Part I.

neighbours, or else terms taken from the localities, as amongst the Fuegians.

We may conclude with the words of W. J. Sollas : " The more we know of these wonderful little people the more we learn to admire and like them. To many solid virtues— untiring energy, boundless patience, and fertile invention, steadfast courage, devoted loyalty, and family affection—they added a native refinement of manners and a rare aesthetic sense. We may learn from them how far the finer excellences of life may be attained in the hunting stage. In their golden age, before the coming of civilised man, they enjoyed their life to the full, glad with the gladness of primeval creatures. The story of their later days, their extermination and the cruel manner of it, is a tale of horror on which we do not care to dwell. They haunt no more the sunlit veldt, their hunting is over, their nation is destroyed ; but they leave behind an imperishable memory, they have immortalised themselves in their art." [1]

[1] *Ancient Hunters*, 1915, p. 425.

CHAPTER V

THE OCEANIC NEGROES : PAPUASIANS (PAPUANS AND MELANESIANS)—NEGRITOES—TASMANIANS

General Ethnical Relations in Oceania—The terms PAPUAN, MELANESIAN and
PAPUASIAN defined—The Papuasian Domain, Past and Present—Papuans
and Melanesians—Physical Characters : Papuan, Papuo-Melanesian, Mela-
nesian—The *New Caledonians*—Physical Characters—Food Question—
General Survey of Melanesian Ethnology—Cultural Problems—Kava-drink-
ing and Betel-chewing—Stone Monuments—The Dual People—Summary of
Culture Strata—Melanesian Culture—Dress—Houses—Weapons—Canoes,
etc.—Social Life—Secret Societies—Clubs—Religion—Western Papuasia—
Ethnical Elements—Region of Transition by Displacements and Crossings
—Papuan and Malay Contrasts—Ethnical and Biological Divides—The
Negritoes—The *Andamanese*—Stone Age—Personal Appearance—Social
Life—Religion—Speech—Method of Counting—Grammatical Structure—
The *Semangs*—Physical Appearance—Usages—Speech—Stone Age—The
Aetas—Head-hunters—*New Guinea Pygmies*—Negrito Culture—The *Tas-
manians*—Tasmanian Culture—Fire Making—Tools and Weapons—Diet—
Dwellings—Extinction.

CONSPECTUS.

Present Range. Papuasian : *East Malaysia, New
Guinea, Melanesia;* Tasmanian : *extinct;* Ne-
grito : *Andamans, Malay Peninsula, Philippines,
New Guinea.*

Distribution in
Past and
Present Times.

Hair. Papuasian : *black, frizzly, mop-like, beard scanty
or absent;* Tasmanian : *black, shorter and less
mop-like than Papuasian;* Negrito : *short, woolly
or frizzly, black, sometimes tinged with brown
or red.*

Physical
Characters.

Colour. All : *very deep shades of chocolate brown, often
verging on black, a very constant character, lighter shades
showing mixture.*

Skull. Papuasian : *extremely dolichocephalic* (68–73)
and high, but very variable in areas of mixture (70–84) ;
Tasmanian : *dolichocephalic or mesaticephalic* (75) ; Negrito :
brachycephalic (80–85).

Jaws. Papuasian : *moderately or not at all prognathous;*
Tasmanian *and* Negrito : *generally prognathous.* **Cheek-**

132

bones. All: *slightly prominent or even retreating.* **Nose.** Papuasian: *large, straight, generally aquiline in true Papuans;* Tasmanian *and* Negrito: *short, flat, broad, wide nostrils (platyrrhine) with large thick cartilage.* **Eyes.** All: *moderately large, round and black or very deep brown, with dirty yellowish cornea, generally deep-set with strong overhanging arches.*

Stature. Papuasian *and* Tasmanian: *above the average, but variable, with rather wide range from 1.62 m. to 1.77 or 1.82 m. (5 ft. 4 in. to 5 ft. 10 in. or 6 ft.);* Negrito: *undersized, but taller than African Negrillo, 1.37 m. to 1.52 m. (4 ft. 6 in. to 5 ft.).*

Temperament. Papuasian: *very excitable, voluble and laughter-loving, fairly intelligent and imaginative;* Tasmanian: *distinctly less excitable and intelligent, but also far less cruel, captives never tortured;* Negrito: *active, quick-witted or cunning within narrow limits, naturally kind and gentle.* [Mental Characters.]

Speech. Papuasian *and* Tasmanian: *agglutinating with postfixes, many stock languages in West Papuasia, apparently one only in East Papuasia (Austronesian);* Negrito: *scarcely known except in Andamans, where agglutination both by class prefixes and by postfixes has acquired a phenomenal development.*

Religion. Papuasian: *reverence paid to ancestors, who may become beneficent or malevolent ghosts; general belief in* mana *or supernatural power; no priests or idols;* Negrito: *exceedingly primitive; belief in spirits, sometimes vague deities.*

Culture. Papuasian: *slightly developed; agriculture somewhat advanced (N. Guinea, N. Caledonia); considerable artistic taste and fancy shown in the wood-carving of houses, canoes, ceremonial objects, etc.* All others: *at the lowest hunting stage, without arts or industries, save the manufacture of weapons, ornaments, baskets, and rarely (Andamanese) pottery.*

Papuasian: I. Western Papuasians (*true Papuans*): *nearly all the New Guinea natives; Aru and other insular groups thence westwards to Flores; Torres Straits and Louisiade Islands.* 2. Eastern [Main Divisions.] Papuasians: *nearly all the natives of Melanesia from Bismarck Archipelago to New Caledonia, with most of Fiji, and part of New Guinea.*

Negritoes: 1. Andamanese *Islanders.* 2. Semangs, *in the Malay Peninsula.* 3. Aetas, *surviving in most of the Philippine Islands.* 4. *Pygmies in New Guinea.*

PAPUASIANS.

From the data supplied in *Ethnology*, Chap. XI. a reconstruction may be attempted of the obscure ethnical relations in Australasia on the following broad lines.

General Ethnical Relations in Oceania.

1. The two main sections of the Ulotrichous division of mankind, now separated by the intervening waters of the Indian Ocean, are fundamentally one.

2. To the Sudanese and Bantu sub-sections in Africa correspond, *mutatis mutandis*, the Papuan and Melanesian sub-sections in Oceania, the former being distinguished by great linguistic diversity, the latter by considerable linguistic uniformity, and both by a rather wide range of physical variety within certain well-marked limits.

3. In Africa the physical varieties are due mainly to Semitic and Hamitic grafts on the Negro stock ; in Oceania mainly to Mongoloid (Malay) and Caucasian (Indonesian) grafts on the Papuan stock.

4. The Negrillo element in Africa has its counterpart in an analogous Negrito element in Oceania (Andamanese, Semangs, Aetas, etc.).

5. In both regions the linguistic diversity apparently presents similar features—a large number of languages differing profoundly in their grammatical structure and vocabularies, but all belonging to the same agglutinative order of speech, and also more or less to the same phonetic system.

6. In both regions the linguistic uniformity is generally confined to one or two geographical areas, Bantuland in Africa and Melanesia in Oceania.

7. In Bantuland the linguistic system shows but faint if any resemblances to any other known tongues, whereas the Melanesian group is but one branch, though the most archaic, of the vast Austronesian Family, diffused over the Indian and Pacific Oceans. The Papuan languages are entirely distinct from the Melanesian. They are in some

respects similar to the Australian, but their exact positions are not yet proved.[1]

8. Owing to their linguistic, geographical, and to some extent their physical and social differences, it is desirable to treat the Papuans and Melanesians as two distinct though closely related sub-groups, and to restrict the use of the terms PAPUAN and MELANESIAN accordingly, while both may be conveniently comprised under the general or collective term PAPUASIAN.[2]

The terms Papuan, Melanesian and Papuasian defined.

9. Here, therefore, by *Papuans* will be understood the true aborigines of New Guinea with its eastern Louisiade dependency,[3] and in the west many of the Malaysian islands as far as Flores inclusive, where the black element and non-Malay speech predominate ; by *Melanesians*, the natives of Melanesia as commonly understood, that is, the Admiralty Isles, New Britain, New Ireland and Duke of York ; the Solomon Islands ; Santa Cruz ; the New Hebrides, New Caledonia, Loyalty, and Fiji, where the black element and Austronesian speech prevail almost exclusively. PAPUASIA will thus comprise the insular world from Flores to New Caledonia.

Such appear to be the present limits of the Papuasian domain, which formerly may have included Micronesia also (the Marianne, Pelew, and Caroline groups), and some writers suggest that it possibly extended over the whole of Polynesia as far as Easter Island.

The Papuasian Domain, Past and Present.

The variation in the inhabitants of New Guinea has often been recognised and is well described by C. G. Seligman

---

[1] Cf. S. H. Ray, *Reports Camb. Anthrop. Exp. Torres Sts.* Vol. III. 1907, pp. 287, 528.   For Melanesian linguistic affinities see also W. Schmidt, *Die Mon-Khmer Völker*, 1906.

[2] C. G. Seligman limits the use of the term *Papuasian* to the inhabitants of New Guinea and its islands, and following a suggestion of A. C. Haddon's (*Geograph. Journ.* XVI. 1900, pp. 265, 414), recognises therein three great divisions, the *Papuans*, the *Western Papuo-Melanesians*, and the *Eastern Papuo-Melanesians*, or *Massim*. Cf. C. G. Seligman, "A Classification of the Natives of British New Guinea," *Journ. Roy. Anthr. Inst.* Vol. XXXIX. 1902, and *The Melanesians of British New Guinea*, 1910.

[3] That is, the indigenous Papuans, who appear to form the great bulk of the New Guinea populations, in contradistinction to the immigrant Melanesians (Motu and others), who are numerous especially along the south-east coast of the mainland and in the neighbouring Louisiade and D'Entrecasteaux Archipelagoes (*Eth.* Ch. XI.).

who remarks[1] that the contrast between the relatively tall,
Papuans and Melanesians, Physical Characters. dark-skinned, frizzly-haired inhabitants of Torres Straits, the Fly River and the neighbouring parts of New Guinea on the one hand, and the smaller lighter coloured peoples to the east, is so striking that the two peoples must be recognised as racially distinct.   He restricts the name Papuan to the congeries of frizzly-haired and often mop-headed peoples whose skin colour is some shade of brownish black, and proposes the term Papuo-Melanesian for the generally smaller, lighter coloured, frizzly-haired races of the eastern peninsula and the islands beyond.   Besides these conspicuous differences "The Papuan is generally taller and is more consistently **Papuan.** dolichocephalic than the Papuo-Melanesian : he is always darker, his usual colour being a dark chocolate or sooty brown ; his head is high and his face, is, as a rule, long with prominent brow-ridges, above which his rather flat forehead commonly slopes backwards.   The Papuo-Melanesian head is usually less high and the brow ridges **Papuo-Melanesian.** less prominent, while the forehead is commonly rounded and not retreating.   The skin colour runs through the whole gamut of shades of *café-au-lait*, from a lightish yellow with only a tinge of brown, to a tolerably dark bronze colour.   The lightest shades are everywhere uncommon, and in many localities appear to be limited to the female sex.   The Papuan nose is longer and stouter and is often so arched as to present the outline known as 'Jewish.'   The character of its bridge varies, typically the nostrils are broad and the tip of the nose is often hooked downwards.   In the Papuo-Melanesian the nose is generally smaller : both races have frizzly hair, but while this is universal among Papuans, curly and even wavy hair is common among both [Eastern and Western] divisions of Papuo-Melanesians."[2]

The Melanesians are as variable as the natives of New Guinea ; the hair may be curly, or even wavy, showing **Melanesian.** evidence of racial mixture, and the skin is chocolate or occasionally copper-coloured.   The stature of the men ranges from 1.50 m. to 1.78 m. (4 ft. 11 in.

---

[1] *The Melanesians of British New Guinea*, 1910, pp. 2, 27.
[2] The curly or wavy hair appears more commonly among women than among men.

to 5 ft. 10 in.), with an average between 1.56 m. and 1.6 m. (5 ft. 1½ in. to 5 ft. 3 in.). The skull is usually dolicho-cephalic, but ranges from 67 to 85 and in certain parts brachycephaly is predominant ; the nose shows great diversity. This type ranges with local variations from the Admiralty Islands and parts of New Guinea through the Bismarck Archipelago, Solomon Islands, and the New Hebrides and other island groups to Fiji and New Caledonia.

The "Kanakas," as the natives of New Caledonia and the Loyalty group are wrongly [1] called by their present rulers, have been described by various French investi-gators. Among the best accounts of them is that of M. Augustin Bernard,[2] based on the observations of de Rochas, Bourgard, Vieillard, Bertillon, Meinicke, and others. Apart from several sporadic Poly-nesian groups in the Loyalties,[3] all are typical Melanesians, long-headed with very broad face at least in the middle, narrow boat-shaped skull (ceph. index 70),[4] large massive lower jaw, often with two supplementary molars,[5] colour a dark chocolate, often with a highly characteristic purple tinge ; but de Rochas' statement that for a few days after birth infants are of a light reddish yellow hue lacks confirmation ; hair less woolly but much longer than the Negro ; beard also longish and frizzly, the peppercorn tufts with simulated bald spaces being an effect

The New Caledonians.

Physical Characters.

---

[1] *Kanaka* is a Polynesian word meaning "man," and should therefore be restricted to the brown Indonesian group, but it is indiscriminately applied by French writers to all South Sea Islanders, whether black or brown. This misuse of the term has found its way into some English books of travel even in the corrupt French form " canaque."

[2] *L'Archipel de la Nouvelle Calédonie*, Paris, 1895.

[3] Lifu, Mare, Uvea, and Isle of Pines. These Polynesians appear to have all come originally from Tonga, first to Uvea Island (Wallis), and thence in the eighteenth century to Uvea in the Loyalties, cradle of all the New Caledonian Polynesian settlements. Cf. C. M. Woodford, " On some Little-known Polynesian Settlements in the Neighbourhood of the Solomon Islands," *Geog. Journ.* XLVIII. 1916.

[4]. This low index is characteristic of most Papuasians, and reaches the extreme of dolichocephaly in the extinct Kai-Colos of Fiji (65°), and amongst some coast Papuans of New Guinea measured by Miklukho-Maclay. But this observer found the characters so variable in New Guinea that he was unable to use it as a racial test. In the New Hebrides, Louisiades, and Bismarck group also he found many of the natives to be broad-headed, with indices as high as 80 and 85 ; and even in the Solomon Islands Guppy records cephalic indices ranging from 69 to 86, but dolichocephaly predominates (*The Solomon Islands*, 1887, pp. 112, 114). Thus this feature is no more constant amongst the Oceanic than it is amongst the African Negroes. (See also M.-Maclay's paper in *Proc. Linn. Soc. New South Wales*, 1882, p. 171 sq.) [5] *Eth.* Ch. VIII.

due to the assiduous use of the comb ; very prominent superciliary arches and thick eyebrows, whence their somewhat
furtive look ; mean height 5 ft. 4 in. ; speech Melanesian with
three marked varieties, that of the south-eastern districts
being considered the most rudimentary member of the whole
Melanesian group.[1]

From the state of their industries, in some respects the
rudest, in others amongst the most advanced in Melanesia, it
may be inferred that after their arrival the New Caledonians,
like the Tasmanians, the Andamanese, and some other insular
groups, remained for long ages almost completely secluded
The Food from the rest of the world. Owing to the
Question. poverty of the soil the struggle for food must
always have been severe. Hence the most
jealously guarded privileges of the chiefs were associated with
questions of diet, while the paradise of the dead was a region
where they had abundance of food and could gorge on yams.

The ethnological history of the whole of the Melanesian
region is obscure, but as the result of recent investigations
General Survey certain broad features may be recognised. The
of Melanesian earliest inhabitants were probably a black,
Ethnology. woolly-haired race, now represented by the
pygmies of New Guinea, remnants of a formerly widely extended Negrito population also surviving in the Andaman
Islands, the Malay Peninsula (Semang) and the Philippines
(Aeta). A taller variety advanced into Tasmania and formed
the Tasmanian group, now extinct, others spread over New
Guinea and the western Pacific as " Papuans," and formed
the basis of the Melanesian populations.[2] The Proto-Poly-
nesians in their migrations from the East Indian Archipelago
to Polynesia passed through this region and imposed their
speech on the population and otherwise modified it. In
later times other migrations have come from the west, and
parts of Melanesia have also been directly influenced by
movements from Polynesia. The result of these supposed
influences has been to form the Melanesian peoples as they
exist to-day.[3] G. Friederici[4] has accumulated a vast amount

[1] Bernard, p. 262.
[2] A. C. Haddon, *The Wanderings of Peoples*, 1911, p. 33.
[3] A. C. Haddon, *The Races of Man*, 1909, p. 21.
[4] *Wissenschaftliche Ergebnisse einer amtlichen Forschungsreise nach dem Bismarck-Archipel im Jahre* 1908 ; *Untersuchungen über eine Melanesische Wanderstrasse*, 1913 ; and *Mitt. aus den deutschen Schutzgebieten, Ergänzungs-*

of evidence based chiefly on linguistics and material culture, to support the theory of Melanesian cultural streams from the west. He regards the Melanesians as having come from that part of Indonesia which extends from the Southern Islands of the Philippine group, through the Minahasa peninsula of Celebes, to the Moluccas in the neighbourhood of Buru and Ceram. From the Moluccan region they passed north of New Guinea to the region about Vitiaz and Dampier Straits, which Friederici regards as the gateway of Melanesia. Here they colonised the northern shores of New Britain, and part of the swarm settled along the eastern and south-eastern shores of New Guinea. Another stream passed to the Northern Louisiades, Southern Solomons, and Northern New Hebrides. The Philippine or sub-Philippine stream took a more northerly route, going by the Admiralty group to New Hanover, East New Ireland and the Solomons.

The first serious attempt to disentangle the complex cha-racter of Melanesian ethnography was made by F. Graebner in 1905,[1] followed by G. Friederici, the references to whose work are given above. More recently W. H. R. Rivers[2] has attacked the cultural problem by means of the genealogical method and the results of his investigations are here briefly summarised. He has discovered several remarkable forms of marriage in Melanesia and has deduced others which have existed previously. He argues that the anomalous forms of marriage imply a former dual organisation (*i.e.* a division of the community into two exogamous groups) with matrilineal descent, and he is driven to assume that in early times there was a state of society in which the elders had acquired so predominant a position that they were able to monopolise all the young women. Some of the relationship systems are of great antiquity, and it is evident that changes have taken place due to cultural in-fluences coming in from without.

Cultural
Problems.

The distribution of kava-drinking and betel-chewing is of great interest. The former occurs all over Poly-nesia (except Easter Island and New Zealand) and throughout southern Melanesia, including

Kava-drinking
and
Betel-chewing.

heft, Nr 5, 1912, Nr 7, 1913. See also S. H. Ray, *Nature*, CLXXII. 1913, and *Man*, XIV. 34, 1914.

[1] *Zeitschr. f. Ethnol.* XXXVII. p. 26, 1905. His later writings should also be consulted, *Anthropos*, IV. 1909, pp. 726, 998 ; *Ethnologie*, 1914, p. 13.

[2] *The History of Melanesian Society*, 1914.

certain Santa Cruz Islands, where it is limited to religious ceremonial. Betel-chewing begins at these islands and extends northwards through New Guinea and Indonesia to India. Kava and betel were introduced into Melanesia by different cultural migrations.

The introduction of betel-chewing was relatively late and restricted and may have taken place from Indonesia after the invasion by the Hindus. With it were associated strongly established patrilineal institutions, marriage with a wife of a father's brother, the special sanctity of the skull and the plank-built canoe. The use of pile dwellings is a more constant element of the betel-culture than of the kava-culture. The religious ritual centres round the skulls of ancestors and relatives, and the cult of the skull has taken a direction which gives the heads of enemies an importance equal to that of relatives, hence head-hunting has become the chief object of warfare. The skull of a relative is the symbol—if not the actual abiding place—of the dead, to be honoured and propitiated, while the skulls of enemies act as the means whereby this honour and propitiation are effected.

The influence of the kava-using peoples was more extensive in time and space than that of the betel-chewing people. Rivers supposes that they had neither clan organisation nor exogamy. Some of them preserved the body after death and respect was paid to the head or skull. It is possible that the custom of payment for a wife came into existence in Melanesia as the result of the need of the immigrant men for women of the indigenous people owing to their bringing few women with them, and the great development of shell money may be due in part to those payments. Contact with the earlier populations also resulted in the development of secret societies. The immigrants introduced the cult of the dead and the institutions of taboo, totemism and chieftainship. They brought with them a form of outrigger canoe and the knowledge of plank-building for canoes (which however was only partially adopted), the rectangular house, and may have known the art of making pile dwellings. They introduced various forms of currency made of shells, teeth, feathers, mats, etc., the drill, the slit drum, or gong, the conch trumpet, the fowl, pig, dog, and megalithic monuments.

There may have been two immigrations of peoples who made monuments of stone: 1. Those who erected the more

dolmen-like structures, probably had aquatic totems, and interred their dead in the extended position.
2. A later movement of people whose stone structures tended to take the form of pyramids, who had bird totems, practised a cult of the sun and cremated their dead. Stone Monuments.

When the kava-using people came into Melanesia they found it already inhabited. The earliest form of social organisation of which we have evidence was on the dual basis, associated with matrilineal descent, the dominance of the old men (gerontocracy) and certain peculiar forms of marriage. These people interred their dead in the contracted or sitting position, which also was employed in most parts of Polynesia. Evidently they feared the ghosts and removed their dead as completely as possible from the living. These people—whom we may speak of as the " dual-people "—were communistic in property and probably practised sexual communism ; the change towards the institution of individual property and individual marriage were assisted by, if not entirely due to, the influence of the kava-people. They practised circumcision. Magic was an indigenous institution. Characteristic is the cult of *vui*, unnamed local spirits with definite haunts or abiding places whose rites are performed in definite localities. In the Northern New Hebrides the offerings connected with *vui* are not made to the *vui* themselves but to the man who owns the place connected with the *vui*. It would seem as if ownership of a locality carried with it ownership of the *vui* connected with the locality. Thus *vui* are local spirits belonging to the indigenous owners of the soil, and there seems no reason to believe that they were ever ghosts of dead men. As totemism occurs among the dual-people of the Bismarck Archipelago (who live in parts of New Britain and New Ireland and Duke of York Island) it is possible that the kava-people were not the sole introducers of totemism into Melanesia. The dual-people were probably acquainted with the bow, which they may have called *busur*, and the dug-out canoe which was used either lashed together in pairs or singly with an outrigger. The Dual-people.

The origin of a dual organisation is generally believed to be due to fission, but it is more reasonable to regard it as due to fusion, as hostility is so frequently manifest between the two groups despite the fact that spouses are always obtained from the other moiety. In New Ireland (and elsewhere) each moiety is associated with a hero ; one acts wisely but unscrupulously, the other is a fool who is always falling an easy victim to the first. Each moiety has a totem bird : one is a fisher, clever and capable, while the second obtains its food by stealing from the other and does not go to sea. One represents the immigrants of superior culture who came by sea, the other the first people, aborigines, of lowly culture who were quite unable to cope with the wiles and stratagems of the people who had settled among them. In the Gazelle Peninsula of New Britain, the dual groups are associated with light and dark coconuts ; affiliated with the former are male objects and the clever bird, which is universally called *taragau*, or a variant of that term. The bird of the other moiety is named *malaba* or *manigulai*, and is associated with female objects. The dark coconuts, the dark colour and flattened noses of the women who were produced by their transformation, and the projecting eyebrows of the *malaba* bird and its human adherents seem to be records in the mythology of the Bismarck Archipelago of the negroid (or, Rivers suggests, an Australoid) character of the aboriginal population. The light coconut which was changed into a light-coloured woman seems to have preserved a tradition of the light colour of the immigrants.

The autochthones of Melanesia were a dark-skinned and ulotrichous people, who had neither a fear of the ghosts of their dead nor a manes cult, but had a cult of local spirits. The Baining of the Gazelle Peninsula of New Britain may be representatives of a stage of Melanesian history earlier than the dual system ; if so, they probably represent in a modified form, the aboriginal element. They are said to be completely devoid of any fear of the dead.

Summary of Culture Strata.

The immigrants whose arrival caused the institution of the dual system were a relatively fair people of superior culture who interred their dead in a sitting position and feared their ghosts. They first introduced the Austronesian language.

All subsequent migrations were of Austronesian-speaking peoples from Indonesia. First came the kava-peoples in various swarms, and more recently the betel-people.

Possibly New Caledonia shows the effects of relative

isolation more than other parts of Melanesia, but, except for Polynesian influence (most directly recognisable in Fiji and southern Melanesia), Melanesia may be regarded as possessing a general culture with certain **Melanesian Culture.** characteristic features which may be thus summarised.[1] The Melanesians are a noisy, excitable, demonstrative, affectionate, cheery, passionate people. They could not be hunters everywhere, as in most of the islands there is no game, nor could they be pastors anywhere, as there are no cattle ; the only resources are fishing and agriculture. In the larger islands there is usually a sharp distinction between the coast people, who are mainly fishers, and the inlanders who are agriculturalists ; the latter are always by far the more primitive, and in many cases are subservient to the former. Both sexes work in the plantations. In parts of New Guinea and the Western Solomons the sago palm is of great importance ; coconut palms grow on the shores of most islands, and bananas, yams, bread-fruit, taro and sweet potatoes supply abundant food. As for dress, the men occasionally wear none, but usually have belts or bands, of bark-cloth, plaits, or strings, and the women almost everywhere have **Dress.** petticoats of finely shredded leaves. The skin is decorated with scars in various patterns, and tattooing is occasionally seen, the former being naturally characteristic of the darker skinned people, and the latter of the lighter. Every portion of the body is decorated in innumerable ways with shell, teeth, feathers, leaves, flowers, and other objects, and plaited bands encircle the neck, body, and limbs. Shell necklaces, which constitute a kind of currency, and artifically deformed boars' tusks are especially characteristic, though each group usually has its peculiar ornaments, distinguishing it from any other group. There is a great variety of houses. The typical Melanesian house has a gable roof, the **Houses.** ridge pole is supported by two main posts, side walls are very low, and the ends are filled in with bamboo screens. Pile dwellings are found in the Bismarck Archipelago, the Solomon Islands and New Guinea, and some New Guinea villages extend out into the sea.

The weapons typical of Melanesia are the club and the spear (though the latter is not found in the Banks Islands),

[1] A. C. Haddon, *The Races of Man*, 1909, pp. 24–8, and *Handbook to the Ethnographical Collections, British Museum*, 1910, pp. 119–139.

each group and often each island possessing its own distinctive pattern.   Stone headed clubs are found
Weapons.   in New Guinea, New Britain and the New
Hebrides.   The spears of the Solomon Islands are finely
decorated and have bone bards ; those of New Caledonia
are pointed with a string-ray spine ; those of the Admiralty
Islands have obsidian heads ; and those of New Britain have
a human armbone at the butt end.   The bow, the chief
weapon of the Papuans, occurs over the greater part of
Melanesia, though it is absent in S.E. New Guinea, and is
only used for hunting in the Admiralty Islands.

The holl wed out tree trunk with or without a plank
gunwale is general, usually with a single outrigger, though
Canoes, etc.   plank-built canoes occur in the Solomons,
characteristically ornamented with shell inlay.
Pottery is an important industry in parts of New Guinea and
in Fiji ; it occurs also in New Caledonia, Espiritu Santo
(New Hebrides) and the Admiralty Islands.   Bark-cloth is
made in most islands, but a loom for weaving leaf strips is
now found only in Santa Cruz.

A division of the community into two exogamous groups
is very widely spread, no intermarriage being permitted within
Social Life.   the group.   Mother-right is prevalent, descent
and inheritance being counted on the mother's
side, while a man's property descends to his sister's children.
At the same time the mother is in no sense the head of the family ;
the house is the father's, the garden may be his, the rule and
government are his, though the maternal uncle sometimes has
more authority than the father.   The transition to father-right
has definitely occurred at various places, and is taking place
elsewhere ; thus, in some of the New Hebrides, the father has
to buy off the rights of his wife's relations or his sister's
children.

Chiefs exist everywhere, being endowed with religious
sanctity in Fiji, where they are regarded as the direct
descendants of the tribal ancestors.   More often, a chief
holds his position solely owing to the fact that he has inherited
the cult of some powerful spirit, and his influence is not very
extensive.   Probably everywhere public affairs are regulated
by discussion among the old or important men, and the more
primitive the society, the more power they possess.   But the
most powerful institutions of all are the secret societies,

occurring with certain exceptions throughout Melanesia. These are accessible to men only, and the candidates on initiation have to submit to treatment **Secret Societies.** which is often rough in the extreme. The members of the societies are believed to be in close association with ghosts and spirits, and exhibit themselves in masks and elaborate dresses in which disguise they are believed by the uninitiated to be supernatural beings. These societies do not practise any secret cult, in fact all that the initiate appears to learn is that the " ghosts " are merely his fellows in disguise, and that the mysterious noises which herald their approach are produced by the bull-roarer and other artificial means. These organisations are most powerful agents for the maintenance of social order and inflict punishment for breaches of customary law, but they are often terrorising and blackmailing institutions. Women are rigorously excluded.

Other social factors of importance are the clubs, especially in the New Hebrides and Banks Islands. These are a means of attaining social rank. They are divided into **Clubs.** different grades, the members of which eat together at their particular fire-place in the club-house. Each rank has its insignia, sometimes human effigies, usually, but wrongly, called " idols." Promotion from one grade to another is chiefly a matter of payment, and few reach the highest. Those who do so become personages of very great influence, since no candidate can obtain promotion without their permission.

Totemism occurs in parts of New Guinea and elsewhere and has marked socialising effects, as totemic solidarity takes precedence of all other considerations, but it is **Religion.** becoming obsolete. The most important religious factor throughout Melanesia is the belief in a supernatural power or influence generally called *mana*. This is what works to effect everything which is beyond the ordinary power of man or outside the common processes of nature ; but this power, though in itself impersonal, is always connected with some person who directs it ; all spirits have it, ghosts generally, and some men. A more or less developed ancestor cult is also universally distributed. Human beings may become beneficent or malevolent ghosts, but not every ghost becomes an object of regard. The ghost who is worshipped is the spirit of a man who in his lifetime had *mana*. Good and

K.

evil spirits independent of ancestors are also abundant every-where. There is no established priesthood, except in Fiji, but as a rule, any man who knows the particular ritual suitable to a definite spirit, acts as intermediary, and a man in com-munication with a powerful spirit becomes a person of great importance. Life after death is universally believed in, and the soul is commonly pictured as undertaking a journey, beset with various perils, to the abode of departed spirits, which is usually represented as lying towards the west. As a rule only the souls of brave men, or initiates, or men who have died in fight, win through to the most desirable abode. Magical practices occur everywhere for the gaining of benefits, plenteous crops, good fishing, fine weather, rain, children or success in love. Harmful magic for producing sickness or death is equally universal.[1]

Returning to the Papuan lands proper, in the insular groups west of New Guinea we enter one of the most

Western Papuasia.

entangled ethnical regions in the world. Here are, no doubt, a few islands such as the Aru group, mainly inhabited by full-blood Papuans, men who furnished Wallace with the models on which he built up his true Papuan type, which has since been vainly assailed by so many later observers. But in others—Ceram, Buru, Timor, and so on to Flores—diverse ethnical and linguistic elements are intermingled in almost hopeless con-fusion. Discarding the term "Alfuro" as of no ethnical value,[2]

Ethnical Elements.

we find the whole area west to about 120° E. longitude[3] occupied in varying proportions by pure and mixed representatives of three distinct stocks: Negro (Papuans), Mongoloid (Malayans), and Cau-casic (Indonesians). From the data supplied by Crawfurd,

---

[1] Besides the earlier works of H. H. Romilly, *The Western Pacific and New Guinea*, 1886, *From My Verandah in New Guinea*, 1889; J. Chalmers, *Work and Adventure in New Guinea*, 1885; O. Finsch, *Samoafahrten! Reisen in Kaiser Wilhelms-Land und Englisch Neu-Guinea*, 1888; C. M. Woodford, *A Naturalist Among the Head-hunters*, 1890; J. P. Thompson, *British New Guinea*, 1892; and R. H. Codrington, *The Melanesians*, 1891, the following more recent works may be consulted:—A. C. Haddon, *Head-hunters, Black, White, and Brown*, 1901, and *Reports of the Cambridge Anthropological Expedition to Torres Straits*, 1901–; R. Parkinson, *Dreissig Jahre in der Südsee*, 1907; G. A. J. van der Sande, *Nova Guinea*, 1907; B. Thompson, *The Fijians*, 1908; G. Brown, *Melanesians and Polynesians*, 1910; F. Speiser, *Südsee Urwald Kannibalen*, 1913.

[2] *Eth. Ch.* XII.

[3] But excluding Celebes, where no trace of Papuan elements has been dis-covered.

Wallace, Forbes, Ten Kate and other trustworthy observers, I have constructed the subjoined table, in which the east Malaysian islands are disposed according to the constituent elements of their inhabitants : [1]

Aru Group — True Papuans dominant ; Indonesians (Korongoei) in the interior.

Kei Group—Malayans ; Indonesians ; Papuan strain everywhere.

Timor ; Wetta ; Timor Laut—Mixed Papuans, Malayans and Indonesians ; no pure type anywhere.

Serwatti Group—Malayans with slight trace of black blood (Papuan or Negrito).

Roti and Sumba—Malayans.

Savu—Indonesians.

Flores ; Solor ; Adonera ; Lomblen ; Pantar ; Allor—Papuans pure or mixed dominant ; Malayans in the coast towns.

Buru—Malayans on coast ; reputed Papuans, but more probably Indonesians in interior.

Ceram—Malayans on coast ; mixed Malayo-Papuans inland.

Amboina ; Banda—Malayans ; Dutch-Malay half-breeds (" Perkeniers ").

Goram—Malayans with slight Papuan strain.

Matabello ; Tior ; Nuso Telo ; Tionfoloka—Papuans with Malayan admixture.

Misol—Malayo-Papuans on coast ; Papuans inland.

Tidor ; Ternate ; Sulla ; Makian—Malayans.

Batjan—Malayans ; Indonesians.

Gilolo—Mixed Papuans ; Indonesians in the north.

Waigiu ; Salwatti ; Batanta—Malayans on the coast ; Papuans inland.

From this apparently chaotic picture, which in some places, such as Timor, presents every gradation from the full-blood Papuan to the typical Malay, Crawfurd concluded that the eastern section of Malaysia constituted a region of transition between the yellowish-brown lank-haired and the dark-brown or black mop-headed stocks. In a sense this is true, but not in the sense intended by Crawfurd, who by " transition " meant the

A Region of Transition by Displacements and Crossings.

---

[1] For details see F. H. H. Guillemard, *Australasia*, Vol. II. and Reclus, Vol. XIV.

actual passage by some process of development from type to type independently of interminglings. But such extreme transitions have nowhere taken place spontaneously, so to say, and in any case could never have been brought about in a small zoological area presenting everywhere the same climatic conditions. Biological types may be, and have been, modified in different environments, arctic, temperate, or tropical zones, but not in the same zone, and if two such marked types as the Mongol and the Negro are now found juxtaposed in the Malaysian tropical zone, the fact must be explained by migrations and displacements, while the intermediate forms are to be attributed to secular intermingling of the extremes. Why should a man, passing from one side to another of an island 10 or 20 miles long, be transformed from a sleek-haired brown to a frizzly-haired black, or from a mercurial laughter-loving Papuan to a Malayan "slow in movement and thoroughly phlegmatic in disposition, rarely seen to laugh or become animated in conversation, with expression generally of vague wonder or weary sadness " ? [1]

Wallace's classical description of these western Papuans, who are here in the very cradleland of the race, can never

Papuan and Malay Contrasts. lose its charm, and its accuracy has been fully confirmed by all later observers. " The typical Papuan race," he writes, " is in many respects the very opposite of the Malay. The colour of the body is a deep sooty-brown or black, sometimes approaching, but never quite equalling, the jet-black of some negro races. The hair is very peculiar, being harsh, dry, and frizzly, growing in little tufts or curls, which in youth are very short and compact, but afterwards grow out to a considerable length, forming the compact, frizzled mop which is the Papuan's pride and glory. . . . The moral characteristics of the Papuan appear to me to separate him as distinctly from the Malay as do his form and features. He is impulsive and demonstrative in speech and action. His emotions and passions express themselves in shouts and laughter, in yells and frantic leapings. . . . The Papuan has a greater feeling for art than the Malay. He decorates his canoe, his house, and almost every domestic utensil with elaborate carving, a habit which is rarely found among tribes of the Malay race. In the

---

[1] S. J. Hickson, *A Naturalist in North Celebes*, 1889, p. 203.

affections and moral sentiments, on the other hand, the Papuans seem very deficient. In the treatment of their children they are often violent and cruel, whereas the Malays are almost invariably kind and gentle."

The ethnological parting-line between the Malayan and Papuasian races, as first laid down by Wallace, nearly coincides with his division between the Indo-Malayan and Austro-Malayan floras and faunas, the chief differences being the positions of Sumbawa and Celebes. Both of these islands are excluded from the Papuasian realm, but included in the Austro-Malayan zoological and botanical regions. *Ethnical and Biological Divides.*

THE OCEANIC NEGRITOES.

Recent discoveries and investigations of the pygmy populations on the eastern border of the Indian Ocean tend to show that the problem is by no means simple. Already two main stocks are recognised, differentiated by wavy and curly hair and dolichocephaly in the Sakai, and so-called woolly hair in the Andamanese Islanders, Semang (Malay Peninsula) and Aeta (Philippines), combined with mesaticephaly or low brachycephaly. In East Sumatra and Celebes a short, curly-haired dark-skinned people occur, racially akin to the Sakai, and Moszkowski suggests that the same element occupied Geelvink Bay (Netherlands New Guinea). These with the Vedda of Ceylon, and some jungle tribes of the Deccan, represent remnants of a once widely distributed pre-Dravidian race, which is also supposed to form the chief element in the Australians.[1] *The Negritoes.*

The " Mincopies," as the Andamanese used to be called, nobody seems to know why, were visited in 1893 by Louis Lapicque, who examined a large kitchen-midden near Port Blair, but some distance from the present coast, hence of great age.[2] Nevertheless he failed to find any worked stone implements, although flint occurs in the island. Indeed, chipped or flaked flints, now replaced by broken glass, were formerly used for shaving and scarification. But, as the present natives use only fishbones, *The Andamanese.*

---

[1] A. C. Haddon, " The Pygmy Question," Appendix B to A. F. R. Wollaston's *Pygmies and Papuans*, 1912, p. 304.
[2] " A la Recherche des Negritos," etc., in *Tour du Monde*, New Series, Livr. 35–8. The midden was 150 ft. round, and over 12 ft. high.

shells, and wood, Lapicque somewhat hastily concluded that
Stone Age. these islanders, like some other primitive groups,
have never passed through a Stone Age at all.
The shell-mounds have certainly yielded an arrow-head and
polished adze " indistinguishable from any of the European or
Indian celts of the so-called Neolithic period."[1]   But there is no
reason to think that the archipelago was ever occupied by a
people different from its present inhabitants.   Hence we may
suppose that their ancestors arrived in their Stone Age, but
afterwards ceased to make stone implements, as less handy
for their purposes and more difficult to make than the shell
or bone-tipped weapons and the nets with which they capture
game and fish more readily " than the most skilful fisherman
with hook and line."[2]   Similarly they would seem to have
long lost the art of making fire, having once obtained it from
a still active volcano in the neighbouring Barren Island.[3]

The inhabitants of the Andaman Islands range in colour
from bronze to sooty black.   Their hair is extremely frizzly,
Personal Appearance. seeming to grow in spiral tufts and is seldom
more than five inches long when untwisted.   The
women usually shave their heads.   Their height
is about 1.48 m. (4 ft. $10\frac{1}{2}$ in.), with well-proportioned body
and small hands.   The cephalic index averages 82.   The
face is broad at the cheek-bones, the eyes are prominent, the
nose is much sunken at the root but straight and small ; the
lips are full but not thick, the chin is small but not retreating,
nor do the jaws project.   The natives are characterised by
honesty, frankness, politeness, modesty, conjugal fidelity,
respect for elders and real affection between relatives and
friends.   The women are on an equal footing with the men
and do their full share of work.   The food is mainly fish
(obtained by netting, spearing or shooting with bow and
arrow), wild yams, turtle, pig and honey.   They do not till
the soil or keep domestic animals.   Instead of clothing both
sexes wear belts, necklaces, leg-bands, arm-bands etc. made
of bones, wood and shell, the women wearing in addition

---

[1] E. H. Man, *Journ. Anthr. Inst.* Vol. XI. 1881, p. 271, and XII. 1883, p. 71.
[2] *Ib.* p. 272.
[3] Close to Barren is the extinct crater of *Narcondam*, i.e. *Narak-andam*
(*Narak* = Hell), from which the *Andaman* group may have taken its name
(Sir H. Yule, *Marco Polo*).   Man notes, however, that the Andamanese were not
aware of the existence of Barren Island until taken past in the settlement steamer
(p. 368).

a rudimentary leaf apron. When fully dressed the men wear bunches of shredded Pandanus leaf at wrists and knees, and a circlet of the same leaf folded on the head. They make canoes, some of which have an outrigger, but never venture far from the shore. They usually live in small encampments round an oval dancing ground, their simple huts are open in front and at the sides, or in a large Social Life. communal hut in which each family has its own particular space, the bachelors and spinsters having theirs. A family consists of a man and his wife and such of their children, own and adopted, as have not passed the period of the ceremonies of adolescence. Between that period and marriage the boys and girls reside in the bachelors' and spinsters' quarters respectively. A man is not regarded as an independent member of the community till he is married and has a child. There is no organised polity. Generally one man excels the rest in hunting, warfare, wisdom and kindliness, and he is deferred to, and becomes, in a sense, chief. A regular feature of Andamanese social life is the meeting at intervals between two or more communities. A visit of a few days is paid and presents are exchanged between hosts and guests, the time being spent in hunting, feasting and dancing.

No forms of worship have been noticed, but there is a belief in various kinds of spirits, the most important of whom is Biliku, usually regarded as female, who is identified with the north-east monsoon and is paired with Tarai Religion. the south-west monsoon. Biliku and Tarai are the producers of rain, storms, thunder and lightning. Fire was stolen from Biliku. There is always great fluidity in native beliefs, so some tribes regard Puluga (Biliku) as a male. Three things make Biliku angry and cause her to send storms ; melting or burning of beeswax, interfering in any way with a certain number of plants, and killing a cicada or making a noise during the time the cicadae are singing. A. R. Brown [1] gives an interesting explanation of this curious belief. Biliku is supposed to have a human form but nobody ever sees her. Her origin is unknown. The idea of her being a creator is local and is probably secondary, she does not concern herself with human actions other than those noted above.

[1] *Folk-Lore*, 1909, p. 257. See also the criticisms of W. Schmidt, " Puluga, the Supreme Being of the Andamanese," *Man*, 2, 1910, and A. Lang, " Puluga," *Man*, 30, 1910 ; A. R. Brown, *The Andaman Islands* (in the Press).

E. H. Man has carefully studied and reduced to writing the Andamanese language, of which there are at least nine distinct

Speech. varieties, corresponding to as many tribal groups. It has no clear affinities to any other tongue,[1] the supposed resemblances to Dravidian and Australian being extremely slight, if not visionary. Its phonetic system is astonishingly rich (no less than 24 vowels and 17 consonants, but no sibilants), while the arithmetic stops at *two*. Nobody ever attempts to count in any way beyond *ten*, which is reached by a singular process. First the nose is tapped with the

Method of Counting. finger-tips of either hand, beginning with the little finger, and saying *úbatúl* (one), then *íkpór* (two) with the next, after which each successive tap makes *anká*, "and this." When the thumb of the second hand is reached, making *ten*, both hands are brought together to indicate 5 + 5, and the sum is clenched with the word *àrdúru* ="all." But this feat is exceptional, and usually after *two* you get only words answering to several, many, numerous, countless, which flight of imagination is reached at about 6 or 7.

Yet with their infantile arithmetic these paradoxical islanders have contrived to develop an astonishingly intricate form of speech characterised by an absolutely bewildering superfluity of pronominal and other elements. Thus the possessive pronouns have as many as sixteen possible variants according to the class of noun (human objects, parts of the body, degrees of kinship, etc.) with which they are in agree-

Grammatical Structure. ment. For instance, *my* is *día dót, dóng, dig, dab, dar, dákà, dóto, dai, dár, ad, ad-en, deb,* with *man, head, wrist, mouth, father, son, step-son, wife,* etc. etc. ; and so with *thy, his, our, your, their !* This grouping of nouns in classes is analogous to the Bantu system, and it is curious to note that the number of classes is about the same. On the other hand there is a wealth of postfixes attached as in normal agglutinating forms of speech, so that "in adding their affixes they follow the principles of the ordinary agglutinative tongues ; in adding their prefixes they follow the well-defined principles of the South African tongues. Hitherto, as far as I know, the two principles in full play have never been found together in any other language . . .

---

[1] " The Andaman languages are one group ; they have no affinities by which we might infer their connection with any other known group " (R. C. Temple, quoted by Man, *Anthrop. Jour.* 1882, p. 123).

In Andamanese both are fully developed, so much so as to interfere with each other's grammatical functions."[1]   The result often is certain *sesquipedalia verba* comparable in length to those of the American polysynthetic languages.   A savage people, who can hardly count beyond two, possessed of about the most intricate language spoken by man, is a psychological puzzle which I cannot profess to fathom.

In the Malay Peninsula the indigenous element is certainly the Negrito, who, known by many names—Semang, Udai, Pangan, Hami, Menik or Mandi—forms a single ethnical group presenting some striking ana- *The Semangs.* logies with the Andamanese.   But, surrounded from time out of mind by Malay peoples, some semi-civilised, some nearly as wild as themselves, but all alike slowly crowding them out of the land, these aborigines have developed defensive quali- ties unneeded by the more favoured insular Negritoes, while their natural development has been arrested at perhaps a somewhat lower plane of culture.   In fact, doomed to ex- tinction before their time came, they never have had a chance in the race, as Hugh Clifford sings in *The Song of the Last Semangs* :

> The paths are rough, the trails are blind
>   The Jungle People tread ;
> The yams are scarce and hard to find
>   With which our folk are fed.
>
> We suffer yet a little space
>   Until we pass away,
> The relics of an ancient race
>   That ne'er has had its day.

In physical features they in many respects resemble the Andamanese.   Their hair is short, universally woolly and black, the skin colour dark chocolate *Physical Appearance.* brown approximating to glossy black,[2] some- times with a reddish tinge.[3]   There is very little evidence for the stature but the 17 males measured by Annandale and Robinson [4] averaged 1.52 m. (5 ft. 0¼ in.).   The average cephalic index is about 78 to 79, extremes ranging from 74 to 84.   The face is round, the forehead rounded, narrow and projecting, or as it were " swollen."   The nose is short and

[1] R. C. Temple, quoted by Man, *Anthrop. Jour.* 1882, p. 123.
[2] W. W. Skeat and C. D. Blagden, *Pagan Races of the Malay Peninsula*, 1906.
[3] R. Martin, *Die Inlandstämme der Malayischen Halbinsel*, 1905.
[4] N. Annandale and H. C. Robinson, "Fasciculi Malayensis," *Anthropology*, 1903.

flattened, with remarkable breadth and distended nostrils. The nasal index of five adult males was 101.2.[1] The cheek-bones are broad and the jaws often protrude slightly ; the lips are as a rule thick. Martin remarks that characteristic both of Semang and Sakai [2] is the great thickening of the integumental part of the upper lip, the whole mouth region projecting from the lower edge of the nose. This convexity occurs in 79 per cent., and is well shown in his photographs.[3]

Hugh Clifford, who has been intimately associated with the " Orang-utan " (Wild-men) as the Malays often call them, describes those of the Plus River valley as " like African Negroes seen through the reverse end of a field-glass. They are sooty-black in colour ; their hair is short and woolly, clinging to the scalp in little crisp curls ; their noses are flat, their lips protrude, and their features are those of the pure negroid type. They are sturdily built and well set upon their legs, but in stature little better than dwarfs. They live by hunting, and have no permanent dwellings, camping in little family groups wherever, for the moment, game is most plentiful." [4]

Their shelters—huts they cannot be called—are exactly like the frailest of the Andamanese, mere lean-to's of matted

Usages.
palm-leaves crazily propped on rough uprights ; clothes they have next to none, and their food is chiefly yams and other jungle roots, fish from the stream, and sun-dried monkey, venison and other game, this term having an elastic meaning. Salt, being rarely obtainable, is a great luxury, as amongst almost all wild tribes. They are a nomadic people living by collecting and hunting ; the wilder ones will often not remain longer than three days in one place. Very few have taken to agriculture. They make use of bamboo rafts for drifting down stream but have no canoes. All men are on an equal footing, but each tribe has a head, who exercises authority. Division of labour is fairly even between men and women. The men hunt, and the women build the shelters and cook the food. They are strictly monogamous and faithful.

---

[1] W. W. Skeat and C. D. Blagden, *loc. cit.*

[2] The Sakai have often been classed among Negritoes, but, although un doubtedly a mixed people, their affinities appear to be pre-Dravidian.

[3] Cf. A. C. Haddon, " The Pygmy Question," Appendix B to A. F. R. Wollaston's *Pygmies and Papuans*, 1912, p. 306.

[4] *In Court and Kampong*, 1897, p. 172.

All the faculties are sharpened mainly in the quest of food and of means to elude the enemy now closing round their farthest retreats in the upland forests. When hard pressed and escape seems impossible, they will climb trees and stretch rattan ropes from branch to branch where these are too wide apart to be reached at a bound, and along such frail aërial bridges women and all will pass with their cooking-pots and other effects, with their babies also at the breast, and the little ones clinging to their mother's heels. For like the Andamanese they love their women-folk and children, and in this way rescue them from the Malay raiders and slavers. But unless the British raj soon intervenes their fate is sealed. They may slip from the Malays, but not from their own traitorous kinsmen, who often lead the hunt, and squat all night long on the tree-tops, calling one to another and signalling from these look-outs when the leaves rustle and the rattans are heaved across, so that nothing can be done, and another family group is swept away into bondage.

From their physical resemblance, undoubted common descent, and geographical proximity, one might also expect to find some affinity in the speech of the Anda- **Speech.** man and Malay Negritoes. But H. Clifford, who made a special study of the dialects on the mainland, discovered no points of contact between them and any other linguistic group.[1] This, however, need cause no surprise, being in no discordance with recognised principles. As in the Andamans, stone implements have been **Stone Age.** found in the Peninsula, and specimens are now in the Pitt-Rivers collection at Oxford.[2] But the present aborigines do not make or use such tools, and there is good reason for thinking that they were the work of their ancestors, arriving, as in the Andamans, in the remotest past. Hence the two groups have been separated for many thousands of years, and their speech has diverged too widely to be now traced back to a common source.

---

[1] Senoi grammar and glossary in *Jour. Straits Branch R. Asiat. Soc.* 1892, No. 24.

[2] See L. Wray's paper "On the Cave Dwellers of Perak," in *Jour. Anthrop. Inst.* 1897, p. 36 sq. This observer thinks "the earliest cave dwellers were most likely the Negritoes" (p. 47), and the great age of the deposits is shown by the fact that "in some of the caves at least 12 feet of a mixture of shells, bones, and earth has been accumulated and subsequently removed again in the floors of the caves. In places two or three layers of solid stalagmite have been formed and removed, some of these layers having been five feet in thickness" (p. 45).

With the Negritoes of the Philippines we enter a region of almost hopeless ethnical complications,[1] amid which, however, **The Aetas.** the dark dwarfish *Aeta* peoples crop out almost everywhere as the indigenous element. The Aeta live in the mountainous districts of the larger islands, and in some of the smaller islands of the Philippines, and the name is conveniently extended to the various groups of Philippine Negritoes, many of whom show the results of mixture with other peoples. Their hair is universally woolly, usually of a dirty black colour, often sun-burnt on the top to a reddish brown. The skin is dark chocolate brown rather than black, sometimes with a yellowish tinge. The average stature of 48 men was 1.46 m. (4 ft. 9 in.), but showed considerable range. The typical nose is broad, flat, and bridgeless, with prominent arched nostrils, the average nasal index for males being 102, and for females 105.[2] The lips are thick, but not protruding, sometimes showing a pronounced convexity between the upper lip and the nose.

John Foreman[3] noted the curious fact that the Aeta were recognised as the owners of the soil long after the arrival of the Malayan intruders.

"For a long time they were the sole masters of Luzon Island, where they exercised seignorial rights over the Tagalogs and other immigrants, until these arrived in such numbers, that the Negritoes were forced to the highlands.

"The taxes imposed upon the primitive Malay settlers by the Negritoes were levied in kind, and, when payment was refused, they swooped down in a posse, and carried off the head of the defaulter. Since the arrival of the Spaniards terror of the white man has made them take definitely to the mountains, where they appear to be very gradually decreasing."[4]

At first sight it may seem unaccountable that a race of such extremely low intellect should be able to assert their

---

[1] See on this point Prof. Blumentritt's paper on the Manguians of Mindoro in *Globus*, LX. No. 14.

[2] One Aeta woman of Zambales had a nasal index of 140.7. W. Allen Reed, "Negritoes of Zambales," *Department of the Interior: Ethnological Survey Publications*, II. 1904, p. 35. For details of physical features see the following :— D. Folkmar, *Album of Philippine Types*, 1904; Dean C. Worcester, "The Non-Christian Tribes of Northern Luzon," *The Philippine Journal of Science*, I. 1906; and A. C. Haddon, "The Pygmy Question," Appendix B to A. F. R. Wollaston's *Pygmies and Papuans*, 1912.

[3] *The Philippine Islands*, etc., London and Hongkong, 1890.

[4] *Op. cit.* p. 210.

supremacy in this way over the intruding Malayans, assumed to be so much their superiors in physical and mental qualities. But it has to be considered that the invasions took place in very remote times, ages before the appearance on the scene of the semi-civilised Muhammadan Malays of history. Whether of Indonesian or of what is called " Malay " stock, the intruders were rude Oceanic peoples, who in the prehistoric period, prior to the spread of civilising Hindu or Moslem influences in Malaysia, had scarcely advanced in general culture much beyond the indigenous Papuan and Negrito populations of that region. Even at present the Gaddanes, Itaves, Igorrotes, and others of Luzon are mere savages, at the head-hunting stage, quite as wild as, and per- Head-hunters. haps even more ferocious than any of the Aetas. Indeed we are told that in some districts the Negrito and Igorrote tribes keep a regular Debtor and Creditor account of heads. Wherever the vendetta still prevails, all alike live in a chronic state of tribal warfare ; periodical head-hunting expeditions are organised by the young men, to present the bride's father with as many grim trophies as possible in proof of their prowess, the victims being usually taken by surprise and stricken down with barbarous weapons, such as a long spear with tridented tips, or darts and arrows carrying at the point two rows of teeth made of flint or sea-shells. To avoid these attacks some, like the Central Sudanese Negroes, live in cabins on high posts or trees 60 to 70 feet from the ground, and defend themselves by showering stones on the marauders.

A physical peculiarity of the full-blood Negritoes, noticed by J. Montano,[1] is the large, clumsy foot, turned slightly inwards, a trait characteristic also of the African Negrilloes ; but in the Aeta the effect is exaggerated by the abnormal divergence of the great toe, as amongst the Annamese.

The presence of a pygmy element in the population of New Guinea had long been suspected, but the actual existence of a pygmy people was first discovered by the British Ornithologists' Union Expedition, New Guinea Pygmies. 1910, at the source of the Mimika river in the Nassau range.[2]

---

[1] *Voyage aux Philippines*, etc., Paris, 1886.
[2] A. F. R. Wollaston, *Pygmies and Papuans*, 1912 ; C. G. Rawling, *The Land of the New Guinea Pygmies*. 1913.

The description of these people, the Tapiro, is as follows.
Their stature averages 1.449 m. (4 ft. 9 in.) ranging from
1.326 m. (4 ft. 4½ in.) to 1.529 (5 ft. 0¼ in.). The skull is very
variable giving indices from 66.9 to 85.1. The skin colour
is lighter than that of the neighbouring Papuans, some individuals being almost yellow. The nose is straight, and though
described as "very wide at the nostrils," the mean of the
indices is only 83, the extremes being 65.5 and 94. The eyes
are noticeably larger and rounder than those of Papuans, and
the upper lip of many of the men is long and curiously convex. A Negrito element has also been recognised in the
Mafulu people investigated by R. W. Williamson in the
Mekeo District,[1] here mixed with Papuan and Papuo-Melanesian. Their stature ranges from 1.47 m. (4 ft. 10 in.) to
1.63 m. (5 ft. 4 in.). The average cephalic index is 80 ranging
from 74.7 to 86.8. The skin colour is dark sooty brown and
the hair, though usually brown or black, is often very much
lighter, "not what we in Europe should call dark." The
average nasal index is 84 with extremes of 71.4 and 100.
Also partly of Negrito origin are the Pĕsĕgĕm of the upper
waters of the Lorentz river.[2]

All these Negrito peoples, as has been pointed out, show
considerable diversity in physical characters, none of the
existing groups, with the exception of the
Andamanese, appearing to be homogeneous
as regards cephalic or nasal index, while the
stature, though always low, shows considerable range. They
have certain cultural features in common,[3] and these as a rule
differentiate them from their neighbours. They seldom
practise any deformation of the person, such as tattooing or
scarification, though the Tapiro and Mafulu wear a nose-
stick. They are invariably collectors and hunters, never,
unless modified by contact with other peoples, undertaking
any cultivation of the soil. Their huts are simple, the pile
dwellings of the Tapiro being evidently copied from their
neighbours. All possess the bow and arrow, though only
the Semang and Aeta use poison. The Andamanese appear
to be one of the very few peoples who possess fire but do

*Negrito
Culture.*

---

[1] *The Mafulu Mountain People of British New Guinea*, 1912.
[2] *Nova Guinea*, VII. 1913, 1915.
[3] A. C. Haddon, "The Pygmy Question," Appendix B to A. F. R. Wollaston's
Pygmies and Papuans, 1912, pp. 314–9.

not know how to make it afresh. There seems a certain amount of evidence that the Negrito method of making fire was that of splitting a dry stick, keeping the ends open by a piece of wood or stone placed in the cleft, stuffing some tinder into the narrow part of the slit and then drawing a strip of rattan to and fro across the spot until a spark sets fire to the tinder.[1] The social structure is everywhere very simple. The social unit appears to be the family and the power of the headman is very limited. Strict monogamy seems to prevail even where, as among the Aeta, polygyny is not prohibited. The dead are buried, but the bodies of those whom it is wished to honour are placed on platforms or on trees.

Related in certain physical characters to the pygmy Negritoes, although not of pygmy proportions,[2] were the aborigines of Tasmania, but their racial affinities are much disputed. Huxley thought   The Tas-
they showed some resemblance to the in-   manians.
habitants of New Caledonia and the Andaman Islands, but Flower was disposed to bring them into closer connection with the Papuans or Melanesians. The leading anthropologists in France do not accept either of these views. Topinard states that there is no close alliance between the New Caledonians and the Tasmanians, while Quatrefages and Hamy remark that " from whatever point of view we look at it, the Tasmanian race presents special characters, so that it is quite impossible to discover any well-defined affinities with any other existing race." Sollas, reviewing these conflicting opinions, concludes that " this probably represents the prevailing opinion of the present day." [3]

The Tasmanians were of medium height, the average for the men being 1.661 m. (5 ft. 5½ in.) with a range from 1.548 m. to 1.732 m. (5 ft. 1 in. to 5 ft. 8 in.) ; the average height for women being 1.503 m. (4 ft. 11 in.) with a range from 1.295 m. to 1.630 m. (4 ft. 3 in. to 5 ft. 4¼ in.). The skin colour was almost black with a brown tinge. The eyes were small and

---

[1] It is not certain however that this method is known to the Semang, and it occurs among peoples who are not Negrito, such as the Kayan of Sarawak, and in other places where a Negrito element has not yet been recorded.

[2] The term pygmy is usually applied to a people whose stature does not exceed 1.5 m. (4 ft. 11 in.).

[3] W. J. Sollas, *Ancient Hunters*, 1915, and W. Turner, " The Aborigines of Australia," *Trans. R. Soc. Edin.* 1908, XLVI. 2, and 1910, XLVII. 3.

deep set beneath prominent overhanging brow-ridges. The nose was short and broad, with a deep notch at the root and widely distended nostrils. The skull was dolichocephalic or low mesaticephalic, with an average index of 75, of peculiar outline when viewed from above. Other peculiarities were the possession of the largest teeth, especially noticeable in comparison with the small jaw, and the smallest known cranial capacity (averaging 1199 c.c. for both sexes, falling in the women to 1093 c.c.).

The aboriginal Tasmanians stood even at a lower level of culture than the Australians. At the occupation the

Tasmanian Culture. scattered bands, with no hereditary chiefs or social organisation, numbered altogether 2000 souls at most, speaking several distinct dialects, whether of one or more stock languages is uncertain. In the absence of sibilants and some other features they resembled the Australian, but were of ruder or less developed structure, and so imperfect that according to Joseph Milligan, our best authority on the subject, " they observed no settled order or

Undeveloped Speech. arrangement of words in the construction of their sentences, but conveyed in a supplementary fashion by tone, manner, and gesture those modifications of meaning which we express by mood, tense, number, etc."[1] Abstract terms were rare, and for every variety of gum-tree or wattle-tree there was a name, but no word for " tree " in general, or for qualities, such as hard, soft, warm, cold, long, short, round, etc. Anything hard was "like a stone," round "like the moon," and so on, " usually suiting the action to the word, and confirming by some sign the meaning to be understood."

They made fire by the stick and groove method, but their acquaintance with the fire-drill is uncertain.[2] The stone

Fire-making. Tools and Weapons. implements are the subject of much discussion. A great number are so rude and uncouth that, taken alone, we should have little reason to suspect that they had been chipped by man : some, on the other hand, show signs of skilful working. They were formerly classed as " eoliths " and compared to the plateau implements of Kent and Sussex, but the comparison cannot be

---

[1] Paper in Brough Smyth's work, II. p. 413.
[2] H. Ling Roth, *The Aborigines of Australia* (2nd. ed.), 1899, Appendix LXXXVIII., and " Tasmanian Firesticks," *Nature*, LIX. 1899, p. 606.

sustained.[1] Sollas illustrates an implement " delusively similar to the head of an axe " and notes its resemblance to a Levallois flake (Acheulean). J. P. Johnson [2] points out the general likeness to pre-Aurignacian forms and there is a remarkable similarity of certain examples to Mousterian types. Weapons were of wood, and consisted of spears pointed and hardened in the fire, and a club or waddy, about two feet long, sometimes knobbed at one end ; the range is said to have been about 40 yards.

In the native diet were included " snakes, lizards, grubs and worms," besides the opossum, wombat, kangaroo, birds and fishes, roots, seeds and fruits, but not human flesh, at least normally. Like the Bushmen, they were **Diet.** gross feeders, consuming enormous quantities of food when they could get it, and the case is mentioned of a woman who was seen to eat from 50 to 60 eggs of the sooty petrel (larger than a duck's), besides a double allowance of bread, at the station on Flinders Island. They had frail bundles of bark made fast with thongs or rushes, half float, half boat, to serve as canoes, but no permanent **Dwellings.** abodes or huts, beyond branches of trees lashed together, supported by stakes, and disposed crescent-shape with the convex side to windward. On the uplands and along the sea-shore they took refuge in caves, rock-shelters and natural hollows. Usually the men went naked, the women wore a loose covering of skins, and personal ornamentation was limited to cosmetics or red ochre, plumbago, and powdered charcoal, with occasionally a necklace of shells strung on a fibrous twine.

Being merely hunters and collectors, with the arrival of English colonists their doom was sealed. " Only in rare instances can a race of hunters contrive to **Extinction.** co-exist with an agricultural people. When the hunting ground of a tribe is restricted owing to its partial occupation by the new arrivals, the tribe affected is compelled to infringe on the boundaries of its neighbours : this is to break the most sacred ' law of the jungle,' and inevitably leads to war : the pressure on one boundary is propagated to the next, the ancient state of equilibrium is profoundly disturbed, and inter-tribal feuds become increasingly frequent.

[1] W. J. Sollas, *Ancient Hunters*, 1915, pp. 90, 106 ff.
[2] *Nature*, XCII. 1913, p. 320.

A bitter feeling is naturally aroused against the original offenders, the alien colonists ; misunderstandings of all kinds inevitably arise, leading too often to bloodshed, and ending in a general conflict between natives and colonists, in which the former, already weakened by disagreements among themselves, must soon succumb. So it was in Tasmania." After the war of 1825 to 1831 the few wretched survivors, numbering about 200, were gathered together into a settlement, and from 1834 onwards every effort was made for their welfare, " but ' the white man's civilisation proved scarcely less fatal than the white man's bullet,' and in 1877, with the death of Truganini, the last survivor, the race became extinct." [1]

[1] W. J. Sollas, *Ancient Hunters*, 1915, pp. 104–5.

CHAPTER VI

THE SOUTHERN MONGOLS

South Mongol Domain—Tibet, the Mongol Cradle-land—Stone Age in Tibet—The Primitive Mongol Type—The Balti and Ladakhi—Balti Type and Origins—The Tibetans Proper—Type—The Bhotiyas—Prehistoric Expansion of the Tibetan Race—Sub-Himalayan Groups : the Gurkhas—Mental Qualities of the Tibetans—Lamaism—The Horsoks—The Tanguts—Polyandry—The Bonbo Religion—Buddhist and Christian Ritualism—The Prayer-Wheel—Language and Letters—Diverse Linguistic Types—Lepcha—Angami-Naga and Kuki-Lushai Speech—Naga Tribes—General Ethnic Relations in Indo-China—Aboriginal and Cultured Peoples—The Talaings—The Manipuri—Religion—The Game of Polo—The Khel System—The Chins—Mental and Physical Qualities—Gods, Nats, and the After-Life—The Kakhyens—Caucasic Elements—The Karens—Type—Temperament—Christian Missions—The Burmese—Type—Character—Buddhism—Position of Woman—Tattooing—The Tai-Shan Peoples—The Ahom, Khamti and Chinese Shans—Shan Cradle-land and Origins—Caucasic Contacts—Tai-Shan Toned Speech—Shan, Lolo, and Mosso Writing Systems—Mosso Origins—Aborigines of South China and Annam—Man-tse Origins and Affinities—Caucasic Aborigines in South-East Asia—The Siamese Shans—Origins and Early Records—Social System—Buddhism—The Annamese—Origins—Physical and Mental Characters—Language and Letters—Social Institutions—Religious Systems—The Chinese—Origins—The Babylonian Theory—Persistence of Chinese Culture and Social System—Letters and Early Records—Traditions of the Stone and Metal Ages—Chinese Cradle and Early Migrations—Absorption of the Aborigines—Survivals : Hok-lo, Hakka, Pun-ti—Confucianism, Taoism, Buddhism—Fung-shui and Ancestry Worship—Islam and Christianity—The Mandarin Class.

CONSPECTUS.

Present Range. *Tibet ; S. Himalayan slopes ; Indo-China to the Isthmus of Kra ; China ; Formosa ; Parts of Malaysia.* Distribution in Past and Present Times.

Hair, *uniformly black, lank, round in transverse section ; sparse or no beard, moustache common.* **Colour,** *generally a dirty yellowish brown, shading off to olive and coppery brown in the south, and to lemon or whitish in N. China.* **Skull,** *normally brachy* (80 to 84), *but in parts of China sub-dolicho* (77) *and high.* **Jaws,** *slightly prognathous.* **Cheek-bones,** *very high and prominent laterally.* **Nose,** *very small, and concave, with* Physical Characters.

163

widish nostrils (mesorrhine), but often large and straight amongst the upper classes. **Eyes,** *small, black, and oblique (outer angle slightly elevated), vertical fold of skin over inner canthus.* **Stature,** *below the average, 1.62 m. (5 ft. 4 in.), but in N. China often tall, 1.77 m. to 1.82 m. (5 ft. 10 in. to 6 ft.).* **Lips,** *rather thin, sometimes slightly protruding.* **Arms, legs,** *and* **feet,** *of normal proportions, calves rather small. A blue patch in lower sacral region is characteristic of new-born.*

Temperament. *Somewhat sluggish, with little initiative, but great endurance ; cunning rather than intelligent ; generally thrifty and industrious, but mostly indolent in Siam and Burma ; moral standard low, with slight sense of right and wrong.*

Mental Characters.

Speech. *Mainly isolating and monosyllabic, due to phonetic decay ; loss of formative elements compensated by tone ; some (south Chinese, Annamese) highly tonic, but others (in Himalayas and North Burma) highly agglutinating and consequently toneless.*

Religion. *Ancestry and spirit-worship, underlying various kinds of Buddhism ; religious sentiment weak in Annam, strong in Tibet ; thinly diffused in China.*

Culture. *Ranges from sheer savagery (Indo-Chinese aborigines) to a low phase of civilisation ; some mechanical arts (ceramics, metallurgy, weaving), and agriculture well developed ; painting, sculpture, and architecture mostly in the barbaric stage ; letters widespread, but true literature and science slightly developed ; stagnation very general.*

Bod-pa. *Tibetan ; Tangut ; Horsok ; Si-fan ; Balti ; Ladakhi ; Gurkha ; Bhotiya ; Miri ; Mishmi ; Abor.*

Main Divisions.

Burmese. *Naga ; Kuki-Lushai ; Chin ; Kakhyen ; Manipuri ; Karen ; Talaing ; Arakanese ; Burmese proper.*

Tai-Shan. *Ahom ; Khamti ; Ngiou ; Lao ; Siamese.*

Giao-Shi. *Annamese ; Cochin-Chinese.*

Chinese. *Chinese proper ; Hakka ; Hok-lo ; Pun-ti.*

The Mongolian stock may be divided into two main branches :[1] the *Mongolo-Tatar*, of the western area, and the *Tibeto-Indo-Chinese* of the eastern area, the latter extending into a secondary branch, *Oceanic Mongols*. These two, that

[1] *Ethnology*, p. 300.

is, the main and secondary branch, which jointly occupy
the greater part of south-east Asia with most of Malaysia,
Madagascar, the Philippines and Formosa, will
form the subject of the present and following   South Mongol
                                                  Domain.
chapters.   Allowing for encroachments and overlappings, especially in Manchuria and North Tibet, the
northern " divide " towards the Mongolo-Tatar domain is
roughly indicated by the Great Wall and the Kuen-lun range
westwards to the Hindu-Kush, and towards the south-west
by the Himalayas from the Hindu-Kush eastwards to Assam.
The Continental section thus comprises the whole of China
proper and Indo-China, together with a great part of Tibet
with Little Tibet (Baltistan and Ladakh), and the Himalayan
uplands including their southern slopes.   This section is
again separated from the Oceanic section by the Isthmus of
Kra—the Malay Peninsula belonging ethnically to the insular
Malay world.   " I believe," writes Warrington Smyth, " that
the Malay never really extended further south than the Kra
isthmus." [1]

From the considerations advanced in *Ethnology*, Chap.
XII., it seems a reasonable assumption that the lacustrine
Tibetan tableland with its Himalayan escarpments, all standing
in pleistocene times at a considerably lower level   Tibet, the
than at present, was the cradle of the Mongol   Mongol
division of mankind.   Here were found all the   Cradle-land.
natural conditions favourable to the development of a new
variety of the species moving from the tropics northwards—
ample space such as all areas of marked specialisation seem
to require ; a different and cooler climate than that of the
equatorial region, though, thanks to its then lower elevation,
warmer than that of the bleak and now barely inhabitable
Tibetan plateau ; extensive plains, nowhere perhaps too
densely wooded, intersected by ridges of moderate height,
and diversified by a lacustrine system far more extensive than
that revealed by the exploration of modern travellers.[2]

Under these circumstances, which are not matter of mere
speculation, but to be directly inferred from the observations
of intelligent explorers and of trained Anglo-Indian surveyors,

[1] *Geogr. Journ.*, May, 1898, p. 491. This statement must of course be taken
as having reference only to the historical Malays and their comparatively late
migrations.
[2] For the desiccation of Asia see P. Kropotkin, *Geogr. Journ.* XXIII. 1904 ;
E. Huntington, *The Pulse of Asia*, 1907.

it would seem not only probable but inevitable that the pleistocene Indo-Malayan should become modified and improved in his new and more favourable Central Asiatic environment.

Later, with the gradual upheaval of the land to a mean altitude of some 14,000 feet above sea-level, the climate deteriorated, and the present somewhat rude and ragged inhabitants of Tibet are to be regarded as the outcome of slow adaptation to their slowly changing surroundings since the occupation of the country by the Indo-Malayan pleistocene precursor. To this precursor Tibet was accessible either from India or from Indo-China, and although
Stone Age in Tibet. few of his implements have yet been reported from the plateau, it is certain that Tibet has passed through the Stone as well as the Metal Ages. In Bogle's time " thunder-stones " were still used for tonsuring the lamas, and even now stone cooking-pots are found amongst the shepherds of the uplands, although they are acquainted both with copper and iron. In India also and Indo-China palaeoliths of rude type occur at various points— Arcot, the Narbada gravels, Mirzapur,[1] the Irawadi valley and the Shan territory—as if to indicate the routes followed by early man in his migrations from Indo-Malaysia northwards.

Thus, where man is silent the stones speak, and so old are these links of past and present that amongst the Shans, as in ancient Greece, their origin being entirely forgotten, they are often mounted as jewellery and worn as charms against mishaps.

Usually the Mongols proper, that is, the steppe nomads who have more than once overrun half the eastern hemisphere, are taken as the typical and original stem of the Mongolian stock. But if Ch. de Ujfalvy's views can be accepted this
The Primitive Mongol Type. honour will now have to be transferred to the Tibetans, who still occupy the supposed cradle of the race. This veteran student of the Central Asiatic peoples describes two Mongol types, a northern round-headed and a southern long-headed, and thinks that the latter, which includes the " Ladakhi, the Champas and Tibetans proper," was " the primitive Mongol type."[2]

---

[1] See J. Cockburn's paper " On Palæolithic Implements," etc., in *Journ. Anthr. Inst.* 1887, p. 57 sq.

[2] " Le type primitif des Mongols est pour nous dolichocéphale " (*Les Aryens au Nord et au Sud de l'Hundou-Kouch*, 1896, p. 50).

the game of polo, which has thence spread to the surrounding peoples as far as Chitral and Irania.

From all these considerations it is inferred that the Balti are the direct descendants of the Sacae, who invaded India about 90 B.C., not from the west (the Kabul valley) as generally stated, but from the north over the Karakorum Passes leading directly to Baltistan.[1]   Thus lives again a name renowned in antiquity, and another of those links is established between the past and the present, which it is the province of the historical ethnologist to rescue from oblivion.

In Tibet proper the ethnical relations have been confused by the loose way tribal and even national names are referred

The Tibetans Proper.

to by Prjevalsky and some other modern explorers.   It should therefore be explained that three somewhat distinct branches of the race have to be carefully distinguished : 1. The *Bod-pa*,[2] " Bodmen," the settled and more or less civilised section, who occupy most of the southern and more fertile provinces of

Bod-pa, Dru-pa, Tanguts.

which Lhasa is the capital, who till the land, live in towns, and have passed from the tribal to the civic state.   2. The *Dru-pa*,[3] peaceful though semi-nomadic pastoral tribes, who live in tents on the northern plateaux, over 15,000 feet above sea-level.   3. The *Tanguts*,[4] restless, predatory tribes, who hover about the north-eastern borderland between Koko-nor and Kansu.

---

[1] *Op. cit.* p. 327.   Here we are reminded that, though the Sacae are called " Scythians " by Herodotus and other ancient writers, under this vague expression were comprised a multitude of heterogeneous peoples, amongst whom were types corresponding to all the main varieties of Mongolian, western Asiatic, and eastern European peoples.   " Aujourd'hui l'ancien type sace, adouci parmi les mélanges, reparaît et constitue le type si caractéristique, si complexe et si différent de ses voisins que nous appelons le type balti " (p. 328).

[2] W. W. Rockhill, our best living authority, accepts none of the current explanations of the widely diffused term *bod* (*bhód, bhot*), which appears to form the second element in the word *Tibet* (*Stod-Bod*, pronounced *Teu-Beu*, " Upper Bod," *i.e.* the central and western parts in contradistinction to *Män-Bod*, " Lower Bod," the eastern provinces).   *Notes on the Ethnology of Tibet*, Washington, 1895, p. 669. This writer finds the first mention of Tibet in the form *Tobbat* (there are many variants) in the Arab Istakhri's works, about 590 A.H., while T. de Lacouperie would connect it with the Tatar kingdom of *Tu-bat* (397–475 A.D.).   This name might easily have been extended by the Chinese from the Tatars of Kansu to the neighbouring Tanguts, and thus to all Tibetans.

[3] *Hbrog-pa, Drok-pa*, pronounced *Dru-pa*.

[4] The Mongols apply the name *Tangut* to Tibet and call all Tibetans *Tangutu,* " which should be discarded as useless and misleading, as the people inhabiting this section of the country are pure Tibetans " (Rockhill, p. 670).   It is curious to note that the Mongol Tangutu is balanced by the Tibetan *Sok-pa,* often applied to all Mongolians.

Owing to the political seclusion of Tibet, the race ha:
hitherto been studied chiefly in outlying provinces beyond the
frontiers, such as Ladakh, Baltistan, and Sikkim,[1]
that is, in districts where mixture with other   The Balti and
races may be suspected. Indeed de Ujfalvy, Ladakhi.
who has made a careful survey of Baltistan and Ladakh,
assures us that, while the Ladakhi represent two varieties of
Asiatic man with ceph. index 77, the Balti are not Tibetans
or Mongols at all, but descendants of the historical Sacae,
although now of Tibetan speech and Moslem faith.[2] They
are of the mean height or slightly above it, with rather low
brow, very prominent superciliary arches, deep
depression at nasal root, thick curved eyebrows, Balti Type and
long, straight or arched nose, thick lips, oval Origins.
chin, small cheek-bones, small flat ears, straight eyes, very
black and abundant ringletty (*bouclé*) hair, full beard, usually
black and silky, robust hairy body, small hands and feet, and
long head (index 72). In such characters it is impossible to
recognise the Mongol, and the contrast is most striking with
the neighbouring Ladakhi, true Mongols, as shown by their
slightly raised superciliary arches, square and scarcely curved
eyebrows, slant eyes, large prominent cheek-bones, lank and
coarse hair, yellowish and nearly hairless body.

Doubtless there has been a considerable intermingling of
Balti and Ladakhi, and in recent times still more of Balti
and Dards (Hindu-Kush " Aryans "), whence Leitner's view
that the Balti are Dards at a remote period conquered by the
Bhóts (Tibetans), losing their speech with their independence.
But of all these peoples the Balti were in former times the
most civilised, as shown by the remarkable rock-carvings still
found in the country, and attributed by the present inhabitants
to a long vanished race. Some of these carvings represent
warriors mounted and on foot, the resemblance being often
very striking between them and the persons figured on the
coins of the Sacae kings both in their physical appearance,
attitudes, arms, and accoutrements. The Balti are still
famous horsemen, and with them is said to have originated

---

[1] Thus Risley's Tibetan measurements were all of subjects from Sikkim and
Nepal (*Tribes and Castes of Bengal*, Calcutta, 1896, *passim*). In the East, however, Desgodins and other French missionaries have had better opportunities
of studying true Tibetans amongst the Si-fan (" Western Strangers "), as the
frontier populations are called by the Chinese.

[2] *Op. cit.* p. 319.

All these are true Tibetans, speak the Tibetan language, and profess one or other of the two national religions, *Bonbo* and Lamaism (the Tibetan form of Buddhism). But the original type is best preserved, not amongst the cultured Bod-pa, who in many places betray a considerable admixture both of Chinese and Hindu elements, but amongst the Dru-pa, who on their bleak upland steppes have for ages had little contact with the surrounding Mongolo-Turki populations. They are described by W. W. Rockhill from personal observation as about five feet five inches high, and round-headed, with wavy hair, clear-brown and even hazel eye, cheek-bone less high than the Mongol, thick nose, depressed at the root, but also prominent and even aquiline and narrow but with broad nostrils, large-lobed ears standing out to a less degree than the Mongol, broad mouth, long black hair, thin beard, generally hairless body, broad shoulders, very small calves, large foot, coarse hand, skin coarse and greasy and of light brown colour, though " frequently nearly white, but when exposed to the weather a dark brown, nearly the colour of our American Indians. Rosy cheeks are quite common amongst the younger women." [1]

Some of these characters—wavy hair, aquiline nose, hazel eye, rosy cheeks—are not Mongolic, and despite W. W. Rockhill's certificate of racial purity, one is led to suspect a Caucasic strain, perhaps through the neighbouring Salars. These are no doubt sometimes called Kara-Tangutans, " Black Tangutans," from the colour of their tents, but we learn from Potanin, who visited them in 1885,[2] that they are Muhammadans of Turki stock and speech, and we already know [3] that from a remote period the Turki people were in close contact with Caucasians. The Salars pitch their tents on the banks of the Khitai and other Yang-tse-Kiang headstreams.

That the national name Bod-pa must be of considerable antiquity is evident from the Sanskrit expression *Bhotiya*, derived from it, and long applied by the Hindus collectively to all southern Tibetans,   **The Bhotiyas.**

---

[1] *Notes on the Ethnology of Tibet*, 1895, p. 675; see also S. Chandra Das, *Journey to Lhasa and Central Tibet*, 1904; F. Grenard, *Tibet: the Country and its Inhabitants*, 1904; G. Sandberg, *Tibet and the Tibetans*, 1906; and L. A. Waddell, *Lhasa and its Mysteries, with a record of the Expedition of 1903–1904*, 1905.

[2] *Isvestia*, XXI. 3.

[3] *Ethnology*, p. 305.

but especially to those of the Himalayan slopes, such as the Rongs (Lepchas) of Sikkim and the *Lho-pa* dominant in Bhutan, properly *Bhót-ánt*, that is, "Land's End"—the extremity of Tibet. Eastwards also the Tibetan race stretches far beyond the political frontiers into the Koko-nor region (Tanguts), and the Chinese province of Se-chuan, where they are grouped with all the other Si-fan aborigines. Towards the south-east are the kindred *Tawangs, Mishmi, Miri, Abor*,[1] *Daflas*, and many others about the Assam borderlands, all of whom may be regarded as true Bhotiyas in the wild state.

Through these the primitive Tibetan race extends into Burma, where however it has become greatly modified and again civilised under different climatic and cultural influences. Thus we see how, in the course of ages, the Bod-pa have widened their domain, radiating in all directions from the central cradle-land about the Upper Brahmaputra (San-po) valley westwards into Kashmir, eastwards into China, southwards down the Himalayan slopes to the Gangetic plains, south-eastwards to Indo-China. In some places they have come into contact with other races and disappeared either by total extinction or by absorption (India, Hindu-Kush), or else preserved their type while accepting the speech, religion, and culture of later intruders. Such are the *Garhwali*, and many groups in Nepal, especially the dominant *Gurkhas* (*Khas*[2]), of whom there are twelve branches, all Aryanised and since the twelfth century speaking the *Parbattia Bhasha*, a Prakrit or vulgar Sanskrit tongue current amongst an extremely mixed population of about 2,000,000.

Prehistoric Expansion of the Tibetan Race.

In other directions the migrations took place in remote prehistoric times, the primitive proto-Tibetan groups becoming

---

[1] *Abor, i.e.* " independent," is the name applied by the Assamese to the East Himalayan hill tribes, the *Minyong, Padam* and *Hrasso*, who are the *Slo* of the Tibetans. These are all affiliated by Desgodins to the Lho-pa of Bhuntan (*Bul. Soc. Géogr.*, October, 1877, p. 431), and are to be distinguished from the *Bori* (*i.e.* " dependent ") tribes of the plains, all more or less Hinduized Bhotiyas (Dalton, *Ethnology of Bengal*, p. 22 sq.). See A. Hamilton, *In Abor Jungles*, 1912.

[2] Not to be confused with the *Khas*, as the wild tribes of the Lao country (Siam) are collectively called. Capt. Eden Vansittart thinks in Nepal the term is an abbreviation of Kshatriya, or else means " fallen." This authority tells us that, although the Khas are true Gurkhas, it is not the Khas who enlist in our Gurkha regiments, but chiefly the Magars and Gurungs, who are of purer Bhotiya race and less completely Hinduized (" The Tribes, Clans, and Castes of Nepal," in *Journ. As. Soc. Bengal*, LXIII. 1, No. 4).

more and more specialised as they receded farther and farther from the cradle-land into Mongolia, Siberia, China, Farther India, and Malaysia. This is at least how I understand the peopling of a great part of the eastern hemisphere by an original nucleus of Mongolic type first differentiated from a pleistocene precursor on the Tibetan tableland.

Strangely contradictory estimates have been formed of the temperament and mental characters of the Bod-pa, some, such as that of Turner,[1] no doubt too favourable, Temperament. while others err perhaps in the opposite direction. Thus Desgodins, who nevertheless knew them well, describes the cultured Tibetan of the south as "a slave towards the great, a despot towards the weak, knavish or treacherous according to circumstances, always on the look-out to defraud, and lying impudently to attain his end," and much more to the same effect.[2]

W. W. Rockhill, who is less severe, thinks that "the Tibetan's character is not as black as Horace della Penna and Desgodins have painted it. Intercourse with these people extending over six years leads me to believe that the Tibetan is kindhearted, affectionate, and law-abiding."[3] He concludes, however, with a not very flattering native estimate deduced from the curious national legend that "the earliest inhabitants of Tibet descended from a king of monkeys and a female hobgoblin, and the character of the race perhaps from those of its first parents. From the king of monkeys [he was an incarnate god] they have religious faith and kindheartedness, intelligence and application, devotion to religion and to religious debate ; from the hobgoblin they get cruelty, fondness for trade and money-making, great bodily strength, lustfulness, fondness for gossip, and carnivorous instinct."[4]

While they are cheerful under a depressing priestly regime, all allow that they are vindictive, superstitious, and cringing in the presence of the lamas, who are at heart more Effects of dreaded than revered. In fact the whole Lamaism on the religious world is one vast organised system Tibetan of hypocrisy, and above the old pagan beliefs Character.

[1] *Embassy to the Court of the Teshoo Lama*, p. 350 sq.
[2] " Voilà, je crois, le vrai Tibetain des pays cultivés du sud, qui se regarde comme bien plus civilisé que les pasteurs ou bergers du nord " (*Le Thibet*, p. 253).
[3] *Notes on the Ethnology*, etc., p. 677. It may here be remarked that the unfriendliness of which travellers often complain appears mainly inspired by the Buddhist theocracy, who rule the land and are jealous of all " interlopers."
[4] *Ibid.* p. 678.

common to all primitive peoples there is merely a veneer of Buddhism, above which follows another and most pernicious veneer of lamaism (priestcraft), under the yoke of which the natural development of the people has been almost completely arrested for several centuries. The burden is borne with surprising endurance, and would be intolerable but for the relief found in secret and occasionally even open revolt against the more oppressive ordinances of the ecclesiastical rule. Thus, despite the prescriptions regarding a strict vegetarian diet expressed in the formula "eat animal flesh eat thy brother," not only laymen but most of the lamas themselves supplement their frugal diet of milk, butter, barley-meal, and fruits with game, yak, and mutton—this last pronounced by Turner the best in the world. The public conscience, however, is saved by a few extra turns of the prayer-wheel at such repasts, and by the general contempt in which is held the hereditary caste of butchers, who like the Jews in medieval times are still confined to a "ghetto" of their own in all the large towns.

These remarks apply more particularly to the settled southern communities living in districts where a little agri-

The Horsoks. culture is possible. Elsewhere the religious cloak is worn very loosely, and the nomad *Horsoks* of the northern steppes, although all nominal Buddhists, pay but scant respect to the decrees supposed to emanate from the Dalai Lama enshrined in Lhasa. Horsok is an almost unique ethnical term,[1] being a curious compound of the two names applied by the Tibetans to the *Hor-pa* and the *Sok-pa* who divide the steppe between them. The Hor-pa, who occupy the western parts, are of Turki stock, and are the only group of that race known to me who profess Buddhism,[2] all the rest being Muhammadans with some Shamanists (Yakuts) in the Lena basin. The Sok-pa, who roam the eastern plains and valleys, although commonly called Mongols, are true Tibetans or more strictly speaking Tanguts, of whom there are here two branches, the *Goliki* and the *Yegrai*, all, like the Hor-pa, of Tibetan speech. The Yegrai, as described by Prjevalsky,

The Tanguts. closely resemble the other North Tibetan tribes, with their long, matted locks falling on their

---

[1] With it may be compared the Chinese province of *Kan-su*, so named from its two chief towns *Kan*-chau and *Su*-chau (Yule's *Marco Polo*, I. p. 222).

[2] "Buddhist Turks," says Sir H. H. Howorth (*Geogr. Journ.* 1887, p. 230).

shoulders, their scanty whiskers and beard, angular head, dark complexion and dirty garb.[1]

Besides stock-breeding and predatory warfare, all these groups follow the hunt, armed with darts, bows, and match-lock guns ; the musk-deer is ensnared, and the only animal spared is the stag, " Buddha's horse." The taste of these rude nomads for liquid blood is insatiable, and the surveyor, Nain Singh, often saw them fall prone on the ground to lick up the blood flowing from a wounded beast. As soon as weaned, the very children and even the horses are fed on a diet of cheese, butter, and blood, kneaded together in a horrible mess, which is greedily devoured when the taste is acquired. On the other hand alcoholic drinks are little consumed, the national beverage being coarse Chinese tea imported in the form of bricks and prepared with *tsampa* (barley-meal) and butter, and thus becoming a food as well as a drink. The lamas have a monopoly of this tea-trade, which could not stand the competition of the Indian growers ; hence arises the chief objection to removing the barriers of seclusion.

Tibet is one of the few regions where polyandrous customs, intimately associated with the matriarchal state, still persist almost in their pristine vigour. The husbands are usually but not necessarily all brothers, and the bride is always obtained by purchase. Tibetan Polyandry. Unless otherwise arranged, the oldest husband is the putative "father," all the others being considered as "uncles." An inevitable result of the institution is to give woman a domi-nant position in society ; hence the "queens" of certain tribes referred to with so much astonishment by the early Chinese chroniclers. Survivors of this "petticoat government" have been noticed by travellers amongst the Lolos, Mossos, and other indigenous communities about the Indo-Chinese frontiers. But it does not follow that polyandry and a matriarchal state always and necessarily preceded polygyny and a patriarchal state. On the contrary, it would appear that polyandry never could have been universal ; possibly it arose from special conditions in particular regions, where the struggle for exist-ence is severe, and the necessity of imposing limits to the increase of population more urgent than elsewhere.[2] Hence

[1] E. Delmar Morgan, *Geogr. Journ.* 1887, p. 226.
[2] " Whatever may have been the origin of polyandry, there can be no doubt that poverty, a desire to keep down population, and to keep property undivided in families, supply sufficient reason to justify its continuance. The same motives

to me it seems as great a mistake to assume a matriarchate as it is to assume promiscuity as the universal antecedent of all later family relations. In Tibet itself polygyny exists side by side with polyandry amongst the wealthy classes, while monogamy is the rule amongst the poor pastoral nomads of the northern steppe.

Great ethnical importance has been attached by some distinguished anthropologists to the treatment of the dead.

Burial Customs. But, as in the New Stone and Metal Ages in Europe cremation and burial were practised side by side,[1] so in Tibet the dead are now simultaneously disposed of in diverse ways. It is a question not so much of race as of caste or social classes, or of the lama's pleasure, who, when the head has been shaved to facilitate the transmigration of the soul, may order the body to be burnt, buried, cast into the river, or even thrown to carrion birds or beasts of prey. Strange to say, the last method, carried out with certain formalities, is one of the most honourable, although the lamas are generally buried in a seated posture, and high officials burnt, and (in Ladakh) the ashes, mixed with a little clay, kneaded into much venerated effigies— doubtless a survival of ancestry worship.

Reference was above made to the primitive Shamanistic ideas which still survive beneath the Buddhist and the later lamaistic systems. In the central and eastern provinces of

The Bonbo Religion. Ui and Tsang this pre-Buddhist religion has again struggled to the surface, or rather persisted under the name of *Bonbo* (*Boa-ho*) side by side with the national creed, from which it has even borrowed many of its present rites. From the colour of the robes usually worn by its priests, it is known as the sect of the " Blacks," in contradistinction to the orthodox " Yellow " and dissenting " Red " lamaists, and as now constituted, its origin is attributed to Shen-rab (Gsen-rabs), who flourished about the fifth century before the new era, and is venerated as the equal of Buddha himself. His followers, who were powerful enough to drive Buddhism from Tibet in the tenth century, worship 18 chief deities, the best known being the red and

---

explain its existence among the lower castes of Malabar, among the Jat (Sikhs) of the Panjab, among the Todas, and probably in most other countries in which this custom prevails " (Rockhill, p. 726).

[1] T. Rice Holmes, *Ancient Britain*, 1907, pp. 110 and 465–6.

black demons, the snake devil, and especially the fiery tiger-god, father of all the secondary members of this truly "diabolical pantheon." It is curious to note that the sacred symbol of the Bonbo sect is the ubiquitous svastika, only with the hooks of the cross reversed, 卍 instead of 卐. This change, which appears to have escaped the diligent research of Thomas Wilson,[1] was caused by the practice of turning the prayer-wheel from right to left as the red lamas do, instead of from left to right as is the orthodox way. The common Buddhist formula of six syllables—*om-ma-ni-pad-me-hum*—is also replaced by one of seven syllables—*ma-tri-mon-tre-sa-ta-dzun*.[2]

Buddhism itself, introduced by Hindu missionaries, is more recent than is commonly supposed. Few conversions were made before the fifth century of our era, and the first temple dates only from the year 698. Reference is often made to the points of contact or "coincidences" which have been observed between this system and that of the Oriental and Latin Christian Churches. There is no question of a common dogma, and the numerous resemblances are concerned only with ritualistic details, such as the cross, the mitre, dalmatica, and other distinctive vestments, choir singing, exorcisms, the thurible, benedictions with outstretched hand, celibacy, the rosary, fasts, processions, litanies, spiritual retreats, holy water, scapulars or other charms, prayer addressed to the saints, relics, pilgrimages, music and bells at the service, monasticism ; this last being developed to a far greater extent in Tibet than at any time in any Christian land, Egypt not excepted. The lamas, representing the regular clergy of the Roman Church, hold a monopoly of all "science," letters, and arts. The block printing-presses are all kept in the huge monasteries which cover the land, and from them are consequently issued only orthodox works and treatises on magic. Religion itself is little better than a system of magic, and the sole aim of all worship, reduced to a mere mechanical system of routine, is to baffle the machinations of the demons who at every turn beset the path of the wayfarer through this "vale of tears."

Buddhism and Lamaism.

Buddhist and Christian Ritualism.

---

[1] At least no reference is made to the Bonbo practice in his almost exhaustive monograph on *The Swastika*, Washington, 1896. The reversed form, however, mentioned by Max Müller and Burnouf, is figured at p. 767 and elsewhere.

[2] Sarat Chandra Das, *Journ. As. Soc. Bengal*, 1881–2.

For this purpose the prayer-wheels—an ingenious con-
trivance by which innumerable supplications, not
The Prayer-
Wheel.   less efficacious because vicarious, may be offered
up night and day to the powers of darkness—
are incessantly kept going all over the land, some being so
cleverly arranged that the sacred formula may be repeated as
many as 40,000 times at each revolution of the cylinder.
These machines, which have also been introduced into Korea
and Japan, have been at work for several centuries without
any appreciable results, although fitted up in all the houses,
by the river banks or on the hill-side, and kept in motion by
the hand, wind, and water ; while others of huge size, 30 to
40 feet high and 15 to 20 in diameter, stand in the temples,
and at each turn repeat the contents of whole volumes of
liturgical essays stowed away in their capacious receptacles.
But despite all these everlasting revolutions, stagnation reigns
supreme throughout the most priest-ridden land under the sun.
   With its religion Tibet imported also its letters from India
by the route of Nepal or Kashmir in the seventh
Language and
Letters.   century. Since then the language has undergone great changes, always, like other members
of the Indo-Chinese family, in the direction from agglutination towards monosyllabism.[1]   But the orthography, apart
from a few feeble efforts at reform, has remained stationary,
so that words are still written as they were pronounced
1200 years ago. The result is a far greater discrepancy
between the spoken and written tongue than in any other
language, English not excepted. Thus the province of Ui
has been identified by Sir A. Cunningham with Ptolemy's
Debasae through its written form *Dbus*, though now always
pronounced *U*.[2]   This bears out de Lacouperie's view that all
words are really uttered as originally spelt, although often
beginning with as many as three consonants. Thus *spra*
(monkey) is now pronounced *deu* in the Lhasa dialect, but
still *streu-go* in that of the province of Kham. The phonetic
disintegration is still going on, so that, barring reform, the
time must come when there will be no correspondence at all
between sound and its graphic expression.

   [1] This point, so important in the history of linguistic evolution, has I think
been fairly established by T. de Lacouperie in a series of papers in the *Oriental
and Babylonian Record*, 1888-90. See G. A. Grierson's *Linguistic Survey of
India*, III. Tibeto-Burman Family, 1906, by Sten Konow.
   [2] *Ladák*, London, 1854.

On the other hand it is a mistake to suppose that all languages in the Indo-Chinese linguistic zone have undergone this enormous extent of phonetic decay. The indefatigable B. H. Hodgson has made us acquainted with several, especially in Nepal, which are of a highly conservative character. Farther east the *Lepcha* (properly *Rong*) of Sikkim presents the remarkable peculiarity of distinct agglutination of the Mongolo-Turki, or perhaps I should say of the Kuki-Lushai type, combined with numerous homophones and a total absence of tone. Thus *pano-sa*, of a king, *pano-sang*, kings, and *pano-sang-sa*, of kings, shows pure agglutination, while *mát* yields no less than twenty-three distinct meanings,[1] which should necessitate a series of discriminating tones, as in Chinese or Siamese. Their absence, however, is readily explained by the persistence of the agglutinative principle, which renders them unnecessary.

Diverse Linguistic Types.

Lepcha.

A somewhat similar feature is presented by the Angami Naga, the chief language of the Naga Hills, of which R. B. McCabe writes that it is " still in a very primitive stage of the agglutinating class," and " peculiarly rich in intonation," although " for one Naga who clearly marks these tonal distinctions twenty fail to do so." [2] It follows that it is mainly spoken without tones, and although said to be " distinctly monosyllabic " it really abounds in polysyllables, such as *merenama*, orphan, *kehutsaporimo*, nowhere, *dukriwáché*, to kill, etc. There are also numerous verbal formative elements given by McCabe himself, so that Angami must clearly be included in the agglutinating order. To this order also belongs beyond all doubt the *Kuki-Lushai* of the neighbouring North Kachar Hills and parts of Nagaland itself, the common speech in fact of the *Rangkhols*,

Angami-Naga Speech.

Kuki-Lushai Language.

[1] G. B. Mainwaring, *A Grammar of the Rong (Lepcha) Language*, etc., Calcutta, 1876, pp. 128–9.

[2] *Outline Grammar of the Angámi-Naga Language*, Calcutta, 1887, pp. 4, 5. For an indication of the astonishing number of distinct languages in the whole of this region see Gertrude M. Godden's paper " On the Naga and other Frontier Tribes of North-East India," in *Journ. Anthr. Inst.* 1897, p. 165. Under the heading Tibeto-Burman Languages Sten Konow recognises *Tibetan, Himalayan, North Assam, Bodo, Naga, Kuki-Chin, Meitei* and *Kachin*. The Naga group comprises dialects of very different kinds ; some approach Tibetan and the North Assam group, others lead over to the Bodo, others connect with Tibeto-Burman. Meitei lies midway between Kuki-Chin and Kachin, and these merge finally in Burmese. Grierson's *Linguistic Survey of India*, Vol. III. 1903–6.

Jansens, Lushai, Roeys and other hill peoples, collectively called *Kuki* by the lowlanders, and *Dzo* by themselves.[1] The highly agglutinating character of this language is evident from the numerous conjugations given by Soppitt,[2] for some of which he has no names, but which may be called *Accelera-tives, Retardatives, Complementatives,* and so on. Thus with the root, *ahong,* come, and infix *jám,* slow, is formed the retardative *náng ahongjámrangmoh,* " will-you-come-slowly ? " (*rang,* future, *moh,* interrogative particle).[3]

The Kuki, the Naga and the Manipuri, none of which claim to be the original occupants of the country, have a tradition of a common ancestor, who had three sons who became the progenitors of the tribes. The Kuki are found almost everywhere throughout Manipur. " We are like the birds of the air," said a Kuki to T. C. Hodson, " we make our nests here this year, and who knows where we shall build next year ? "[4] The following description is given of the Naga tribes, *Tangkhuls, Mao* and *Maram Nagas (Angami Nagas), Kolya,* or *Mayang Khong* group, *Kabuis, Quoirengs, Chirus* and *Marrings.* " Differences of stature, dress, coiffure and weapons make it easy to distinguish between the members of these tribes. In colour they are all brown with but little variety, though some of the Tangkhuls who earn their living by salt making seem to be darker. Among them all, as among the Manipuris, there are persons who have a tinge of colour in their cheeks when still young. The nose also varies, for there are cases where it is almost straight, while in the majority of individuals it is flattened at the nostril. Here and there one may see noses which in profile are almost Roman. The eyes are usually brown, though black eyes are sometimes found to occur. The jaw is generally clean, not

Naga Tribes.

---

[1] Almost hopeless confusion continues to prevail in the tribal nomenclature of these multitudinous hill peoples. The official sanction given to the terms *Kuki* and *Lushai* as collective names may be regretted, but seems now past remedy. *Kuki* is unknown to the people themselves, while *Lushai* is only the name of a single group proud of their head-hunting proclivities, hence they call themselves, or perhaps are called *Lu-Shai,* " Head-Cutters," from *lu* head, *sha* to cut (G. H. Damant). Other explanations suggested by C. A. Soppitt (*Kuki-Lushai Tribes, with an Outline Grammar of the Rangkhol-Lushai Language,* Shillong, 1887) cannot be accepted.   [2] *Op cit.*

[3] See G. A. Grierson and Sten Konow in Grierson's *Linguistic Survey of India,* Vol. III. Part II. Bodo, Nāgā and Kachin, 1903, Part III. Kuki-Chin and Burma, 1904.

[4] *The Naga Tribes of Manipur,* 1911, p. 2. Cf. J. Shakespear, " The Kuki-Lushai Clans," *Journ. Roy. Anthr. Inst.* XXXIX. 1909.

heavy, and the hair is of some variety, as there are many persons whose hair is decidedly curly, and in most there is a wave. Beards are very uncommon, and hair on the face is very rare, so much so that the few who possess a moustache are known as *khoi-hao-bas* (Meithei words, meaning moustache grower). I am informed that the ladies do not like hirsute men, and that the men therefore pull out any stray hairs. The cheekbones are often prominent and the slope of the eye is not very marked." [1] The stature is moderate varying from the slender lightly built Marrings to the tall sturdy finely proportioned Maos. The women are all much shorter than the men, but strongly built with a muscular development of which the men would not be ashamed. The land is thickly peopled with local deities and at Maram the case is recorded of a Rain Deity who was once a man of the village specially cunning in rain making. Among the points of special interest in this region are the stone monuments still erected in honour of the dead, and the custom of head-hunting, connected with simple blood feud, with agrarian rites, with funerary rites and eschatological belief, and in some cases no more than a social duty.[2]

Through these Naga and Kuki aborigines we pass without any break of continuity from the Bhotiya populations of the Himalayan slopes to those of Indo-China. Here also, as indeed in nearly all semi-civilised lands, peoples at various grades of culture are found dwelling for ages side by side—rude and savage groups on the uplands or in the more dense wooded tracts, settled communities with a large measure of political unity (in fact nations and peoples in the strict sense of those terms) on the lowlands, and especially along the rich alluvial riverine plains of this well watered region. The common theory is that the wild tribes represent the true aborigines driven to the hills and woodlands by civilised invaders from India and other lands, who are now represented by the settled communities.

The general Ethnical Relations in Indo-China.

Whether such movements and dislocations have elsewhere taken place we need not here stop to inquire ; indeed their probability, and in some instances their certainty may be frankly

---

[1] *Op. cit.* p. 5.
[2] *Op. cit.* p. 122. A custom of human sacrifice among the Naga is described in the *Journal of the Burma Research Society,* 1911, " Human Sacrifices near the Upper Chindwin."

admitted.   But I cannot think that the theory expresses the
true relations in most parts of Farther India.   Here the
Aborigines and Cultured Peoples of one Stock. civilised peoples, and *ex hypothesi* the intruders,
are the Manipuri, Burmese, Arakanese, and the
nearly extinct or absorbed Talaings or Mons in
the west ;   the Siamese, Shans or Laos, and
Khamti in the centre ;   the Annamese (Tonkinese and Cochin-
Chinese), Cambojans, and the almost extinct Champas in the
east.   Nearly all of these I hold to be quite as indigenous as
the hillmen, the only difference being that, thanks to their
more favourable environment, they emerged at an early date
from the savage state and thus became more receptive to
foreign civilising influences, mostly Hindu, but also Chinese
(in Annam).   All are either partly or mainly of Mongolic or
Indonesian type, and all speak toned Indo-Chinese languages,
except the Cambojans and Champas, whose linguistic relations
are with the Oceanic peoples, who are not here in question.
The cultivated languages are no doubt full of Sanskrit or
Prakrit terms in the west and centre, and of Chinese in the
east, and all, except Annamese, which uses a Chinese ideographic system, are written with alphabets derived through
the square Pali characters from the Devanagari.   It is also
true that the vast monuments of Burma, Siam, and Camboja
all betray Hindu influences, many of the temples being covered
with Brahmanical or Buddhist sculptures and inscriptions.
But precisely analogous phenomena are reproduced in Java,
Sumatra, and other Malaysian lands, as well as in Japan and
partly in China itself.   Are we then to conclude that there
have been Hindu invasions and settlements in all these regions,
the most populous on the globe ?

During the historic period a few Hinduized Dravidians,
especially Telingas (Telugus) of the Coromandel coast, have
The Talaings. from time to time   emigrated to Indo-China
(Pegu), where the name survives amongst the
" Talaings," that is, the Mons, by whom they
were absorbed, just as the Mons themselves are now being
absorbed by the Burmese.   Others of the same connection
have gained a footing here and there in Malaysia, especially
the Malacca coastlands, where they are called " Klings,"[1]
i.e. Telings, Telingas.

[1] It is a curious phonetic phenomenon that the combinations *kl* and *tl* are
indistinguishable in utterance, so that it is immaterial whether this term be written

But beyond these partial movements, without any kind of influence on the general ethnical relations, I know of no Hindu (some have even used the term " Aryan," and have brought Aryans to Camboja) invasions except those of a moral order— the invasions of the zealous Hindu missionaries, both Brahman and Buddhist, which, however, amply suffice to account for all the above indicated points of contact between the Indian, the Indo-Chinese, and the Malayan populations.

That the civilised lowlanders and rude highlanders are generally of the same aboriginal stocks is well seen in the Manipur district with its fertile alluvial plains and encircling Naga and Lushai Hills on the north The Manipuri. and south. The Hinduized Manipuri of the plains, that is, the politically dominant *Meithis*, as they call themselves, are considered by George Watt to be " a mixed race between the Kukies and the Nagas." [1] The Meithis are described as possessing in general the facial characteristics of Mongolian type, but with great diversity of feature. " It is not uncommon to meet with girls with brownish-black hair, brown eyes, fair complexions, straight noses and rosy cheeks." [2] In spite of the veneer of civilisation acquired by the Meithis, the old order of things has by no means passed away. " The *maiba*, the doctor and priest of the animistic system, still finds a livelihood despite the competition on the one hand of the Brahmin, and on the other of the hospital Assistant. Nevertheless the *maibas* frequently adapt their methods to the altered circumstances in which they now find themselves, and realize that the combination of croton oil and a charm is more efficacious than the charm alone." [3]

" It is possible to discover at least four definite orders of spiritual beings who have crystallized out from the amorphous mass of animistic Deities. There are the *Lam Lai*, gods of the country-side who shade off into Religion. Nature Gods controlling the rain, the primal necessity of an agricultural community; the *Umang Lai* or Deities of the Forest Jungle; the *Imung Lai*, the Household Deities, Lords of the lives, the births and the deaths of individuals, and there are Tribal Ancestors, the ritual of whose worship is a strange

Kling or *Tling*, though the latter form would be preferable, as showing its origin from *Telinga*.

[1] " The Aboriginal Tribes of Manipur," *Journ. Anthr. Inst.* 1887, p. 350.
[2] R. Brown, *Statistical Account of Manipur*, 1874.
[3] T. C. Hodson, *The Meitheis*, 1908, p. 96.

compound of magic and Nature-worship. Beyond these
Divine beings, who possess in some sort a majesty of orderly
decent behaviour, there are spirits of the mountain passes,
spirits of the lakes and rivers, vampires and all the horrid
legion of witchcraft. . . . It is difficult to estimate the precise
effect of Hinduism on the civilisation of the people, for to the
outward observer they seem to have adopted only the festivals,
the outward ritual, the caste marks and the exclusiveness
of Hinduism, while all unmindful of its spirit and inward
essentials. Colonel McCulloch remarked nearly fifty years
ago that ' In fact their observances are only for appearance
sake, not the promptings of the heart.' " [1]

It is noteworthy that the Manipuri are also devoted to the
game of polo, which R. C. Temple tells us they play much in
the same way as do the Balti and Ladakhi at the opposite
extremity of the Himalayas. Another remarkable link with

The Khel System. the " Far West " is the term *Khel*, which has
travelled all the way from Persia or Parthia
through Afghanistan to Nagaland, where it
retains the same meaning of clan or section of a village, and
produces the same disintegrating effects as amongst the
Afghans. In Angamiland each village is split into two or
more Khels, and " it is no unusual state of affairs to find
Khel A of one village at war with Khel B of another, while
not at war with Khel B of its own village. The Khels are
often completely separated by great walls, the people on either
side living within a few yards of each other, yet having no
dealings whatever. Each Khel has its own headman, but
little respect is paid to the chief : each Khel may be described
as a small republic." [2]   There appears to be no trace even of
a *jirga*, or council of elders, by which some measure of cohesion
is imparted to the Afghan Khel system.

From the Kuki-Nagas the transition is unbroken to the
large group of *Chins* of the Chindwin valley, named from them,

The Chins. and thence northwards to the rude *Kakhyens*
(*Kachins*) about the Irawadi headstreams and
southwards to the numerous *Karen* tribes, who occupy the
ethnical parting-line between Burma and Siam all the way
down to Tenasserim.

For the first detailed account of the Chins we are indebted

[1] T. C. Hodson, *The Meitheis*, 1908, pp. 96–7.
[2] G. Watt, *loc. cit.* p. 362.

to S. Carey and H. N. Tuck,[1] who accept B. Houghton's theory that these tribes, as well as the Kuki-Lushai, " originally lived in what we now know as Tibet, and are of one and the same stock ; their form of government, method of cultivation, manners and customs, beliefs and traditions, all point to one origin." The term Chin, said to be a Burmese form of the Chinese *jin*, " men," is unknown to these aborigines, who call themselves *Yo* in the north and *Lai* in the south, while in Lower Burma they are *Shu*.

In truth there is no recognised collective name, and *Shendu* (*Sindhu*) often so applied is proper only to the once formidable Chittagong and Arakan frontier tribes, *Klang-klangs* and *Hakas*, who with the *Sokté, Tashons,* Confused Tribal *Siyins*, and others are now reduced and ad- Nomenclature. ministered from Falam. Each little group has its own tribal name, and often one or two others, descriptive, abusive and so on, given them by their neighbours. Thus the *Nwengals* (*Nun*, river, *ngal*, across) are only that section of the Soktés now settled on the farther or right bank of the Manipur, while the Soktés themselves (*Sok*, to go down, *té*, men) are so called because they migrated from Chin Nwe (9 miles from Tiddim), cradle of the Chin race, down to Molbem, their earliest settlement, which is the Mobingyi of the Burmese. So with Siyin, the Burmese form of *Sheyanté* (*she*, alkali, *yan*, side, *té*, men), the group who settled by the alkali springs east of Chin Nwe, who are the *Tauté* (" stout " or " sturdy " people) of the Lushai and southern Chins. Let these few specimens suffice as a slight object-lesson in the involved tribal nomenclature which prevails, not only amongst the Chins, but everywhere in the Tibeto-Indo-Chinese domain, from the north-western Himalayas to Cape St James at the south-eastern extremity of Farther India. I have myself collected nearly a thousand such names of clans, septs, and fragmentary groups within this domain, and am well aware that the list neither is, nor ever can be, complete, the groups themselves often being unstable quantities in a constant state of fluctuation.

Most of the Chin groups have popular legends to explain either their origin or their present reduced state. Thus the Tawyans, a branch of the Tashons, claim to be Torrs, that is, the people of the Rawvan district, who were formerly

---

[1] *The Chin Hills*, etc., Vol. I., Rangoon, 1896.

very powerful, but were ruined by their insane efforts to capture the sun. Building a sort of Jacob's **Creation Legends.** ladder, they mounted higher and higher ; but growing tired, quarrelled among themselves, and one day, while half of them were clambering up the pole, the other half below cut it down just as they were about to seize the sun. So the Whenohs, another Tashon group, said to be Lushais left behind in a district now forming part of Chinland, tell a different tale. They say they came out of the rocks at Sepi, which they think was their original home. They share, however, this legend of their underground origin with the Soktés and several other Chin tribes.

Amid much diversity of speech and physique the Chins present some common mental qualities, such as " slow speech, **Mental and** serious manner, respect for birth and knowledge **Physical Quali-** of pedigrees, the duty of revenge, the taste for **ties.** a treacherous method of warfare, the curse of drink, the virtue of hospitality, the clannish feeling, the vice of avarice, the filthy state of the body, mutual distrust, impatience under control, the want of power of combination and of continued effort, arrogance in victory, speedy discouragement and panic in defeat." [1]

Physically they are a fine race, taller and stouter than the surrounding lowlanders, men 5 feet 10 or 11 inches being common enough among the independent southerners. There are some " perfectly proportioned giants with a magnificent development of muscle." Yet dwarfs are met with in some districts, and in others " the inhabitants are a wretched lot, much afflicted with goître, amongst whom may be seen cretins who crawl about on all fours with the pigs in the gutter. At Dimlo, in the Sokté tract, leprosy has a firm hold on the inhabitants."

Although often described as devil-worshippers, the Chins really worship neither god nor devil. The northerners believe **Gods, Nats, and** there is no Supreme Being, and although the **the After-Life.** southerners admit a " Kozin " or head god, to whom they sacrifice, they do not worship him, and never look to him for any grace or mercy, except that of withholding the plagues and misfortunes which he is capable of working on any in this world who offend him. Besides

[1] *Op. cit.* p. 165.

Kozin, there are *nats* or spirits of the house, family, clan, fields ; and others who dwell in particular places in the air, the streams, the jungle, and the hills. Kindly *nats* are ignored ; all others can and will do harm unless propitiated.[1]

The departed go to *Mithikwa*, " Dead Man's Village," which is divided into *Pwethikwa*, the pleasant abode, and *Sathikwa*, the wretched abode of the *unavenged*. Good or bad deeds do not affect the future of man, who must go to Pwethikwa if he dies a natural or accidental death, and to Sathikwa if killed, and there bide till avenged by blood. Thus the vendetta receives a sort of religious sanction, strengthened by the belief that the slain becomes the slave of the slayer in the next world. " Should the slayer himself be slain, then the first slain is the slave of the second slain, who in turn is the slave of the man who killed him."

Whether a man has been honest or dishonest in this world is of no consequence in the next existence ; but, if he has killed many people in this world, he has many slaves to serve him in his future existence ; if he has killed many wild animals, then he will start well-supplied with food, for all that he kills on earth are his in the future existence. In the next existence hunting and drinking will certainly be practised, but whether fighting and raiding will be indulged in is unknown.

Cholera and small-pox are spirits, and when cholera broke out among the Chins who visited Rangoon in 1895 they carried their *dahs* (knives) drawn to scare off the *nat*, and spent the day hiding under bushes, so that the spirit should not find them. Some even wanted to sacrifice a slave boy, but were talked over to substitute some pariah dogs. They firmly believe in the evil eye, and the Hakas think the Sujins and others are all wizards, whose single glance can bewitch them, and may cause lizards to enter the body and devour the entrails. A Chin once complained to Surgeon-Major Newland that a *nat* had entered his stomach at the glance of a Yahow, and he went to hospital quite prepared to die. But an emetic brought him round, and he went off happy in the belief that he had vomited the *nat*.

---

[1] R. C. Temple, Art. " Burma," Hastings, *Ency. Religion and Ethics*, 1910.

Ethnically connected with the Kuki-Naga groups are the *Kakhyens* of the Irawadi headstreams, and the *Karens*, who

The Kakhyens. form numerous village communities about the Burma-Siamese borderland. The Kakhyens, so called abusively by the Burmese, are the *Cacobees* of the early writers,[1] whose proper name is *Singpho* (*Chingpaw*), i.e. " Men,"[2] and whose curious semi-agglutinating speech, spoken in an ascending tone, each sentence ending in a long-drawn *î* in a higher key (Bigandet), shows affinities rather with the Mishmi and other North Assamese tongues than with the cultured Burmese. They form a very widespread family, stretching from the Eastern Himalayas right into Yunnan, and presenting two somewhat marked physical types: (1) the

Caucasic Elements. true Chingpaws, with short round head, low forehead, prominent cheek-bones, slant eye, broad nose, thick protruding lips, very dark brown hair and eyes, dirty buff colour, mean height (about 5 ft. 5 or 6 in.) with disproportionately short legs ; (2) a much finer race, with regular Caucasic features, long oval face, pointed chin, aquiline nose. One Kakhyen belle met with at Bhamo, " with large lustrous eyes and fair skin, might almost have passed for a European."[3]

It is important to note this Caucasic element, which we first meet here going eastwards from the Himalayas, but which is found either separate or interspersed amongst the Mongoloid populations all over the south-east Asiatic uplands from Tibet to Cochin-China, and passing thence into Oceanica.[4]

The kinship of the Kakhyens with the still more numerous Karens is now generally accepted, and it is no

The Karens. longer found necessary to bring the latter all the way from Turkestan. They form a large section, perhaps one-sixth, of the whole population of Burma,

---

[1] Dalton, *Ethnology of Bengal*, p. 9.
[2] Prince Henri d'Orléans writes " que les Singphos et les Katchins [Kakhyens] ne font qu'un, que le premier mot est *thai* et le second birman." *Du Tonkin aux Indes*, 1898, p. 311. This is how the ethnical confusion in these borderlands gets perpetuated. *Singpho* is not *Thai*, i.e. Shan or Siamese, but a native word as here explained.
[3] John Anderson, *Mandalay to Momein*, 1876, p. 131.
[4] Three skulls discovered by M. Mansuy in a cave at Pho-Binh-Gia (Indo-China) associated with Neolithic culture were markedly dolichocephalic, resembling in some respects the Cro-Magnon race of the Reindeer period. Cf. R. Verneau, *L'Anthropologie*, xx. 1909.

and overflow into the west Siamese borderlands. Their sub-divisions are endless, though all may be reduced to three main branches, *Sgaws*, *Pwos* and *Bwais*, these last including the somewhat distinct group of *Karenni*, or " Red Karens." Although D. M. Smeaton calls the language " monosyllabic," it is evidently agglutinating, of the normal sub-Himalayan type.[1]

The Karens are a short, sturdy race, with straight black and also brownish hair, black, and even hazel eyes, and light or yellowish brown complexion, so that here also a Caucasic strain may be suspected.

Type.

Despite the favourable pictures of the missionaries, whose propaganda has been singularly successful amongst these aborigines, the Karens are not an amiable or particularly friendly people, but rather shy, reticent and even surly, though trustworthy and loyal to those chiefs and guides who have once gained their confidence. In warfare they are treacherous rather than brave, and strangely cruel even to little children. Their belief in a divine Creator who has deserted them resembles that of the Kuki people, and to the *nats* of the Kuki correspond the *la* of the Karens, who are even more numerous, every mountain, stream, rapid, crest, peak or other conspicuous object having its proper indwelling *la*. There are also seven specially baneful spirits, who have to be appeased by family offerings. " On the whole their belief in a personal god, their tradition as to the former possession of a ' law,' and their expectation of a prophet have made them susceptible to Christianity to a degree that is almost unique. Of this splendid opportunity the American mission has taken full advantage, educating, civilising, welding together, and making a people out of the downtrodden Karen tribes, while Christianising them." [2]

Temperament.

Flourishing Christian Missions.

In the Burmese division proper are comprised several groups, presenting all grades of culture, from the sheer savagery of the Mros, Kheongs, and others of the Arakan Yoma range, and the agricultural Mugs of the Arakan plains, to the dominant historical Burmese nation of the Irawadi valley. Here also the terminology is perplexing, and it may be well to explain that

The Burmese.

[1] *The Loyal Karens of Burma*, 1887.
[2] R. C. Temple, *Academy*, Jan. 29, 1887, p. 72.

Yoma, applied by Logan collectively to all the Arakan Hill
Perplexing   tribes, has no ethnic value at all, simply meaning
Tribal Nomen-   a mountain range in Burmese.[1] *Toung-gnu*,
clature.   one of Mason's divisions of the Burmese family,
was merely a petty state founded by a younger branch of the
Royal House, and " has no more claim to rank as a separate
tribe than any other Burman town." [2] *Tavoyers* are merely
the people of the Tavoy district, Tenasserim, originally from
Arakan, and now speaking a Burmese dialect largely affected
by Siamese elements ; *Taungthas*, like Yoma, means " Highlander," and is even of wider application ; the Tipperahs,
Mrungs, Kumi, Mros, Khemis, and Khyengs are all Taungthas
of Burmese stock, and speak rude Burmese dialects.

The correlative of Taungthas is *Khyungthas*, " River
People," that is, the Arakan Lowlanders comprising the
more civilised peoples about the middle and lower course of
the rivers, who are improperly called *Mugs* (*Maghs*) by the
Bengali, and whose real name is *Rakhaingtha*, *i.e.* people of
Rakhaing (Arakan). They are undoubtedly of the same
stock as the cultured Burmese, whose traditions point to
Arakan as the cradle of the race, and in whose chronicles the
Rakhaingtha are called *M'ranmákríh*, " Great M'ranmas," or
" Elder Burmese." Both branches call themselves *M'ranma*,
M'rama (the correct form of *Barma*, *Burma*, but now usually
pronounced Myamma), probably from a root *mro*, *myo*, " man,"
though connected by Burnouf with Brahma, the Brahmanical
having preceded the Buddhist religion in this region. In any
case the M'rama may claim a respectable antiquity, being
already mentioned in the national records so early as the first
century of the new era, when the land " was said to be overrun
with fabulous monsters and other terrors, which are called to
this day by the superstitious natives, the five enemies. These
were a fierce tiger, an enormous boar, a flying dragon, a
prodigious man-eating bird, and a huge creeping pumpkin,
which threatened to entangle the whole country." [3]

The Burmese type has been not incorrectly described as
intermediate between the Chinese and the Malay, more
Type.   refined, or at least softer than either, of yellowish
brown or olive complexion, often showing very

---

[1] Forbes, *Languages of Further India*, p. 61.
[2] *Ibid.* p. 55.
[3] G. W. Bird, *Wanderings in Burma*, 1897, p. 335.

dark shades, full black and lank hair, no beard, small but straight nose, weak extremities, pliant figure, and a mean height.[1]

Most Europeans speak well of the Burmese people, whose bright genial temperament and extreme friendliness towards strangers more than outweigh a natural indolence which hurts nobody but themselves, and a little arrogance or vanity inspired by the still remembered glories of a nation that once ruled over a great part of Indo-China. Perhaps the most remarkable feature of Burmese society is the almost democratic independence and equality of all classes developed under an exceptionally severe Asiatic autocracy. "They are perfectly republican in the freedom with which all ranks mingle together and talk with one another, without any marked distinction in regard to difference of rank or wealth."[2] Scott attributes this trait, I think rightly, to the great leveller, Buddhism, the true spirit of which has perhaps been better preserved in Burma than in any other land.

Character.

Burmese Buddhism.

The priesthood has not become the privileged and oppressive class that has usurped all spiritual and temporal functions in Tibet, for in Burma everybody is or has been a priest for some period of his life. All enter the monasteries— which are the national schools—not only for general instruction, but actually as members of the sacerdotal order. They submit to the tonsure, take "minor orders," so to say, and wear the yellow robe, if only for a few months or weeks or days. But for the time being they must renounce "the world, the flesh and the devil," and must play the mendicant, make the round of the village at least once with the begging-bowl hung round their neck in company with the regular members of the community. They thus become initiated, and it becomes no longer possible for the confraternity to impose either on the rulers or on the ruled. "Teaching is all that the brethren of the order do for the people. They have no spiritual powers whatever. They simply become members of a holy society that they may observe the precepts of the

---

[1] The Burmese is the most mixed race in the province. "Originally Dravidians of some sort, they seem to have received blood from various sources—Hindu, Musalmān, Chinese, Shān, Talaing, European and others." W. Crooke, "The Stability of Caste and Tribal Groups in India," *Journ. Roy. Anthr. Soc.* XLIV. 1914, p. 279, quoting the *Ethnographic Survey of India*, 1906.

[2] J. G. Scott, *Burma*, etc., 1886, p. 115.

Master more perfectly, and all they do for the alms lavished on them by the pious laity is to instruct the children in reading, writing, and the rudiments of religion."[1]

R. Grant Brown denies the common report which " has appeared in almost every work in which religion in Burma is dealt with " that Burman Buddhism is superficial. "The Burman Buddhist is at least as much influenced by his religion as the average Christian. The monks are probably as strict in their religious observances as any large religious body in the world. . . . Most laymen, too, obey the prohibitions against alcohol and the taking of life, though these run counter both to strong human instincts and to animistic practice."[2]

Nor is the personal freedom here spoken of confined to the men. In no other part of the world do the women enjoy a larger measure of independent action than in Burma, with the result that they are acknow-ledged to be far more virtuous, thrifty, and intelligent than those of all the surrounding lands. Their capacity for business and petty dealings is rivalled only by their Gallic sisters ; and H. S. Hallett tells us that in every town and village " you will see damsels squatted on the floor of the verandah with diminutive, or sometimes large, stalls in front of them, covered with vegetables, fruit, betel-nut, cigars and other articles. However numerous they may be, the price of everything is known to them ; and such is their idea of probity, that pilfering is quite unknown amongst them. They are entirely trusted by their parents from their earliest years ; even when they blossom into young women, *chaperons* are never a necessity ; yet immorality is far less customary amongst them, I am led to believe, than in any country in Europe."[3]

Position of Woman.

This observer quotes Bishop Bigandet, a forty years' resident amongst the natives, to the effect that " in Burmah and Siam the doctrines of Buddhism have produced a striking, and to the lover of true civilization a most interesting result —the almost complete equality of the condition of the women with that of the men. In these countries women are seen

---

[1] *Op. cit.* p. 118.
[2] "The Taungbyôn Festival, Burma," *Journ. Roy. Anthr. Soc.* XLV. 1915, p. 355.
[3] *Amongst the Shans*, etc., 1885, p. 233.

circulating freely in the streets ; they preside at the *comptoir*, and hold an almost exclusive possession of the bazaars. Their social position is more elevated, in every respect, than in the regions where Buddhism is not the predominating creed. They may be said to be men's companions, and not their slaves."

Burma is one of those regions where tattooing has acquired the rank of a fine art. Indeed the intricate designs and general pictorial effect produced by the Burmese artists on the living body are rivalled Tattooing. only by those of Japan, New Zealand, and some other Polynesian groups. Hallett, who states that "the Burmese, the Shans, and certain Burmanized tribes are the only peoples in the south of Asia who are known to tattoo their body," tells us that the elaborate operation is performed only on the male sex, the whole person from waist to knees, and amongst some Shan tribes from neck to foot, being covered with heraldic figures of animals, with intervening traceries, so that at a little distance the effect is that of a pair of dark-blue breeches.[1] The pigments are lamp-black or vermilion, and the pattern is usually first traced with a fine hair pencil and then worked in by a series of punctures made by a long pointed brass style.[2]

East of Burma we enter the country of the *Shans*, one of the most numerous and widespread peoples of Asia, who call themselves *Tai* (*T'hai*), "Noble" or "Free," although slavery in various forms has from time The Tai-Shan Peoples. immemorial been a social institution amongst all the southern groups. Here again tribal and national terminology is somewhat bewildering ; but it will help to notice that *Shan*, said to be of Chinese origin,[3] is the collective Burmese name, and therefore corresponds to *Lao*, the collective Siamese name. These two terms are therefore rather

---

[1] Cf. the Shans of Yunnan, who are nearly all " tatoués, depuis la ceinture jusqu'au genou, de dessins bleus si serrés qu'ils paraissent former une vraie culotte," Pr. Henri d'Orléans, *Du Tonkin aux Indes*, 1898, p. 83.

[2] For recent literature on Burma and the Burmese consult besides the *Ethnographic Survey of India*, 1906, and the *Census Report* of 1911, J. G. Scott, *The Burman*, 1896, and *Burma*, 1906 ; A. Ireland, *The Province of Burma*, 1907 ; H. Fielding Hall, *The Soul of a People*, 1898, and *A People at School*, 1906.

[3] Probably *for Shan-tsĕ, Shan-yen*, " highlanders " (*Shan*, mountain), *Shan* itself being the same word as *Siam*, a form which comes to us through the Portuguese *Siāo*.

political than ethnical, Shan denoting all the Tai peoples formerly subject to Burma and now mostly British subjects, Lao all the Tai peoples formerly subject to Siam, and now (since 1896) mostly French subjects.[1] The Siamese group them all in two divisions, the *Lau-pang-dun*, " Black-paunch Lao," so called because they clothe themselves as it were in a dark skin-tight garb by the tattooing process ; and the *Lau-pang-kah*, " White-paunch Lao," who do not tattoo. The Burmese groups call themselves collectively *Ngiou*,[2] while the most general Chinese name is *Paï (Pa-y)*. Prince Henri d'Orléans, who is careful to point out that Paï is only another name for Lao,[3] constantly met Paï groups all along the route from Tonking to Assam, and the bulk of the lowland population in Assam itself belongs originally [4] to the same family, though now mostly assimilated to the Hindus in speech, religion, and general culture. Assam in fact takes

The Ahom, Khamti, and Chinese Shans. its name from the *Ahoms*, the " peerless," the title first adopted by the Mau Shan chief, Chukupha, who invaded the country from north-east Burma, and in 1228 A.D. founded the Ahom dynasty, which was overthrown in 1810 by the Burmese, who were ejected in 1827 by the English.[5]

These Ahoms came from the Khamti (Kampti) district

---

[1] For the Laos see L. de Reinach, *Le Laos*, 1902, with bibliography.

[2] Carl Bock, MS. note. This observer notes that many of the Ngiou have been largely assimilated in type to the Burmese and in one place goes so far as to assert that " the Ngiou are decidedly of the same race as the Burmese. I have had opportunities of seeing hundreds of both countries, and of closely watching their features and build. The Ngiou wear the hair in a topknot in the same way as the Burmese, but they are easily distinguished by their tattooing, which is much more elaborate " (*Temples and Elephants*, 1884, p. 297). Of course all spring from one primeval stock, but they now constitute distinct ethnical groups, and, except about the borderlands, where blends may be suspected, both the physical and mental characters differ considerably. Bock's *Ngiou* is no doubt the same name as *Ngnio*, which H. S. Hallett applies in one place to the Mossé Shans north of Zimme, and elsewhere to the Burmese Shans collectively (*A Thousand Miles on an Elephant*, 1890, pp. 158 and 358).

[3] " Les Paï ne sont autres que des Laotiens " (Prince Henri, p. 42).

[4] One Shan group, the Deodhaings, still persist, and occupy a few villages near Sibsagar (S. E. Peal, *Nature*, June 19, 1884, p. 169). Dalton also mentions the *Kamjangs*, a Khamti (Tai) tribe in the Sadiya district, Assam (*Ethnology of Bengal*, p. 6).

[5] Much unexpected light has been thrown upon the early history of these Ahoms by E. Gait, who has discovered and described in the *Journ. As. Soc. Bengal*, 1894, a large number of *puthis*, or MSS. (28 in the Sibsagar district alone), in the now almost extinct Ahom language, some of which give a continuous history of the Ahom rajas from 568 to 1795 A.D. Most of the others appear to be treatises on religious mysticism or divination, such as " a book on the calculation of future events by examining the leg of a fowl " (*ib.*).

about the sources of the Irawadi, where Prince Henri was surprised to find a civilised and lettered Buddhist people of Paï (Shan) speech still enjoying political autonomy in the dangerous proximity of *le léopard britannique*. They call themselves *Padao*, and it is curious to note that both *Padam* and *Assami* are also tribal names amongst the neighbouring Abor Hillmen. The French traveller was told that the Padao, who claimed to be *T'hais* (Tai) like the Laotians,[1] were indigenous, and he describes the type as also Laotian— straight eyes rather wide apart, nose broad at base, forehead arched, superciliary arches prominent, thick lips, pointed chin, olive colour, slightly bronzed and darker than in the Lao country ; the men ill-favoured, the young women with pleasant features, and some with very beautiful eyes.

Passing into China we are still in the midst of Shan peoples, whose range appears formerly to have extended up to the right bank of the Yang-tse-Kiang, and whose cradle has been traced by de Lacouperie to "the Kiu-lung mountains north of Sechuen and south of Shensi in China proper."[2]   This authority holds that they constitute a chief element in the Chinese race itself, which, as it spread southwards beyond the Yang-tse-Kiang, amalgamated with the Shan aborigines, and thus became profoundly modified both in type and speech, the present Chinese language comprising over thirty per cent. of Shan ingredients.   Colquhoun also, during his explorations in the southern provinces, found that "most of the aborigines, although known to the Chinese by various nicknames, were Shans ; and that their propinquity to the Chinese was slowly changing their habits, manners, and dress, and gradually incorporating them with that people."[3]

Shan Cradle- land and Origins.

This process of fusion has been in progress for ages, not only between the southern Chinese and the Shans, but also between the Shans and the Caucasic aborigines, whom we first met amongst the Kakhyens, but who are found scattered mostly in small groups over all the uplands between Tibet and the Cochin-Chinese coast range.   The result is that the Shans are generally of finer physique than either the kindred Siamese and Malays

Shan and Caucasic Contacts.

[1] *Op. cit.* p. 309.
[2] A. R. Colquhoun, *Amongst the Shans*, 1885, Introduction, p. lv.
[3] *Op. cit.* p. 328.

in the south, or the more remotely connected Chinese in the north. The colour, says Bock, " is much lighter than that of the Siamese," and " in facial expression the Laotians are better-looking than the Malays, having good high foreheads, and the men particularly having regular well-shaped noses, with nostrils not so wide as those of their neighbours." [1]   Still more emphatic is the testimony of Kreitner of the Szechenyi expedition, who tells us that the Burmese Shans have " a nobler head than the Chinese ; the dark eyes are about horizontal, the nose is straight, the whole expression approaches that of the Caucasic race." [2]

Notwithstanding their wide diffusion, interminglings with other races, varied grades of culture, and lack of political cohesion, the Tai-Shan groups acquire a certain
Tai-Shan Toned Speech. ethnical and even national unity from their generally uniform type, social usages, Buddhist religion, and common Indo-Chinese speech. Amidst a chaos of radically distinct idioms current amongst the surrounding indigenous populations, they have everywhere preserved a remarkable degree of linguistic uniformity, all speaking various more or less divergent dialects of the same mother-tongue. Excluding a large percentage of Sanskrit terms introduced into the literary language by their Hindu educators, this radical mother-tongue comprises about 1860 distinct words or rather sounds, which have been reduced by phonetic decay to so many monosyllables, each uttered with five tones, the natural tone, two higher tones, and two lower.[3]   Each term thus acquires five distinct meanings, and in fact represents five different words, which were phonetically distinct dissyllables, or even polysyllables in the primitive language.

The same process of disintegration has been at work throughout the whole of the Indo-Chinese linguistic area, where all the leading tongues—Chinese, Annamese, Tai-Shan, Burmese—belong to the same isolating form of speech, which, as explained in *Ethnology*, Chap. IX., is not a primitive condition, but a later development, the outcome of profound phonetic corruption.

---

[1] *Temples and Elephants*, p. 320.
[2] " Der Gesichtsausdruck überhaupt nähert sich der kaukasischen Race " (*Im fernen Osten*, p. 959).
[3] Low's *Siamese Grammar*, p. 14.

The remarkable uniformity of the Tai-Shan member of this order of speech may be in part due to the conservative effects of the literary standard. Probably over 2000 years ago most of the Shan groups were brought under Hindu influences by the Brahman, and later by the Buddhist missionaries, who reduced their rude speech to written form, while introducing a large number of Sanskrit terms inseparable from the new religious ideas. The writing systems, all based on the square Pali form of the Devanagari syllabic characters, were adapted to the phonetic requirements of the various dialects, with the result that the Tai-Shan linguistic family is encumbered with four different scripts. " The Western Shans use one very like the Burmese ; the Siamese have a character of their own, which is very like Pali ; the Shans called Lü have another character of their own ; and to the north of Siam the Lao Shans have another." [1]

Shan and other Indo-Chinese Writing Systems.

These Shan alphabets of Hindu origin are supposed by de Lacouperie to be connected with the writing systems which have been credited to the Mossos, Lolos, and some other hill peoples about the Chinese and Indo-Chinese borderlands. At Lan-Chu in the Lolo country Prince Henri found that MSS. were very numerous, and he was shown some very fine specimens " enluminés." Here, he tells us, the script is still in use, being employed jointly with Chinese in drawing up legal documents connected with property. He was informed that this Lolo script comprised 300 characters, read from top to bottom and from left to right,[2] although other authorities say from right to left.

Of the Lolo he gives no specimens,[3] but reproduces two

[1] R. G. Woodthorpe, " The Shans and Hill Tribes of the Mekong," in *Journ. Anthr. Inst.* 1897, p. 16.

[2] *Op. cit.* p. 55.

[3] This omission, however, is partly supplied by T. de Lacouperie, who gives us an account of a wonderful Lolo MS. on satin, red on one side, blue on the other, containing nearly 5750 words written in black, " apparently with the Chinese brush." The MS. was obtained by E. Colborne Baber from a Lolo chief, forwarded to Europe in 1881, and described by de Lacouperie, *Journ. R. As. Soc.* Vol. xiv. Part i. " The writing runs in lines from top to bottom and from left to right, as in Chinese " (p. 1), and this authority regards it as the link that was wanting to connect the various members of a widely diffused family radiating from India (Harapa seal, Indo-Pali, Vatteluttu) to Malaysia (Batta, Rejang, Lampong, Bugis, Makassar, Tagal), to Indo-China (Lao, Siamese, Lolo), Korea and Japan, and also including the Siao-chuen Chinese system " in use a few centuries B.C." (p. 5). It would be premature to say that all these connections are established.

or three pages of a Mosso book with transliteration and translation. Other specimens, but without explanation, were already known through Gill and Desgodins, and their decipherment had exercised the ingenuity of several Chinese scholars. Their failure to interpret them is now accounted for by Prince Henri, who declares that, " strictly speaking the Mossos have no writing system. The magicians keep and still make copy-books full of hieroglyphics ; each page is divided into little sections (*cahiers*) following horizontally from left to right, in which are inscribed one or more somewhat rough figures, heads of animals, men, houses, conventional signs representing the sky or lightning, and so on." Some of the magicians expounded two of the books, which contained invocations, beginning with the creation of the world, and winding up with a catalogue of all the evils threatening mortals, but to be averted by being pious, that is, by making gifts to the magicians. The same ideas are always expressed by the same signs ; yet the magicians declared that there was no alphabet, the hieroglyphs being handed down bodily from one expert to another. Nevertheless Prince Henri looks on this as one of the first steps in the history of writing ; " originally many of the Chinese characters were simply pictorial, and if the Mossos, instead of being hemmed in, had acquired a large expansion, their sacred books might also perhaps have given birth to true characters." [1]

Although now " hemmed in," the Mossos are a historical and somewhat cultured people, belonging to the same group **Mosso Origins.** as the *Iungs* (*Njungs*), who came from the regions north-east of Tibet, and appeared on the Chinese frontiers about 600 B.C. They are referred to in the Chinese records of 796 A.D., when they were reduced by the king of Nanchao. After various vicissitudes they recognised the Chinese suzerainty in the fourteenth century, and were finally subdued in the eighteenth. De Lacouperie [2] thinks they are probably of the same origin as the Lolos, the two languages having much in common, and the names of both being Chinese, while the Lolos and the Mossos call themselves respectively *Nossu* (*Nesu*) and *Nashi* (*Nashri*).

---

[1] *Op. cit.* p. 193.
[2] *Beginnings of Writing in Central and Eastern Asia, passim.* For the Lolos see A. F. Legendre, " Les Lolos. Étude ethnologique et anthropologique," *T'oung Pao II.* Vol. x. 1909.

Everywhere amongst these border tribes are met groups of aborigines, who present more or less regular features which are described by various travellers as "Caucasic" or "European." Thus the *Kiu-tse*, who are the *Khanungs* of the English maps, and are akin to the large *Lu-tse* family (*Melam, Anu, Diasu*, etc.), reminded Prince Henri of some Europeans of his acquaintance,[1] and he speaks of the light colour, straight nose and eyes, and generally fine type of the Yayo (Yao), as the Chinese call them, but whose real name is *Lin-tin-yu*.

Aborigines of South China and Annam.

The same Caucasic element reappears in a pronounced form amongst the indigenous populations of Tonking, to whom A. Billet has devoted an instructive monograph.[2] This observer, who declares that these aborigines are quite distinct both from the Chinese and the Annamese, groups them in three main divisions—*Tho, Nong*, and *Man*[3]—all collectively called *Moi, Muong*, and *Myong* by the Annamese. The Thos, who are the most numerous, are agriculturists, holding all the upland valleys and thinning off towards the wooded heights. They are tall compared to the Mongols (5 ft. 6 or 7 in.), lighter than the Annamese, round-headed, with oval face, deep-set straight eyes, low cheek-bones, straight and even slightly aquiline nose not depressed at root, and muscular frames. They are a patient, industrious, and frugal people, now mainly subject to Chinese and Annamese influences in their social usages and religion. Very peculiar nevertheless are some of their surviving customs, such as the feast of youth, the pastime of swinging, and especially chess played with living pieces, whose movements are directed by two players. The language appears to be a Shan dialect, and to this family the writer affiliates both the Thos and the

---

[1] "Quelques-uns de ces Kiou-tsés me rappellent des Européens que je connais." (*Op. cit.* p. 252.)

[2] *Deux Ans dans le Haut-Tonkin*, etc., Paris, 1896.

[3] With regard to *Man* (*Man-tse*) it should be explained that in Chinese it means "untameable worms," that is, *wild* or *barbarous*, and we are warned by Desgodins that "il ne faut pas prendre ces mots comme des noms propres de tribus" (*Bul. Soc. Géogr.* XII. p. 410). In 1877 Capt. W. Gill visited a large nation of *Man-tse* with 18 tribal divisions, reaching from West Yunnan to the extreme north of Sechuen, a sort of federacy recognising a king, with Chinese habits and dress, but speaking a language resembling Sanskrit (?). These were the *Sumu*, or "White Man-tse," apparently the same as those visited in 1896 by Mrs Bishop, and by her described as semi-independent, ruled by their own chiefs, and in appearance "quite Caucasian, both men and women being very handsome," strict Buddhists, friendly and hospitable, and living in large stone houses (Letter to *Times*, Aug, 18, 1896).

Nongs. The latter are a much more mixed people, now largely assimilated to the Chinese, although the primitive type still persists, especially amongst the women, as is so often the case. A. Billet tells us that he often met Nong women " with light and sometimes even red hair." [1]

It is extremely interesting to learn that the Mans came traditionally " from a far-off western land where their fore-

Man-tse Origins and Affinities. fathers were said to have lived in contact with peoples of white blood thousands of years ago." This tradition, which would identify them with the above-mentioned Man-tse, is supported by their physical appearance—long head, oval face, small cheek-bones, eyes without the Mongol fold, skin not yellowish but rather " browned by the sun," regular features—in nothing recalling the traits of the yellow races.

Let us now turn to M. R. Verneau's comments on the

Caucasic Aborigines in South-East Asia. rich materials brought together by A. Billet, in whom, " being not only a medical man, but also a graduate in the natural sciences, absolute confidence may be placed." [2]

" The Máns-Tien, the Máns-Coc, the Máns-Meo (Miao, Miao-tse, or Mieu) present a pretty complete identity with the Pan-y and the Pan-yao of South Kwang-si ; they are the debris of a very ancient race, which with T. de Lacouperie may be called pre-Chinese. This early race, which bore the name of *Pan-hu* or *Ngao*, occupied Central China before the arrival of the Chinese. According to M. d'Hervey de Saint-Denys, the mountains and valleys of Kwei-cháu where these Miao-tse still survive were the cradle of the Pan-hu. In any case it seems certain that the T'hai and the Man race came from Central Asia, and that, from the anthropological stand-point, they differ altogether from the Mongol group repre-sented by the Chinese and the Annamese. The Man especially presents striking affinities with the Aryan type."

Thus is again confirmed by the latest investigations, and by the conclusions of some of the leading members of the French school of anthropology, the view first advanced by me in 1879, that peoples of the Caucasic (here called " Aryan ") division had already spread to the utmost confines

---

[1] " Des paysannes nóngs dont les cheveux étaient blonds, quelquefois même roux." *Op. cit.*

[2] *L'Anthropologie*, 1896, p. 602 sq.

of south-east Asia in remote prehistoric times, and had in this region even preceded the first waves of Mongolic migration radiating from their cradle-land on the Tibetan plateau.[1]

Reference was above made to the singular lack of political cohesion at all times betrayed by the Tai-Shan peoples. The only noteworthy exception is the Siamese branch, which forms the bulk of the population in the Menam basin. In this highly favoured region of vast hill-encircled alluvial plains of inexhaustible fertility, traversed by numerous streams navigable for light craft, and giving direct access to the inland waters of Malaysia, the Southern Shans were able at an early date to merge the primitive tribal groups in a great nationality, and found a powerful empire, which at one time dominated most of Indo-China and the Malay Peninsula.

The Siamese Shans.

Siam, alone of all the Shan states, even still maintains a precarious independence, although now again reduced by European aggression to little more than the natural limits of the fluvial valley, which is usually regarded by the Southern Shans as the home of their race. Yet they appear to have been here preceded by the Caucasic Khmers (Cambojans), whose advent is referred in the national chronicles to the year 543 B.C. and who, according to the Hindu records, were expelled about 443 A.D. It was through these Khmers, and not directly from India, that the "Sayamas" received their Hindu culture, and the Siamese annals, mingling fact with fiction, refer to the miraculous birth of the national hero, Phra-Ruang, who threw off the foreign yoke, declared the people henceforth T'hai, "Freemen," invented the present Siamese alphabet, and ordered the Khom (Cambojan) to be reserved in future for copying the sacred writings.

The introduction of Buddhism is assigned to the year 638 A.D., one of the first authentic dates in the native records. The ancient city of Labong had already been founded (575), and other settlements now followed rapidly, always in the direction of the south, according as the Shan race steadily advanced towards the seaboard, driving before them or mingling with Khmers, Lawas, Karens, and other aborigines,

---

[1] "On the Relations of the Indo-Chinese and Inter-Oceanic Races and Languages." Paper read at the Meeting of the Brit. Association, Sheffield, 1879, and printed in the *Journ. Anthr. Inst.*, February, 1880.

some now extinct, some still surviving on the wooded uplands and plateaux encircling the Menam valley. Ayuthia, the great centre of national life in later times, dates only from the year 1350, when the empire had received its greatest expansion, comprising the whole of Camboja, Pegu, Tenasserim, and the Malay Peninsula, and extending its conquering arms across the inland waters as far as Java.[1]   Then followed the disastrous wars with Burma, which twice captured and finally destroyed Ayuthia (1767), now a picturesque elephant-park visited by tourists from the present capital, Bangkok, founded in 1772 a little lower down the Menam.

But the elements of decay existed from the first in the institution of slavery or serfdom, which was not restricted to **Siamese Social System.** a particular class, as in other lands, but, before the modern reforms, extended in principle to all the kings' subjects in mockery declared " Freemen " by the founders of the monarchy.   This, however, may be regarded as perhaps little more than a legal fiction, for at all times class distinctions were really recognised, comprising the members of the royal family—a somewhat numerous group—the nobles named by the king, the *leks* or vassals, and the people, these latter being again subdivided into three sections, those liable to taxation, those subject to forced labour, and the slaves proper.   But so little developed was the sentiment of personal dignity and freedom, that anybody from the highest noble to the humblest citizen might at any moment lapse into the lowest category.   Like most Mongoloid peoples, the Siamese are incurable gamblers, and formerly it was an everyday occurrence for a freeman to stake all his goods and chattels, wives, children, and self, on the hazard of the die.

Yet the women, like their Burmese sisters, have always held a somewhat honourable social position, being free to **Status of Woman.** walk abroad, go shopping, visit their friends, see the sights, and take part in the frequent public feastings without restriction.   Those, however, who brought no dower and had to be purchased,

---

[1] In the Javanese annals the invaders are called " Cambojans," but at this time (about 1340) Camboja had already been reduced, and the Siamese conquerors had brought back from its renowned capital, Angkor Wat, over 90,000 captives. These were largely employed in the wars of the period, which were thus attributed to Camboja instead of to Siam by foreign peoples ignorant of the changed relations in Indo-China.

might again be sold at any time, and many thus constantly fell from the dignity of matrons to the position of the merest drudges without rights or privileges of any kind. These strange relations were endurable, thanks to the genial nature of the national temperament, by which the hard lot of the thralls was softened, and a little light allowed to penetrate into the darkest corners [1] of the social system. The open slave-markets, which in the vassal Lao states fostered systematic raiding-expeditions amongst the unreduced aborigines, were abolished in 1873, and since 1890 all born in slavery are free on reaching their 21st year.

Siamese Buddhism is a slightly modified form of that prevailing in Ceylon, although strictly practised but by few. There are two classes or " sects," the reformers who attach more importance to the observance   Buddhism. of the canon law than to meditation, and the old believers, some devoted to a contemplative life, others to the study of the sunless wilderness of Buddhist writings. But, beneath it all, spirit or devil-worship is still rife, and in many districts pure animism is practically the only religion. Even temples and shrines have been raised to the countless gods of land and water, woods, mountains, villages and households. To these gods are credited all sorts of calamities, and to prevent them from getting into the bodies of the dead the latter are brought out, not through door or window, but through a breach in the wall, which is afterwards carefully built up. Similar ideas prevail amongst many other peoples, both at higher and lower levels of culture, for nothing is more ineradicable than such popular beliefs associated with the relations presumed to exist between the present and the after life.

Incredible sums are yearly lavished in offerings to the spirits, which give rise to an endless round of feasts and

---

[1] How very dark some of these corners can be may be seen from the sad picture of maladministration, vice, and corruption still prevalent so late as 1890, given by Hallett in *A Thousand Miles on an Elephant*, Ch. xxxv. ; and even still later by H. Warington Smyth in *Five Years in Siam, from 1891 to 1896* (1898). This observer credits the Siamese with an undeveloped sense of right and wrong, so that they are good only by accident. " To do a thing because it is right is beyond them ; to abstain from a thing because it is against their good name, or involves serious consequences, is possibly within the power of a few ; the question of right and wrong does not enter the calculation." But he thinks they may possess a high degree of intelligence, and mentions the case of a peasant, who from an atlas had taught himself geography and politics. P. A. Thompson, *Lotus Land*, 1906, gives an account of the country and people of Southern Siam.

revels, and also in support of the numerous Buddhist temples, convents, and their inmates. The treasures accumulated in the " royal cloisters " and other shrines represent a great part of the national savings—investments of the other world, among which are said to be numerous gold statues glittering with rubies, sapphires, and other priceless gems. But in these matters the taste of the *talapoins*,[1] as the priests were formerly called, is somewhat catholic, including pictures of reviews and battle-scenes from the European illustrated papers, and sometimes even statues of Napoleon set up by the side of Buddha.

So numerous, absurd, and exacting are the rules of the monastic communities that, but for the aid of the temple servants and novices, existence would be im-

Monasticism and Pessimism. possible. A list of such puerilities occupies several pages in A. R. Colquhoun's work *Amongst the Shans* (219–231), and from these we learn that the monks must not dig the ground, so that they can neither plant nor sow ; must not boil rice, as it would kill the germ ; eat corn for the same reason ; climb trees lest a branch get broken ; kindle a flame, as it destroys the fuel ; put out a flame, as that also would extinguish life ; forge iron, as sparks would fly out and perish ; swing their arms in walking ; wink in speaking ; buy or sell ; stretch the legs when sitting ; breed poultry, pigs, or other animals ; mount an elephant or palanquin ; wear red, black, green, or white garments ; mourn for the dead, etc., etc. In a word all might be summed up by a general injunction neither to do anything, nor not to do anything, and then despair of attaining *Nirvana* ; for it would be impossible to conceive of any more pessimistic system in theory.[2] Practically it is otherwise, and in point of fact the utmost religious indifference prevails amongst all classes.

Within the Mongolic division it would be difficult to imagine any more striking contrast than that presented by the gentle, kindly, and on the whole not ill-favoured Siamese, and their hard-featured, hard-hearted, and grasping Annamese

---

[1] Probably a corruption of *talapat*, the name of the palm-tree which yields the fan-leaf constantly used by the monks.

[2] " In conversation with the monks M'Gilvary was told that it would most likely be countless ages before they would attain the much wished for state of Nirvana, and that one transgression at any time might relegate them to the lowest hell to begin again their melancholy pilgrimage " (Hallett, *A Thousand Miles on an Elephant*, p. 337).

neighbours. Let anyone, who may fancy there is little or nothing in blood, pass rapidly from the bright, genial—if somewhat listless and corrupt—social The Annamese. life of Bangkok to the dry, uncongenial moral atmosphere of Ha-noi or Saigon, and he will be apt to modify his views on that point. Few observers have a good word to say for the Tonkingese, the Cochin-Chinese, or any other branch of the Annamese family, and some even of the least prejudiced are so outspoken that we must needs infer there is good ground for their severe strictures on these strange, uncouth materialists. Buddhists of course they are nominally ; but of the moral sense they have little, unless it be (amongst the lettered classes) a pale reflection of the pale Chinese ethical code. The whole region in fact is a sort of attenuated China, to which it owes its arts and industries, its letters, moral systems, general culture, and even a large part of its inhabitants. *Giao-shi* (*Kiao-shi*), the name of the aborigines, said to mean " Bifurcated," or " Cross-toes," [1] in reference to the wide space between the great toe and the Origins. next, occurs in the legendary Chinese records so far back as 2285 B.C., since which period the two countries are supposed to have maintained almost uninterrupted relations, whether friendly or hostile, down to the present day. At first the Giao-shi were confined to the northern parts of Lu-kiang, the present Tonking, all the rest of the coastlands being held by the powerful Champa (Tsiampa) people, whose affinities are with the Oceanic populations. But in 218 B.C., Lu-kiang having been reduced and incorporated with China proper, a large number of Chinese emigrants settled in the country, and gradually merged with the Giao-shi in a single nationality, whose twofold descent is still reflected in the Annamese physical and mental characters.

This term Annam,[2] however, did not come into use till the seventh century, when it was officially applied to the frontier river between China and Tonking, and afterwards extended to the whole of Tonking and Cochin-China. Tonking itself, meaning the " Eastern Court," [3] was originally the name only

[1] " Le gros orteil est très développé et écarté des autres doigts du pied. A ce caractère distinctif, que l'on retrouve encore aujourd'hui chez les indigènes de race pure, on peut reconnaître facilement que les Giao-chi sont les ancêtres des Annamites " (*La Cochinchine française en* 1878, p. 231). See also a note on the subject by C. F. Tremlett in *Journ. Anthr. Inst.* 1879, p. 460.

[2] Properly *An-nan*, a modified form of *ngan-nan*, " Southern Peace."

[3] Cf. *Nan-king*, *Pe-king*, " Southern " and " Northern " Courts (Capitals).

of the city of Ha-noi when it was a royal residence, but was later extended to the whole of the northern kingdom, whose true name is *Yüeh-nan*. To this corresponded the southern Kwe-Chen-Ching, " Kingdom of Chen-Ching," which was so named in the ninth century from its capital Chen-Ching, and of which our Cochin-China appears to be a corrupt form.

But, amid all this troublesome political nomenclature, the dominant Annamese nation has faithfully preserved its homogeneous character, spreading, like the Siamese Shans, steadily southwards, and gradually absorbing the whole of the Champa domain to the southern extremity of the peninsula, as well as a large part of the ancient kingdom of Camboja about the Mekhong delta. They thus form at present the almost exclusive ethnical element throughout all the lowland and cultivated parts of Tonking, upper and lower Cochin-China and south Camboja, with a total population in 1898 of about twenty millions.

The Annamese are described in a semi-official report [1] as characterised by a high broad forehead, high cheek-bones,

Physical and Mental Characters. small crushed nose, rather thick lips, black hair, scant beard, mean height, coppery complexion, deceitful (*rusée*) expression, and rude or insolent bearing. The head is round (index 83 to 84) and the features are in general flat and coarse, while to an ungainly exterior corresponds a harsh unsympathetic temperament. The Abbé Gagelin, who lived years in their midst, frankly declares that they are at once arrogant and dishonest, and dead to all the finer feelings of human nature, so that after years of absence the nearest akin will meet without any outward sign of pleasure or affection. Others go further, and J. G. Scott summed it all up by declaring that " the fewer Annamese there are, the less taint there is on the human race." No doubt Lord Curzon gives a more favourable picture, but this traveller spent only a short time in the country, and even he allows that they are " tricky and deceitful, disposed to thieve when they get the chance, mendacious, and incurable gamblers." [2]

Yet they have one redeeming quality, an intense love of personal freedom, strangely contrasting with the almost abject slavish spirit of the Siamese. The feeling extends to all

---

[1] *La Gazette Géographique*, March 12, 1885.
[2] *Geogr. Journ.*, Sept. 1893, p. 194.

classes, so that servitude is held in abhorrence, and, as in Burma, a democratic sense of equality permeates the social system.[1] Hence, although the State has always been an absolute monarchy, each separate commune constitutes a veritable little oligarchic commonwealth. This has come as a great surprise to the present French administrators of the country, who frankly declare that they cannot hope to improve the social or political position of the people by substituting European for native laws and usages. The Annamese have in fact little to learn from western social institutions.

Their language, spoken everywhere with remarkable uniformity, is of the normal Indo-Chinese isolating type, possessing six tones, three high, and three low, and written in ideographic characters based on the Chinese, but with numerous modifications *Language and Letters.* and additions. But, although these are ill-suited for the purpose, the attempt made by the early Portuguese missionaries to substitute the so-called *quôc-ngừ*, or Roman phonetic system, has been defeated by the conservative spirit of the people. Primary instruction has long been widely diffused, and almost everybody can read and write as many of the numerous hieroglyphs as are needed for the ordinary purpose of daily intercourse. Every village has its free school, and a higher range of studies is encouraged by the public examinations to which, as in China, all candidates for government appointments are subjected. Under such a scheme surprising results might be achieved, were the course of studies not based exclusively on the empty formulas of Chinese classical literature. The subjects taught are for the most part puerile, and true science is replaced by the dry moral precepts of Confucius. One result amongst the educated classes is a scoffing, sceptical spirit, free from all religious prejudice, and unhampered by theological creeds or dogmas, combined with a lofty moral tone, not always however in harmony with daily conduct.

Even more than in China, the family is the true base of the social system, the head of the household being not only the high-priest of the ancestral cult, but also a kind of patriarch enjoying almost absolute *Religious Systems.* control over his children. In this respect the

[1] " Parmi les citoyens règne la plus parfaite égalité. Point d'esclavage, la servitude est en horreur. Aussi tout homme peut-il aspirer aux emplois, se plaindre aux mêmes tribunaux que son adversaire " (*op. cit.* p. 6).

relations are somewhat one-sided, the father having no recognised obligations towards his offspring, while these are expected to show him perfect obedience in life and veneration after death. Besides this worship of ancestry and the Confucian ethical philosophy, a national form of Buddhism is prevalent. Some even profess all three of these so-called "religions," beneath which there still survive many of the primitive superstitions associated with a not yet extinct belief in spirits and the supernatural power of magicians. While the Buddhist temples are neglected and the few bonzes [1] despised, offerings are still made to the genii of agriculture, of the waters, the tiger, the dolphin, peace, war, diseases, and so forth, whose rude statues in the form of dragons or other fabulous monsters are even set up in the pagodas. Since the early part of the seventeenth century Roman Catholic missionaries have laboured with considerable success in this unpromising field, where the congregations were estimated in 1898 at about 900,000.

From Annam the ethical transition is easy to China [2] and its teeming multitudes, regarding whose origins, racial and cultural, two opposite views at present hold the field. What may be called the old, but by no means the obsolete school, regards the Chinese populations as the direct descendants of the aborigines who during the Stone Ages entered the Hoang-ho valley probably from the Tibetan plateau, there developed their peculiar culture independently of foreign influences, and thence spread gradually southwards to the whole of China proper, extirpating, absorbing, or driving to the encircling western and southern uplands the ruder aborigines of the Yang-tse-Kiang and Si-Kiang basins.

The Chinese.

[1] From *bonzo*, a Portuguese corruption of the Japanese *busso*, a devout person, applied first to the Buddhist priests of Japan, and then extended to those of China and neighbouring lands.

[2] This name, probably the Chinese *jin*, men, people, already occurs in Sanskrit writings in its present form: चीन, *China*, whence the Hindi چين, *Chín*, and the Arabo-Persian صين, *Sín*, which gives the classical *Sinae*. The most common national name is Chûng-kûe, "middle kingdom" (presumably the centre of the universe), whence Chûng-kûe-Jín, the Chinese people. Some have referred *China* to the *Chin* (*Tsin*) dynasty (909 B.C.), while Marco Polo's *Kataia* (Russian *Kitai*) is the *Khata* (North China) of the Mongol period, from the Manchu *K'i-tan*, founders of the Liâo dynasty, which was overthrown 1115 A.D. by the Nü-Chăn Tatars. Ptolemy's *Thinae* is rightly regarded by Edkins as the same word as *Sinae*, the substitution of *t* for *s* being normal in Annam, whence this form may have reached the west through the southern seaport of Kattigara.

In direct opposition to this view the new school, championed especially by T. de Lacouperie,[1] holds that the civilisation of China was due to relatively late intruders from south-western Asia, who arrived not as rude aborigines, but as a cultured people with a considerable knowledge of letters, science, and the arts, all of which they acquired either directly or indirectly from the civilised Akkado-Sumerian inhabitants of Babylonia.

The Babylonian Theory.

Not merely analogies and resemblances, but what are called actual identities, are pointed out between the two cultures, and even between the two languages, sufficient to establish a common origin of both, Mesopotamia being the fountain-head, whence the stream flowed by channels not clearly defined to the Hoang-ho valley. Thus the Chin. *yu*, originally *go*, is equated with Akkad *gu*, to speak ; *ye* with *ge*, night, and so on. Then the astronomic and chronologic systems are compared, Berossus and the cuneiform tablets dividing the prehistoric Akkad epoch into 10 periods of 10 kings, lasting 120 Sari, or 432,000 years, while the corresponding Chinese astronomic myth also comprises 10 kings (or dynasties) covering the same period of 432,000 years. The astronomic system credited to the emperor Yao (2000 B.C.) similarly corresponds with the Akkadian, both having the same five planets with names of like meaning, and a year of 12 months and 30 days, with the same cycle of intercalated days, while several of the now obsolete names of the Chinese months answer to those of the Babylonians. Even the name of the first Chinese emperor who built an observatory, Nai-Kwang-ti, somewhat resembles that of the Elamite king, Kuder-na-hangti, who conquered Chaldaea about 2280 B.C.

All this can hardly be explained away as a mere series of coincidences ; nevertheless neither Sinologues nor Akkadists are quite convinced, and it is obvious that many of the resemblances may be due to trade or intercourse both by the old overland caravan routes, and by the seaborne traffic from Eridu at the head of the Persian Gulf, which was a flourishing emporium 4000 or 5000 years ago.

But, despite some verbal analogies, an almost insurmountable difficulty is presented by the Akkadian and Chinese

---

[1] *Western Origin of the Early Chinese Civilization, from 2300 B.C. to 200 A.D., or Chapters on the Elements Derived from the Old Civilizations of West Asia in the Formation of the Ancient Chinese Culture*, London, 1894.

languages, which no philological ingenuity can bring into such relation as is required by the hypothesis. T. G. Pinches has shown that at a very early period, say some 5000 years ago, Akkadian already consisted, "for the greater part, of words of one syllable," and was "greatly affected by phonetic decay, the result being that an enormous number of homophones were developed out of roots originally quite distinct."[1] This Akkadian scholar sends me a number of instances, such as *tu* for *tura*, to enter ; *ti* for *tila*, to live ; *du* for *dumu*, son ; *du* for *dugu*, good, as in *Eridu*, for *Gurudugu*, "the good city," adding that "the list could be extended indefinitely."[2] But de Lacouperie's Bak tribes, that is, the first immigrants from south-west Asia, are not supposed to have reached North China till about 2500 or 3000 B.C., at which time the Chinese language was still in the untoned agglutinating state, with but few monosyllabic homophones, and consequently quite distinct from the Akkadian, as known to us from the Assyrian syllabaries, bilingual lists, and earlier tablets from Nippur or Lagash.

Hence the linguistic argument seems to fail completely, while the Babylonian origin of the Chinese writing system, or rather, the derivation of Chinese and Sumerian from some common parent in Central Asia, awaits further evidence. Many of the Chinese and Akkadian "line forms" collated by C. J. Ball[3] are so simple and, one might say, obvious, that they seem to prove nothing. They may be compared with such infantile utterances as *pa, ma, da, ta,* occurring in half the languages of the world, without proving a connection or affinity between any of them. But even were the common origin of the two scripts established, it would prove nothing as to the common origin of the two peoples, but only show cultural influences, which need not be denied.

But if Chinese origins cannot be clearly traced back to Babylonia, Chinese culture may still, in a sense, claim to be

Chinese Culture and Social System.

the oldest in the world, inasmuch as it has persisted with little change from its rise some 4500 years ago down to present times. All other early civilisations—Mesopotamian, Egyptian, Assyrian,

---

[1] "Observations upon the Languages of the Early Inhabitants of Mesopotamia," in *Journ. R. As. Soc.* XVI. Part 2.

[2] MS. note, May 7, 1896.

[3] C. J. Ball, *Chinese and Sumerian*, 1913.

Persian, Hellenic—have perished, or live only in their monuments, traditions, oral or written records. But the Chinese, despite repeated political and social convulsions, is still as deeply rooted in the past as ever, showing no break of continuity from the dim echoes of remote prehistoric ages down to the last revolution, and the establishment of the Republic. These things touch the surface only of the great ocean of Chinese humanity, which is held together, not by any general spirit of national sentiment (all sentiment is alien from the Chinese temperament), nor by any community of speech, for many of the provincial dialects differ profoundly from each other, but by a prodigious power of inertia, which has hitherto resisted all attempts at change either by pressure from without, or by spontaneous impulse from within.

What they were thousands of years ago, the Chinese still are, a frugal, peace-loving, hard-working people, occupied mainly with tillage and trade, cultivating few arts beyond weaving, porcelain and metal work, but with a widely diffused knowledge of letters, and a writing system which still remains at the cumbrous ideographic stage, **Letters and Early Records.** needing as many different symbols as there are distinct concepts to be expressed. Yet the system has one advantage, enabling those who speak mutually unintelligible idioms to converse together, using the pencil instead of the tongue. For this very reason the attempts made centuries ago by the government to substitute a phonetic script had to be abandoned. It was found that imperial edicts and other documents so written could not be understood by the populations speaking dialects different from the literary standard, whereas the hieroglyphs, like our ciphers 1, 2, 3 . . ., could be read by all educated persons of whatever allied form of speech.

Originally the Chinese system, whether developed on the spot or derived from Akkadian or any other foreign source, was of course pictographic or ideographic, and it is commonly supposed to have remained at that stage ever since, the only material changes being of a graphic nature. The pictographs were conventionalised and reduced to their present form, but still remained ideograms supplemented by a limited number of phonetic determinants. But de Lacouperie has shown that this view is a mistake, and that the evolution from the pictograph to the phonetic symbol had been practically completed in China many centuries before the new era. The

Ku-wen style current before the ninth century B.C. " was really the phonetic expression of speech." [1] But for the reason stated it had to be discontinued, and a return made to the earlier ideographic style. The change was effected about 820 B.C. by She Chöu, minister of the Emperor Süen Wang, who introduced the *Ta-chuen* style in which " he tried to speak to the eye and no longer to the ear," that is, he reverted to the earlier ideographic process, which has since prevailed. It was simplified about 227 B.C. (*Siao Chuen* style), and after some other modifications the present caligraphic form (*Kiai Shu*) was introduced by Wang Hi in 350 A.D. Thus one consequence of the " Expansion of China " was a reversion to barbarism, in respect at least of the national graphic system, by which Chinese thought and literature have been hampered for nearly 3000 years.

Written records, though at first mainly of a mythical character, date from about 3000 B.C.[2] Reference is made in the early documents to the rude and savage times, which in China as elsewhere certainly preceded the historic period. Three different prehistoric ages are even discriminated, and tradition relates how Fu-hi introduced wooden, Thin-ming stone, and Shi-yu metal implements.[3] Later, when their origin and use were forgotten, the jade axes, like those from Yunnan, were looked on as bolts hurled to the earth by the god of thunder, while the arrow-heads, supposed to be also of

---

[1] *History of the Archaic Chinese Writing and Texts*, 1882, p. 5.

[2] The first actual date given is that of Tai Hao (Fu-hi), 2953 B.C., but this ruler belongs to the fabulous period, and is stated to have reigned 115 years. The first certain date would appear to be that of Yau, first of the Chinese sages and reformer of the calendar (2357 B.C.). The date 2254 B.C. for Confucius's model king Shun seems also established. But of course all this is modern history compared with the now determined Babylonian and Egyptian records.

[3] Amongst the metals reference is made to iron so early as the time of the Emperor Ta Yü (2200 B.C.), when it is mentioned as an article of tribute in the *Shu-King*. F. Hirth, who states this fact, adds that during the same period, if not even earlier, iron was already a flourishing industry in the Liang district (Paper on the " History of Chinese Culture," Munich Anthropological Society, April, 1898). At the discussion which followed the reading of this paper Montelius argued that iron was unknown in Western Asia and Egypt before 1500 B.C., although the point was contested by Hommel, who quoted a word for iron in the earliest Egyptian texts. Montelius, however, explained that terms originally meaning " ore " or " metal" were afterwards used for " iron." Such was certainly the case with the Gk. χαλκός, at first " copper," then metal in general, and used still later for σίδηρος, " iron " ; hence χαλκεύς=coppersmith, blacksmith, and even goldsmith. So also with the Lat. *aes* (Sanskrit *ayas*, akin to *aurora*, with simple idea of brightness), used first especially for copper (*aes cyprium*, *cuprum*), and then for *bronze* (Lewis and Short). For Hirth's later views see his *Ancient History of China*, 1908 (from the fabulous ages to 221 B.C.).

divine origin, were endowed in the popular fancy with special virtues and even regarded as emblems of sovereignty. Thus may perhaps be explained the curious fact that in early times, before the twelfth century B.C., tribute in flint weapons was paid to the imperial government by some of the reduced wild tribes of the western uplands.

These men of the Stone and Metal Ages are no doubt still largely represented, not only amongst the rude hill tribes of the southern and western borderlands, but also amongst the settled and cultured lowlanders   Early of the great fluvial valleys. The " Hundred   Migrations. Families," as the first immigrants called themselves, came traditionally from the north-western regions beyond the Hoang-ho. According to the Yu-kung their original home lay in the south-western part of Eastern Turkestan, whence they first migrated east to the oases north of the Nan-Shan range, and then, in the fourth millennium before the new era, to the fertile valleys of the Hoang-ho and its Hoeï-ho tributary. Thence they spread slowly along the other great river valleys, partly expelling, partly intermingling with the aborigines, but so late as the seventh century B.C. were still mainly confined to the region between   Absorption of the Peï-ho and the lower Yang-tse-Kiang. Even   the Aborigines. here several indigenous groups, such as the Hoeï, whose name survives in that of the Hoeï river, and the Laï of the Shantong Peninsula, long held their ground, but all were ultimately absorbed or assimilated throughout the northern lands as far south as the left bank of the Yang-tse-Kiang.

Beyond this river many were also merged in the dominant people continually advancing southwards ; but others, collectively or vaguely known as Si-fans, Mans, Miao-   Survivals— tse, Paï, Tho, Y-jen,[1] Lolo, etc., were driven to   Hok-lo ; the south-western highlands which they still   Hakka; Pun-ti. occupy. Even some of the populations in the settled districts, such as the *Hok-los*,[2] and *Hakkas*,[3] of Kwang-tung, and the

---

[1] This term *Y-jen* (*Yi-jen*), meaning much the same as *Man, Man-tse*, savage, rude, untameable, has acquired a sort of diplomatic distinction. In the treaty of Tien-tsin (1858) it was stipulated that it should no longer, as heretofore, be applied in official documents to the English or to any subjects of the Queen.

[2] See J. Edkins, *China's Place in Philology*, p. 117. The Hok-los were originally from Fo-kien, whence their alternative name, *Fo-lo*. The *lo* appears to be the same word as in the reduplicated *Lo-lo*, meaning something like the Greek and Latin *Bar-bar*, stammerers, rude, uncultured.

[3] The *Hakkas, i.e.* " strangers," speak a well-marked dialect current on the

Pun-ti[1] of the Canton district, are scarcely yet thoroughly assimilated. They differ greatly in temperament, usages, appearance, and speech from the typical Chinese of the Central and Northern provinces, whom in fact they look upon as " foreigners," and with whom they hold intercourse through " Pidgin English,"[2] the *lingua franca* of the Chinese seaboard.[3]

Nevertheless a general homogeneous character is imparted to the whole people by their common political, social, and religious institutions, and by that principle of convergence in virtue of which different ethnical groups, thrown together in the same era and brought under a single administration, tend to merge in a uniform new national type. This general uniformity is conspicuous especially in the religious ideas which, except in the sceptical lettered circles, everywhere underlies the three recognised national religions, or " State Churches," as they might almost be called : *ju-kiao*, Confucianism ; *tao-kiao*, Taoism ; and *fo-kiao*, Buddhism (Fo = Buddha). The first, confined mainly to the educated upper classes, is not so much a religion as a philosophic system, a frigid ethical code based on the moral and matter-of-fact teachings of Confucius.[4] Confucius was essen-

Confucianism.

tially a social and political reformer, who taught by example and precept ; the main inducement to virtue being, not rewards or penalties in the after-life, but well- or ill-being in the present. His system is summed up in the expression " worldly wisdom," as embodied in such popular sayings as : A friend is hardly made in a year, but unmade in a moment ; When safe remember danger, in peace forget not war ; Filial father, filial son, unfilial father, unfilial son ; In washing up, plates and dishes may get broken ; Don't do what you would

uplands between Kwang-tung, Kiang-si, and Fo-kien. J. Dyer Ball, *Easy Lessons in the Hakka Dialect*, 1884.

[1] Numerous in the western parts of Kwang-tung and in the Canton district. J. Dyer Ball, *Cantonese Made Easy*, Hongkong, 1884.

[2] In this expression " Pidgin " appears to be a corruption of the word *business* taken in a very wide sense, as in such terms as *talkee-pidgin*=a conversation, discussion ; *sing-song pidgin*=a concert, etc. It is no unusual occurrence for persons from widely separated Chinese provinces meeting in England to be obliged to use this common jargon in conversation.

[3] For the aboriginal peoples, with bibliography, see M. Kennelly's translation of L. Richard's *Comprehensive Geography of the Chinese Empire and its Dependencies*, 1908, pp. 371–3.

[4] *Kung-tse*, " Teacher Kung," or more fully *Kung-fu-tse*, " the eminent teacher Kung," which gives the Latinised form *Confucius*.

not have known ; Thatch your roof before the rain, dig the well before you thirst ; The gambler's success is his ruin ; Money goes to the gambling den as the criminal to execution (never returns) ; Money hides many faults ; Stop the hand, stop the mouth (stop work and starve) ; To open a shop is easy, to keep it open hard ; Win your lawsuit and lose your money.

Although he instituted no religious system, Confucius nevertheless enjoined the observance of the already existing forms of worship, and after death became himself the object of a widespread cult, which still persists. " In every city there is a temple, built at the public expense, containing either a statue of the philosopher, or a tablet inscribed with his titles. Every spring and autumn worship is paid to him in these temples by the chief official personages of the city. In the schools also, on the first and fifteenth of each month, his title being written on red paper and affixed to a tablet, worship is performed in a special room by burning incense and candles, and by prostrations." [1]

Taoism, a sort of pantheistic mysticism, called by its founder, Lao-tse (600 B.C.), the *Tao*, or " way of salvation," was embodied in the formula " matter and the visible world are merely manifestations of a   Taoism. sublime, eternal, incomprehensible principle." It taught, in anticipation of Sakya-Muni, that by controlling his passions man may escape or cut short an endless series of transmigrations, and thus arrive by the Tao at everlasting bliss— sleep ? unconscious rest or absorption in the eternal essence ? Nirvana ? It is impossible to tell from the lofty but absolutely unintelligible language in which the master's teachings are wrapped.

But it matters little, because his disciples have long forgotten the principles they never understood, and Taoism has almost everywhere been transformed to a system of magic associated with the never-dying primeval superstitions. Originally there was no hierarchy of priests, the only specially religious class being the Ascetics, who passed their lives

---

[1] *Kwong Ki Chiu*, 1881, p. 875. Confucius was born in 550 and died in 477 B.C., and to him are at present dedicated as many as 1560 temples, in which are observed real sacrificial rites. For these sacrifices the State yearly supplies 26,606 sheep, pigs, rabbits and other animals, besides 27,000 pieces of silk, most of which things, however, become the " perquisites " of the attendants in the sanctuaries.

absorbed in the contemplation of the eternal verities.   But
out of this class, drawn together by their common interests, was
developed a kind of monasticism, with an organised brotherhood of astrologers, magicians, Shamanists, somnambulists,
" mediums," " thought-readers," charlatans and impostors of
all sorts, sheltered under a threadbare garb of religion.

    Buddhism also, although of foreign origin, has completely
conformed to the national spirit, and is now a curious blend
of Hindu metaphysics with the primitive Chinese
Buddhism. belief in spirits and a deified ancestry.   In every
district are practised diverse forms of worship between which
no clear dividing line can be drawn, and, as in Annam, the
same persons may be at once followers of Confucius, Lao-tse,
and Buddha.   In fact such was the position of the Emperor,
who belonged *ex officio* to all three of these State religions,
and scrupulously took part in their various observances.
There is even some truth in the Chinese view that " all three
make but one religion," the first appealing to man's moral
nature, the second to the instinct of self-preservation, the
third to the higher sphere of thought and contemplation.

    But behind, one might say above it all, the old animism still
prevails, manifested in a multitude of superstitious practices,
Fung-shui and whose purport is to appease the evil and secure
Ancestry the favour of the good spirits, the *Feng-shui* or
Worship. *Fung-shui,* " air and water " genii, who have to
be reckoned with in all the weightiest as well as the most
trivial occurrences of daily life.   These with the ghosts of
their ancestors, by whom the whole land is haunted, are the
bane of the Chinaman's existence.   Everything depends on
maintaining a perfect balance between the Fung-shui, that is,
the two principles represented by the " White Tiger " and
the " Azure Dragon," who guard the approaches of every
dwelling, and whose opposing influences have to be nicely
adjusted by the well-paid professors of the magic arts.   At
the death of the emperor Tung Chih (1875) a great difficulty
was raised by the State astrologers, who found that the realm
would be endangered if he were buried, according to rule, in
the imperial cemetery 100 miles west of Pekin, as his father
reposed in the other imperial cemetery situated the same
distance east of the capital.   For some subtle reason the
balance would have been disturbed between Tiger and Dragon,
and it took nine months to settle the point, during which, as

reported by the American Legation, the whole empire was stirred, councils of State agitated, and £50,000 expended to decide where the remains of a worthless and vicious young man should be interred.

Owing to the necessary disturbance of the ancestral burial places, much trouble has been anticipated in the construction of the railways, for which concessions have now been granted to European syndicates. But an Englishman long resident in the country has declared that there will be no resistance on the part of the people. " The dead can be removed with due regard to Fung Shui ; a few dollars will make that all right." This is fully in accordance with the thrifty character of the Chinese, which overrides all other considerations, as expressed in the popular saying : " With money you may move the gods ; without it you cannot move men." But the gods may even be moved without money, or at least with spurious paper money, for it is a fixed belief of their votaries that, like mortals, they may be outwitted by such devices. When rallied for burning flash notes at a popular shrine, since no spirit-bank would cash them, a Chinaman retorted : " Why me burn good note ? Joss no can savvy." In a similar spirit the god of war is hoodwinked by wooden boards hung on the ramparts of Pekin and painted to look like heavy ordnance.

In fact appearance, outward show, observance of the " eleventh commandment," in a word " face," as it is called, is everything in China. " To understand, however imperfectly, what is meant by ' face,' we must take account of the fact that as a race the Chinese have a strong dramatic instinct. Upon very slight provocation any Chinese regards himself in the light of an actor in a drama. A Chinese thinks in theatrical terms. If his troubles are adjusted he speaks of himself as having ' got off the stage ' with credit, and if they are not adjusted he finds no way to ' retire from the stage.' The question is never of facts, but always of form. Once rightly apprehended, ' face ' will be found to be in itself a key to the combination-lock of many of the most important characteristics of the Chinese." [1]

[1] Arthur H. Smith, *Chinese Characteristics*, New York, 1895. The good, or at least the useful, qualities of the Chinese are stated by this shrewd observer to be a love of industry, peace, and social order, a matchless patience and for-bearance under wrongs and evils beyond cure, a happy temperament, no nerves, and " a digestion like that of an ostrich." See also H. A. Giles, *China and the*

Of foreign religions Islam, next to Buddhism, has made most progress. Introduced by the early Arab and Persian traders, and zealously preached throughout the Jagatai empire in the twelfth century, it has secured a firm footing especially in Kan-su, Shen-si, and Yunnan, and is of course dominant in Eastern (Chinese) Turkestan. Despite the wholesale butcheries that followed the repeated insurrections between 1855 and 1877, the *Hoeï-Hoeï, Panthays*, or *Dungans*, as the Muhammadans are variously called, were still estimated, in 1898, at about 22,000,000 in the whole empire.

Islam and Christianity.

Islam was preceded by Christianity, which, as attested by the authentic inscription of Si-ngan-fu, penetrated into the western provinces under the form of Nestorianism about the seventh century. The famous Roman Catholic missions with headquarters at Pekin date from the close of the sixteenth century, and despite internal dissensions have had a fair measure of success, the congregations comprising altogether over one million members. Protestant missions date from 1807 (London Missionary Society) and in 1910 claimed over 200,000 church members and baptized Christians, the total having more than doubled since 1900.[1]

The above-mentioned dissensions arose out of the practices associated with ancestry worship, offerings of flowers, fruits and so forth, which the Jesuits regarded merely as proofs of filial devotion, but were denounced by the Dominicans as acts of idolatry. After many years of idle controversy, the question was at last decided against the Jesuits by Clement XI in the famous Bull, *Ex illa die* (1715), and since then, neophytes having to renounce the national cult of their forefathers, conversions have mainly been confined to the lower classes, too humble to boast of any family tree, or too poor to commemorate the dead by ever-recurring costly sepulchral rites.

In China there are no hereditary nobles, indeed no nobles at all, unless it be the rather numerous descendants of Confucius who dwell together and enjoy certain social privileges, in this somewhat resembling the *Shorfa* (descendants of the Prophet) in Muhammadan lands. If any titles have to be awarded for

Chinese, 1902 ; E. H. Parker, *John Chinaman and a Few Others*, 1901 ; J. Dyer Ball, *Things Chinese*, 1903 ; and M. Kennelly in Richard's *Comprehensive Geography of the Chinese Empire and its Dependencies*, 1908.
[1] See *Contemporary Review*, Feb. 1908, "Report on Christian Missions in China," by Mr F. W. Fox, Professor Macalister and Sir Alexander Simpson.

great deeds they fall, not on the hero, but on his forefathers, and thus at a stroke of the vermilion pencil are ennobled countless past generations, while the last of the line remains unhonoured until he goes over to the majority. Between the Emperor, " patriarch of his people," and the people themselves, however, there stood an aristocracy of talent, or at least of Chinese scholarship, the governing Mandarin [1] class, which was open to the highest and the lowest alike. All nominations to office were conferred exclusively on the successful competitors at the public examinations, so that, like the French conscript with the hypothetical Marshal's bâton in his knapsack, every Chinese citizen carried the buttoned cap of official rank in his capacious sleeve. Of these there are nine grades, indicated respectively in descending order by the ruby, red coral, sapphire, opaque blue, crystal, white shell, gold (two), and silver button, or rather little globe, on the cap of office, with which correspond the nine birds—manchu crane, golden pheasant, peacock, wild goose, silver pheasant, egret, mandarin duck, quail, and jay—embroidered on the breast and back of the State robe.

The Mandarin Class.

Theoretically the system is admirable, and at all events is better than appointments by Court favour. But in practice it was vitiated, first by the narrow, antiquated course of studies in the dry Chinese classics, calculated to produce pedants rather than statesmen, and secondly by the monopoly of preference which it conferred on a lettered caste to the exclusion of men of action, vigour, and enterprise. Moreover, appointments being made for life, barring crime or blunder, the Mandarins, as long as they approved themselves zealous supporters of the reigning dynasty, enjoyed a free hand in amassing wealth by plunder, and the wealth thus acquired was used to purchase further promotion and advancement, rather than to improve the welfare of the people.

They have the reputation of being a courteous people, as punctilious as the Malays themselves ; and they are so amongst each other. But their attitude towards strangers is the embodiment of aggressive self-righteousness, a complacent feeling of superiority which nothing can disturb. Even the upper classes, with all their efforts to be at least polite, often

[1] A happy Portuguese coinage from the Malay *mantri*, a state minister, which is the Sanskrit *mantrin*, a counsellor, from *mantra*, a sacred text, a counsel, from Aryan root *man*, to think, know, whence also the English *mind*.

betray the feeling in a subdued arrogance which is not always to be distinguished from vulgar insolence. " After the courteous, kindly Japanese, the Chinese seem indifferent, rough, and disagreeable, except the well-to-do merchants in the shops, who are bland, complacent, and courteous. Their rude stare, and the way they hustle you in the streets and shout their 'pidjun' English at you is not attractive."[1] But the stare, the hustling and the shouting may not be due to incivility. No doubt the Chinaman regards the foreigner as a "devil," but he has reason, and he never ceases to be astonished at foreign manners and customs " extremely ferocious and almost entirely uncivilised."[2]

[1] Miss Bird (Mrs Bishop), *The Golden Chersonese*, 1883, p. 37.
[2] H. A. Giles, *The Civilisation of China*, 1911, p. 237. See especially Chap XI., " Chinese and Foreigners," for the etiquette of street regulations and the habit of shouting conversation.

CHAPTER VII

THE OCEANIC MONGOLS

CONSPECTUS.

Present Range. *Indonesia, Philippines, Formosa, Nicobar Is., Madagascar.* Distribution.

Hair, *same as Southern Mongols, scant or no beard.* **Colour,** *yellowish or olive brown, yellow tint sometimes very faint or absent, light leathery hue* Physical Characters. *common in Madagascar.*

Skull, *brachy or sub-brachycephalic (78 to 85).* **Jaws,** *slightly projecting.* **Cheek-bones,** *prominent, but less so than true Mongol.* **Nose,** *rather small, often straight with widish nostrils (mesorrhine).* **Eyes,** *black, medium size, horizontal or slightly oblique, often with Mongol fold.* **Stature,** *undersized, from 1.52 m. to 1.65 m. (5 ft. to 5 ft. 5 in.).* **Lips,** *thickish, slightly protruding, and kept a little apart in repose.* **Arms** *and* **legs,** *rather small, slender and delicate ;* **feet,** *small.*

Temperament. *Normally quiet, reserved and taciturn,*

but under excitement subject to fits of blind fury; fairly in-
telligent, polite and ceremonious, but uncertain,
Mental *untrustworthy, and even treacherous; daring,*
Characters. *adventurous and reckless; musical; not distinctly*
cruel, though indifferent to physical suffering in others.

Speech, *various branches of a single stock language—*
the **Austronesian** (**Oceanic** *or* **Malayo-Polynesian**), *at*
different stages of agglutination.

Religion, *of the primitive Malayans somewhat un-*
developed—a vague dread of ghosts and other spirits, but rites
and ceremonies mainly absent, although human sacrifices to the
departed occurred in Borneo; the cultured Malayans formerly
Hindus (Brahman and Buddhist), now mostly Moslem, but in
the Philippines and Madagascar Christian; belief in witch-
craft, charms, and spells everywhere prevalent.

Culture, *of the primitive Malayans very low—head-hunting,*
mutilation, common in Borneo; hunting, fishing; no agri-
culture; simple arts and industries; the Moslem and Christian
Malayans semi-civilised; the industrial arts—weaving, dyeing,
pottery, metal-work, also trade, navigation, house and boat-
building—well developod; architecture formerly flourishing in
Java under Hindu influences; letters widespread even amongst
some of the rude Malayans, but literature and science rudi-
mentary; rich oral folklore.

Malayans (**Proto-Malays**): *Lampongs, Rejangs, Battas,*
Achinese, and Palembangs in Sumatra; Sundanese, Javanese
proper, and Madurese in Java; Dayaks in Borneo;
Main Divisions. *Balinese; Sassaks (Lombok); Bugis and Mang-*
kassaras in Celebes; Tagalogs, Visayas, Bicols, Ilocanos and
Pangasinanes in Philippines; Aborigines of Formosa; Nicobar
Islanders; Hovas, Betsimisarakas, and Sakalavas in Mada-
gascar.

Malays Proper (*Historical Malays*): *Menangkabau*
(*Sumatra*); *Malay Peninsula; Pinang; Singapore, Lingga,*
Bangka; Borneo Coastlands; Tidor, Ternate; Amboina;
Parts of the Sula Archipelago.

In the Oceanic domain, which for ethnical purposes begins
at the neck of the Malay Peninsula, the Mongol peoples range
Range of the from Madagascar eastwards to Formosa and
Oceanic Micronesia, but are found in compact masses
Mongols. chiefly on the mainland, in the Sunda Islands

(Sumatra, Java, Bali, Lombok, Borneo, Celebes) and in the Philippines. Even here they have mingled in many places with other populations, forming fresh ethnical groups, in which the Mongol element is not always conspicuous. Such fusions have taken place with the Negrito aborigines in the Malay Peninsula and the Philippines ; with Papuans in Micronesia, Flores, and other islands east of Lombok ; with dolichocephalic Indonesians in Sumatra, Borneo, Celebes, Halmahera (Jilolo), parts of the Philippines,[1] and perhaps also Timor and Ceram ; and with African negroes (Bantu) in Madagascar. To unravel some of these racial entanglements is one of the most difficult tasks in anthropology, and in the absence of detailed information cannot yet be everywhere attempted with any prospect of success.

The problem has been greatly, though perhaps inevitably complicated by the indiscriminate extension of the term " Malay " to all these and even to other mixed Oceanic populations farther east, as, for instance, **The term "Malay."** in the expression " Malayo-Polynesian," applied by many writers not only in a linguistic, but also in an ethnical sense, to most of the insular peoples from Madagascar to Easter Island, and from Hawaii to New Zealand. It is now of course too late to hope to remedy this misuse of terms by proposing a fresh nomenclature. But much of the consequent confusion will be avoided by restricting *Malayo-Polynesian* [2] altogether to linguistic matters, and carefully distinguishing between *Indonesian*, the pre-Malay dolichocephalic element in Oceania,[3] *Malayan* or *Proto-Malayan*, collective name of

[1] Here E. T. Hamy finds connecting links between the true Malays and the Indonesians in the Bicols of Albay and the Bisayas of Panay (" Les Races Malaïques et Américaines," in *L'Anthropologie*, 1896, p. 136). Used in this extended sense, Hamy's *Malaique* corresponds generally to our *Malayan* as defined presently.

[2] Ethnically Malayo-Polynesian is an impossible expression, because it links together the Malays, who belong to the Mongol, and the Polynesians, who belong to the Caucasic division. But as both undoubtedly speak languages of the same linguistic stock the expression is permitted in philology, although, as P. W. Schmidt points out, " Malay " and " Polynesian " are not of equal rank : and the combination is as unbalanced as " Indo-Bavarian " for " Indo-Germanic " ; it is best therefore to adopt Schmidt's term *Austronesian* for this family of languages (*Die Mon-Khmer Völker*, 1906, p. 69).

[3] Indonesian type : undulating black hair, often tinged with red ; tawny skin, often rather light ; low stature, 1.54 m.—1.57 m. (5 ft. 0½ in.—5 ft. 1¾ in.) ; mesaticephalic head (76–78) probably originally dolichocephalic ; cheek-bones sometimes projecting ; nose often flattened, sometimes concave. It is difficult to isolate this type as it has almost everywhere been mixed with a brachycephalic Proto-Malay stock, but the Muruts of Borneo (cranial index 73) are probably typical (A. C. Haddon, *The Races of Man*, 1909, p. 14).

all the Oceanic Mongols, who are brachycephals, and *Malay*, a particular branch of the Malayan family, as fully explained in *Ethnology*, pp. 326–30.[1]

The essential point to remember is that the true Malays— who call themselves *Orang-Maláyu*, speak the standard but
The Historical Malays. quite modern Malay language, and are all Muhammadans—are a historical people who appear on the scene in relatively recent times, ages after the insular world had been occupied by the Mongol peoples to whom their name has been extended, but who never call themselves Malays. The Orang-Maláyu, who have acquired such an astonishing predominance in the Eastern Archipelago, were originally an obscure tribe who rose to power in the Menangkabau district, Sumatra, not before the twelfth century, and whose migrations date only from about the year 1160 A.D. At this time, according to the native records,[2] was founded the first foreign settlement, Singapore, a pure Sanskrit name meaning the " Lion City," from which it might be inferred that these first settlers were not Muhammadans, as is commonly assumed, but Brahmans or Buddhists, both these forms of Hinduism having been propagated throughout Sumatra and the other Sunda Islands centuries
Migrations and Present Range. before this time. It is also noteworthy that the early settlers on the mainland are stated to have been pagans, or to have professed some corrupt form of Hindu idolatry, till their conversion to Islam by the renowned Sultan Mahmud Shah about the middle of the thirteenth century. It is therefore probable enough that the earlier movements were carried out under Hindu influences, and may have begun long before the historical date 1160. Menangkabau, however, was the first Mussulman State that acquired political supremacy in Sumatra, and this district thus became the chief centre for the later diffusion of the cultured Malays, their language, usages, and religion, throughout the Peninsula and the Archipelago. Here they are now found in compact masses chiefly in south Sumatra (Menangkabau, Palembang, the Lampongs) ; in all the insular groups between Sumatra and Borneo ; in the Malay Peninsula as far north as

---

[1] Recent literature on this area includes F. A. Swettenham, *The Real Malay*, 1900, *British Malaya*, 1906 ; W. W. Skeat, *Malay Magic*, 1900 ; N. Annandale and H. C. Robinson, *Fasciculi Malayenses*, 1903 ; W. W. Skeat and C. O. Blagden, *Pagan Races of the Malay Peninsula*, 1903.
[2] J. Leyden, *Malay Annals*, 1821, p. 44.

the Kra Isthmus, here intermingling with the Siamese as "Sam-Sams," partly Buddhists, partly Muhammadans; round the coast of Borneo and about the estuaries of that island; in Tidor, Ternate, and the adjacent coast of Jilolo; in the Banda, Sula, and Sulu groups; in Batavia, Singapore, and all the other large seaports of the Archipelago. In all these lands beyond Sumatra the Orang-Maláyu are thus seen to be comparatively recent arrivals,[1] and in fact intruders on the other Malayan populations, with whom they collectively constitute the Oceanic branch of the Mongol division. Their diffusion was everywhere brought about much in the same way as in Ternate, where A. R. Wallace tells us that the ruling people "are an intrusive Malay race somewhat allied to the Macassar people, who settled in the country at a very early epoch, drove out the indigenes, who were no doubt the same as those of the adjacent island of Gilolo, and established a monarchy. They perhaps obtained many of their wives from the natives, which will account for the extraordinary language they speak—in some respects closely allied to that of the natives of Gilolo, while it contains much that points to a Malayan [Malay] origin. To most of these people the Malay language is quite unintelligible."[2]

The Malayan populations, as distinguished from the Malays proper, form socially two very distinct classes—the *Orang Benua*, "Men of the Soil," rude aborigines, numerous especially in the interior of the Malay Peninsula, Borneo, Celebes, Jilolo, Timor, Ceram, the Philippines, Formosa, and Madagascar; and the cultured peoples, formerly Hindus but now mostly Muhammadans, who have long been constituted in large communities and nationalities with historical records, and flourishing arts and industries. They speak cultivated languages of the Austronesian family, generally much better preserved and of richer grammatical structure than the simplified modern speech of the Orang-Maláyu. Such are the Achinese, Rejangs, and Passumahs of Sumatra; the

The Malayans—two Classes; Rude and Cultured.

---

[1] In some places quite recent, as in Rembau, Malay Peninsula, whose inhabitants are mainly immigrants from Sumatra in the seventeenth century; and in the neighbouring group of petty Negri Sembilan States, where the very tribal names, such as *Anak Acheh*, and *Sri Lemak Menangkabau*, betray their late arrival from the Sumatran districts of Achin and Menangkabau.

[2] *The Malay Archipelago*, p. 310.

Bugis, Mangkassaras and some Minahasans of Celebes ;[1] the Tagalogs and Visayas of the Philippines ; the Sassaks and Balinese of Lombok and Bali (most of these still Hindus); the Madurese and Javanese proper of Java ; and the Hovas of Madagascar. To call any of these " Malays,"[2] is like calling the Italians " French," or the Germans " English," because of their respective Romance and Teutonic connections.

Pre-eminent in many respects amongst all the Malayan peoples are the *Javanese—Sundanese* in the west, *Javanese proper* in the centre, *Madurese* in the east—who
The Javanese.
were a highly civilised nation while the Sumatran Malays were still savages, perhaps head-hunters and cannibals like the neighbouring Battas. Although now almost exclusively Muhammadans, they had already adopted some form of Hinduism probably over 2000 years ago, and under the guidance of their Indian teachers had rapidly developed a very advanced state of culture. " Under a completely organised although despotic government, the arts of peace and war were brought to considerable perfection, and the natives of Java became famous throughout the East as accomplished musicians and workers in gold, iron and copper, none of which metals were found in the island itself. They possessed a regular calendar with astronomical eras, and a metrical literature, in which, however, history was inextricably blended with romance. Bronze and stone inscriptions in the Kavi, or old Javanese language, still survive from the eleventh or twelfth century, and to the same dates may be referred the vast ruins of Brambanam and the stupendous temple of Boro-budor in the centre of the island. There are few statues of Hindu divinities in this temple, but many are found in its immediate vicinity, and from the various archaeological objects collected in

---

[1] For Celebes see Von Paul und Fritz Sarasin, *Reisen in Celebes ausgeführt in den Jahren 1893–6 und 1902–3*, 1905, and *Versuch einer Anthropologie der Insel Celebes*, 1905.

[2] In 1898 a troop of Javanese minstrels visited London, and one of them, whom I addressed in a few broken Malay sentences, resented in his sleepy way the imputation that he was an Orang-Maláyu, explaining that he was *Orang Java*, a Javanese, and (when further questioned) *Orang Solo*, a native of the Solo district, East Java. It was interesting to notice the very marked Mongolic features of these natives, vividly recalling the remark of A. R. Wallace, on the difficulty of distinguishing between a Javanese and a Chinaman when both are dressed alike. The resemblance may to a small extent be due to " mixture with Chinese blood " (B. Hagen, *Jour. Anthrop. Soc.* Vienna, 1889) ; but occurs over such a wide area that it must mainly be attributed to the common origin of the Chinese and Javanese peoples.

the district it is evident that both the Buddhist and Brahmanical forms of Hinduism were introduced at an early date.

"But all came to an end by the overthrow of the chief Hindu power in 1478, after which event Islam spread rapidly over the whole of Java and Madura. Brahmanism, however, still holds its ground in Bali and Lombok, the last strongholds of Hinduism in the Eastern Archipelago."[1]

On the obscure religious and social relations in these Lesser Sundanese Islands much light has been thrown by Capt. W. Cool, an English translation of whose work *With the Dutch in the East* was issued by E. J. Taylor in 1897. Here it is shown how Hinduism, formerly dominant throughout a great part of Malaysia, gradually yielded in some places to a revival of the never extinct primitive nature-worship, in others to the spread of Islam, which in Bali alone failed to gain a footing. In this island a curious mingling of Buddhist and Brahmanical forms with the primordial heathendom not only persisted, but was strong enough to acquire the political ascendancy over the Mussulman Sassaks of the neighbouring island of Lombok. Thus while Islam reigns exclusively in Java—formerly the chief domain of Hinduism in the Archipelago—Bali, Lombok, and even Sumbawa, present the strange spectacle of large communities professing every form of belief, from the grossest heathendom to pure monotheism.

Balinese and Sassaks.

Primitive and later Religions and Cultures.

As I have elsewhere pointed out,[2] it is the same with the cultures and general social conditions, which show an almost unbroken transition from the savagery of Sumbawa to the relative degrees of refinement reached by the natives of Lombok and especially of Bali. Here, however, owing to the unfavourable political relations, a retrograde movement is perceptible in the crumbling temples, grass-grown highways, and neglected homesteads. But it is everywhere evident enough that "just as Hinduism has only touched the outer surface of their religion, it has failed to penetrate into their social institutions, which, like their gods, originate from the time when Polynesian heathendom was all powerful."[3]

A striking illustration of the vitality of the early beliefs is

[1] A. H. Keane, *Eastern Geography*, 2nd ed. 1892, p. 121.
[2] *Academy*, May 1, 1897, p. 469.
[3] Cool, p. 139.

K.

presented by the local traditions, which relate how these foreign
gods installed themselves in the Lesser Sundanese
Hindu Legends in Bali. Islands after their expulsion from Java by the
Muhammadans in the fifteenth century. Being
greatly incensed at the introduction of the Koran, and also
anxious to avoid ·contact with the " foreign devils," the
Hindu deities moved eastwards with the intention of setting
up their throne in Bali. But Bali already possessed its
own gods, the wicked Rakshasas, who fiercely resented the
intrusion, but in the struggle that ensued were annihilated,
all but the still reigning Mraya Dewana. Then the new
thrones had to be erected on heights, as in Java ; but at
that time there were no mountains in Bali, which was a very
flat country. So the difficulty was overcome by bodily trans-
ferring the four hills at the eastern extremity of Java to the
neighbouring island. Gunong Agong, highest of the four,
was set down in the east, and became the Olympus of Bali,
while the other three were planted in the west, south, and north,
and assigned to the different gods according to their respective
ranks. Thus were at once explained the local theogony and
the present physical features of the island.

Despite their generally quiet, taciturn demeanour, all these
Sundanese peoples are just as liable as the Orang-Maláyu
Running Amok. himself, to those sudden outbursts of demoniacal
frenzy and homicidal mania called by them *měng-
ámok*, and by us " running amok." Indeed A. R. Wallace
tells us that such wild outbreaks occur more frequently (about
one or two every month) amongst the civilised Mangkassaras
and Bugis of south Celebes than elsewhere in the Archipelago.
" It is the national and therefore the honourable mode of
committing suicide among the natives of Celebes, and is the
fashionable way of escaping from their difficulties. A Roman
fell upon his sword, a Japanese rips up his stomach, and an
Englishman blows out his brains with a pistol. The Bugis
mode has many advantages to one suicidally inclined. A
man thinks himself wronged by society—he is in debt and
cannot pay—he is taken for a slave or has gambled away his
wife or child into slavery—he sees no way of recovering what
he has lost, and becomes desperate. He will not put up with
such cruel wrongs, but will be revenged on mankind and die
like a hero. He grasps his kris-handle, and the next moment
draws out the weapon and stabs a man to the heart. He runs

on, with bloody kris in his hand, stabbing at everyone he meets. 'Amok! Amok!' then resounds through the streets. Spears, krisses, knives and guns are brought out against him. He rushes madly forward, kills all he can—men, women, and children—and dies overwhelmed by numbers amid all the excitement of a battle."[1]

Possibly connected with this blind impulse may be the strange nervous affection called *látah*, which is also prevalent amongst the Malayans, and which was first clearly described by the distinguished Malay scholar, Sir Frank Athelstane Swettenham.[2] No attempt has yet been made thoroughly to diagnose this uncanny disorder,[3] which would seem so much more characteristic of the high-strung or shattered nervous system of ultra-refined European society, than of that artless upsophisticated child of nature, the Orang-Maláyu. Its effects on the mental state are such as to disturb all normal cerebration, and Swettenham mentions two látah-struck Malays, who would make admirable " subjects " at a séance of theosophic psychists. Any simple device served to attract their attention, when by merely looking them hard in the face they fell helplessly in the hands of the operator, instantly lost all self-control, and went passively through any performance either verbally imposed or even merely suggested by a sign.

The Látah Malady.

A peculiar feminine strain has often been imputed to the Malay temperament, yet this same Oceanic people displays in many respects a curiously kindred spirit with the ordinary Englishman, as, for instance, in his love of gambling, boxing, cock-fighting, field sports,[4] and adventure. No more fearless explorers of the high seas, formerly rovers and corsairs, at all times enterprising traders, are anywhere to be found than the Menangkabau Malays and their near kinsmen, the renowned Bugis " Merchant Adventurers " of south Celebes. Their clumsy but seaworthy praus are met in every seaport from Sumatra to the Aru Islands, and they have established permanent trading stations and even settlements in Borneo, the Philippines, Timor, and as far east as New Guinea. On one occasion Wallace sailed from Dobbo

The Malayan Seafarers and Rovers.

[1] *The Malay Archipelago*, p. 175.
[2] In *Malay Sketches*, 1895.
[3] Cf. M. A. Czaplicka on Arctic Hysteria in *Aboriginal Siberia*, 1914, p. 307.
[4] On these national pastimes see Sir Hugh Clifford, *In Court and Kampong*, 1897, p. 46 sq.

in company with fifteen large Makassar praus, each with a cargo
worth about £1000, and as many of the Bugis settle amongst
the rude aborigines of the eastern isles, they thus co-operate
with the Sumatran Malays in extending the area of civilising
influences throughout Papuasia.

Formerly they combined piracy with legitimate trade, and'
long after the suppression of the North Bornean corsairs by
Keppel and Brooke, the inland waters continued to be infested
especially by the *Bajau* rovers of Celebes, and by the *Balagnini*
of the Sulu Archipelago, most dreaded of all the *Orang-Laut,*
" Men of the Sea," the " Sea Gypsies " of the English.   These
were the " Cellates " (*Orang-Selat,* " Men of the Straits ") of
the early Portuguese writers, who described them as from
time immemorial engaged in fishing and plundering on the
high seas.[1]

In those days, and even in comparatively late times, the
relations in the Eastern Archipelago greatly resembled those

Malaysia and
Pelasgia—
a Historical
Parallel.

prevailing in the Aegean Sea at the dawn of
Greek history, while the restless seafaring populations were still in a state of flux, passing from
island to island in quest of booty or barter before
permanently settling down in favourable sites.[2]   With the
Greek historian's philosophic disquisition on these Pelasgian
and proto-Hellenic relations may be compared A. R. Wallace's
account of the Batjan coastlands when visited by him in the
late fifties.   " Opposite us, and all along this coast of Batchian,
stretches a row of fine islands completely uninhabited.   Whenever I asked the reason why no one goes to live in them, the
answer always was ' For fear of the Magindano pirates.' [3]
Every year these scourges of the Archipelago wander in one
direction or another, making their rendezvous on some
uninhabited island, and carrying devastation to all the small
settlements around ;   robbing, destroying, killing, or taking

---

[1] *Cujo officio he rubar e pescar,* " whose business it is to rob and fish " (Barros).
Many of the Bajaus lived entirely afloat, passing their lives in boats from the
cradle to the grave, and praying Allah that they might die at sea.

[2] Thucydides, *Pel. War,* I. 1–16.

[3] These are the noted *Illanuns,* who occupy the south side of the large
Philippine island of Mindanao, but many of whom, like the Bajaus of Celebes and
the Sulu Islanders, have formed settlements on the north-east coast of Borneo.
" Long ago their warfare against the Spaniards degenerated into general piracy.
Their usual practice was not to take captives, but to murder all on board any boat
they took.   Those with us [British North Borneo] have all settled down to a more
orderly way of life " (W. B. Pryer, *Journ. Anthr. Inst.* 1886, p. 231).

captive all they meet with.   Their long, well-manned praus escape from the pursuit of any sailing vessel by pulling away right in the wind's eye, and the warning smoke of a steamer generally enables them to hide in some shallow bay, or narrow river, or forest-covered inlet, till the danger is passed." [1]   Thus, like geographical surroundings, with corresponding social conditions, produce like results in all times amongst all peoples.

This fundamental truth receives further illustration from the ideas prevalent amongst the Malayans regarding witchcraft, the magic arts, charms and spells, and especially the belief in the power of certain malevolent human beings to transform them- selves into wild beasts and prey upon their fellow-creatures. Such superstitions girdle the globe, taking their local colouring from the fauna of the different regions, so that the were-wolf of medieval Europe finds its counterpart in the human jaguar of South America, the human lion or leopard of Africa,[2] and the human tiger of the Malay Peninsula.   Hugh Clifford, who relates an occurrence known to himself in connection with a " were-tiger " story of the Perak district, aptly remarks that " the white man and the brown, the yellow and the black, independently, and without receiving the idea from one another, have all found the same explanation for the like phenomena, all apparently recognising the truth of the Malay proverb, that we are like unto the *táman* fish that preys upon its own kind." [3]   The story in question turns upon a young bride, whose husband comes home late three nights following, and the third time, being watched, is discovered by her in the form of a full-grown tiger stretched on the ladder, which, as in all Malay houses, leads from the ground to the threshold of the door.   " Patímah gazed at the tiger from a distance of only a foot or two, for she was too paralysed with fear to move or cry out, and as she looked a gradual transformation took place in the creature at her feet.   Slowly, as one sees a ripple of wind pass over the surface of still water, the tiger's

Malayan Folklore—The Were-tiger.

---

[1] *The Malay Archipelago*, p. 341.

[2] In Central Africa " the belief in ' were ' animals, that is to say in human beings who have changed themselves into lions or leopards or some such harmful beasts, is nearly universal.   Moreover there are individuals who imagine they possess this power of assuming the form of an animal and killing human beings in that shape."   Sir H. H. Johnston, *British Central Africa*, p. 439.

[3] *In Court and Kampong*, p. 63.

features palpitated and were changed, until the horrified girl saw the face of her husband come up through that of the beast, much as the face of a diver comes up to the surface of a pool.   In another moment Patímah saw that it was Haji Ali who was ascending the ladder of his house, and the spell that had hitherto bound her was snapped."

These same Malays of Perak, H. H. Rajah Dris tells us, are still specially noted for many strange customs and superstitions " utterly opposed to Muhammadan teaching, and savouring strongly of devil-worship.   This enormous belief in the supernatural is possibly a relic of the pre-Islam State." [1]

We do not know who were the primitive inhabitants of Borneo.   One would expect to find Negritoes in the interior, but despite the assertion of A. de Quatrefages [2]

Borneo.

it is impossible to overlook the conclusions of A. B. Meyer [3] that no authoritative evidence of their occurrence is forthcoming, and A. C. Haddon [4] confidently states that there are none in Sarawak.   It might be supposed that the Pre-Dravidian element found in Sumatra and Celebes might occur also in Borneo, but the only indication of such influence is the " black skin " noticed among certain Ulu Ayar of the Upper Kapuas in Western Dutch Borneo.[5]   With the exception of certain peoples such as Europeans, Indians, Chinese, and Orang-Maláyu, whose foreign origin is obvious, the population as a whole may be regarded as being composed of two main races, the Indonesian and Proto-Malay.   Probably all tribes are of mixed origin, but some, such as the *Murut, Dusun, Kalabit,* and *Land Dayak* are more Indonesian while the *Iban (Sea Dayak)* are distinctly Proto-Malay.   The *Land Dayak* have doubtless been crossed with Indo-Javans.

Scattered over a considerable part of the jungle live the nomad *Punan* and *Ukit.*   They are a slender pale people with a slightly broad head.   They are grouped

Punan.

in small communities and inhabit the dense jungle at the head waters of the principal rivers of Borneo.

<hr>

[1] *Journ. Anthr. Inst.* 1886, p. 227.   The Rajah gives the leading features of the character of his countrymen as " pride of race and birth, extraordinary observance of punctilio, and a bigoted adherence to ancient custom and tradition."
[2] *The Pygmies* (Translation), 1895, p. 26, fig. 15.
[3] *The Distribution of the Negritos,* 1899, p. 50.
[4] In the Appendix to C. Hose and W. McDougall, *The Pagan Tribes of Borneo* 1912, p. 311.
[5] J. H. Kohlbrugge, *L'Anthropologie,* IX. 1898.

They live on whatever they can find in the jungle, and do not cultivate the soil, nor live in permanent houses. Their few wants are supplied by barter from friendly settled peoples, or in return for iron implements, calico, beads, tobacco, etc., they offer jungle produce, mainly gutta, indiarubber, camphor, dammar and ratans. They are very mild savages, not head-hunters, they are generous to one another, moderately truthful, kind to the women and very fond of their children.

Hose and Haddon have introduced the term *Klemantan* (*Kalamantan*) for the weak agricultural tribes such as the *Murut, Kalabit, Land Dayak, Sebop, Barawan, Milanau*, etc.[1] Brook Low,[2] who knew the **Klemantan.** Land Dayak well, gives a very favourable account of the people and this opinion has been confirmed by other travellers. They are described as amiable, honest, grateful, moral and hospitable. Crimes of violence, other than head-hunting, are unknown. The circular *panga* is a "house set apart for the residence of young unmarried men, in which the trophy-heads are kept, and here also all ceremonial receptions take place."[3] The *baloi* of the Ot Danom of the Kahajan river is very similar.[4] The very energetic and dominating *Bahau-Kenyah-Kayan* group are rather short in **Bahau-Kenyah-Kayan.** stature, with slightly broad heads. They occupy the best tracts of land which lie in the undulating hills at the upper reaches of the rivers, between the swampy low country and the mountains. The Kayan more especially have almost exterminated some of the smaller tribes. The Klemantan and Kenyah-Kayan tribes are agriculturists. They clear the jungle off the low hills that flank the tributaries of the larger rivers, but always leave a few scattered trees standing; irrigation is attempted by the Kalabits only, as *padi* rice is grown like any other cereals on dry ground; swamp *padi* is also grown on the low land. In their gardens they grow yams, pumpkins, sugar cane, bananas, and sometimes coconuts and other produce. They hunt all land animals that serve as food, and fish, usually with nets, in the rivers, or spear those

[1] A. C. Haddon, "A Sketch of the Ethnography of Sarawak," *Archivio per l' Antropologia e l' Etnologia*, XXXI. 1901 ; C. Hose and W. McDougall, *The Pagan Tribes of Borneo*, 1912, Appendix, p. 314.
[2] H. Ling Roth, *The Natives of Sarawak and British North Borneo*, 1896.
[3] O. Beccari, *Wanderings in the Great Forests of Borneo*, 1904, p. 54.
[4] Schwaner, in H. Ling Roth, *The Natives of Sarawak*, etc., 1896.

fish that have been stupefied with *tuba* ; river prawns are also a favourite article of diet.

They all live in long communal houses which are situated on the banks of the rivers.   Among the Klemantan tribes the headman has not much influence, unless he is a man of exceptional power and energy, but among the larger tribes and especially among the Kayan and Kenyah the headmen are the real chiefs and exercise undisputed sway.   The Kenyah are perhaps the most advanced in social evolution, holding their own by superior solidarity and intelligence against the turbulent Kayan.

All the agricultural tribes are artistic, but in varying degrees ; they are also musical and sing delightful chorus songs.   In some tribes the ends of the beams. of the houses are carved to represent various animals, in some the verandah is decorated with boldly carved planks, or with painted boards and doors.   The bamboo receptacles carved in low relief, the bone handles of their swords and the minor articles of daily life, are decorated in a way that reveals the true artistic spirit. Both Kenyah and Kayan smelt iron and make spear heads and sword blades, the former being especially noted for their good steel.   The forge with two bellows is the form widely spread in Malaysia.

The truculent *Iban* (*Sea Dayak*) have spread from a restricted area in Sarawak.[1]   They are short and have

Iban (Sea Dayak). broader heads than the other tribes ; the colour is on the whole darker than among the cinnamon coloured inland tribes.   They have the same long, slightly wavy, black hair showing a reddish tinge in certain lights, that is characteristic of the Borneans generally. Most of the Iban inhabit low lying land ; they prefer to live on the low hills, but as this is not always practicable they plant swamp *padi* ; all those who settle at the heads of rivers plant *padi* on the hills in the same manner as the up-river natives.   They also cultivate maize, sugar cane, sweet potatoes, gourds, pumpkins, cucumbers, melons, mustard, ginger and other vegetables.   Generally groups of relations work together in the fields.   Although essentially agricultural, they are warlike and passionately devoted to head-hunting. The Iban of the Batang Lupar and Saribas in the olden days joined the Malays in their large war praus on piratical raids

[1] A. C. Haddon, *Head-Hunters, Black, White and Brown*, 1901, p. 324.

along the coast and up certain rivers and they owe their name of Sea Dayaks to this practice. The raids were organised by Malays who went for plunder but they could always ensure the aid of Iban by the bribe of the heads of the slain as their share. The Iban women weave beautiful cotton cloths on a very simple loom. Intricate patterns are made by tying several warp strands with leaves at varying intervals, then dipping the whole into the dye which does not penetrate the tied portions. This process is repeated if a three-colour design is desired. The pattern is produced solely in the warp, the woof threads are self-coloured and are not visible in the fabric, which is therefore a cotton rep. Little tattooing is seen among the Iban women though the men have adopted the custom from the Kayan.

It is probable that the Iban belong to the same stock as the original Malay, and if so, their migration may be regarded as the first wave of the movement that culminated in the Malay Empire. The Malays must have came to Borneo not later than the early part of the fifteenth century as Brunei was a large and wealthy town in 1521. Probably the Malays came directly from the Malay Peninsula, but they must have mixed largely with the *Kadayan, Milanau,* and other coastal people. The Sarawak and Brunei Malays are probably mainly coastal Borneans with some Malay blood, but they have absorbed the Malay culture, spirit and religion.

From the sociological point of view the Punan, living by the chase and on exploitation of jungle produce, represent the lowest grade of culture in Borneo. Without social organisation they are alike incapable of real **Summary.** endemic improvement or of seriously affecting other peoples. The purely agricultural tribes that cultivate *padi* on the low hills or in the swamps from the next social stratum. These indigenous tillers of the soil have been hard pressed by various swarms of foreigners.

The Kenyah-Kayan migration was that of a people of a slightly higher grade of culture. They were agriculturists, but the social organisation was firmer and they were probably superior in physique. If they introduced iron weapons, this would give them an enormous advantage. These immigrant agricultural artisans, directed by powerful chiefs, had no difficulty in taking possession of the most desirable land.

From an opposite point of the compass in early times

came another agricultural people who strangely enough have strong individualistic tendencies, the usually peaceable habits of tillers of the soil having been complicated by a lust for heads and other warlike propensities. But the Iban do not appear to have gained much against the Kenyah and Kayan. Conquest implies a strong leader, obedience to authority and concerted action. The Iban appear to be formidable only when led and organised by Europeans.

The Malay was of a yet higher social type. His political organisation was well established, and he had the advantage of religious enthusiasm, for Islam has no small share in the expansion of the Malay. He is a trader, and still more an exploiter, having a sporting element in his character not altogether compatible with steady trade. Then appeared on the scene the Anglo-Saxon overlord. The quality of firmness combined with justice made itself felt. At times the lower social types hurled themselves, but in vain, against the instrument that had been forged and tempered in a similar turmoil of Iberian, Celt, Angle and Viking in Northern Europe. Now they acknowledge that safety of life and property and almost complete liberty are fully worth the very small price that they have to pay for them.[1]

The cult of omen animals, most frequently birds, is indigenous to Borneo. These are possessed with the spirit of certain invisible beings above, and bear their names, and are invoked to secure good crops, freedom from accident, victory in war, profit in exchange, skill in discourse, and cleverness in all native craft. The Iban have a belief in *Ngarong* or spirit-helpers, somewhat resembling that of the *Manitu* of North America. The *Ngarong* is the spirit of a dead relative who visits a dreamer, who afterwards searches for the outward and visible sign of his spiritual protector, and finds it in some form, perhaps a natural object, or some one animal, henceforth held in special respect.[2]

Religion.

In Sumatra there occur some remains of Hindu temples,[3]

[1] A. C. Haddon, *Head-Hunters, Black, White and Brown*, 1901, pp. 327–8.
[2] For further literature on Borneo see W. H. Furness, *The Home-life of the Borneo Head-Hunters*, 1902 ; A. W. Nieuwenhuis, *Quer durch Borneo*, 1904 ; E. H. Gomes, *Seventeen Years among the Sea-Dyaks of Borneo*, 1911 ; C. Hose and W. McDougall, *Journ. Anthr. Inst.*, xxxi. 1901, and *The Pagan Tribes of Borneo*, 1912.
[3] Not only in the southern districts for centuries subject to Javanese influences, but also in Battaland, where they were first discovered by H. von Rosenberg in

as well as other mysterious monuments in the Passumah lands inland from Benkulen, relics of a former culture, which goes back to prehistoric times. They take the form Early Man and of huge monoliths, which are roughly shaped to his Works in the likeness of human figures, with strange Sumatra. features very different from the Malay or Hindu types. The present Sarawi natives of the district, who would be quite incapable of executing such works, know nothing of their origin, and attribute them to certain legendary beings who formerly wandered over the land, turning all their enemies into stone. Further research may possibly discover some connection between these relics of a forgotten past and the numerous prehistoric monuments of Easter Island and other places in the Pacific Ocean. Of all the Indonesian peoples still surviving in Malaysia, none present so many points of contact with the Eastern Polynesians, The Mentawi as do the natives of the Mentawi Islands which Islanders. skirt the south-west coast of Sumatra. " On a closer inspection of the inhabitants the attentive observer at once perceives that the Mentawi natives have but little in common with the peoples and tribes of the neighbouring islands, and that as regards physical appearance, speech, customs, and usages they stand almost entirely apart. They bear such a decided stamp of a Polynesian tribe that one feels far more inclined to compare them with the inhabitants of the South Sea Islands." [1]

The survival of an Indonesian group on the western verge of Malaysia is all the more remarkable since the *Nias* islanders, a little farther north, are of Mongol stock, like most if not all of the inhabitants of the Sumatran mainland. Here the typical Malays of the central districts (Menangkabau, Korinchi, and Siak) merge southwards in the Javanese and mixed Malayo-Javanese peoples of the *Rejang,* Hindu *Palembang,* and *Lampong* districts. Although Influences.

1853, and figured and described in *Der Malayische Archipel,* Leipzig, 1878, Vol. I. p. 27 sq. " Nach ihrer Form und ihren Bildwerken zu urtheilen, waren die Gebäude Tempel, worin der Buddha-Kultus gefeiert wurde " (p. 28). These are all the more interesting since Hindu ruins are otherwise rare in Sumatra, where there is nothing comparable to the stupendous monuments of Central and East Java.

[1] Von Rosenberg, *op. cit.* Vol. I. p. 189. Amongst the points of close resemblance may be mentioned the outriggers, for which Mentawi has the same word (*abak*) as the Samoan (*va'r=vaka*) ; the funeral rites ; taboo ; the facial expression ; and the language, in which the numerical systems are identical ; cf. Ment. *limongapula* with Sam. *limagafulu,* the Malay being *limapulah* (fifty), where the Sam. infix *ga* (absent in Malay) is pronounced *gna,* exactly as in Ment.

Muhammadans probably since the thirteenth century, all these peoples had been early brought under Hindu influences by missionaries and even settlers from Java, and these influences are still apparent in many of the customs, popular traditions, languages, and letters of the South Sumatran settled communities. Thus the Lampongs, despite their profession of

Indian Origin of the Malaysian Alphabets. Islam, employ, not the Arabic characters, like the Malays proper, but a script derived from the peculiar Javanese writing system. This system itself, originally introduced from India probably over 2000 years ago, is based on some early forms of the Devanagari, such as those occurring in the rock inscriptions of the famous Buddhist king As'oka (third century B.C.).[1] From Java, which is now shown beyond doubt to be the true centre of dispersion,[2] the parent alphabet was under Hindu influences diffused in pre-Muhammadan times throughout Malaysia, from Sumatra to the Philippines.

But the thinly-spread Indo-Javanese culture, in few places penetrating much below the surface, received a rude shock from the Muhammadan irruption, its natural development being almost everywhere arrested, or else either effaced or displaced by Islam. No trace can any longer be detected of graphic signs in Borneo, where the aborigines have retained the savage state even in those southern districts where Buddhism or Brahmanisn had certainly been propagated long before the arrival of the Muhammadan Malays. But elsewhere the Javanese stock alphabet has shown extraordinary vitality, persisting under diverse forms down to the present day, not only amongst the semi-civilised Mussulman peoples, such as the Sumatran Rejangs,[3] Korinchi, and Lampongs, the Bugis and Mangkassaras of Celebes, and the (now Christian)

[1] See Fr. Müller, *Ueber den Ursprung der Schrift der Malaiischen Völker*, Vienna, 1865; and my Appendix to Stanford's *Australasia*, First Series, 1879, p. 624.

[2] *Die Mangianenschrift von Mindoro, herausgegeben von A. B. Meyer u. A. Schadenberg*, speciell bearbeitet von W. Foy, Dresden, 1895; see also my remarks in *Journ. Anthr. Inst.* 1896, p. 277 sq.

[3] The Rejang, which certainly belongs to the same Indo-Javanese system as all the other Malaysian alphabets, has been regarded by Sayce and Renan as " pure Phoenician," while Neubauer has compared it with that current in the fourth and fifth centuries B.C. The suggestion that it may have been introduced by the Phoenician crews of Alexander's admiral, Nearchus (*Archaeol. Oxon.* 1895. No. 6), could not have been made by anyone aware of its close connection with the Lampong of South, and the Batta of North Sumatra (see also Prof. Kern, *Globus*, 70, p. 116).

Tagalogs and Visayas of the Philippines, but even amongst the somewhat rude and pagan Palawan natives, the wild Manguianes of Mindoro, and the cannibal Battas [1] of North Sumatra.

These Battas, however, despite their undoubted canni-balism,[2] cannot be called savages, at least without some reserve. They are skilful stock-breeders and agriculturists, raising fine crops of maize and rice ; they dwell together in large, settled communities with an organised government, hereditary chiefs, popular assemblies, and a written civil and penal code. There is even an effective postal system, which utilises for letter-boxes the hollow tree-trunks at all the cross-roads, and is largely patronised by the young men and women, all of whom read and write, and carry on an animated correspondence in their degraded Devanagari script, which is written on palm-leaves in vertical lines running upwards and from right to left. The Battas also excel in several industries, such as pottery, weaving, jewellery, iron work, and house-building, their picturesque dwellings, which resemble Swiss chalets, rising to two stories above the ground-floor reserved for the live stock. For these arts they are no doubt largely indebted to their Hindu teachers, from whom also they have inherited some of their religious ideas, such as the triune deity—Creator, Preserver, and Destroyer—besides other inferior divinities collectively called *diebata*, a modified form of the Indian *devaté*.[3]

The Battas— Cultured Cannibals.

[1] Sing. *Batta*, pl. *Battak*, hence the current form *Battaks* is a solecism, and we should write either *Battas* or *Battak*. Lassen derives the word from the Sanskrit *b'háta*, " savage."

[2] Again confirmed by Volz and H. von Autenrieth, who explored Battaland early in 1898, and penetrated to the territory of the " Cannibal Pakpaks " (*Geogr. Journ.*, June, 1898, p. 672) ; not however " for the first time," as here stated. The Pakpaks had already been visited in 1853 by Von Rosenberg, who found cannibalism so prevalent that " Niemand Anstand nimmt das essen von Men-schenfleisch einzugestehen " (*op. cit.* I. p. 56).

[3] It is interesting to note that by the aid of the Lampong alphabet, South Sumatra, John Mathew reads the word *Daibattah* in the legend on the head-dress of a gigantic figure seen by Sir George Grey on the roof of a cave on the Glenelg river, North-west Australia (" The Cave Paintings of Australia," etc., in *Journ. Anthr. Inst.* 1894, p. 44 sq.). He quotes from Coleman's *Mythology of the Hindus* the statement that "the Battas of Sumatra believe in the existence of one supreme being, whom they name *Debati Hasi Asi*. Since completing the work of creation they suppose him to have remained perfectly quiescent, having wholly committed the government to his three sons, who do not govern in person, but by vakeels or proxies." Here is possibly another confirmation of the view that early Malayan migrations or expeditions, some even to Australia, took place in pre-Muhammadan times, long before the rise and diffusion of the Orang-Maláyu in the Archipelago.

In the strangest contrast to these survivals of a foreign culture which had probably never struck very deep roots, stand the savage survivals from still more ancient times. Conspicuous amongst these are the cannibal practices, which if not now universal still take some peculiarly revolting forms. Thus captives and criminals are, under certain circumstances, condemned to be eaten alive, and the same fate **Cannibalism.** is or was reserved for those incapacitated for work by age or infirmities. When the time came, we are told by the early European observers and by the reports of the Arabs, the " grandfathers " voluntarily suspended themselves by their arms from an overhanging branch, while friends and neighbours danced round and round, shouting, " when the fruit is ripe it falls." And when it did fall, that is, as soon as it could hold on no longer, the company fell upon it with their krisses, hacking it to pieces, and devouring the remains seasoned with lime-juice, for such feasts were generally held when the limes were ripe.[1]

Grouped chiefly round about Lake Toba, the Battas occupy a very wide domain, stretching south to about the parallel of Mount Ophir, and bordering northwards on the **The Achinese.** territory of the Achin people. These valiant natives, who have till recently stoutly maintained their political independence against the Dutch, were also at one time Hinduized, as is evident from many of their traditions, their Malayan language largely charged with Sanskrit terms, and even their physical appearance, suggesting a considerable admixture of Hindu as well as of Arab blood. **Early Records.** With the Arab traders and settlers came the Koran, and the Achinese people have been not over-zealous followers of the Prophet since the close of the twelfth century. The Muhammadan State, founded in 1205, acquired a dominant position in the Archipelago early in the sixteenth century, when it ruled over about half of Sumatra, exacted tribute from many vassal princes, maintained powerful armaments by land and sea, and entered into political and commercial relations with Egypt, Japan, and several European States.

There are two somewhat distinct ethnical groups, the *Orang-Tunong* of the uplands, a comparatively homogeneous Malayan people, and the mixed *Orang-Baruh* of the lowlands,

---

[1] *Memoir of the Life, etc. of Sir T. S. Raffles*, by his widow, 1830.

who are described by A. Lubbers [1] as taller than the average
Malay (5 feet 5 or 6 in.), also less round-headed (index 80.5),
with prominent nose, rather regular features, and muscular
frames ; but the complexion is darker than that of the Orang-
Maláyu, a trait which has been attributed to a larger infusion
of Dravidian blood (Klings and Tamuls) from southern India.
The charge of cruelty and treachery brought against them by
the Dutch may be received with some reserve, such terms as
" patriot " and " rebel " being interchangeable according to
the standpoints from which they are considered.   In any case
no one denies them the virtues of valour and love of freedom,
with which are associated industrious habits and a remarkable
aptitude for such handicrafts as metal work, jewellery, weaving,
and ship-building.   The Achinese do not appear to be very
strict Muhammadans; polygamy is little practised,   Islam and
their women are free to go abroad unveiled, nor   Hindu Re-
are they condemned to the seclusion of the harem,   miniscences.
and a pleasing survival from Buddhist times is the *Kanduri*,
a solemn feast, in which the poor are permitted to share.
Another reminiscence of Hindu philosophy may perhaps have
been an outburst of religious fervour, which took the form of
a pantheistic creed, and was so zealously preached, that it had
to be stamped out with fire and sword by the dominant
Moslem monotheists.[2]

Since the French occupation of Madagascar, the Malagasy
problem has naturally been revived.   But it may   Ethnical
be regretted that so much time and talent have   Relations in
been spent on a somewhat thrashed-out question   Madagascar.
by a number of writers, who did not first take the trouble to
read up the literature of the subject.

By what race Madagascar was first peopled it is no longer
possible to say.   The local reports or traditions of primitive
peoples, either extinct or still surviving in the
interior, belong rather to the sphere of Malagasy   Prehistoric
folklore than to that of ethnological research.   Peoples.
In these reports mention is frequently made of the *Kimos*,
said to be now or formerly living in the Bara country, and of
the *Vazimbas*, who are by some supposed to have been Gallas
(*Ba-Simba*)—though they had no knowledge of iron—whose
graves are supposed to be certain monolithic monuments

---

[1] " Anthropologie des Atjehs," in *Rev. Med.*, Batavia, xxx. 6, 1890.
[2] See C. Snouck Hurgronje, *The Achenese*, 1906.

which take the form of menhirs disposed in circles, and are believed by the present inhabitants of the land to be still haunted by evil spirits, that is, the ghosts of the long extinct Vazimbas.

Much of the confusion prevalent regarding the present ethnical relations may be avoided if certain points (ably summarised by T. A. Joyce [1]) are borne in mind. **Oceanic Immigrants.** The greater part of the population is negroid ; the language spoken over the whole of the island and many institutions and customs are Malayo-Polynesian. A small section (Antimerina commonly called Hovas)—forming the dominant people in the nineteenth century—is of fairly pure Malay (or Javanese) blood, but is composed of sixteenth-century immigrants, whereas the language belongs to a very early branch of the Malayo-Polynesian (Austronesian) family. It would be natural to suppose that the negroid element was African,[2] **Negroid Element.** for in later times large numbers of Africans have been brought over by Arabs and other slavers ; but there are several objections to this view. In the first place, the natives of the neighbouring coast are not seamen, and the vogage to Madagascar offers peculiar difficulties owing to the strong currents. In the second place, it seems impossible that the first inhabitants, supposing them to be African, should have abandoned their own language in favour of one introduced by a small minority of immigrants ; the few Bantu words found in Madagascar may well have been adopted from the slaves. In the third place, the culture exhibits no distinctively African features, but is far more akin to that of south-east Asia. There is much to be said, therefore, for the view that the earliest and negroid inhabitants of Madagascar were Oceanic negroids, who have always been known as expert seamen.

Since the coming of the negroid population, which probably arrived in very early days, various small bands of immigrants or castaways have landed on the shores of Madagascar and imposed themselves as reigning dynasties on the surrounding villages, each thus forming the nucleus of what now appears as a tribe. Among these were immigrants from Arabia, and

---

[1] *Handbook to the Ethnographical Collections, British Museum*, 1910, p. 245.
[2] This opinion is still held by many competent authorities. Cf. J. Deniker, *The Races of Man*, 1900, p. 469 ff.

J. T. Last, who identifies Madagascar with the island of *Menuthias* described by Arrian in the third century A.D.,[1] suggests the " possibility that Madagascar may have been reached by Arabs before the Christian era." This " possibility " is converted almost into a certainty by the analysis of the Arabo-Malagasy terms made by Dahle, who clearly shows that such terms " are comparatively very few," and also " very ancient," in fact that, as already suggested by Fleischer of Leipzig, many, perhaps the majority of them, " may be traced back to Himyaritic influence," [2] that is, not merely to pre-Muhammadan, but to pre-Christian times, just like the Sanskritic elements in the Oceanic tongues.

Arabic Element.

The evidence that Malagasy is itself one of these Oceanic tongues, and not an offshoot of the comparatively recent standard Malay is overwhelming, and need not here detain us.[3] The diffusion of this Austronesian language over the whole island—even amongst distinctly Negroid Bantu populations, such as the Betsileos and Tanalas—to the absolute exclusion of all other forms of speech, is an extraordinary linguistic phenomenon more easily proved than explained. There are, of course, provincialisms and even what may be called local dialects, such as that of the Antankarana people at the northern extremity of the island who, although commonly included in the large division of the western Sakalavas, really form a separate ethnical group, speaking a somewhat marked variety of Malagasy. But even this differs much less from the normal form than might be supposed by comparing, for instance, such a term as *maso-mahamay*, sun, with the Hova *maso-andro*, where *maso* in both means " eye," *mahamay* in

Uniformity of the Language.

---

[1] " His remarks would scarcely apply to any other island off the East African coast, his descriptions of the rivers, crocodiles, land-tortoises, canoes, sea-turtles, and wicker-work weirs for catching fish, apply exactly to Madagascar of the present day, but to none of the other islands " (*Journ. Anthr. Inst.* 1896, p. 47).

[2] *Loc. cit.* p. 77. Thus to take the days of the week, we have :—Malagasy *alahady, alatsinainy* ; old Arab. (Himyar.) *al-áhadu, al-itsnáni* ; modern Arab. *el-áhad, el-etnén* (Sunday, Monday), where the Mal. forms are obviously derived not from the present, but from the ancient Arabic. From all this it seems reasonable to infer that the early Semitic influences in Madagascar may be due to the same Sabaean or Minaean peoples of South Arabia, to whom the Zimbabwe monuments in the auriferous region south of the Zambesi were accredited by Theodore Bent.

[3] Those who may still doubt should consult M. Aristide Marre, *Les Affinités de la Langue Malgache*, Leyden, 1884 ; Last's above quoted Paper in the *Journ. Anthr. Inst.* and R. H. Codrington's *Melanesian Languages*, Oxford, 1885.

both=" burning," and *andro* in both = " day." Thus the
only difference is that one calls the sun " burning eye," while
the Hovas call it the " day's eye," as do so many peoples in
Malaysia.[1]

So also the fish-eating *Anorohoro* people, a branch of the
Sihanakas in the Alaotra valley, are said to have " quite
a different dialect from them." [2] But the state-
**Malagasy
Gothamites.** ment need not be taken too seriously, because
these rustic fisherfolk, who may be called the
Gothamites of Madagascar, are supposed, by their scornful
neighbours, to do everything " contrariwise." Of them it is
told that once when cooking eggs they boiled them for hours
to make them soft, and then finding they got harder and
harder threw them away as unfit for food. Others having
only one slave, who could not paddle the canoe properly, cut
him in two, putting one half at the prow, the other at the
stern, and were surprised at the result. It was not to be expected that such simpletons should speak Malagasy properly,
which nevertheless is spoken with surprising uniformity by all
the Malayan and Negro or Negroid peoples alike.

In Madagascar, however, the fusion of the two races is
far less complete than is commonly supposed. Various shades
Partial Fusion of transition between the two extremes are no
of the Malayan doubt presented by the *Sakalavas* of the west,
and Negro and the *Betsimisarakas*, *Sitanakas*, and others
Races. of the east coast. But, strange to say, on the
central tableland the two seem to stand almost completely
apart, so that here the politically dominant Hovas still present
all the essential characteristics of the Oceanic Mongol, while
their southern neighbours, the *Betsileos*, as well as the *Tanalas*
and *Ibaras*, are described as " African pure and simple, allied
to the south-eastern tribes of that continent." [3]

Specially remarkable is the account given by a careful
observer, G. A. Shaw, of the Betsileos, whose " average
height is not less than six feet for the men, and a few inches
less for the women. They are large-boned and muscular, and
their colour is several degrees darker than that of the Hovas,
approaching very close to a black. The forehead is low and

---

[1] Malay *mata-ari*; Bajau *mata-lon*; Menado *mata-roū*; Salayer *mato-allo*,
all meaning literally " day's eye " (*mata, mato*=Malagasy *maso*=eye ; *ari, allo*,
etc.=day, with normal interchange of *r* and *l*).

[2] J. Sibree, *Antananarivo Annual*, 1877, p. 62.

[3] W. D. Cowan, *The Bara Land*, Antananarivo, 1881, p. 67.

broad, the nose flatter, and the lips thicker than those of their conquerors, whilst their hair is *invariably* crisp and woolly. No pure Betsileo is to be met with having the smooth long hair of the Hovas. In this, as in other points, there is a very clear departure from the Malayan type, and a close approximation to the Negro races of the adjacent continent."[1]

Now compare these brawny negroid giants with the wiry undersized Malayan Hovas. As described by A. Vouchereau,[2] their type closely resembles that of the Javanese —short stature, yellowish or light leather com- **Hova Type.** plexion, long, black, smooth and rather coarse hair, round head (85.25), flat and straight forehead, flat face, prominent cheek-bones, small straight nose, tolerably wide nostrils, small black and slightly oblique eyes, rather thick lips, slim lithesome figure, small extremities, dull restless expression, cranial capacity 1516 c.c., superior to both Negro and Sakalava.[3]

Except in respect of this high cranial capacity, the measurements of three Malagasy skulls in the Cambridge University Anatomical Museum, studied by W. L. H. Duckworth,[4] correspond fairly well with these descriptions. Thus the cephalic index of the reputed Betsimisaraka (Negroid) and that of the Betsileo (Negro) are respectively 71 and 72.4, while that of the Hova is 82.1 ; the first two, therefore, are long-haired, the third round-headed, as we should expect. But the cubic capacity of the Hova (presumably Mongoloid) is only 1315 as compared with 1450 and 1480 **The Black** of two others, presumably African Negroes. **Element from** Duckworth discusses the question whether the **Africa.** black element in Madagascar is of African or Oceanic (Melanesian-Papuan) origin, about which much diversity of opinion still prevails, and on the evidence of the few cranial specimens available he decides in favour of the African.

---

[1] " The Betsileo, Country and People," in *Antananarivo Annual*, 1877, p. 79.

[2] " Note sur l'Anthropologie de Madagascar," etc., in *L'Anthropologie*, 1897, p. 149 sq.

[3] The contrast between the two elements is drawn in a few bold strokes by Mrs Z. Colvile, who found that in the east coast districts the natives (Betsimisarakas chiefly) were black " with short, curly hair and negro type of feature, and showed every sign of being of African origin. The Hovas, on the contrary, had complexions little darker than those of the peasantry of Southern Europe, straight black hair, rather sharp features, slim figures, and were unmistakably of the Asiatic type " (*Round the Black Man's Garden*, 1893, p. 143). But even amongst the Hovas a strain of black blood is betrayed in the generally rather thick lips, and among the lower classes in the wavy hair and dark skin.

[4] *Journ. Anthr. Inst.* 1897, p. 285 sq.

Despite the low cubic capacity of Duckworth's Hova, the mental powers of these, and indeed of the Malagasy

Mental Qualities of the Malagasy. generally, are far from despicable. Before the French occupation the London Missionary Society had succeeded in disseminating Christian principles and even some degree of culture among considerable numbers both in the Hova capital and surrounding districts.

Spread of Christianity. The local press had been kept going by native compositors, who had issued quite an extensive literature both in Malagasy and English. Agricultural and industrial methods had been improved, some engineering works attempted, and the Hova craftsmen had learnt to build but not to complete houses in the European style, because, although they could master European processes, they could not, Christians though they were, get the better of the old superstitions, one of which is that the owner of a house always dies within a year of its completion. Longevity is therefore ensured by not completing it, with the curious result that the whole city looks unfinished or dilapidated. In the house where Mrs Colvile stayed, " one window was framed and glazed, the other nailed up with rough boards ; part of the stair-banister had no top-rail ; outside only a portion of the roof had been tiled ; and so on throughout."[1]

The culture has been thus summarised by T. A. Joyce.[2] Clothing is entirely vegetable, and the Malay *sarong* is found

Culture. throughout the east ; bark-cloth in the south-east and west. Hairdressing varies considerably, and among the Bara and Sakalava is often elaborate. Silver ornaments are found amongst the Antimerina and some other eastern tribes, made chiefly from European coins dating from the sixteenth century. Circumcision is universal. In the east the tribes are chiefly agricultural ; in the north, west and south, pastoral. Fishing is important among those tribes situated on coast, lake or river. Houses are all rectangular and pile-dwellings are found locally. Rice is the staple crop and the cattle are of the humped variety. The Antimerina excel the rest in all crafts. Weaving, basket-work (woven variety) and iron-working are all good ; the use of iron is said to have been unknown to the Bara and Vazimba until comparatively recent times. Pottery is poor. Carvings in the

[1] *Journ. Anthr. Inst.* 1897, p. 153.
[2] *Handbook to the Ethnological Collection, British Museum,* 1910, pp. 246–7.

round (men and animals) are found amongst the Sakalava and Bara, in relief (arabesques, etc.) among the Betsileo and others.   Before the introduction of firearms, the spear was the universal weapon ;   bows are rare and possibly of late introduction ;   slings and the blowgun are also found.   Shields are circular, made of wood covered with hide.   The early system of government was patriarchal, and villages were independent ;   the later immigrants introduced a system of feudal monarchy with themselves as a ruling caste.   Thus the Antimerina have three main castes ; *Andriana* or nobles (*i.e.* pure-blooded descendants of the conquerors), *Hova,* or freemen (descendants of the incorporated Vazimba more or less mixed with the conquerors), and *Andevo* or slaves.   The king was regarded almost as a god.   An institution thoroughly suggestive of Malayo-Polynesian sociology is that of *fadi* or tabu, which enters into every sphere of human activity.   An indefinite creator-god was recognised, but more important were a number of spirits and fetishes, the latter with definite functions.   Signs of tree worship and of belief in transmigration are sporadic.   At the present time, half the population of the island is, at least nominally, Christian.

A good deal of fancy is displayed in the oral literature, comprising histories, or at least legends, fables, songs, riddles, and a great mass of folklore, much of which has already been rescued from oblivion by the **Malagasy Folklore.** "Malagasy Folklore Society."   Some of the stories present the usual analogies to others in widely separated lands, stories which seem to be perennial, and to crop up wherever the surface is a little disturbed by investigators. One of those in Dahle's extensive collection, entitled the "History of Andrian arisaina bonia masobonia manoro" might be described as a variant of our "Beauty and the Beast." Besides this prince with the long name, called *Bonia* "for short," there is a princess "Golden Beauty," both being of miraculous birth, but the latter a cripple and deformed, until found and wedded by Bonia.   Then she is so transfigured that the "Beast" is captivated and contrives to carry her off. Thereupon follows an extraordinary series of adventures, resulting of course in the rescue of Golden Beauty by Bonia, when everything ends happily, not only for the two lovers, but for all other people whose wives had also been abducted. These are now restored to their husbands by the hero, who vanquishes and slays the monster in a fierce fight, just as in our nursery tales of knights and dragons.

In the Philippines, where the ethnical confusion is probably greater than in any other part of Malaysia, the great bulk of the inhabitants appear to be of Indonesian and proto-Malayan stocks. Except in the southern island of Mindanao, which is still mainly Muhammadan or heathen, most of the settled populations have long been nominal Roman Catholics under a curious theocratic administration, in which the true rulers are not the civil functionaries, but the priests, and especially the regular clergy.[1] One result has been over three centuries of unstable political and social relations, ending in the occupation of the archipelago by the United States (1898). Another, with which we are here more concerned, has been such a transformation of the subtle Malayan character that those who have lived longest amongst the natives pronounce their temperament unfathomable. Having to comply outwardly with the numerous Christian observances, they seek relief in two ways, first by making the most of the Catholic ceremonial and turning the many feast-days of the calendar into occasions of revelry and dissipation, connived at if not even shared in by the padres ;[2] secondly by secretly cherishing the old beliefs and disguising their true feelings, until the opportunity is presented of throwing off the mask and declaring themselves in their true colours. A Franciscan friar, who had spent half his life amongst them, left on record that " the native is an incomprehensible phenomenon, the mainspring of whose line of thought and the guiding motive of whose actions have never yet been, and perhaps never will be, discovered. A native will serve a master satisfactorily for years, and then suddenly abscond, or commit some such hideous crime as conniving with a brigand band to murder the family and pillage the house."[3]

In fact nobody can ever tell what a Tagal, and especially a Visaya, will do at any moment. His character is a succession of surprises ; " the experience of each year brings

The Philippine Natives.

---

[1] Augustinians, Dominicans, Recollects (Friars Minor of the Strict Observance), and Jesuits.

[2] In fact there is no great parade of morality on either side, nor is it any reflection on a woman to have children by the priest.

[3] J. Foreman, *The Philippine Islands*, 1899, p. 181.

one to form fresh conclusions, and the most exact definition of such a kaleidoscopic creature is, after all, hypothetical."

After centuries of misrule, it was perhaps not surprising that no kind of sympathy was developed between the natives and the whites. Foreman tells us that everywhere in the archipelago he found mothers teaching their little ones to look on their white rulers as demoniacal beings, evil spirits, or at least something to be dreaded. "If a child cries, it is hushed by the exclamation, *Castila!* (Spaniard) ; if a white man approaches a native dwelling, the watchword always is *Castila!* and the children hasten to retreat from the dreadful object."

For administrative purposes the natives were classed in three social divisions—*Indios, Infieles,* and *Moros*—which, as aptly remarked by F. H. H. Guillemard, is "an ecclesiastical rather than a scientific classification."[1] The *Indios* were the Christian-ised and more or less cultured populations of all the towns and of the settled agricultural districts, speaking a distinct Malayo-Polynesian language of much more archaic type than the standard Malay. According to the census of 1903 the total population of the islands was 7,635,428, of whom nearly 7,000,000 were classed as civilised, and the rest as wild, including 23,000 Negritoes (*Aeta,* see p. 156). At the time of the Spanish occupation in the six-teenth century the *Visayas* of the central islands and part of Mindanao were the most advanced among the native tribes, but this distinction is now claimed for the *Tagalogs*, who form the bulk of the population in Manila and other parts of Luzon, and also in Mindanao, and whose language is gradually displacing other dialects throughout the archipelago. Other civilised tribes are the *Ilocano, Bicol, Pangasinan, Pampangan* and *Cagayan*, all of Luzon. Less civilised tribes are the *Manobo, Mandaya, Subano* and *Bagobo* of Mindanao, the *Bukidnon* of Mindanao and the central islands, the *Tagbanua* and *Batak* of Palawan, and the *Igorots* of Luzon, some of whom are industrious farmers, while among others, head-hunting is still prevalent. These have been described by A. E. Jenks in a monograph.[2] The head form is very

Three Social Groups.

The Indios.

---

[1] *Australasia,* 1894, II. p. 49.
[2] *The Bontoc Igorot,* Eth. Survey Pub. Vol. I. 1904. Further information concerning the Philippines is published in the *Census Report in* 1903, 1905 ;

variable. Of 32 men measured by Jenks the extremes of cephalic index were 91.48 and 67.48. The stature is always low, averaging 1.62 m. (5 ft. 4 in.) but with an appearance of greater height. The hair is black, straight, lank, coarse and abundant but " I doubt whether to-day an entire tribe of perfectly straight-haired primitive Malayan people exists in the archipelago." [1]

Under *Moros* (" Moors ") are comprised the Muhammadans exclusively, some of whom are Malayans (chiefly in Mindanao, Basilan, and Palawan), some true Malays (chiefly in the Sulu archipelago). Many of these are still independent, and not a few, if not actually wild, are certainly but little removed from the savage state. Yet, like the Sumatran Battas, they possess a knowledge of letters, the Sulu people using the Arabic script, as do all the Orang-Maláyu, while the Palawan natives employ a variant of the Devanagari prototype derived directly from the Javanese, as above explained. They number nearly 280,000, of whom more than one half are in Mindanao, and they form the bulk of the population in some of the islands of the Sulu archipelago.

The Moros.

Some of these Sulu people, till lately fierce sea-rovers, get baptized now and then ; but, says Foreman, " they appeared to be as much Christian as I was Mussulman." [2] They keep their harems all the same, and when asked how many gods there are, answer " four," presumably Allah plus the Athanasian Trinity. So the Ba-Fiots of Angola add crucifying to their " penal code," and so in King M'tesa's time the Baganda scrupulously kept two weekly holidays, the Mussulman Friday, and the Christian Sunday. Lofty creeds superimposed too rapidly on primitive beliefs are apt to get " mixed " ; they need time to become assimilated.

That in the aborigines of Formosa are represented both Mongol (proto-Malayan) and Indonesian elements may now probably be accepted as an established fact. The long-standing reports of Negritoes also, like the Philippine Aeta, have never been confirmed, and may be dismissed from the present consideration. Probably five-sixths of the whole population are

Malayans and Indonesians in Formosa.

Ethnological Survey Publications, 1904– ; C. A. Koeze, *Crania Ethnica Philippinica, ein Beitrag zur Anthropologie der Philippinen*, 1901– ; Henry Gannett, *People of the Philippines*, 1904 ; R. B. Bean, *The Racial Anatomy of the Philippine Islanders*, 1910 ; Fay-Cooper Cole, *Wild Tribes of Davao District, Mindanao*, 1913.
[1] A. E. Jenks, *The Bontoc Igorot*, 1904, p. 41.   [2] *Op. cit.* p. 247.

Chinese immigrants, amongst whom are a large number of Hakkas and Hok-los from the provinces of Fo-Kien and Kwang-tung.[1] They occupy all the **The Chinese Settlers.** cultivated western lowlands, which from the ethnological standpoint may be regarded as a seaward outpost of the Chinese mainland. The rest of the island, that is, the central highlands and precipitous eastern slopes, may similarly be looked on as a north-eastern outpost of Malaysia, being almost exclusively held by Indonesian and Malayan aborigines from Malaysia (especially the Philippines), with possibly some early intruders both from Polynesia and from the north (Japan). All are classed by the Chinese settlers after their usual fashion in three social divisions :—

1. The *Pepohwans* of the plains, who although called " Barbarians," are sedentary agriculturists and quite as civilised as their Chinese neighbours themselves, with whom they are gradually merging in a single ethnical group. The Pepohwans are described by P. Ibis as a fine race, very tall, and " fetishists," though the mysterious rites are left to the women. Their national feasts, dances, and other usages forcibly recall those of the Micronesians and Polynesians. They may therefore, perhaps, be regarded as early immigrants from the South Sea Islands, distinct in every respect from the true aborigines.

2. The *Sekhwans*, " Tame Savages," [2] who are also settled agriculturists, subject to the Chinese (since 1895 to the Japanese) administration, but physically distinct from all the other Formosans—light complexion, large mouth, thick lips, remarkably long and prominent teeth, weak constitution. P. Ibis suspects a strain of Dutch blood dating from the seventeenth century. This is confirmed by the old books and other curious documents found amongst them, which have given rise to so much speculation, and, it may be added, some mystification, regarding a peculiar writing system and a literature formerly current amongst the Formosan aborigines.[3]

[1] Girard de Rialle, *Rev. d'Anthrop.*, Jan. and April, 1885. These studies are based largely on the data supplied by M. Paul Ibis and earlier travellers in the island. Nothing better has since appeared except G. Taylor's valuable contributions to the *China Review* (see below). The census of 1904 gave 2,860,574 Chinese, 51,770 Japanese and 104,334 aborigines.

[2] Lit. " ripe barbarians " (*barbares mûrs*, Ibis).

[3] See facsimiles of bilingual and other MSS. from Formosa in T. de Lacouperie's *Formosa Notes on MSS., Languages, and Races*, Hertford, 1887. The whole question is here fully discussed, though the author seems unable to arrive at any definite conclusion even as to the *bona* or *mala fides* of the noted impostor George Psalmanazar.

3. The *Chinhwans*, '' Green Barbarians ''—that is, utter savages—the true independent aborigines, of whom there are an unknown number of tribes, but regarding whom the Chinese possess but little definite information.   Not so their Japanese successors, one of whom, Kisak Tamai,[1] tells us that the Chinhwans show a close resemblance to the Malays of the Malay Peninsula and also to those of the Philippines, and in some respects to the Japanese themselves.   When dressed like Japanese and mingling with Japanese women, they can hardly be distinguished from them.   The vendetta is still rife amongst many of the ruder tribes, and such is their traditional hatred of the Chinese intruders that no one can either be tattooed or permitted to wear a bracelet until he has carried off a Celestial head or two.   In every household there is a frame or bracket on which these heads are mounted, and some of their warriors can proudly point to over seventy of such trophies.   It is a relief to hear that with their new Japanese masters they have sworn friendship, these new rulers of the land being their '' brothers and sisters.''   The oath of eternal alliance is taken by digging a hole in the ground, putting a stone in it, throwing earth at each other, then covering the stone with the earth, all of which means that '' as the stone in the ground keeps sound, so do we keep our word unbroken.''

It is interesting to note that this Japanese ethnologist's remarks on the physical resemblances of the aborigines are

Racial
Affinities.

fully in accord with those of European observers.   Thus to Hamy '' they recalled the Igorrotes of North Luzon, as well as the Malays of Singapore.'' [2]   G. Taylor also, who has visited several of the wildest groups in the southern and eastern districts [3] (*Tipuns, Paiwans, Diaramocks, Nickas, Amias* and many others), traces some '' probably '' to Japan (Tipuns) ; others to Malaysia (the cruel, predatory Paiwan head-hunters) ; and others to the Liu-Kiu archipelago (the Pepohwans now of Chinese speech).   He describes the Diaramocks as the most dreaded of all the

---

[1] *Globus*, 70, p. 93 sq.

[2] '' Les Races Malaïques,'' etc., in *L'Anthropologie*, 1896.

[3] '' The Aborigines of Formosa,'' in *China Review*, XIV. p. 198 sq., also XVI. No. 3 ('' A Ramble through Southern Formosa ''). The services rendered by this intelligent observer to Formosan ethnology deserve more general recognition than they have hitherto received. See also the *Report on the control of the Aborigines of Formosa*, Bureau of Aboriginal Affairs, Formosa, 1911.

southern groups, but doubts whether the charge of cannibalism brought against them by their neighbours is quite
justified.

Whether the historical Malays from Singapore or elsewhere, as above suggested, are really represented in Formosa
may be doubted, since no survivals either of Hindu or
Muhammadan rites appear to have been detected amongst
the aborigines. It is of course possible that they may have
reached the island at some remote time, and since relapsed
into savagery, from which the Orang-laut were never very
far removed. But in the absence of proof, it will be safer to
regard all the wild tribes as partly of Indonesian, partly of
proto-Malayan origin.

This view is also in conformity with the character of the
numerous Formosan dialects, whose affinities are either with
the Gyarung and others of the Asiatic Indonesian
tongues, or else with the Austronesian organic   Linguistic
speech generally, but not specially with any   Affinities.
particular member of that family, least of all with the comparatively recent standard Malay. Thus Arnold Schetelig
points out that only about a sixth part of the Formosan
vocabulary taken generally corresponds with modern Malay.[1]
The analogies of all the rest must be sought in the various
branches of the Oceanic stock language, and in the Gyarung
and the non-Chinese tongues of Eastern China.[2] Formosa
thus presents a curious ethnical and linguistic connecting link
between the Continental and Oceanic populations.

In the Nicobar archipelago are distinguished two ethnical
groups, the coast people, *i.e.* the *Nicobarese*[3] proper, and the
Shom Pen, aborigines of the less accessible inland
districts in Great Nicobar. But the distinction   The
appears to be rather social than racial, and we   Nicobarese.
may now conclude with E. H. Man that all the islanders
belong essentially to the Mongolic division, the inlanders
representing the pure type, the others being " descended from

[1] " Sprachen der Ureinwohner Formosa's," in *Zeitschr. f. Völkerpsychologie*, etc.,
v. p. 437 sq. This anthropologist found to his great surprise that the Polynesian
and Maori skulls in the London College of Surgeons presented striking analogies
with those collected by himself in Formosa. Here at least is a remarkable
harmony between speech and physical characters.

[2] De Lacouperie, *op. cit.* p. 73.

[3] The natives of course know nothing of this word, and speak of their island
homes as *Mattai*, a vague term applied equally to land, country, village, and even
the whole world.

a mongrel Malay stock, the crosses being probably in the majority of cases with Burmese and occasionally with natives of the opposite coast of Siam, and perchance also in remote times with such of the Shom Pen as may have settled in their midst." [1]

Among the numerous usages which point to an Indo-Chinese and Oceanic connection are pile-dwellings ; the chewing of betel, which appears to be here mixed with some earthy substance causing a dental incrustation so thick as even to prevent the closing of the lips ; distention of the ear-lobe by wooden cylinders ; aversion from the use of milk ; and the *couvade*, as amongst some Bornean Dayaks. The language, which has an extraordinarily rich phonetic system (as many as 25 consonantal and 35 vowel sounds), is polysyllabic and untoned, like the Austronesian, and the type also seems to resemble the Oceanic more than the Continental Mongol subdivision. Mean height 5 ft. 3 in. (Shom Pen one inch less) ; nose wide and flat ; eyes rather obliquely set ; cheek-bones prominent ; features flat, though less so than in the normal Malayan ; complexion mostly a yellowish or reddish brown (Shom Pen dull brown) ; hair a dark rusty brown, rarely quite black, straight, though not seldom wavy and even ringletty, but Shom Pen generally quite straight.

On the other hand they approach nearer to the Burmese in their mental characters ; in their frank, independent spirit, inquisitiveness, and kindness towards their women, who enjoy complete social equality, as in Burma ; and lastly in their universal belief in spirits called *iwi* or *síya*, who, like the *nats* of Indo-China, cause sickness and death unless scared away or appeased by offerings. Like the Burmese, also, they place a piece of money in the mouth or against the cheek of a corpse before burial, to help in the other world.

One of the few industries is the manufacture of a peculiar kind of rough painted pottery, which is absolutely confined to the islet of Chowra, 5 miles north of Teressa. The reason of this restriction is explained by a popular legend, according to which in remote ages the Great Unknown decreed that, on pain of sudden death, an earthquake, or some such calamity, the making of earthenware was to be carried on only in Chowra, and all the work of preparing the clay, moulding

---

[1] " The Nicobar Islanders," in *Journ. Anthr. Inst.* 1889, p. 354 sq.   Cf. C. B. Kloss, *In the Andamans and Nicobars*, 1903.

and firing the pots, was to devolve on the women. Once, a long time ago, one of these women, when on a visit in another island, began, heedless of the divine injunction, to make a vessel, and fell dead on the spot. Thus was confirmed the tradition, and no attempt has since been made to infringe the " Chowra monopoly." [1]

All things considered, it may be inferred that the archipelago was originally occupied by primitive peoples of Malayan stock now represented by the Shom Pen of Great Nicobar, and was afterwards re-settled on the coastlands by Indo-Chinese and Malayan intruders, who intermingled, and either extirpated or absorbed, or else drove to the interior the first occupants. Nicobar thus resembles Formosa in its intermediate position between the continental and Oceanic Mongol populations. Another point of analogy is the absence of Negritoes from both of these insular areas, where anthropologists had confidently anticipated the presence of a dark element like that of the Andamanese and Philippine Aeta.

[1] E. H. Man, *Journ. Anthr. Inst.* 1894, p. 21.

CHAPTER VIII

THE NORTHERN MONGOLS

Domain of the Mongolo-Turki Section—Early Contact with Caucasic Peoples—Primitive Man in Siberia—and Mongolia—Early Man in Korea and Japan—in Finland and East Europe—Early Man in Babylonia—The Sumerians—The *Akkadians*—Babylonian Chronology—Elamite Origins—Historical Records—Babylonian Religion—Social System—General Culture—The Mongols Proper—Physical Type—Ethnical and Administrative Divisions—Buddhism—The Tunguses—Cradle and Type—Mental Characters—Shamanism—The Manchus—Origins and Early Records—Type—The Dauri—Mongolo-Turki Speech—Language and Racial Characters—Mongol and Manchu Script—The Yukaghirs—A Primitive Writing System—Chukchis and Koryaks—Chukchi and Eskimo Relations—Type and Social State—Koryaks and Kamchadales—The Gilyaks—The Koreans—Ethnical Elements—Korean Origins and Records—Religion—The Korean Script—The Japanese—Origins—Constituent Elements—The Japanese Type—Japanese and Liu-Kiu Islanders—Their Languages and Religions—Cult of the Dead—Shintoism and Buddhism.

CONSPECTUS.

Present Range. *The Northern Hemisphere from Japan to Lapland, and from the Arctic Ocean to the Great Wall and* Tibet ; *Aralo-Caspian Basin ; Parts of Irania ;* **Distribution.** *Asia Minor ; Parts of East Russia, Balkan Peninsula, and Lower Danube.*

Hair, *generally the same as South Mongol, but in Mongolo-Caucasic transitional groups brown, chestnut, and even towy or light flaxen, also wavy and ringletty ; beard* **Physical Characters.** *mostly absent except amongst the Western Turks and some Koreans.*

Colour, *light or dirty yellowish amongst all true Mongols and Siberians ; very variable (white, sallow, swarthy) in the transitional groups (Finns, Lapps, Magyars, Bulgars, Western Turks), and many Manchus and Koreans ; in Japan the un-exposed parts of the body also white.*

Skull, *highly brachycephalic in the true Mongol (80 to 85) ; variable (sub-brachy and sub-dolicho) in most transitional groups and even some Siberians (Ostyaks and Voguls 77).* **Jaws, cheek-bones, nose,** *and* **eyes** *much the same as in South*

254

Mongols ; but nose often large and straight, and eyes straight, greyish, or even blue in Finns, Manchus, Koreans, and some other Mongolo-Caucasians.

Stature, *usually short (below 1.68 m., 5 ft. 6 in.), but many Manchus and Koreans tall, 1.728 m. to 1.778 m. (5 ft. 8 or 10 in.).* **Lips, arms, legs,** *and* **feet,** *usually the same as South Mongols ; but Japanese legs disproportionately short.*

Temperament, *of all true Mongols and many Mongoloids, dull, reserved, somewhat sullen and apathetic ; but in some groups (Finns, Japanese) active and energetic ;* Mental Characters. *nearly all brave, warlike, even fierce, and capable of great atrocities, though not normally cruel ; within the historic period the character has almost everywhere undergone a marked change from a rude and ferocious to a milder and more humane disposition ; ethical tone higher than South Mongol, with more developed sense of right and wrong.*

Speech, *very uniform ; apparently only one stock language* (**Finno-Tatar** *or* **Ural-Altaic Family**) *a highly typical agglutinating form with no prefixes, but numerous postfixes attached loosely to an unchangeable root, by which their vowels are modified in accordance with subtle laws of vocalic harmony ; the chief members of the family (Finnish, Magyar, Turkish, Mongol, and especially Korean and Japanese) diverge greatly from the common prototype.*

Religion, *originally spirit-worship through a mediator* (Shaman), *perhaps everywhere, and still exclusively prevalent amongst Siberian and all other uncivilised groups ; all Mongols proper, Manchus, and Koreans nominal Buddhists ; all Turki peoples Moslem ; Japanese Buddhists and Shintoists ; Finns, Lapps, Bulgars, Magyars, and some Siberians real or nominal Christians,*

Culture, *rude and barbaric rather than savage amongst the Siberian aborigines, who are nearly all nomadic hunters and fishers with half-wild reindeer herds but scarcely any industries ; the mongols proper, Kirghiz, Uzbegs and Turkomans semi-nomadic pastors ; the Anatolian and Balkan Turks, Manchus, and Koreans settled agriculturists, with scarcely any arts or letters and no science ; Japanese, Finns, Bulgars and Magyars civilised up to, and in some respects beyond the European average (Magyar and Finnish literature, Japanese art).*

Mongol Proper. *Sharra (Eastern), Kal-* **Main Divisions.** *mak (Western), Buryat (Siberian) Mongol.*

Tungus. *Tungus proper, Manchu, Gold, Oroch, Lamut.*

Korean ; Japanese *and* **Liu-Kiu.**

Turki. *Yakut ; Kirghiz ; Uzbeg ; Taranchi ; Kara-Kalpak ; Nogai ; Turkoman ; Anatolian ; Osmanli.*

Finno-Ugrian. *Baltic Finn ; Lapp ; Samoyed ; Cheremiss ; Votyak ; Vogul ; Ostyak ; Bulgar ; Magyar.*

East Siberian. *Yukaghir ; Chukchi ; Koryak ; Kamchadale ; Gilyak.*

By " Northern Mongols " are here to be understood all those branches of the Mongol Division of mankind which are usually comprised under the collective geographical expression *Ural-Altaic*, to which corresponds the ethnical designation *Mongolo-Tatar*, or more properly *Mongolo-Turki*.[1] Their domain is roughly separated from that of the Southern Mongols (Chap. VI.) by the Great Wall and the Kuen-lun range, beyond which it spreads out westwards over most of Western Asia, and a considerable part of North Europe, with many scattered groups in Central and South Russia, the Balkan Peninsula, and the Middle Danube basin. In the extreme north their territory stretches from the shores of the Pacific with Japan and parts of Sakhalin continually westwards across Korea, Siberia, Central and North Russia to Finland and Lapland. But its southern limits can be indicated only approximately by a line drawn from the Kuen-lun range westwards along the northern escarpments of the Iranian plateau, and round the southern shores of the Caspian to the Mediterranean. This line, however, must be drawn in such a way as to include Afghan Turkestan, much of the North Persian and Caucasian steppes, and nearly the whole of Asia Minor, while excluding Armenia, Kurdestan, and Syria.

Nor is it to be supposed that even within these limits the North Mongol territory is everywhere continuous. In East Europe especially, where they are for the most part comparatively recent intruders, the Mongols are found only in isolated and vanishing groups in the Lower and Middle Volga basin, the Crimea, and the North Caucasian steppe, and in more compact bodies in Rumelia, Bulgaria, and Hungary. Throughout all these districts, however, the process of absorption or assimilation to

Domain of the Northern Mongols.

Early Contact with Caucasic Peoples.

---

[1] As fully explained in *Eth.* p. 303.

the normal European physical type is so far completed that many of the Nogai and other Russian "Tartars," as they are called, the Volga and Baltic Finns, the Magyars, and Osmanli Turks, would scarcely be recognised as members of the North Mongol family but for their common Finno-Turki speech, and the historic evidence by which their original connection with this division is established beyond all question.

In Central Asia also (North Irania, the Aralo-Caspian and Tarim basins) the Mongols have been in close contact with Caucasic peoples probably since the New Stone Age, and here intermediate types have been developed, by which an almost unbroken transition has been brought about between the yellow and the white races.

During recent years much light has been shed on the physiographical conditions of Central Asia in early times. Stein's[1] explorations in 1900–1 and 1906–8 in Chinese Turkestan, the Pumpelly Expeditions[2] in 1903 and 1904 in Russian Turkestan, the travels of Sven Hedin[3] in 1899–1902, and 1906–8, of Carruthers[4] in N.W. Mongolia, and the researches of Ellsworth Huntington[5] (a member of the first Pumpelly Expedition) in 1905–7 all bear testimony to the variation in climate which the districts of Central Asia have undergone since glacial times. There has been a general trend towards arid conditions, alternating with periods of greater humidity, when tracts, now deserted, were capable of maintaining a dense population. Abundant evidence of man's occupation has been found in delta oases formed by snow-fed mountain streams, or on the banks of vanished rivers, where now-a-days all is desolation, though, as T. Peisker[6] points out, climate was not the sole or even the main factor in many areas. In some places, as at Merv, the earliest occupation was only a few centuries before the Christian era, but at Anau near Askhabad some 300 miles east of the Caspian, explored by the Pumpelly Expedition, the earliest strata contained remains of Stone Age culture. The North

Primitive Man in Siberia and Mongolia.

[1] Mark Aurel Stein, *Sand-buried Cities of Khotan*, 1903, and *Geog. Journ.*, July, Sept. 1909.
[2] R. Pumpelly, *Explorations in Turkestan*, 1905, and *Explorations in Turkestan ; Expedition of 1904*, 1908.
[3] Sven Hedin, *Scientific Results of a Journey in Central Asia, 1899–1902*, 1906, and *Geog. Journ.*, April, 1909.
[4] Douglas Carruthers, *Unknown Mongolia*, 1913 (with bibliography).
[5] Ellsworth Huntington, *The Pulse of Asia*, 1910.
[6] "The Asiatic Background," *Cambridge Medieval History*, Vol. I. 1911.

Kurgan or tumulus, rising some 40 or 50 feet above the plain, showed a definite stratification of structures in sun-dried bricks, raised by successive generations of occupants. H. Schmidt, who was in charge of the excavations, was able to collect a valuable series of potsherds, showing a gradual evolution in form, technique and ornamentation, from the earliest to the latest periods. One point of great significance for establishing cultural if not physical relationships in this obscure region is the resemblance between the geometrical designs on pots of the early period and similar pottery found by MM. Gautier and Lampre [1] at Mussian, and by M. J. de Morgan [1] at Susa, while clay figurines from the South Kurgan (copper culture) are clearly of Babylonian type, the influence of which is seen much later in terra-cotta figurines discovered by Stein [2] at Yotkan.

With the progress of archaeological research, it becomes daily more evident that the whole of the North Mongol domain, from Finland to Japan, has passed through the Stone and Metal Ages, like most other habitable parts of the globe. During his wanderings in Siberia and Mongolia in the early nineties, Hans Leder [3] came upon countless prehistoric stations, kurgans (barrows), stone circles, and many megalithic monuments of various types. In West Siberia the barrows, which consist solely of earth without any stone-work, are by the present inhabitants called *Chudskiye Kurgani*, " Chudish Graves," and, as in North Russia, this term " Chude " is ascribed to a now vanished unknown race which formerly inhabited the land. To them, as to the " Toltecs " in Central America, all ancient monuments are credited, and while some regard them as prehistoric Finns, others identify them with the historic Scythians, the Scythians of Herodotus.

There are reasons, however, for thinking that the Chudes may represent an earlier race, the men of the Stone Age, who, migrating from north Europe eastwards, had reached the Tom valley (which drains to the Obi) before the extinction of the mammoth, and later spread over the whole of northern Asia, leaving everywhere evidence of their presence in the megalithic monuments now being daily brought to light in East Siberia,

---

[1] *Mémoires de la Délégation en Perse; Recherches archéologiques* (from 1899).
[2] *Sand-buried Cities of Khotan*, 1903.
[3] " Ueber Alte Grabstätten in Sibirien und der Mongolei," in *Mitt. d. Anthrop. Ges.*, Vienna, 1895, xxv. 9.

Mongolia, Korea, and Japan.   This view receives support from the characters of two skulls found in 1895 by A. P. Mostitz in one of the five prehistoric stations on the left bank of the Sava affluent of the Selenga river, near Ust-Kiakta in Trans-Baikalia.   They differ markedly from the normal Buryat (Siberian Mongol) type, recalling rather the long-shaped skulls of the South Russian kurgans, with cephalic indices 73.2 and 73.5, as measured by M. J. D. Talko-Hryncewicz.[1]   Thus, in the very heart of the Mongol domain, the characteristically round-headed race would appear to have been preceded, as in Europe, by a long-headed type.

In East Siberia, and especially in the Lake Baikal region, Leder found extensive tracts strewn with kurgans, many of which have already been explored, and their contents deposited in the Irkutsk museum.   Amongst these are great numbers of stone implements, and objects made of bone and mammoth tusks, besides carefully worked copper ware, betraying technical skill and some artistic taste in the designs.   In Trans-Baikalia, still farther east, with the kurgans are associated the so-called *Kameni Babi*, " Stone Women," monoliths rough-hewn in the form of human figures.   Many of these monoliths bear inscriptions, which, however, appear to be of recent date (mostly Buddhist prayers and formularies), and are not to be confounded with the much older rock inscriptions deciphered by W. Thomsen through Turki language.

Continuing his investigations in Mongolia proper, Leder here also discovered earthen kurgans, which, however, differed from those of Siberia by being for the most part surmounted either with circular or rectangular stone structures, or else with monoliths.   They are called *Kürüktsír* by the present inhabitants, who hold them in great awe, and never venture to touch them.   Unfortunately strangers also are unable to examine their contents, all disturbance of the ground with spade or shovel being forbidden under pain of death by the Chinese officials, for fear of awakening the evil spirits, now slumbering peacefully below the surface.   The Siberian burial mounds have yielded no bronze, a fact which indicates considerable antiquity, although no date can be set for its introduction into these regions.   Better evidence of antiquity is found in the climatic changes resulting in recent desiccation,

---

[1] Th. Volkov, in *L'Anthropologie*, 1896, p. 82.

which must have taken place here as elsewhere, for the burials bear witness to the existence of a denser population than could be supported at the present time.[1]

Such an antiquity is indeed required to explain the spread of neolithic remains to the Pacific seaboard, and especially

Early Man in Korea and Japan.

to Korea and Japan. In Korea W. Gowland examined a dolmen 30 miles from Seul, which he describes and figures,[2] and which is remarkable especially for the disproportionate size of the capstone, a huge undressed megalith 14½ by over 13 feet. He refers to four or five others, all in the northern part of the peninsula, and regards them as "intermediate in form between a cist and a dolmen." But he thinks it probable that they were never covered by mounds, but always stood as monuments above ground, in this respect differing from the Japanese, the majority of which are all buried in tumuli. In some of their features these present a curious resemblance to the Brittany structures, but no stone implements appear to have been found in any of the burial mounds, and the Japanese chambered tombs, according to Hamada, Professor of Archaeology in Kyoto University, are usually attributed to the Iron age (fifth to seventh centuries A.D.).[3]

In many districts Japan contains memorials of a remote past—shell mounds, cave-dwellings, and in Yezo certain pits, which are not occupied by the present Ainu population, but are by them attributed to the *Koro-pok-guru*, "People of the Hollows," who occupied the land before their arrival, and lived in huts built over these pits. Similar remains on an islet near Nemuro on the north-east coast of Yezo are said by the Japanese to have belonged to the *Kobito*, a dwarfish race exterminated by the Ainu, hence apparently identical with the Koro-pok-guru. They are associated by John Milne with some primitive peoples of the Kurile Islands, Sakhalin, and Kamchatka, who, like the Eskimo of the American coast, had extended formerly much farther south than at present.

---

[1] Too much stress must not, however, be laid upon the theory of gradual desiccation as a factor in depopulation. There are many causes such as earthquake, water-spouts, shifting of currents, neglect of irrigation and, above all, the work of enemies to account for the sand-buried ruins of populous cities in Central Asia. See T. Peisker, " The Asiatic Background," *Cambridge Medieval History*, Vol. I. 1911, p. 326.

[2] *Journ. Anthr. Inst.* 1895, p. 318 sq.

[3] Cf. *Archæologia Cambrensis*, 6th Ser. XIV. Part 1, 1914, p. 131, and *Zeitschr. f. Ethnol.* 1910, p. 601.

In a kitchen-midden, 330 by 200 feet, near Shiidzuka in the province of Ibaraki, the Japanese antiquaries S. Yagi and M. Shinomura [1] have found numerous objects belonging to the Stone Age of Japan. Amongst them were flint implements, worked bones, ashes, pottery, and a whole series of clay figures of human beings. The finders suggest that these remains may have belonged to a homogeneous race of the Stone Period, who, however, were not the ancestors of the Ainu—hitherto generally regarded as the first inhabitants of Japan. In the national records vague reference is made to other aborigines, such as the "Long Legs," and the "Eight Wild Tribes," described as the enemies of the first Japanese settlers in Kiu-shiu, and reduced by Jimmu Tenno, the semi-mythical founder of the present dynasty; the *Ebisu*, who are probably to be identified with the Ainu; and the *Seki-Manzi*, "Stone-Men," also located in the southern island of Kiu-shiu. The last mentioned, of whom, however, little further is known, seem to have some claim to be associated with the above described remains of early man in Japan.[2]

In the extreme west the present Mongol peoples, being quite recent intruders, can in no way be connected with the abundant prehistoric relics daily brought to light in that region (South Russia, the Balkan Penin-sula, Hungary). The same remark applies even to Finland itself, which was at one time supposed to be the cradle of the Finnish people, but is now shown to have been first occupied by Germanic tribes. From an exhaustive study of the bronze-yielding tumuli A. Hackman [3] concludes that the population of the Bronze Period was Teutonic, and in this he agrees both with Montelius and with W. Thomsen. The latter holds on linguistic grounds that at the beginning of the new era the Finns still dwelt east of the Gulf of Finland, whence they moved west in later times.

Early Man in Finland and East Europe.

It is unfortunate that, owing probably to the character of the country, remains of the Stone Age in Babylonia are wanting so that no comparison can yet be made with the neolithic cultures of Egypt and the Aegean. The constant floods to which Babylonia was ever subject swept away all traces of early occupations until the advent of the Sumerians, who built

---

[1] " Zur Prähistorik Japans," *Globus*, 1896, No. 10.
[2] The best account of the archaeology of Japan will be found in *Prehistoric Japan*, by N. G. Munro, 1912.
[3] *Die Bronzezeit Finnlands*, Helsingfors, 1897.

their cities on artificial mounds. The question of Akkado-Sumerian [1] origins is by no means clear, for many important cities are unexplored and even unidentified, but the general trend of recent opinion may be noted. The linguistic problem is peculiarly complicated by the fact that almost all the Sumerian texts show evidence of Semitic influence, and consist to a great extent of religious hymns and incantations which often appear to be merely translations of Semitic ideas turned by Semitic priests into the formal religious Sumerian language. J. Halévy, indeed, followed by others, regarded Sumerian as no true language, but merely a priestly system of cryptography,[2] based on Semitic. As regards linguistic affinities, K. A. Hermann [3] endeavoured to establish a connection between the early texts and Ural-Altaic, more especially with Ugro-Finnish. A more recent suggestion that the language is of Indo-European origin and structure rests on equally slight resemblances. The comparison with Chinese has already been noticed. J. D. Prince [4] utters a word of caution against comparing ancient texts with idioms of more recent peoples of Western Asia, in spite of many tempting resemblances, and claims that until further light has been shed on the problem Sumerian should be regarded as standing quite alone, " a prehistoric philological remnant."

Early Man in Babylonia.

E. Meyer [5] claims for the Sumerians not only linguistic but also physical isolation. The Sumerian type as represented on the monuments shows a narrow pointed nose, with straight bridge and small nostrils, cheeks and lips not fleshy, like the Semites, with prominent cheek-bones, small mouth, narrow lips finely curved, the lower jaw very short, with angular sharply projecting chin, oblique Mongolian eyes, low forehead, usually sloping away directly from the root of the nose. In fact the nose has almost the appearance of a bird's beak, projecting far in advance of mouth and chin, while the forehead almost disappears. The hair

The Sumerians.

---

[1] " Akkadian," first applied by Rawlinson to the non-Semitic texts found at Nineveh, is still often used by English writers in place of the more correct *Sumerian*, the Akkadians being now shown to be Semitic immigrants into Northern Babylonia (p. 264).

[2] Cf. L. W. King, *History of Sumer and Akkad*, 1910, pp. 5, 6.

[3] *Ueber die Summerische Sprache*, Paper read at the Russian Archaeological Congress, Riga, 1896.

[4] " Sumer and Sumerian," *Ency. Brit.* 1911, with references.

[5] *Geschichte des Altertums*, I. 2, 2nd ed. 1909, p. 404.

and beard are closely shaven. The Sumerians were undoubtedly a warlike people, fighting not like the Semites in
loosely extended battle array, but in close phalanx, their large
shields protecting their bodies from neck to feet, forming
a rampart beyond which projected the inclined spears of the
foremost rank. Battle axe and javelin were also used. Helmets
protected head and neck. Besides lance or spear the royal
leaders carried a curved throwing weapon, formed of three
strands bound together at intervals with thongs of leather or
bands of metal ; this seems to have developed later into a sign
of authority and hence into a sceptre. The bow, the typical
weapon of the Semites and the mountainous people to the east,
was unrepresented. The gods carried clubs with stone heads.
It is important to notice that, in direct contrast to the
Sumerians themselves, their gods had abundant hair on their
heads, carefully curled and dressed, and a long curly beard on
the chin, though cheeks and lips were closely shaven ; these
fashions recall those of the Semites. Thus, although the
general view is to regard the Sumerians as the autochtones and
the Semites as the later intruders in Babylonia, the Semitic
character of the Sumerian gods points to an opposite conclusion.
But the time has not yet come for any definite conclusion
to be reached. All that can be said is that according to our
present knowledge the assumption that the earliest population
was Sumerian and that the Semites were the conquering
intruders is only slightly more probable than the reverse.[1]

Recent archaeological discoveries make Sumerian origins
a little clearer. Explorations in Central Asia (as mentioned
above, p. 257) show that districts once well watered, and
capable of supporting a large population, have been subject to
periods of excessive drought, and this no doubt is the prime
cause of the racial unrest which has ever been characteristic
of the dwellers in these regions. A cycle of drought may well
have prompted the Sumerian migration of the fourth millennium B.C., as it is shown to have prompted the later invasions
of the last two thousand years.[2] Although there is no evidence
to connect the original home of the Sumerians with any of the

---

[1] E. Meyer, *Geschichte des Altertums*, I. 2, 2nd ed. 1909, p. 406. L. W. King
(*History of Sumer and Akkad*, 1910) discusses Meyer's arguments and points out
that the earliest Sumerian gods appear to be free from Semitic influence (p. 51).
He is inclined, however, to regard the Sumerians as displacing an earlier Semitic
people (Hutchinson's *History of the Nations*, 1914, pp. 221 and 229).
[2] Ellsworth Huntington, *The Pulse of Asia*, 1910, p. 382.

oases yet excavated in Central Asia, yet signs of cultural contact are not wanting, and it may safely be inferred that their civilisation was evolved in some region to the east of the Euphrates valley before their entrance into Babylonia.[1]

Since Semitic influence was first felt in the north of Babylonia, at Akkad, it is assumed that the immigration was **The Akkadians.** from the north-west from Arabia by way of the Syrian coastlands, and in this case also the impulse may have been the occurrence of an arid period in the centre of the Arabian continent. The Semites are found not as barbarian invaders, but as a highly cultivated people. They absorbed several cultural elements of the Sumerians, notably their script, and were profoundly influenced by Sumerian religion. The Akkadians are represented with elaborately curled hair and beard, and hence, in contradistinction to the shaven Sumerians, are referred to as "the black-headed ones." Their chief weapon was the bow, but they had also lances and battle axes. As among the Sumerians the sign of kingship was a boomerang-like sceptre.[2] Except for Babylon and Sippar, which throw little light on the early periods, no systematic excavation has been undertaken in northern Babylonia, and the site of Akkad is still unidentified.

The chronology of this early age of Babylonia is much disputed. The very high dates of 5000 or 6000 B.C. formerly **Babylonian Chronology.** assigned by many writers to the earliest remains of the Sumerians and the Babylonian Semites, depended to a great extent on the statement of Nabonidus (556 B.C.) that 3200 years separated his own age from that of Naram-Sin, the son of Sargon of Agade ; for to Sargon, on this statement alone, a date of 3800 has usually been assigned.[3] This date presents many difficulties, leaving many centuries unrepresented by any royal names or records. Even the suggested emendation of the text reducing the estimate by a thousand years is not generally acceptable. Most authorities hesitate to date any Babylonian records before 3000 B.C.[4] and agree that the time has not arrived for fixing any definite dates for the early period.

[1] L. W. King, *History of Sumer and Akkad*, 1910, p. 357.
[2] E. Meyer, *Geschichte des Altertums*, I. 2, 2nd ed. 1909, p. 463.
[3] L. W. King, *History of Sumer and Akkad*, 1910, p. 61, and the article, "Chronology. Babylonia and Assyria," *Ency. Brit.* 1911. Cf. also E. Meyer, *Geschichte des Altertums*, I. 2, 2nd ed. 1909, §§ 329 and 383.
[4] The cylinder-seals and tablets of Fara, excavated by Koldewey, Andrae and Noeldeke in 1902–3 may go back to 3400 B.C. Cf. L. W. King, *loc. cit.* p. 65.

Despite the legendary matter associated with his memory, Shar-Gani-sharri, commonly called Sargon of Akkad, about 2500 B.C. (Meyer), 2650 B.C. (King), was beyond question a historical person though it seems that there has been some confusion with Sharru-gi, or Sharrukîn, also called Sargon, earliest king of Kish.[1] Tradition records how his mother, a royal princess, concealed his birth by placing him in a rush basket closed with bitumen and sending him adrift on the stream, from which he was rescued by Akki the water-carrier, who brought him up as his own child. The incident, about which there is nothing miraculous, presents a curious parallel to, if it be not the source of, similar tales related of Moses, Cyrus, and other ancient leaders of men. Sargon also tells us that he ruled from his capital, Agade, for 45 years over Upper and Lower Mesopotamia, governed the black-headed ones, as the Akkads are constantly called, rode in bronze chariots over rugged lands, and made expeditions thrice to the sea-coast. The expeditions are confirmed by inscriptions from Syria, though the cylinder of his son, Naram-Sin, found by Cesnola in Cyprus, is now regarded as of later date.[2] As they also penetrated to Sinai their influence appears to have extended over the whole of Syria and North Arabia. They erected great structures at Nippur, which was at that time so ancient that Naram-Sin's huge brick platform stood on a mass 30 feet thick of the accumulated debris of earlier buildings. Among the most interesting of recent discoveries at Nippur are pre-Semitic tablets containing accounts similar to those recorded in the book of Genesis, from which in some cases the latter have clearly been derived. The " Deluge Fragment " published in 1910 relates the warning given by the god Ea to Utnapishtim, the Babylonian Noah, and the directions for building a ship by means of which he and his family may escape, together with the beasts of the field and the birds of heaven.[3] A still later discovery agrees more closely with the Bible version, giving the name of the one pious man as Tagtog, Semitic Nûhu, and assigning nine months as the period of the duration of the flood. The same tablet also contains an account of the

---

[1] C. H. W. Johns, *Ancient Babylonia*, 1913, regards Sharrukîn as " Sargon of Akkad," p. 39.

[2] L. W. King, *History of Sumer and Akkad*, 1910, pp. 234, 343, where the seal is referred to a period not much earlier than the First Dynasty of Babylon.

[3] H. V. Hilprecht, *The Babylonian Expedition of the University of Pennsylvania*, Series D, Vol. v. 1. 1910.

Fall of Man ; but it is Noah, not Adam, who is tempted and falls, and the forbidden fruit is cassia.[1]

Sennacherib's grandson, Ashurbanipal, who belongs to the late Assyrian empire when the centre of power had been shifted from Babylonia to Nineveh, has left re-corded on his brick tablets how he overran Elam and destroyed its capital, Susa (645 B.C.). He states that from this place he brought back the effigy of the goddess Nana, which had been carried away from her temple at Erech by an Elamite king by whom Akkad had been con-quered 1635 years before, *i.e.* 2280 B.C. Over Akkad Elam ruled 300 years, and it was a king of this dynasty, Khudur-Lagamar, who has been identified by T. G. Pinches with the "Chedorlaomer, king of Elam" routed by Abraham (Gen. xiv. 14-17).[2] Thus is explained the presence of Elamites at this time so far west as Syria, their own seat being amid the Kurdish mountains in the Upper Tigris basin.

Elamite Origins.

The Elamites do not appear to have been of the same stock as the Sumerians. They are described as peaceful, in-dustrious, and skilful husbandmen, with a surprising knowledge of irrigating processes. The non-Semitic language shows possible connections with Mitanni.[3] Yet the type would appear to be on the whole rather Semitic, judging at least from the large arched nose and thick beard of the Susian god, Ramman, brought by Ashurbanipal out of Elam, and figured in Layard's *Monuments of Nineveh*, 1st Series, Plate 65. This, however, may be ex-plained by the fact that the Elamites were subdued at an early date by intruding Semites, although they afterwards shook off the yoke and became strong enough to conquer Mesopo-tamia and extend their expeditions to Syria and the Jordan. The capital of Elam was the renowned city of Susa (Shushan, whence Susiana, the modern Khuzistan). Recent

Historical Records.

---

[1] See *The Times*, June 24, 1914.

[2] "Babylonia and Elam Four Thousand Years Ago," in *Knowledge*, May 1, 1896, p. 116 sq. and elsewhere.

[3] The term "Elam" is said to have the same meaning as "Akkad" (*i.e.* High-land) in contradistinction to "Sumer" (Lowland). It should be noted that neither Akkad nor Sumer occurs in the oldest texts, where Akkad is called *Kish* from the name of its capital, and Sumer *Kiengi* (*Kengi*), probably a general name meaning "the land." Kish has been identified with the Kush of Gen. x., one of the best abused words in Palethnology. For this identification, however, there is some ground, seeing that Kush is mentioned in the closest connection with "Babel, and Erech, and Accad, and Calneh, in the land of Shinar" (Mesopotamia), *v.* 10.

excavations show that the settlement dates from neolithic times.[1]

Even after the capture of Susa by Ashurbanipal, Elam again rose to great power under Cyrus the Great, who, how-ever, was no Persian adventurer, as stated by Herodotus, but the legitimate Elamite ruler, as inscribed on his cylinder and tablet now in the British Museum :—" Cyrus, the great king, the king of Babylon, the king of Sumir and Akkad, the king of the four zones, the son of Kambyses, the great king, the king of Elam, the grandson of Cyrus the great king," who by the favour of Merodach has overcome the black-headed people (*i.e.* the Akkads) and at last entered Babylon in peace. On an earlier cylinder Nabonidus, last king of Babylon, tells us how this same Cyrus subdued the Medes—here called *Mandas*, " Barbarians "—and captured their king Astyages and his capital Ekbatana. But although Cyrus, hitherto supposed to be a Persian and a Zoroastrian monotheist, here appears as an Elamite and a polytheist, " it is pretty certain that although descended from Elamite kings, these were [at that time] kings of Persian race, who, after the destruction of the old [Elamite] monarchy by Ashurbanipal, had established a new dynasty at the city of Susa. Cyrus always traces his descent from Achæmenes, the chief of the leading Persian clan of Pasar-gadæ." [2] Hence although wrong in speaking of Cyrus as an adventurer, Herodotus rightly calls him a Persian, and at this late date Elam itself may well have been already Aryanised in speech,[3] while still retaining its old Sumerian religion. The

[1] J. de Morgan, *Mémoires de la Délégation en Perse*, 1899–1906.
[2] S. Laing, *Human Origins*, p. 74.
[3] And it has remained so ever since, the present Lur and Bakhtiari inhabitants of Susiana speaking, not the standard Neo-Persian, but dialects of the ruder Kurdish branch of the Iranian family, as if they had been Aryanised from Media, the capital of which was Ekbatana. We have here, perhaps, a clue to the origin of the Medes themselves, who were certainly the above-mentioned Mandas of Nabonidus, their capital being also the same Ekbatana. Now Sayce (*Academy*, Sept. 7, 1895, p. 189) identified the Kimmerians with these Manda nomads, whose king Tukdammé (Tugdammé) was the Lygdanis of Strabo (I. 3, 16), who led a horde of Kimmerians into Lydia and captured Sardis. We know from Esar-haddon's inscriptions that by the Assyrians these Kimmerians were called Manda, their prince Teupsa (Teispe) being described as " of the people of the Manda." An oracle given to Esar-haddon begins : " The Kimmerian in the mountains has set fire in the land of Ellip," *i.e.* the land where Ekbatana was afterwards founded, which is now shown to have already been occupied by the Kimmerian or Manda hordes. It follows that Kimmerians, Mandas, Medes with their modern Kurd and Bakhtiari representatives, were all one people, who were almost certainly of Aryan speech, if not actually of proto-Aryan stock. " The Kurds are the descendants of Aryan invaders and have maintained their type and their language for more than

Babylonian pantheon survived, in fact, till the time of Darius Hystaspes, who introduced Zoroastrianism with its supreme gods, Ahura-Mazda, creator of all good, and Ahriman, author of all evil.

It is now possible to gain some idea of the gradual growth of the city states of Babylonia. Beginning with a mere collection of rude reed huts, these were succeeded by structures of sun-dried bricks, built in a group for mutual protection, probably around a centre of a local god, and surrounded by a wall. The land around the settlement was irrigated by canals, and here the corn and vegetables were grown and the flocks and herds were tended for the maintenance of the population. The central figure was always the god, who occasionally gave his name to the site, and who was the owner of all the land, the inhabitants being merely his tenants who owed him rent for their estates. It was the god who waged wars with the neighbours, and with whom treaties were made. The treaty between Lagash and Umma fixing the limitations of their boundaries, a constant matter of dispute, was made by Ningirsu, god of Lagash, and the city god of Umma, under the arbitration of Enlil, the chief of the gods, whose central shrine was at Nippur.

Babylonian Religion.

With the growth of the cities disputes of territory were sure to arise, and either by conquest or amalgamation, cities became absorbed into states. The problem then was the adjustment of the various city gods, each reigning supreme in his own city, but taking a higher or lower place in the Babylonian pantheon. When one city gained a supremacy over all its neighbours, its governor might assume the title of king. But the king was merely the *patesi*, the steward of the city god. Even when the supremacy was sufficiently permanent for the establishment of a dynasty, this was a dynasty of the city rather than of a family, for the successive kings were not necessarily of the same family.[1]

Among the city gods who developed into powerful deities were Anu of Uruk (Erech), Enlil of Nippur and Ea of Eridu (originally a sea-port). These became the supreme triad, Anu ruling over the heavens, enthroned on the northern pole, as

3300 years," F. v. Luschan, " The Early Inhabitants of Western Asia," *Journ. Roy. Anthr. Inst.* XLI. 1911, p. 230. For a classification of Kurds see Mark Sykes, " The Kurdish Tribes of the Ottoman Empire," *Journ. Roy. Anthr. Inst.* XXXVIII. 1908, p. 451. Cf. also D. G. Hogarth, *The Nearer East*, 1902.

[1] C. H. W. Johns, *Ancient Babylonia*, 1913, p. 27.

king and father of the gods ; Enlil, the Semitic Bel, god of earth, lord of the lands, formerly chief of all the gods ; and Ea, god of the water-depths, whose son was ultimately to eclipse his father as Marduk of Babylon. A second triad is composed of the local deities who developed into Sin, the moon-god of Ur, Shamash the sun-god of Larsa, and the famous Ishtar, the great mother, goddess of love and queen of heaven. The realm of the dead was a dark place under the earth, where the dead lived as shadows, eating the dust of the earth. Their lot depended partly on their earlier lives, and partly on the devotion of their surviving relatives. Although their dead kings were deified there seems to be no evidence for a belief in a general resurrection or in the transmigration of souls. The hymns and prayers to the gods however show a very high religious level in spite of the important part played by soothsaying and exorcism, relics of earlier culture. The permanence of these may be partly ascribed to the essentially theocratic character of Babylonian government. The king was merely the agent of the god, whose desires were interpreted by the priestly soothsayers and exorcists, and no action could be undertaken in worldly or in religious concerns without their superintendence. The kings occasionally attempted to free themselves from the power of the priests, but the attempt was always vain. The power of the priests had often a sound economic basis, for the temples of the great cities were centres of vast wealth and of far-reaching trade, as is proved by the discovery of the commercial contracts stored in the temple archives.[1]

How the family expands through the clan and tribe into the nation, is clearly seen in the Babylonian social system, in which the inhabitants of each city were still "divided into clans, all of whose members claimed Social System. to be descended from a common ancestor who had flourished at a more or less remote period. The members of each clan were by no means all in the same social position, some having gone down in the world, others having raised themselves ; and amongst them we find many different callings—from agricultural labourers to scribes, and from merchants to artisans. No natural tie existed among the majority of these members except the remembrance of their common origin, perhaps also

---

[1] Cf. H. Zimmern, article " Babylonians and Assyrians," *Ency. Religion and Ethics*, 1909.

a common religion, and eventual rights of succession or claims upon what belonged to each one individually." [1]   The god or goddess, it is suggested, who watched over each man, and of whom each was the son, was originally the god or goddess of the clan (its totem).   So also in Egypt, the members of the community were all supposed to come of the same stock (*páit*), and to belong to the same family (*páitu*), whose chiefs (*ropáitu*) were the guardians of the family, several groups of such families being under a *ropáitú-há*, or head chief.[2]

Amongst the local institutions, it is startling to find a fully developed ground-landlord system, though not quite so bad as that still patiently endured in England, already flourishing ages ago in Babylonia.   " The cost of repairs fell usually on the lessee, who was also allowed to build on the land he had leased, in which case it was declared free of all charges for a period of about ten years ; but the house and, as a rule, all he had built, then reverted to the landlord." [3]

In many other respects great progress had been made, and it is the belief of von Ihring,[4] Hommel [5] and others that from **General Culture.** Babylonia was first diffused a knowledge of letters, astronomy, agriculture, navigation, architecture, and other arts, to the Nile valley, and mainly through Egypt to the Western World, and through Irania to China and India.   In this generalisation there is probably a large measure of truth, although it will be seen farther on that the Asiatic origin of Egyptian culture is still far from being proved.[6]

One element the two peoples certainly had in common— a highly developed agricultural system, which formed the foundation of their greatness, and was maintained in a rainless climate by a stupendous system of irrigation works.   Such works were carried out on a prodigious scale by the ancient Babylonians six or eight thousand years ago.   The plains of the Lower Euphrates and Tigris, since rendered desolate under Turkish misrule, are intersected by the remains of an intricate network of canalisation covering all the space between the two rivers, and are strewn with the ruins of many great cities, whose inhabitants, numbering scores of thousands, were

---

[1] G. Maspero, *Dawn of Civilisation*, p. 733.
[2] *Ibid.* p. 71.
[3] *Ibid.* p. 752.
[4] *Vorgeschichte*, etc., Book ii. *passim.*
[5] *Geschichte Babyloniens u. Assyriens.*
[6] G. Maspero, *The Struggle of the Nations, Egypt, Syria and Assyria*, 1910.

supported by the produce of a highly cultivated region, which is now an arid waste varied only by crumbling mounds, stagnant waters, and the camping-grounds of a few Arab tent-dwellers.

Those who attach weight to distinctive racial qualities have always found a difficulty in attributing this wonderful civilisation to the same Mongolic people, who in their own homes have scarcely anywhere advanced beyond the hunting, fishing, or pastoral states. But it has always to be remembered that man, like all other zoological forms, necessarily reflects the character of his environment. The Mongols might in time become agriculturists in the alluvial Mesopotamian lands, though the kindred people who give their name to the whole ethnical division and present its physical characters in an exaggerated form, ever remain tented nomads on the dry Central Asiatic steppe, which yields little but herbage, and is suitable for tillage only in a few more favoured districts. Here the typical Mongols, cut off from the arable lands of South Siberia by the Tian-shan and Altai ranges, and to some extent denied access to the rich fluvial valleys of the Middle Kingdom by the barrier of the Great Wall, have for ages led a pastoral life in the inhabitable tracts and oases of the Gobi wilderness and the Ordos region within the great bend of the Hoang-ho. During the historic period these natural and artificial ramparts have been several times surmounted by fierce Mongol hordes, pouring like irresistible flood-waters over the whole of China and many parts of Siberia, and extending their predatory or conquering expeditions across the more open northern plains westwards nearly to the shores of the Atlantic. But such devastating torrents, which at intervals convulsed and caused dislocations amongst half the settled populations of the globe, had little effect on the tribal groups that remained behind. These continued and continue to occupy the original camping-grounds, as changeless and uniform in their physical appearance, mental characters, and social usages as the Arab bedouins and all other inhabitants of monotonous undiversified steppe lands.

The Mongols Proper.

De Ujfalvy's suggestion that the typical Mongols of the plains, with whom we are now dealing, were originally a long-headed race, can scarcely be taken seriously. At present and, in fact, throughout historic times, all

Physical Type.

true Mongol peoples are and have been distinguished by a high degree of brachycephaly, with cephalic index generally from 87 upwards, and it may be remembered that the highest known index of any undeformed skull was that of Huxley's Mongol (98.21). But, as already noticed, those recovered from prehistoric, or neolithic kurgans, are found to be dolichocephalous like those of palaeolithic and early neolithic man in Europe.

Taken in connection with the numerous prehistoric remains above recorded from all parts of Central Asia and Siberia, this fact may perhaps help to bring de Ujfalvy's view into harmony with the actual conditions. Everything will be explained by assuming that the proto-Mongolic tribes, spreading from the Tibetan plateau over the plains now bearing their name, found that region already occupied by the long-headed Caucasic peoples of the Stone Ages, whom they either exterminated or drove north to the Altai uplands, and east to Manchuria and Korea, where a strong Caucasic strain still persists. De Ujfalvy's long-heads would thus be, not the proto-Mongols who were always round-headed, but the long-headed neolithic pre-Mongol race expelled by them from Mongolia who may provisionally be termed proto-Nordics.

That this region has been their true home since the first migrations from the south there can be no doubt. Here land and people stand in the closest relation one to the other ; here every conspicuous physical feature recalls some popular memory ; every rugged crest is associated with the name of some national hero, every lake or stream is still worshipped or held in awe as a local deity, or else the abode of the ancestral shades. Here also the Mongols proper form two main divisions, *Sharra* in the east and *Kalmúk* in the west, while a third group, the somewhat mixed *Buryats*, have long been settled in the Siberian provinces of Irkutsk and Trans-Baikalia. Under the Chinese semi-military administration all except the Buryats, who are Russian subjects, are constituted since the seventeenth century in 41 *Aimaks* (large tribal groups or principalities with hereditary khans) and 226 *Koshungs*, " Banners," that is, smaller groups whose chiefs are dependent on the khans of their respective Aimaks, who are themselves directly responsible to the imperial government. Subjoined is a table of these administrative divisions, which present a curious

Ethnical and
Administrative
Divisions.

but effective combination of the tribal and political systems, analogous to the arrangement in Pondoland and some other districts in Cape Colony, where the hereditary tribal chief assumes the functions of a responsible British magistrate.

Tribal or Territorial Divisions	Aimaks (Principalities)	Koshungs (Banners)
Khalkas	4	86
Inner Mongolia with Ordos	25	51
Chakars	1	8
Ala-Shan	1	3
Koko-nor and Tsaidam	5	29
Sungaria	4	32
Uriankhai	1	17
	41	226

Since their organisation in Aimaks and Koshungs, the Mongols have ceased to be a terror to the surrounding peoples. The incessant struggles between these tented warriors and the peaceful Chinese populations, which began long before the dawn of history, were brought to a close with the overthrow of the Sungarian power in the eighteenth century, when their political cohesion was broken, and the whole nation reduced to a state of abject helplessness, from which they cannot now hope to recover. The arm of Chinese rule could be replaced only by the firmer grip of the northern autocrat, whose shadow already lies athwart the Gobi wilderness.

Thus the only escape from the crushing monotony of a purely pastoral life, no longer relieved by intervals of warlike or predatory expeditions, lies in a survival of the old Shamanist superstitions, or a further development of the degrading Tibetan lamaism represented at Urga by the *Kutukhtu*, an incarnation of the Buddha only less revered **Buddhism.** than the Dalai Lama himself.[1] Besides this High Priest at Urga, there are over a hundred smaller incarnations—*Gigens*, as they are called—and these saintly beings possess unlimited means of plundering their votaries. The smallest favour, the touch of their garments, a pious ejaculation or blessing, is

[1] It is noteworthy that *Dalai*, " Ocean," is itself a Mongol word, though *Lama*, " Priest," is Tibetan. The explanation is that in the thirteenth century a local incarnation of Buddha was raised by the then dominant Mongols to the first rank, and this title of *Dalai Lama*, the " Ocean Priest," *i.e.* the Priest of fathomless wisdom, was bestowed on one of his successors in the sixteenth century, and still retained by the High Pontiff at Lhasa.

regarded as a priceless spiritual gift, and must be paid for with costly offerings.   Even the dead do not escape these exactions. However disposed of, whether buried or cremated, like the khans and lamas, or exposed to beasts and birds of prey, as is the fate of the common folk, " masses," which also command a high price, have to be said for forty days to relieve their souls from the torments of the Buddhist purgatory.

It is a singular fact, which, however, may perhaps admit of explanation, that nearly all the true Mongol peoples have been Buddhists since the spread of Sakya-Muni's teachings throughout Central Asia, while their Turki kinsmen are zealous followers of the Prophet.   Thus is seen, for instance, the strange spectacle of two Mongolic groups, the Kirghiz of the Turki branch and the Kalmuks of the West Mongol branch, en-camped side by side on the Lower Volga plains, the former all under the banner of the Crescent, the latter devout wor-shippers of all the incarnations of Buddha.   But analogous phenomena occur amongst the European peoples, the Teutons being mainly Protestants, those of neo-Latin speech mainly Roman Catholics, and the Eastern Orthodox.   From all this, however, nothing more can be inferred than that the religions are partly a question of geography, partly determined by racial temperament and political conditions ;   while the religious sentiment, being universal, is above all local or ethnical considerations.

Under the first term of the expression *Mongolo-Turki* (p. 256) are comprised, besides the Mongols proper, nearly all those branches of the division which lie to the east and north-east of Mongolia, and are in most respects more closely allied with the Mongol than with the Turki section.   Such are the *Tunguses*, with the kindred *Manchus, Golds, Orochons, Lamuts*, and others of the Amur basin, the Upper Lena head-streams, the eastern affluents of the Yenisei, and the shores of the Sea of Okhotsk ; the *Gilyaks* about the Amur estuary and in the northern parts of Sakhalin ; the *Kamchadales* in South Kam-chatka ; in the extreme north-east the *Koryaks, Chukchis*, and *Yukaghirs* ; lastly the *Koreans, Japanese*, and *Liu-Kiu (Lu-Chu) Islanders*.   To the Mongol section thus belong nearly all the peoples lying between the Yenisei and the Pacific (including most of the adjacent archipelagos), and between the Great Wall and the Arctic Ocean.   The only two ex-ceptions are the *Yakuts* of the middle and Lower Lena and neighbouring Arctic rivers, who are of Turki stock ; and the *Ainus* of Yezo, South Sakhalin, and some of the Kurile Islands, who belong to the Caucasic division.

M. A. Czaplicka proposes a useful classification of the various peoples of Siberia, usually grouped on account of linguistic affinities as Ural-Altaians, and as " no other part of the world presents a racial problem of such complexity and in regard to no other part of the world's inhabitants have ethnologists of the last hundred years put forward such widely differing hypotheses of their origin," [1] her tabulation may serve to clear the way. She divides the whole area [2] into *Palaeo-Siberians*, representing the most ancient stock of dwellers in Siberia, and *Neo-Siberians*, comprising the various tribes of Central Asiatic origin who are sufficiently differentiated from the kindred peoples of their earlier homes as to deserve a generic name of their own. The Palaeo-Siberians thus include the *Chukchi, Koryak, Kamchadale, Ainu, Gilyak, Eskimo, Aleut, Yukaghir, Chuvanzy* and *Ostyak* of Yenisei. The Neo-Siberians include the Finnic Tribes (Ugrian *Ostyak*, and *Vogul*), Samoyedic Tribes, Turkic Tribes (*Yakut* and Turko-Tatars of Tobolsk and Tomsk Governments), Mongolic Tribes (Western Mongols or *Kalmuk*, Eastern Mongols, and *Buryat*), and Tungusic Tribes (*Tungus, Chapogir, Gold, Lamut, Manchu, Manyarg, Oroch, Orochon* (" Reindeer Tungus "), *Oroke*).

A striking illustration of the general statement that the various cultural states are a question not of race, but of environment, is afforded by the varying social conditions of the widespread Tungus family, who **The Tunguses.** are fishers on the Arctic coast, hunters in the East Siberian woodlands, and for the most part sedentary tillers of the soil and townspeople in the rich alluvial valleys of the Amur and its southern affluents. The Russians, from whom we get the term Tungus,[3] recognise these various pursuits, and speak of

---

[1] *Aboriginal Siberia*, 1914, p. 13.   [2] *Loc. cit.* pp. 18–21.
[3] Either from the Chinese *Tunghu*, " Eastern Barbarians," or from the Turki *Tinghiz*, as in Isaac Massa : *per interpretes se Tingoesi vocari dixerunt* (*Descriptio*, etc., Amsterdam, 1612). But there is no collective national name, and at present they call themselves *Don-ki, Boia, Boie*, etc., terms all meaning " Men," " People." In the Chinese records they are referred to under the name of *I-lu* so early as 263 A.D., when they dwelt in the forest region between the Upper Temen and Yalu rivers on the one hand and the Pacific Ocean on the other, and paid tribute in kind—sable furs, bows, and stone arrow-heads. Arrows and stone arrow-heads were also the tribute paid to the emperors of the Shang dynasty (1766–1154 B.C.) by the *Su-shen*, who dwelt north of the Liao-tung peninsula, so that we have here official proof of a Stone Age of long duration in Manchuria. Later, the Chinese

Horse, Cattle, Reindeer, Dog, Steppe, and *Forest* Tunguses, besides the settled farmers and stock-breeders of the Amur.

Their original home appears to have been the Shan-alin uplands, where they dwelt with the kindred *Niu-chi* (Manchus) till the thirteenth century, when the disturbances brought about by the wars and conquests of Jenghiz-Khan drove them to their present seat in East Siberia. The type, although essentially Mongolic in the somewhat flat features, very prominent cheek-bones, slant eyes, long lank hair, yellowish brown colour and low stature, seems to show admixture with a higher race in the shapely frame, the nimble, active figure, and quick, intelligent expression, and especially in the variable skull. While generally round (indices 80° to 84°), the head is sometimes flat on the top, like that of the true Mongol, sometimes high and short, which, as Hamy tells us, is specially characteristic of the Turki race.[1]

Cradle and Type.

All observers speak in enthusiastic language of the temperament and moral qualities of the Tunguses, and particularly of those groups that roam the forests about the Tunguska tributaries of the Yenisei, which take their name from these daring hunters and trappers. "Full of animation and natural impulse, always cheerful even in the deepest misery, holding themselves and others in like respect, of gentle manners and poetic speech, obliging without servility, unaffectedly proud, scorning falsehood, and indifferent to suffering and death, the Tunguses are unquestionably an heroic people."[2]

Mental Characters.

A few have been brought within the pale of the Orthodox Church, and in the extreme south some are classed as Buddhists. But the great bulk of the Tungus nation are still Shamanists. Indeed the very word *Shaman* is of Tungus origin, though current also amongst the Buryats and Yakuts. It is often taken to be the equivalent of priest; but in point of fact it represents a stage in the development of natural religion which has scarcely yet reached the sacerdotal

Shamanism.

chronicles mention the *U-ki* or *Mo-ho*, a warlike people of the Sungari valley and surrounding uplands, who in the 7th century founded the kingdom of *Pu-hai*, overthrown in 925 by the Khitans of the Lower Sungari below its Noni confluence, who were themselves Tunguses and according to some Chinese authorities the direct ancestors of the Manchus.

[1] " C'est la tendance de la tête à se développer en hauteur, juste en sens inverse de l'aplatissement vertical du Mongol. La tête du Turc est donc à la fois plus haute et plus courte " (*L'Anthropologie*, VI. 3, p. 8).

[2] Reclus, VI. ; Eng. ed. p. 360.

state. " Although in many cases the shamans act as priests, and take part in popular and family festivals, prayers, and sacrifices, their chief importance is based on the performance of duties which distinguish them sharply from ordinary priests." [1] Their functions are threefold, those of the medicine-man (the leech, or healer by supernatural means) ; of the soothsayer (the prophet through communion with the invisible world) ; and of the priest, especially in his capacity as exorcist, and in his general power to influence, control, or even coerce the good and evil spirits on behalf of their votaries. But as all spirits are, or were originally, identified with the souls of the departed, it follows that in its ultimate analysis Shamanism resolves itself into a form of ancestry-worship.

The system, of which there are many phases reflecting the different cultural states of its adherents, still prevails amongst all the Siberian aborigines,[2] and generally amongst all the un-civilised Ural-Altaic populations, so that here again the religions strictly reflect the social condition of the peoples. Thus the somewhat cultured Finns, Turks, Mongols, and Manchus are all either Christians, Muhammadans, or Buddhists ; while the uncultured but closely related Samoyeds, Ostyaks, Orochons, Tunguses, Golds, Gilyaks, Koryaks, and Chukchi, are almost without exception Shamanists.

The shamans do not appear to constitute a special caste or sacerdotal order, like the hierarchies of the Christian Churches. Some are hereditary, some elected by popular vote, so to say. They may be either men, or women (*shamanka*), married or single ; and if " rank " is spoken of, it simply means greater or less proficiency in the performance of the duties imposed on them. Everything thus depends on their personal merits, which naturally gives rise to much jealousy between the members of the craft. Thus amongst the " whites " and the " blacks," that is, those whose dealings are with the good and the bad spirits respectively, there is in some districts a standing feud, often resulting in fierce encounters and bloodshed. The Buryats tell how the two factions throw axes at each other at great distances, the struggle usually ending in the death of one of the combatants. The blacks, who serve the evil spirits,

---

[1] V. M. Mikhailovskii, *Shamanism in Siberia and European Russia*, translated by Oliver Wardrop, *Journ. Anthr. Inst.* 1895, p. 91.
[2] M. A. Czaplicka, *Aboriginal Siberia*, 1914. Part III. discusses Shamanism, pp. 166–255.

bringing only disease, death, or ill-luck, and even killing people by eating up their souls, are of course the least popular, but also the most dreaded. Many are credited with extraordinary and even miraculous powers, and there can be no doubt that they often act up to their reputation by performing almost incredible conjuring tricks in order to impose on the credulity of the ignorant, or outbid their rivals for the public favour. Old Richard Johnson of Chancelour's expedition to Muscovy records how he saw a Samoyed shaman stab himself with a sword, then make the sword red hot and thrust it through his body, so that the point protruded at the back, and Johnson was able to touch it with his finger. They then bound the wizard tight with a reindeer-rope, and went through some performances curiously like those of the Davenport brothers and other modern conjurers.[1]

To the much-discussed question whether the shamans are impostors, the best answer has perhaps been given by Castrèn, who, speaking of the same Samoyed magicians, remarks that if they were merely cheats, we should have to suppose that they did not share the religious beliefs of their fellow-tribesmen, but were a sort of rationalists far in advance of the times. Hence it would seem much more probable that they deceived both themselves and others,[2] while no doubt many bolster up a waning reputation by playing the mountebank where there is no danger of detection.

"Shamanism amongst the Siberian peoples," concludes our Russian authority, " is at the present time in a moribund condition ; it must die out with those beliefs among which alone such phenomena can arise and flourish. Buddhism on the one hand, and Muhammadanism on the other, not to mention Christianity, are rapidly destroying the old ideas of the tribes among whom the shamans performed. Especially has the more ancient Black Faith suffered from the Yellow Faith preached by the lamas. But the shamans, with their dark mysterious rites, have made a good struggle for life, and are still frequently found among the native Christians and Muhammadans. The mullahs and lamas have even been obliged to become shamans to a great extent, and many Siberian tribes, who are nominally Christians, believe in shamans, and have recourse to them."

[1] Hakluyt, 1809 ed., I. p. 317 sq.
[2] Quoted by Mikhailovskii, p. 144.

Of all members of the Tungusic family the Manchus alone can be called a historical people. If they were really descended from the *Khitans* of the Sungari valley, then their authentic records will date from the tenth century A.D., when these renowned warriors,   The Manchus. after overthrowing the Pu-haï (925), founded the Liao dynasty and reduced a great part of North China and surrounding lands. The Khitans, from whom China was known to Marco Polo as *Khitai* (Cathay), as it still is to the Russians, were conquered in 1125 by the *Niu-chi* (*Yu-chi, Nu-chin*) of the Shan-alin uplands, reputed cradle of the Manchu race. These Niu-chi, direct ancestors of the Manchus, founded (1115)   Origins and the State known as that of the " Golden Tartars,"   Early from *Kin*, " gold," the title adopted by their   Records. chief Aguta, " because iron (in reference to the *Liao*, ' Iron ' dynasty) may rust, but gold remains ever pure and bright." The Kins, however, retained their brightness only a little over a century, having been eclipsed by Jenghiz-Khan in 1234. But about the middle of the fourteenth century the Niu-chi again rose to power under Aishiu-Gioro, who, although of miraculous birth and surrounded by other legendary matter, appears to have been a historical person. He may be regarded as the true founder of the Manchu dynasty, for it was in his time that this name came into general use. Sing-tsu, one of his descendants, constructed the palisade, a feeble imitation of the Great Wall, sections of which still exist. Thai-tsu, a still more famous member of the family, greatly extended the Manchu Kingdom (1580-1626), and it was his son Tai-dsung who first assumed the imperial dignity under the title of Tai-Tsing. After his death, the Ming dynasty having been overthrown by a rebel chief, the Manchus were invited by the imperialists to aid in restoring order, entered Peking in triumph, and, finding that the last of the Mings had committed suicide, placed Tai-dsung's nephew on the throne, thus founding the Manchu dynasty (1644) which lasted down to 1912.

Such has been the contribution of the Manchu people to history ; their contributions to arts, letters, science, in a word, to the general progress of mankind, have been *nil*. They found the Middle Kingdom, after ages of a sluggish growth, in a state of absolute stagnation, and there they have left it. On the other hand their assumption of the imperial administration brought about their own ruin, their effacement, and almost their

very extinction as a separate nationality.[1]   Manchuria, like
Mongolia, is organised in a number of half military, half civil
divisions, the so-called *Paki*, or " Eight Banners," and the constant demand made on these reserves, to support the dynasty
and supply trustworthy garrisons for all the strongholds of the
empire, has drawn off the best blood of the people, in fact sapped
its vitality at the fountain-head.   Then the rich arable tracts
thus depleted were gradually occupied by agricultural settlers
from the south, with the result that the Manchu race has nearly
disappeared.   From the ethnical standpoint the whole region
beyond the Great Wall as far north as the Amur has practically
become an integral part of China, and from the political standpoint since 1898 an integral part of the Russian empire.   Towards the middle of the nineteenth century the Eight Banners
numbered scarcely more than a quarter of a million, and about
that time the Abbé Huc declared that " the Manchu nationality
is destroyed beyond recovery.   At present we shall look in vain
for a single town or a single village throughout Manchuria
which is not exclusively inhabited by Chinese.   The local colour
has been completely effaced, and except a few nomad groups
nobody speaks Manchu." [2]

Similar testimony is afforded by later observers, and Henry
Lansdell, amongst others, remarks that " the Manchu, during
the two centuries they have reigned in China, may be said to
have been working out their own annihilation.   Their manners,
language, their very country has become Chinese, and some
maintain that the Manchu proper are now extinct." [3]

But the type, so far from being extinct, may be said to have
received a considerable expansion, especially amongst the populations of north-east China.   The taller stature

Type.

and greatly superior physical appearance of the
inhabitants of Tien-tsin and surrounding districts [4] over those
of the southern provinces (Fokien, Kwang-tung), who are the

---

[1] Cf. H. A. Giles, *China and the Manchus*, 1912.
[2] *Souvenirs d'un voyage dans la Tartarie*, 1853, I. 162.
[3] *Through Siberia*, 1882, Vol. II. p. 172.
[4] European visitors often notice with surprise the fine physique of these natives,
many of whom average nearly six feet in height.   But there is an extraordinary
disparity between the two sexes, perhaps greater than in any other country.   The
much smaller stature and feebler constitution of the women is no doubt due to the
detestable custom of crippling the feet in childhood, thereby depriving them of
natural exercise during the period of growth.   It may be noted that the anti-foot-
bandaging movement is making progress throughout China, the object being to
abolish the cruel practice by making the *kin lien* (" golden lilies ") unfashionable,
and the *ti mien*, the " heavenly feet "—*i.e.* the natural—popular in their stead.

chief representatives of the Chinese race abroad, seem best explained by continual crossings with the neighbouring Manchu people, at least since the twelfth century, if not earlier.

Closely related to the Manchus (of the same stock, says Sir H. H. Howorth, the distinction being purely political) are the *Dauri*, who give their name to the extensive Daur plateau, and formerly occupied both sides of **The Dauri.** the Upper Amur. Daur is, in fact, the name applied by the Buryats to all the Tungus peoples of the Amur basin. The Dauri proper, who are now perhaps the best representatives of the original Manchu type, would seem to have intermingled at a remote time with the long headed pre-Mongol populations of Central Asia. They are " taller and stronger than the Oronchons [Tungus groups lower down the Amur] ; the countenance is oval and more intellectual, and the cheeks are less broad. The nose is rather prominent, and the eyebrows straight. The skin is tawny, and the hair brown."[1] Most of these characters are such as we should expect to find in a people of mixed Mongolo-Caucasic descent, the latter element being derived from the long-headed race who had already reached the present Mongolia, Manchuria, Korea, and the adjacent islands during neolithic times. Thus may be explained the tall stature, somewhat regular features, brown hair, light eyes, and even florid complexion so often observed amongst the present inhabitants of Manchuria, Korea, and parts of North China.

But no admixture, except of Chinese literary terms, is seen in the Manchu language, which, like Mongolic, is a typical member of the agglutinating Ural-Altaic family. Despite great differences, lexical, phonetic, and even **Mongolo-Turki** structural, all the members of this widespread **Speech.** order of speech have in common a number of fundamental features, which justify the assumption that all spring from an original stock language, which has long been extinct, and the germs of which were perhaps first developed on the Tibetan plateau. The essential characters of the system are :—(1) a " root " or notional term, generally a closed syllable, nominal or verbal, with a vowel or diphthong, strong or weak (hard or soft) according to the meaning of the term, hence incapable of change ; (2) a number of particles or relational terms somewhat loosely postfixed to the root, but incorporated with it by the

[1] H. Lansdell, *Through Siberia*, 1882, II. p. 172.

principle of (3) vowel harmony, a kind of vocal concordance, in virtue of which the vowels of all the postfixes must harmonise with the unchangeable vowel of the root. If this is strong all the following vowels of the combination, no matter what its length, must be strong ; if weak they must conform in the same way. With nominal roots the postfixes are necessarily limited to the expression of a few simple relations ; but with verbal roots they are in principle unlimited, so that the multifarious relations of the verb to its subject and object are all incorporated in the verbal compound itself, which may thus run at times to inordinate lengths. Hence we have the expression " incorporating," commonly applied to this agglutinating system, which sometimes goes so far as to embody the notions of causality, possibility, passivity, negation, intensity, condition, and so on, besides the direct pronominal objects, in one interminable conglomerate, which is then treated as a simple verb, and run through all the secondary changes of number, person, tense, and mood. The result is an endless number of theoretically possible verbal forms, which, although in practice naturally limited to the ordinary requirements of speech, are far too numerous to allow of a complete verbal paradigm being constructed of any fully developed member of the Ural-Altaic group, such, for instance, as Yakut, Tungus, Turki, Mordvinian, Finnish, or Magyar.

In this system the vowels are classed as strong or hard (*a, o, u*), weak or soft (the same *umlauted* : *ä, ö, ü,*), and neutral (generally *e, i*), these last being so called because they occur indifferently with the two other classes. Thus, if the determining root vowel is *a* (strong), that of the postfixes may be either *a* (strong), *e* or *i* (neutral) ; if *ä* (weak), that of the postfixes may be either *ä* (weak), or *e* or *i* as before. The postfixes themselves no doubt were originally notional terms worn down in form and meaning, so as to express mere abstract relation, as in the Magyar *vel*=with, from *veli*=companion. Tacked on to the root *fa*=tree, this will give the ablative case, first unharmonised, *fa-vel*, then harmonised, *fa-val*=tree-with, with a tree. In the early Magyar texts of the twelfth century inharmonic compounds, such as *halál-nek*, later *halák-nak*=at death, are numerous, from which it has been inferred that the principle of vowel harmony is not an original feature of the Ural-Altaic languages, but a later development, due in fact to phonetic decay, and still scarcely known in some members of the group, such as Votyak and Highland Cheremissian (Volga Finn). But M. Lucien Adam holds that these idioms have lost the principle through foreign (Russian) influence, and that the few traces still perceptible are survivals from a time when all the Ural-Altaic tongues were subject to progressive vowel harmony.[1]

But however this be, Dean Byrne is disposed to regard the alternating energetic utterance of the hard, and indolent utterance of the soft vowel series, as an expression of the alternating active and lethargic temperament of the race, such alternations being themselves due to the climatic conditions of their environment. "Certainly the life of the great nomadic races involves a twofold experience of this kind, as they must during their abundant summer provide for their rigorous winter, when little can be done. Their character, too, involves a striking combination of intermittent indolence and energy ; and it is very remarkable that this distinction of roots is peculiar to the languages spoken originally where this great distinction of seasons exists. The fact that the distinction [between hard and soft] is imparted to all the suffixes of a root proves that the radical characteristic which it expresses is thought with these ; and consequently that the radical idea is retained in the consciousness while these are added to it."[2]

Language and Racial Characters.

This is a highly characteristic instance of the methods followed by Dean Byrne in his ingenious but hopeless attempt to explain the subtle structure of speech by the still more subtle temperament of the speaker, taken in connection with the alternating nature of the climate. The feature in question cannot be due to such alternation of mood and climate, because it is persistent throughout all seasons, while the hard and soft elements occur simultaneously, one might say, promiscuously, in conversation under all mental states of those conversing.

The true explanation is given by Schleicher, who points out that progressive vocal assimilation is the necessary result of agglutination, which by this means binds together the idea and its relations in their outward expression, just as they are already

---

[1] *De l'Harmonie des Voyelles dans les Langues Uralo-Altaïques*, 1874, p. 67 sq.
[2] *General Principles of the Structure of Language*, 1885, Vol. I. p. 357. The evidence here chiefly relied upon is that afforded by the Yakutic, a pure Turki idiom, which is spoken in the region of extremest heat and cold (Middle and Lower Lena basin), and in which the principle of progressive assonance attains its greatest development.

inseparably associated in the mind of the speaker. Hence it is that such assonance is not confined to the Ural-Altaic group, analogous processes occurring at certain stages of their growth in all forms of speech, as in Wolof, Zulu-Xosa, Celtic (expressed by the formula of Irish grammarians : " broad to broad, slender to slender "), and even in Latin, as in such vocalic concordance as : *annus, perennis* ; *ars, iners* ; *lego, diligo*. In these examples the root vowel is influenced by that of the prefix, while in the Mongolo-Turki family the root vowel, coming first, is unchangeable, but, as explained, influences the vowels of the postfixes, the phonetic principle being the same in both systems.

Both Mongol and Manchu are cultivated languages employing modified forms of the Uiguric (Turki) script, which is based on the Syriac introduced by the Christian (Nestorian) missionaries in the seventh century. It was first adopted by the Mongols about 1280, and perfected by the scribe Tsorji Osir under Jenezek Khan (1307–1311). The letters, connected together by continuous strokes, and slightly modified, as in Syriac, according to their position at the beginning, middle, or end of the word, are disposed in vertical columns from left to right, an arrangement due no doubt to Chinese influence. This is the more probable since the Manchus, before the introduction of the Mongol system in the sixteenth century, employed the Chinese characters ever since the time of the Kin dynasty.

Mongol and Manchu Script.

None of the other Tungusic or north-east Siberian peoples possess any writing system except the Yukaghirs of the Yasachnaya affluent of the Kolyma river, who were visited in 1892 by the Russian traveller, S. Shargorodsky. From his report,[1] it appears that this symbolic writing is carved with a sharp knife out of soft fresh birch-bark, these simple materials sufficing to describe the tracks followed on hunting and fishing expeditions, as well as the sentiments of the young women in their correspondence with their sweethearts. Specimens are given of these curious documents, some of which are touching and even pathetic. " Thou goest hence, and I bide alone, for thy sake still to weep and moan," writes one disconsolate maid to her parting lover. Another with a touch of jealousy : " Thou goest forth thy Russian flame to seek, who stands 'twixt thee and me, thy heart from me apart to keep. In a new home joy wilt thou find, while I must ever

The Yukaghirs.

[1] Explained and illustrated by General Krahmer in *Globus*, 1896, p. 208 sq.

grieve, as thee I bear in mind, though another yet there be who loveth me." Or again : " Each youth his mate doth find ; my fate alone it is of him to dream, who to another wedded is, and I must fain contented be, if only he forget not me." And with a note of wail : " Thou hast gone hence, and of late it seems this place for me is desolate ; and I too forth must fare, that so the memories old I may forget, and from the pangs thus flee of those bright days, which here I once enjoyed with thee."

Details of domestic life may even be given, and one accomplished maiden is able to make a record in her note-book of the combs, shawls, needles, thimble, cake of soap, lollipops, skeins of wool, and other sundries, which she has received from a Yakut packman, in exchange for some clothes she has made him. Without illustrations no description of the process would be intelligible. Indeed it would seem these primitive documents are not always understood by the young folks themselves. They gather at times in groups to watch the process of composition by some expert damsel, the village " notary," and much merriment, we are told, is caused by the blunders of those who fail to read the text aright.

It is not stated whether the system is current amongst the other Yukaghir tribes, who dwell on the banks of the Indigirka, Yana, Kerkodona, and neighbouring districts. They thus skirt the Frozen Ocean from near the Lena delta to and beyond the Kolyma, and are conterminous landwards with the Yakuts on the south-west and the Chukchi on the north-east. With the Chukchi, the Koryaks, the Kamchadales, and the Gilyaks they form a separate branch of the Mongolic division sometimes grouped together as " Hyperboreans," but distinguished from other Ural-Altaic peoples perhaps strictly on linguistic grounds. Although now reduced to scarcely 1500, the Yukaghirs were formerly a numerous people, and the popular saying that their hearths on the banks of the Kolyma at one time outnumbered the stars in the sky seems a reminiscence of more prosperous days. But great inroads have been made by epidemics, tribal wars, the excessive use of coarse Ukraine tobacco and of bad spirits, indulged in even by the women and children. " A Yukaghir, it is said, never intoxicates himself alone, but calls upon his family to share the drink, even children in arms being supplied with a portion." [1] Their language, which

[1] H. Lansdell, *Through Siberia*, 1882, I. p. 299.

A. Schiefner regards as radically distinct from all others,[1] is disappearing even more rapidly than the people themselves, if it be not already quite extinct. In the eighties it was spoken only by about a dozen old persons, its place being taken almost everywhere by the Turki dialect of the Yakuts.[2]

There appears to be a curious interchange of tribal names between the Chukchi and their Koryak neighbours, the term

Koryak being the Chukchi *Khorana*, "Rein-
Chukchi and Koryaks. deer," while the Koryaks are said to call them-
selves *Chauchau*, whence some derive the word *Chukchi*. Hooper, however, tells us that the proper form of Chukchi is *Tuski*, "Brothers," or "Confederates," [3] and in any case the point is of little consequence, as Dittmar is probably right in regarding both groups as closely related, and sprung originally from one stock.[4] Jointly they occupy the north-east extremity of the continent between the Kolyma and Bering Strait, together with the northern parts of Kamchatka ; the Chukchi lying to the north, the Koryaks to the south, mainly round about the north-eastern inlets of the Sea of Okhotsk. Reasons have already been advanced for supposing that the Chukchi were a Tungus people who came originally from the Amur basin. In their arctic homes they appear to have waged long wars with the Onkilon (Ang-kali) aborigines, gradually merging with the survivors and also mingling both with the Koryaks and Chuklukmiut Eskimo settled on the Asiatic side of Bering Strait.

But their relations to all these peoples are involved in great obscurity, and while some connect them with the Itelmes of

Chukchi and Eskimo Relations. Kamchatka,[5] by others they have been affiliated to the Eskimo, owing to the Eskimo dialect said to be spoken by them. But this "dialect" is only a trading jargon, a sort of "pidgin Eskimo" current all round the coast, and consisting of Chukchi, Innuit, Koryak, English,

[1] "Ueber die Sprache der Jukagiren," in *Mélanges Asiatiques*, 1859, III. p. 595 sq.

[2] W. I. Jochelson recently discovered two independent Yukaghir dialects. "Essay on the Grammar of the Yukaghir Language," *Annals N. Y. Ac. Sc.* 1905 ; *The Yukaghir and the Yukaghirized Tungus. Memoir of the Jesup North Pacific Expedition*, Vol. IX. 1910. For the Koryak see his monograph in the same series, Vol. VI. 1905–8.

[3] *Ten Months among the Tents of the Tuski.*

[4] "Ueber die Koriaken u. ihnen nahe verwandten Tchouktchen," in *Bul. Acad. Sc.*, St Petersburg, XII. p. 99.

[5] Peschel, *Races of Man*, p. 391, who says the Chukchi are "as closely related to the Itelmes in speech as are Spaniards to Portuguese."

and even Hawaii elements, mingled together in varying proportions. The true Chukchi language, of which Nordenskiöld collected 1000 words, is quite distinct from Eskimo, and probably akin to Koryak,[1] and the Swedish explorer aptly remarks that " this race, settled on the primeval route between the Old and New World, bears an unmistakable stamp of the Mongols of Asia and the Eskimo and Indians of America." He was much struck by the great resemblance of the Chukchi weapons and household utensils to those of the Greenland Eskimo, while Signe Rink shows that even popular legends have been diffused amongst the populations on both sides of Bering Strait.[2] Such common elements, however, prove little for racial affinity, which seems excluded by the extremely round shape of the Chukchi skull, as compared with the long-headed Eskimo. But the type varies considerably both amongst the so-called " Fishing Chukchi," who   Type and occupy permanent stations along the seaboard,   Social State. and the " Reindeer Chukchi," who roam the inland districts, shifting their camping-grounds with the seasons. There are no hereditary chiefs, and little deference is paid to the authority even of the owner of the largest reindeer herds, on whom the Russians have conferred the title of *Jerema*, regarding him as the head of the Chukchi nation, and holding him responsible for the good conduct of his rude subjects. Although nominal Christians, they continue to sacrifice animals to the spirits of the rivers and mountains, and also to practise Shamanist rites. They believe in an after-life, but only for those who die a violent death. Hence the resignation and even alacrity with which the hopelessly infirm and the aged submit, when the time comes, to be dispatched by their kinsfolk, in accordance with the tribal customs of *kamitok*, which still survives in full vigour amongst the Chukchi, as amongst the Sumatran Battas, and may be traced in many other parts of the world.

" The doomed one," writes Harry de Windt, " takes a lively interest in the proceedings, and often assists in the preparation for his own death. The execution is always preceded by a feast, where seal and walrus meat are greedily devoured, and whisky consumed till all are intoxicated. A spontaneous burst of singing and the muffled roll of walrus-hide drums then herald

---

[1] *Petermann's Mitt.* Vol. 25, 1879, p. 138.
[2] " The Girl and the Dogs, an Eskimo Folk-tale," *Amer. Anthropologist,* June 1898, p. 181 sq.

the fatal moment. At a given signal a ring is formed by the relations and friends, the entire settlement looking on from the background. The executioner (usually the victim's son or brother) then steps forward, and placing his right foot behind the back of the condemned, slowly strangles him to death with a walrus thong. A kamitok took place during the latter part of our stay." [1]

This custom of " voluntary death " is sometimes due to sorrow at the death of a near relative, a quarrel at home, or merely weariness of life, and Bogoras thinks that the custom of killing old people does not exist as such, but is voluntarily chosen in preference to the hard life of an invalid. [2]

Most recent observers have come to look upon the Chukchi and *Koryaks* as essentially one and the same people, the chief difference being that the latter are if possible even more degraded than their northern neighbours. [3]

Koryaks and Kamchadales.

Like them they are classed as sedentary fisher-folk or nomad reindeer-owners, the latter, who call themselves Tumugulu, " Wanderers," roaming chiefly between Ghiyiginsk Bay and the Anadyr river. Through them the Chukchi merge gradually in the *Itelmes*, who are better known as Kamchadales, from the Kamchatka river, where they are now chiefly concentrated. Most of the Itelmes are already Russified in speech and—outwardly at least—in religion ; but they still secretly immolate a dog now and then, to propitiate the malevolent beings who throw obstacles in the way of their hunting and fishing expeditions. Yet their very existence depends on their canine associates, who are of a stout, almost wolfish breed, inured to hunger and hardships, and excellent for sledge work.

Somewhat distinct both from all these Hyperboreans and from their neighbours, the Orochons, Golds, Manegrs and other Tungus peoples, are the *Gilyaks*, formerly widespread, but now confined to the Amur delta and the northern parts of Sakhalin. [4] Some observers have

The Gilyaks.

[1] *Through the Gold Fields of Alaska to Bering Strait*, 1898.
[2] Cf. W. Bogoras, *The Chukchee, Memoir of the Jesup North Pacific Expedition*, Vol. VII. 1904–10.
[3] This, however, applies only to the fishing Koryaks, for G. Kennan speaks highly of the domestic virtues, hospitality, and other good qualities of the nomad groups (*Tent Life in Siberia*, 1871).
[4] See L. Sternberg, *The Tribes of the Amur River, Memoirs of the Jesup North Pacific Expedition*, Vol. IV. 1900.

connected them with the Ainu and the Korean aborigines, while
A. Anuchin detects two types—a Mongoloid with sparse beard,
high cheek-bones, and flat face, and a Caucasic with bushy
beard and more regular features.[1]   The latter traits have been
attributed to Russian mixture, but, as conjectured by H. von
Siebold, are more probably due to a.fundamental connection
with their Ainu neighbours.[2]

Mentally the Gilyaks take a low position—H. Lansdell
thought the lowest of any people he had met in Siberia.[3]
Despite the zeal of the Russian missionaries, and the induce-
ments to join the fold, they remain obdurate Shamanists, and
even fatalists, so that " if one falls into the water the others
will not help him out, on the plea that they would thus be
opposing a higher power, who wills that he should perish. . . .
The soul of the Gilyak is supposed to pass at death into his
favourite dog, which is accordingly fed with choice food ; and
when the spirit has been prayed by the shamans out of the dog,
the animal is sacrificed on his master's grave.   The soul is then
represented as passing underground, lighted and guided by its
own sun and moon, and continuing to lead there, in its spiritual
abode, the same manner of life and pursuits as in the flesh." [4]

A speciality of the Gilyaks, as well as of their Gold neighbours, is the fish-skin costume, made from the skins of two
kinds of salmon, and from this all these aborigines are known
to the Chinese as *Yupitatse,* " Fish-skin-clad-People."   " They
strip it off with great dexterity, and by beating with a mallet
remove the scales, and so render it supple.   Clothes thus made
are waterproof.   I saw a travelling-bag, and even the sail of a
boat, made of this material." [5]

Like the Ainu, the Gilyaks may be called bear-worshippers.
At least this animal is supposed to be one of their chief gods,
although they ensnare him in winter, keep him in confinement,
and when well fattened tear him to pieces, devouring his
mangled remains with much feasting and jubilation.

Since the opening up of Korea, some fresh light has been
thrown upon the origins and ethnical relations of its present
inhabitants.   In his monograph on the Yellow Races[6] Hamy

---

[1] *Mem. Imp. Soc. Nat. Sc.* xx. Supplement, Moscow, 1877.
[2] " Scheinen grosse Aenlichkeit in Sprache, Gesichtsbildung und Sitten mit
den Aino zu haben " (*Ueber die Aino,* Berlin, 1881, p. 12).
[3] *Through Siberia,* 1882, ii. p. 227.
[4] *Ibid.* p. 235.   [5] *Ibid.* p. 221.
[6] *L'Anthropologie,* vi. No. 3.

had included them in the Mongol division, but not without
reserve, adding that "while some might be
taken for Tibetans, others look like an Oceanic
cross; hence the contradictory reports and theories of modern
travellers." Since then the study of some skulls forwarded to
Paris has enabled him to clear up some of the confusion, which
is obviously due to interminglings of different elements dating
from remote (neolithic) times. On the data supplied by these
skulls Hamy classes the Koreans in three groups :—1. The
natives of the northern provinces (Ping-ngan-tao and Hien-
king-tao), strikingly like their Mongol [Tungus] neighbours;
2. Those of the southern provinces (Kling-
chang-tao and Thsiusan-lo-tao), descendants of
the ancient Chinhans and Pien-hans, showing
Japanese affinities; 3. Those of the inner provinces (Hoang-
hae-tao and Ching-tsing-tao), who present a transitional form
between the northerns and southerns, both in their physical
type and geographical position.[1]

The Koreans.

Ethnical Elements.

Caucasic features—light eyes, large nose, hair often brown,
full beard, fair and even white skin, tall stature—are conspicuous, especially amongst the upper classes and many of the
southern Koreans.[2] They are thus shown to be a mixed race,
the Mongol element dominating in the north, as might be
expected, and the Caucasic in the south.

These conclusions seem to be confirmed by what is known
of the early movements, migrations, and displacements of the
populations in north-east Asia about the dawn
of history. In these vicissitudes the Koreans, as
they are now called,[3] appear to have first taken
part in the twelfth century B.C., when the peninsula was already
occupied, as it still is, by Mongols, the *Sien-pi*, in the north,

Korean Origins and Records.

---

[1] *Bul. du Muséum d'Hist. Nat.* 1896, No. 4. All the skulls were brachy or
sub-brachy, varying from 81 to 83.8 and 84.8. The author remarks generally that
" photographes et crânes diffèrent, du tout au tout, des choses similaires venues
jusqu'à présent de Mongolie et de Chine, et font plutôt penser au Japon, à Formose, et d'une manière plus générale à ce vaste ensemble de peuples maritimes
que Lesson désignait jadis sous le nom de ' Mongols-pélasgiens,' " p. 3.

[2] On this juxtaposition of the yellow and blond types in Korea V. de Saint-
Martin's language is highly significant : " Cette dualité de type, un type tout à
fait caucasique à côté du type mongol, est un fait commun à toute le ceinture d'îles
qui couvre les côtes orientales de l'Asie, depuis les Kouriles jusqu'à Formose, et
même jusqu'à la zone orientale de l'Indo-Chine " (*Art. Corée,* p. 800).

[3] From *Koraï,* in Japanese *Kome* (Chinese *Kaoli*), name of a petty state, which
enjoyed political predominance in the peninsula for about 500 years (tenth to fourteenth century A.D.). An older designation still in official use is *Tsio-sien,* that is,
the Chinese *Chao-sien,* " Bright Dawn " (Klaproth, *Asia Polyglotta,* p. 334 sq.).

and in the south by several branches of the *Hans* (*San-San*), of whom it is recorded that they spoke a language unintelligible to the Sien-pi, and resembled the Japanese in appearance, manners, and customs.   From this it may be inferred that the Hans were the true aborigines, probably direct descendants of the Caucasic peoples of the New Stone Age, while the Sien-pi were Mongolic (Tungusic) intruders from the present Manchuria.   For some time these Sien-pi played a leading part in the political convulsions prior and subsequent to the erection of the Great Wall by Shih Hwang Ti, founder of the Tsin dynasty (221–209 B.C.).[1]   Soon after the completion of this barrier, the *Hiung-nu*, no longer able to scour the fertile plains of the Middle Kingdom, turned their arms against the neighbouring *Yuè-chi*, whom they drove westwards to the Sungarian valleys.   Here they were soon displaced by the *Usuns* (*Wu-sun*), a fair, blue-eyed people of unknown origin, who have been called " Aryans," and even " Teutons," and whom Ch. de Ujfalvy identifies with the tall long-headed western blonds (de Lapouge's *Homo Europaeus*), mixed with brown round-headed hordes of white complexion.[2]   Accepting this view, we may go further, and identify the Usuns, as well as the other white peoples of the early Chinese records, with the already described Central Asiatic Caucasians of the Stone Ages, whose osseous remains we now possess, and who come to the surface in the very first Chinese documents dealing with the turbulent populations beyond the Great Wall.   The white element, with all the correlated characters, existed beyond all question, for it is continuously referred to in those documents.   How is its presence in East Central Asia, including Manchuria and Korea,

---

[1] This stupendous work, on which about 1,000,000 hands are said to have been engaged for five years, possesses great ethnical as well as political importance. Running for over 1500 miles across hills, valleys, and rivers along the northern frontier of China proper, it long arrested the southern movements of the restless Mongolo-Turki hordes, and thus gave a westerly direction to their incursions many centuries before the great invasions of Jenghiz-Khan and his successors.   It is strange to reflect that the ethnological relations were thus profoundly disturbed throughout the eastern hemisphere by the work of a ruthless despot who reigned only twelve years, and in that time waged war against all the best traditions of the empire, destroying the books of Confucius and the other sages, and burying alive 460 men of letters for their efforts to rescue those writings from total extinction.

[2] *Les Aryens au Nord et au Sud de l'Hindou-Kouch*, 1896, p. 25.   This writer does not think that the Usuns should be identified with the tall race of horse-like face, large nose, and deep-set eyes mentioned in the early Chinese records, because no reference is made to " blue eyes," which would not have been omitted had they existed.   But, if I remember, " green eyes " are spoken of, and we know that none of the early writers use colour terms with strict accuracy.

to be explained ?   Only on two assumptions—*proto-historic*
migrations from the Far West, barred by the proto-historic
migrations from the Far East, as largely determined by the
erection of the Great Wall ; or *prehistoric* (neolithic) migrations, also from the Far West, but barred by no serious obstacle,
because antecedent to the arrival of the proto-Mongolic tribes
from the Tibetan plateau.   The true solution of the endless
ethnical complications in the extreme East, as in the Oceanic
world, will still be found in the now-demonstrated presence of
a Caucasic element antecedent to the Mongol in those regions.

When the Hiung-nu [1] power was weakened by their westerly
migrations to Sungaria and south-west Siberia (Upper Irtysh
and Lake Balkash depression), and broken into two sections
during their wars with the two Han dynasties (201 B.C.–
220 A.D.), the Korean Sien-pi became the dominant nation north
of the Great Wall.   After destroying the last vestiges of the
unstable Hiung-nu empire, and driving the Mongolo-Turki
hordes still westwards, the Yuan-yuans, most powerful of all
the Sien-pi tribes, remained masters of East Central Asia for
about 400 years and then disappeared from history.[2]   At least
after the sixth century A.D. no further mention is made of the
Sien-pi principalities either in Manchuria or in Korea.   Here,
however, they appear still to form a dominant element in the
northern   (Mongol)   provinces,   calling   themselves   Ghirin
(Khirin), from the Khirin (Sungari) valley of the Amur, where
they once held sway.

[1] I have not thought it desirable to touch on the interminable controversy
respecting the ethnical relations of the Hiung-nu, regarding them, not as a distinct
ethnical group, but like the Huns, their later western representatives, as a heterogeneous collection of Mongol, Tungus, Turki, and perhaps even Finnish hordes
under a Mongol military caste.   At the same time I have little doubt that Mon-
golo-Tungus elements greatly predominated in the eastern regions (Mongolia
proper, Manchuria) both amongst the Hiung-nu and their Yuan-yuan (Sien-pi)
successors, and that all the founders of the first great empires prior to that of the
Turki Assena in the Altai region (sixth century A.D.) were full-blood Mongols, as
indeed recognised by Jenghiz-Khan himself.   For the migrations of these and
neighbouring peoples, consult A. C. Haddon, *The Wanderings of Peoples*, 1911,
pp. 16 and 28.

[2] On the authority of the Wei-Shu documents contained in the Wei-Chï,
E. H. Parker gives (in the *China Review* and *A Thousand Years of the Tartars*,
Shanghai, 1895) the dates 386–556 A.D. as the period covered by the " Sien-pi
Tartar dynasty of Wei."   This is not to be confused with the Chinese dynasty of
Wei (224–264, or according to Kwong Ki-Chiu 234–274 A.D.).   The term " Tartar "
(Ta-Ta), it may be explained, is used by Parker, as well as by the Chinese
historians generally, in a somewhat wide sense, so as to include all the nomad
populations north of the Great Wall, whether of Tungus (Manchu), Mongol, or
even Turki stock.   The original tribes bearing the name were Mongols, and
Jenghiz-Khan himself was a Tata on his mother's side.

Since those days Korea has been alternately a vassal State and a province of the Middle Kingdom, with interludes of Japanese ascendancy, interrupted only by the four centuries of Koraï ascendancy (934–1368). This was the most brilliant epoch in the national records, when Korea was rather the ally than the vassal of China, and when trade, industry, and the arts, especially porcelain and bronze work, flourished in the land. But by centuries of subsequent misrule, a people endowed with excellent natural qualities have been reduced to the lowest state of degradation. Before the reforms introduced by the political events of 1895–96, " the country was eaten up by officialism. It is not only that abuses without number prevailed, but the whole system of government was an abuse, a sea of corruption, without a bottom or a shore, an engine of robbery, crushing the life out of all industry."[1] But an improvement was speedily remarked. " The air of the men has undergone a subtle and real change, and the women, though they nominally keep up their habits by seclusion, have lost the hang-dog air which distinguished them at home. The alacrity of movement is a change also, and has replaced the conceited swing of the *yang-ban* [nobles] and the heartless lounge of the peasant." This improvement was merely temporary. The last years of the century were marked by the waning of Japanese influence, due to Russian intrigues, the restoration of absolute monarchy together with its worst abuses, the abandonment of reforms and a retrograde movement throughout the kingdom. The successes of Japan in 1904–5 resulted in the restoration of her ascendancy, culminating in 1910 in the cession of sovereignty by the emperor of Korea to the emperor of Japan.

The religious sentiment is perhaps less developed than among any other Asiatic people. Buddhism, introduced about 380 A.D., never took root, and while the *literati* are satisfied with the moral precepts of Confucius, the rest have not progressed beyond the nature-worship which was the ancient religion of the land. Every mountain, pass, ford or even eddy of a river has a spirit to whom offerings are made. Honour is also paid to ancestors, both royal and domestic, at their temples or altars, and chapels are built and dedicated to men who have specially distinguished themselves in loyalty, virtue or lofty teaching.

Religion.

Philologists now recognise some affinity between the Korean

[1] Mrs Bishop, *Korea and Her Neighbours*, 1898.

and Japanese languages, both of which appear to be remotely
connected with the Ural-Altaic family. The
The Korean Script. Koreans possess a true alphabet of 28 letters,
which, however, is not a local invention, as is
sometimes asserted. It appears to have been introduced by
the Buddhist monks about or before the tenth century, and to
be based on some cursive form of the Indian (Devanagari)
system,[1] although scarcely any resemblance can now be traced
between the two alphabets. This script is little used except
by the lower classes and the women, the *literati* preferring to
write either in Chinese, or else in the so-called *nido*, that is, an
adaptation of the Chinese symbols to the phonetic expression
of the Korean syllables. The *nido* is exactly analogous to the
Japanese *Katakana* script, in which modified forms of Chinese
ideographs are used phonetically to express 47 syllables (the
so-called *I-ro-fa* syllabary), raised to 73 by the *nigori* and *maru*
diacritical marks.

The present population of Japan, according to E. Baelz,
shows the following types. The first and most important is the
The Japanese. Manchu-Korean type, characteristic of North
China and Korea, and most frequent among the
upper classes in Japan. The stature is conspicuously tall, the
effect being heightened by slender and elegant figure. The
face is long, with more or less oblique eyes but no marked
prominence of the cheek-bones. The nose is aquiline, the chin
slightly receding. With this type is associated a narrow chest,
giving an air of elegance rather than of muscularity, an effect
which is enhanced by the extremely delicate hands with long
slender fingers. The second type is the Mongol, and presents
a distinct contrast, with strong and squarely built figure, broad
face, prominent cheek-bones, oblique eyes, flat nose and wide
mouth. This type is not common in the Japanese Islands.
The third type, more conspicuous than either of the preceding,
is the Malay. The stature is small, with well-knit frame, and
broad, well-developed chest. The face is generally round, the
nose short, jaws and chin frequently projecting. None of these
three types represents the aboriginal race of Japan, for there
seems to be no doubt that the Ainu, who now survive in parts

---

[1] T. de Lacouperie says on "a Tibeto-Indian base" (*Beginnings of Writing in Central and Eastern Asia*, 1894, p. 148); and E. H. Parker: "It is demonstrable that the Korean letters are an adaptation from the Sanskrit," *i.e.* the Devanagari (*Academy*, Dec. 21, 1895, p. 550).

of the northern island of Yezo, occupied a greater area in earlier times and to them the prehistoric shell-mounds and other remains are usually attributed.[1]   The Ainu are thickly and strongly built, but differ from all other Oriental types in the hairiness of face and body.   The head is long, with a cephalic index of 77.8.   Face and nose are broad, and the eyes are horizontal, not oblique, lacking the Mongolian fold.

It is generally assumed that this population represents the easterly migration of that long-headed type which can be traced across the continents of Europe and Asia in the Stone Age, and that their entrance into the islands was effected at a time when the channel separating them from the mainland was neither so wide nor so deep as at the present time.   Later Manchu-Korean invaders from the West, Mongols from the South, and Malays from the East pressed the aborigines further and further north, to Yezo, Sakhalin and the Kuriles.   But it is possible that the Ainu were not the earliest inhabitants of Japan, for they themselves bear witness to predecessors, the *Koro-pok-guru*, mentioned above (p. 260).   Neither is the assumption of kinship between the Ainu and prehistoric populations of Western Europe accepted without demur.   Deniker, while acknowledging the resemblance to certain European types, classes the Ainu as a separate race, the *Palaeasiatics*.   For while in head-length, prominent superciliary ridges, hairiness and the form of the nose they may be compared to Russians, Todas, and Australians, their skin colour, prominent cheek-bones, and other somatic features make any close affinity impossible.[2]

Origins— Constituent Elements.

In spite of these various ingredients the Japanese people may be regarded as fairly homogeneous.   Apart from some tall and robust persons [amongst the upper classes, and athletes, acrobats, and wrestlers, the general impression that the Japanese are a short finely moulded race is fully borne out by the now regularly recorded military measurements of recruits, showing for height an average of 1.585 m. (5 ft. 2½ in.) to 1.639 m. (5 ft. 4½ in.), for chest 33 in., and disproportionately short legs.   Other distinctive characters, all tending to stamp a certain individuality on the people, taken as a whole and

Japanese Type.

---

[1] See p. 261.   Also Koganei, " Ueber die Urbewohner von Japan," *Mitt. d. Deutsch. Gesell. f. Natur- u. Völkerkunde Ostasiens*, IX. 3, 1903, containing an exhaustive review of recent literature, and N. G. Munro, *Prehistoric Japan*, 1912.

[2] J. Deniker, *Races of Man*, 1900, pp. 371–2.   See also J. Batchelor, *The Ainu of Japan*, 1892, and the article " Ainus " in *Ency. of Religion and Ethics*, 1908.

irrespective of local peculiarities, are a flat forehead, great distance between the eyebrows, a very small nose with raised nostrils, no glabella, no perceptible nasal root ; [1] an active, wiry figure ; the exposed skin less yellow than the Chinese, and rather inclining to a light fawn, but the covered parts very light, some say even white ; the eyes also less oblique, and all other characteristically Mongol features generally softened, except the black lank hair, which in transverse section is perhaps even rounder than that of most other Mongol peoples. [2]

With this it will be instructive to compare F. H. H. Guillemard's graphic account of the Liu-Kiu islanders, whose Koreo-Japanese affinities are now placed beyond all doubt : " They are a short race, probably even shorter than the Japanese, but much better proportioned, being without the long bodies and short legs of the latter people, and having as a rule extremely well-developed chests. The colour of the skin varies of course with the social position of the individual. Those who work in the fields, clad only in a waist-cloth, are nearly as dark as a Malay, but the upper classes are much fairer, and are at the same time devoid of any of the yellow tint of the Chinaman. To the latter race indeed they cannot be said to bear any resemblance, and though the type is much closer to the Japanese, it is nevertheless very distinct. . . . In Liu-Kiu the Japanese and natives were easily recognised by us from the first, and must

Japanese and Liu-Kiu Islanders.

therefore be possessed of very considerable differences. The Liu-Kiuan has the face less flattened, the eyes are more deeply set, and the nose more prominent at its origin. The forehead is high and the cheekbones somewhat less marked than in the Japanese ; the eyebrows are arched and thick, and the eyelashes long. The expression is gentle and pleasing, though somewhat sad, and is apparently a true index of their character." [3]

This description is not accepted without some reserve by Chamberlain, who in fact holds that " the physical type of the Luchuans resembles that of the Japanese almost to identity." [4] In explanation however of the singularly mild, inoffensive, and " even timid disposition " of the Liu-Kiuans, this observer suggests " the probable absence of any admixture of Malay

[1] G. Baudens, *Bul. Soc. Geogr.* x. p. 419.
[2] See especially E. Baelz, " Die körperlichen Eigenschaften der Japaner," in *Mitt. der Deutsch. Gesell, f. Natur- u. Völkerkunde Ostasiens,* 28 and 32.
[3] *Cruise of the Marchesa,* 1886, I. p. 36.
[4] *Geogr. Journ.* 1895, II. p. 318.

blood in the race." [1]   But everybody admits a Malay element
in Japan.   It would therefore appear that Guillemard must be
right, and that, as even shown by all good photographs, differences do exist, due in fact to the presence of this very Malay
strain in the Japanese race.

Elsewhere [2] Chamberlain has given us a scholarly account
of the Liu-Kiu language, which is not merely a " sister," as he
says, but obviously an *elder* sister, more archaic
in structure and partly in its phonetics, than the   The Languages
oldest known form of Japanese.   In the verb, for   and Religions.
instance, Japanese retains only one past tense of the indicative,
with but one grammatical form, whereas Liu-Kiuan preserves
the three original past tenses, each of which possesses a five-
fold inflection.   All these racial, linguistic, and even mental
resemblances, such as the fundamental similarity of many of
their customs and ways of thought, he would explain with much
probability by the routes followed by the first emigrants from
the mainland.   While the great bulk spread east and north
over the great archipelago, everywhere " driving the aborigines
before them," a smaller stream may have trended southward
to the little southern group, whose islets stretch like stepping-
stones the whole way from Japan to Great Liu-Kiu. [3]

Amongst the common mental traits, mention is made of the
Shinto religion, " the simplest and most rustic form " of which
still survives in Liu-Kiu.   Here, as in Japan, it
was originally a rude system of nature-worship,   Cult of the
the normal development of which was arrested   Dead.
by Chinese and Buddhist influences.   Later it became associated
with spirit-worship, the spirits being at first the souls of the
dead, and although there is at present no cult of the dead, in the
strict sense of the expression, the Liu-Kiu islanders probably
pay more respect to the departed than any people in the
world.

In Japan, Shintoism, as reformed in recent times, has become much more a political institution than a religious system.
The *Kami-no-michi*, that is, the Japanese form
of the Chinese *Shin-to*, " way of the Gods," or   Shintoism.
" spirits," is not merely the national faith, but is inseparably
bound up with the interests of the reigning dynasty, holding
the Mikado to be the direct descendant of the Sun-goddess.

[1] *Geogr. Journ.* 1895, II. p. 460.
[2] *Journ. Anthrop. Soc.* 1897, p. 47 sq.   [3] *Ibid.* p. 58.

Hence its three cardinal precepts now are :—1. Honour the *Kami* (spirits), of whom the emperor is the chief representative on earth ; 2. Revere him as thy sovereign ; 3. Obey the will of his Court, and that is the whole duty of man. There is no moral code, and loyal expositors have declared that the Mikado's will is the only test of right and wrong.

But apart from this political exegesis, Shintoism in its higher form may be called a cultured deism, in its lower a " blind obedience to governmental and priestly dictates." [1] There are dim notions about a supreme creator, immortality, and even rewards and penalties in the after-life. Some also talk vaguely, as a pantheist might, of a sublime being or essence pervading all nature, too vast and ethereal to be personified or addressed in prayer, identified with the *tenka*, " heavens," from which all things emanate, to which all return. Yet, although a personal deity seems thus excluded, their are Shinto temples, apparently for the worship of the heavenly bodies and powers of nature, conceived as self-existing personalities—the so-called *Kami*, " spirits," " gods," of which there are " eight millions," that is, they are countless.

One cannot but suspect that some of these notions have been grafted on the old national faith by Buddhism, which

Buddhism. was introduced about 550 A.D. and for a time had great vogue. It was encouraged especially by the Shoguns, or military usurpers of the Mikado's [2] functions, obviously as a set-off against the Shinto theocracy. During their tenure of power (1192–1868 A.D.) the land was covered with Buddhist shrines and temples, some of vast size and quaint design, filled with hideous idols, huge bells, and colossal statues of Buddha.

But with the fall of the Shogun the little prestige still enjoyed by Buddhism came to an end, and the temples, spoiled of their treasures, have more than ever become the resort of pleasure-seekers rather than of pious worshippers. " To all the larger temples are attached regular spectacles, playhouses, panoramas, besides lotteries, games of various sorts, including the famous ' fan-throwing,' and shooting-galleries, where the bow and arrow and the blow-pipe take the place of the rifle.

---

[1] Ripley and Dana, *Amer. Cyc.* IX. 538.

[2] *Shogun* from *Sho*=general, and *gún*=army, hence Commander-in-chief ; *Mikado* from *mi*=sublime, and *kado*=gate, with which cf. the " Sublime Porte " (J. J. Rein, *Japan nach Reisen u. Studien*, 1881, I. p. 245). But Mikado has become somewhat antiquated, being now generally replaced by the title *Kotei*, " Emperor."

The accumulated treasures of the priests have been confiscated, the monks driven from their monasteries, and many of these buildings converted into profane uses.   Countless temple bells have already found their way to America, or have been sold for old metal." [1]

Besides these forms of belief, there is a third religious, or rather philosophic system, the so-called *Siza*, based on the ethical teachings of Confucius, a sort of refined materialism, such as underlies the whole religious thought of the nation. Siza, always confined to the *literati*, has in recent years found a formidable rival in the " English Philosophy," represented by such writers as Buckle, Mill, Herbert Spencer, Darwin, and Huxley, most of whose works have already been translated into Japanese.

Thus this highly gifted people are being assimilated to the western world in their social and religious, as well as their political institutions.   Their intellectual powers, already tested in the fields of war, science, diplomacy, and self-government, are certainly superior to those of all other Asiatic peoples, and this is perhaps the best guarantee for the stability of the stupendous transformation that a single generation has witnessed from an exaggerated form of medieval feudalism to a political and social system in harmony with the most advanced phases of modern thought.   The system has doubtless not yet penetrated to the lower strata, especially amongst the rural populations.   But their natural receptivity, combined with a singular freedom from " insular prejudice," must ensure the ultimate acceptance of the new order by all classes of the community.

[1] Keane's *Asia*, I. p. 487.

CHAPTER IX

THE NORTHERN MONGOLS (*continued*)

The Finno-Turki Peoples—Assimilation to the Caucasic Type—Turki Cradle—
Ural-Altaian Invasions—The Scythians—Parthians and Turkomans—Massa-
getae and Yué-chi—Indo-Scythians and Graeco-Baktrians—Dahae, Ját, and
Rájput Origins—The " White Huns "—The Uigurs—Orkhon Inscriptions—
The Assena Turki Dynasty—Toghuz-Uigur Empire—Kashgarian and Sun-
garian Populations—The Oghuz Turks and their Migrations—Seljuks and
Osmanli—The Yakuts—The Kirghiz—Kazák and Kossack—The Kara-
Kirghiz—The Finnish Peoples—Former and Present Domain—Late West-
ward Spread of the Finns—The Bronze and Iron Ages in the Finnish Lands—
The Baltic Finns—Relations to Goths, Letts, and Slavs—Finno-Russ Origins
—Tavastian and Karelian Finns—The Kwæns—The Lapps—Samoyeds and
Permian Finns—Lapp Origins and Migrations—Temperament—Religion—
The Volga Finns—The Votyak Pagans—Human Sacrifices—The Bulgars—
Origins and Migrations—An Ethnical Transformation—Great and Little
Bulgaria—Avars and Magyars—Magyar Origins and early Records—Present
Position of the Magyars—Ethnical and Linguistic Relations in Eastern
Europe.

IN a very broad way all the western branches of the North
Mongol division may be comprised under the collective designation of Finno-Turki Mongols. Jointly they
constitute a well-marked section of the family,
being distinguished from the eastern section by
several features which they have in common, and the most
important of which is unquestionably a much larger infusion
of Caucasic blood than is seen in any of the Mongolo-Tungusic
groups. So pronounced is this feature amongst many Finnish
as will as Turkish peoples, that some anthropologists have felt
inclined to deny any direct connection between the eastern
and western divisions of Mongolian man and to regard the
Baltic Finns, for instance, rather as " Allophylian Whites "
than as original members of the yellow race. Prichard, to
whom we owe this now nearly obsolete term
" Allophylian," held this view,[1] and even Sayce
is " more than doubtful whether we can class the
Mongols physiologically with the Turkish-Tatars [the Turki
peoples], or the Ugro-Finns." [2]

The Finno-
Turki Peoples.

Assimilation to
the Caucasic
Type.

[1] *Natural History of Man*, 1865 ed. pp. 185–6.
[2] *Science of Language*, 1879, II. p. 190.

It may, indeed, be allowed that at present the great majority of the Finno-Turki populations occupy a position amongst the varieties of mankind which is extremely perplexing for the strict systematist. When the whole division is brought under survey, every shade of transition is observed between the Siberian Samoyeds of the Finnic branch and the steppe Kirghiz of the Turki branch on the one hand, both of whom show Mongol characters in an exaggerated form, and on the other the Osmanli Turks and Hungarian Magyars, most of whom may be regarded as typical Caucasians. Moreover, the difficulty is increased by the fact, already pointed out, that these mixed Mongolo-Caucasic characters occur not only amongst the late historic groups, but also amongst the earliest known groups—" Chudes," Usuns, Uigurs and others—who may be called Proto-Finnish and Proto-Turki peoples. But precisely herein lies the solution of the problem. Most of the region now held by Turki and Finnish nations was originally occupied by long-headed Caucasic men of the late Stone Ages (see above). Then followed the Proto-Mongol intruders from the Tibetan table-land, who partly submerged, partly intermingled with their neolithic neighbours, many thus acquiring those mixed characters by which they have been distinguished from the earliest historic times. Later, further interminglings took place according as the Finno-Turki hordes, leaving their original seats in the Altai and surrounding regions, advanced westwards and came more and more into contact with the European populations of Caucasic type.

We may therefore conclude that the majority of the Finno-Turki were almost from the first a somewhat mixed race, and that during historic times the original Mongol element has gradually yielded to the Caucasic in the direction from east to west. Such is the picture now presented by these heterogeneous populations, who in their primeval eastern seats are still mostly typical Mongols, but have been more and more assimilated to the European type in their new Anatolian, Baltic, Danubian, and Balkan homes.

Observant travellers have often been impressed by this progressive conformity of the Mongolo-Turki to Europeans. During his westward journey through Central Asia Younghusband, on passing from Mongolia to Eastern Turkestan, found that the people, though tall and fine-looking, had at first more of the Mongol cast of feature than he had expected.

" Their faces, however, though somewhat round, were slightly more elongated than the Mongol, and there was considerably more intelligence about them.   But there was more roundness, less intelligence, less sharpness in the outlines than is seen in the inhabitants of Kashgar and Yarkand."   Then he adds : " As I proceeded westwards I noticed a gradual, scarcely per- ceptible, change from the round of a Mongolian type to a sharper and yet more sharp type of feature. . . . As we get farther away from Mongolia, we notice that the faces become gradually longer and narrower ; and farther west still, among some of the inhabitants of Afghan Turkestan, we see that the Tartar or Mongol type of feature is almost entirely lost." [1]   To com- plete the picture it need only be added that still further west, in Asia Minor, the Balkan Peninsula, Hungary, and Finland, the Mongol features are often entirely lost.   " The Turks of the west have so much Aryan and Semitic blood in them, that the last vestiges of their original physical characters have been lost, and their language alone indicates their previous descent." [2]

Before they were broken up and dispersed over half the northern hemisphere by Mongol pressure from the east, **Turki Cradle.** the primitive Turki tribes dwelt, according to Howorth, mainly between the Ulugh-dagh moun- tains and the Orkhon river in Mongolia, that is, along the southern slopes and spurs of the Altai-Sayan system from the head waters of the Irtysh to the valleys draining north to Lake Baikal.   But the Turki cradle is shifted farther east by Richt- hofen, who thinks that their true home lay between the Amur, the Lena, and the Selenga, where at one time they had their camping-grounds in close proximity to their Mongol and Tungus kinsmen.   There is nothing to show that the Yakuts, who are admittedly of Turki stock, ever migrated to their present northern homes in the Lena basin, which has more probably always been their native land.[3]

But when they come within the horizon of history the Turki are already a numerous nation, with a north-western and south-

---

[1] *The Heart of a Continent*, 1896, p. 118.
[2] O. Peschel, *Races of Man*, 1894, p. 380.
[3] See Ch. de Ujfalvy, *Les Aryens*, etc., 1896, p. 25. Reference should perhaps be also made to E. H. Parker's theory (*Academy*, Dec. 21, 1895) that the Turki cradle lay, not in the Altai or Altun-dagh (" Golden Mountains ") of North Mon- golia, but 1000 miles farther south in the " Golden Mountains " (*Kin-shan*) of the present Chinese province of Kansu. But the evidence relied on is not satis- factory, and indeed in one or two important instances is not evidence at all.

eastern division,[1] which may well have jointly occupied the whole region from the Irtysh to the Lena, and both views may thus be reconciled. In any case the Turki domain lay west of the Mongol, and the Altai uplands, taken in the widest sense, may still be regarded as the most probable zone of specialisation for the Turki physical type. The typical characteristics are a yellowish white complexion, a high brachycephalic head, often almost cuboid, due to parieto-occipital flattening (especially noticeable among the Yakuts), an elongated oval face, with straight, somewhat prominent nose, and non-Mongolian eyes. The stature is moderate, with an average of 1.675 m. (5 ft. 6 in.), and a tendency to stoutness.

Intermediate between the typical Turki and the Mongols Hamy places the Uzbegs, Kirghiz, Bashkirs, and Nogais ; and between the Turks and Finns those extremely mixed groups of East Russia commonly but wrongly called " Tartars," as well as other transitions between Turk, Slav, Greek, Arab, Osmanli of Constantinople, Kurugli of Algeria and others, whose study shows the extreme difficulty of accurately determining the limits of the Yellow and the White races.[2]

Analogous difficulties recur in the study of the Northerr (Siberian) groups—Samoyeds, Ostyaks, Voguls and othei Ugrians—who present great individual variations, leading almost without a break from the Mongol to the Lapp, from the Lapp to the Finn, from Finn to Slav and Teuton. Thus may be shown a series of observations continuous between the most typical Mongol, and those aberrant Mongolo-Caucasic groups which answer to Prichard's " Allophylian races." Thus also is confirmed by a study of details the above broad generalisation in which I have endeavoured to determine the relation of the Finno-Turki peoples to the primary Mongol and Caucasic divisions.

Peisker's description of the Scythian invasions of Irania[3] may be taken as typical of the whole area, and explains the complexity of the ethnological problems. The steppes and deserts of Central Asia are an impas-   Ural-Altaian sable barrier for the South Asiatics, the Aryans,   Invasions. but not for the North Asiatic, the Altaian ; for him they are an open country, providing him with the indispensable winter

---

[1] J. B. Bury, *English Historical Rev.*, July, 1897.

[2] *L'Anthropologie*, vi. No. 3.

[3] T. Peisker, " The Asiatic Background," *Cambridge Medieval History*, Vol. i. 1911, p. 354.

pastures. On the other hand, for the South Asiatic Aryan these deserts are an object of terror, and besides he is not impelled towards them as he has winter pastures near at hand. It is this difference in the distance of summer and winter pastures that makes the North Asiatic Altaian an ever-wandering herdsman, and the grazing part of the Indo-European race cattle-rearers settled in limited districts. Thus, while the native Iranian must halt before the trackless region of steppes and deserts and cannot follow the well-mounted robber-nomad thither, Iran itself is the object of greatest longing to the nomadic Altaian. Here he can plunder and enslave to his heart's delight, and if he succeeds in maintaining himself for a considerable time among the Aryans, he learns the language of the subjugated people and, by mingling with them, loses his Mongol characteristics more and more. If the Iranian is now fortunate enough to shake off the yoke, the dispossessed iranised Altaian intruder inflicts himself upon other lands. So it was with the Scythians. Leaving their families behind in the South Russian steppes, the Scythians invaded Media *c.* B.C. 630, and advanced into Mesopotamia as far as Egypt.

The Scythians. In Media they took Median wives and learned the Median language. After being driven out by Cyaxares, on their return, some 28 years later, they met with a new generation, the offspring of the wives and daughters whom they had left behind, and slaves of an alien race. A hundred and fifty years later Hippocrates remarked their yellowish red complexion, corpulence, smooth skins, and their consequent eunuch-like appearance—all typically Mongol characteristics. Hippocrates was the most celebrated physician and natural philosopher of the ancient world. His evidence is unshakeable and cannot be invalidated by the Aryan speech of the Scythians. Their Mongol type was innate in them, whereas their Iranian speech was acquired and is no refutation of Hippocrates' testimony. On the later Greek vases from South Russian excavations they already appear strongly demongolised and the Altaian is only suggested by their hair, which is as stiff as a horse's mane— hence Aristotle's epithet εὐθύτριχες—the characteristic that survives longest among all Ural-Altaian hybrid peoples.

E. H. Parker unfortunately lent the weight of his authority to the statement that the word " Türkö " [Turki] " goes no farther back than the fifth century of our era," and that " so far as recorded history is concerned the name of Turk dates from this time."[1] But Turki tribes bearing this national name had penetrated into East Europe hundreds of years before that time, and were already seated on the Tanais (Don) about the new era. They are mentioned by name both by Pomponius Mela[2] and by Pliny,[3] and to the same connection belonged, beyond all doubt, the warlike *Parthians*, who 300 years earlier were already seated on the confines of Iran and Turan, routed the legions of Crassus and Antony, and for five centuries (250 B.C.–229 A.D.) usurped the throne of the " King of Kings," holding sway from the Euphrates to the Ganges, and from the Caspian to the Indian Ocean. Direct descendants of the Parthians are the fierce Turkoman nomads, who for ages terrorised over all the settled populations encircling the Aralo-Caspian depression. Their power has at last been broken by the Russians, but they are still politically dominant in Persia.[4] They have thus been for many ages in the closest contact with Caucasic Iranians, with the result that the present Turkoman type is shown by J. L. Yavorsky's observations to be extremely variable.[5]

Parthians and Turkomans.

Both the Parthians and the *Massagetae* have been identified with the *Yué-chi*, who figured so largely in the annals of the Han dynasties, and are above mentioned as having been driven west to Sungaria by the Hiung-nu after the erection of the Great Wall. It has been said that, could we follow the peregrinations of the Yué-chi bands from their early seats at the foot of the Kinghan mountains to their disappearance amid the snows of the Western Himalayas, we should hold the key to the solution of the

Massagetae and Yué-chi.

---

[1] *Academy*, Dec. 21, 1895, p. 548.

[2] " Budini Gelonion urbem ligneam habitant ; juxta Thyssagetae *Turcaeque* vastas silvas occupant, alunturque venando " (I. 19, p. 27 of Leipzig ed. 1880).

[3] " Dein Tanain amnem gemino ore influentem incolunt Sarmatae...Tindari, Thussagetae, *Tyrcae*, usque ad solitudines saltuosis convallibus asperas, etc." (Bk. VIII. 7, Vol. I. p. 234 of Berlin ed. 1886). The variants *Turcae* and *Tyrcae* are noteworthy, as indicating the same vacillating sound of the root vowel (*u* and *y=ü*) that still persists.

[4] Not only was the usurper Nadir Shah a Turkoman of the Afshàr tribe but the present reigning family belongs to the rival clan of Qajar Turkomans long settled in Khorasan, the home of their Parthian forefathers.

[5] Of 59 Turkomans the hair was generally a dark brown ; the eyes brown (45) and light grey (14) ; face orthognathous (52) and prognathous (7) ; eyes mostly *not* oblique ; cephalic index 68.69 to 81.76, mean 75.64 ; dolicho 28, sub-dolicho 18, 9 mesati, 4 sub-brachy. Five skulls from an old graveyard at Samarkand were also very heterogeneous, cephalic index ranging from 77.72 to 94.93. This last, unless deformed, exceeds in brachycephaly " le célèbre crâne d'un Slave vende qu'on cite dans les manuels d'anthropologie " (Th. Volkov, *L'Anthropologie*, 1897, pp. 355–7).

K.

obscure problems associated with the migrations of the Mongolo-Turki hordes since the torrent of invasion was diverted
westwards by Shih Hwang Ti's mighty barrier.   One point,
however, seems clear enough, that the Yué-chi were a different
people both from the Parthians who had already occupied
Hyrcania (Khorasan) at least in the third century B.C., if not
earlier, and from the Massagetae.   For the latter were seated
on the Yaxartes (Sir-darya) in the time of Cyrus (sixth century
B.C.), whereas the Yué-chi still dwelt east of Lake Lob (Tarim
basin) in the third century.   After their defeat by the Hiung-nu
and the Usuns (201 and 165 B.C.), they withdrew to Sogdiana
(Transoxiana), reduced the *Ta-Hia* of Baktria, and in 126 B.C.

Indo-Scythians   overthrew the Graeco-Baktrian kingdom, which
and Graeco-   had been founded after the death of Alexander to-
Baktrians.   wards the close of the fourth century.   But in the
Kabul valley, south of the Hindu-Kush, the Greeks still held
their ground for over 100 years, until Kadphises I., king of the
Kushans—a branch of the Yué-chi—after uniting the whole
nation in a single Indo-Scythian state, extended his conquests
to Kabul and succeeded Hermaeus, last of the Greek dynasty
(40–20 B.C. ?).   Kadphises' son Kadaphes (10 A.D.) added to
his empire a great part of North India, where his successors
of the Yué-chi dynasty reigned from the middle of the first to
the end of the fourth century A.D.   Here they are supposed by

Dahae, Ját, and   some authorities to be still represented by the
Rájput Origins.   *Játs* and *Rájputs*, and even Prichard allows that
the supposition " does not appear altogether pre-
posterous," although " the physical characters of the Játs are
very different from those attributed to the Yuetschi [Yué-chi]
and the kindred tribes [Suns, Kushans, etc,] by the writers
cited by Klaproth and Abel Remusat, who say that they are
of sanguine complexion with blue eyes." [1]

We now know that these characters present little difficulty
when the composite origin of the Turki people is borne in mind.
On the other hand it is interesting to note that the above-
mentioned Ta-Hia have by some been identified with the warlike
Scythian Dahae,[2] and these with the Dehiya or Dhé, one of the

---

[1] Quoted by W. Crooke, who points out that " the opinion of the best Indian
authorities seems to be gradually turning to the belief that the connection between
Játs and Rájputs is more intimate than was formerly supposed " (*The Tribes and
Castes of the North-Western Provinces and Oudh*, Calcutta, 1896, III. p. 27).

[2] Virgil's " indomiti Dahae " (*Aen.* VIII. 728) : possibly the Dehavites (Dievi)
of Ezra iv. 9.

great divisions of the Indian Játs. But if Rawlinson [1] is right, the term *Dahae* was not racial but social, meaning *rustici*,—the peasantry are opposed to the nomads ; hence the Dahae are heard of everywhere throughout Irania, just as *Dehwar* [2] is still the common designation of the Tajik (Persian) peasantry in Afghanistan and Baluchistan. This is also the view taken by de Ujfalvy, who identifies the Ta-Hia, not with the Scythian Dahae, or with any other particular tribe, but with the peaceful rural population of Baktriana,[3] whose reduction by the Yué-chi, possibly Strabo's Tokhari, was followed by the overthrow of the Graeco-Baktrians. The solution of the puzzling Yué-chi-Ját problem would therefore seem to be that the Dehiya and other Játs, always an agricultural people, are descended from the old Iranian peasantry of Baktriana, some of whom followed the fortunes of their Greek rulers into Kabul valley, while others accompanied the conquering Yué-chi founders of the Indo-Scythian empire into northern India.

Then followed the overthrow of the Yué-chi themselves by the *Yé-tha* (*Ye-tha-i-li-to*) of the Chinese records, that is, the *Ephthalites*, or so-called " White Huns," of the Greek and Arab writers, who about 425 A.D. overran Transoxiana, and soon afterwards penetrated through the moun-tain passes into the Kabul and Indus valleys. The "White Huns." Although confused by some contemporary writers (Zosimus, Am. Marcellinus) with Attila's Huns, M. Drouin has made it clear that the Yé-tha were not Huns (Mongols) at all, but, like the Yué-chi, a Turki people, who were driven westwards about the same time as the Hiung-nu by the Yuan-yuans (see above). Of Hun they had little but the name, and the more accurate Procopius was aware that they differed entirely from " the Huns known to us, not being nomads, but settled for a long time in a fertile region." He speaks also of their white colour and regular features, and their sedentary life [4] as in the Chinese accounts, where they are described as warlike conquerors of twenty kingdoms, as far as that of the A-si (Arsacides, Par-thians), and in their customs resembling the Tu-Kiu (Turks), being in fact " of the same race." On the ruins of the Indo-Scythian (Yué-chi) empire, the White Huns ruled in India

[1] *Herodotus*, Vol. i. p. 413.
[2] From Pers. دہ, *dih, dah,* village (Parsi *dahi*).
[3] *Les Aryens*, etc., p. 68 sq.
[4] *De Bello Persico, passim.*

and the surrounding lands from 425 to the middle of the sixth
centuiy. A little later came the Arabs, who in 706 captured
Samarkand, and under the Abassides were supreme in Central
Asia till scattered to the winds by the Oghuz Turki hordes.

From all this it has been suggested that—while the Baktrian
peasants entered India as settlers, and are now represented by
the agricultural Játs—the Yué-chi and Yé-tha, both of fair
Turki stock, came as conquerors, and are now represented by
the Rájputs, " Sons of Kings," the warrior and land-owning
race of northern India. It is significant that these Thákur,
" feudal lords," mostly trace their genealogies from about the beginning of the seventh century, as if they had become Hinduised
soon after the fall of the foreign Yé-tha dynasty, while on the
other hand " the country legends abound with instances of the
conflict between the Rájput and the Bráhman in prehistoric
times."[1] This supports the conjecture that the Rájputs entered
India, not as " Aryans " of the Kshatriya or military caste, as
is commonly assumed, but as aliens (Turki), the avowed foes
of the true Aryans, that is, the Bráhman or theocratic (priestly)
caste. Thus also is explained the intimate association of the
Rájputs and the Játs from the first—the Rájputs being the
Turki leaders of the invasions ; and the Játs their peaceful
Baktrian subjects following in their wake.

The theory that the haughty Rájputs are of unsullied
" Aryan blood " is scarcely any longer held even by the Rájputs
themselves ; they are undoubtedly of mixed origin. But the
definite physical type which H. H. Risley [2] describes as characteristic of Rájputs and Játs in the Kashmir Valley, Punjab
and Rajputana, shows them to be wavy-haired dark-skinned
dolichocephals, linked rather with the " Caucasic " than the
" Mongolian " division.

Nearly related to the White Huns were the *Uigurs*, the
Kao-che of the Chinese annals, who may claim to be the first

The Uigurs.

Turki nation that founded a relatively civilised
State in Central Asia. Before the general com-
motion caused by the westward pressure of the Hiung-nu, they
appear to have dwelt in eastern Turkestan (Kashgaria) between
the Usuns and the Sacae, and here they had already made
considerable progress under Buddhist influences about the
fourth or fifth century of the new era. Later, the Buddhist

[1] Crooke, *op. cit.* IV. p. 221.
[2] *The Tribes and Castes of Bengal,* 1892 ; *The People of India,* 1908.

missionaries from Tibet were replaced by Christian (Nestorian) evangelists from western Asia, who in the seventh century reduced the Uigur language to written form, adapting for the purpose the Syriac alphabet, which was afterwards borrowed by the Mongols and the Manchus.

This Syriac script—which, as shown by the authentic inscription of Si-ngan-fu, was introduced into China in 635 A.D. —is not to be confused with that of the Orkhon inscriptions [1] dating from 732 A.D., and bearing a certain resemblance to some of the Runic characters, as also to the Korean, at least in form, but never in sound. Yet although differing from the Uiguric, Prof. Thomsen, who has successfully deciphered the Orkhon text, thinks that this script may also be derived, at least indirectly through some of the Iranian varieties, from the same Aramean (Syriac) form of the Semitic alphabet that gave birth to the Uiguric.[2]

The Orkhon Inscriptions.

It is more important to note that all the non-Chinese inscriptions are in the Turki language, while the Chinese text refers by name to the father, the grandfather, and the great-grandfather of the reigning Khan Bilga, which takes us back nearly to the time when Sinjibu (Dizabul), Great Khan of the Altai Turks, was visited by the Byzantine envoy, Zimarchus, in 569 A.D. In the still extant report of this embassy [3] the Turks (Τοῦρκοι) are mentioned by name, and are described as nomads who dwelt in tents mounted on wagons, burnt the dead, and raised to their memory monuments, statues, and cairns with as many stones as the foes slain by the deceased in battle. It is also stated that they had a peculiar writing system, which must have been that of these Orkhon inscriptions, the Uiguric having apparently been introduced somewhat later.

---

[1] Discovered in 1889 by N. M. Yadrintseff in the Orkhon valley, which drains to the Selenga affluent of Lake Baikal. The inscriptions, one in Chinese and three in Turki, cover the four sides of a monument erected by a Chinese emperor to the memory of Kyul-teghin, brother of the then reigning Turki Khan Bilga (Mogilan). In the same historical district, where stand the ruins of Karakoram— long the centre of Turki and later of Mongol power—other inscribed monuments have also been found, all apparently in the same Turki language and script, but quite distinct from the glyptic rock carvings of the Upper Yenisei river, Siberia. The chief workers in this field were the Finnish archaeologists, J. R. Aspelin, A. Snellman and Axel O. Heikel, the results of whose labours are collected in the *Inscriptions de l'Jénisséi recuellies et publiées par la Société Finlandaise d'Archéologie*, Helsingfors, 1889 ; and *Inscriptions de l'Orkhon*, etc., Helsingfors, 1892.

[2] "La source d'où est tirée l'origine de l'alphabet turc, sinon immédiatement, du moins par intermédiaire, c'est la forme de l'alphabet sémitique qu'on appelle araméenne " (*Inscriptions de l'Orkhon déchiffrées*, Helsingfors, 1894).

[3] See Klaproth, *Tableau Historique de l'Asie*, p. 116 sq.

Originally the Uigurs comprised nineteen clans, which at a remote period already formed two great sections :—the On-Uigur ("Ten Uigurs ") in the south, and the Toghuz-Uigur ("Nine Uigurs ") in the north. The former had penetrated westwards to the Aral Sea [1] as early as the second century A.D., and many of them undoubtedly took part in Attila's invasion of Europe.

Later, all these Western Uigurs, mentioned amongst the hordes that harassed the Eastern Empire in the fifth and sixth centuries, in association especially with the Turki Avars, disappear from history, being merged in the Ugrian and other Finnish peoples of the Volga basin. The Toghuz section also, after throwing off the yoke of the Mongol or Tungus Geugen

The Assena Turki Dynasty. (Jeu-Jen) in the fifth century, were for a time submerged in the vast empire of the Altai Turks, founded in 552 by Tumen of the House of Assena (A-shi-na), who was the first to assume the title of Kha-Khan, " Great Khan," and whose dynasty ruled over the united Turki and Mongol peoples from the Pacific to the Caspian, and from the Frozen Ocean to the confines of China and Tibet. Both the above-mentioned Sinjibu, who received the Byzantine envoy, and the Bilga Khan of the Orkhon *stele*, belonged to this dynasty, which was replaced in 774 by Pei-lo (Huei-hu), chief of the Toghuz-Uigurs. This is how we are to understand the statement that all the Turki peoples who during the somewhat unstable rule of the Assena dynasty from 552 to 774 had undergone many vicissitudes, and about 580 were even broken into two great sections (Eastern Turks of the Karakoram region and Western Turks of the Tarim basin), were again united

Toghuz-Uigur Empire. in one vast political system under the Toghuz-Uigurs. These are henceforth known in history simply as Uigurs, the On branch having, as stated, long disappeared in the West. The centre of their power seems to have oscillated between Karakoram and Turfan in Eastern Turkestan, the extensive ruins of which have been explored by D. A. Klements, Sven Hedin and M. A. Stein. Their vast dominions were gradually dismembered, first by the *Hakas*, or *Ki-li-Kissé*, precursors of the present Kirghiz, who overran the eastern (Orkhon) districts about 840, and then by the Muhammadans of Máwar-en-Nahar (Transoxiana), who over-

---

[1] They are the *Onoi*, the " Tens," who at this time dwelt beyond the Scythians of the Caspian Sea (Dionysius Periegetes).

threw the " Lion Kings," as the Uigur Khans of Turfan were called, and set up several petty Mussulman states in Eastern Turkestan. Later they fell under the yoke of the Kara-Khitais, and were amongst the first to join the devastating hordes of Jenghiz-Khan; their name, which henceforth vanishes from history,[1] has been popularly recognised under the form of "Ogres," in fable and nursery tales, but the derivation lacks historical foundation.

At present the heterogeneous populations of the Tarim basin (Kashgaria, Eastern Turkestan), where the various elements have been intermingled, offer a striking contrast to those of the Ili valley (Sungaria), where one invading horde has succeeded and been superimposed on another. Hence the complexity of the Kashgarian type, in which the original " horse-like face " everywhere crops out, absorbing the later Mongolo-Turki arrivals. But in Sungaria the Kalmuk, Chinese, Dungan, Taranchi, and Kirghiz groups are all still sharply distinguished and perceptible at a glance. " Amongst the Kashgarians—a term as vague ethnically as ' Aryan '—Richthofen has determined the successive presence of the Su, Yué-chi, and Usun hordes, as described in the early Chinese chronicles." [2]

The recent explorations of M. A. Stein have thrown some light on the ethnology of this region, and a preliminary survey of results was prepared and published by T. A. Joyce. He concludes that the original inhabitants were of Alpine type, with, in the west, traces of the Indo-Afghan, and that the Mongolian has had very little influence upon the population.[3]

In close proximity to the Toghuz-Uigurs dwelt the *Oghuz* (*Ghuz, Uz*), for whom eponymous heroes have been provided in the legendary records of the Eastern Turks, although all these terms would appear to be merely shortened forms of Toghuz.[4] But whether true Uigurs, or a distinct branch of

---

[1] It still persists, however, as a tribal designation both amongst the Kirghiz and Uzbegs, and in 1885 Potanin visited the *Yegurs* of the Edzin-gol valley in south-east Mongolia, said to be the last surviving representatives of the Uigur nation (H. Schott, " Zur Uigurenfrage," in *Abhandl. d. k. Akad. d. Wiss.*, Berlin, 1873, pp. 101–21).

[2] Ch. de Ujfalvy, *Les Aryens au Nord et au Sud de l'Hindou-Kouch*, p. 28.

[3] " Notes on the Physical Anthropology of Chinese Turkestan and the Pamirs," *Journ. Roy. Anthr. Inst.* XLII. 1912.

[4] " The Uzi of the Greeks are the Gozz [Ghuz] of the Orientals. They appear on the Danube and the Volga, in Armenia, Syria, and Chorasan, and their name seems to have been extended to the whole Turkoman [Turki] race " [by the Arab writers] ; Gibbon, Ch. LVII.

the Turki people, the Ghuz, as they are commonly called by
The Oghuz   the Arab writers, began their westward migra-
Turks and their   tions about the year 780.   After occupying Trans-
Migrations.   oxiana, where they are now represented by the
Uzbegs [1] of Bokhara and surrounding lands, they gradually
spread as conquerors over all the northern parts of Irania, Asia
Minor, Syria, the Russian and Caucasian steppes, Ukrainia,
Dacia, and the Balkan Peninsula.   In most of these lands they
formed fresh ethnical combinations both with the Caucasic
aborigines, and with many kindred Turki as well as Mongol
peoples, some of whom are settled in these regions since
neolithic times, while others had either accompanied Attila's
expeditions, or followed in his wake (Pechenegs, Komans,
Alans, Kipchaks, Kara-Kalpaks), or else arrived later in company with Jenghiz-Khan and his successors (Karan and Nogai
" Tatars ").[2]

In Russia, Rumania (Dacia), and most of the Balkan Peninsula these Mongolo-Turki blends have been again submerged
by the dominant Slav and Rumanian peoples (Great and Little
Russians, Servo-Croatians, Montenegrini, Moldavians, and
Walachians).   But in south-western Asia they still constitute
perhaps the majority of the population between the Indus and
Constantinople, in many places forming numerous compact
communities, in which the Mongolo-Turki physical and mental
characters are conspicuous. Such, besides the already mentioned
Turkomans of Parthian lineage, are all the nomad and many
of the settled inhabitants of Khiva, Ferghana, Karategin, Bokhara, generally comprised under the name of Uzbegs and
" Sartes."   Such also are the Turki peoples of Afghan Turkestan, and of the neighbouring uplands (Hazaras and Aimaks
who claim Mongol descent, though now of Persian speech); the
Aderbaijani and many other more scattered groups in Persia ;
the Nogai and Kumuk tribes of Caucasia, and especially most
of the nomad and settled agricultural populations of Asia Minor.
The Anatolian peasantry form, in fact, the most numerous and
compact division of the Turki family still surviving in any part
of their vast domain between the Bosporus and the Lena.

---

[1] Who take their name from a mythical Uz-beg, " Prince Uz " (*beg* in Turki=a
chief, or hereditary ruler).
[2] Both of these take their name, not from mythical but from historical chiefs :
—*Kazan Khan* of the Volga, " the rival of Cyrus and Alexander," who was however of the house of Jenghiz, consequently not a Turk, like most of his subjects,
but a true Mongol (*ob.* 1304) ; and *Noga*, the ally and champion of Michael

Out of this prolific Oghuz stock arose many renowned chiefs, founders of vast but somewhat unstable empires, such as those of the Gasnevides, who ruled from Persia to the Indus ; the Seljuks, who first wrested the Asiatic provinces from Byzantium ; the Osmanli, so named from Othman, the Arabised form of Athman, who prepared the way for Orkhan (1326–60), true builder of the Ottoman power, which has alone survived the shipwreck of all the historical Turki states.   The vicissitudes of these monarchies, looked on perhaps with too kindly an eye by Gibbon, belong to the domain of history, and it will suffice here to state that from the ethical standpoint the chief interest centres in that of the Seljukides, covering the period from about the middle of the eleventh to the middle of the thirteenth century. It was under Togrul-beg of this dynasty (1038–63) that " the whole body of the Turkish nation embraced with fervour and sincerity the religion of Mahomet."[1]   A little later began the permanent Turki occupation of Asia Minor, where, after the conquest of Armenia (1065–68) and the overthrow of the Byzantine emperor Romanus Diogenes (1071), numerous military settlements, followed by nomad Turkoman encampments, were established by the great Seljuk rulers, Alp Arslan and Malek Shah (1063–92), at all the strategical points.   These first arrivals were joined later by others fleeing before the Mongol hosts led by Jenghiz-Khan's successors down to the time of Timur-beg.   But the Christians (Greeks and earlier aborigines) were not exterminated, and we read that, while great numbers apostatised, " many thousand children were marked by the knife of circumcision ;   and many thousand captives were devoted to the service or the pleasures of their masters " (*ib.*). In other words, the already mixed Turki intruders were yet more modified by further interminglings with the earlier inhabitants of Asia Minor.   Those who, following the fortunes of the Othman dynasty, crossed the Bosporus and settled in Rumelia and some other parts of the Balkan Peninsula, now prefer to call themselves *Osmanli*, even repudiating the national name " Turk " still retained with pride by the ruder peasant

Seljuks and Osmanli.

Palaeologus against the Mongols marching under the terrible Holagu almost to the shores of the Bosporus.

[1] Gibbon, Chap. LVII.   By the " Turkish nation " is here to be understood the western section only.   The Turks of Máwar-en-Nahar and Kashgaria (Eastern Turkestan) had been brought under the influences of Islam by the first Arab invaders from Persia two centuries earlier.

classes of Asia Minor. The latter are often spoken of as
" Seljuk Turks," as if there were some racial difference between
them and the European Osmanli, and for the distinction there
is some foundation. As pointed out by Arminius Vambéry,[1]
the Osmanli have been influenced and modified by their closer
association with the Christian populations of the Balkan lands,
while in Anatolia the Seljuks have been able better to preserve
the national type and temperament. The true Turki spirit
(" das Türkentum ") survives especially in the provinces of
Lykaonia and Kappadokia, where the few surviving natives
were not only Islamised but ethnically fused, whereas in Europe
most of them (Bosnians, Albanians) were only Islamised, and
here the Turki element has always been slight.

At present the original Turki type and temperament are
perhaps best preserved amongst the remote *Yakuts* of the Lena,
and the *Kirghiz* groups (*Kirghiz Kazaks* and

The Yakuts.

Kara Kirghiz) of the West Siberian steppe and
the Pamir uplands. The Turki connection of the Yakuts, about
which some unnecessary doubts had been raised, has been set
at rest by V. A. Sierochevsky,[2] who, however, describes them
as now a very mixed people, owing to alliances with the Tunguses and Russians. They are of short stature, averaging
scarcely 5 ft. 4 in., and this observer thought their dark but not
brilliant black eyes, deeply sunk in narrow orbits, gave them
more of a Red Indian than of a Mongol cast. They are almost
the only progressive aboriginal people in Siberia, although
numbering not more than 200,000 souls, concentrated chiefly
along the river banks on the plateau between the Lena and the
Aldan.

In the Yakuts we have an extreme instance of the capacity
of man to adapt himself to the *milieu*. They not merely exist,
but thrive and display a considerable degree of energy and
enterprise in the coldest region on the globe. Within the
isothermal of $-72°$ Fahr., Verkhoyansk, in the heart of their
territory, is alone included, for the period from November to
February, and in this temperature, at which the quicksilver
freezes, the Yakut children may be seen gambolling naked in
the snow. In midwinter R. Kennan met some of these " men

---

[1] " Die Stellung der Türken in Europa," in *Geogr. Zeitschrift*, Leipzig, 1897,
Part 5, p. 250 sq.

[2] " Ethnographic Researches," edited by N. E. Vasilofsky for the *Imperial
Geogr. Soc.* 1896, quoted in *Nature*, Dec. 3, 1896, p. 97.

of iron," as Wrangel calls them, airily arrayed in nothing but a shirt and a sheepskin, lounging about as if in the enjoyment of the balmy zephyrs of some genial sub-tropical zone.

Although nearly all are Orthodox Christians, or at least baptized as such, they are mere Shamanists at heart, still conjuring the powers of nature, but offering no worship to a supreme deity, of whom they have a vague notion, though he is too far off to hear, or too good to need their supplications. The world of good and evil spirits, however, has been enriched by accessions from the Russian calendar and pandemonium. Thanks to their commercial spirit, the Yakut language, a very pure Turki idiom, is even more widespread than the race, having become a general medium of intercourse for Tungus, Russian, Mongol and other traders throughout East Siberia, from Irkutsk to the Sea of Okhotsk, and from the Chinese frontier to the Arctic Ocean.[1]

To some extent W. Radloff is right in describing the great Kirghiz Turki family as " of all Turks most nearly allied to the Mongols in their physical characters, and by their family names such as Kyptshak [Kipchak], Argyn, **The Kirghiz.** Naiman, giving evidence of Mongolian descent, or at least of intermixture with Mongols."[2] But we have already been warned against the danger of attaching too much importance to these tribal designations, many of which seem, after acquiring renown on the battle-field, to have passed readily from one ethnic group to another. There are certain Hindu-Kush and Afghan tribes who think themselves Greeks or Arabs, because of the supposed descent of their chiefs from Alexander the Great or the Prophet's family, and genealogical trees spring up like the conjurer's mango plant in support of such illustrious lineage. The Chagatai (Jagatai) tribes, of Turki stock and speech, take their name from a full-blood Mongol, Chagatai, second son of Jenghiz-Khan, to whom fell Eastern Turkestan in the partition of the empire.

In the same way many Uzbeg and Kirghiz Turki tribes are named from famous Mongol chiefs, although no one will deny a strain of true Mongol blood in all these heterogeneous groups. This is evident enough from the square and somewhat flat Mongol features, prominent cheek-bones, oblique eyes, large mouth, feet and hands, yellowish brown complexion, ungainly obese figures and short stature, all of which are charac-

---

[1] A. Erman, *Reise um die Erde*, 1835, Vol. III. p. 51.
[2] Quoted by Peschel, *Races of Man*, p. 383.

teristic of both sections, the Kara-Kirghiz highlanders, and the Kazaks of the lowlands. Some ethnologists regard these Kirghiz groups, not as a distinct branch of the Mongolo-Turki race, but rather as a confederation of several nomad tribes stretching from the Gobi to the Lower Volga, and mingled together by Jenghiz-Khan and his successors.[1]

The true national name is *Kazák*, " Riders," and as they were originally for the most part mounted marauders, or free
Kasak and Kossack.
lances of the steppe, the term came to be gradually applied to all nomad and other horsemen engaged in predatory warfare. It thus at an early date reached the South Russian steppe, where it was adopted in the form of *Kossack* by the Russians themselves. It should be noted that the compound term Kirghiz-Kazak, introduced by the Russians to distinguish these nomads from their own
The Kara-Kirghiz.
Cossacks, is really a misnomer. The word " Kirghiz," whatever its origin, is never used by the Kazaks in reference to themselves, but only to their near relations, the Kirghiz, or Kara-Kirghiz,[2] of the uplands.

These highlanders, who roam the Tian-Shan and Pamir valleys, form two sections :—*On*, " Right," or East, and *Sol*, " Left," or West. They are the *Diko Kamennyi*, that is, " Wild Rock People," of the Russians, whence the expression " Block Kirghiz " still found in some English books of travel. But they call themselves simply Kirghiz, claiming descent from an original tribe of that name, itself sprung from a legendary Kirghiz-beg, from whom are also descended the Chiliks, Kitars and others, all now reunited with the Ons and the Sols.

The Kazaks also are grouped in long-established and still jealously maintained sections—the *Great, Middle, Little*, and *Inner Horde*—whose joint domain extends from Lake Balkash round the north side of the Caspian down to the Lower Volga.[3] All accepted the teachings of Islam many centuries ago, but their Muhammadanism [4] is of a somewhat negative

---

[1] M. Balkashin in *Izvestia Russ. Geogr. Soc.*, April, 1883.

[2] *Kara*=" Black," with reference to the colour of their round felt tents.

[3] On the obscure relations of these Hordes to the Kara-Kirghiz and prehistoric Usuns some light has been thrown by the investigations of N. A. Aristov, a summary of whose conclusions is given by A. Ivanovski in *Centralblatt für Anthropologie*, etc., 1896, p. 47.

[4] Although officially returned as Muhammadans of the Sunni sect, Levchine tells us that it is hard to say whether they are Moslem, Pagan (Shamanists), or Manichean, this last because they believe God has made good angels called

character, without mosques, mollahs, or fanaticism, and in practice not greatly to be distinguished from the old Siberian Shamanism. Kumiss, fermented mare's milk, their universal drink, as amongst the ancient Scythians, plays a large part in the life of these hospitable steppe nomads.

One of the lasting results of Castrèn's labours has been to place beyond reasonable doubt the Altai origin of the Finnish peoples.[1] Their cradle may now be localised with some confidence about the head waters of the **The Finns.** Yenisei, in proximity to that of their Turki kinsmen. Here is the seat of the *Soyotes* and of the closely allied *Koibals, Kamassintzi, Matores, Karagasses* and others, who occupy a considerable territory along both slopes of the Sayan range, and may be regarded as the primitive stock of the widely diffused Finnish race. Some of these groups have intermingled with the neighbouring Turki peoples, and even speak Turki dialects. But the original Finnish type and speech are well represented by the Soyotes, who are here indigenous, and "from these their . . . kinsmen, the Samoyeds have spread as breeders of reindeer to the north of the continent from the White Sea to the Bay of Chatanga."[2] Others, following a westerly route along the foot of the Altai and down the Irtysh to the Urals, appear to have long occupied both slopes of that range, where they acquired some degree of culture, and especially that knowledge of, and skill in working, the precious and other metals, for which the " White-eyed Chudes " were famous, and to which repeated reference is made in the songs of the *Kalevala*.[3] As

Mankir and bad angels called *Nankir*. Two of these spirits sit invisibly on the shoulders of every person from his birth, the good on the right, the bad on the left, each noting his actions in their respective books, and balancing accounts at his death. It is interesting to compare these ideas with those of the Uzbeg prince who explained to Lansdell that at the resurrection, the earth being flat, the dead grow out of it like grass ; then God divides the good from the bad, sending these below and those above. In heaven nobody dies, and every wish is gratified ; even the wicked creditor may seek out his debtor, and in lieu of the money owing may take over the equivalent in his good deeds, if there be any, and thus be saved (*Through Central Asia*, 1887, p. 438).

[1] See especially his *Reiseberichte u. Briefe aus den Jahren 1845-49*, p. 401 sq. ; and *Versuch einer Koibalischen u. Karagassischen Sprachlehre*, 1858, Vol. I. *passim*. But cf. J. Szinnyei, *Finnisch-ugrische Sprachwissenschaft*, 1910, pp. 19–20.

[2] Peschel, *Races of Man*, p. 386.

[3] In a suggestive paper on this collection of Finnish songs C. U. Clark (*Forum*, April, 1898, p. 238 sq.) shows from the primitive character of the mythology, the frequent allusions to copper or bronze, and the almost utter absence of Christian ideas and other indications, that these songs must be of great antiquity. " There seems to be no doubt that some parts date back to at least 3000 years ago, before the Finns and the Hungarians had become distinct peoples ; for the names of the

there are no mines or minerals in Finland itself, it seems obvious that the legendary heroes of the Finnish national epic must have dwelt in some metalliferous region, which could only be the Altai or the Urals, possibly both.

In any case the Urals became a second home and point of dispersion for the Finnish tribes (*Ugrian Finns*), whose migrations—some prehistoric, some historic—can be followed thence down the Pechora and Dvina to the Frozen Ocean,[1] and down the Kama to the Volga. From this artery, where permanent settlements were formed (*Volga Finns*), some conquering hordes went south and west (*Danubian Finns*), while more peaceful wanderers ascended the great river to Lakes Ladoga and Onega, and thence to the shores of the Baltic and Lapland (*Baltic and Lake Finns*).

Thus were constituted the main branches of the widespread Finnish family, whose domain formerly extended from the

Former and Present Domain. Katanga beyond the Yenisei to Lapland, and from the Arctic Ocean to the Altai range, the Caspian, and the Volga, with considerable *enclaves* in the Danube basin. But throughout their relatively short historic life the Finnish peoples, despite a characteristic tenacity and power of resistance, have in many places been encroached upon, absorbed, or even entirely eliminated, by more aggressive races, such as the Siberian " Tatars " in their Altai cradleland, the Turki Kirghiz and Bashkirs in the West Siberian steppes and the Urals, the Russians in the Volga and Lake districts, the Germans and Lithuanians in the Baltic Provinces (Kurland, Livonia, Esthonia), the Rumanians, Slavs, and others in the Danube regions, where the Ugrian Bulgars and Magyars have been almost entirely assimilated in type (and the former also in speech) to the surrounding European populations.

Few anthropologists now attach much importance to the views not yet quite obsolete regarding a former extension of

divinities, many of the customs, and even particular incantations and bits of superstitions mentioned in the Kalevala are curiously duplicated in ancient Hungarian writings."

[1] When Ohthere made his famous voyage round North Cape to the Cwen Sea (White Sea) all this Arctic seaboard was inhabited, not by Samoyeds, as at present, but by true Finns, whom King Alfred calls *Beormas, i.e.* the *Biarmians* of the Norsemen, and the *Permiaki* (*Permians*) of the Russians (*Orosius, i.* 13). In medieval times the whole region between the White Sea and the Urals was often called Permia ; but since the withdrawal southwards of the Zirynians and other Permian Finns this Arctic region has been thinly occupied by Samoyed tribes spreading slowly westward from Siberia to the Pechora and Lower Dvina.

the Finnish race over the whole of Europe and the British Isles. Despite the fact that all the Finns are essentially round-headed, they were identified first with the long-headed cavemen, who retreated north with the reindeer, as was the favourite hypothesis, and then with the early neolithic races who were also long-headed. Elaborate but now forgotten essays were written by learned philologists to establish a common origin of the Basque and the Finnic tongues, which have nothing in common, and half the myths, folklore, and legendary heroes of the western nations were traced to Finno-Ugrian sources.

Late Westward Spread of the Finns.

Now we know better, and both archaeologists and philologists have made it evident that the Finnish peoples are relatively quite recent arrivals in Europe, that the men of the Bronze Age in Finland itself were not Finns but Teutons, and that at the beginning of the new era all the Finnish tribes still dwelt east of the Gulf of Finland.[1]

Not only so, but the eastern migrations themselves, as above roughly outlined, appear to have taken place at a relatively late epoch, long after the inhabitants of West Siberia had passed from the New Stone to the Metal Ages. J. R. Aspelin, "founder of Finno-Ugrian archaeology," points out that the Finno-Ugrian peoples originally occupied a geographical position between the Indo-Germanic and the Mongolic races, and that their first Iron Age was most probably a development, between the Yenisei and the Kama, of the so-called Ural-Altai Bronze Age, the last echoes of which may be traced westwards to Finland and North Scandinavia. In the Upper Yenisei districts iron objects had still the forms of the Bronze Age, when that ancient civilisation, associated with the name of the "Chudes," was interrupted by an invasion which introduced the still persisting Turki Iron Age, expelled the aboriginal inhabitants, and thus gave rise to the great migrations first of the Finno-Ugrians, and then of the Turki peoples (Bashkirs,

The Iron and Bronze Ages in the Finnish Lands.

[1] See A. Hackman, *Die Bronzezeit Finnlands*, Helsingfors, 1897 ; also M. Aspelin, O. Montelius, V. Thomsen and others, who have all, on various grounds, arrived at the same conclusion. Even D. E. D. Europaeus, who has advanced so many heterodox views on the Finnish cradleland, and on the relations of the Finnic to the Mongolo-Turki languages, agrees that " vers l'époque de la naissance de J. C., c'est-à-dire bien longtemps avant que ces tribus immigrassent en Finlande, elles [the western Finns] étaient établies immédiatement au sud des lacs d'Onéga et de Ladoga." (*Travaux Géographiques exécutés en Finlande jusqu'en 1895*, Helsingfors, 1895, p. 141.)

Volga " Tatars " and others) to and across the Urals. It was here, in the Permian territory between the Irtysh and the Kama, that the West Siberian (Chudish) Iron Age continued its normal and unbroken evolution. The objects recovered from the old graves and kurgans in the present governments of Tver and Iaroslav, and especially at Ananyino on the Kama, centre of this culture, show that here took place the transition from the Bronze to the Iron Age some 300 years before the new era, and here was developed a later Iron Age, whose forms are characteristic of the northern Finno-Ugrian lands. The whole region would thus appear to have been first occupied by these immigrants from Asia after the irruption of the Turki hordes into Western Siberia during the first Iron Age, at most some 500 or 600 years before the Christian era. The Finno-Ugrian migrations are thus limited to a period of not more than 2600 years from the present time, and this conclusion, based on archaeological grounds, agrees fairly well with the historical, linguistic, and ethnical data.

It is especially in this obscure field of research that the eminent Danish scholar, Vilhelm Thomsen, has rendered inestimable services to European ethnology. By the light of his linguistic studies A. H. Snellman [1] has elucidated the origins of the Baltic Finns, the Proto-Esthonians, the now all but extinct Livonians, and the quite extinct Kurlanders, from the time when they still dwelt east and south-east of the Baltic lands, under the influence of the surrounding Lithuanian and Gothic tribes, till the German conquest of the Baltic provinces. We learn from Jordanes, to whom is due the first authentic account of these populations, that the various Finnish tribes were subject to the Gothic king Hermanarich, and Thomsen now shows that all the Western Finns (Esthonians, Livonians, Votes, Vepses, Karelians, Tavastians, and others of Finland) must in the first centuries of the new era have lived practically as one people in the closest social union, speaking one language, and following the same religious, tribal, and political institutions. Earlier than the Gothic was the Letto-Lithuanian contact, as shown by the fact that its traces are perceptible in the language of the Volga Finns, in which German loan-words are absent. From these investigations it becomes clear that the Finnish domain must

The Baltic Finns.

---

[1] *Finska Forminnesföreningens Tidskrift, Journ. Fin. Antiq. Soc.* 1896, p. 137 sq.

at that time have stretched from the present Esthonia, Livonia, and Lake Ladoga south to the western Dvina.

The westward movement was connected with the Slav migrations. When the Slavs south of the Letts moved west, other Slav tribes must have pushed north, thus driving both Letts and Finns west to the Baltic provinces, which had previously been occupied by the Germans (Goths). Some of the Western Finns must have found their way about 500 A.D., scarcely earlier, into parts of this region, where they came into hostile and friendly contact with the Norsemen. These relations would even appear to be reflected in the Norse mythology, which may be regarded as in great measure an echo of historic events. The wars of the Swedish and Danish kings referred to in these oral records may be interpreted as plundering expeditions rather than permanent conquests, while the undoubtedly active intercourse between the east and west coasts of the Baltic may be explained on the assumption that, after the withdrawal of the Goths, a remnant of the Germanic populations remained behind in the Baltic provinces.

Relations to Goths, Letts, and Slavs.

From Nestor's statement that all three of the Varangian princes settled, not amongst Slavish but amongst Finnish peoples, it may be inferred that the Finnish element constituted the most important section in the newly founded Russian State; and it may here be mentioned that the term " Russ " itself has now been traced to the Finnish word *Ruost* (*Ruosti*), a " Norseman." But although at first greatly outnumbering the Slavs, the Finnish peoples soon lost the political ascendancy, and their subsequent history may be summed up in the expression—gradual absorption in the surrounding Slav populations. This inevitable process is still going on amongst all the Volga, Lake and Baltic Finns, except in Finland and Lapland, where other conditions obtain.[1]

Finno-Russ Origins.

Most Finnish ethnologists agree that however much they may now differ in their physical and mental characters and usages, Finns and Lapps were all originally one people. Some

---

[1] " Les Finnois et leurs congénères ont occupé autrefois, sur d'immenses espaces, les vastes régions forestières de la Russie septentrionale et centrale, et de la Sibérie occidentale ; mais plus tard, refoulés et divisés par d'autres peuples, ils furent réduits à des tribus isolées, dont il ne reste maintenant que des débris épars " (*Travaux Géographiques*, p. 132).

variant of *Suoma*[1] enters into the national name of all the Baltic groups—*Suomalaiset*, the Finns of Finland, *Somelaïzed*, those of Esthonia, *Samelats* (Sabmelad), the Lapps, *Samoyad*, the Samoyeds. In Ohthere's time the Norsemen called all the Lapps " Finnas " (as the Norwegians still do), and that early

Tavastian and Karelian Finns. navigator already noticed that these " Finns " seemed to speak the same language as the Beormas, who were true Finns.[2] Nor do the present inhabitants of Finland, taken as a whole, differ more in outward appearance and temperament from their Lapp neighbours than do the Tavastians and the Karelians, that is, their western and eastern sections, from each other. The Tavastians, who call themselves Hémelaiset, " Lake People," have rather broad, heavy frames, small and oblique blue or grey eyes, towy hair and white complexion, without the clear florid colour of the North Germanic and English peoples. The temperament is somewhat sluggish, passive and enduring, morose and vindictive, but honest and trustworthy.

Very different are the tall, slim, active Karelians (*Karia-laiset*, " Cowherds," from *Kari*, " Cow "), with more regular features, straight grey eyes, brown complexion, and chestnut hair, like that of the hero of the Kalevala, hanging in ringlets down the shoulders. Many of the Karelians, and most of the neighbouring *Ingrians* about the head of the Gulf of Finland, as well as the Votes and Vepses of the great lakes, have been assimilated in speech, religion, and usages to the surrounding Russian populations. But the more conservative Tavastians have hitherto tenaciously preserved the national sentiment, language, and traditions. Despite the pressure of Sweden on the west, and of Russia on the east, the Finns still stand out as a distinct European nationality, and continue to cultivate with success their harmonious and highly poetical language. Since the twelfth century they have been Christians, converted to the Catholic faith by " Saint " Eric, King of Sweden, and later to Lutheranism, again by the Swedes.[3] The national university, removed in 1827 from Abo to Helsingfors, is a centre of much scientific and literary work, and here E. Lönnrot,

---

[1] A word of doubtful meaning, commonly but wrongly supposed to mean *swamp* or *fen*, and thus to be the original of the Teutonic *Finnas*, " Fen People " (see Thomsen, *Einfluss d. ger. Spr. auf die finnisch-lappischen*, p. 14).

[2] " Þa Finnas, him þuhte, and þa Beormas sprǣcon neah án geðeode " (Orosius, I. 14).

[3] See my paper on the Finns in Cassell's *Storehouse of Information*, p. 296.

father of Finnish literature, brought out his various editions of the *Kalevala*, that of 1849 consisting of some 50,000 strophes.[1]

A kind of transition from these settled and cultured Finns to the Lapps of Scandinavia and Russia is formed by the still almost nomad, or at least restless *Kwæns*, who formerly roamed as far as the White Sea, which The Kwaens. in Alfred's time was known as the *Cwen Sæ* (Kwæn Sea). These Kwæns, who still number nearly 300,000, are even called nomads by J. A. Friis, who tells us that there is a continual movement of small bands between Finland and Scandinavia. " The wandering Kwæns pass round the Gulf of Bothnia and up through Lappmarken to Kittalä, where they separate, some going to Varanger, and others to Alten. They follow the same route as that which, according to historians, some of the Norsemen followed in their wanderings from Finland."[2] The references of the Sagas are mostly to these primitive Bothnian Finns, with whom the Norsemen first came in contact, and who in the sixth and following centuries were still in a rude state not greatly removed from that of their Ugrian forefathers. As shown by Almqvist's researches, they lived almost exclusively by hunting and fishing, had scarcely a rudimentary knowledge of agriculture, and could prepare neither butter nor cheese from the milk of their half-wild reindeer herds.

Such were also, and in some measure still are, the kindred Lapps, who with the allied *Yurak Samoyeds* of Arctic Russia are the only true nomads still surviving in Europe. The Lapps, A. H. Cocks, who travelled amongst all these Samoyeds and rude aborigines in 1888, describes the Kwæns Permian Finns. who range north to Lake Enara, as " for the most part of a very rough class," and found that the Russian Lapps of the Kola Peninsula, " except as to their clothing and the addition of coffee and sugar to their food supply, are living now much the same life as their ancestors probably lived 2000 or more years ago, a far more primitive life, in fact, than the Reindeer Lapps [of Scandinavia]. They have not yet begun to use tobacco, and reading and writing are entirely unknown among them. Unlike the three other divisions of the race [the Norwegian, Swedish, and Finnish Lapps], they are a very cheerful,

---

[1] The fullest information concerning Finland and its inhabitants is found in the *Atlas de Finlande*, with *Texte* (2 vols.) published by the *Soc. Géog. Finland* in 1910.

[2] *Laila*, Earl of Ducie's English ed., p. 58. The Swedish *Bothnia* is stated to be a translation of *Kwæn*, meaning low-lying coastlands ; hence *Kainulaiset*, as they call themselves, would mean " Coastlanders."

light-hearted people, and have the curious habit of expressing their thoughts aloud in extempore sing-song." [1]

Similar traits have been noticed in the Samoyeds, whom F. G. Jackson describes as an extremely sociable and hospitable people, delighting in gossip, and much given to laughter and merriment.[2] He gives their mean height as nearly 5 ft. 2 in., which is about the same as that of the Lapps (Von Düben, 5 ft. 2 in., others rather less), while that of the Finns averages 5 ft. 5 in. (Topinard). Although the general Mongol appearance is much less pronounced in the Lapps than in the Samoyeds, in some respects—low stature, flat face with peculiar round outline—the latter reminded Jackson of the Ziryanians, who are a branch of the Beormas (Permian Finns), though like them now much mixed with the Russians. The so-called prehistoric " Lapp Graves," occurring throughout the southern parts of Scandinavia, are now known from their contents to have belonged to the Norse race, who appear to have occupied this region since the New Stone Age, while the Lapp domain seems never to have reached very much farther south than Trondhjem.

All these facts, taken especially in connection with the late arrival of the Finns themselves in Finland, lend support to **Lapp Origins and Migrations.** the view that the Lapps are a branch, not of the Suomalaiset, but of the Permian Finns, and reached their present homes, not from Finland, but from North Russia through the Kanin and Kola Peninsulas, if not round the shores of the White Sea, at some remote period prior to the occupation of Finland by its present inhabitants. This assumption would also explain Ohthere's statement that Lapps and Permians seemed to speak nearly the same language. The resemblance is still close, though I am not competent to say to which branch of the Finno-Ugrian family Lapp is most nearly allied.

Of the Mongol physical characters the Lapp still retains the round low skull (index 83), the prominent cheek-bones, **Temperament— Religion.** somewhat flat features, and ungainly figure. The temperament, also, is still perhaps more Asiatic than European, although since the eighteenth century they have been Christians—Lutherans in Scandinavia, Orthodox in Russia. In pagan times Shamanism had nowhere acquired a greater development than among the Lapps. A great

[1] *A Boat Journey to Inari*, Viking Club, Feb. 1, 1895.
[2] *The Great Frozen Land*, 1895, p. 61.

feature of the system were the " rune-trees," made of pine or birch bark, inscribed with figures of gods, men, or animals, which were consulted on all important occasions, and their mysterious signs interpreted by the Shamans. Even foreign potentates hearkened to the voice of these renowned magicians, and in England the expression " Lapland witches" became proverbial, although it appears that there never were any witches, but only wizards, in Lapland. Such rites have long ceased to be practised, although some of the crude ideas of a material after-life still linger on. Money and other treasures are often buried or hid away, the owners dying without revealing the secret, either through forgetfulness, or more probably of set purpose in the hope of thus making provision for the other world.

Amongst the kindred Samoyeds, despite their Russian orthodoxy, the old pagan beliefs enjoy a still more vigorous existence. " As long as things go well with him, he is a Christian ; but should his reindeer die, or other catastrophe happen, he immediately returns to his old god *Num* or *Chaddi*. . . . He conducts his heathen services by night and in secret, and carefully screens from sight any image of Chaddi." [1] Jackson noticed several instances of this compromise between the old and the new, such as the wooden cross supplemented on the Samoyed graves by an overturned sledge to convey the dead safely over the snows of the under-world, and the rings of stones, within which the human sacrifices were perhaps formerly offered to propitiate Chaddi ; and although these things have ceased, " it is only a few years ago that a Samoyad living on Novaia Zemlia sacrificed a young girl." [2]

Similar beliefs and practices still prevail not only amongst the Siberian Finns—Ostyaks of the Yenisei and Obi rivers, Voguls of the Urals—but even amongst the Votyaks, Mordvinians, Cheremisses and other scattered groups still surviving in the Volga basin.

The Volga Finns.

So recently as the year 1896 a number of Votyaks were tried and convicted for the murder of a passing mendicant, whom they had beheaded to appease the wrath of Kiremet, Spirit of Evil and author of the famine raging at that time in Central Russia. Besides Kiremet, the Votyaks—who appear to have migrated from the Urals to their present homes between the

---

[1] *The Great Frozen Land*, p. 84.
[2] Cf. M. A. Czaplicka, *Aboriginal Siberia*, 1914, pp. 162, 289 n.

Kama and the Viatka rivers about 400 A.D., and are mostly heathens—also worship Inmar, God of Heaven, to whom they sacrifice animals as well as human beings whenever it can be safely done. We are assured by Baron de Baye that even the few who are baptized take part secretly in these unhallowed rites.[1]

To the Ugrian branch, rudest and most savage of all the Finnish peoples, belong these now moribund Volga groups, as well as the fierce Bulgar and Magyar hordes, if not also their precursors, the *Jazyges* and *Rhoxolani*, who in the second century A.D. swarmed into Pannonia from the Russian steppe, and in company with the Germanic Quadi and Marcomanni twice (168 and 172) advanced to the walls of Aquileia, and were twice arrested by the legions of Marcus Aurelius and Verus. Of the once numerous Jazyges, whom Pliny calls Sarmates, there were several branches—*Maeotae, Metanastae, Basilii* (" Royal ")—who were first reduced by the Goths spreading from the Baltic to the Euxine and Lower Danube, and then overwhelmed with the Dacians, Getae, Bastarnae, and a hundred other ancient peoples in the great deluge of the Hunnish invasion.

From the same South Russian steppe—the plains watered by the Lower Don and Dnieper—came the *Bulgars*, first in

The Bulgars —Origins and Migrations.

association with the Huns, from whom they are scarcely distinguished by the early Byzantine writers, and then as a separate people, who, after throwing off the yoke of the Avars (635 A.D.), withdrew before the pressure of the Khazars westwards to the Lower Danube (678). But their records go much farther back than these dates, and while philologists and archaeologists are able to trace their wanderings step by step north to the Middle Volga and the Ural Mountains, authentic Armenian documents carry their history back to the second century B.C. Under the Arsacides numerous bands of Bulgars, driven from their homes about the Kama confluence by civil strife, settled on the banks of the Aras, and since that time (150-114 B.C.) the Bulgars were known to the Armenians as a great nation dwelling away to the north far beyond the Caucasus.

Originally the name, which afterwards acquired such an

---

[1] *Notes sur les Votiaks payens des Gouvernements de Kazan et Viatka*, Paris, 1897. They are still numerous, especially in Viatka, where they numbered 240,000 in 1897.

odious notoriety amongst the European peoples, may have been more geographical than ethnical, implying not so much a particular nation as all the inhabitants of the *Bulga* (Volga) between the Kama and the Caspian.   But at that time this section of the great river seems to have been mainly held by more or less homogeneous branches of the Finno-Ugarian family, and palethnologists have now shown that to this connection beyond all question belonged in physical appearance, speech, and usages those bands known as Bulgars, who formed permanent settlements in Moesia south of the Lower Danube towards the close of the seventh century.[1]   Here " these bold and dexterous archers, who drank the milk and feasted on the flesh of their fleet and indefatigable horses ; whose flocks and herds followed, or rather guided, the motions of their roving camps ; to whose inroads no country was remote or impervious, and who were practised in flight, though incapable of fear," [2] established a powerful state, which maintained its independence for over seven hundred years (678–1392).

Acting at first in association with the Slavs, and then assuming " a vague dominion " over their restless Sarmatian allies, the Bulgars spread the terror of their hated name throughout the Balkan lands, and were prevented only by the skill of Belisarius from anticipating their Turki kinsmen in the overthrow of the Byzantine Empire itself.   Procopius and Jornandes have left terrible pictures of the ferocity, debasement, and utter savagery, both of the Bulgars and of their Slav confederates during the period preceding the foundation of the Bulgar dynasty in Moesia.   Wherever the Slavs (Antes, Slavini) passed, no soul was left alive ; Thrace and Illyria were strewn with unburied corpses ; captives were shut up with horse and cattle in stables, and all consumed together, while the brutal hordes danced to the music of their shrieks and groans.   Indescribable was the horror inspired by the Bulgars, who killed for killing's sake, wasted for sheer love of destruction, swept away all works of the human hand, burnt, razed cities, left in their wake nought but a picture of their own cheerless native steppes.   Of all the barbarians that harried the Empire, the Bulgars have left the most detested name, although closely rivalled by the Slavs.

[1] See especially Schafarik's classical work *Slavische Alterthümer*, ii. p. 159 sq. and V. de Saint-Martin, *Études de Géographie Ancienne et d'Etnographie asiatique*, ii. p. 10 sq., also the still indispensable Gibbon, Ch. XLII., etc.
[2] *Decline and Fall*, XLII.

To the ethnologist the later history of the Bulgarians is of exceptional interest. They entered the Danubian lands in the seventh century as typical Ugro-Finns, repulsive alike in physical appearance and mental characters. Their dreaded chief, Krum, celebrated his triumphs with sanguinary rites, and his followers yielded in no respects to the Huns themselves in coarseness and brutality. Yet an almost complete moral if not physical transformation had been effected by the middle of the ninth century, when the Bulgars were evangelised by Byzantine missionaries, exchanged their rude Ugrian speech for a Slavonic tongue, the so-called " Church Slav," or even " Old Bulgarian," and became henceforth merged in the surrounding Slav populations. The national name " Bulgar " alone survives, as that of a somewhat peaceful southern " Slav " people, who in our time again acquired the political independence of which they had been deprived by Bajazet I. in 1392.

Nor did this name disappear from the Volga lands after the great migration of Bulgar hordes to the Don basin during the third and fourth centuries A.D. On the contrary, here arose another and a greater Bulgar empire, which was known to the Byzantines of the tenth century as " Black Bulgaria," and later to the Arabs and Western peoples as " Great Bulgaria," in contradistinction to the " Little Bulgaria " south of the Danube.[1] It fell to pieces during the later " Tatar " wars, and nothing now remains of the Volga Bulgars, except the Volga itself from which they were named.

Great and Little Bulgaria.

In the same region, but farther north,[2] lay also a " Great Hungary," the original seat of those other Ugrian Finns known as Hungarians and Magyars, who followed later in the track of the Bulgars, and like them formed permanent settlements in the Danube basin, but higher up in Pannonia, the present kingdom of Hungary. Here, however, the Magyars had been preceded by the kindred

Avars and Magyars.

[1] Rubruquis (thirteenth century): " We came to the Etil, a very large and deep river four times wider than the Seine, flowing from ' Great Bulgaria,' which lies to the north." Farther on he adds: " It is from this Great Bulgaria that issued those Bulgarians who are beyond the Danube, on the Constantinople side " (quoted by V. de Saint-Martin).

[2] Evidently much nearer to the Ural Mountains, for Jean du Plan Carpin says this " Great Hungary was the land of *Bascart*," that is, *Bashkir*, a large Finno-Turki people, who still occupy a considerable territory in the Orenburg Government about the southern slopes of the Urals.

(or at least distantly connected) Avars, the dominant people in the Middle Danube lands for a great part of the period between the departure of the Huns and the arrival of the Magyars.[1] Rolling up like a storm cloud from the depths of Siberia to the Volga and Euxine, sweeping everything before them, reducing Kutigurs, Utigurs, · Bulgars, and Slavs, the Avars presented themselves in the sixth century on the frontiers of the empire as the unwelcome allies of Justinian. Arrested at the Elbe by the Austrasian Franks, and hard pressed by the Gepidae, they withdrew to the Lower Danube under the ferocious Khagan Bayan, who, before his overthrow by the Emperor Mauritius and death in 602, had crossed the Danube, captured Sirmium, and reduced the whole region bordering on the Byzantine empire. Later the still powerful Avars with their Slav followers, " the Avar viper and the Slav locust," overran the Balkan lands, and in 625 nearly captured Constantinople. They were at last crushed by Pepin, king of Italy, who reoccupied Sirmium in 799, and brought back such treasure that the value of gold was for a time enormously reduced.

Then came the opportunity of the *Hunagars* (Hungarians), who, after advancing from the Urals to the Volga (550 A.D.), had reached the Danube about 886. Here they were invited to the aid of the Germanic king Arnulf, threatened by a formidable coalition of the western Slavs under the redoubtable Zventibolg, a nominal Christian who would enter the church on horseback followed by **Magyar Origins and early Records.** his wild retainers, and threaten the priest at the altar with the lash. In the upland Transylvanian valleys the Hunagars had been joined by eight of the derelict Khazar tribes, amongst whom were the *Megers* or *Mogers*, whose name under the form of *Magyar* was eventually extended to the united Hunagar-Khazar nation. Under their renowned king Arpad, son of Almuth, they first overthrew Zventibolg, and then with the help of the surviving Avars reduced the surrounding Slav populations. Thus towards the close of the ninth century was founded in Pannonia the present kingdom of Hungary, in which

---

[1] With them were associated many of the surviving fugitive On-Uigurs (Gibbon's " Ogors or Varchonites "), whence the report that they were not true Avars. But the Turki genealogies would appear to admit their claim to the name, and in any case the Uigurs and Avars of those times cannot now be ethnically distinguished. *Kandish*, one of their envoys to Justinian, is clearly a Turki name, and *Varchonites* seems to point to the Warkhon (Orkhon), seat in successive ages of the eastern Turks, the Uigurs, and the true Mongols.

were absorbed all the kindred Mongol and Finno-Turki elements that still survived from the two previous Mongolo-Turki empires, established in the same region by the Huns under Attila (430–453), and by the Avars under Khagan Bayan (562–602).

After reducing the whole of Pannonia and ravaging Carinthia and Friuli, the Hunagars raided Bavaria and Italy (899–900), imposed a tribute on the feeble successor of Arnulf (910), and pushed their plundering expeditions as far west as Alsace, Lorraine, and Burgundy, everywhere committing atrocities that recalled the memory of Attila's savage hordes. Trained riders, archers and javelin-throwers from infancy, they advanced to the attack in numerous companies following hard upon each other, avoiding close quarters, but wearing out their antagonists by the persistence of their onslaughts. They were the scourge and terror of Europe, and were publicly proclaimed by the Emperor Otto I. (955) the enemies of God and humanity.

This period of lawlessness and savagery was closed by the conversion of Saint Stephen I. (997–1038), after which the Magyars became gradually assimilated in type and general culture, but not in speech, to the western nations.[1] Their harmonious and highly cultivated language still remains a typical member of the Ural-Altaic family, reflecting in its somewhat composite vocabulary the various Finno-Ugric and Turki elements (Ugrians and Permians from the Urals, Volga Finns, Turki Avars and Khazars), of which the substratum of the Magyar nation is constituted.[2]

"The modern Magyars," says Peisker, "are one of the most varied race-mixtures on the face of the earth, and one of the two chief Magyar types of to-day—traced to the Arpad era [end of ninth century] by tomb-findings—is dolichocephalic with a narrow visage. There we have before us Altaian origin, Ugrian speech and Indo-European type combined."[3]

Politically the Magyars continue to occupy a position of vital importance in Eastern Europe, wedged in between the

[1] *Ethnology*, p. 309.

[2] Vambéry, perhaps the best authority on this point, holds that in its structure Magyar leans more to the Finno-Ugric, and in its vocabulary to the Turki branch of the Ural-Altaic linguistic family. He attributes the effacement of the physical type partly to the effects of the environment, partly to the continuous interminglings of the Ugric, Turki, Slav, and Germanic peoples in Pannonia ("Ueber den Ursprung der Magyaren," in *Mitt. d. K. K. Geograph. Ges.*, Vienna, 1897, XL. Nos. 3 and 4).

[3] T. Peisker, "The Asiatic Background," *Cambridge Medieval History*, Vol. I. 1911, p. 356.

northern and southern Slav peoples, and thus presenting an insurmountable obstacle to the aspirations of the Panslavist dreamers.   The fiery and vigorous Magyar nationality, a compact body of about 8,000,000 (1898), holds the boundless plains watered by the Middle Danube and the Theiss, and thus permanently separates the Chechs, Moravians, and Slovaks of Bohemia and the northern Carpathians from their kinsmen, the Yugo-Slavs (" Southern Slavs ") of Servia and the other now Slavonised Balkan lands.   These Yugo-Slavs are in their turn severed by the Rumanians of Neo-Latin speech from their northern and eastern brethren, the Ruthenians, Poles, Great and Little Russians. Had the Magyars and Rumanians adopted any of the neighbouring Slav idioms, it is safe to say that, like the Ugrian Bulgarians, they must have long ago been absorbed in the surrounding Panslav world, with consequences to the central European nations which it would not be difficult to forecast.   Here we have a striking illustration of the influence of language in developing and preserving the national sentiment, analogous in many respects to that now witnessed on a larger scale amongst the English-speaking populations on both sides of the Atlantic and in the Austral lands.   From this point of view the ethnologist may unreservedly accept Ehrenreich's trenchant remark that " the nation stands and falls with its speech." [1]

[1] " Das Volk steht und fällt mit der Sprache " (*Urbewohner Brasiliens*, 1897, p. 14).

CHAPTER X

THE AMERICAN ABORIGINES

CONSPECTUS.

Present Range. *N.W. Pacific Coastlands ; the shores of the Arctic Ocean, Labrador, and Greenland ; the unsettled*

Distribution in Past and Present Times. *parts of Alaska and the Dominion ; Reservations and Agencies in the Dominion and the United States ; parts of Florida, Arizona, and New Mexico ; most of Central and South America with Fuegia either wild and full-blood, or semi-civilised half-breeds.*

Hair, *black, lank, coarse, often very long, nearly round in transverse section ; very scanty on face and practically absent on body ;* **Colour,** *differs, according to localities,*

Physical Characters. *from dusky yellowish white to that of solid chocolate, but the prevailing colour is brown ;* **Skull,** *generally mesaticephalous (79), but with wide range from 65 (some Eskimo) to 89 or 90 (some British Columbians, Peruvians) ; the* **os Incae** *more frequently present than amongst other races, but the* **os linguae** *(hyoid bone) often imperfectly developed ;* **Jaws,** *massive, but moderately profecting ;* **Cheekbone**, *as a rule rather prominent laterally, and also high :*

Nose, *generally large, straight or even aquiline, and mesorrhine ;* **Eyes,** *nearly always dark brown, with a yellowish conjunctiva, and the eye-slits show a prevailing tendency to a slight upward slant ;* **Stature,** *usually above the medium 1.728 m. (5 ft. 8 or 10 in.), but variable—under 1.677 m. (5 ft. 6 in.) on the western plateaux (Peruvians, etc.), also in Fuegia and Alaska ; 1.829 m. (6 ft., and upwards in Patagonia (Tehuelches), Central Brazil (Bororos) and Prairie (Algonquians, Iroquoians) ; the relative proportions of the two elements of the arms and of the legs (radio-humeral and tibio-femoral indices) are intermediate between those of whites and negroes.*

Temperament, *moody, reserved, and wary ; outwardly impassive and capable of enduring extreme physical pain ; considerate towards each other, kind and gentle towards their women and children, but not in a* Mental Characters. *demonstrative manner ; keen sense of justice, hence easily offended, but also easily pacified. The outward show of dignity and a lofty air assumed by many seems due more to vanity or ostentation than to a feeling of true pride. Mental capacity considerable, much higher than the Negro, but on the whole inferior to the Mongol.*

Speech, *exclusively polysynthetic, a type unknown elsewhere ; is not a primitive condition, but a highly specialised form of agglutination, in which all the terms of the sentence tend to coalesce in a single polysyllabic word ; stock languages very numerous, perhaps more so than all the stock languages of all the other orders of speech in the rest of the world.*

Religion, *various grades of spirit and nature worship, corresponding to the various cultural grades ; a crude form of shamanism prevalent amongst most of the North American aborigines, polytheism with sacrifice and priestcraft amongst the cultured peoples (Aztecs, Mayas, etc.) ; the monotheistic concept nowhere clearly evolved ; belief in a natural after-life very prevalent, if not universal.*

Culture, *highly diversified, ranging from the lowest stages of savagery through various degrees of barbarism to the advanced social state of the more or less civilised Mayas, Aztecs, Chibchas, Yungas, Quichuas, and Aymaras ; amongst these pottery, weaving, metal-work, agriculture, and especially architecture fairly well developed ; letters less so, although the Maya script seems to have reached the true phonetic state ; navigation and science rudimentary or absent ; savagery generally far more prevalent*

I. *Eskimo.*

II. *Mackenzie Area.*   Déné tribes.

> 1 Yellow Knives, 2 Dog Rib, 3 Hares, 4 Slavey, 5 Chipewyan, 6 Beaver, 7 Nahane, 8 Sekani, 9 Babine, 10 Carrier, 11 Loucheux, 12 Ahtena, 13 Khotana.

III. *North Pacific Area.*

> 14 Tlingit, 15 Haida, 16 Kwakiutl, 17 Bellacoola, 18 Coast Salish, 19 Nootka, 20 Chinook, 21 Kalapooian.

IV. *Plateau Area.*

> 22 Shahapts or Nez Percés, 23 Shoshoni, 24 Interior Salish, Thompson, 25 Lillooet, 26 Shushwap.

V. *Californian Area.*

> 27 Wintun, 28 Pomo, 29 Miwok, 30 Yokut.

VI. *Plains Area.*

> 31 Assiniboin, 32 Arapaho, 33 Siksika or Blackfoot, 34 Blood, 35 Piegan, 36 Crow, 37 Cheyenne, 38 Comanche, 39 Gros Ventre, 40 Kiowa, 41 Sarsi, 42 Teton-Dakota (Sioux), 43 Arikara, Hidatsa, Mandan, 44 Iowa, 45 Missouri, 46 Omaha, 47 Osage, 48 Oto, 49 Pawnee, 50 Ponca, 51 Santee-Dakota (Sioux), 52 Yankton-Dakota (Sioux), 53 Wichita, 54 Wind River Shoshoni, 55 Plains-Ojibway, 56 Plains-Cree.

VII. *Eastern Woodland Area.*

> 57 Ojibway, 58 Saulteaux, 59 Wood Cree, 60 Montagnais, 61 Naskapi, 62 Huron, 63 Wyandot, 64 Erie, 65 Susquehanna, 66 Iroquois, 67 Algonquin, 68 Ottawa, 69 Menomini, 70 Sauk and Fox, 71 Potawatomi, 72 Peoria, 73 Illinois, 74 Kickapoo, 75 Miami, 76 Abnaki, 77 Micmac.

VIII. *South-eastern Area.*

> 78 Shawnee, 79 Creek, 80 Chickasaw, 81 Choctaw, 82 Seminole, 83 Cherokee, 84 Tuscarora, 85 Yuchi, 86 Powhatan, 87 Tunican, 88 Natchez.

IX. *South-western Area.*   Pueblo tribes.

> 89 Hopi, 90 Zuñi, 91 Rio Grande, 92 Navaho, 93 Pima, 94 Mohave, 95 Jicarilla, 96 Mescalero.

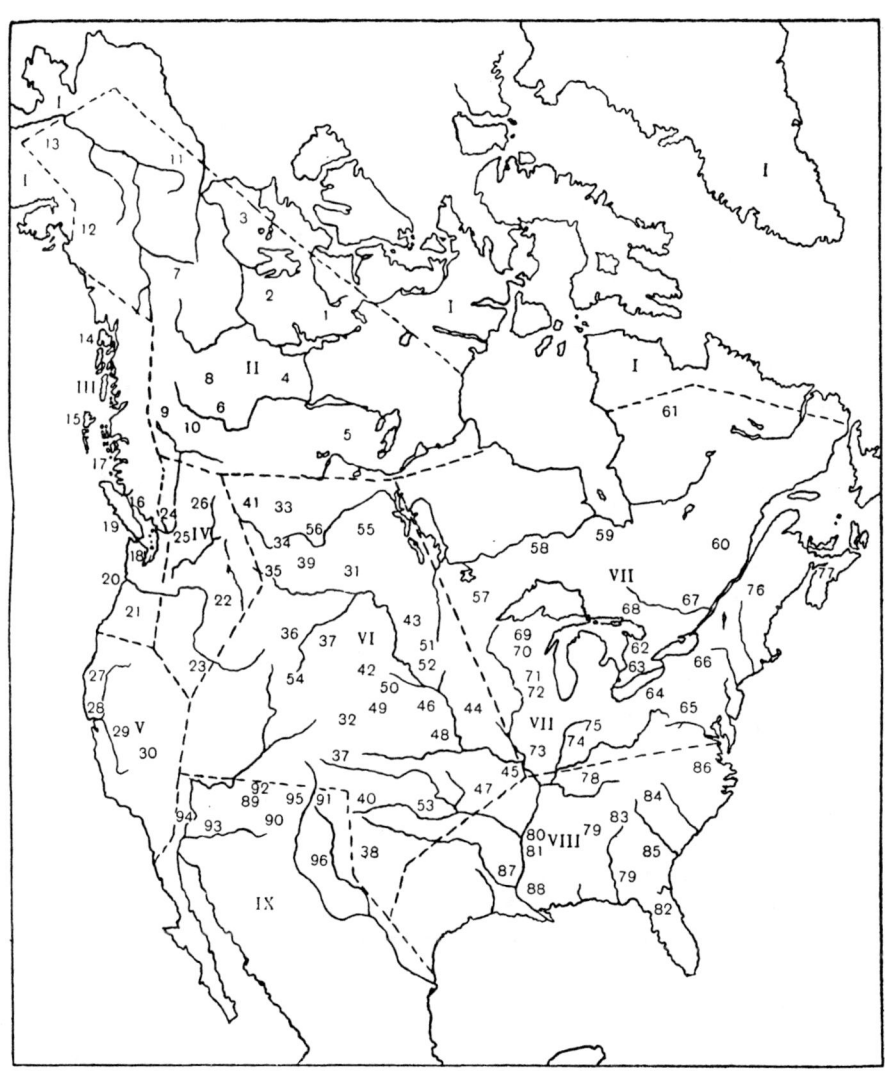

MAP OF AREAS OF MATERIAL CULTURE IN NORTH AMERICA (after C. Wissler, *Am. Anth.* XVI. 1914).

and intense in South than in North America, but the tribal state almost everywhere persistent.

North America : *Eskimauan* (Innuit, Aleut, Karalit) ; *Athapascan* (Déné, Pacific division, Apache, Navaho) ; *Kolu-* Main Divisions. *schan ; Algonquian* (Delaware, Abnaki, Ojib- way, Shawnee, Arapaho, Sauk and Fox, Black- feet) ; *Iroquoian* (Huron, Mohawk, Tuscarora, Seneca, Cayuga, Onondaga) ; *Siouan* (Dakota, Omaha, Crow, Iowa, Osage, Assiniboin) ; *Shoshonian* (Comanche, Ute) ; *Salishan ; Shahap-tian ; Caddoan ; Muskhogean* (Creek, Choctaw, Chickasaw, Seminole) ; *Pueblo* (Zuñian, Keresan, Tanoan).

Central America : *Nahuatlan* (Aztec, Pipil, Niquiran) ; *Huaxtecan* (Maya, Quiché) ; *Totonac ; Miztecan ; Zapotecan ; Chorotegan ; Tarascan ; Otomitlan ; Talanamcan ; Choco.*

South America : *Muyscan* (Chibcha) ; *Quichuan* (Inca, Aymara) ; *Yungan* (Chimu) ; *Antisan ; Jivaran ; Zaparan ; Betoyan; Maku; Pana* (Cashibo, Karipuna, Setebo) ; *Ticunan; Chiquitan ; Arawakan* (Arua, Maypure, Vapisiana, Ipurina, Mahinaku, Layana, Kustenau, Moxo) ; *Cariban* (Bakaïri, Na-huqua, Galibi, Kalina, Arecuna, Macusi, Ackawoi) ; *Tupi-Guaranian* (Omagua, Mundurucu, Kamayura, Emerillon) ; *Gesan* (Botocudo, Kayapo, Cherentes) ; *Charruan ; Bororo ; Karayan ; Guaycuruan* (Abipones, Mataco, Toba) ; *Araucanian* or *Moluchean ; Patagonian* or *Tehuelchean* (Pilma, Yacana, Ona) ; *Enneman* (Lengua, Sanapana, Angaites) ; *Fuegian* (Yahgan, Alakaluf).

It is impossible to dissociate the ethnological history of the New World from that of the Old. The absence from America at any period of the world's history not only of anthropoid apes but also of the *Cercopithecidae*, in other words American Origins. of the Catarrhini, entirely precludes the possibility of the independent origin of man in the western hemisphere. Therefore the population of the Americas must have come from the Old World. In prehistoric times there were only two possible routes for such immigration to have taken place. For the mid-Atlantic land connection was severed long ages before the appearance of man, and the connection of South America with Antarctica had also long disappeared.[1] We are therefore compelled to look to a farther extension of land be-tween North America and northern Europe on the one hand,

[1] A. C. Haddon, *The Wanderings of Peoples*, 1911, p. 72.

and between north-west America and north-east Asia on the other. We know that in late Tertiary times there was a land-bridge connecting north-west Europe with Greenland, and Scharff [1] believes that the Barren-ground reindeer took this route to Norway and western Europe during early glacial times, but that " towards the latter part of the Glacial period the land-connection . . . broke down." Other authorities are of opinion that the continuous land between the two continents in higher latitudes remained until post-glacial times. Brinton [2] considered that it was impossible for man to have reached America from Asia, because Siberia was covered with glaciers and not peopled until late Neolithic times, whereas man was living in both North and South America at the close of the Glacial Age. He acknowledged frequent communication in later times between Asia and America, but maintained that the movement was rather from America to Asia than otherwise. He was therefore a strong advocate of the European origin of the American race. There is no doubt that North America was connected with Asia in Tertiary times, though some geologists assert that " the far North-west did not rise from the waves of the Pacific ocean (which once flowed with a boundless expanse to the North Pole) until after the glacial period." In that case " the first inhabitants of America certainly did not get there in this way, for by that time the bones of many generations were already bleaching on the soil of the New World." [3] The " Miocene Bridge," as the land connecting Asia and America in late geological times has been called, was probably very wide, one side would stretch from Kamchatka to British Columbia, and the other across Behring Strait. If, as seems probable, this connection persisted till, or was reconstituted during, the human period, tribes migrating to America by the more northerly route would enter the land east of the great barrier of the Rocky Mountains. The route from the Old World to the New by the Pacific margin probably remained nearly always open. Thus, while not denying the possibility of a very early migration from North Europe to North America through Greenland, it appears more probable that America received its population from North Asia.

We have next to determine what were the characteristics

---

[1] R. F. Scharff, *The History of the European Fauna*, 1899, pp. 155, 186.
[2] D. G. Brinton, *The American Race*, 1891.
[3] K. Haebler, *The World's History* (ed. Helmolt), I. 1901, p. 181.

of the earliest inhabitants of America, and the approximate
date of their arrival.   There have been many sen-
Fossil Man in   sational accounts of the discoveries of fossil man
America.   in America, which have not been able to stand
the criticism of scientific investigation.   It must always be
remembered that the evidence is primarily one of stratigraphy.
Assuming, of course, that the human skeletal remains found in
a given deposit are contemporaneous with the formation of
that deposit and not subsequently interred in it, it is for the
geologist to determine the age.   The amount of petrifaction
and the state of preservation of the bones are quite fallacious
nor can much reliance be placed upon the anatomical character
of the remains.   Primordial human remains may be expected
to show ancestral characters to a marked degree, but as we
have insufficient data to enable us to determine the rate of
evolution, anatomical considerations must fit into the time-
scale granted by the geologist.

Apart from pure stratigraphy associated animal remains
may serve to support or refute the claims to antiquity, while
the presence of artifacts, objects made or used by man, may
afford evidence for determining the relative date if the cultural
stratigraphy of the area has been sufficiently established.

Fortunately the fossil human remains of America have been
carefully studied by a competent authority who says, " Irrespective of other considerations, in every instance where enough
of the bones is preserved for comparison the somatological
evidence bears witness against the geological antiquity of the
remains and for their close affinity to, or identity with those of
the modern Indian.   Under these circumstances but one conclusion is justified, which is that thus far on this continent, no
human bones of undisputed geological antiquity are known." [1]
Hrdlička subsequently studied the remains of South America
and says, " A conscientious, unbiased study of all the available
facts has shown that the whole structure erected in support of
the theory of geologically ancient man on that continent rests
on very imperfectly and incorrectly interpreted data and in
many instances on false premises, and as a consequence of
these weaknesses must completely collapse when subjected to
searching criticism.—As to the antiquity of the various archaeological remains from Argentina attributed to early man, all

[1] A. Hrdlička, " Skeletal Remains suggesting or attributed to Early Man in
North America," *Bureau Am. Eth. Bull.* 33, 1907, p. 98.

those to which particular importance has been attached have been found without tenable claim to great age, while others, mostly single objects, without exception fall into the category of the doubtful." [1]

The conclusions of W. H. Holmes, Bailey Willis, F. E. Wright and C. N. Fenner, who collaborated with Hrdlička, with regard to the evidence thus far furnished, are that "it fails to establish the claim that in South America there have been brought forth thus far tangible traces of either geologically ancient man himself or of any precursors of the human race." [2] Hrdlička is careful to add, however, "This should not be taken as a categorical denial of the existence of early man in South America, however improbable such a presence may now appear."

According to J. W. Gidley [3] the evidence of vertebrate paleontology indicates (1) That man did not exist in North America at the beginning of the Pleistocene although there was a land connection between Asia and North America at that time permitting a free passage for large mammals. (2) That a similar land connection was again in existence at the close of the last glacial epoch, and probably continued up to comparatively recent times, as indicated by the close resemblance of related living mammalian species on either side of the present Behring Strait. (3) That the first authentic records of prehistoric man in America have been found in deposits that are not older than the last glacial epoch, and probably of even later date, the inference being that man first found his way into North America at some time near the close of the existence of this last land bridge. (4) That this land bridge was broad and vegetative, and the climate presumably mild, at least along its southern coast border, making it habitable for man.

Rivet [4] points out that from Brazil to Terra del Fuegia on the Atlantic slope, in Bolivia and Peru, on the high plateaux of the Andes, on the Pacific coast and perhaps in the south of California, traces of a distinct race are met with, sometimes in single individuals, sometimes in whole groups. This race of Lagoa Santa is an

The Lagoa-Santa Race.

[1] A. Hrdlička, "Early Man in South America," *Bureau Am. Eth. Bull.* 52, 1912.
[2] *Loc. cit.* pp. 385–6.
[3] *American Anthropologist*, XIV. 1912, p. 22.
[4] P. Rivet, "La Race de Lagoa-Santa chez les populations précolombiennes de l'Équateur," *Bull. Soc. d'Anth.* v. 2, 1908, p. 264.

important primordial element in the population of South America, and has been termed by Deniker the Palaeo-American sub-race.[1]

The men were of low stature but considerable strength, the skull was long, narrow and high, of moderate size, prognathous, with strong brow ridges, but not a retreating forehead. There is no reliable evidence as to the age of these remains. Hrdlička, after reviewing all the evidence says, " Besides agreeing closely with the dolichocephalic American type, which had an extensive representation throughout Brazil, including the Province of Minas Geraes, and in many other parts of South America, it is the same type which is met with farther north among the Aztec, Tarasco, Otomi, Tarahumare, Pima, Californians, ancient Utah cliff dwellers, ancient north-eastern Pueblos, Shoshoni, many of the Plains Tribes, Iroquois, Eastern Siouan, and Algonquian. But it is apart from the Eskimo, who form a distinct subtype of the yellow-brown strain of humanity." [2]

Rivet [3] adds that an examination of the present distribution of the descendants of the Lagoa-Santa type shows that they are all border peoples, in East Brazil, and the south of Patagonia and Terra del Fuegia, where the climate is rigorous, in desert islands of west and southern Chili, on the coast of Ecuador, and perhaps in California. This suggests that they have been driven out in a great eccentric movement from their old habitat, into new environment producing fresh crossings.

There is an absence of this high narrow-headed type throughout the northern part of South America, and a prevalence of medium or sub-brachycephalic heads which are always low in the crown. These are now represented by the Caribs and Arawaks, but there was more than one migration of brachycephalic peoples from the north.

To return to North America. As we have just seen Hrdlička recognises a dolichocephalic element in North **Physical Type** America, and various ethnic groups range to pro-**in North** nounced brachycephaly. Nevertheless he believes **America.** in the original unity of the Indian race in America, basing his conclusions on the colour of the skin, which ranges from yellowish white to dark brown, the straight black hair, scanty beard, hairless body, brown and often more or less slanting

[1] J. Deniker, *The Races of Man*, 1900, p. 512.
[2] *Bur. Am. Eth. Bull.* 52, 1912, pp. 183–4.
[3] *Loc. cit.* p. 267.

eye, mesorrhine nose, medium prognathism, skeletal proportions and other essential features.   In all these characters the
American Indians resemble the yellowish brown peoples of
eastern Asia and a large part of Polynesia.[1]   He also believes
that there were many successive migrations from Asia.

The differences of opinion between Hrdlička and other
students is probably more a question of nomenclature than of
fact.   The eastern Asiatics and Polynesians are mixed peoples,
and if there were numerous migrations from Asia, spread over
a very long period of time, people of different stocks would
have found their way into America.   " It is indeed probable,"
Hrdlička adds, " that the western coast of America, within the
last two thousand years, was on more than one occasion reached,
by small parties of Polynesians, and that the eastern coast was
similarly reached by small groups of whites ; but these ac-
cretions have not modified greatly, if at all, the mass of the
native population." [2]

The inhabitants of the plains east of the Rocky Mountains
and the eastern wooded area are characterised by a head which
varies about the lower limit of brachycephaly, and by tall
stature.   This stock probably arrived by the North Pacific
Bridge before the end of the last Glacial period, and extended
over the continent east of the great divide.   Finally bands from
the north, east and south migrated into the prairie area.   The
markedly brachycephalic immigrants from Asia appear to have
proceeded mainly down the Pacific slope and to have populated
Central and South America, with an overflow into the south
of North America.   It is probable that there were several
migrations of allied but not similar broad-headed peoples from
Asia in early days, and we know that recently there have been
racial and cultural drifts between the neighbouring portions of
America and Asia.[3]   Indeed Bogoras [4] suggests that ethno-
graphically the line separating Asia and America should lie
from the lower Kolyma River to Gishiga Bay.

Owing to these various immigrations and subsequent
minglings the cranial forms show much variation, and are not
sufficiently significant to serve as a basis of classification.   In
parts of North America the round-headed mound-builders and

[1] A. Hrdlička, *Am. Anth.* xiv. 1912, p. 10.
[2] *Ibid.* p. 12.
[3] A. C. Haddon, *The Wanderings of Peoples*, 1911, pp. 78–9.
[4] W. Bogoras, *Am. Anth.* iv. 1902, p. 577.

others were encroached upon by populations of increasingly dolichocephalic type—Plains Indians and Cherokees, Chichimecs, Tepanecs, Acolhuas. Even still dolichocephaly is characteristic of Iroquois, Coahuilas, Sonorans, while the intermediate indices met with on the prairies and plateaux undoubtedly indicate the mixture between the long-headed invaders and the round-heads whom they swept aside as they advanced southwards. Thus the Minnetaris are highly dolicho; the Poncas and Osages sub-brachy; the Algonquians variable, while the Siouans oscillate widely round a mesaticephalous mean.

The Athapascans alone are homogeneous, and their sub-brachycephaly recurs amongst the Apaches and their other

Cranial Deformation. southern kindred, who have given it an exaggerated form by the widespread practice of artificial deformation, which dates from remote times. The most typical cases both of brachy and dolicho deformation are from the Cerro de las Palmas graves in south-west Mexico. Deformation prevails also in Peru and Bolivia, as well as in Ceara and the Rio Negro on the Atlantic side. The flat-head form, so common from the Columbia estuary to Peru, occurs amongst the broad-faced Huaxtecs, their near relations the Maya-Quichés, and the Nahuatlans. It is also found amongst

The " Toltecs." the extinct Cebunys of Cuba, Hayti and Jamaica, and the so-called " Toltecs," that is, the people of Tollan (Tula), who first founded a civilised state on the Mexican table-land (sixth and seventh centuries A.D.), and whose name afterwards became associated with every ancient monument throughout Central America. On this " Toltec question " the most contradictory theories are current; some hold that the Toltecs were a great and powerful nation, who after the overthrow of their empire migrated southwards, spreading their culture throughout Central America; others regard them as " fabulous," or at all events " nothing more than a sept of the Nahuas themselves, the ancestors of those Mexicans who built Tenochtitlan," *i.e.* the present city of Mexico. A third view, that of Valentini, that the Toltecs were not Nahuas but Mayas, is now supported both by E. P. Dieseldorff[1] and by Förstemann.[2] T. A. Joyce[3] suggests that the vanguard of the Nahuas on reaching the Mexican valley adopted and improved the culture

[1] *Bur. Am. Eth. Bull.* 28, 1904, p. 535.
[2] *Globus*, LXX. No. 3.
[3] *Mexican Archaeology*, 1914, p. 7 ff.

of an agricultural people of Tarascan affinities whose culture was in part due to Mayan inspiration, whom they found settled there.   Later migrations of Nahua were greatly impressed with the " Toltec " culture which had thus arisen through the impact of a virile hunting people on more passive agriculturalists.

On the North-west Pacific Coast similar ethnical inter-minglings recur, and Franz Boas [1] here distinguishes as many as four types, the Northern (Tsimshian and others), the Kwakiutl, the Lillooet of the Harrison Lake region and the inland Salishan (Flat-heads, Shuswaps, etc.).   All are brachycephalic, but while the Tsimshians are of medium height 1.675 m. (5 ft. 6 in.) with low, concave nose, very large head, and enormously broad face, exceeding the average for North America by 6 mm., the Kwakiutls are shorter 1.645 m. (5 ft. 4¾ in.) with very high and relatively narrow hooked nose, and quite exceptionally high face ; the Harrison Lake very short 1.600 m. (5 ft. 3 in.) with exceedingly short and broad head (c. 1. nearly 89), "surpassing in this respect all other forms known to exist in North America "; lastly, the inland Salish of medium height 1.679 m. (5 ft. 6 in.) with high and wide nose of the characteristic Indian form and a short head.

Type of North-west Coast Indians Variable.

It would be difficult to find anywhere a greater contrast than that which is presented by some of these British Columbian natives, those, for instance, of Harrison Lake with almost cir-cular heads (88.8), and some of the Labrador Eskimo with a degree of dolichocephaly not exceeded even by the Fijian Kai-Colos (65).[2]   But this violent contrast is somewhat toned by the intermediate forms, such as those of the Tlingits, the Aleutian islanders, and the western (Alaskan) Eskimo, by which the transition is effected between the Arctic and the more southern populations.   It is not possible at present to indicate even in outline the chronology of any of the ethnic movements outlined above.   Warren K. Moore-head [3] agrees with the great majority of American archaeologists in holding the existence of palaeolithic man in North America as not proven,[4] the so-called palaeoliths being

Date of Migra-tions.

---

[1] " The Social Organization, etc. of the Kwakiutl Indians," *Rep. U.S. Nat. Mus.* 1895, Washington (1897), p. 321 sq. and *Ann. Arch. Rep.* 1905, Toronto, 1906, p. 84.

[2] W. L. H. Duckworth, *Journ. Anthr. Inst.*, August, 1895.

[3] *The Stone Age in North America*, 1911.

[4] On the other hand there are a few American archaeologists who believe in

either rejects or rude tools for rough purposes. When man migrated to America from North and East Asia whenever that period may have been, he appears to have been in that stage of culture—or rather of stone technique—which we term Neolithic, and the drifting movement ceased before he had learnt the use of metals.

A further proof of the antiquity of the migrations is afforded by linguistics. A. F. Chamberlain asserts[1] that "it may be said with certainty, so far as all data hitherto presented are concerned, that no satisfactory proof whatever has been put forward to induce us to believe that any single American Indian tongue or group of tongues has been derived from any Old World form of speech now existing or known to have existed in the past. In whatever way the multiplicity of American Indian languages and dialects may have arisen, one can be reasonably sure that the differentiation and divergence have developed here in America and are in no sense due to the occasional intrusion of Old World tongues individually or *en masse*. . . . Certain real relationships between the American Indians and the peoples of north-eastern Asia, known as ' Paleo-Asiatics,' have, however, been revealed as a result of the extensive investigations of the Jesup North Pacific Expedition. . . . . The general conclusion to be drawn from the evidence is that the so-called ' Paleo-Asiatic ' peoples of north-eastern Asia, *i.e.* the Chukchee, Koryak, Kamchadale, Gilyak, Yukaghir, etc. really belong physically and culturally with the aborigines of north-western America. . . . Like the modern Asiatic Eskimo they represent a reflex from America and Asia, and not *vice versa*. . . . It is the opinion of good authorities also that the ' Paleo-Asiatic ' peoples belong linguistically with the American Indians rather than with the other tribes and stocks of northern or southern Asia. Here we have then the only real relationship of a linguistic character that has ever been convincingly argued between tongues of the New World and tongues of the Old."

Evidence from Linguistics.

It is not merely that the American languages differ from other forms of speech in their general phonetic, structural and lexical features ; they differ from them in their very morphology, as much, for instance, as in the zoological world class differs

the occurrence of implements of palaeolithic type in the United States, but there is no corroborative evidence on the part of contemporaneous fossils. See N. H. Winchell, " The weathering of aboriginal stone artifacts," No. 1. *Collection of the Minnesota Hist. Soc.* Vol. XVI. 1913.

[1] *Am. Anth.* XIV. 1912, p. 55.

from class, order from order. They have all of them developed on the same polysynthetic lines, from which if a few here and there now appear to depart, it is only because in the course of their further evolution they have, so to say, broken away from that prototype.[1] Take the rudest or the most highly cultivated anywhere from Alaska to Fuegia—Eskimauan, Iroquoian, Algonquian, Aztec, Tarascan, Ipurina, Peruvian, Yahgan—and you will find each and all giving abundant evidence of this universal polysynthetic character, not one true instance of which can be found anywhere in the eastern hemisphere. There is incorporation with the verb, as in Basque, many of the Caucasus tongues, and the Ural-Altaic group; but it is everywhere limited to pronominal and purely relational elements.

But in the American order of speech there is no such limitation, and not merely the pronouns, which are restricted in number, but the nouns with their attributes, which are practically numberless, all enter necessarily into the verbal paradigm. Thus in Tarascan (Mexico): *hopocuni*=to wash the hands; *hopodini*=to wash the ears, from *hoponi*=to wash, which cannot be used alone.[2] So in Ipurina (Amazonia): *nicuçacatçaurumatinit*=I draw the cord tight round your waist, from *ni*, I; *cuçaca*, to draw tight; *tça*, cord; *túruma*, waist; *tini*, characteristic verbal affix; *t*, thy, referring to waist.[3]

We see from such examples that polysynthesis is not a primitive condition of speech, as is often asserted, but on the contrary a highly developed system, in which the original agglutinative process has gone so far as to attract all the elements of the sentence to the verb, round which they cluster like swarming bees round their queen. In Eskimauan the tendency is shown in the construction of nouns and verbs, by which other classes of words are made almost unnecessary, and one

---

[1] Such disintegration is clearly seen in the Carib still surviving in Dominica, of which J. Numa Rat contributed a somewhat full account to the *Journ. Anthr. Inst.* for Nov. 1897, p. 293 sq. Here the broken form *arametakuahátina buka* appears to represent the polysynthetic *arametakuanientibubuka* (root *arameta*, to hide), as in Père Breton's *Grammaire Caraibe*, p. 45, where we have also the form *arametakualubatibubasubutuiruni*=know that he will conceal thee (p. 48). It may at the same time be allowed that great inroads have been made on the principle of polysynthesis even in the continental (South American) Carib, as well as in the Colombian Chibcha, the Mexican Otomi and Pima, and no doubt in some other linguistic groups. But that the system must have formerly been continuous over the whole of America seems proved by the persistence of extremely polysynthetic tongues in such widely separated regions as Greenland (Eskimo), Mexico (Aztec), Peru (Quichuan), and Chili (Araucanian).

[2] R. de la Grasserie and N. Léon, *Langue Tarasque*, Paris, 1896.

[3] J. E. R. Polak, *Ipurina Grammar*, etc., London, 1894.

word, sometimes of interminable length, is able to express a whole sentence with its subordinate clauses. H. Rink, one of the first Eskimo scholars of modern times, gives the instance : " Suérúkame-autdlásassoq-tusaramiuk-tuningingmago-iluarin-gilát=they did not approve that he (*a*) had omitted to give him (*b*) something, as he (*a*) heard that he (*b*) was going to depart on account of being destitute of everything." [1] Such monstrosities " are so complicated that in daily speech they could hardly ever occur ; but still they are correct and can be understood by intelligent people." [2]

He gives another and much longer example, which the reader may be spared, adding that there are altogether about 200 particles, as many as ten of which may be piled up on any given stem. The process also often involves great phonetic changes, by which the original form of the elements becomes disguised, as, for instance, in the English *hap'oth*=half-penny-worth. The attempt to determine the number of words that might be formed in this way on a single stem, such as *igdlo*, a house, had to be given up after getting as far as the compound *igdlorssualiortugssarsiumavoq*=he wants to find one who will build a large house.

It is clear that such a linguistic evolution implies both the postulated isolation from other influences, which must have disturbed and broken up the cumbrous process, and also the postulated long period of time to develop and consolidate the system throughout the New World. But time is still more imperiously demanded by the vast number of stock languages, many already extinct, many still current all over the continent, all of which differ profoundly in their vocabulary, often also in their phonesis, and in fact have nothing in common except this extraordinary polysynthetic groove in which they are cast. There are probably about 75 stock languages in North America, of which 58 occur north of Mexico.

Stock Languages.

But even that conveys but a faint idea of the astonishing diversity of speech prevailing in this truly linguistic Babel.

---

[1] *The Eskimo Tribes, their Distribution and Characteristics*, Copenhagen, 1887, I. p. 62 sq.

[2] In fact this very word was first given " as an ordinary example " by Klein-schmidt, *Gram. d. Grönlandischen Sprache*, Sect. 99, and is also quoted by Byrne, who translates : " They disapproved of him, because he did not give to him, when he heard that he would go off, because he had nothing " (*Principles*, etc., I. p. 140).

J. W. Powell [1] points out that the practically distinct idioms are far more numerous than might be inferred even from such a large number of mother tongues. Thus, in the Algonquian [2] linguistic family he tells us there are about 40, no one of which could be understood by a people speaking another ; in Athapascan from 30 to 40 ; in Siouan over 20 ; and in Shoshonian a still greater number.[3] The greatest linguistic diversity in a relatively small area is found in the state of California, where, according to Powell's classification, 22 distinct stocks of languages are spoken. R. B. Dixon and A. L. Kroeber [4] show however that these fall into three morphological groups which are also characterised by certain cultural features. It is the same, or perhaps even worse, in Central and in South America, where the linguistic confusion is so great that no complete classification of the native tongues seems possible. Clements R. Markham in the third edition of his exhaustive list of the Amazonian tribes [5] has no less than 1087 entries. He concludes that these may be referred to 485 distinct tribes in all the periods, since the days of Acuña (1639). Deducting some 111 as extinct or nearly so, the total amounts to " 323 at the outside " (p. 135). But for such linguistic differences, large numbers of these groups would be quite indistinguishable from each other, so great is the prevailing similarity in physical appearance and usages in many districts. Thus Ehrenreich tells us that, " despite their ethnico-linguistic differences, the tribes about the head waters of the Xingu present complete uniformity in their daily habits, in the conditions of their existence, and their general culture," [6] though it is curious to note that the art of making pottery is restricted here to the Arawak tribes.[7]

---

[1] " Indian Linguistic Families of America north of Mexico," *Seventh Ann. Rept. Bureau of Ethnology*, 1885–6 (1891). See also the " Handbook of American Indian Languages," Part 1 by Franz Boas and others, *Bureau of American Ethnology, Bulletin* 40, 1911. The Introduction by F. Boas gives a good general idea of the characteristics of these languages and deals shortly with related problems.

[2] Following this ethnologist's convenient precedent, I use both in *Ethnology* and here the final syllable *an* to indicate stock races and languages in America. Thus *Algonquin*=the particular tribe and language of that name ; *Algonquian* =the whole family ; *Iroquois, Iroquoian, Carib, Cariban*, etc.

[3] *Forum*, Feb. 1898, p. 683.

[4] Studies of these languages by Kroeber and others will be found in *University of California Publications*; *American Archaeology and Ethnology*, L. 1903 onwards. Cf. also A. L. Kroeber, " The Languages of the American Indians," *Pop. Sci. Monthly*. LXXVIII. 1911.

[5] *Journ. Roy. Anthr. Inst.* XL. 1910, p. 73.

[6] *Urbewohner Brasiliens*, 1897, p. 46.

[7] Karl v. d. Steinen, *Unter den Naturvölkern Zentral-Brasiliens*, 1894, p. 215.

Yet amongst them are represented three of the radically distinct linguistic groups of Brazil, some (Bakaïri and Nahuqua) belonging to the Carib, some (Auetö and Kamayura) to the Tupi-Guarani, and some (Mehinaku and Vaura) to the Arawak family. Obviously these could not be so discriminated but for their linguistic differences. On the other hand the opposite phenomenon is occasionally presented of tribes differing considerably in their social relations, which are nevertheless of the same origin, or, what is regarded by Ehrenreich as the same thing, belong to the same linguistic group. Such are the Ipurina, the Paumari and the Yamamadi of the Purus valley, all grouped as Arawaks because they speak dialects of the Arawakan stock language. At the same time it should be noted that the social differences observed by some modern travellers are often due to the ever-increasing contact with the whites, who are now encroaching on the Gran Chaco plains, and ascending every Amazonian tributary in quest of rubber and the other natural produce abounding in these regions. The consequent displacement of tribes is discussed by G. E. Church.[1]

In the introduction to his valuable list Clements Markham observes that the evidence of language favours the theory that the Amazonian tribes, " now like the sands on the sea-shore for number, originally sprang from two or at most three parent stocks. Dialects of the *Tupi* language extend from the roots of the Andes to the Atlantic, and southward into Paraguay . . . and it is established that the differences in the roots, between the numerous Amazonian languages, are not so great as was generally supposed." [2] This no doubt is true, and will account for much. But when we see it here recorded that of the Carabuyanas (Japura river) there are or were 16 branches, that the Chiquito group (Bolivia) comprises 40 tribes speaking "seven different languages"; that of the Juris (Upper Amazons) there are ten divisions ; of the Moxos (Beni and Mamoré rivers) 26 branches, " speaking nine or, according to Southey, thirteen languages " ; of the Uaupés (Rio Negro) 30 divisions, and so on, we feel how much there is still left to be accounted for. Attempts have been made to weaken the force of the linguistic argument by the assumption, at one time much in favour, that the American tongues are of a somewhat evanescent nature, in an unstable condition, often changing their form and structure

[1] *Aborigines of South America*, 1912.
[2] *Loc. cit.* p. 75.

within a few generations. But, says Powell, "this widely spread opinion does not find warrant in the facts discovered in the course of this research. The author has everywhere been impressed with the fact that savage tongues are singularly persistent, and that a language which is dependent for its existence upon oral tradition is not easily modified."[1] A test case is the Delaware (Leni Lenapé), an Algonquian tongue which, judging from the specimens collected by Th. Campanius about 1645, has undergone but slight modification during the last 250 years.

In this connection the important point to be noticed is the fact that some of the stock languages have an immense range, while others are crowded together in indescribable confusion in rugged upland valleys, or about river estuaries, or in the recesses of trackless woodlands, and this strangely irregular distribution prevails in all the main divisions of the continent. Thus of Powell's 58 linguistic families in North America as many as 40 are restricted to the relatively narrow strip of coastland between the Rocky Mountains and the Pacific, ten are dotted round the Gulf of Mexico from Florida to the Rio Grande, and two disposed round the Gulf of California, while nearly all the rest of the land—some six million square miles— is occupied by the six widely diffused Eskimauan, Athapascan, Algonquian, Iroquoian, Siouan, and Shoshonian families. The same phenomenon is presented by Central and South America, where less than a dozen stock languages—Opatan, Nahuatlan, Huastecan, Chorotegan, Quichuan, Arawakan, Gesan (Tapuyan), Tupi-Guaranian, Cariban—are spread over millions of square miles, while many scores of others are restricted to extremely narrow areas. Here the crowding is largely determined, as in Caucasia, by the altitude (Andes in Colombia, Ecuador, Peru, and Bolivia ; Sierras in Mexico).

It is strongly held by many American ethnologists that the various cultures of America are autochthonous, nothing being borrowed from the Old World. J. W. Powell,[2] **Culture.** who rendered such inestimable services to American anthropology, affirmed that " the aboriginal peoples of America cannot be allied preferentially to any one branch of the human race in the Old World "; that " there is no evidence that any of the arts of the American Indians were borrowed from the Orient"; that " the industrial arts of America

[1] *Indian Linguistic Families*, p. 141.
[2] "Whence came the American Indians?" *Forum*, Feb. 1898.

were born in America, America was inhabited by tribes at the time of the beginning of industrial arts. They left the Old World before they had learned to make knives, spear and arrowheads, or at least when they knew the art only in its crudest state. Thus primitive man has been here ever since the invention of the stone knife and the stone hammer." He further contended that " the American Indian did not derive his forms of government, his industrial or decorative arts, his languages, or his mythological opinions from the Old World, but developed them in the New ; " and that " in the demotic characteristics of the American Indians, all that is common to tribes of the Orient is universal, all that distinguishes one group of tribes from another in America distinguishes them from all other tribes of the world."

This view has been emphasised afresh by Fewkes,[1] though of recent years it has met with vigorous opposition. At the conclusion of his article " Die melanesische Bogenkultur und ihre Verwandten "[2] Graebner attempts to trace the cultural connection of South America with South-east Asia rather than with the South Seas, the main links being represented by head-hunting, certain types of skin-drum and of basket, and in particular three types of crutch-handled paddle. According to him the spread of culture has taken place by the land route and Behring Strait, not across the Pacific by way of the South Seas, a view to which he adheres in his later work. An ingenious and detailed attempt has also been made by Pater Schmidt[3] to trace the various cultures determined for Oceania and Africa in South America. Apart from the great linguistic groups usually adopted as the basis of classification, Schmidt would divide the South American Indians according to their stage of economic development into collectors, cultivators, and civilised peoples of the Andean highlands. Though this series may have the appearance of evolution, in point of fact " each group is composed of peoples differing absolutely in language and race, who brought with them to South America in historically distinct migrations at all events the fundamentals of their respective cultures. . . . As we pass in review the cultural elements of the

---

[1] J. Walter Fewkes, " Great Stone Monuments in History and Geography," *Pres. Add. Anthrop. Soc., Washington*, 1912.

[2] F. Graebner, *Anthropos*, IV. 1909, esp. pp. 1013–24. Cf. also his *Ethnologie*, 1914.

[3] W. Schmidt, " Kulturkreise und Kulturschichten in Südamerika," *Zeitschrift für Ethnologie*, Jg. 45, 1913, p. 1014 ff.

separate groups, their weapons, implements, dwellings, their sociology, mythology, and religion we discover the innate similarity of these groups to the culture-zones of the Old World in all essential features."[1] The author proceeds to work out his theory in great detail; the earlier cultures he too considers have travelled by the enormously lengthy land route by way of North America, only the "free patrilineal culture" (Polynesia and Indonesia) having reached the west coast directly by sea.[2]

W. H. Holmes[3] draws attention to analogies between American and foreign archaeological remains, for example the stone gouge of New England and Europe. He hints at influences coming from the Mediterranean and even from Africa. "Even more remarkable and diversified are the correspondences between the architectural remains of Yucatan and those of Cambodia and Java in the far East. On the Pacific side of the American continent strange coincidences occur in like degree, seeming to indicate that the broad Pacific has not proved a complete bar to intercourse of peoples of the opposing continents ... it seems highly probable considering the nature of the archeological evidence, that the Western World has not been always and wholly beyond the reach of members of the white, Polynesian, and perhaps even the black races."

Walter Hough[4] gives various cultural parallels between America and the other side of the Pacific but does not commit himself. S. Hagar[5] brings forward some interesting correspondences between the astronomy of the New and of the Old Worlds, but adopts a cautious attitude.

More recently the problem has been attacked with great energy by G. Elliot Smith.[6] His investigations into the processes of mummification and the tombs of ancient Egypt led him to comparative studies, and he notes that certain customs seem to be found in association, forming what is known as a culture-complex. For example, "in most regions the people who introduced the habit of megalithic building and sun worship also brought with them the practice of mummification." Also associated with these are :—stories of dwarfs and giants, belief in the indwelling of gods and great men in megalithic monu-

---

[1] *Loc. cit.* pp. 1020, 1021.
[2] *Ibid.* p. 1093 ; cf. also p. 1098 where the Peruvian sailing balsa is traced to Polynesia, sailing rafts being still used in the Eastern Paumotu islands.
[3] *Am. Anth.* XIV. 1912, pp. 34–6.
[4] *Loc. cit.* p. 39.   [5] *Loc. cit.* p. 43.
[6] G. Elliot Smith, *The Migrations of Early Culture*, 1915.

ments, the use of these structures in a particular manner for special council, the practice of hanging rags on trees in association with such monuments, serpent worship, tattooing, distension of the lobe of the ear, the use of pearls, the conch-shell trumpet, etc. In a map showing the distribution of this "heliolithic" culture-complex he indicates the main lines of migration to America, one across the Aleutian chain and down the west coast to California, the other and more important one, across the Pacific to Peru, and thence to various parts of South America, through Central America to the southern half of the United States. Contrary to Schmidt, Elliot Smith postulates contact of cultures rather than actual migrations of people ; he considers it possible that a small number of aliens arriving by sea in Peru, for example, might introduce customs of a highly novel and subversive character which would take root and spread far and wide. The Peruvian custom of embalming the dead certainly presents analogies to that of ancient Egypt, and Elliot Smith is convinced that " the rude megalithic architecture of America bears obvious evidence of the same inspiration which prompted that of the Old World." In a later paper Elliot Smith [1] adduces further evidence in support of his thesis "that the essential elements of the ancient civilization of India, Further Asia, the Malay Archipelago, Oceania, and America were brought in succession to each of these places by mariners, whose oriental migrations (on an extensive scale) began as trading intercourse between the Eastern Mediterranean and India some time after 800 B.C. and continued for many centuries." This dissemination was in the first instance due to the Phoenicians and there are "unmistakable tokens that the same Phoenician methods which led to the diffusion of this culture-complex in the Old World also were responsible for planting it in the New [2] some centuries after the Phoenicians themselves had ceased to be " (*l. c.* p. 27). Further evidence along the same lines is offered by W. J. Perry [3] who has noted the geographical distribution of terraced cultivation and irrigation and finds that it corresponds to a remarkable extent with that of the "heliolithic" culture-complex, and by J. Wilfrid

---

[1] G. Elliot Smith, " The Influence of Ancient Egyptian Civilization in the East and in America," *Bull. of the John Rylands Library*, Jany.—March, 1916, pp. 3, 4.

[2] Cf. W. J. Perry, " The Relationship between the Geographical Distribution of Megalithic Monuments and Ancient Mines," reprinted from *Manchester Memoirs*, Vol. LX. (1915), pt. I ; " The Megalithic Culture of Indonesia," 1918.

[3] W. J. Perry, *Mem. and Proc. Manchester Lit. and Phil. Soc.* LX. 1916, No. 6.

Jackson [1] who has investigated the Aztec Moon-cult and its relation to the Chank cult of India, the money cowry as a sacred object among North American Indians,[2] shell trumpets and their distribution in the Old and New World [3] and the geographical distribution of the shell purple industry.[4]   He points out that we have ample evidence of the practice of this ancient industry in several places in Central America, and refers to Zelia Nuttall's interesting paper on the subject.[5]   Elliot Smith also discusses " Pre-Columbian Representations of the Elephant in America " [6] and remarks " coincidences of so remarkable a nature cannot be due to chance.   They not only confirm the identification of the elephant in designs in America, but also incidentally point to the conclusion that the Hindu god Indra was adopted in Central America with practically all the attributes assigned to him in his Asiatic home."   Elliot Smith believes that practically every element of the early civilisation of America was derived from the Old World.   Small groups of immigrants from time to time brought certain of the beliefs, customs, and inventions of the Mediterranean area, Egypt, Ethiopia, Arabia, Babylonia, Indonesia, Eastern Asia' and Oceania, and the confused jumble of practices became assimilated and " Americanised " in the new home across the Pacific as the result of the domination of the great uncultured aboriginal populations by small bands of more cultured foreigners.   These highly suggestive studies will force adherents of the theory of the indigenous origin of American culture to reconsider the grounds for their opinions and will lead them to turn once more to the writings of Bancroft,[7] Tylor,[8] Nuttall,[9] Macmillan Brown,[10] Enoch [11] and others.

There is no satisfactory scheme of classification of the American peoples.   Although there is a good deal of scattered information about the physical anthropology of the natives it has not yet been systematised and no   Classification.

[1] *Loc. cit.* No. 5.   [2] *Loc. cit.* No. 4.
[3] *Loc. cit.* No. 8.   [4] *Loc. cit.* No. 7.
[5] *Putnam Anniversary Volume*, 1909, p. 365.
[6] *Nature*, Nov. 25 and Dec. 16, 1915.
[7] H. H. Bancroft, *The Native Races of the Pacific States of North America*, 1875.
[8] E. B. Tylor, " On the game of Patolli in Ancient Mexico and its probably Asiatic origin," *Journ. Anthr. Inst.* VIII. 1878, p. 116.   *Rep. Brit. Ass.* 1894, p. 774.
[9] Zelia Nuttall, " The Fundamental Principles of Old and New World Civilisations," *Arch. and Eth. Papers, Peabody Mus. Cambridge, Mass.* II. 1901.
[10] J. Macmillan Brown, *Maori and Polynesian*, 1907.
[11] C. R. Enoch, *The Secret of the Pacific*, 1912.

classification can at present be based thereon. A linguistic classification is therefore usually adopted, but a geographical or cultural grouping, or a combination of the two, has much practical convenience. As Farrand [1] points out " It must never be forgotten that the limits of physical, linguistic and cultural groups do not correspond ; and the overlapping of stocks determined by those criteria is an unavoidable complication."

An inspection of the map of the distribution of linguistic stocks of North America prepared by J. W. Powell [2] which represents the probable state of affairs about **Linguistic Classification.** 1500 A.D. shows that a few linguistic stocks have a wide distribution while there is a large number of restricted stocks crowded along the Pacific slope. The following are the better known tribes of the more important stocks together with their distribution.

Eskimauan (Eskimo), along the Arctic coasts from 60° N. lat. in the west, to 50° in the east. *Athapascan*, northern group, Déné or Tinneh (including many tribes), interior of Alaska, northern British Columbia and the Mackenzie basin, and the Sarsi of south-eastern Alberta and northern Montana ; southern group, Navaho and Apache in Arizona, New Mexico and northern Mexico ; the Pacific group, a small band in southern British Columbia, others in Washington, Oregon and northern California. *Algonquian*, south and west of Canada, the United States east of the Mississippi, the whole valley of the Ohio, and the states of the Atlantic coast. Blackfoot of Montana, Alberta, south and further east, Cheyenne and Arapaho of Minnesota. The main group of dialects is divided into the Massachusett, Ojibway (Ojibway, Ottawa, Illinois, Miami, etc.) and Cree types. The latter include the Cree, Montagnais, Sauk and Fox, Menomini, Shawnee, Abnaki, etc. *Iroquoian*, in the provinces of Ontario and Quebec ; Hurons in the valley of the St Lawrence and lake Simcoe. Neutral confederacy in western New York and north and west of lake Erie. The great confederacy of the Iroquois or " Five Nations " (Seneca, Cayuga, Oneida, Onondaga and Mohawk, to which the Tuscarora were added in 1712) in central New York ; the Conestoga and Susquehanna to the south. A southern group was located in eastern Virginia and north Carolina, and the Cherokee, centred in the southern Appalachians from parts of Virginia

[1] Livingston Farrand, *Basis of American History*, 1904, pp. 88–9.
[2] *7th Ann. Rep. Bur. Am. Eth.* 1885–6 (1891).

and Kentucky to northern Alabama. *Muskhogean* of Georgia, Alabama and Mississippi, including the Choctaw, Chickasaw, Creek, Seminole, etc. and the Natchez. There are several small groups about the mouth of the Mississippi. *Caddoan.* The earliest inhabitants of the central and southern plains beyond the Missouri belonged to this stock, the largest group occupied parts of Louisiana, Arkansas, Oklahoma and Texas, it consists of the Caddo, Wichita, etc. and the Kichai, the Pawnee tribes in parts of Nebraska and Kansas and an offshoot, the Arikara in North Dakota. *Siouan*, a small group in Virginia, Carolina, Catawba, etc. and a very large group, practically occupying the basins of the Missouri and Arkansas, with a prolongation through Wisconsin, where were the Winnebago. The main tribes are the Mandan, Crow, Dakota, Assiniboin, Omaha and Osage. *Shoshonian* of the Great Plateau and southern California. The two outlying tribes were the Hopi of north Arizona and the Comanche who ranged over the southern plains. Among the plateau tribes are the Ute, Shoshoni, Mono and Luiseño. *Yuman*, from Arizona to Lower California.

From the data available J. R. Swanton and R. B. Dixon draw the following conclusions.[1] " It appears that the origin of the tribes of several of our stocks may be referred back to a swarming ground, usually of rather indefinite size but none the less roughly indicated. That for the Muskhogeans, including probably some of the smaller southern stocks, must be placed in Louisiana, Arkansas and perhaps the western parts of Mississippi and Tennessee, although a few tribes seem to have come from the region of the Ohio. That for the Iroquoians would be along the Ohio and perhaps farther west, and that of the Siouans on the lower Ohio and the country to the north including part at least of Wisconsin. The dispersion area for the Algonquians was farther north about the Great Lakes and perhaps also the St Lawrence, and that for the Eskimo about Hudson Bay or between it and the Mackenzie river. The Caddoan peoples seem to have been on the southern plains from earliest times. On the north Pacific coast we have indications that the flow of population has been from the interior to the coast. This seems certain in the case of the Indians of the Chimmesayan stock and some Tlinglit subdivisions. Some Tlinglit clans, however,

Ethnic Movements.

---

[1] " Primitive American History," *Am. Anth.* XVI. 1914, pp. 410–11.

have moved from the neighbourhood to the Nass northward. Looking farther south we find evidence that the coast Salish have moved from the inner side of the coast ranges, while a small branch has subsequently passed northward to the west of it.   The Athapascan stock in all probability has moved southward, sending one arm down the Pacific coast, and a larger body presumably through the Plains which reached as far as northern Mexico.   Most of the stocks of the Great Plateau and of Oregon and California show little evidence of movement, such indications as are present, however, pointing toward the south as a rule.   The Pueblo Indians appear to have had a mixed origin, part of them coming from the north, part from the south.   In general there is to be noted a striking contrast between the comparatively settled condition of those tribes west of the Rocky mountains and the numerous movements, particularly in later times, of those to the east."

With regard to the Pacific coast Dixon [1] notes that it " has apparently been occupied from the earliest times by peoples differing but little in their culture from the tribes found in occupancy in the sixteenth century.   Cut off from the rest of the country by the great chain of the Cordilleras and the inhospitable and arid interior plateaus, the tribes of this narrow coastal strip developed in comparative seclusion their various cultures, each adopted to the environment in which it was found. . . .

" In several of the ingenious theories relating to the development and origin of American cultures in general, it has been contended that considerable migrations both of peoples and of cultural elements passed along this coastal highway from north to south.   If, however, the archaeological evidence is to be depended on, such great sweeping movements, involving many elements of foreign culture, could hardly have taken place, for no trace of their passage or modifying effect is apparent. . . . We can feel fairly sure that the prehistoric peoples of each area were in the main the direct ancestors of the local tribes of to-day. . . .

" In comparison with the relative simplicity of the archaeological record on the Pacific coast, that of the eastern portion of the continent is complex, and might indeed be best described as a palimpsest.   This complexity leads inevitably to the con-

---

[1] Roland B. Dixon, *Am. Anth.* xv. 1913, pp. 538–9.

clusion that here there have been numerous and far-reaching ethnic movements, resulting in a stratification of cultures."

W. H. Holmes has compiled a map marking the limits of eleven areas which can be recognised by their archaeological remains.[1]   He points out that the culture units are, as a matter of course, not usually well-defined.   **Archaeological Classification.**   Cultures are bound to over-lap and blend along the borders and more especially along lines of ready communication. In some cases evidence has been reported of early cultures radically distinct from the type adopted as characteristic of the areas, and ancestral forms grading into the later and into the historic forms are thought to have been recognised.   Holmes frankly acknowledges the tentative character of the scheme, which forms part of a synthesis that he is preparing of the antiquities of the whole American continent.

North America is customarily divided into nine areas of material culture, and though this is convenient, a more correct method, as C. Wissler points out,[2] is to locate the respective groups of typical tribes as culture   **Cultural Classification.**   centres, classifying the other tribes as intermediate or transitional.   The geographical stability of the material culture centres is confirmed by archaeological evidence which suggests that the striking individuality they now possess resulted from a more or less gradual expansion along original lines. The material cultures of these centres possess great vitality and are often able completely to dominate intrusive cultural unity.   Thus tribes have passed from an intermediate state to a typical, as when the Cheyenne were forced into the Plains centre, and the Shoshonian Hopi adopted the typical Pueblo culture.   Wissler comes to the conclusion that "the location of these centres is largely a matter of ethnic accident, but once located and the adjustments made, the stability of the environment doubtless tends to hold each particular type of material culture to its initial locality, even in the face of many changes in blood and language."   It is from his valuable paper that the material culture traits of the following areas have been obtained.

I. Eskimo Area.   The fact that the Eskimo live by the sea and chiefly upon sea food does not differentiate them from

[1] " Areas of American culture characterisation tentatively outlined as an aid in the study of the Antiquities," *Am. Anth.* XVI. 1914, pp. 413–46.

[2] Clark Wissler, " Material Cultures of the North American Indians," *Am. Anth.* XVI. 1914, pp. 447–505.

the tribes of the North Pacific coast, but they are distinguished from the latter by the habit of camping in winter upon sea

Eskimo : Material Culture.

ice and living upon seal, and in the summer upon land animals. The kayak and "woman's boat," the lamp, harpoon, float, woman's knife, bow-drill, snow goggles, trussed-bow, and dog traction are almost universal. The type of winter shelter varies considerably, but the skin tent is general in summer and the snow house, as a more or less permanent winter house, prevails east of Point Barrow.

The mode of life of all the Eskimo, as F. Boas [1] has pointed out, is fairly uniform and depends on the distribution of food at the different seasons. The migrations of game compel the natives to move their habitations from time to time, and as the inhospitable country does not produce vegetation to an extent sufficient to support human life they are forced to depend entirely upon animal food. The abundance of seals in Arctic America enables man to withstand the inclemency of the climate and the sterility of the soil. The skins of seals furnish the materials for summer garments and for the tent, their flesh is almost their only food, and their blubber their indispensable fuel during the long dark winter when they live in solid snow houses. When the ice breaks up in the spring the Eskimo establish their settlements at the head of the fiords where salmon are easily caught. When the snow on the land has melted in July the natives take hunting trips inland in order to obtain the precious skins of the reindeer, or of the musk-ox, of whose heavy pelts the winter garments are made. Walrus and the ground seal also arrive and birds are found in abundance and eaten raw.

The Eskimo [2] occupy more than 5000 miles of sea-board from north-east Greenland to the mouth of the Copper river

Origin and Affinities.

in western Alaska. Many views have been advanced as to the position of their centre of dispersion ; most probably it lay to the west of Hudson Bay. Rink [3] is of opinion that they originated as a distinct people in Alaska, where they developed an Arctic

[1] " The Central Eskimo," *6th Ann. Rep. Bur. Am. Eth.* 1884–5 (1888), p. 419.
[2] The name is said to come from the Abnaki *Esquimantsic,* or from *Ashkimeq,* the Ojibway equivalent meaning " eaters of raw flesh." They call themselves Innuit, meaning " people."
[3] H. Rink, " The Eskimo Tribes, their Distribution and Characteristics," *Meddelelser om Grönland,* II. 1887.

culture ; but Boas[1] regards them " as, comparatively speaking, new arrivals in Alaska, which they reached from the east." A westward movement is supported by myths and customs, and by the affinities of the Eskimo with northern Asiatics. There was always hostility between the Eskimo and the North American Indians, which, apart from their very specialised mode of life, precluded any Eskimo extension southwards. The expansion of the Eskimo to Greenland is explained by Steensby[2] as follows :—the main southern movement would have followed the west coast from Melville Bay, rounded the southern point and proceeded some distance up the east coast. From the Barren Grounds north-west of Hudson Bay the Polar Eskimo followed the musk-ox, advanced due north to Ellesmere Land, then crossed to Greenland, and, still hunting the musk-ox, advanced along the north coast and down the east coast towards Scoresby Sound.   Another line of migration apparently started from the vicinity of Southampton Island and pursued the reindeer northwards into Baffin Land ; on reaching Ponds Inlet these reindeer-hunting Eskimo for the most part turned along the east coast.

Physically the Eskimo constitute a distinct type.   They are of medium stature, but possess uncommon strength and endurance ; their skin is light brownish yellow with a ruddy tint on the exposed parts ; hands and feet are small and well formed ; their heads **Physical Type.** are high, with broad faces, and narrow high noses, and eyes of a Mongolian character.   But great varieties are found in different parts of the vast area over which they range.   The Polar Eskimo of Greenland, studied by Steensby, were more of American Indian than of Asiatic type.[3]   Of their psychology this writer says, " For the Polar Eskimos life is deadly real and sober, a constant striving for food and warmth which is borne with good humour, and all dispensations are accepted as natural consequences, about which it is of no use to reason or complain."   " The hard struggle for existence has not permitted the Polar Eskimo to become other than a confirmed egoist, who knows nothing of disinterestedness.   Towards his enemies he is crafty and deceitful—he does not attack them

---

[1] F. Boas, " Ethnological Problems in Canada," *Journ. Roy. Anthr. Inst.* XL. 1910, p. 529.

[2] H. P. Steensby, " Contributions to the Ethnology and Anthropogeography of the Polar Eskimos," *Meddelelser om Grönland*, XXXIV. 1910.

[3] H. P. Steensby, *loc. cit.* p. 384.

openly, but indulges in backbiting. . . . It is only during the hunt that a common interest and a common danger engender a deeper feeling of comradeship." [1]

Still less Mongolian in type are the " blond Eskimo " recently encountered by Stefánsson in south-west Victoria Island,[2] who are regarded by him as very possibly the mixed descendants of Scandinavian ancestors who had drifted there from west Greenland. It is known that Eric the Red discovered Greenland in the year 982 and that three years later settlers went there from the Norse colony in Iceland.

The winter snow houses, which are about 12 × 15 ft. in diameter and 12 ft. high, usually with annexes, are always **Social Life.** occupied by two families, each woman having her own lamp and sitting on the ledge in front of it. If more families join in making a snow house, they make two main rooms. Whenever it is possible the men spend the short days in hunting and each woman prepares the food for her husband. The long nights are mainly spent in various recreations. The social life in the summer settlement is somewhat different. The families do not cook their own meals, but a single one suffices for the whole settlement. The day before it is her turn to cook the woman goes to the hills to fetch enough shrubs for the fire. When a meal is ready the master of the house calls out and everybody comes out of his tent with a knife, the men sit in one circle and the women in another. These dinners, which are always held in the evening, are almost always enlivened by a mimic performance. The great religious feasts take place just before the beginning of winter.

There are three forms of social grouping : the Family, House-mates, and Place-mates. (1) The family consists of a man, his wife or wives, their children and adopted children ; widows and their children may be adopted, but the woman retains her own fireplace. Sometimes men are adopted, such as bachelors without any relatives, cripples, or impoverished men. Joint ownership and use of a boat and house, and common labour and toil in obtaining the means of support define the real community of the family. (2) House-mates are families that join together to build and occupy and maintain the same house. This form of establishment is especially common in

---

[1] *Loc. cit.* pp. 366, 376.
[2] V. Stefánsson, *My Life with the Eskimo*, 1913, p. 194 ff.

Greenland, but each family keeps its separate establishment inside the common house. (3) Place-fellows. The inhabitants of the same hamlet or winter establishment form one community although no chief is elected or authority acknowledged.

Generally children are betrothed when very young. The newly married pair usually live at first with the wife's family. Both polygyny and polyandry occur. A man may lend or exchange his wife for a whole season or longer, as a sign of friendship. On certain occasions it is even commanded by religious law. There is no government, but there is a kind of chief in the settlement, though his authority is very limited. He is called the " pimain," *i.e.* he who knows everything best. He decides the proper time to shift the huts from one place to another, he may ask some men to go sealing, others to go deer hunting, but there is not the slightest obligation to obey him. The men in a community may form themselves into an informal council for the regulation of affairs. The decorative art of the Eskimo is not remarkably developed, but the pictorial art consists of clever sketches of everyday scenes and there is a well developed plastic art. Many of the carvings are toys and are made for the pleasure of the work. " The religious views and practices of the Eskimo while, on the whole, alike in their fundamental traits, show a considerable amount of differentiation in the extreme east and in the extreme west. It would seem that the characteristic traits of shamanism are common to all the Eskimo tribes. The art of the shaman (angakok) is acquired by the acquisition of guardian spirits. . . . Besides the spirits which may become guardian spirits of men, the Eskimo believes in a great many others which are hostile and bring disaster and death. . . . The ritualistic development of Eskimo religion is very slight." [1]

II. Mackenzie Area. Skirting the Eskimo area is a belt of semi-Arctic lands almost cut in two by Hudson Bay. To the west are the Déné tribes, who are believed **Déné :** to fall into three culture groups, an eastern group, **Material** Yellow Knives, Dog Rib, Hares, Slavey, Chi- **Culture.** pewyan and Beaver ; a south-western group, Nahane, Sekani, Babine and Carrier ; and a north-western group, comprising the Kutchin, Loucheux, Ahtena and Khotana. The material

[1] F. Boas, "The Eskimo," *Annual Archaeological Report*, 1905, Toronto (1906), p. 112 ff.

culture of the south-western group is deduced from the writings of Father Morice.[1]   All the tribes are hunters of large or small game, caribou are often driven into enclosures, small game taken in snares or traps ; various kinds of fish are largely used, and a few of the tribes on the head waters of the Pacific take salmon ; large use of berries is made, they are mashed and dried by a special process ; edible roots and other vegetable foods are used to some extent ; utensils are of wood and bark ; there is no pottery ; bark vessels are used for boiling with or without stones ; travel in summer is largely by canoe, in winter by snowshoe ; dog sleds are used to some extent, but chiefly since trade days, the toboggan form prevailing ; clothing is of skins ; mittens and caps are worn ; there is no weaving except rabbit-skin garments, but fine network occurs on snowshoes, bags, and fish nets, materials being of bark fibre, sinew and babiche ; there is also a special form of woven quill work ; the typical habitation seems to be the double lean-to, though many intrusive forms occur ; other material culture traits include the making of fish-hooks and spears ; a limited use of copper ; and poorly developed work in stone.

The physical characteristics vary very much from tribe to tribe.   The Sekani, according to Morice, are slender and bony,

Physical Type.   in stature rather below the average, with a narrow forehead, hollow cheeks, prominent cheekbones, small eyes deeply sunk in their orbit, the upper lip very thin and the lower somewhat protruding, the chin very small and the nose straight.   The Carriers, on the contrary, are tall and stout, without as a rule being too corpulent.   The men average 1.66 m. in height.   Their forehead is much broader than that of the Sekani, and less receding than is usual with American aborigines.   The face is full, and the nose aquiline.   All the tribes are remarkably unwarlike, timid, and even cowardly.   Weapons are seldom used and in personal combat, which consists in a species of wrestling, knives are previously laid aside.   The fear of enemies is a marked feature, due in part, doubtless, to traditional recollection of the raids of earlier days.   Their honesty is noted by all travellers.   Morice records that among the Sekani a trader will sometimes go on a trapping expedition, leaving his store

---

[1] A. G. Morice, " Notes on the Western Dénes," *Trans. Canadian Inst.* IV. 1895 ; " The Western Dénes," *Proc. Canadian Inst.* XXV. (3rd Series, VII.) 1890 ; " The Canadian Dénes," *Ann. Arch. Rep.* 1905 (1906), p. 187.

unlocked, without fear of any of its contents going amiss. Meantime a native may call in his absence, help himself to as much powder and shot or any other item as he may need, but he will never fail to leave there an exact equivalent in furs.

The eastern Déné are nomad hunters who gather berries and roots, while the western are semi-sedentary, living for most of the year in villages when they subsist largely on salmon. The former are patrilineal Social Life. and the latter are grouped into matrilineal exogamic totemic clans. The headmen of the clans formed a class of privileged nobles who alone owned the hunting grounds. Morice speaks of clan, honorific and personal totems. The first two were adopted from coastal tribes, the honorific was assumed by some individuals in order to attain a rank to which they were not entitled by heredity. The " personal totem " is the guardian spirit or genius, the belief in which is common to nearly all North American peoples. Shamanism prevails throughout the area. The mythology almost always refers to a " Transformer " who visited the world when incomplete and set things in order. They have the custom of the potlatch.[1] If a man desires another man's wife he can challenge the husband to a wrestling match, the winner keeps the woman.[2]

III. North Pacific Coast Area. This culture is rather complex with tribal variations, but it can be treated under three subdivisions, a northern group, Tlingit, N. Pacific Haida and Tsimshian; a central group, the Coast : Material Kwakiutl tribes and the Bellacoola; and a Culture. southern group, the Coast Salish, Nootka, Chinook, Kalapooian, Waiilatpuan, Chimakuan and some Athapascan tribes. The first of these seem to be the type and are characterised by : the great dependence upon sea food, some hunting upon the mainland, large use of berries (dried fish, clams and berries are the staple food) ; cooking with hot stones in boxes and baskets ; large rectangular gabled houses of upright cedar planks with carved posts and totem poles ; travel chiefly by water in large seagoing dug-out canoes some of which had

[1] From the Nootka word *potlatsh*, " giving " or " a gift," so called because these great winter ceremonials were especially marked by the giving away of quantities of goods, commonly blankets. Cf. J. R. Swanton in *Handbook of American Indians* (F. W. Hodge, editor), 1910.

[2] Besides C. Wissler, *loc. cit.* p. 457 and A. G. Morice, *loc. cit.*, cf. J. Jette, *Journ. Roy. Anthr. Inst.* XXXVII. 1907, p. 157 ; C. Hill-Tout, *British North America*, 1907 ; and G. T. Emmons, " The Tahltan Indians," *Anthr. Pub. University of Pennsylvania*, IV. I, 1911.

sails ; no pottery nor stone vessels, except mortars ; baskets in checker, those in twine reaching a high state of excellence among the Tlingit ; coil basketry not made ; mats of cedar bark and soft bags in abundance ; no true loom, the warp hanging from a bar and weaving with the fingers downwards ; clothing rather scanty, chiefly of skin, a wide basket hat (the only one of the kind on the continent, apparently for protection against rain) ; feet usually bare, but skin moccasins and leggings occasionally made ; for weapons the bow, club and a peculiar dagger, no lances ; slat, rod and skin armour ; wooden helmets, no shields ; practically no chipped stone tools, but nephrite or green stone used ; wood work highly developed ; work in copper possibly aboriginal but, if so, weakly developed. The central group differs in a few minor points ; twisted and loosely woven bark or wool takes the place of skins for clothing and baskets are all in checkerwork. Among the southern group appears a strong tendency to use stone arrowheads, and a peculiar flat club occurs, vaguely similar to the New Zealand type.[1]

Physically the typical North Pacific tribes are of medium stature, with long arms and short bodies. Among the northern branches the stature averages 1.675 m. (5 ft. 6 in.), the head is very large with an average index of 82.5. The face is very broad, the nose concave or straight, seldom convex, with slight elevation. Among the southern tribes, notably the Kwakiutl, the stature averages 1.645 m. (5 ft. 4¾ in.), the cephalic index is 84.5, the face very broad but also of great length, the nose very high, rather narrow and frequently convex.

Physical Type.

The social relations of these peoples vary from tribe to tribe, but on the whole they fall into a sequence from north to south. In the northern portion descent is matrilineal, but patrilineal in the south. J. G. Frazer does not accept the view of Boas " that the Northern Kwakiutl have borrowed both the rule of maternal descent and the division into totemic clans from their more northerly neighbours of alien stocks ; in other words, that totemism and mother-kin have spread southward among a people who had father-kin and no totemic system."[2] He inclines " to the other view, formerly favoured by Boas himself, namely, that

Social Life.

[1] C. Wissler, *loc. cit.* p. 454.
[2] J. G. Frazer, *Totemism and Exogamy*, III. 1910, p. 319.

the Kwakiutl are in a stage of transition from mother-kin to father-kin." [1]

Each village is autonomous and originally may have been restricted to a single totem clan. The population is divided into three ranks, nobles, common people and a low caste consisting of poor people and serfs who cannot participate in the secret societies. In addition there is a totemic grouping. There may be several totemic clans in one village and the same totem may not only occur in every village, but may extend from one tribe to another. This suggests that there were originally two, or in some cases more than two, totemic clans which in process of time became subdivided into sub-clans; these, while retaining the crest of the original clan, acquired fresh ones, and the families contained in each sub-clan may have their special crest or crests in addition. New crests and names are constantly being introduced. Marriage is forbidden between people of the same crest, irrespective of the tribe. The natives according to Boas do not consider themselves descendants from their totem. A wife brings her father's position, crest and privileges as a dower to her husband, who is not allowed to use them himself, but acquires them for the use of his son, in other words this inheritance is in the female line.

The widely spread American custom of a youth acquiring a guardian spirit is far more prevalent among the southern section than the northern, but among the Kwakiutl he can only obtain as his patron, one or more of a limited number of spirits which are hereditary in his clan. In the northern tribes the secret societies are co-extensive with the totemic clans; among the Kwakiutl they are connected with guardian spirits and it is significant that during the summer, when the people are scattered, society is based on the old clan system, but when the people live together in villages in the winter, society is reorganised on the basis of the secret societies. There is a highly developed system of barter of which the blanket is now the unit of value, formerly the units were elk-skins, canoes or slaves. Certain symbolic objects have attained fanciful values. A vast credit system has grown up based on the custom of loaning property at high interest, at the great festivals called "potlatch" and by it the giver gains great honour. The religion is closely related to the totemic beliefs; supernatural aid

---

[1] *Loc. cit.* p. 333.

is given by the spirits to those who win their favour. The raven is the chief figure in the mythology ; he regulates the phenomena of nature, procures fire, daylight, and fresh water, and teaches men the arts.

To the south, and extending inland to the divide, forming a much less characteristic group are the Salish or Flat-heads who are allied to the Athapascans. The coastal Salish assimilate the culture just described, but the plateau Salish are more democratic, less settled and more individualistic in religious matters.[1] The Chinooks or Flat-heads of the lower reaches of the Columbia river are nearly extinct. They deformed the heads of infants. These tribes and the Shahapts or Nez Percés are differentiated by garments of raw hides, cranial deformation, absence of tattooing and plain bows, but they still have communal houses though without totem posts. They cook by means of heated stones and have zoomorphic masks.[2]

IV. Plateau Area. The Plateau area lies between the North Pacific Coast area and the Plains. It is far less uniform than either in its topography, the south being a veritable desert while the north is moist and fertile. The traits may be summarised as : extensive use of salmon, deer, roots (especially camas) and berries; the use of a handled digging stick, cooking with hot stones in holes and baskets ; the pulverisation of dried salmon and roots for storage ; winter houses, semi-subterranean, a circular pit with a conical roof and smoke hole entrance ; summer houses, movable or transient, mat or rush-covered tents and the lean-to, double and single ; the dog sometimes used as a pack animal ; water transportation weakly developed, crude dug-outs and bark canoes being used ; pottery not known ; basketry highly developed, coil, rectangular shapes, imbricated technique; twine weaving in flexible bags and mats ; some simple weaving of bark fibre for clothing ; clothing for the entire body usually of deerskins ; skin caps for the men, and in some cases basket caps for women ; blankets of woven rabbit-skin ; the sinew-backed bow prevailed ; clubs, lances, and knives, and rod and slat armour were used in war, also heavy leather shirts ; fish spears, hooks, traps and bag nets were used ; dressing of deerskins highly developed ; upright stretching frames and straight

Plateau Area : Material Culture.

---

[1] See p. 367.
[2] F. Boas, *Brit. Ass. Reports*, 1885–98 ; *Social Organisation of the Kwakiutl Indians*, 1897 ; A. P. Niblack, " The Coast Indians," *U.S. Nat. Mus. Report*, 1898.

long handled scrapers ; wood work more advanced than among
Plains tribes, but insignificant compared to North Pacific Coast
area ; stone work confined to the making of tools and points,
battering and flaking ; work in bone, metal, and feathers very
weak.[1]

Of the tribes of this area, the interior Salish, the Thompson,
Shushwap and Lillooet, appear to be the most typical of those
concerning which any information is available.
The Shahapts or Nez Percés, and the Shoshoni   The Interior
show some marked Plains traits.   " The interior   Salish.
Salish are landsmen and hunters, and from time immemorial
have been accustomed to follow their game over mountainous
country.   This mode of life has engendered among them an
active, slender, athletic type of men ; they are considerably
taller and possess a much finer physique than their congeners
of the coastal region, who are fishermen, passing the larger
portion of their time on the water squatting in their canoes,
never walking to any place if they can possibly reach it by
water.   The typical coast Salish are a squat thick-set people,
with disproportionate legs and bodies, slow and heavy in their
movements, and as unlike their brothers of the interior as it
is possible for them to be." [2]

The Thompsons represented the Salish at their highest
and best, both morally and physically, and their ethical precepts
and teaching set a very high standard of virtue before the
advent of the Europeans.   Hill-Tout says that receptiveness
and a wholesale adoption of foreign fashions and customs are
their striking qualities, and " if they have fallen away from
these high standards, as we fear they have, the fault is not
theirs but ours. . . . We assumed a grave responsibility when
we undertook to civilise these races." [3]

The simplest form of social organisation is found among
the interior hunting tribes, where a state of pure anarchy may

---

[1] For this area consult J. Teit, " The Thompson Indians of British Columbia,"
" The Lillooet Indians," and " The Shushwap," in *Memoirs, Am. Mus. Nat. Hist.*
Vol. ii. 4, 1900 ; Vol. iv. 5, 1906 ; and Vol. iv. 7, 1909 ; F. Boas, " The Salish
Tribes of the Interior of British Columbia," *Ann. Arch. Rep.* 1905 (Toronto,
1906) ; C. Hill-Tout, " The Salish Tribes of the Coast and Lower Fraser Delta,"
Ann. Arch. Rep. 1905 (Toronto, 1906) ; H. J. Spinden, " The Nez Percés Indians,"
Memoirs, Am. Anth. Ass. ii. 3, 1908 ; R. H. Lowie, " The Northern Shoshone,"
Anth. Papers, Am. Mus. Nat. Hist. ii. 2, 1908 ; A. B. Lewis, " Tribes of the
Columbia Valley," etc., *Memoirs, Am. Anth. Ass.* i. 2, 1906.

[2] C. Hill-Tout, *British North America*, 1907, p. 37.

[3] *Loc. cit.* p. 50.

be said to have formerly prevailed, each family being a law
unto itself and acknowledging no authority save
that of its own elderman. Each local community was composed of a greater or less number
of these self-ruling families. There was a kind of headship or
nominal authority given to the oldest and wisest of the elder-
men in some of the larger communities, where occasion called
for it or where circumstances arose in which it became necessary
to have a central representative. This led in some centres to
the regular appointing of local chiefs or heads whose business
it was to look after the material interest of the commune over
which they presided ; but the office was always strictly elective
and hedged with manifold limitations as to authority and
privilege. For example, the local chief was not necessarily
the head of all undertakings. He would not lead in war or
the chase unless he happened to be the best hunter or the
bravest and most skilful warrior among them ; and he was
subject to deposition at a moment's notice if his conduct did
not meet with the approval of the elders of the commune.
His office or leadership was therefore purely a nominal one.
All hunting, fishing, root, and berry grounds were common
property and shared in by all alike. . . . In one particular tribe
even the food was held and meals were taken in common, the
presiding elder or headman calling upon a certain family each
day to provide and prepare the meals for all the rest, every one,
more or less, taking it in turn to discharge this social duty.[1]

V. Californian Area. Of the four sub-culture areas noted
by Kroeber[2] the central group is the most extensive and typical.
Its main charactistics are : acorns as the chief
vegetable food, supplemented by wild seeds,
while roots and berries are scarcely used ; the
acorns are made into bread by a roundabout process ; hunting
is mostly of small game, fishing wherever possible ; the houses
are of many forms, all simple shelters of brush or tule, or more
substantial conical lean-to structures of poles ; the dog was not
used for packing and there were no canoes, but rafts of tule
were used for ferrying ; no pottery but high development of
basketry both coil and twine ; bags and mats scanty ; cloth or

*Social Or-
ganisation.*

*California :
Material
Culture.*

---

[1] *Loc. cit.* pp. 158–9.
[2] A. L. Kroeber, " Types of Indian Culture in California," *University of California Publications Am. Arch. and Eth.* II. 3, 1904 ; cf. also the special anthropological publications of the University of California.

other weaving of simple elements not known ; clothing simple and scanty ; feet usually bare ; the bow the only weapon, usually sinew-backed ; work in skins, wood, bone, etc. weak, in metals absent, in stone work not advanced. In the south modifications enter with large groups of Yuman and Shoshonian tribes where pottery, sandals and wooden war clubs are intrusive. The extinct Santa Barbara were excellent workers in stone, bone and shell, and made plank canoes.

Topographical variation produces consequent changes in mode of life as the well watered and wooded country of Oregon and Northern California gradually merges into Social Life. the warm dry climate of South California with decreasing moisture towards the tropics. As Kroeber says,[1] "From the time of the first settlement of California, its Indians have been described as both more primitive and more peaceful than the majority of the natives of North America. . . . The practical arts of life, the social institutions and the ceremonies of the Californian Indians are unusually simple and undeveloped. There was no war for its own sake, no confederation of powerful tribes, no communal stone pueblos, no totems, or potlatches. The picturesqueness and the dignity of the Indians are lacking. In general rudeness of culture the Californian Indians are scarcely above the Eskimo. . . . If the degree of civilisation attained by people depends in any large measure on their habitat, as does not seem likely, it might be concluded from the case of the Californian Indians that natural advantages were an impediment rather than an incentive to progress. . . . It is possible to speak of typical Californian Indians and to recognise a typical Californian culture area. A feature that should not be lost sight of is the great stability of population. . . . The social organisation was both simple and loose. . . . Beyond the family the only bases of organisation were the village and the language." In so simple a condition of society difference of rank naturally found but little scope. The influence of chiefs was comparatively small, and distinct classes, as of nobility or slaves, were unknown. Individual property rights were developed and what organisation of society there was, was largely on the basis of property. The ceremonies are characterised by a very slight development of the extreme ritualism that is so characteristic of the American Indians, and by an almost

[1] *Loc. cit.* p. 81 ff.

entire absence of symbolism of any kind. Fetishism is also unusual. One set of ceremonies was usually connected with a secret religious society ; during initiation members were disguised by feathers and paint, but masks were not worn. There was also an annual tribal spectacular ceremony held in remembrance of the dead. In the north-west portion of the state a somewhat more highly developed and specialised culture existed which has some affinities with that of the north-west tribes, as is indicated by a greater advance in technology, a social organisation largely upon a property basis and a system of mythology that is suggestive of those further north. The now extinct tribes of the Santa Barbara islands and adjacent mainland were more advanced. They alone employed a plank-built canoe instead of the balsas or canoe-shaped bundles of rushes of the greater part of California. They made stone bowls and did inlaid work. Like the North Californians and tribes further north they buried instead of burning their dead. The eastern tribes shade off into their neighbours. The Luiseño, the southernmost of the Shoshonians, had puberty rites for girls and boys.[1] The belief in a succession of births " is reminiscent of Oceanic and Asiatic ways of thought." [2] [About] 1788 a secret cult arose inculcating, with penalties, obedience, fasting, and self-sacrifice on initiates.[3]

VI. Plains Area. The chief traits of this culture are the dependence upon the bison (" buffalo ") and the very limited

Plains Area : Material Culture.

use of roots and berries ; absence of fishing ; lack of agriculture ; the *tipi* or tent as the movable dwelling and transportation by land only, with the dog and the travois (in historic times, with the horse) ; no baskets, pottery, or true weaving ; clothing of bison and deer-skins ; there is high development of work in skins and special bead technique and raw-hide work (parfleche, cylindrical bag, etc.), and weak development of work in wood, stone and bone. This typical culture is manifested in the Assiniboin, Arapaho, Blackfoot, Crow, Cheyenne, Comanche, Gros Ventre, Kiowa, Kiowa-Apache, Sarsi and Teton-Dakota.[4] Among the tribes

[1] P. S. Spartman, *University of California Publications, Am. Arch. and Eth.* VIII. 1908, p. 221 ff. ; A. L. Kroeber, " Types of Indian Culture in California," *ibid.* II. 1904, p. 81 ff.

[2] A. L. Kroeber, *ibid.* VIII. 1908, p. 72.

[3] C. G. DuBois, " The Religion of the Luiseño Indians," *tom. cit.* p. 73 ff.

[4] Dakota is the name of the largest division of the Siouan linguistic family, commonly called Sioux ; Santee, Yankton and Teton constituting, with the Assiniboin, the four main dialects.

of the eastern border a limited use of pottery and basketry may be added, some spinning and weaving of bags, and rather extensive agriculture. Here the tipi alternates with larger and more permanent houses covered with grass, bark or earth, and there was some attempt at water transportation. These tribes are the Arikara, Hidatsa, Iowa, Kansa, Mandan, Missouri, Omaha, Osage, Oto, Pawnee, Ponca, Santee-Dakota,[1] Yankton-Dakota[1] and Wichita.

On the western border other tribes (Wind River Shoshoni, Uinta and Uncompahgre Ute) lack pottery but produce a rather high type of basketry, depending far less on the bison but more on deer and small game, making large use of wild grass seeds.

On the north-eastern border the Plains-Ojibway and Plains-Cree combine many traits of the forest hunting tribes with those found in the Plains.

The Dakota or Sioux are universally conceded to be of the highest type, physically, mentally and probably morally of any of the western tribes. Their bravery has never been questioned by white or Indian and they conquered or drove out every rival except the Ojibway. Their physical characteristics are as follows: dark skin faintly tinged with red, facial features more strongly marked than those of the Pacific Coast Indians, nose and lower jaw particularly prominent and heavy, head generally meso-cephalic and not artificially deformed. They are a free and dominant race of hunters and warriors, necessarily strong and active. Their weapons of stone, wood, bone and horn are toma-hawk, club, flint knife, and bow and arrow. All their habits centre in the bison, which provided the staple materials of nutrition and industry. Drawing and painting were done on prepared bison skins and elaborately carved pipes were made for ceremonial use.

The Dakota (Sioux).

They are divided into kinship groups, with inheritance as a rule in the male line. The woman is autocrat of the home. Exogamy was strictly enforced in the clan but marriage within the tribe or with related tribes was encouraged. The marriage was arranged by the parents and polygyny was common where means would permit. Government consisted in chieftainship acquired by personal merit, and the old men exercised con-siderable influence.

[1] See note 4, p. 370.

Religious conceptions were based on a belief in *Wakonda*
or *Manito*,[1] an all-pervading spirit force, whose cult involved
Religion.   various shamanistic ceremonials consisting of
dancing, chanting, feasting and fasting.   Most
distinctive of these is the Sun dance, practised by almost all
the tribes of the plains except the Comanche.   It is an annual
festival lasting several days, in honour of the sun, for the
purpose of obtaining abundant produce throughout the
year.

The Sun dance was not only the greatest ceremony of the
Plains tribe but was a condition of their existence.   More than
any other ceremony or occasion, it furnished the
The Sun   tribe the opportunity for the expression of emotion
Dance.   in rhythm, and was the occasion of the tribe becoming more closely united.   It gave opportunity for the
making and renewing of common interests, the inauguration of
tribal policies, and the renewing of the rank of the chiefs ; for
the exhibition, by means of mourning feasts, of grief over the
loss of members of families ; for the fulfilment of social obligations by means of feasts; and, finally, for the exercise and
gratification of the emotions of love on the part of the young
in the various social dances which always formed an interesting
feature of the ceremony.[2]

Being strongly opposed by the missionaries because it was
utterly misunderstood,[3] and finding no favour in official circles,
the Sun dance has been for many years an object of persecution,
and in consequence is extinct among the Dakota, Crows, Mandan, Pawnee, and Kiowa, but it is still performed by the Cree,
Siksika (Blackfoot), Arapaho, Cheyenne, Assiniboin, Ponca,
Shoshoni and Ute, though in many of these tribes its disappearance is near at hand, for it has lost part of its rites and

---

[1] *Wakonda* is the term employed " when the power believed to animate all
natural forms is spoken to or spoken of in supplications or rituals " by many tribes
of the Siouan family.   *Manito* is the Algonquian name for " the mysterious and
unknown potencies and powers of life and of the universe."   " *Wakonda*," says
Miss Fletcher, " is difficult to define, for exact terms change it from its native un-
crystallized condition to something foreign to aboriginal thought.   Vague as the
concept seems to be to one of another race, to the Indian it is as real and as
mysterious as the starry night or the flush of the coming day," " Handbook of
American Indians " (ed. F. W. Hodge), *Bur. Am. Eth. Bull.* 30, 1907.
[2] See G. A. Dorsey, " Handbook of American Indians " (ed. F. W. Hodge),
Bur. Am. Eth. Bull. 30, 1907.
[3] G. B. Grinnell points out that the personal torture often associated with the
ceremonies has no connection with them, but represents the fulfilment of individual vows.   " The Cheyenne Medicine Lodge," *Am. Anth.* XVI. 1914, p. 245.

has become largely a spectacle for gain rather than a great religious ceremony.[1]

The Pawnee do not differ at all widely from the Dakota, but have a somewhat finer cast of features. They are more given to agriculture, raising crops of maize, pump- **The Pawnee.** kins, etc. The Pawnee type of hut is character- istic, consisting of a circular framework of poles or logs, covered with brush, bark and earth. Their religious ceremonies were connected with the cosmic forces and the heavenly bodies. The dominating power was Tirawa generally spoken of as " Father." The winds, thunder, lightning and rain were his messengers. Among the Skidi the morning and evening stars represented the masculine and feminine elements, and were connected with the advent and perpetuation on earth of all living forms. A series of ceremonies relative to the bringing of life and its increase began with the first thunder in the spring and culminated at the summer solstice in human sacrifice, but the series did not close until the maize, called " mother corn," was harvested. At every stage of the series certain shrines or " bundles " became the centre of a ceremony. Each shrine was in charge of an hereditary keeper, but its rituals and ceremonies were in the keeping of a priesthood open to all proper aspirants. Through the sacred and symbolic articles of the shrines and their rituals and ceremonies a medium of communication was believed to be opened between the people and the supernatural powers, by which food, long life and prosperity were obtained. The mythology of the Pawnee is remarkably rich in symbolism and poetic fancy and their re- ligious system is elaborate and cogent. The secret societies, of which there were several in each tribe, were connected with the belief in supernatural animals. The functions of these societies were to call the game, to heal diseases, and to give occult powers. Their rites were elaborate and their ceremonies dramatic.[2]

The Blackfeet or Siksika,[3] an Algonquian confederacy of

---

[1] See G. A. Dorsey, " Arapaho Sun Dance," *Pub. Field Col. Mus. Anth.* iv. 4 (Chicago), 1903 ; " The Cheyenne," *tom. cit.* ix. 1905.

[2] A. C. Fletcher, in " Handbook of American Indians " (ed. F. W. Hodge), *Bur. Am. Eth.*, Bull. 30, 1907 ; *Am. Anth.* iv. 4, 1902 ; " The Hako, a Pawnee Cere- mony," *22nd Ann. Rep. Bur. Am. Eth.* 1900–1, 2 (1904) ; G. A. Dorsey, " Tradi- tions of the Skidi Pawnee," *Mem. Am. Folklore Soc.* viii. 1904.

[3] From *siksinam* " black," and *ka*, the root of *oqkatsh* " foot." The origin of the name is commonly given as referring to the blackening of their moccasins by the ashes of the prairie fires.

the northern plains, agree in culture with the Plains tribes
generally, though there is evidence of an earlier
The Black-feet. culture, approximately that of the eastern woodland tribes.   They are divided into the Siksika
proper, or Blackfeet, the Kainah or Bloods, and the Piegan,
the whole being popularly known as Blackfoot or Blackfeet.
Formerly bison and deer were their chief food and there is no
evidence that they ever practised agriculture, though tobacco
was grown and used entirely for ceremonial purposes.   The
doors of their tipis always faced east.   They have a great
number of dances—religious, war and social—besides secret
societies for various purposes, together with many "sacred
bundles" around every one of which centres a ritual.   Practically every adult has his personal "medicine."   The principal
deities are the Sun, and a supernatural being known as *Napi*
"Old Man," who may be an incarnation of the same idea.
The religious activity of a Blackfoot consists in putting himself·
into a position where the cosmic power will take pity upon him
and give him something in return.   There was no conception
of a single personal god.[1]

The Arapaho, another Algonquian Plains tribe, were once
according to their own traditions a sedentary agricultural people
The Arapaho. far to the north of their present range, apparently
in North Minnesota.   They have been closely
associated with the Cheyenne for many generations.[2]   The
annual Sun dance is their greatest tribal ceremony, and they
were active propagators of the ghost-dance religion of the last
century which centred in the belief in the coming of a messiah
and the restoration of the country to the Indians.[3]

The Cheyenne, also of agricultural origin, have been for
generations a typical prairie tribe, living in skin tipis, following
The Cheyenne. the bison over large areas, travelling and fighting
on horseback.   In character they are proud, con-
tentious, and brave to desperation, with an exceptionally high
standard for women.   Under the old system they had a council
of 44 elective chiefs, of whom four constituted a higher body,

[1] J. Mooney, "Handbook of American Indians" (ed. F. W. Hodge), *Bur. Am. Eth.*, Bull. 30, 1907 ; C. Wissler, "Material culture of the Blackfoot Indians," *Anth. Papers, Am. Mus. Nat. Hist.* v. 1, 1910 ; J. W. Schultz, *My Life as an Indian*, 1907.
[2] A. L. Kroeber, "The Arapaho," *Bull. Am. Mus. Nat. Hist.* XVIII. 1900 ; G. A. Dorsey and A. L. Kroeber, "Traditions of the Arapaho," *Pub. Field Col. Mus. Anth.* v. 1903 ; G. A. Dorsey, "Arapaho Sun Dance," *ib.* IV. 1903.
[3] J. Mooney, "The Ghost Dance Religion," *14th Ann. Rep. Bur. Am. Eth.* 1896.

with power to elect one of their number as head chief of the tribe. In all councils that concerned the relations with other tribes, one member of the council was appointed to argue as proxy or " devil's advocate " for the alien people. The council of 44 is still symbolised by a bundle of 44 invitation sticks, kept with the sacred medicine-arrows, and formerly sent round when occasion arose to convene the assembly. The four medicine-arrows constitute the tribal palladium which they claim to have had from the beginning of the world. It was exposed once a year with appropriate rites, and is still religiously preserved. No woman, white man, or even mixed blood of the tribe has ever been allowed to come near the sacred arrows. In priestly dignity the keepers of the medicine-arrows and the priests of the Sun dance rites stood first and equal.[1]

VII. Eastern Woodland Area.[2] The culture north of the Great Lakes and east of the St Lawrence is comparable to that of the Déné (see p. 361), the main traits being : the taking of caribou in pens ; the snaring of game ; the importance of small game and fish, also of berries ; the weaving of rabbit-skins ; the birch canoe ; the toboggan ; the conical skin or bark-covered shelter ; the absence of basketry and pottery and the use of bark and wooden utensils. To this northern group belong the Ojibway north of the lakes, including the Saulteaux, the Wood Cree, the Montagnais and the Naskapi. Further south the main body falls into three large divisions : Iroquoian tribes (Huron, Wyandot, Erie, Susquehanna and Five Nations) ; Central Algonquian to the west of the Iroquois (some Ojibway, Ottawa, Menomini, Sauk and Fox,[3] Potawatomi, Peoria, Illinois, Kickapoo, Miami, Piankashaw, Shawnee and Siouan Winnebago) ; Eastern Algonquian (Abnaki group and Micmac).

The Central group west of the Iroquois appears to be the

Eastern Woodlands : Material Culture.

[1] G. A. Dorsey, " The Cheyenne," *Pub. Field Col. Mus. Anth.* IX. 1905 ; G. B. Grinnell, " Social organisation of the Cheyennes," *Rep. Int. Cong. Am.* XIII. 1902.

[2] Consult the following : A. C. Parker, " Iroquois uses of Maize and other Food Plants," Bull. 144, *University of California Pub., Arch. and Eth.* VII. 4, 1909 ; W. J. Hoffman, " The Menomini Indians," 14*th Ann. Rep. Bur. Am. Eth.* 1892–3, I (1896) ; A. E. Jenks, " The Wild Rice Gatherers of the Upper Lakes," 19*th Ann. Rep. Bur. Am. Eth.* 1897–8, II. (1912) ; A. F. Chamberlain, " The Kootenay Indians and Indians of the Eastern Provinces of Canada," *Ann. Arch. Rep.* 1905 (1906) ; A. Skinner, " Notes on the Eastern Cree and Northern Saulteaux," *Anth. Papers, Am. Mus. Nat. Hist.* IX. I, 1911 ; *The Indians of Greater New York*, 1914 ; J. N. B. Hewitt, " Iroquoian Cosmology," 21*st Ann. Rep. Bur. Am. Eth.* 1899–1900 (1903), etc.

[3] For the Foxes (properly Musquakie) see M. A. Owen, *Folklore of the Musuakie Indians*, 1904.

most typical and the best known and the following are the

Central Group. main culture traits : maize, squashes and bean were cultivated, wild rice where available was a great staple, and maple sugar was manufactured ; deer, bear and even bison were hunted ; also wild fowl ; fishing was fairly developed, especially sturgeon fishing on the lakes ; pottery poor, but formerly used for cooking vessels, vessels of wood and bark common ; some splint basketry ; two types of shelter prevailed, a dome-shaped bark or mat-covered lodge for winter and a rectangular bark house for summer, though the Ojibway used the conical type of the northern border group ; dug-out and bark canoes and snowshoes were used, occasionally the toboggan and dog traction ; weaving was of bark fibre (downward with fingers), and soft bags, pack lines and fish nets were made ; clothing was of skins ; soft-soled moccasins with drooping flaps, leggings, breech-cloth and sleeved shirts for men, for women a skirt and jacket, though a one-piece dress was known ; robes of skin or woven rabbit-skin ; no armour or lances ; bows of plain wood and clubs ; in trade days, the tomahawk ; work in wood, stone and bone weakly developed ; probably considerable use of copper in prehistoric times ; feather-work rare.

In the eastern group agriculture was more intensive (except in the north) and pottery was more highly developed.

Eastern Group. Woven feather cloaks were common, there was a special development of work in steatite, and more use was made of edible roots.

The Iroquoian tribes were even more intensive agriculturalists and potters. They made some use of the blow-gun,

Iroquoian Tribes. developed cornhusk weaving, carved elaborate masks from wood, lived in rectangular houses of peculiar pattern, built fortifications and were superior in bone work.[1]

In physical type the Ojibways,[2] who may be taken as typical of the central Algonquians, were 1.73 m. (5 ft. 8 in.) in height,

The Ojibway. with brachycephalic heads (82 in the east, 80 in the west, but variable), heavy strongly developed cheek-bones and heavy and prominent nose. They were hard fighters and beat back the raids of the Iroquois on the east and of the Foxes on the south, and drove the Sioux before them

---

[1] C. Wissler, *loc. cit.* p. 459.
[2] Ojibway, meaning " to roast till puckered up," referred to the puckered seam on the moccasins. Chippewa is the popular adaptation of the word.

out upon the Plains.   According to Schoolcraft, who was personally acquainted with them and married a woman of the tribe, the warriors equalled in physical appearance the best formed of the North-West Indians, with the possible exception of the Foxes.

They were organised in many exogamous clans; descent was patrilineal although it was matrilineal in most Algonquian tribes.   The clan system was totemic.   There was a clan chief and generally a tribal chief as well, chosen from one clan in which the office was hereditary.   His authority was rather indefinite.

As regards religion W. Jones [1] notes their belief in a cosmic mystery present throughout all Nature, called "Manito."   It was natural to identify the Manito with both animate and inanimate objects and the impulse   **Religion.** was strong to enter into personal relations with the mystic power.   There was one personification of the cosmic mystery; and this was an animate being called the Great Manito.   Although they have long been in friendly relations with the whites Christianity has had but little effect on them, largely owing to the conservatism of the native medicine-men.   The *Medewiwin*, or grand medicine society, was a powerful organisation, which controlled all the movements of the tribe.[2]

The Iroquois [3] are not much differentiated in general culture from the stocks around them, but in political development they stand unique.   The Five Nations, Mo-   **The Iroquois.** hawk, Onondaga, Oneida, Cayuga and Seneca (subsequently joined by the Tuscarora), formed the famous League of the Iroquois about the year 1570.   Each tribe remained independent in matters of local concern, but supreme authority was delegated to a council of elected sachems.   They were second to no other Indian people north of Mexico in political organisation, statecraft and military prowess, and their astute diplomats were a match for the wily French and English statesmen with whom they treated.   So successful was this confederacy that for centuries it enjoyed complete supremacy over its neighbours, until it controlled the country from Hudson Bay to North Carolina.   The powerful Ojibway at the end of

[1] W. Jones, *Ann. Arch. Rep.* 1905 (Toronto), 1906, p. 144.   Cf. note on p. 372.
[2] W. J. Hoffman, "The Midewiwin or 'grand medicine society' of the Ojibwa," *7th Ann. Rep. Bur. Am. Eth.* 1886 (1891).
[3] From the Algonkin word meaning "real adders" with French suffix.

Lake Superior checked their north-west expansion, and their own kindred the Cherokee stopped their progress southwards.

The social organisation was as a rule much more complex and cohesive than that of any other Indians, and the most notable difference was in regard to the important position accorded to the women. Among the Cherokee, the Iroquois and the Hurons the women performed important and essential functions in their government. Every chief was chosen and retained his position and every important measure was enacted by the consent and co-operation of the child-bearing women, and the candidate for a chieftainship was nominated by the suffrages of the matrons of this group. His selection from among their sons had to be confirmed by the tribal and the federal councils respectively, and finally he was installed into office by federal officers. Lands and the "long houses" of related families belonged solely to the women.

VIII. South-eastern Area. This area is conveniently divided by the Mississippi, the typical culture occurring in the east. The Powhatan group and the Shawnee are intermediate, and the chief tribes are the Muskhogean (Creek, Choctaw, Chickasaw, Seminole, etc.) and Iroquian tribes (Cherokee and Tuscarora) with the Yuchi, Eastern Siouan, Tunican and Quapaw. The main culture traits are : great use of vegetable food and intensive agriculture ; maize, cane (a kind of millet), pumpkins, watermelons and tobacco being raised. Large use of wild vegetables, the dog, the only domestic animal, eaten ; later chickens, hogs, horses and cattle quickly adopted ; large game, deer, bear and bison, in the west ; turkeys and small game also hunted ; some fishing (with fish poison) ; of manufactured foods bears' oil, hickory-nut oil, persimmon bread and hominy are noteworthy, together with the famous black drink ;[1] houses generally rectangular with curved roofs, covered with thatch or bark, often with plaster walls, reinforced with wicker work ; towns were fortified with palisades ; dug-out canoes were used for transport. Clothing chiefly of deerskins and bison robes, shirt-like garments for men, skirts and toga-like upper garments for women, boot-like moccasins in winter ;

(margin note: South-eastern Area : Material Culture.*)*

---

[1] A decoction made by boiling the leaves of *Ilex cassine* in water, employed as "medicine" for ceremonial purification. It was a powerful agent for the production of the nervous state and disordered imagination necessary to "spiritual" power.

there were woven fabrics of bark fibre, fine netted feather
cloaks, and some bison hair weaving in the west (the weaving
being downwards with the fingers) ; baskets of cane and splints,
the double or netted basket and the basket meal sieve being
special forms ; knives of cane, darts of cane and bone ; blow-
guns in general use ; pottery good, coil process, with paddle
decorations ; a particular method of skin dressing (macerated
in mortars), good work in stone, but little in metal.[1]

The Creek women were short though well formed, while
the warrior according to Picket [2] was " larger than the ordinary
race of Europeans, often above 6 ft. in height,   The Creeks.
but was invariably well formed, erect in his carriage, and graceful in every movement. They were proud,
haughty and arrogant, brave and valiant in war." As a people
they were more than usually devoted to decoration and ornament ; they were fond of music and ball play was their most
important game. Each Creek town had its independent
government, under an elected chief who was advised by the
council of the town in all important matters. Certain towns
were consecrated to peace ceremonies and were known as
" white towns," while others, set apart for war ceremonials,
were known as " red towns." The solemn annual festival of
the Creeks was the " busk " or *puskita*, a rejoicing over the
first-fruits of the year. Each town celebrated its busk whenever
the crops had come to maturity. All the worn-out clothes,
household furniture, pots and pans and refuse, grain and other
provisions were gathered together into a heap and consumed.
After a fast, all the fires in the town were extinguished and
a priest kindled a new fire from which were made all the
fires in the town. A general amnesty was proclaimed, all
malefactors might return to their towns and their offences
were forgiven. Indeed the new fire meant the new life,
physical and moral, which had to begin with the new year.[3]

The Yuchi houses are grouped round a square plot of
ground which is held as sacred, and here the religious ceremonies and social gatherings take place. On the   The Yuchi.
edges stand four ceremonial lodges, in conformity
with the four cardinal points, in which the different clan groups

---

[1] C. Wissler, *loc. cit.* pp. 462–3.
[2] A. J. Pickett, *Hist. of Alabama*, 1851 (ed. 1896), p. 87.
[3] Cf. A. S. Gatschet, " A migration legend of the Creek Indians," *Trans. Acad.
Sci. St Louis*, v. 1888.

have assigned places. The square ground symbolises the rain-bow, where in the sky-world, Sun, the mythical culture-hero, underwent the ceremonial ordeals which he handed down to the first Yuchi. The Sun, as chief of the sky-world, author of the life, the ceremonies and the culture of the people, is by far the most important figure in their religious life. Various animals in the sky-world and vegetation spirits are recognised, besides the totemic ancestral spirits, who play an important part.

According to Speck [1] " the members of each clan believe that they are relatives and, in some vague way, the descendants of certain pre-existing animals whose names and identity they now bear. The animal ancestors are accordingly totemic. In regard to the living animals, they, too, are the earthly types and descendants of the pre-existing ones, hence, since they trace their descent from the same sources as the human clans, the two are consanguinely related." Thus the members of a clan feel obliged not to do violence to the wild animals having the form or name of their tutelaries, though the flesh and fur may be obtained from the members of other clans who are under no such obligations. The different individuals of the clan inherit the protection of the clan totems at the initiatory rites, and thenceforth retain them as their protectors through life.

Public religious worship centres in the complex annual ceremony connected with the corn harvest and includes the making of new fire, clan dances impersonating totemic ances-tors, dances to propitiate maleficent spirits and acknowledge the assistance of beneficent ones in the hope of a continuance of their benefits, scarification of the males for sacrifice and purification, taking an emetic as a purifier, the partaking of the first green corn of the season, and the performance of a characteristic ball game with two sticks.

The middle and lower portions of the Mississippi valley with out-lying territories exhibit archaeological evidence of a remarkable culture, higher than that of any other
Mound Builders. area north of Mexico. This culture was charac-terised by " well established sedentary life, ex-tensive practice of agricultural pursuits, and construction of

---

[1] F. G. Speck, " Some outlines of Aboriginal Culture in the S.E. States," *Am. Anth.* N.S. IX. 1907 ; " Ethnology of the Yuchi Indians," *Anth. Pub. Mus. Univ. Pa.* I. I, 1909.

permanent works—domiciliary, religious, civic, defensive and mortuary, of great magnitude and much diversity of form." The people, some, if not all of whom were mound-builders, were of numerous linguistic stocks, Siouan, Algonquian, Iroquoian, Muskhogean, Tunican, Chitimachan, Caddoan and others, and "these historic peoples, remnants of which are still found within the area, were doubtless preceded by other groups not of a distinct race but probably of the same or related linguistic families. This view, in recent years, has gradually taken the place of the early assumption that the mound culture belonged to a people of high cultural attainments who had been succeeded by Indian tribes. That mound building continued down to the period of European occupancy is a well established fact, and many of the burial mounds contain as original conclusions articles of European make." [1]

These general conclusions are in no way opposed to De Nadaillac's suggestion that the mounds were certainly the work of Indians, but of more civilised tribes than the present Algonquians, by whom they were driven south to Florida, and there found with their towns, council-houses, and other structures by the first white settlers.[2] It would appear, however, from F. H. Cushing's investigations, that these tribal council-houses of the Seminole Indians were a local development, growing up on the spot under conditions quite different from those prevailing in the north. Many of the vast shell-mounds, especially between Tampa and Cape Sable, are clearly of artificial structure, that is, made with definite purpose, and carried up symmetrically into large mounds comparable in dimensions with the Indian mounds of the interior. They originated with pile dwellings in shallow water, where the kitchen refuse, chiefly shells, accumulates and rises above the surface, when the building appears to stand on posts in a low mound. Then this type of structure comes to be regarded as the normal for house-building everywhere. "Through this natural series of changes in type there is a tendency to the development of mounds as sites for habitations and for the council-house of the clan or tribe, the sites being either separate mounds or single large mounds, according to circumstances. Thus the study of the living Seminole Indians and of the shell-mounds in the same

---

[1] W. H. Holmes, "Areas of American Culture," etc., *Am. Anth.* XVI. 1914, p. 424.
[2] *L'Anthropologie*, 1897, p. 702 sq.

vicinity . . . suggests a possible origin for a custom of mound-building at one time so prevalent among the North American Indians." [1] But if this be the genesis of such structures, the custom must have spread from the shores of the Gulf inland, and not from the Ohio valley southwards to Florida.

IX. South-western Area. On account of its highly developed state and its prehistoric antecedents, the Pueblo South-western culture appears as the type, though this is by no Area : Material means uniform in the different villages. Three Culture. geographical groups may be recognised, the Hopi,[2] the Zuñi,[3] and the Rio Grande.[4]

The culture of the whole may be characterised by : main dependence upon maize and other cultivated foods (men doing the cultivating and cloth-weaving instead of women) ; use of a grinding stone instead of a mortar ; the art of masonry ; loom or upward weaving ; cultivated cotton as a textile material ; pottery decorated in colour ; unique style of building and the domestication of the turkey. Though the main dependence was on vegetable food there was some hunting ; the eastern villages hunted bison and deer, especially Taos. Drives of rabbits and antelopes were practised, the unique hunting weapon being the curved rabbit stick. Woven robes were usual. Men wore aprons and a robe when needed. Women wore a garment reaching from shoulder to knee fastened on the right shoulder only. In addition to cloth robes some were woven of rabbit-skin and some netted with turkey feathers. Hard-soled moccasins were worn, those for women having long strips of deerskin wound round the leg. Pottery was highly developed, not only for practical use. Basketry was known but not so highly developed as among the non-Pueblo tribes. The dog was not used for transportation and there were no boats. Work in stone and wood not superior to that of other areas ; some work in turquoise, but none in metal.

Many tribes appear to be transitional to the Pueblo type. Thus the Pima once lived in adobe houses, though not of Pueblo type, they developed irrigation but also made ex-

---

[1] 16*th Ann. Rep. Bur. Am. Eth.*, Washington, 1897, p. lvi sq.

[2] Walpi, Sichumovi, Hano (Tewa), Shipaulovi, Mishongnovi, Shunopovi and Oraibi.

[3] Zuñi proper, Pescado, Nutria and Ojo Caliente.

[4] Taos, Picuris, San Juan, Santa Clara, San Ildefonso, Tesuque, Pojoaque, Nambe, Jemez, Pecos, Sandia, Isleta, all of Tanoan stock ; San Felipe, Cochiti, Santo Domingo, Santa Ana, Sia Laguna and Acoma, of Keresan stock.

tensive use of wild plants, raised cotton, wove cloth, were indifferent potters but experts in basketry. The Mohave, Yuma, Cocopa, Maricopa and Yavapai built a square flat-roofed house of wood, had no irrigation, were not good basket-makers (except the Yavapai) but otherwise resembled the Pima. The Walapai and Havasupai were somewhat more nomadic. Transitional or Intermediate Tribes.

The Athapascan tribes to the east show intermediate cultures. The Jicarilla and Mescalero used the Plains tipi, gathered wild vegetable food, hunted bison, had no agriculture or weaving, but dressed in skins, and had the glass-bead technique of the Plains. The western Apache differed little from these, but rarely used tipis and gave a little more attention to agriculture. In general the Apache have certain undoubted Pueblo traits, they also remind one of the Plains, the Plateaus, and, in a lean-to like shelter, of the Mackenzie area. The Navaho seem to have taken their most striking features from European influence, but their shelter is of the northern type, while costume, pottery and feeble attempts at basketry and formerly at agriculture suggest Pueblo influence.[1]

Pueblo culture takes its name from the towns or villages of stone or adobe houses which form the characteristic feature of the area. These vary according to the locality, those in the north being generally of sandstone, while adobe or sun-dried brick was employed to the south. The groups of dwellings were generally compact structures of several stories, with many small rooms, built in terrace fashion, the roof of one storey forming a promenade for the storey next above. Thus from the front the structure is like a gigantic staircase, from the back a perpendicular wall. The upper houses were and still are reached by means of movable ladders and a hatchway in the roof. Mainly in the north but scattered throughout the area are the remains of dwellings built in natural recesses of cliffs, while in some places the cliff face is honeycombed with masonry to provide habitations. The Pueblos.

Although doubtless designed for purposes of hiding and

---

[1] For this area see A. F. Bandelier, " Final Report of Investigations among the Indians of the S.W. United States," *Arch. Inst. of Am. Papers*, 1890–2 ; P. E. Goddard, " Indians of the Southwest," *Handbook Series, Am. Mus. Nat. Hist.* 2, 1913 ; F. Russell, " The Pima Indians," *26th Ann. Rep. Bur. Am. Eth.* 1904–5 (1908) ; G. Nordenskiöld, *The Cliff Dwellers of Mesa Verde, S.W. Colorado*, 1893 ; C. Mindeleff, " Aboriginal Remains in Verde Valley, Arizona," *13th Ann. Rep. Bur. Am. Eth.* 1891–2 (1896). For chronology cf. L. Spier, *Am. Mus. Nat. Hist. Anth.* xviii.

defence, many of the cliff houses were near streams and fields
Cliff Dwellings.   and were occupied because they afforded shelter
and were natural dwelling places; many were
storage places for maize and other property : others again
were places for outlook from which the fields could be watched
or the approach of strangers observed. In some districts
evidence of post-Spanish occupancy exists. From intensive
investigation of the cliff dwellings it is evident that the inhabitants had the same material culture as that of existing
Pueblo Indians, and from the ceremonial objects which have
been discovered and the symbolic decoration that was employed it is equally clear that their religion was essentially
similar. Moreover the various types of skulls that have been
recovered are similar to those of the present population of the
district. It may therefore be safely said that there is no evidence of the former general occupancy of the region by peoples
other than those now classed as Pueblo Indians or their
neighbours.

J. W. Fewkes points out that the district is one of arid
plateaus, separated and dissected by deep cañons, frequently
composed of flat-lying rock strata forming ledge-marked cliffs
by the erosive action of the rare storms. " Only along the few
streams heading in the mountains does permanent water exist,
and along the cliff lines slabs of rock suitable for building
abound ; and the primitive ancients, dependent as they were
on environment, naturally produced the cliff dwellings. The
tendency toward this type was strengthened by intertribal
relations ; the cliff dwellers were probably descended from
agricultural or semi-agricultural villagers who sought protection
against enemies, and the control of land and water through
aggregation in communities. . . . Locally the ancient villages of
Canyon de Chelly are known as Aztec ruins, and this designation
is just so far as it implies relationship with the aborigines of
moderately advanced culture in Mexico and Central America,
though it would be misleading if regarded as indicating essential
difference between the ancient villagers and their modern descendants and neighbours still occupying the pueblos." [1]

Each Pueblo contains at least one *kiva*, either wholly or
partly underground, entered by means of a ladder and hatchway, forming a sacred chamber for the transaction of civil or

[1] 16*th Ann. Report*, p. xciv. Cf. E. Huntington, " Desiccation in Arizona,"
Geog. Journ., Sept. and Oct. 1912.

religious affairs, and also a club for the men. In some villages each totemic clan has its own *kiva*. The Indians   Religion. are eminently a religious people and much time is devoted to complicated rites to ensure a supply of rain, their main concern, and the growth of crops. Among the Hopi from four to sixteen days in every month are employed by one society or another in the carrying out of religious rites. The secret portions of these complicated ceremonies take place in the *kiva*, while the so-called " dances " are performed in the open.

The clan ancestors may be impersonated by masked men, called *katcinas*, the name being also applied to the religious dramas in which they appear.[1]

In reference to J. Walter Fewkes' account of the " Tusayan Snake Ceremonies," it is pointed out that " the Pueblo Indians adore a plurality of deities, to which various po-   Snake Dances. tencies are ascribed. These zoic deities, or beast gods, are worshipped by means of ceremonies which are sometimes highly elaborate ; and, so far as practicable, the mystic zoic potency is represented in the ceremony by a living animal of similar species or by an artificial symbol. Prominent among the animate representatives of the zoic pantheon throughout the arid region is the serpent, especially the venomous and hence mysteriously potent rattlesnake. To the primitive mind there is intimate association, too, between the swift-striking and deadly viper and the lightning, with its attendant rain and thunder ; there is intimate association, too, between the moisture-loving reptile of the subdeserts and the life-giving storms and freshets ; and so the native rattlesnake plays an important rôle in the ceremonies, especially in the invocations for rain, which characterise the entire arid region." [2]

---

[1] For the religion consult F. H. Cushing, " Zuñi Creation Myths," 13*th Ann. Rep. Bur. Am. Eth.* 1891–2 (1896) ; *Zuñi Folk Tales*, 1901 ; Matilda C. Stevenson, " The Religious Life of the Zuñi Child," 5*th Ann. Rep. Bur. Am. Eth.* 1887 ; " The Zuñi Indians, their mythology, esoteric fraternities, and ceremonies," 23*rd Rep.* 1904 ; J. W. Fewkes, " Tusayan Katcinas," 15*th Ann. Rep. Bur. Am. Eth.* 1893–4 (1897) ; " Tusayan Snake Ceremonies," 16*th Rep.* 1894–5 (1897) ; " Tusayan Flute and Snake Ceremonies," 19*th Rep.* 1897–8, II. (1900) ; " Hopi Katcinas," 21*st Rep.* 1899–1900 (1903), and other papers. For dances see W. Hough, *Moki Snake dance*, 1898 ; G. A. Dorsey and H. R. Voth, " Mishongnovi Ceremonies of the Snake and Antelope Fraternities," *Pub. Field Col. Mus. Anth.* III. 3, 1902 ; J. W. Fewkes, " Snake Ceremonials at Walpi," *Jour. Am. Eth. and Arch.* IV. 1894 and " Tusayan Snake Ceremonies," 16*th Ann. Rep. Bur. Am. Eth.* 1897 ; H. Hodge, " Pueblo Snake Ceremonies," *Am. Anth.* IX. 1896.
[2] p. xcvii.

Fewkes pursues the same fruitful line of thought in his monograph on *The Feather Symbol in Ancient Hopi Designs*,[1] showing how amongst the Tusayan Pueblos, although they have left no written records, there survives an elaborate paleography, the feather *motif* in the pottery found in the old ruins, which is in fact " a picture writing often highly symbolic and complicated," revealing certain phases of Hopi thought in remote times. " Thus we come back to a belief, taught by other reasoning, that ornamentation of ancient pottery was something higher than simple effort to beautify ceramic wares. The ruling motive was a religious one, for in their system everything was under the same sway. Esthetic and religious feelings were not differentiated, the one implied the other, and to elaborately decorate a vessel without introducing a religious symbol was to the ancient potter an impossibility." [2]

Physically the Pueblo Indians are of short stature, with long, low head, delicate face and dark skin. They are mus-
Physical Type. cular and of great endurance, able to carry heavy burdens up steep and difficult trails, and to walk or even run great distances. It is said to be no uncommon thing for a Hopi to run 40 miles over a burning desert to his cornfield, hoe his corn, and return home within 24 hours. Distances of 140 miles are frequently made within 36 hours.[3] In disposition they are mild and peaceable, industrious, and extraordinarily conservative, a trait shown in the fidelity with which they retain and perpetuate their ancient customs.[4] Labour is more evenly divided than among most
Social Life. Indian tribes. The men help the women with the heavier work of house-building, they collect the fuel, weave blankets and make moccasins, occupations usually regarded as women's work. The women carry the water, and make the pottery for which the region is famous.[5]

A. L. Kroeber has made a careful study of Zuñi sociology [6] and come to the conclusion that the family is fundamental and the clan secondary, though kinship terms are applied to clan mates in a random fashion, and even the true kinship

[1] *Amer. Anthropologist*, Jan. 1898.　　　　[2] p. 13.
[3] G. W. James, *Indians of the Painted Desert Region*, 1903, p. 90.
[4] L. Farrand, *Basis of American History*, 1904, p. 184.
[5] W. H. Holmes, " Pottery of the ancient Pueblos," *4th Ann. Rep. Bur. Am. Eth.* 1882–3 (1886) ; F. H. Cushing, " A study of Pueblo Pottery," etc., *ib.* ; J. W. Fewkes, " Archaeological expedition to Arizona," *17th Rep.* 1895–6 (1898) ; W. Hough, " Archaeological field work in N.E. Arizona " (1901), *Rep. U.S. Nat. Mus.* 1903.
[6] " Zuñi Kin and Clan," *Anth. Papers, Am. Mus. Nat. Hist.* XVIII. 1917, p. 39.

terms are applied loosely. In view of the obvious pre-eminence of the woman, who receives the husband into her and her mother's house, it is worthy of note that she and her children recognise her husband's relatives as their kin as fully as he adopts hers. The Zuñi are not a woman-ruled people. As regards government, women neither claim nor have any voice whatever, nor are there women priests, nor fraternity officers. Even within the house, so long as a man is a legitimate inmate thereof, he is master of it and of its affairs. They are a monogamous people. Divorce is more easy than marriage, and most men and women of middle age have been married to several partners. Marriage in the mother's clan is forbidden ; in the father's clan, disapproved. The phratries have no social significance, there is no central clan house, no recognised head, no meeting, council or any organisation, nor does the clan as such ever act as a body. The clans have little connection with the religious societies or fraternities. There are no totemic tabus nor is there worship of the clan totem. People are reckoned as belonging to the father's clan almost as much as to that of the mother. If one of the family of a person who belongs to a fraternity falls sick the fraternity is called in to cure the patient, who is subsequently received into its ranks. The Zuñi fraternity is largely a body of religious physicians, membership is voluntary and not limited by sex. At Hopi we hear of rain-making more than of doctoring, more of " priests " than of " theurgists." The religious functions of the Zuñi are most marked in the ceremonies of the Ko-tikkyanne, the " god-society " or " masked-dancer society," and it is with these that the *kivas* are associated. They are almost wholly concerned with rain. Only men can become members and entrance is compulsory. Kroeber believes that " the truest understanding of Zuñi life, other than its purely practical manifestation, can be had by setting the ettowe [' fetish '] as a centre. Around these, priesthoods, fraternities, clan organisation, as well as most esoteric thinking and sacred tradition, group themselves ; while, in turn, kivas, dances, and acts of public worship can be construed as but the outward means of expression of the inner activities that radiate around the nucleus of the physical fetishes and the ideas attached to them." [1]

[1] p. 167.

CHAPTER XI

THE AMERICAN ABORIGINES (*continued*)

Mexican and Central American Cultures—Aztec and Maya Scripts and Calendars—Nahua and Shoshoni—Chichimec and Aztec Empires—Uncultured Mexican Peoples: *Otomi; Seri*—Early Man in Yucatan—The Maya to-day—Transitions from North to South America—*Chontal* and *Choco*—The *Catio*—Cultures of the Andean area—The Colombian *Chibcha*—Empire of the Inca—*Quichuan* Race and Language—Inca Origins and History—The *Aymara*—*Chimu* Culture—Peruvian Politico-Social System—The *Araucanians*—The *Pampas Indians*—The *Gauchos*—*Patagonians* and *Fuegians*—Linguistic Relations—The *Yahgans*—The *Cashibo*—The *Pana Family*—The *Caribs*—*Arawakan Family*—The *Ges* (*Tapuyan*) *Family*—The *Botocudo*—The *Tupi-Guaranian Family*—The *Chiquito*—*Mataco* and *Toba* of the Gran Chaco.

In Mexico and Central America interest is centred chiefly in two great ethnical groups—the *Nahuatlan* and *Huaxtecan* —whose cultural, historical, and even geographical relations are so intimately interwoven that they can scarcely be treated apart. Thus, although their civilisations are concentrated respectively in the Anahuac (Mexican) plateau and Yucatan and Guatemala, the two domains overlap completely at both ends, so that there are isolated branches of the Huaxtecan family in Mexico (the Huaxtecs (Totonacs) of Vera Cruz, from whom the whole group is named, and of the Nahuatlan in Nicaragua (Pipils, Niquirans, and others).[1]

This very circumstance has no doubt tended to increase the difficulties connected with the questions of their origins, migrations, and mutual cultural influences. Some of these difficulties disappear if the "Toltecs" be eliminated (see p. 342), who had hitherto been a great disturbing element in this connection, and all the rest have in my opinion been satisfactorily

Mexican and Central American Cultures.

[1] Some Nahuas, whom the Spaniards called "Mexicans" or "Chichimecs," were met by Vasquez de Coronado even as far south as the Chiriqui lagoon, Panama. These Seguas, as they called themselves, have since disappeared, and it is no longer possible to say how they strayed so far from their northern homes.

disposed of by E. Förstemann, a leading authority on all Aztec-Maya questions.[1]   This eminent archaeologist refers first to the views of Seler,[2] who assumes a southern movement of Maya tribes from Yucatan, and a like movement of Aztecs from Tabasco to Nicaragua, and even to Yucatan.   On the other hand Dieseldorff holds that Maya art was independently developed, while the link between it and the Aztec shows that an interchange took place, in which process the Maya was the giver, the Aztec the recipient.   He further attributes the over-throw of the Maya power 100 or 200 years before the conquest to the Aztecs, and thinks the Aztecs or Nahuas took their god Quetzalcoatl from the "Toltecs," who were a Maya people. Ph. J. Valentini also infers that the Maya were the original people, the Aztecs "mere parasites." [3]

Now Förstemann lays down the principle that any theory, to be satisfactory, should fit in with such facts as :—(1) the agreement and diversity of both cultures ;   (2) the antiquity and disappearance of the mysterious Toltecs ;   (3) the complete isolation at 22° N. lat. of the Huaxtecs from the other Maya tribes, and their difference from them ;   (4) the equally complete isolation of the Guatemalan Pipils, and of the other southern (Nicaraguan) Aztec groups from the rest of the Nahua peoples ; (5) the remarkable absence of Aztec local names in Yucatan, while they occur in hundreds in Chiapas, Guatemala, Honduras and Nicaragua, where scarcely any trace is left of Maya names.

To account for these facts he assumes that in the earliest known times Central America from about 23° to 10° N. was mainly inhabited by Maya tribes, who had even reached Cuba. While these Mayas were still at quite a low stage of culture, the Aztecs advanced from as far north as at least 26° N. but only on the Pacific side, thus leaving the Huaxtecs almost untouched in the east.   The Aztecs called the Mayas "Toltecs" because they first came in contact with one of their northern branches living in the region about Tula (north of Mexico city).[4]   But when all the relations became clearer, the Toltecs

[1] "Recent Maya Investigations," *Bur. Am. Eth. Bull.* 28, 1904, p. 555.

[2] *Alterthümer aus Guatemala*, p. 24.

[3] *Analysis of the Pictorial Text inscribed on two Palenque Tablets*, N. York, 1896.

[4] H. Beuchat however considers that "the Toltec question remains insoluble"; though the hypothesis that the Toltecs formed part of the north to south move-ment is attractive, it is not yet proved, *Manuel d'Archéologie américaine*, Paris, 1912, pp. 258–61.

fell gradually into the background, and at last entered the domain of the fabulous.

Now the Aztecs borrowed much from the Mayas, especially gods, whose names they simply translated. A typical case is that of Cuculcan, which becomes Quetzalcoatl, where *cuc*= *quezal*=the bird *Trogon resplendens*, and *can*=*coatl*=snake.[1] With the higher culture developed in Guatemala the Aztecs came first in contact after passing through Mixtec and Zapotec territory, not long before Columbian times, so that they had no time here to consolidate their empire and assimilate the Mayas. On the contrary the Aztecs were themselves merged in these, all but the Pipils and the settlements on Lake Nicaragua, which retained their national peculiarities.

But whence came the hundreds of Aztec names in the lands between Chiapas and Nicaragua ? Here it should be noted that these names are almost exclusively confined to the more important stations, while the less prominent places have everywhere names taken from the tongues of the local tribes. But even the Aztec names themselves occur properly only in official use, hence also on the charts, and are not current to-day amongst the natives who have kept aloof from the Spanish-speaking populations. Hence the inference that such names were mainly introduced by the Spaniards and their Mexican troops during the conquest of those lands, say, up to about 1535, and do not appear in Yucatan which was not conquered from Mexico. Förstemann reluctantly accepts this view, advanced by Sapper,[2] having nothing better to suggest.

The coastal towns of Yucatan visited by Spaniards from Cuba in 1517 and onwards were decidedly inferior architecturally to the great temple structures of the interior, though doubtless erected by the same people. The inland cities of Chichen-Itza and Uxmal by that time had fallen from their ancient glory though still religious centres.[3]

The Maya would thus appear to have stood on a higher plane of culture than their Aztec rivals, and the same conclusion

---

[1] Quetzalcoatl, the " Bright-feathered Snake," was one of the three chief gods of the Nahuan pantheon. He was the god of wind and inventor of all the arts, round whom clusters much of the mythology, and of the pictorial and plastic art of the Mexicans.

[2] *Globus*, LXVI. pp. 95–6.

[3] Herbert J. Spinden, " A Study of Maya Art," *Mem. Peabody Mus.* VI., Cambridge, Mass. 1913, p. 3 ff., and *Proc. Nineteenth Internat. Congress Americanists*, 1917, p. 165.

may be drawn from their respective writing systems. Of all
the aborigines these two alone had developed what may fairly
be called a script in the strict sense of the term, although
neither of them had reached the same level of efficiency as
the Babylonian cuneiforms, or the Chinese or the Egyptian
hieroglyphs, not to speak of the syllabic and alphabetic systems
of the Old World.   Some even of the barbaric peoples, such
as most of the prairie Indians, had reached the stage of graphic
symbolism, and were thus on the threshold of writing at the
discovery.   " The art was rudimentary and limited to crude
pictography.   The pictographs were painted or sculptured on
cliff-faces, boulders, the walls of caverns, and even on trees,
as well as on skins, bark, and various artificial objects.   Among
certain Mexican tribes, also, autographic records were in use,
and some of them were much better differentiated
than any within the present area of the United   Aztec and
States.   The records were not only painted and   Maya Scripts,
sculptured on stone and moulded in stucco, but were inscribed
in books or codices of native parchment and paper ; while the
characters were measurably arbitrary, *i.e.* ideographic rather
than pictographic." [1]

The Aztec writing may be best described as pictographic,
the pictures being symbolical or, in the case of names, combined
into a rebus.   No doubt much diversity of opinion prevails as
to whether the Maya symbols are phonetic or ideographic,
and it is a fact that no single text, however short, has yet
been satisfactorily deciphered.   It seems that many of the
symbols possessed true phonetic value and were used to express sounds and syllables, though it cannot be claimed that
the Maya scribes had reached that advanced stage where they
could indicate each letter sound by a glyph or symbol.[2]   According to Cyrus Thomas, a symbol was selected because the
name or word it represented had as its chief phonetic element
a certain consonant sound or syllable.   If this were *b* the symbol
would be used where *b* was the prominent element of the word

[1] J. W. Powell, *16th Ann. Rep. Bur. Am. Eth.* 1894, p. xcv.
[2] Sylvanus Griswold Morley (" An Introduction to the Study of the Maya
hieroglyphs," *Bur. Am. Eth. Bull.* 57, 1915), briefly summarises the theories
advanced for the interpretation of Maya writing (pp. 26–30).   " The theory now
most generally accepted is, that while chiefly ideographic, the glyphs are sometimes phonetic."   This author is of opinion " that as the decipherment of Maya
writing progresses, more and more phonetic elements will be identified, though
the idea conveyed by a glyph will always be found to overshadow its phonetic
value " (p. 30).

to be indicated, no reference, however, to its original signification being necessarily retained.   Thus the symbol for *cab*,
'earth,' might be used in writing *Caban*, a day name, or *cabil*,
'honey,' because *cab* is their chief phonetic element. . . . One
reason why attempts at decipherment have failed is a misconception of the peculiar character of the writing, which is
in a transition stage from the purely ideographic to the
phonetic.[1]   From the example here given, the Maya script
would appear to have in part reached the rebus stage, which
also plays so large a part in the Egyptian hieroglyphic system.
Cab is obviously a rebus, and the transition from the rebus to
true syllabic and alphabetic systems has already been explained.[2]   The German Americanists on the other hand have
always regarded Maya writing as more ideographic, and H.
Beuchat adopts this view, for " no symbol has ever been read
phonetically with a different meaning from that which it
possesses as an ideogram." [3]

But not only were the Maya day characters phonetic ; the
Maya calendar itself, afterwards borrowed by the Aztecs, has
and Calendars. been described as even more accurate than the
Julian itself.   " Among the Plains Indians the
calendars are simple, consisting commonly of a record of
winters ('winter counts'), and of notable events occurring
either during the winter or during some other season ; while
the shorter time divisions are reckoned by 'nights' (days),
'dead moons' (lunations), and seasons of leafing, flowering,
or fruiting of plants, migrating of animals, etc., and there is
no definite system of reducing days to lunations or lunations
to years.   Among the Pueblo Indians calendric records are
inconspicuous or absent, though there is a much more definite
calendric system which is fixed and perpetuated by religious
ceremonies ; while among some of the Mexican tribes there
are elaborate calendric systems combined with complete
calendric records.   The perfection of the calendar among
the Maya and Nahua Indians is indicated by the fact that
not only were 365 days reckoned as a year, but the bissextile
was recognised." [4]

[1] "Day Symbols of the Maya Year," *16th Ann. Rep. Bur. Am. Eth.* 1894, p. 205.
[2] p. 32 ff.
[3] *Manuel d'Archéologie américaine*, p. 506.
[4] *16th Ann. Rep. Bur. Am. Eth.* 1894, p. xcvi. In " The Maya Year " (1894)
Cyrus Thomas shows that " the year recorded in the Dresden codex consisted of 18
months of 20 days each, with 5 supplemental days, or of 365 days " (*ib.*). S. G.

In another important respect the superiority of the Maya-Quiché peoples over the northern Nahuans is incontestable. When their religious systems are compared, it is at once seen that at the time of the discovery the Mexican Aztecs were little better than ruth-less barbarians newly clothed in the borrowed robes of an advanced culture, to which they had not had time to adapt themselves properly, and in which they could but masquerade after their own savage fashion.

Nahua and Shoshoni.

It has to be remembered that the Aztecs were but one branch of the Nahuatlan family, whose affinities Buschmann [1] has traced northwards to the rude Shoshonian aborigines who roamed from the present States of Montana, Idaho, and Oregon down into Utah, Texas, and California.[2] To this Nahuatlan stock belonged the barbaric hordes who overthrew the civilisation which flourished on the Anahuac (Mexican) table-land about the sixth century A.D. and is associated with the ruins of Tula and Cholula. It now seems clear that the so-called " Toltecs," the " Pyramid-builders," were not Nahuatlans but Huaxtecans, who were absorbed by the immigrants or driven southwards.

Morley points out (*Bur. Am. Eth. Bull.* 57, pp. 44–5) that though the Maya doubt-less knew that the true length of the year exceeded 365 days by 6 hours, yet no interpolation of intercalary days was actually made, as this would have thrown the whole calendar into confusion. The priests apparently corrected the calendar by additional calculations to show how far the recorded year was ahead of the true year. Those who have persistently appealed to these Maya-Aztec calendric systems as convincing proofs of Asiatic influences in the evolution of American cultures will now have to show where these influences come in. As a matter of fact the systems are fundamentally distinct, the American showing the clearest indica-tions of local development, as seen in the mere fact that the day characters of the Maya codices were phonetic, *i.e.* largely rebuses explicable only in the Maya language, which has no affinities out of America. A careful study of the Maya calendric system based both on the codices and the inscriptions has been made by C. P. Bowditch, *The Numeration, Calendar Systems and Astronomical Knowledge of the Mayas*, Cambridge, Mass. 1910. The Aztec month of 20 days is also clearly indicated by the 20 corresponding signs on the great Calendar Stone now fixed in the wall of the Cathedral tower of Mexico. This basalt stone, which weighs 25 tons and has a diameter of 11 feet, is briefly described and figured by T. A. Joyce, *Mexican Archaeology*, 1914, pp. 73, 74 ; cf. Pl. VIII. fig. 1. See also the account by Alfredo Chavero in the *Anales del Museo Nacional de Mexico*, and an excellent reproduction of the Calendar Stone in T. U. Brocklehurst's *Mexico To-day*, 1883, p. 186 ; also Zelia Nuttall's study of the " Mexican Calendar System," *Tenth Internat. Congress of Americanists*, Stockholm, 1894. " The regular rotation of market-days and the day of enforced rest every 20 days were the prominent and permanent features of the civil solar year " (*ib.*).

[1] *Spuren der Aztek. Sprache*, 1859, *passim.*

[2] Linguistic and mythological affinities also exist according to Spence between the Nahuan people and the Tsimshian-Nootka group of Columbia. Cf. *The Civili-sation of Ancient Mexico*, 1912, p. 6.

To north and north-west of the settled peoples of the valley lived nomadic hunting tribes called Chichimec,[1] merged
in a loose political system which was dignified in
the local traditions by the name of the "Chichimec
Empire." The chief part was played by tribes
of Nahuan origin,[2] whose ascendancy lasted from about the eleventh to the fifteenth century, when they were in their turn overthrown and absorbed by the historical Nahuan confederacy of the *Aztecs*[3] whose capital was Tenochtitlan (the present city of Mexico), the *Acolhuas* (capital Tezcuco), and the *Tepanecs* (capital Tlacopan).

Chichimec and Aztec Empires.

Thus the Aztec Empire reduced by the Conquistadores in 1520 had but a brief record, although the Aztecs themselves as well as many other tribes of Nahuatl speech, must have been in contact with the more civilised Huaxtecan peoples for centuries before the appearance of the Spaniards on the scene. It was during these ages that the Nahuas "borrowed much from the Mayas," as Förstemann puts it, without greatly benefiting by the process. Thus the Maya gods, for the most part of a relatively mild type like the Maya themselves, become in the hideous Aztec pantheon ferocious demons with an insatiable thirst for blood, so that the teocalli, "god's houses," were transformed to human shambles, where on solemn occasions the victims were said to have numbered tens of thousands.[4]

[1] "Chiefly of the Nahuatl race" (De Nadaillac, p. 279). It should, however, be noted that this general name of Chichimec (meaning little more than "nomadic hunters") comprised a large number of barbarous tribes—Pames, Pintos, etc.— who are described as wandering about naked or wearing only the skins of beasts. living in caves or rock-shelters, armed with bows, slings, and clubs, constantly at war amongst themselves or with the surrounding peoples, eating raw flesh, drinking the blood of their captives or treating them with unheard-of cruelty, altogether a horror and terror to all the more civilised communities. "Chichimec Empire" may therefore be taken merely as a euphemistic expression for the reign of barbarism raised up on the ruins of the early Toltec civilisation. Yet it had its dynasties and dates and legendary sequence of events, according to the native historian, Ixtlilxochitl, himself of royal lineage, and he states that Xolotl, founder of the empire, had under orders 3,202,000 men and women, that his decisive victory over the Toltecs took place in 1015, that he assumed the title of "Chichimecatl Tecuhti," Great Chief of the Chichimecs, and that after a succession of revolts, wars, conspiracies, and revolutions, Maxtla, last of the dynasty, was overthrown in 1431 by the Aztecs and their allies.

[2] H. Beuchat, *Manuel d'Archéologie américaine*, pp. 262–6.

[3] Named from the shadowy land of Aztlan away to the north, where they long dwelt in the seven legendary caves of Chicomoztoc, whence they migrated at some unknown period to the lacustrine region, where they founded Tenochtitlan, seat of their empire.

[4] "The gods of the Mayas appear to have been less sanguinary than those of the Nahuas. The immolation of a dog was with them enough for an occasion

Besides the Aztecs and their allies, the elevated Mexican plateaus were occupied by several other relatively civilised nations, such as the *Miztecs* and *Zapotecs* of   Uncultured Oajaca, the *Tarasco* and neighbouring *Matlalt-*   Mexican *zinca* of Michoacan,[1] all of whom spoke inde-   Peoples. pendent stock languages, and the *Totonacs* of Vera Cruz, who were of Huaxtecan speech, and were in touch to the north with the Huaxtecs, a primitive Maya people. The high degree of civilisation attained by some of these nations before their reduction by the Aztecs is attested by the magnificent ruins of Mitla, capital of the Zapotecs, which was captured and destroyed by the Mexicans in 1494.[2] Of the royal palace Viollet-le-Duc speaks in enthusiastic terms, declaring that " the monuments of the golden age of Greece and Rome alone equal the beauty of the masonry of this great building."[3] In general their usages and religious rites resembled those of the Aztecs, although the Zapotecs, besides the civil ruler, had a High Priest who took part in the government. " His feet were never allowed to touch the ground ; he was carried on the shoulders of his attendants ; and when he appeared all, even the chiefs themselves, had to fall prostrate before him, and none dared to raise their eyes in his presence."[4] The Zapotec language is still spoken by about 260 natives in the State of Oajaca.

Farther north the plains and uplands continued to be inhabited by a multitude of wild tribes speaking an unknown number of stock languages, and thus presenting a chaos of ethnical and linguistic elements comparable to that which prevails along the north-west coast. Of these rude popula-tions one of the most widespread are the Otomi   Otomi—Seri. of the central region, noted for the monosyllabic

that would have been celebrated by the Nahuas with hecatombs of victims. Human sacrifices did however take place " (De Nadaillac, p. 266), though they were as nothing compared with the countless victims demanded by the Aztec gods. " The dedication by Ahuizotl of the great temple of Huitzilopochtli in 1487 is alleged to have been celebrated by the butchery of 72,344 victims," and " under Montezuma II. 12,000 captives are said to have perished " on one occasion (*ib.* p. 297) ; all no doubt gross exaggerations, but leaving a large margin for perhaps the most terrible chapter of horrors in the records of natural religions. Cf. T. A. Joyce, *Mexican Archaeology*, pp. 261–2.

    [1] A popular and well-illustrated account of Huichols and Tarascos, as also of the Tarahumare farther north, is given by Carl Lumholtz, *Unknown Mexico*, 2 vols. New York, 1902.

    [2] Cf. Hans Gadow, *Through Southern Mexico*, 1908, map p. 296, also p. 314.

    [3] Quoted by De Nadaillac, p. 365.   [4] p. 363.

tendencies of their language, which Najera, a native grammarian, has on this ground compared with Chinese, from
which, however, it is fundamentally distinct. Still more
primitive are the Seri Indians of Tiburon island in the Gulf
of California and the adjacent mainland, who were visited in
1895 by W. J. McGee, and found to be probably more isolated
and savage than any other tribe remaining on the North
American Continent. They hunt, fish, and collect vegetable
food, and most of their food is eaten raw, they have no
domestic animals save dogs, they are totally without agriculture, and their industrial arts are few and rude. They use
the bow and arrow but have no knife. Their houses are
flimsy huts. They make pottery and rafts of canes. The
Seri are loosely organised in a number of exogamic, matrilineal, totemic clans. Mother-right obtains to a greater extent
perhaps than in any other people. At marriage the husband
becomes a privileged guest in the wife's mother's household,
and it is only in the chase or on the war-path that men take
an important place. Polygyny prevails. The most conspicuous
ceremony is the girl's puberty feast. The dead are buried in
a contracted position. " The strongest tribal characteristic is
implacable animosity towards aliens. . . . In their estimation
the brightest virtue is the shedding of alien blood, while the
blackest crime in their calendar is alien conjugal union." [1]

It is noteworthy that but few traces of such savagery have
yet been discovered in Yucatan. The investigations of Henry
Mercer [2] in this region lend strong support to Förstemann's
views regarding the early Huaxtecan migrations and the
general southward spread of Maya culture from the Mexican
table-land. Nearly thirty caves examined by this
Early Man in Yucatan. explorer failed to yield any remains either of the
mastodon, mammoth, and horse, or of early man,
elsewhere so often associated with these animals. Hence
Mercer infers that the Mayas reached Yucatan already in an
advanced state of culture, which remained unchanged till the
conquest. In the caves were found great quantities of good
pottery, generally well baked and of symmetrical form, the
oldest quite as good as the latest where they occur in stratified
beds, showing no progress anywhere.

The caves of Loltun (Yucatan) and Copan (Honduras),

[1] *17th Ann. Rep. Bur. Am. Eth.* 1895–6, Pt. 1 (1898), p. 11.
[2] *The Hill Caves of Yucatan*, New York, 1903.

examined by E. H. Thompson and G. Byron-Gordon, yielded pre-Mayan débris from the deep strata. Perhaps this very ancient population was of the same race as the little known tribes still living in the forests of Honduras and San Salsvador.[1]

Since the conquest the Aztecs, and other cultured nations of Anahuac, have yielded to European influences to a far greater extent than the Maya-Quiché of Yucatan and Guatemala. In the city of Mexico the Nahuatl tongue has almost died out, and this place has long been a leading centre of Spanish arts and letters ;[2] yet the Mexicans yearly celebrate a feast in memory of their great ancestors who died in defence of their country.[3] But Merida, standing on the site of the ancient Ti-hoó, has almost again become a Maya town, where the white settlers themselves have been largely assimilated in speech and usages to the natives. The very streets are still indicated by the carved images of the hawk, flamingo, or other tutelar deities, while the houses **The Maya to-day.** of the suburbs continue to be built in the old Maya style, two or three feet above the street level, with a walled porch and stone bench running round the enclosure.

One reason for this remarkable contrast may be that the Nahua culture, as above seen, was to a great extent borrowed in relatively recent times, whereas the Maya civilisation is now shown to date from the epoch of the Tolan and Cholulan pyramid-builders. Hence the former yielded to the first shock, while the latter still persists to some extent in Yucatan. Here about 1000 A.D. the cities of Chichen-Itza, Uxmal and Mayapan formed a confederacy in which each was to share equally in the government of the country. Under the peaceful conditions of the next two centuries followed the second and last great Maya epoch, the Age of Architecture, as it has been termed, as opposed to the first epoch, the Age of Sculpture, from the second to the sixth century A.D. During this earlier epoch flourished the great cities of the south, Palenque, Quirigua, Copan, and others.[4] Despite their more gentle disposition,

---

[1] H. Beuchat, *Manuel d'Archéologie américaine*, 1912, p. 407.

[2] " In the city of Mexico everything has a Spanish look " (Brocklehurst, *Mexico To-day*, p. 15). The Aztec language however is still current in the surrounding districts and generally in the provinces forming part of the former Aztec empire.

[3] C. Lumholtz, *Unknown Mexico*, II. p. 480 ; cf. pp. 477–80.

[4] Sylvanus Griswold Morley, " An Introduction to the Study of the Maya Hieroglyphs," *Bur. Am. Eth. Bull.* 57, 1915, pp. 2–5.

as expressed in the softer and almost feminine lines of their features, the Mayas held out more valiantly than the Aztecs against the Spaniards, and a section of the nation occupying a strip of territory between Yucatan and British Honduras, still maintains its independence. The " barbarians," as the inhabitants of this district are called, would appear to be scarcely less civilised than their neighbours, although they have forgotten the teachings of the padres, and transformed the Catholic churches to wayside inns. Even as it is the descendants of the Spaniards have to a great extent forgotten their mother-tongue, and Maya-Quiché dialects are almost everywhere current except in the Campeachy district. Those also who call themselves Catholics preserve and practise many of the old rites. After burial the track from the grave to the house is carefully chalked, so that the soul of the departed may know the way back when the time comes to enter the body of some new-born babe. The descendants of the national astrologers everywhere pursue their arts, determining events, forecasting the harvests and so on by the conjunctions of the stars, and every village has its native " Zadkiel " who reads the future in the ubiquitous crystal globe. Even certain priests continue to celebrate the " Field Mass," at which a cock is sacrificed to the Mayan Aesculapius, with invocations to the Trinity and their associates, the four genii of the rain and crops. " These tutelar deities, however, have taken Christian names, the Red, or God of the East, having become St Dominic ; the White, or God of the North, St Gabriel ; the Black, or God of the West, St James ; and the ' Yellow Goddess ' of the South, Mary Magdalene." [1]

To the observer passing from the northern to the southern division of the New World no marked contrasts are at first **Transitions** perceptible, either in the physical appearance, **from North to** or in the social condition of the aborigines. The **South America.** substantial uniformity, which in these respects prevails from the Arctic to the Austral waters, is in fact well illustrated by the comparatively slight differences presented by the primitive populations dwelling north and south of the Isthmus of Panama.

At the discovery the West Indies were inhabited by two

[1] E. Reclus, *Universal Geography*, XVII. p. 156.

distinct peoples, both apparently of South American origin.
The populations of the greater Antilles, Cuba, Jamaica, Santo
Domingo and Porto Rico were of Arawak stock, as were also
the Lucayans of the Bahamas. The Lesser Antilles were
peopled by Caribs, whose culture had been somewhat modified
by the Arawaks who had preceded them. As regards influences from the north-west and west, Joyce considers that
intercourse between Yucatan and Western Cuba was confined to occasional trading voyages and did not long antedate
the arrival of the Spaniards. The same applies to Florida
where, however, Antillean influences may be traced, especially
in pottery designs.[1] According to Beuchat, however, the
Guacanabibes of Cuba are of common origin with the Tekestas
of Florida. Other tribes from Florida spread to the Bahamas,
Cuba,[2] and perhaps Hayti, but were checked by Arawaks from
South America who mastered the whole of the West Indies.
Last came the more vigorous but less advanced Caribs, also
from the southern mainland (of Arawak origin according to
Joyce and Beuchat). The statement of Columbus that the
Lucayans[3] were " of good size, with large eyes and broader
foreheads than he had ever seen in any other race of men " is
fully borne out by the character of some old skulls from the
Bahamas measured by W. K. Brooks, who regarded them as
belonging to " a well-marked type of the North American
Indian race which was at that time distributed over the
Bahama Islands, Hayti, and the greater part of Cuba. As
these islands are only a few miles from the peninsula of
Florida, this race must at some time have inhabited at least
the south-eastern extremity of the continent, and it is therefore extremely interesting to note that the North American
crania which exhibit the closest resemblance to those from

---

[1] T. A. Joyce, *Central American and West Indian Archaeology*, 1916, pp. 157,
256–7. An admirable account is given of the material culture and mode of life of
these peoples at the time of the discovery.

[2] The rapid disappearance of the Cuban aborigines has been the subject of
much comment. Between the years 1512–32 all but some 4000 had perished,
although they are supposed to have originally numbered about a million, distributed in 30 tribal groups, whose names and territories have all been carefully
preserved. But they practically offered no resistance to the ruthless Conquistadores, and it was a Cuban chief who even under torture refused to be baptized,
declaring that he would never enter the same heaven as the Spaniard. One is
reminded of the analogous cases of Jarl Hakon, the Norseman, and the Saxon
Witikind, who rejected Christianity, preferring to share the lot of their pagan forefathers in the next world.

[3] H. Beuchat, pp. 507–11, 526–8.

the Bahama Islands have been obtained from Florida." [1] This observer dwells on the solidity and massiveness of the Lucayan skulls, which bring them into direct relation with the races both of the Mississippi plains and of the Brazilian and Venezuelan coast-lands, though the general ethnography of Panama and Costa Rica reveals no active influence exerted by tribes of Colombia and Venezuela, except in eastern Panama.[2]

Equally close is the connection established between the surviving Isthmian and Colombian peoples of the Atrato and Magdalena basins. The Chontal of Nicaragua are scarcely to be distinguished from some of the Santa Marta hillmen, while the Choco and perhaps the Cuna of Panama have been affiliated to the Choco of the Atrato and San Juan rivers. The cultural connection between the tribes of the Isthmus and of Colombia appears especially in the gold-work and pottery of the Chiriqui ; at the Chiriqui Lagoon, however, Nahuan influence is perceptible.[3] Attempts, which however can hardly be regarded as successful, have even been made to establish linguistic relations between the Costa Rican Guatuso and the Timote of the Merida uplands of Venezuela, who are themselves a branch of the formerly widespread Muyscan family.

Chontal and Choco.

But with these Muyscans we at once enter a new ethnical and cultural domain, in which may be studied the resemblances due to the common origin of all the American aborigines, and the divergences due obviously to long isolation and independent local developments in the two continental divisions. In general the southern populations present more violent contrasts than the northern in their social and intellectual developments, so that while the wild tribes touch a lower depth of savagery, some at least of the civilised peoples rise to a higher degree of excellence, if not in letters—where the inferiority is manifest—certainly in the arts of engineering, architecture, agriculture, and political organisation. Thus we need not travel many miles inland from the Isthmus without meeting the Catio, a wild tribe between the Atrato and the

---

[1] Paper read before the National Academy of Sciences, America, 1890.

[2] T. A. Joyce, p. 2, who deals with the archaeology, as far as it is known as yet, of Nicaragua, Costa Rica and Panama. Cf. especially linguistic map at p. 30 for distribution of tribes.

[3] T. A. Joyce, *South American Archaeology*, 1912, p. 7.

Cauca, more degraded even than the Seri of Tiburon island, most debased of all North American hordes. **The Catio.** These Catio, a now nearly extinct branch of the Choco stock, were said to dwell like the anthropoid apes, in the branches of trees ; they mostly went naked, and were reported, like the Mangbattus and other Congo negroes, to "fatten their captives for the table." Their Darien neighbours of the Nore valley, who gave an alternative name to the Panama peninsula, were accustomed to steal the women of hostile tribes, cohabit with them, and carefully bring up the children till their fourteenth year, when they were eaten with much rejoicing, the mothers ultimately sharing the same fate ; [1] and the Cocoma of the Marañon "were in the habit of eating their own dead relations, and grinding their bones to drink in their fermented liquor. They said it was better to be inside a friend than to be swallowed up by the cold earth." [2] In fact of the Colombian aborigines Herrera tells us that "the living are the grave of the dead ; for the husband has been seen to eat his wife, the brother his brother or sister, the son his father ; captives also are eaten roasted." [3]

Thus is raised the question of cannibalism in the New World, where at the discovery it was incomparably more prevalent south than north of the equator. Compare the Eskimo and the Fuegians at the two extremes, the former practically exonerated of the charge, and in distress sparing wives and children and eating their dogs ; the latter sparing their dogs because useful for catching otters, and smoking and eating their old women because useless for further purposes.[4] In the north the taste for human flesh had declined, and the practice survived only as a ceremonial rite, chiefly amongst the British Columbians and the Aztecs, except of course in case of famine, when even the highest races are capable of devouring their fellows. But in the south cannibalism in some of its most repulsive forms was common enough almost everywhere. Killing and eating feeble and aged

[1] "The travels of P. de Cieza de Leon" (Hakluyt Soc. 1864, p. 50 f.).
[2] Sir C. R. Markham, "List of Tribes," etc., *Journ. Roy. Anth. Inst.* XI. 1910, p. 95. "This idea was widespread, and many Amazonian peoples declared they preferred to be eaten by their friends than by worms."
[3] Quoted by Steinmetz, *Endokannibalismus*, p. 19.
[4] C. Darwin, *Journal of Researches*, 1889, p. 155. Thanks to their frequent contact with Europeans since the expeditions of Fitzroy and Darwin, the Fuegians have given up the practice, hence the doubts or denials of Bridges, Hyades, and other later observers.

members of the tribe in kindness is still general ; but the
Mayorunas of the Upper Amazon waters do not wait till they
have grown lean with years or wasted with disease ; [1] and it
was a baptized member of the same tribe who complained on
his death-bed that he would not now provide a meal for his
Christian friends, but must be devoured by worms.[2]

In the southern continent the social conditions illustrated
by these practices prevailed everywhere, except on the
elevated plateaus of the western Cordilleras,
which for many ages before the discovery had
been the seats of several successive cultures, in
some respects rivalling, but in others much inferior to those
of Central America.   When the Conquistadores reached this
part of the New World, to which they were attracted by the
not altogether groundless reports of fabulous wealth embodied
in the legend of *El Dorado*, the " Man of Gold," they found
it occupied by a cultural zone which extended almost continuously from the present republic of Colombia through
Ecuador, Peru, and Bolivia right into Chili.   In
the north the dominant people were the semi-
civilised Chibcha, already mentioned under the name of
Muysca,[3] who had developed an organised system of government on the Bogota table-land, and had succeeded in extending
their somewhat more refined social institutions to some of the
other aborigines of Colombia, though not to many of the out-
lying members of their own race.   As in Mexico many of the
Nahuatlan tribes remained little better than savages to the
last, so in Colombia the civilised Muyscans were surrounded by
numerous kindred tribes—Coyaima, Natagaima, Tocaima and
others, collectively known as Panches—who were real savages
with scarcely any tribal organisation, wearing no clothes, and
according to the early accounts still addicted to cannibalism.

The Muysca proper had a tradition that they owed their
superiority to their culture-hero Bochica, who came from the
east long ago, taught them everything, and was then placed
with Chiminigagua, the creator, at the head of their pantheon,

Cultures of the Andean Area.

The Chibcha.

[1] V. Martius, *Zur Ethnographie Brasiliens*, 1867, p. 430.
[2] Herbert Spencer, *The Principles of Ethics*, 1892, I. p. 330.
[3] The national name was *Muysca*, " Men," " Human Body," and the number
twenty (in reference to the ten fingers and ten toes making up that score).
Chibcha was a mimetic name having allusion to the sound *ch* (as in Charles),
which is of frequent recurrence in the Muysca language.   With man = 20, cf. the
Bellacoola (British Columbia) 19 = 1 man - 1 ; 20 = 1 man, etc. ; and this again with
Lat. *undeviginti*.

and worshipped with solemn rites and even human sacrifices. Amongst the arts thus acquired was that of the goldsmith, in which they surpassed all other peoples of the New World. The precious metal was even said to be minted in the shape of discs, which formed an almost solitary instance of a true metal currency amongst the American aborigines.[1] Brooches, pendants, and especially grotesque figurines of gold, often alloyed with silver and copper, have been found in great numbers and still occasionally turn up on the plateau.   These finds are partly accounted for by the practice of offering such objects in the open air to the personified constellations and forces of nature, for the primitive religion of all the Andean tribes consisted of nature-, in particular sun-cults. Near Bogota was a temple of the sun, where children were reared for sacrifice.[2]   Any mysterious sound emanating from a forest, a rock, a mountain pass, or gloomy gorge, was accepted as a manifestation of some divine presence ; a shrine was raised to the embodied spirit, and so the whole land became literally crowded with local deities.   This world itself was upborne on the shoulders of Chibchacum, a national Atlas, who now and then eased himself by shifting the burden, and thus caused earthquakes.   In most lands subject to underground disturbances analogous ideas prevail, and when their source is so obvious, it seems unreasonable to seek for explanations in racial affinities, contacts, foreign influences, and so forth.

It has often been remarked that at the advent of the whites the native civilisations seemed generally stricken as if by the hand of death, so that even if not suddenly arrested by the intruders they must sooner or later have perished of themselves.   Such speculations are seldom convincing, because we never know what recuperative forces may be at work to ward off the evil day.   When the Spaniards arrived in Colombia they found at one end of the scale naked and savage cannibals, at the other a people with a feudal form of government, whose political system was progressive, who, though possessing no form of writing, had a system of measures and a calendar, and who were skilled in the arts of weaving, pottery, and metallurgy.[3]   The chiefs of the Chibcha were all absolute monarchs and the appointment of priests rested with them.

---

[1] W. Bollaert, *Antiquarian, Ethnological, and other Researches in New Granada*, etc., 1860, *passim*.

[2] T. A. Joyce, *South American Archaeology*, 1912, p. 28.   [3] *Ibid.* p. 44.

Succession to the chieftainship was matrilineal, and installation in the office was attended by much ceremony.   A great gulf separated nobles and commoners ; slavery existed as an institution but slaves were well treated.   Polygyny was permitted, but relatives within certain degrees might not marry.[1]   This feebly organised political system broke to pieces at the first shock from without, and so disheartened had the people become under their half theocratic rulers, that they scarcely raised a hand in defence of the government which in their minds was associated only with tyranny and oppression.   The conquest was in any case facilitated by the civil war at the time raging between the northern and southern kingdoms which with several other semi-independent states constituted the Muyscan empire.   This empire was almost conterminous southwards with that of the Incas.   At least the numerous terms occurring in the dialects of the Paes, Coconucos, and other South Colombian tribes, show that Peruvian influences had spread beyond the political frontiers far to the north, without, however, quite reaching the confines of the Muyscan domain.

But for several centuries prior to the discovery the sway of the Peruvian Incas had been established throughout nearly
Empire of the Inca. the whole of the Andean lands, and the territory directly ruled by them extended from the Quito district about the equator for some 2500 miles southwards to the Rio Maule in Chili, with an average breadth of 400 miles between the Pacific and the eastern slopes of the Cordilleras.   Their dominion thus comprised a considerable part of the present republics of Ecuador, Peru, Bolivia, Chili, and Argentina, with a roughly estimated area of 1,000,000 square miles, and a population of over 10,000,000.   Here the
Quichuan Race and Speech. ruling race were the Quichua, whose speech, called by themselves *ruma-simi*, "the language of men," is still current in several well-marked dialects throughout all the provinces of the old empire.   In Lima and all the seaports and inland towns Spanish prevails, but in the rural districts Quichuan remains the mother-tongue of over 2,000,000 natives, and has even become the *lingua franca* of the written regions, just as Tupi-Guarani is the *lingoa geral*, "general language," of the eastern section of South America.   The attempts to find affinities with Aryan (especially Sanskrit), and other linguistic families of the

[1] T. A. Joyce, *loc. cit.* pp. 18–22.

eastern hemisphere, have broken down before the application of sound philological principles to these studies, and Quichuan is now recognised as a stock language of the usual American type, unconnected with any other except that of the Bolivian Aymaras. Even this connection is regarded by some students as verbal rather than structural, an interchange of a considerable number of terms being easily explained by the close contact in which the two peoples have long dwelt.

As to the origin of the Incas we cannot do better than follow the views of Sir Clements Markham, who has made a careful study of the various early authorities. His account (*The Incas of Peru*, 1910) is based largely on the works of Spanish military **Inca Origins and History.** writers such as Ciezo de Leon and Pedro Pizarro (cousin of the conqueror), of priests like Molina, Montesinos, and the half-breed Blas Valera, and on those of the Inca Garcilasso de la Vega, son of a Spanish knight and an Inca princess. The megalithic ruins of Tiahuanacu, at the southern end of lake Titicaca, mark the earliest known centre of culture in southern Peru. They are situated on a lofty plateau, over 13,000 feet above the sea, and are the remains of a great city built by highly skilled masons who used enormous stones. The placing of such monoliths, unrivalled except by those of ancient Egypt, indicates a dense and well-organised population. The famous monolithic doorway is elaborately carved, the central figure apparently representing the deity, while on either side are figures, human- or bird-headed, kneeling in adoration (*op. cit.*, pls. at pp. 26, 28). Now it seems probable that the builders of this megalithic city were the ancestors of the Incas, assuming that a substratum of truth underlies the Paccari-tampu myth.

The end of the early civilisation is stated to have been caused by a great invasion from the south, when the king was killed in a battle in the Collao, north of Lake Titicaca. A state of barbarism ensued. A remnant of the royal house took refuge in a district called Tampu-Toccò (" Window Tavern ") [1] and there preserved a vestige of their ancient traditions and civilisation. Elsewhere religion deteriorated to nature worship, here the kings declared themselves to be children of the sun.

[1] Markham locates it in the province of Paruro, department of Cuzco ; Hiram Bingham, director of the Peruvian Expeditions of the Nat. Geog. Soc. and Yale University, identifies it with Machu Picchu (*Nat. Geog. Mag.*, Washington, D.C., Feb. 1915, p. 172).

Montesinos' list of kings gives 27 names for this period of
Tampu-Tocco, which may cover 650 years.

The myth, which is "certainly the outcome of a real
tradition, . . . the fabulous version of a distant historical
event," tells how Manco Ccapac and the three other Ayars, his
brothers, the children of the sun, came forth with their wives
from the central opening or window in the hill Tampu-Tocco.
They advanced slowly at the head of several *ayllus* (lineages).
Ayar Manco took the lead, and he had with him a falcon-like
bird revered as sacred, and a golden staff which he flung
ahead ; when it reached soil so fertile that the whole length
sank in, there the final halt was to be made. This happened
in the fertile vale of Cuzco. The date of these events would
be about four centuries before the Spanish conquest.

Farther north at about 15° S. lat. the Inca civilisation was
preceded, according to Uhle, by the very ancient one of Ica
and Nazca, where dwelt a people who made pottery but were
ignorant of weaving. The same authority has also discovered
about Lima the remains of a tall people, who made rude
pottery, nets, and objects of bone.[1]

Manco established himself in the Cuzco valley, his third
successor finally subjugating the tribes there. The early
position of the Incas, cemented by judicious marriages, seems
to have been one of priority in a very loose confederacy. The
rise of the Incas was due to the ambition of the lady Siuyacu
whose son, Inca Rocca, appears to have been the pioneer of
empire ; material prosperity began under him, schools were
erected and irrigation works begun. Then from a strip of
land 250 miles long between the gorge of the Apurimac and
the wide fertile valley of Vilcamayu, the empire was extended
to form the Ttahua-ntin-suyu, " the four provinces," of which
the northern one, Chinchay-suyu, reached to Quito, and the
southern, Colla-suyu, into Chili. This southward extension
was due to the efforts of Pachacuti who succeeded after hard
fighting in annexing the region around Lake Titicaca, and
the new territory was named after the Collas, the largest and
most powerful tribe thereabouts. In order to pacify the region
permanently large numbers of Collas were sent as *mitimaes*,
or colonists, as far as the borders of Quito, while their places

[1] H. Beuchat, pp. 573–5. For culture sequences in the Andean area see
P. A. Means, *Proc. Nineteenth Internat. Congress of Americanists*, 1917, p. 236 ff.,
and *Man*, 1918, No. 91.

were filled by loyal colonists from Inca districts.   Among these
were a number of Aymaras from the Quichuan
region of the Pachachaca, a left bank tributary   The Aymara.
of the Apurimac, who were settled among the remaining
Lupacas on the west shore of Lake Titicaca at Juli.   Thither
came Jesuit fathers in 1572 and learnt the language of the
Lupacas from these Aymara colonists, who had been there
three generations ; the name Aymara was given by the priests
not only to the Lupaca language but to those spoken by Collas
and other Titicacan tribes.   Thus the name Aymara is now
generally but quite erroneously applied to the language and
people of this region ; it was first so used in 1575.   It must
be pointed out, however, that other authorities regard the
Aymara and Quichua as entirely distinct.   A. Chervin [1] discusses the physical differences at great length and concludes
that they are two separate brachycephalic peoples.

The Peruvians were primarily agriculturists, maize and at
higher altitudes the potato being their chief crops.   Their
aqueducts and irrigation systems moved the admiration of
early chroniclers, as did also their roads and suspension
bridges.[2]   The supreme deity and creator was Uira-cocha,
who was worshipped by the more intellectual and had a temple
at Cuzco.   The popular religion was the worship of the founder
of each *ayllu*, or clan, and all joined in adoration of the sun as
ancestor of the sovereign Incas.   Sun-worship was attended
by a magnificent ritual, the high priest was an official
of highest rank, often a brother of the sovereign, and there
were over 3000 Virgins of the Sun (*aclla*) connected with the
cult at Cuzco.   The peasants put their trust in *conopas*, or
household gods, which controlled their crops and their llamas.
The calendar had been calculated with considerable ingenuity,
and certain festivals took place annually and were usually
accompanied with much chicha-drinking.   It is remarkable
that so advanced a people kept all their elaborate records by
means of *quipus* (coloured strings with knots).

Here is not the place to enter into the details of the astonishing architectural, engineering, and artistic remains, often
assigned to the Incas, whose empire had absorbed
in the north the old civilisation of the *Chimu*,   The Chimu.

---

[1] *Anthropologie Bolivienne*, 3 vols., Paris, 1907–8.
[2] An admirable account of the material culture of Peru is given by T. A. Joyce,
South American Archaeology, 1912, cap. VI.

perhaps of the *Atacameño*, and other cultured peoples whose very names have perished. The Yunga (Mochica or Chimu), conquered by the Inca Tupac Yupanqui, had a language radically distinct from Quichuan, but have long been assimilated to their conquerors.

The ruins of Grand Chimu (modern Trujillo) cover a vast area, nearly 15 miles by 6, which is everywhere strewn with the remains of palaces, reservoirs, aqueducts, ramparts, and especially *huacas*, that is, truncated pyramids not unlike those of Mexico, whence the theory that the Chimus, of unknown origin, were " Toltecs " from Central America. One of these huacas is described by Squier as 150 feet high with a base 580 feet square, and an area of 8 acres, presenting from a distance the appearance of a huge crater.[1] Still larger is the so-called " Temple of the Sun," 800 by 470 feet, 200 feet high, and covering an area of 7 acres. An immense population of hundreds of thousands was assigned to this place in pre-Inca times ; but from some rough surveys made in 1897 it would appear that much of the space within the enclosures consists of waste lands, which had never been built over, and it is calculated that at no time could the number of inhabitants have greatly exceeded 50,000.

We need not stop to describe the peculiar civil and social institutions of the Peruvians, which are of common knowledge.

Peruvian Political System. Enough to say that here everything was planned in the interests of the theocratic and all-powerful Incas, who were more than obeyed, almost honoured with divine worship by their much bethralled and priest-ridden subjects. " The despotic authority of the Incas was the basis of government ; that authority was founded on the religious respect yielded to the descendant of the sun, and supported by a skilfully combined hierarchy." [2] From remote antiquity the peoples of this area were organised into *ayllus* each occupying part of a valley or a limited area. It was a patriarchal system, land belonging to the *ayllu*, which was a group of families. The Incas systematised this institution, the *ayllu* was made to compromise 100 families under a village officer who annually allotted land to the heads of families. Each family was divided by the head into 10 classes based on age. Ten *ayllus* (now termed *pachacas*) formed a *huaranca*.

[1] *Peru*, p. 120.
[2] De Nadaillac, *Pre-Historic America*, 1885, p. 438.

A valley with a varying number of *huarancas* was termed a *hunu* ; over four *hunus* there was an imperial officer. " This was indeed Socialism," Markham observes, " existing under an inexorable despotism " (p. 169).

Beyond the Maule, southernmost limits of all these effete civilisations, man reasserted himself in the " South American Iroquois," as those Chilian aborigines   The Arauca-
have been called who called themselves *Molu-che*,   nians.
" Warriors," but are better known by their Quichuan designation of *Aucaes*, "Rebels," whence the Spanish Aucans (Araucan, Araucanian). These " Rebels," who have never hitherto been overcome by the arms of any people, and whose heroic deeds in the long wars waged by the white intruders against their freedom form the topic of a noble Spanish epic poem,[1] still maintain a measure of national autonomy as the friends and faithful allies of the Chilian republic. Individual freedom and equality were leading features of the social system which was in the main patriarchal. The Araucanians were led by four independent chiefs, each supported by five *ulmen*, or district chiefs, whose office was hereditary but whose authority was little more than nominal. It was only in time of national warfare that the tribes united under a war-chief.[2] Not only are all the tribes absolutely free, but the same is true of every clan, sept, and family group. Needless to say, there are no slaves or serfs. " The law of retaliation was the only one understood, although the commercial spirit of the Araucano led him to forgo personal revenge for its accruing profit. Thus every injury had its price." [3]

The basis of their belief is a rude form of nature worship, the principal deities being malignant and requiring propitiation. The chief god was Pillan, the thunder god. Spirits of the dead go west over the sea to a place of abundance where no evil spirits have entry.[4] And this simple belief is almost the only substitute for the rewards and punishments which supply the motive for the observance of an artificial ethical code in so many more developed religious systems.

In the sonorous Araucanian language, which is still spoken by about 40,000 full-blood natives, the term *che*, meaning

[1] Alonzo de Ercilla's *Araucana*.
[2] T. A. Joyce, *South American Archaeology*, 1912, p. 243 ; R. E. Latham, " Ethnology of the Araucanos," *Journ. Roy. Anth. Inst.* XXXIX. 1909, p. 355.
[3] Latham, p. 356.   [4] *Ibid.* pp. 344–50.

" people," occurs as the postfix of several ethical groups, which, however, are not tribal but purely territorial divisions. Thus, while *Molu-che* is the collective name of the whole nation, the *Picun-che*, *Huilli-che*, and *Puel-che* are simply the North, South, and East men respectively. The Central and most numerous division are the *Puen-che*, that is, people of the pine district, who are both the most typical and most intelligent of all the Araucanian family. Ehrenreich's remark that many of the American aborigines resemble Europeans as much as or even more than the Asiatic Mongols, is certainly borne out by the facial expression of these Puenche. The resemblance is even extended to the mental characters, as reflected in their oral literature. Amongst the specimens of the national folklore preserved in the Puenche dialect and edited with Spanish translations by Rodolfo Lenz,[1] is the story of a departed lover, who returns from the other world to demand his betrothed and carries her off to his grave. Although this might seem an adaptation of Bürger's " Lenore," Lenz is of opinion that it is a genuine Araucanian legend.

Of the above-mentioned groups the Puelche are now included politically in Argentina. Their original home seems to have been north of the Rio Negro, but they raided westwards and some adopted the Araucanian language [2] and to them also the Chilian affix *che* has also been extended. Indeed the term Puelche, meaning simply " Easterns," is applied not only to the Argentine Moluche, whose territory stretches east of the Cordilleras as far as the Mendoza in Cuyo, but also to all the aborigines commonly called *Pampeans* (*Pampas Indians*) by the Europeans and *Penek* by the Patagonians. Under the designation of Puelche would therefore be comprised the now extinct *Ranqualche* (Ranqueles), who formerly raided up to Buenos-Ayres and the other Spanish settlements on the Plate River, the *Mapoche* of the Lower Salado, and generally all the nomads as far south as the Rio Negro.

The Pampas Indians.

These aborigines are now best represented by the *Gauchos*, who are mostly Spaniards on the father's side and Indians on the mother's, and reflect this double descent in their half-nomadic, half-civilised life. These Gauchos, who are now also disappearing before the encroach-

Gauchos.

---

[1] In the *Anales de la Universidad de Chile* for 1897.
[2] T. A. Joyce, p. 240.

ments of the " Gringos,"[1] *i.e.* the white immigrants from almost every country in Europe, have been enveloped in an ill-deserved halo of romance, thanks mainly to their roving habits, splendid horsemanship, love of finery, and genial disposition combined with that innate grace and courtesy which belongs to all of Spanish blood. But those who knew them best described them as of sordid nature, cruel to their womenkind, reckless gamblers and libertines, ruthless political partisans, at times even religious fanatics without a spark of true religion, and at heart little better than bloodthirsty savages.

Beyond the Rio Negro follow the gigantic Patagonians, that is, the *Tehuelche* or *Chuelche* of the Araucanians, who have no true collective name unless it be *Tsoneca*, a word of uncertain use and origin. Most of the tribal groups—*Yacana*, *Pilma*, *Chao* and others —are broken up, and the former division between the Northern Tehuelche (Tehuelhet), comprising the *Callilehet* (Serranos or Highlanders) of the Upper Chupat, with the Calilan between the Rios Chupat and Negro, and the Southern Tehuelche (Yacana, Sehuan, etc.), south to Fuegia, no longer holds good since the general displacement of all these fluctuating nomad hordes. A branch of the Tehuelche are unquestionably the *Ona* of the eastern parts of Fuegia, the true aborigines of which are the *Yahgans* of the central and the *Alakalufs* of the western islands.

The Patagonians.

Hitherto to the question whence came these tall Patagonians, no answer could be given beyond the suggestion that they may have been specialised in their present habitat, where nevertheless they seem to be obviously intruders. Now, however, one may perhaps venture to look for their original home amongst the *Bororo* of Matto Grosso, a once powerful race who held the region between the Rios Cuyaba and Paraguay. These Bororo, who had been heard of by Martius were visited by Ehrenreich[2] and by Karl von den Steinen,[3] who found them to be a nomadic hunting people with a remarkable social organisation centring in the men's clubhouse (*baitó*). Their physical characters, as described by the former observer, correspond closely with those of the Pata-

---

[1] Properly *Griegos*, " Greeks," so called because supposed to speak " Greek," *i.e.* any language other than Spanish.
[2] *Urbewohner Brasiliens*, 1897, pp. 69, 110, 125.
[3] *Unter den Naturvölkern Zentral-Brasiliens*, 1894, pp. 441-3, 468 ff.

gonians : " An exceptionally tall race rivalling the South Sea
Islanders, Patagonians, and Redskins ; by far the tallest
Indians hitherto discovered within the tropics," their stature
ranging nearly up to 6 ft. 4 in., with very large and rounded
heads (men 81.2 ; women 77.4). With this should be compared the very large round old Patagonian skull from the
Rio Negro, measured by Rudolf Martin.[1] The account reads
like the description of some forerunner of a prehistoric Bororo
irruption into the Patagonian steppe lands.

To the perplexing use of the term Puelche above referred
to is perhaps due the difference of opinion still prevailing on
the number of stock languages in the southern section of
the Continent. D'Orbigny's emphatic statement [2] that the
Puelche spoke a language fundamentally distinct both from
the Araucanian and the Patagonian has been
questioned on the strength of some Puelche
words, which were collected by Hale at Carmen
on the Rio Negro, and differ but slightly from Patagonian.
But the Rio Negro lies on the ethnical divide between the
two races, which sufficiently accounts for the resemblances,
while the words are too few to prove anything. Hale calls
them " Southern Puelche," but they were in fact Tehuelche
(Patagonian), the true Pampean Puelche having disappeared
from that region before Hale's time.[3] I have now the un-
impeachable authority of T. P. Schmid, for many years a
missionary amongst these aborigines, for asserting that
d'Orbigny's statement is absolutely correct. His Puelche
were the Pampeans, because he locates them in the region
between the Rios Negro and Colorado, that is, north of
Patagonian and east of Araucanian territory, and Schmid
assures me that all three—Araucanian, Pampean, and Patagonian—are undoubtedly stock languages, distinct both in their
vocabulary and structure, with nothing in common except their
common polysynthetic form. In a list of 2000 Patagonian
and Araucanian words he found only two alike, *patac*=100,
and *huarunc*=1000, numerals obviously borrowed by the rude

*Linguistic
Relations.*

[1] *Quarterly Journal of Swiss Naturalists*, Zurich, 1896, p. 496 ff. ; cf. T. A.
Joyce, *South American Archaeology*, 1912, pp. 241-2.
[2] *L'Homme Américain*, II. p. 70.
[3] They were replaced or absorbed partly by the Patagonians, but chiefly by the
Araucanian Puelche, who many years ago migrated down the Rio Negro as far
as El Carmen and even to the coast at Bahia Blanca. Hence Hale's Puelche
were in fact Araucanians with a Patagonian strain.

Tehuelche from the more cultured Moluche. In Fuegia there is at least one radically distinct tongue, the Yahgan, studied by Bridges. Here the Ona is probably a Patagonian dialect, and Alakaluf perhaps remotely allied to Araucanian. Thus in the whole region south of the Plate River the stock languages are not known to exceed four : Araucanian ; Pampean (Puelche) ; Patagonian (Tehuelche) ; and Yahgan.

Few aboriginal peoples have been the subject of more glaringly discrepant statements than the Yahgans, to whom several lengthy monographs have been devoted during the last few decades. How contradictory **The Yahgans.** are the statements of intelligent and even trained observers, whose good faith is beyond suspicion and who have no cause to serve except the truth, will best be seen by placing in juxtaposition the accounts of the family relations by G. Bove, a well-known Italian observer, and P. Hyades of the French Cape Horn Expedition, both summarised : [1]—

Bove.	*Hyades.*
The women are treated as slaves. The greater the number of wives or slaves a man has the easier he finds a living ; hence polygamy is deep-rooted and four wives common. Owing to the rigid climate and bad treatment the mortality of children under 10 years is excessive; the mother's love lasts till the child is weaned, after which it rapidly wanes, and is completely gone when the child attains the age of 7 or 8 years. The Fuegian's only lasting love is the love of self. As there are no family ties, the word " authority " is devoid of meaning.	The Fuegians are capable of great love which accounts for the jealousy of the men over their wives and the coquetry sometimes manifested by women and girls. Some men have two or more wives, but monogamy is the rule. Children are tenderly cared for by their parents, who in return are treated by them with affection and deference. The Fuegians are of a generous disposition and like to share their pleasures with others. The husbands exercise due control, and punish severely any act of infidelity.

These seeming contradictions may be partly explained by the general improvement in manners due to the beneficent action of the English missionaries in recent years, and great progress has certainly been made since the accounts of King, Fitz-Roy and Darwin.[2]

But even in the more favoured regions of the Parana and Amazon basins many tribes are met which yield little if at

---

[1] *Mission Scientifique de Cap Horn*, VII., par P. Hyades et J. Deniker, 1891, pp. 238, 243, 378.
[2] For the latest information and full bibliography see J. M. Cooper, *Bureau Am. Eth. Bull.* 63, 1917, and *Proc. Nineteenth Internat. Congress Americanists*, 1917, p. 445 ; also, C. W. Furlong, *ibid.* pp. 420 ff., 432 ff.

all to the Fuegians of the early writers in sheer savagery and
debasement. Thus the *Cashibo* or *Carapache*
of the Ucayali, who are described as " white as
Germans, with long beards,"[1] may be said to answer almost
better than any other human group to the old saying, *homo
homini lupus.* They roam the forests like wild beasts, living
almost entirely upon game, in which is included man himself.
" When one of them is pursuing the chase in the woods and
hears another hunter imitating the cry of an animal, he immediately makes the same cry to entice him nearer, and, if
he is of another tribe, he kills him if he can, and (as is alleged)
eats him." Hence they are naturally " in a state of hostility
with all their neighbours." [2]

The Cashibo.

These Cashibo, *i.e.* " Bats," are members of a widespread
linguistic family which in ethnological writings bears the name
of *Pano*, from the Pano of the Huallaga and
Marañon, who are now broken up or greatly
reduced, but whose language is current amongst
the Cashibo, the Conibo, the Karipuna, the Setebo, the
Sipivio (Shipibo) and others about the head waters of the
Amazons in Peru, Bolivia, and Brazil, as far east as the
Madeira. Amongst these, as amongst the Moxo and so
many other riverine tribes in Amazonia, a slow transformation
is in progress. Some have been baptized, and while still
occupying their old haunts and keeping up the tribal organisation, have been induced to forgo their savage ways and
turn to peaceful pursuits. They are beginning to wear clothes,
usually cotton robes of some vivid colour, to till the soil, take
service with the white traders, or even trade themselves in
their canoes up and down the tributaries of the Amazons.
Beyond the Rubber Belt, however, many tribes are quite
untouched by outside influences. The cannibal Boro and
Witoto, living between the Issa and Japura, are ignorant of
any method of producing fire, and their women go entirely
nude, though some of their arts and crafts exhibit considerable
skill, notably the plaitwork and blow-pipes of the Boro.[3]

The Pano Family.

In this boundless Amazonian region of moist sunless
woodlands fringed north and east by Atlantic coast ranges,
diversified by the open Venezuelan llanos, and merging

[1] Markham, " List of Tribes," etc., *Journ. Roy. Anth. Inst.* XI. 1910, pp. 89–90.
[2] *Ibid.*
[3] T. Whiffen, *The North-West Amazons*, 1915, pp. 48, 78, 91, etc.

southwards in the vast alluvial plains of the Parana-Para-
guay basin, much light has been brought to bear   Ethnical
on the obscure ethnical relations by the recent   Relations in
explorations especially of Paul Ehrenreich and   Amazonia.
Karl von den Steinen about the Xingu, Purus, Madeira and
other southern affluents of the great artery.[1]   These observers
comprise the countless Brazilian aborigines in four main
linguistic divisions, which in conformity with Powell's terminology may here be named the CARIBAN, ARAWAKAN, GESAN and
TUPI-GUARANIAN families.   There remain, however, numerous
groups which cannot be so classified, such as the Bororo and
Karaya of Matto Grosso, while in the relatively small area
between the Japura and the Waupes Koch-Grünberg found
two other language groups, Betoya and Maku in addition to
Carib and Arawak.[2]

Hitherto the Caribs were commonly supposed to have had
their original homes far to the north, possibly in the Alleghany
uplands, or in Florida, where they have been   The Caribs.
doubtfully identified with the extinct Timuqua-
nans, and whence they spread through the Antilles southwards
to Venezuela, the Guianas, and north-east Brazil, beyond
which they were not known to have ranged anywhere south
of the Amazons.   But this view is now shown to be untenable, and several Carib tribes, such as the Bakaïri and
Nahuqua[3] of the Upper Xingu, all speaking archaic forms
of the Carib stock language, have been met by the German
explorers in the very heart of Brazil ; whence the inference
that the cradle of this race is to be sought rather in the centre
of South America, perhaps on the Goyaz and Matto Grosso
table-lands, from which region they moved northwards, if not
to Florida, at least to the Caribbean Sea which is named from
them.[4]   The wide diffusion of this stock is evidenced by the
existence of an unmistakably Carib tribe in the basin of the
Rio Magdalena beyond the Andes.[5]

In the north the chief groups are the Makirifare of

[1] For the material culture of the Araguayan tribes, cf. Fritz Krause, *In den
Wildnissen Brasiliens*, 1911.
[2] T. Koch-Grünberg, *Zwei Jahre unter den Indianern*, 2 vols., Berlin, 1910.
See Vol. II. map after p. 319.
[3] Ehrenreich, *loc. cit.* p. 45 ff. ; von den Steinen, *loc. cit.* p. 153 ff.
[4] It should be stated that a like conclusion was reached by Lucien Adam from
the vocabularies brought by Crevaux from the Upper Japura tribes—Witotos,
Corequajes, Kariginas and others—all of Carib speech.
[5] A. C. Haddon, *The Wanderings of Peoples*, Cambridge, 1911, p. 109.

Venezuela and the Macusi, Kalina, and Galibi of British, Dutch, and French Guiana [1] respectively. In general all the Caribs present much the same physical characters, although the southerners are rather taller (5 ft. 4 in.) with less round heads (index 79.6) than the Guiana Caribs (5 ft. 2 in., and 81.3).

Perhaps even a greater extension has been given by the German explorers to the Arawakan family, which, like the Cariban, was hitherto supposed to be mainly confined to the region north of the Amazons, but is now known to range as far south as the Upper Paraguay, about 20° S. lat. (*Layana, Kwana*, etc.), east to the Amazons estuary (*Aruan*), and north-west to the Goajira peninsula. To this great family—which von den Steinen proposes to call *Nu-Aruak* from the pronominal prefix *nu* = I, common to most of the tribes—belong also the *Maypures* of the Orinoco; the *Atarais* and *Vapisiana* of British Guiana; the *Manao* of the Rio Negro; the *Yumana*; the *Paumari* and *Ipurina* of the Ipuri basin; the *Moxo* of the Upper Mamoré, and the *Mehinaku* and *Kustenau* of the Upper Xingu.

The Arawakan Family.

Physically the Arawaks differ from the Caribs scarcely, if at all, more than their Amazonian and Guiana sections differ from each other. In fact, but for their radically distinct speech it would be impossible to constitute these two ethnical divisions, which are admittedly based on linguistic grounds. But while the Caribs had their cradle in Central Brazil and migrated northwards, the Arawaks would appear to have originated in eastern Bolivia, and spread thence east, north-east and south-east along the Amazons and Orinoco and into the Paraguay basin.[2]

Our third great Brazilian division, the Gesan family, takes its name from the syllable *ges* which, like the Araucan *che*, forms the final element of several tribal names in East Brazil. Of this the most characteristic are the *Aimores* of the Serra dos Aimores coast range, who are better known as Botocudo, and it was to the kindred tribes of the province of Goyaz that the arbitrary collective name of " Ges " was first applied by Martius. A

The Gesan Family.

---

[1] Described by E. F. im Thurn, *Among the Indians of Guiana*, London, 1883.
[2] A. C. Haddon, *The Wanderings of Peoples*, pp. 110–11.

better general designation would perhaps have been *Tapuya,*
"Strangers," "Enemies," a term by which the Tupi people
called all other natives of that region who were not of their
race or speech, or rather who were not "Tupi," that is,
"Allies" or "Associates." Tapuya had been adopted somewhat in this sense by the early Portuguese writers, who however applied it rather loosely not only to the Aimores, but
also to a large number of kindred and other tribes as far north
as the Amazons estuary.

To the same connection belong several groups in Goyaz
already described by Milliet and Martius, and more recently
visited by Ehrenreich, von den Steinen and Krause. Such
are the Kayapo or Suya, a large nation with several divisions between the Araguaya and Xingu rivers ; and the
Akua, better known as Cherentes, about the upper course
of the Tocantins. Isolated Tapuyan tribes, such as the
Kamés or Kaingangs, wrongly called "Coroados," and the
Chogleng of Santo Catharina and Rio Grand do Sul, are
scattered over the southern provinces of Brazil.

The Tapuya would thus appear to have formerly occupied
the whole of East Brazil from the Amazons to the Plate River
for an unknown distance inland. Here they must be regarded
as the true aborigines, who were in remote times already encroached upon, and broken into isolated fragments, by tribes
of the Tupi-Guarani stock spreading from the interior sea-
wards.[1]

But in their physical characters and extremely low cultural
state, or rather the almost total absence of anything that can
be called "culture," the Tapuya are the nearest representatives and probably the direct descendants of the primitive race,
whose osseous remains have been found in the Lagoa Santa
caves, and the Santa Catharina shell-mounds (*sambaqui*). On
anatomic grounds the Botocudo are allied both   The Botocudo.
to the Lagoa Santa fossil man and to the *sam-*
baqui race by J. R. Peixoto, who describes the skull as marked
by prominent glabella and superciliary arches, keel or roof-
shaped vault, vertical lateral walls, simple sutures, receding
brow, deeply depressed nasal root, high prognathism, massive

---

[1] V. d. Steinen, *Unter den Naturvölkern Zentral-Brasiliens*, p. 157. "D'après
Gonçalves Dias les tribus brésiliennes descendraient de deux races absolument
distinctes : la race conquérante des Tupi . . . et la race vaincue, pourchassée, des
Tapuya..."; V. de Saint-Martin, p. 517, *Nouveau Dictionnaire de Géographie
Universelle*, 1879, A—C.

lower jaw, and long head (index 73.30) with cranial capacity
1480 c.c. for men, and 1212 for women.[1] It is also noteworthy that some of the Botocudo[2] call themselves *Nac-
nanuk, Nac-poruc,* "Sons of the Soil," and they have no
traditions of ever having migrated from any other land. All
their implements—spears, bow and arrows, mortars, water-
vessels, bags—are of wood or vegetable fibre, so that they
may be said not to have yet reached even the stone age.
They are not, however, in the promiscuous state, as has been
asserted, for the unions, though temporary, are jealously
guarded while they last, and, as amongst the Fuegians whom
they resemble in so many respects, the women are constantly
subject to the most barbarous treatment, beaten with clubs
or hacked about with bamboo knives. One of those in
Ribeiro's party, who visited London in 1883, had her arms,
legs, and whole body covered with scars and gashes inflicted
during momentary fits of brutal rage by her ephemeral partner.
Their dwellings are mere branches stuck in the ground, bound
together with bast, and though seldom over 4 ft. in height
accommodating two or more families. The Botocudo are
pure nomads, roaming naked in the woods in quest of the
roots, berries, honey, frogs, snakes, grubs, man, and other
larger game which form their diet, and are eaten raw or else
cooked in huge bamboo canes. Formerly they had no ham-
mocks, but slept without any covering, either on the ground
strewn with bast, or in the ashes of the fire kindled for the
evening meal. About their cannibalism, which has been
doubted, there is really no question. They wore the teeth
of those they had eaten strung together as necklaces, and ate
not only the foe slain in battle, but members of kindred
tribes, all but the heads, which were stuck as trophies on
stakes and used as butts for the practice of archery.

At the graves of the dead, fires are kept up for some time
to scare away the bad spirits, from which custom the Botocudo might be credited with some notions concerning the
supernatural. All good influences are attributed by them to
the "day-fire" (sun), all bad things to the "night-fire" (moon),

[1] *Novos Estudios Craniologicos sobre os Botocudos,* Rio Janeiro, 1882, *passim.*
[2] Possibly so called from the Portuguese *botoque,* a barrel plug, from the wooden
plug or disc formerly worn by all the tribes both as a lip ornament and an ear-
plug, distending the lobes like great leathern bat's-wings down to the shoulders.
But this embellishment is called *tembeitera* by the Brazilians, and Botocudo may
perhaps be connected with *betó-apoc,* the native name of the ear-plug.

which causes the thunderstorm, and is supposed itself at times to fall on the earth, crushing the hill-tops, flooding the plains and destroying multitudes of people. During storms and eclipses arrows are shot up to scare away the demons or devouring dragons, as amongst so many Indo-Chinese peoples. But beyond this there is no conception of a supreme being, or creative force, the terms *yanchong, tapan*, said to mean " God," standing merely for spirit, demon, thunder, or at most the thunder god.

Owing to the choice made by the missionaries of the Tupi language as the *lingoa geral*, or common medium of intercourse amongst the multitudinous populations of Brazil and Paraguay, a somewhat exaggerated idea has been formed of the range of the Tupi-Guarani family. Many of the tribes about the stations, after being induced by the padres to learn this convenient *lingua franca*, were apt in course of time to forget their own mother-tongue, and thus came to be accounted members of this family. But allowing for such a source of error, there can be no doubt that at the discovery the Tupi or Eastern, and the Guarani or Western, section occupied jointly an immense area, which may perhaps be estimated at about one-fourth of the southern continent. Tupi tribes were met as far west as Peru, where they were represented by the Omagua ("Flatheads "[1]), in French Guiana the Emerillons and the Oyampi belong to this stock, as do the Kamayura and Auetö on the Upper Xingu, and the Mundurucu of the middle Tapajoz.

Some attention has been paid to the speech of the Ticuna of the Marañon, which appears to be a stock language with strong Pana and weak Aymara[2] affinities. Although its numeral system stops at 2, it is still in advance of a

___

[1] They are the *Cambebas* of the Tupi, a term also meaning Flatheads, and they are so called because " apertão aos recemnacidos as cabeças entre duas taboas afim de achatál-as, costume que actualmente han perdido " (Milliet, II. p. 174).

[2] Such " identities " as Tic. *drejà*=Aym. *chacha* (man) ; *etai*=*utax* (house) etc., are not convincing, especially in the absence of any scientific study of the laws of *Lautverschiebung*, if any exist between the Aymara-Ticuna phonetic systems. And then the question of loan words has to be settled before any safe conclusions can be drawn from such assumed resemblances. The point is important in the present connection, because current statements regarding the supposed reduction of the number of stock languages in South America are largely based on the unscientific comparison of lists of words, which may have nothing in common except perhaps a letter or two like the *m* in Macedon and Monmouth. Two languages (cf. Turkish and Arabic) may have hundreds or thousands of words in common, and yet belong to fundamentally different linguistic families.

neighbouring *Chiquito* tongue, which is said to have no
numerals at all, *etama*, supposed to be 1, really meaning
"alone."

Yet it would be a mistake to infer that these Bolivian
Chiquito, who occupy the southernmost headstreams of the

The Chiquito. Madeira, are a particularly stupid people. On
the contrary, the Naquiñoñeis, "Men," as they
call themselves, are in some respects remarkably clever, and,
strange to say, their otherwise rich and harmonious language
(presumably the dominant *Moncoca* dialect is meant) has
terms to express such various distinctions as the height of a
tree, of a house, of a tower, and other subtle shades of difference disregarded in more cultured tongues.[1]   But it is to be
considered that, *pace* Max Müller, the range of thought and
of speech is not the same, and all peoples have no doubt
many notions for which they have no equivalents in their
necessarily defective languages. The Chiquito, *i.e.* " Little
Folks," were so named because, " when the country was first
invaded, the Indians fled to the forests ; and the Spaniards
came to their abandoned huts, where the doorways were so
exceedingly low that the Indians who had fled were supposed
to be dwarfs."[2]   They are a peaceful industrious nation, who
ply several trades, manufacture their own copper boilers for
making sugar, weave ponchos and straw hats, and when they
want blue trousers they plant a row of indigo, and rows of
white and yellow cotton when striped trousers are in fashion.
Hence the question arises, whether these clever little people
may not after all have originally possessed some defective
numeral system, which was merely superseded by the Spanish
numbers.

The Gran Chaco is another area of considerable modification induced by European influence, and there only remain

Mataco and Toba. hybridised descendants of many of the ancient
peoples, for example, the Abipone of the Guay-
curu family.   Pure survivals of this family are
the Mataco and Toba of the Vermejo and Pilcomayo rivers.
These two tribes were visited by Ehrenreich, who noticed
their disproportionately short arms and legs, and excessive

---

[1] A. Balbi, *Atlas Ethnographique du Globe*, XXVII. With regard to the
numerals this authority tells us that " il a emprunté à l'espagnol ses noms de
nombres " (*ib.*).

[2] Markham, *List of the Tribes*, p. 92.

development of the thorax.[1] The daily life, customs, and beliefs of these and other Chaco Indians have been admirably described and illustrated by Erland Nordenskiöld,[2] who lived and travelled among them. The Toba and Mataco frequently fall out with the neighbouring Choroti and Ashluslays of the Pilcomayo anent fishing rights and so on, but the conflict consists in ambuscades and treachery rather than in pitched battles. Weapons consist of bows and arrows and clubs, and lances are used on horseback. Enemies are scalped and these trophies are greatly prized, being hung outside the victor's hut when fine and playing a part on great occasions. On the conclusion of peace both sides pay the blood-price for those slain by them in sheep, horses, etc. Within the Choroti or Ashluslay village all are equal, and though property is held individually, the fortunate will always share with those in want, so that theft is unknown. To kill old people or young children is regarded as no crime.[3]

[1] *Urbewohner Brasiliens*, p. 101.

[2] " La vie des Indiens dans le Chaco," trans. by H. Beuchat, *Rev. de Géog. annuelle*, t. VI. Paris, 1912. Cf. also the forthcoming book by R. Karsten of Helsingfors who has recently visited some of these tribes.

[3] While this account of Central and South America was in the Press Clark Wissler's valuable book was published, *The American Indian*, New York, 1917. He describes (pp. 227–42) the following culture areas :

    X.   The Nahua area (the ancient Maya and the later Aztec cultures).

    XI.   The Chibcha area (from the Chibcha-speaking Talamanca and Chiriqui of Costa Rica to and including Colombia and western Venezuela).

    XII.   The Inca area (Ecuador, Peru and northern Chili).

    XIII.   The Guanaco area (lower half of Chili, Argentine, Patagonia, Tierra del Fuego).

    XIV.   The Amazon area (all the rest of South America).

    XV.   The Antilles (West Indies, linking on to the Amazon area).

CHAPTER XII

THE PRE-DRAVIDIANS : JUNGLE TRIBES OF THE DECCAN, VEDDA, SAKAI, AUSTRALIANS

The Pre-Dravidians—The *Kadir*—The *Paniyan*—The *Irula*—The *Kurumba*— The *Vedda*—The *Sakai*—The *Toala*—Australia : Physical Conditions— Physical Type—Australian Origins—Evidence from Language and Culture— Four Successive Immigrations—Earlier Views—Material Culture—Sociology —Initiation Ceremonies—Totemism—The Family—Kinship—Property and Trade—Magic and Religion.

CONSPECTUS.

Present Range. *Jungle tribes, Deccan ; Vedda, Ceylon ;*
Distribution. *Sakai, Malay Peninsula and East Sumatra ; Australians, unsettled parts of Australia and reservations.*

Hair, *wavy to curly, long, usually black.*

Colour, *dark brown.* **Skull,** *typically dolichocephalic. Vedda skull dolichocephalic (70.5) and very small, Sakai*
Physical Characters. *mesaticephalic (78), Toala (mixed) low brachy-cephalic (82).* **Jaws,** *orthognathous. Australians, generally prognathous.* **Nose,** *usually* platyrrhine. **Stature,** *low. Vedda* 1.53 *m.* (5 *ft.* 0½ *in.*) *to Australian* 1.575 m. (5 *ft.* 2 *in.*).

Speech, *Jungle tribes, usually borrowed from neighbours.*
Mental Characters. *Australian languages agglutinative, not uniform throughout the continent and unconnected with any other group.*

Culture, *lowest hunting stage, simple agriculture has been adopted by a few tribes from their neighbours.*

The term Pre-Dravidian, the first use of which seems to be due to Lapicque, is now employed to include certain jungle
The Pre-Dravidians. tribes of South India, the Vedda of Ceylon, the Sakai of the southern Malay Peninsula, the basal element in certain tribes in the East India Archipelago and the main element in the Australians. Pre-Dravidian

characters are coarse hair, more or less wavy or curly, a narrow head, a very broad nose, dark brown skin and short stature.

The following may be taken as examples of the Pre-Dravidian jungle tribes of Southern India.[1]   The *Kadir* of the Anaimalai Hills and the mountain ranges south into Tra- The Kadir. vancore, are of short stature (1.577 m. 5 ft. 2 in.), with a dark skin, dolichocephalic and platyrrhine.   They chip their incisor teeth, as do the *Mala-Vadan*, and dilate the lobes of their ears, but do not tattoo.   They wear bamboo combs similar to those of the Sakai.   They speak a Tamil patois. " The Kadirs," according to Thurston, " afford a typical example of happiness without culture " ; they are nomad hunters and collectors of jungle products, with scarcely any tillage ; they do not possess land but have the right to collect all minor forest produce and sell it to the Government.   They deal most extensively in wax and honey.   They are polygynous.   Their dead are buried in the jungle, the head is entirely covered with leaves and placed towards the east ; there are no monuments. Their religion is a crude polytheism with a vague worship of stone images or invisible gods ; it is " an ejaculatory religion."

The *Paniyan*, who live in Malabar, the Wynad and the Nilgiris, have thick and sometimes everted lips and the hair is in some a mass of short curls, in others long The Paniyan. wavy curls.   They are dark skinned, dolicho- cephalic (index 74), platyrrhine and of short stature (1.574 m. 5 ft. 2 in.).   They sometimes tattoo, and the lobes of the ears are dilated.   Fire is made by the sawing method.   They are agriculturalists and were practically serfs ; they are bold and reckless and were formerly often employed as thieves.   They speak a debased Malayalam patois.   Their dead are buried ; they practise monogamy and have beliefs in various spirits.

The *Irula* are the darkest of the Nilgiri tribes.   They are dolichocephalic (index 75.8), platyrrhine and of low stature (1.598 m. nearly 5 ft. 3 in.).   No tattooing is re- The Irula. corded, but they dilate the lobes of their ears. Their language is a corrupt form of Tamil.   They are agriculturalists and eat all kinds of meat except that of buffaloes and cattle.   They are as a rule monogamous.   Their dead are buried in a sitting posture and the grave is marked by a stone.   Professedly they are worshippers of Vishnu.

[1] E. Thurston, *Castes and Tribes of Southern India*, 1909.

The jungle *Kurumba* of the Nilgiris appear to be remnants of a great and widely spread people who erected dolmens.

The Kurumba. They have slightly broader heads (index 77) than allied tribes, but resemble them in their broad nose, dark skin and low stature (1.575 m. 5 ft. 2 in.). They cultivate the ground a little, but are essentially wood-cutters, hunters, and collectors of jungle produce. There is said to be no marriage rite, and several brothers share a wife. Some bury their dead. After a death a long waterworn stone is usually placed in one of the old dolmens which are scattered over the Nilgiri plateau, but occasionally a small dolmen is raised to mark the burial. They have a great reputation for magical powers. Some worship Siva, others worship Kuribattraya (Lord of many sheep), and the wife of Siva. They also worship a rough stone, setting it up in a cave or in a circle of stones to which they make *puja* and offer cooked rice at the sowing time. The Kadu Kurumba of Mysore bury children but cremate adults ; there is a separate house in each village for unmarried girls and another at the end of the village for unmarried males.

The *Vedda* of Ceylon have long black coarse wavy or slightly curly hair. The cephalic index is 70.5, the nose is

The Vedda. depressed at the root, almost platyrrhine ; the broad face is remarkably orthognathous and the forehead is slightly retreating with prominent brow arches ; the lips are thin, and the skin is dark brown. The stature is extremely low, only 1.533 m. (5 ft. 0½ in.). The Coast and less pure Vedda average 43 mm. (1¾ in.). taller and have broader heads. The true Vedda are a grave but happy people, quiet, upright, hospitable with a strong love of liberty. Lying and theft are unknown. They are timid and have a great fear of strangers. The bow and arrow are their only weapons and the arrow tipped with iron obtained from the Sinhalese forms a universal tool. They speak a modified Sinhali, but employ only one numeral and count with sticks. They live under rock shelters or in simple huts made of boughs. They are strictly monogamous and live in isolated families with no chiefs and have no regular clan meetings. Each section of the Vedda had in earlier days its own hunting grounds where fish, game, honey, and yams constituted their sole food. The wild Vedda simply leave their dead in a cave, which is then deserted. The three things that loom largest

in the native mind are hunting, honey, and the cult of the
dead. The last constitutes almost the whole of the religious
life and magical practices of the people ; it is the *motif* of
almost every dance and may have been the source of all.
After a death they perform certain dances and rites through a
shaman in connection with the recently departed ghost, *yaka*.
They also propitiate powerful *yaku*, male and female, by
sacrifices and ceremonial dances.[1]

The *Sakai* or *Senoi* are jungle folk, some of whom have
mixed with Semang and other peoples. Their skin is of a
medium brown colour. Their hair is long, mainly
wavy or loosely curly, and black with a reddish   The Sakai.
tinge. The average stature may be taken to be from 1.5 m.
to 1.55 m. (59 to 61 inches), the head index varies from about
77 to 81. The face is fairly broad, with prominent cheek-bones
and brow ridges ; the low broad nose has spreading alae and
short concave ridge ; the lips are thick but not everted. They
are largely nomadic, and their agriculture is of the most primitive description, their usual implement being the digging stick.
Their houses are built on the ground and as a rule are rectangular in plan though occasionally conical, and huts are
sometimes built in trees as refuges from wild beasts. A scanty
garment of bark cloth was formerly worn, and, like the Semang,
they make fringed girdles from a black thread-like fungus.
Their distinctive weapon is the blow-pipe which they have
brought to great perfection, and their food consists in jungle
produce, including many poisonous roots and tubers which
they have learnt how to treat, so as to render them innocuous.
They do not make canoes and rarely use rafts. In the marriage
ceremony the man has to chase the girl round a mound of
earth and catch her before she has encircled it a third time.
The marriage tie is strictly observed. Each village has a
petty chief, whose influence is purely personal. Individual
property does not exist, only family property. Cultivation is
also communal. The inhabitants of the upper heaven consist
of Tuhan or Peng, the " god " of the Sakai and a giantess
named " Granny Long-breasts " who washes sin-blackened
human souls in hot water ; the good souls ultimately go to a
cloud-land. There are numerous demons and whenever the

---

[1] P. and F. Sarasin, *Ergebnisse Naturwissenschaftlicher Forschungen auf Ceylon.
Die Steinzeit auf Ceylon,* 1908 ; H. Parker, *Ancient Ceylon,* 1909. The most
complete account is given by C. G. and B. Z. Seligman, *The Veddas,* 1911.

Sakai have done wrong Tuhan gives the demons leave to attack them, and there is no contending against his decree. He is not prayed to, as his will is unalterable.[1]

The *Toala* of the south-west peninsula of the Celebes are at base, according to the Sarasins,[2] a Pre-Dravidian people,

The Toala. though some mixture with other races has taken place. The hair is very wavy and even curly, the skin darkish brown, the head low brachycephalic (index 82) and the stature 1.575 m. (5 ft. 2 in.). The face is somewhat short with very broad nose and thick lips. Possibly the *Ulu Ayar* of west Borneo who are related to the Land Dayaks may be partly of Pre-Dravidian origin and other traces of this race will probably be found in the East India Archipelago.[3]

Australia resembles South Africa in the arid conditions characterising the interior, the eastern range of mountains

Australia: Physical Conditions. precipitating the warm moisture-laden winds from the Pacific. As a result of the restricted rainfall there is no river system of importance except that of the Murray and its tributary the Darling. In the north and north-east, owing to heavier rainfall, there are numerous water-courses, but they do not open up the interior of the country. The lack of uniformity in the water supply has a far-reaching effect on all living beings. The arid conditions, the irregularity and short duration of the rainfall oblige the natives to be continually migrating, and prevent these unsettled bands from ever attaining any size, indeed they are sometimes hard pressed to obtain enough food to keep alive.

It may be assumed that the backwardness of the culture of the Australians is due partly to the low state of culture of their ancestors when they arrived in the country, and partly to the peculiar character of the country as well as of its flora and fauna, since Australia has never been stocked with wild animals dangerous to human life, or with any suitable for domestication. The relative isolation from other peoples has had a retarding effect and the Australian has developed largely along his own lines without the impetus given by competition with other peoples. Records of simple migration are rare.

---

[1] W. W. Skeat and C. O. Blagden, *Pagan Races of the Malay Peninsula*, 1906 ; R. Martin, *Die Inlandstämme der Malayischen Halbinseln*, 1905.

[2] Fritz Sarasin, *Versuch einer Anthropologie der Insel Celebes. Zweiter Teil : Die Varietäten des Menschen auf Celebes*, 1906.

[3] A. C. Haddon, Appendix to C. Hose and W. McDougall, *The Pagan Tribes of Borneo*, II. 1912.

There have been no waves of aggression, and intertribal feuds are not very serious affairs. The Australians have never influenced any other peoples and they are doomed gradually to disappear.

Baldwin Spencer says "In the matter of personal appearance while conforming generally to what is known as the Australian type, there is considerable variation. The man varies from, approximately, a maximum of 6 ft. 3 in. to a minimum of 5 ft. 2 in. . . . As a general rule, few of them are taller than 5 ft. 8 in. The women vary between 5 ft. 9 in. and 4 ft. 9 in. Their average height is not more than 5 ft. 2 in. The brow ridges are strongly marked, especially in the man, and the forehead slopes back. The nose is broad with the root deep set. In colour the native is dark chocolate brown, not black. The hair . . . may be almost straight, decidedly wavy—its usual feature—or almost, but never really, frizzly. . . . The beard also may be well developed or almost absent." [1] The skull is dolichocephalic with an average cranial index of 72, prognathous and platyrrhine.

Physical
Type.

There has been much speculation with regard to the origin of the present Australian race. According to Baldwin Spencer "There can be no doubt but that in past times the whole of the continent, including Tasmania, was occupied by one race. This original, and probably Negritto [2] population, at an early period, was widely spread over Malaysia and Australia including Tasmania, which at that time was not shut off by Bass Strait. The Tasmanians had no boats capable of crossing the latter and [it is assumed that their ancestors] must have gone over on land." [3]

Australian
Origins.

Subsequently when the land sank a remnant of the old ulotrichous population " was thus left stranded in Tasmania, where *Homo tasmanianus* survived until he came in contact with Europeans and was exterminated." He had frizzly hair. " His weapons and implements were of the most primitive kind ; long pointed unbarbed spears, no spear thrower, no boomerang, simple throwing stick and only the crudest form of chipped stone axes, knives and scrapers that were never

[1] *Federal Handbook, Brit. Ass. for Advancement of Science*, 1914, p. 36.
[2] The Tasmanians can scarcely be termed Negritoes. The important point to be noted is that this early population was ulotrichous, cf. p. 159.
[3] *Loc. cit.* p. 34. Or the Strait may then have been very narrow.

hafted. Unfortunately of his organisation, customs, and beliefs we know but little in detail."[1]

It is now generally held that at a later date an immigration of a people in a somewhat higher stage of culture took place; these are regarded by some as belonging to the Dravidian, and by others, and with more probability, to the Pre-Dravidian race. J. Mathew[2] suggests that " the two races are represented by the two primary classes, or phratries, of Australian society, which were generally designated by names indicating a contrast of colour, such as eaglehawk and crow. The crow, black cockatoo, etc., would represent the Tasmanian element; the eaglehawk, white cockatoo, etc., the so-called Dravidian." Baldwin Spencer does not think that the moiety names lend any serious support to the theory of the mixture of two races differing in colour. He goes on to say, "Mr Matthew also postulates a comparatively recent slight infusion of Malay blood in the northern half of Australia. There is, however, practically no evidence of Malay infusion. One of the most striking features of the Malay is his long, lank hair, and yet it is just in these north parts that the most frizzly hair is met with."[1]

As concerns linguistics S. H. Ray says, "There is no evidence of an African, Andaman, Papuan, or Malay con-

Evidence from Language and Culture. nection with the Australian languages. There are reasons for regarding the Australian as in a similar morphological stage to the Dravidian, but there is no genealogical relationship proved."[3] No connection has yet been proved between the Australian languages and the Austronesian or Oceanic branch of the Austric family of languages, first systematically described by W. Schmidt.[4] The study of Australian languages is particularly difficult owing to the very few serviceable grammars and dictionaries, and the large number of very incomplete vocabularies scattered about in inaccessible works and journals. The main conclusion to which Schmidt has arrived[5] is that the Australian languages are not, as had been supposed, a mainly uniform group. Though

---

[1] *Loc. cit.* p. 34.

[2] *Two Representative Tribes of Queensland*, 1910, p. 30.

[3] *Reports Camb. Exped. to Torres Straits*, III. 1907, p. 528.

[4] *Die Mon-Khmer Völker*, 1906. Schmidt has for many years studied the Australian languages and has published his results in *Anthropos*, Vols. VII., VIII. 1912, 1913, from which, and also from *Man*, No. 8, 1908, the following summarised extracts are taken.

[5] See *Man*, No. 8, 1908, pp. 184–5.

over the greater part of Australia languages possess strong common elements, North Australia has languages showing no similarities in vocabulary and very few in grammar with that larger group or with each other. The area of the North Australian languages is included in a line from south of Roebuck Bay in the west to Cape Flattery in the east, with a southward bend to include Arunta (Aranda), interrupted by a branch of southern languages running up north down Flinders and Leichhardt rivers.[1] The area contains two or three linguistic groups, best distinguished by their terminations which consist respectively of vowels and consonants, the oldest group ; vowels alone, the latest group ; and vowels and liquids, probably representing a transition between the two.

In South Australia, though differences occur, the languages possess common features both in grammar and vocabulary, having similar personal pronouns, and certain words for parts of the body in common. Linguistic differences are associated with differences in social grouping, the area of purely vowel endings coinciding with the area of the 2-class system and matrilinear descent, while the area of liquid endings is partly coterminous with the 4-class system and (often) patrilinear succession.

Schmidt endeavours to trace the connection between the distribution of languages with that of types of social groupings, more particularly in connection with the culture zones which Graebner [2] has traced throughout the Pacific area, representing successive waves **Four successive Immigrations.** of migration. The first immigration, corresponding with Graebner's *Ur-period*, is represented by languages with postposed genitive, the earliest stratum being pure only in Tasmania ; remnants of the first stratum and a second stratum occur in Victoria, and remnants of the second stratum to the north and north-east. According to Schmidt this cultural stratum is characterised by absence of group or marriage totemism, and presence of sex patrons (" sex-totemism "). The second immigration is represented by languages with preposition of the genitive, initial *r* and *l*, vowel and explosive

---

[1] See the map constructed by P. W. Schmidt and P. K. Streit, *Anthropos*, VII. 1912.

[2] See *Globus,* XC. 1906, and " Die sozialen Systeme d. Südsee," *Ztschr. f. Sozialwissenschaft*, XI. 1908. Schmidt's divergence from Graebner's views are dealt with in *Zeitschr. f. Ethnologie*, 1909, pp. 372–5, and *Anthropos*, VII. 1912, p. 246 ff.

endings, and is found fairly pure only in the extreme north-west and north, and in places in the north-east.   The great multiplicity of languages belonging to this stratum may be attributed to the predominance of the strictly local type of totem-groups.   These are the languages of Graebner's "totem-culture."   The third immigration is represented by languages with preposition of the genitive, no initial *r* and *l*, and purely vowel terminations.   These are the languages of the south central group of tribes with a 2-class system and matrilinear descent.   This uniform group has the largest area and has influenced the whole mass of Australian languages, only North Australia and Tasmania remaining immune.   Their sociological structure with no localisation of totems and classes contributed to their power of expansion.   The fourth immigration is represented by languages of an intermediate type, with vowel and liquid endings but no initial *r* and *l*.   These are the tribes with 4-class and 8-class systems, universal father-right (proving the strong influence of older totemic ideas), curious fertility rites, conception ideas and migration myths.

It will be seen that Schmidt's conclusions confute the evolutionary theory developed by Frazer, Hartland, Howitt,

Earlier Views.   Spencer and Gillen, Durkheim and (in part) Andrew Lang, that Australia was essentially homogeneous in fundamental ideas which have developed differently on account of geographic and climatic variation. Schmidt's view is that Australia was entered successively by a number of entirely different tribes, so that the variation now met with is due to radical diversities and to the numerous intermixtures arising from migrations and stratifications of peoples.   The linguistic data dispose of the idea that the oldest tribes with mother-right, 2-class system, traces of group-marriage, and lack of moral and religious ideas live in the centre, and that from thence advancement radiated towards the coast bringing about father-right, abandonment of class system and totemism, individual marriage, and higher ethical and religious ideas.   On the contrary it would appear that the centre of the continent is the great channel in which movements are still taking place ; the older peoples are driven out towards the margin and there preserve the old sociological, ethical and religious conditions.   In fact, the older the people, judging from their linguistic stratum, the less one finds among them what has been assumed to be the initial stage for Central

Australia.[1] These are Schmidt's views and they confirm the cultural results established by Graebner. But as the whole question of the culture layers in the Pacific is still under discussion it is inadvisable at this stage of our knowledge to make any definite statements. It is worth noting, however, that [2] the distribution of simple burial of the dead coincides in the main with Schmidt's South Australian language area, and the area roughly enclosed on the east by long. 140° E. and the north by lat. 20° S. appears to form a technological province distinct from the rest of Australia.[3]

Rarely can the Australian depend on regular supplies of food. He feeds on flesh, fish, grubs and insects, and wild vegetable food ; probably everything that is edible is eaten. Cannibalism is widely spread, but human flesh is nowhere a regular article of food. Clothing, apart from ornament, is rarely worn, but in the south, skin cloaks and fur aprons are fairly common. Scarification of the body is frequent and conspicuous. The men usually let their hair grow long, and the women keep theirs short. Dwellings are of the simplest character, usually merely breakwinds or slight huts, but where there is a large supply of vegetable food, huts are made of boughs covered with bark or grass and are sometimes coated with clay. Implements are made of shell, bone, wood and stone. Baldwin Spencer remarks, " It is not too much to say that at the present time we can parallel amongst Australian stone weapons all the types known in Europe under the names Chellean, Mousterian, Aurignacian, etc. . . . The terms Eolithic, Palaeolithic, and Neolithic do not apply in Australia as indicating either time periods or levels of culture." [4] Spears and wooden clubs are universal, and the use of the spear-thrower is generally distributed. The boomerang is found almost throughout Australia ; the variety that returns when it is thrown is as a rule only a plaything or for throwing at birds. The forms of the various implements vary in different parts of the country and in some districts certain implements may be entirely absent. For example the boomerang is not found in the northern parts of Cape York peninsula or of the Northern Territory, and the

Material Culture.

[1] *Anthropos*, VII. 1912, pp. 247, 248.
[2] N. W. Thomas, " The Disposal of the Dead in Australia," *Folklore*, XIX. 1908.
[3] A. R. Brown, MS.
[4] *Federal Handbook, British Association for the Advancement of Science*, 1914, p. 76.

spear-thrower is absent from south-east Queensland. Bows
and arrows are unknown and pottery making does not occur.
Rafts are made of one or more logs, and the commonest form
of canoe is that made of a single sheet of bark. Dug-outs
occur in a few places, and both single and double outriggers are
found only on the Queensland coast. These sporadic occurrences give additional support to the modern view that the
racial and cultural history of Australia is by no means so
simple as has till lately been assumed.[1]

Students of Australian sociology have been so much impressed with certain prominent features of social organisation
that they have paid insufficient attention to
kinship and the family ; the former has however
recently been investigated by A. R. Brown,[2] while information
concerning the latter has been carefully sifted by B. Malinowski.[3]
The main features of social groupings are the tribe, the local
groups, the classes, the totemic clans and the families. A tribe
is composed of a number of local groups and these are perpetuated in the same tracts by the sons, who hunt over the
grounds of their fathers ; this is the " local organisation."
The local group is the only political unit, and *intra*-group
justice has been extended to *inter*-group justice, where the
units of reference are not based on kinship ; this may be regarded as the earliest stage of what is known as International
Law.[4] In the so-called " social organisation," the tribe as a
community is divided into two parts (moieties or phratries),
which are quite distinct from the local groups, though rarely
they may be coincident. Each moiety may be sub-divided
into two or four exogamous sections which are generally called
" classes " and are peculiar to Australia. Descent in the classes
is as a rule indirect matrilineal or indirect patrilineal, that is to
say, while the child still belongs to its mother's or father's
moiety (as the case may be) it is assigned to the class to which
the mother or the father does not belong ; but the grand-
children belong to the class of a grandmother or grandfather.
In diagram I (below) *A* and *C* are classes of one moiety,
B and *D* those of the other. Thus when *A* man marries

Sociology.

---

[1] A. C. Haddon, " The Outrigger Canoes of Torres Straits and North Queensland," *Essays and Studies Presented to W. Ridgeway*, 1913, p. 621, and W. H. R.
Rivers, " The Contact of Peoples," in the same volume, p. 479.
[2] *Man*, No. 32, 1910.
[3] *The Family among the Australian Aborigines*, 1913.
[4] G. C. Wheeler, *The Tribe, and intertribal relations in Australia*, 1910, p. 163.

B woman the children are D. B man marries A woman and
the children are C and so on.   When there are four classes in
each moiety the diagram works out as follows (II) : [1]

$$\begin{pmatrix} A & = & B \\ C & = & D \end{pmatrix} \qquad \begin{pmatrix} \begin{pmatrix} A' & = & B' \\ A'' & = & B'' \\ C' & = & D' \\ C'' & = & D'' \end{pmatrix} \end{pmatrix}$$

I   II

Very important in social life are the initiation ceremonies
by means of which a youth is admitted to the status of tribal
manhood.   These ceremonies vary greatly from tribe to tribe
but they agree in certain fundamental points.   " (1) They
begin at the age of puberty.   (2) During the initiation ceremonies the women play an important part.   (3) At the close
of the first part of the ceremonies, such as that of tooth
knocking out or circumcision, a definite performance is enacted
emblematic of the fact that the youths have passed out of
the control of the women.   (4) During the essential parts the
women are typically absent and the youths are shown the bull-
roarer, have the secret beliefs explained to them and are
instructed in the moral precepts and customs, including food
restrictions, that they must henceforth observe under severe
penalties.   (5) The last grade is not passed through until a
man is quite mature." [2]

Practically universal is the existence of a grouping of
individuals under the names of plants, animals or various
objects ; these are termed totems and the human
groups are termed totem clans.   The members   Totemism.
of a totem clan commonly believe themselves to be actually
descended from or related to their totem, and all members of
a clan, whatever tribe they may belong to, are regarded as
brethren, who have mutual duties, prohibitions and privileges.
Thus a member of a totem clan must help and never injure
any fellow member.   " Speaking generally it may be said that
every totemic group has certain ceremonies associated with it
and that these refer to old totemic ancestors.   In all tribes
they form part of a secret ritual in which only the initiated
may take part.   In most tribes a certain number are shown

[1] A. R. Brown, "Marriage and Descent in North Australia," *Man*, No. 32, 1910.
[2] W. Baldwin Spencer, *loc. cit.* p. 50.

to the youths during the early stages of initiation, but at a later period he sees many more." [1]

In several tribes, and probably it was very general, certain magical ceremonies were performed to render the totem abundant or efficacious. The sex patron (" sex totem "), when the women have one animal, such as the owlet night-jar associated with them, and the men another, such as the bat; and the guardian genius (mis-called "individual totem"), acquired by dreaming of some animal, are of rare occurrence.

The individual family has been shown by Malinowski [2] to be " a unit playing an important part in the social life of the **The Family.** natives and well defined by a number of moral, customary and legal norms; it is further determined by the sexual division of labour, the aboriginal mode of living, and especially by the intimate relation between the parents and children. The individual relation between husband and wife (marriage) is rooted in the unity of the family . . . and in the well-defined, though not always exclusive, sexual right the husband acquires over his wife." All sexual licence is regulated by and subject to strict rules. The *Pirrauru* custom, by which individuals are allocated accessory spouses, " proves that the relationship involved does not possess the character of marriage. For it completely differs from marriage in nearly all the essential points by which marriage in Australia is defined. And above all the Pirrauru relation does not seem to involve the facts of family life in its true sense " (p. 298).

A. R. Brown [3] asserts that so far as our information goes, the only method of regulating marriage is by means of the **Kinship.** relationship system. In every tribe there is a law to the effect that a man may only marry women who stand to him in a certain relationship, and there is no evidence that there is any other method of regulating marriage. The so-called class rule by which a man of a special division or group is required to marry a woman of another division is merely the law of relationship stated in a less exact form. It is the fact that a man may only marry a relative of a certain kind that necessitates the marrying into a particular relationship division. The rule of totemic exogamy, according to A. R. Brown, is equally seen to have no existence apart from the

[1] W. Baldwin Spencer, *loc. cit.* p. 44.
[2] *The Family among the Australian Aborigines*, 1913, p. 304.
[3] MS.

relationship rule. Where a totemic group is a clan and consists of relations all of one line of descent, a man is prohibited from marrying a woman of his own group by the ordinary rule of relationship. On the other hand, where the totemic group is not a clan, but is a local group (as in the Burduna tribe) or a cult society (as in the Arunta tribe) there is no rule prohibiting a man from marrying a woman of the same totemic group as himself. The so-called rule of local exogamy in some tribes (perhaps in all) is merely a result of the fact that the local group is a clan, *i.e.* a group of persons related in one line of descent only. Only two methods of regulating marriage are known to exist in the greater part of Australia : [1] Type I. A man marries the daughter of one of the men he denotes by the same term as his mother's brother. Type II. A man marries a woman who is the daughter's daughter of some man whom he denotes by the same term as his mother's mother's brother. In either case he may not marry any other kind of relative. The existence of two phratries or moieties or four named divisions (" classes ") in a tribe conveys no information whatever as to the marriage rule of the tribe. The term " class " and " sub-class," according to A. R. Brown, had better be discarded as writers use them to denote several totally distinct kinds of divisions.

The tribe has collecting and hunting rights over an area with recognised limits, smaller communities down to the family unit having similar rights within the tribal boundaries. In some cases a tribe which had no stone suitable for making stone implements within its own boundaries was allowed to send tribal messengers to a quarry to procure what was needed without molestation, though Howitt speaks of family ownership of quarries.[2] Implements are personal property. An extensive system of intertribal communication and exchange is carried on, apparently by recognised middlemen, and tribes meet on certain occasions at established trade centres for a regulated barter.

Property and Trade.

Beneficent and malevolent magic are universally practised and totemism possesses a religious besides a social aspect. An emotional relation often exists between the members of a totem clan and their totem, and the latter are believed at times to warn or protect

Magic and Religion.

[1] A. R. Brown, " Three Tribes of Western Australia," *Journ. Roy. Anthr. Inst.* XLIII. 1913.

[2] A. W. Howitt, *The Native Tribes of South-east Australia*, 1904, p. 311.

their human kinsmen. It may be noted that the widely spread and elaborate ceremonies designed to render the totem prolific or to ensure its abundance, though performed solely by members of the totem clan concerned, are less for their own benefit than for that of the community.[1] Owing *perhaps to the* difficulty of distinguishing between the purely social and the religious institutions of primitive peoples great diversity of opinion prevails even amongst the best observers regarding the religious views of the Australian aborigines. The existence of a " tribal All-Father " is perhaps most clearly emphasised by A. W. Howitt,[2] who finds this belief widespread in the whole of Victoria and New South Wales, up to the eastern boundaries of the tribes of the Darling River. Amongst those of New South Wales are the Euahlayi, whom K. Langloh Parker describes[3] as having a more advanced theology and a more developed worship (including prayers, pp. 79–80) than any other Australian tribe. These now eat their hereditary totem without scruple—a sure sign that the totemic system is dying out, although still outwardly in full force. Amongst the Arunta, Kaitish, and the other Central and Northern tribes studied by Spencer and Gillen, totemism still survives, and totems are even assigned to the mysterious *Iruntarinia* entities, vague and invisible incarnations of the ghosts of ancestors who lived in the *Alcheringa* time, the dim remote past at the beginning of everything. These are far more powerful than living men, because their spirit part is associated with the so-called *churinga*, consisting of stones, pieces of wood or any other objects which are deemed sacred as possessing a kind of *mana* which makes the yams and grass to grow, enables a man to capture game, and so forth. " That the *churinga* are simply objects endowed with *mana* is the happy suggestion of Sidney Hartland[4] whose explanation has dispelled the dense fog of mystification hitherto enveloping the strange beliefs and observances of these Central and Northern tribes."[5] N. W. Thomas[6] reviews the whole question of Australian religion, and after describing Twanjiraka,

---

[1] W. Baldwin Spencer and F. J. Gillen, *The Native Tribes of Central Australia,* 1899, Chap. vi., and *The Northern Tribes of Central Australia,* 1904, Chap. ix.

[2] *The Native Tribes of South-east Australia,* 1904, p. 500.

[3] *The Euahlayi Tribe,* 1905.

[4] Presidential Address (Section H) Brit. Ass. York, 1906.

[5] A. H. Keane, Art. " Australasia," in Hastings' *Encyclopaedia of Religion and Ethics,* 1909, p. 244.

[6] *The Natives of Australia,* 1906, Chap. xiii. Religion.

Malbanga and Ulthaana, of the Arunta, Baiame or Byamee, famous in anthropological controversy,[1] Daramulun of the Yuin, Mungan-ngaua (our father) of the Kurnai, Nurrundere of the Narrinyeri, Bunjil or Pundjel, often called Mamingorak (our father) of Victoria, and others, he concludes, "These are by no means the only gods known to Australian tribes; on the contrary it can hardly be definitely asserted that there is or was any tribe which had not some such belief." [2]

[1] E. B. Tylor, *Journ. Anthr, Inst.* XXI. p. 292 ; A. Lang, *Magic and Religion*, p. 25 ; *Myth, Ritual and Religion*, Chap. XII. ; K. Langloh Parker, *The Euahlayi Tribe*, 1905, Chap. II. ; M. F. v. Leonhardi, *Anthropos*, IV. 1909, p. 1065, and many others.

[2] The following should be consulted :
Original memoirs : C. Strehlow, *Die Aranda- und Loritza-Stämme in Zentral-Australien*, 1907 ; W. E. Roth, *Ethnological Studies among the north-west-central Queensland Aborigines*, 1897 ; *North Queensland Ethnography, Bulletins* 1–8, 1901–6, and *Bulletins* 9–18 ; *Records of the Australian Museum*, VI.–VIII. Sydney, 1890–1910.
Compilations and discussions : E. Durkheim, *The Elementary Forms of the Religious Life : a Study in Religious Sociology* (translated by J. W. Swain), a very suggestive study based on Australian custom and belief ; J. G. Frazer, *Exogamy and Totemism*, I. 1910 ; *The Belief in Immortality and the Worship of the Dead*, I. pp. 67–169, 1913.

CHAPTER XIII

THE CAUCASIC PEOPLES

CONSPECTUS.

Present Range. *All the extra-tropical habitable lands,
except Chinese empire, Japan, and the Arctic zone ; inter-
tropical America, Arabia, India, and Indonesia ;*
Distribution. *sporadically everywhere.*

Three main types :—1. Southern dolichocephals, **Mediter-
ranean;** *2. Northern Dolichocephals,* **Nordic;**
Physical
Characters. *3. Brachycephals,* **Alpine.**

Hair : *1. Very dark brown or black, wiry, curly or ringletty. 2. Very light brown, flaxen, or red, rather long, straight
or wavy, smooth and glossy. 3. Light chestnut or reddish brown,
wavy, rather short and dull. All oval in section ; beard of all
full, bushy, straight, or wavy, often lighter than hair of head,
sometimes very long.* **Colour :** *1. Very variable—white, light
olive, all shades of brown and even blackish (Eastern Hamites
and others). 2 Florid. 3. Pale white, swarthy or very light
brown.* **Skull :** *1 and 2 long (72 to 79) ; 3 round (85 to 87
and upwards) ; all orthognathous. Cheek-bone of all small,
never projecting laterally, sometimes rather high (some Berbers*

438

and Scotch). **Nose,** *mostly large, narrow, straight, arched or hooked, sometimes rather broad, heavy, concave and short.* **Eyes :** 1. *Black or deep brown, but also blue.* 2. *Mainly blue.* 3. *Brown, hazel-grey and black.*

Stature : 1. *Undersized (mean 1.630 m. 5 ft. 4 in.), but variable (some Hamites, Hindus, and others medium or tall).* 2. *Tall (mean 1.728 m. 5 ft. 8 or 9 in.).* 3. *Medium (mean 5 ft. 6 in.), but also very tall (Indonesians 1.750 m. to 1.830 m. 5 ft. 9 to 6 ft.).* **Lips,** *mostly rather full and well-shaped, but sometimes thin, or upper lip very long (many Irish), and under lip pendulous (many Jews).* **Arms,** *rather short as compared with Negro.* **Legs,** *shapely, with calves usually well developed.* **Feet :** 1 *and* 3 *small with high instep ;* 2 *rather large.*

Temperament : 1 *and* 3. *Brilliant, quick-witted, excitable, and impulsive ; sociable and courteous, but fickle, untrustworthy, and even treacherous (Iberian, South Italian) ;* Mental
Characters. *often atrociously cruel (many Slavs, Persians, Semites, Indonesians and even South Europeans) ; æsthetic sense highly, ethic·slightly developed. All brave, imaginative, musical, and richly endowed intellectually.* 2. *Earnest, energetic, and enterprising ; steadfast, solid, and stolid ; outwardly reserved, thoughtful, and deeply religious ; humane, firm; but not normally cruel.*

Speech, *mostly of the inflecting order with strong tendency towards analytical forms ; very few stock languages (Aryan, Ibero-Hamito-Semitic), except in the Caucasus, where stock languages of highly agglutinating types are numerous, and in Indonesia, where one agglutinating stock language prevails.*

Religion, *mainly Monotheistic, with or without priesthood and sacrifice (Jewish, Christian, Muhammadan) ; polytheistic and animistic in parts of Caucasus, India, Indonesia, and Africa. Gross superstitions still prevalent in many places.*

Culture, *generally high—all arts, industries, science, philosophy and letters in a flourishing state now almost everywhere except in Africa and Indonesia, and still progressive. In some regions civilisation dates from an early period (Egypt, South Arabia, Babylonia ; the Minoan, Hellenic, Hittite, and Italic cultures). Indonesians and many Hamites still rude, with primitive usages, few arts, no science or letters, and cannibalism prevalent in some places (Gallaland).*

Mediterranean type : *most Iberians, Corsicans, Sards,*

*Sicilians, Italians; some Greeks; Berbers and other Ha-
mites; Arabs and other Semites; some Hindus;*
**Main
Divisions.** *Dravidians, Todas, Ainus, Indonesians, some
Polynesians.*

Nordic type: *Scandinavians, North-west Germans,
Dutch, Flemings, most English, Scotch, some Irish, Anglo-
Americans, Anglo-Australasians, English and Dutch of
S. Africa; Thrako-Hellenes. true Kurds, most West Persians,
Afghans, Dards and Siah-post Kafirs.*

Alpine type: *most French, South Germans, Swiss and
Tyrolese; Russians, Poles, Chekhs, Yugo-Slavs; some Al-
banians and Rumanians; Armenians, Tajiks (East Persians),
Galchas.*

It is a remarkable fact that the Caucasic division of the
human family, of which nearly all students of the subject are
**General
Considerations.** members, with which we are in any case, so to
say, on the most intimate terms, and with the
constituent elements of which we might consequently be supposed to be best acquainted, is the most
debatable field in the whole range of anthropological studies.
Why this should be so is not at first sight quite apparent,
though the phenomenon may perhaps be partly explained by
the consideration that the component parts are really of a more
complex character, and thus present more intricate problems
for solution, than those of any other division. But to some
extent this would also seem to be one of those cases in which
we fail to see the wood for the trees. To put it plainly, few
will venture to deny that the inherent difficulties of the subject
have in recent times been rather increased than diminished by
the bold and often mutually destructive theories, and, in some
instances one might add, the really wild speculations put
forward in the earnest desire to remove the endless obscurities
in which the more fundamental questions are undoubtedly still
involved. Controversial matter which seemed thrashed out
has been reopened, several fresh factors have been brought
into play, and the warfare connected with such burning topics
as Aryan origins, Ibero-Pelasgic relations, European round-
heads and long-heads, has acquired renewed intensity amid
the rival theories of eminent champions of new ideas.
The question is not made any simpler by the frequent
attacks that have been directed from more than one quarter

against the long-established Caucasic terminology, and well-supported objections are raised to the use of such time-honoured names as " Hamitic," " Semitic," and even " Caucasic " itself. But no really satisfactory substitute for "Caucasic" has yet been suggested, and it is doubtful if any name could be found sufficiently comprehensive to include all the races, long-headed and short-headed, fair and dark, tall and short, that we are at present content to group under this non-committal heading. Undoubtedly the term " Caucasic " cannot be defended on ethnical grounds. " Nowhere else in the world probably is so heterogeneous a lot of people, languages and religions gathered together in one place as along the chain of the Caucasus mountains." [1] But we are no more called upon to believe that the " Caucasic " peoples originated in the Caucasus, than that the Semites are all descendants of Shem or Hamites of Ham. " Caucasic " has one claim that can never be disputed, that of priority, and it would be well if innovators in these matters were to take to heart the sober language of Ehrenreich, who reminds us that the accepted names are, what they ought to be, " purely conventional," and " historically justified," and " should be held as valid until something better can be found to take their place." [2] It was considerations such as these, weighing so strongly in favour of current usage, that induced me *stare per vias antiquas* in the *Ethnology*, and consequently also in the present work. Hence, here as there, the Caucasic Division retains its title, together with those of its main subdivisions—Hamitic, Semitic, Keltic, Slavic, Hellenic, Teutonic, Iranic, Galchic and so on.

The chief exception is "Aryan," a linguistic expression forced by the philologists into the domain of Ethnology, where it has no place or meaning. There was of course a time when a community, or group of communities, existed probably in the steppe region between the Carpathians and the Hindu-Kush,[3]

---

[1] *The Races of Europe : A Sociological Study*, W. Z. Ripley, 1900, p. 437.

[2] " Diese Namen sind natürlich rein conventionell. Sie sind historisch berechtigt . . . und mögen Geltung behalten, so lange wir keine zutrefferenden an ihre Stelle setzen können " (*Anthropologische Studien*, etc., p. 15).

[3] E. Meyer, *Geschichte des Altertums*, 1909, l. 2, discussing the original home of the Indo-Europeans (§ 561, *Das Problem der Heimat und Ausbreitung der Indogermanen*) remarks (p. 800) that the discovery of Tocharish (Sieg und Siegling, " Tocharish, die Sprache der Indo-skythen," *Sitz. d. Berl. Ak.* 1908, p. 915 ff.), a language belonging apparently to the *centum* (Western and European) group, overthrows all earlier conceptions as to the distribution of the Indogermans and gives weight to the hypothesis of their Asiatic origin.

by whom the Aryan mother-tongue was evolved, and who still for a time presented a certain uniformity in their physical characters, were, in fact, of Aryan speech and type. But while their Aryan speech persists in endlessly modified forms, they have themselves long disappeared as a distinct race, merged in the countless other races on whom they, perhaps as conquerors, imposed their Aryan language. Hence we can and must speak of Aryan tongues, and of an Aryan linguistic family, which continues to flourish and spread over the globe. But of an Aryan race there can be no further question since the absorption of the original stock in a hundred other races in remote prehistoric times. Where comprehensive references have to be made, I therefore substitute for Aryans and Aryan race the expression peoples of Aryan speech, at least wherever the unqualified term Aryan might lead to misunderstandings.

This way of looking at the question, which has now become more thorny than ever, has the signal advantage of being indifferent to any preconceived theories regarding the physical characters of that long vanished proto-Aryan race. How great this advantage is may be judged from the mere statement that, while German anthropologists are still almost to a man loyal to the traditional view that the first Aryans were best represented by the tall, long-headed, tawny-haired, blue-eyed Teutonic barbarians of Tacitus—who, Virchow tells us, have completely disappeared from sight in the present population —the Italian school, or at least its chief exponent, Sergi, was equally convinced that the picture was a myth, that such Aryans never existed, that "the true primitive Aryans were not long, but round-headed, not fair but dark, not tall but short, and are in fact to-day best represented by the round-headed Kelts, Slavs, and South Germans."[1]

The fact is that the Aryan prototype has vanished as completely as has the Aryan mother-tongue, and can be conjecturally restored only by processes analogous to those by which Schleicher and other philologists have endeavoured with dubious success to restore the organic Aryan speech as constituted before the dispersion.

But here arises the more important question, by what right are so many and such diverse peoples grouped together and ticketed "Caucasians"? Are they to be really taken as

[1] " Io non dubito di denominare *aria* questa stirpe, etc." (*Umbri, Italici, Arii*, Bologna, 1897, p. 14, and elsewhere).

objectively one, or are they merely artificial groupings, arbitrarily arranged abstractions ?   Certainly this
Caucasic division consists apparently of the   **Constituent Elements.**
most heterogeneous elements, more so than
perhaps any other.   Hence it seems to require a strong
mental effort to sweep into a single category, however elastic,
so many different peoples—Europeans, North Africans, West
Asiatics, Iranians and others all the way to the Indo-Gangetic
plains and uplands, whose complexion presents every shade of
colour, except yellow, from white to the deepest brown or
even black.

But they are grouped together in a single division, because
of certain common characteristics, and because, as pointed out
by Ehrenreich, who himself emphasises these objections, their
substantial uniformity speaks to the eye that sees below the
surface.   At the first glance, except perhaps in a few extreme
cases for which it would be futile to create independent categories, we recognise a common racial stamp in the facial
expression, the structure of the hair, partly also the bodily
proportions, in all of which points they agree more with each
other than with the other main divisions.   Even in the case
of certain black or very dark races, such as the Beja, Somali,
and a few other Eastern Hamites, we are reminded instinctively
more of Europeans or Berbers than of negroes, thanks to their
more regular features and brighter expression.   " Those who
will accept nothing unless it can be measured, weighed, and
numbered, may think perhaps that according to modern notions
this appeal to the outward expression is unscientific.   Nevertheless nobody can deny the evidence of the obvious physical
differences between Caucasians, African Negroes, Mongols,
Australians, and so on.   After all, physical anthropology itself
dates only from the moment when we became conscious of
these differences, even before we were able to give them exact
expression by measurements.   It was precisely the general
picture that spoke powerfully and directly to the eye." [1]   The
argument need not here be pursued further, as it will receive
abundant illustration in the details to follow.

Since the discovery of the New and the Austral Worlds,
the Caucasic division as represented by the chief European

[1] *Anthrop. Studien,* p. 15, " Diese Gemeinsamkeit der Charakteren beweist uns
die Blutverwandtschaft " (*ib.*).

nations has received an enormous expansion. Here of course it is necessary to distinguish between political and ethnical conquests, as, for instance, those of India, held by military tenure, and of Australia by actual settlement. Politically the whole world has become Caucasic with the exception of half-a-dozen states such as China, Turkey, Japan, Siam, Morocco, still enjoying a real or fictitious autonomy. But, from the ethnical standpoint, those regions in which the Caucasic peoples can establish themselves and perpetuate their race as colonists are alone to be regarded as fresh accessions to the original and later (historical) Caucasic domains. Such fresh accessions are however of vast extent, including the greater part of Siberia and adjoining regions, where Slav branches of the Aryan-speaking peoples are now founding permanent new homes; the whole of Australia, Tasmania, and New Zealand, which have become the inheritance of the Caucasic inhabitants of the British Isles; large tracts in South Africa, already occupied by settlers chiefly from Holland and Great Britain; lastly the New World, where most of the northern continent is settled by full-blood Europeans, mainly British, French and German, while in the rest (Central and South America) the Caucasic immigrants (chiefly from the Iberian peninsula) have formed new ethnical groups by fusion with the aborigines. These new

Past and Present Range. accessions, all acquired within the last 400 years, may be roughly estimated at about 28 million square miles, which with some 12 millions held throughout the historic period (Africa north of Sudan, most of Europe, South-West and parts of Central and South Asia, Indonesia) gives an extent of 40 million square miles to the present Caucasic domain, either actually occupied or in process of settlement. As the whole of the dry land scarcely exceeds 52 millions, this leaves not more than about 12 millions for the now reduced domains of all the other divisions, and even of this a great part (*e.g.* Tibetan table-land, Gobi, tundras, Greenland) is barely or not at all inhabitable. This, it may be incidentally remarked, is perhaps the best reply to those who have in late years given expression to gloomy forebodings regarding the ultimate fate of the Caucasic races. The "yellow scare" may be dismissed with the reflection that the Caucasian populations, who have inherited or acquired nearly four-fifths of the earth's surface besides the absolute dominion of the high seas, is not destined to be submerged by any conceivable combination of all the other elements, still less by the Mongol alone.[1]

Where have we to seek the primeval home of this most vigorous and dominant branch of the human family ? Since no direct evidence can be cited, the answer necessarily takes the form of a hypothesis, and must rely mainly on the indirect evidence supplied by our vague knowledge of geographical conditions in pleistocene times, on past and present zoological distributions, with here and there, the assistance of a hint gleaned from archaeological discoveries. We may deal first with the arguments brought forward in favour of Africa north of Sudan. Here were found in quaternary times all the physical elements which zoologists demand for great specialisations—ample space, a favourable climate and abundance of food, besides continuous land connection at two or three points across the Mediterranean, by which the pliocene and early pleistocene faunas moved freely between the two continents.

Caucasic Cradle —North Africa.

Many of the speculations on the subject failed to convince, largely because the writers took, so to say, the ground from under their own feet, by submerging most of the land under a vast " Quaternary Sahara Sea," which had no existence, and which, moreover, reduced the whole of North Africa to a Mauretanian island, a mere " appendix of Europe," as it is in one place expressly called. Then this inconvenient inland basin was got rid of, not by an outflow—being on the same level as the Atlantic, of which it was, in fact figured as an inlet—but by " evaporation," which process is however somehow confined to this inlet, and does not affect either the Mediterranean or the Altantic itself. Nor is it explained how the oceanic waters were prevented from rushing in according " as the Sahara sea evaporated to become a desert." The attempt to evolve a " Eurafrican race " in such an impossible area necessarily broke down, other endless perplexities being involved in the initial geological misconception.

The " Quaternary Sahara."

Not only was the Sahara dry land in pleistocene times, but it stood then at a considerably higher altitude than at present, although its mean elevation is still estimated by

---

[1] Sir W. Crooke's anticipation of a possible future failure of the wheat supply as affecting the destinies of the Caucasic peoples (*Presidential Address at Meeting Br. Assoc.* Bristol, 1898) is an economic question which cannot here be discussed.

Chavanne at 1500 feet above sea-level. " Quaternary deposits cover wide areas, and were at one time supposed to be of marine origin. It was even held that the great sand dunes must have been formed under the sea ; but at this date it is scarcely necessary to discuss such a view. The advocates of a Quaternary Sahara Sea argued chiefly from the discovery of marine shells at several points in the middle of the Sahara. But Tournouër has shown that to call in the aid of a great ocean in order to explain the presence of one or two shells is a needless expenditure of energy." [1]

At an altitude of probably over 2000 feet the Sahara must have enjoyed an almost ideal climate during late pliocene and pleistocene times, when Europe was exposed to more than one glacial invasion, and to a large extent covered at long intervals by a succession of solid ice-caps. We now know that these stony and sandy wastes were traversed in all directions by great rivers, such as the Massarawa trending south to the Niger, or the Igharghar [2] flowing north to the Mediterranean, and that these now dry beds may still be traced for hundreds of miles by chains of pools or lakelets, by long eroded valleys and by other indications of the action of running waters.

Nor could there be any lack of vegetable or animal life in a favoured region, which was thus abundantly supplied with natural irrigation arteries, while the tropical heats were tempered by great elevation and at times by the refreshing breezes from sub-arctic Europe.

From these well-watered and fertile lands, some of which continued even in Roman times to be the granary of the empire, came that succession of southern animals—hippopotamus, hyaena, rhinoceros, elephant, cave-lion—which made Europe seem like a " zoological appendix of Africa." In association with this fauna may have come man himself, for although North Africa has not yet yielded evidence of a widespread culture comparable to that of the Palaeolithic Age in Europe,

---

[1] Ph. Lake, " The Geology of the Sahara," in *Science Progress*, July, 1895.
[2] This name, meaning in Berber " running water," has been handed down from a time when the Igharghar was still a mighty stream with a northerly course of some 800 miles, draining an area of many thousand square miles, in which there is not at present a single perennial brooklet. It would appear that even crocodiles still survive from those remote times in the so-called Lake Miharo of the Tassili district, where von Bary detected very distinct traces of their presence in 1876. A. E. Pease also refers to a Frenchman " who had satisfied himself of the existence of crocodiles cut off in ages long ago from watercourses that have disappeared " (*Contemp. Review*, July, 1896).

yet the negroid characters of the Grimaldi skeletons have been held to prove an early connection between the opposite shores of the Mediterranean. The hypothesis of African origin is supported by archaeological evidence of the presence of early man all over North Africa from the shores of the Mediterranean through Egypt to Somaliland. Thus one of J. de Morgan's momentous conclusions was that the existence of civilised men in Egypt might be reckoned by thousands, and of the aborigines by myriads of years. These aborigines he identified with the men of the old Stone Age, of whom he believed four stations to have been discovered—Dahshur, Abydos, Tukh, and Thebes.[1]

Of Tunisia Arsène Dumont declared that "the immense period of time during which man made use of stone implements is nowhere so strikingly shown." Here some of the flints were found in abundance under a thick bed of quaternary limestone deposited by the waters of a stream that has disappeared. Hence " the origin of man in Mauretania must be set back to a remote age which deranges all chronology and confounds the very fables of the mythologies."[2]

The skeleton found in 1914 by Hans Reck at Oldoway (then German East Africa) was claimed to be of Pleistocene Age, but according to A. Keith " the evidence . . . cannot be accepted as having finally proved this degree of antiquity."[3]

The doctrine of the specialisation of the dolichocephalic European types in Africa, before their migrations northwards, lies at the base of Sergi's views regarding the African origin of those types. Arguing against the Asiatic origin of the Hamites, as held by Prichard, Virchow, Sayce and others, he points out that this race, scarcely if at all represented in Asia, has an immense range in Africa, where its several sub-varieties must have been evolved before their dispersion over a great part of that continent and of Europe. Then, regarding Hamites and Semites as essentially one, he concludes that Africa is the cradle whence this primitive stock " spread northwards to Europe, where it still persists, especially in the

---

[1] *Recherches sur les Origines de l'Egypte : L'Age de la Pierre et des Métaux,* 1897.
[2] *Bul. Soc. d'Anthrop.* 1896, p. 394. This indefatigable explorer remarks, in reference to the continuity of human culture in Tunisia throughout the Old and New Stone Ages, that " ces populations fortement mélangées d'éléments néander-thaloïdes de la Kromirie fabriquent encore des vases de tous points analogues à la poterie néolithique " (*ib.*).
[3] *The Antiquity of Man,* 1915, p. 255.

Mediterranean and its three principal peninsulas, and east-wards to West Asia." [1]

The theory of an African cradle for the dolichocephalic Mediterranean type does not lack supporters, but when, re-lying on the undeniable presence of brachycephals, some writers would derive the Alpine type from the same area, the larger aspect of continental migrations appears to be overlooked (see pp. 451–2 below). To constitute a distinct race, says Zabo-rowski, a wide geographical area is needed, such as is presented by both shores of the Mediterranean " with the whole of North Africa including the Sahara, which was till lately still thickly peopled." [2]   Then to the question by whom has this North African and Mediterranean region been inhabited since qua-ternary times, he answers " by the ancestors of our Libyans, Egyptians, Pelasgians, Iberians " ; and after rejecting the Asiatic theory, he elsewhere arrives at " the grand generalisa-tion that the whole of North Africa, connected by land with Europe in the Quaternary epoch, formed part of the geo-graphical area of the ancient white race, of which the Egyptians, so far from being the parent stem, would appear to be merely a branch." [3]

Coming to details, Bertholon,[4] from the human remains found by Carton at Bulla-Regia, determined for Tunisia and **Early European** surrounding lands two main long-headed types, **and Mauretanian** one like the Neanderthal (occurring both in **types.** Kuhmeria, and in the stations abounding in palaeoliths), the other like the later Cro-Magnon dolmen-builders, whom De Quatrefages had already identified with the tall, long-headed, fair, and even blue-eyed Berbers still met in various parts of Mauretania, and formerly represented in the Canary Islands.[5]   Bertholon agrees with Collignon that the Mauretanian megalith-builders are of the same race as those of Europe, and besides the two long-headed races

---

[1] *Africa, Antropologia della Stirpe Camitica*, Turin, 1897, p. 404 sq.

[2] " Le nord de l'Afrique entière, y compris le Sahara naguère encore fort peuplé," *i.e.* of course relatively speaking, " Du Dniester à la Caspienne," in *Bul. Soc. d'Anthrop.* 1896, p. 81 sq.

[3] *Ibid.* p. 654 sq.

[4] *Résumé de l'Anthropologie de la Tunisie*, 1896, p. 4 sq.

[5] This identity is confirmed by the characters of three skulls from the dolmens of Madracen near Batna, Algeria, now in the Constantine Museum, found by Letourneau and Papillaut to present striking affinities with the long-headed Cro-Magnon race (Ceph. Index 70, 74, 78) ; leptoprosope with prominent glabella, notable alveolar prognathism, and sub-occipital bone projecting chignon-fashion at the back (*Bul. Soc. d'Anthrop.* 1896, p. 347).

describes (1) a short round-headed type in Gerba Island and East Tunisia [1] representing the Libyans proper, and (2) a blond type of the Sahel, Khumeria, and other parts, whom he identifies with the Mazices of Herodotus, with the " Afri," whose name has been extended to the whole continent, and the blond Getulians of the Aures Mountains.

It has been objected that, as established by de Lapouge and Ripley, there are three distinct ethnical zones in Europe : —(1) Nordic : the tall, fair, long-headed northern The Three Great European Ethnical Groups. type, commonly identified by the Germans with the race represented by the osseous remains from the " Reihengräber," *i.e.* the " Germanic," which the French call Kymric or Aryan, for which de Lapouge reserves Linné's *Homo europaeus*, and to which Ripley applies the term " Teutonic," because the whole combination of characters " accords exactly with the descriptions handed down to us by the ancients. Such were the Goths, Ostrogoths, Visigoths, Vandals, Lombards, together with the Danes, Norsemen, Saxons. . . . History is thus corroborated by natural science." (2) Mediterranean : the southern zone of short, dark, long-heads, *i.e.* the primitive element in Iberia, Italy, South France, Sicily, Corsica, Sardinia, and Greece, called Iberians by the English and identified by many with the Ligurians, Pelasgians, and allied peoples, grouped together by Ripley as Mediter-raneans.[2] (3) Alpine : the central zone of short, medium-sized round-heads with light or chestnut hair, and gray or hazel eye, de Lapouge's and Ripley's *Homo alpinus*, the Kelts or Kelto-Slavs of the French, the Ligurians or Arvernians of Beddoe and other English writers. Here belong the tall Armenoids, the Armenians being descendants of the Hittites.

The question is, Can all these have come from North

---

[1] He shows (" Exploration Anthropologique de l'Ile de Gerba," in *L'Anthropologie*, 1897, p. 424 sq.) that the North African brown brachycephalics, forming the substratum in Mauretania, and very pure in Gerba, resemble the European populations the more they have avoided contact with foreign races. He quotes H. Martin : " Le type brun qui domine dans la Grande Kabylie du Jurjura ressemble singulière-ment en majorité au type français brun. Si l'on habillait ces hommes de vêtements européens, vous ne les distingueriez pas de paysans ou de soldats français." He compares them especially to the Bretons, and agrees with Martin that "il y a parmi les Berbères bruns des brachycéphales; je croirais volontiers que les brachycéphales bruns sont des Ligures. Libyens et Ligures paraissent avoir été originairement de la même race." He thinks the very names are the same : " Λιβύες est exactement le même mot que Λιγύες; rien n'était plus fréquent dans les dialectes primitifs que la mutation du *b* en *g*."
[2] *The Races of Europe*, 1900, *passim*.

K.   29

Africa? We have seen that this region has yielded the remains of one round-headed and two long-headed prehistoric types. Henri Malbot pointed out that, as far back as we can go, we meet the two quite distinct long-headed Berber types, and he holds that this racial duality is proved by the megalithic tombs (dolmens) of Roknia between Jemmapes and Guelma, possibly some 4000 or 5000 years old. The remains here found by L. L. C. Faidherbe belong to two different races, both dolichocephalic, but one tall, with prominant zygomatic arches and very strong nasal spine (it reads almost like the description of a brawny Caledonian), the other short, with well-balanced skull and small nasal spine.[1] The earliest (Egyptian) records refer to brown and blond populations living in North Africa some 5000 years ago, and it has been claimed that the raw materials, so to say, were here to hand both of the fair northern and dark southern European long-heads.

These different races were represented even amongst the extinct Guanches of the Canary Islands, as shown by a study

The Guanches— Types and Affinities.

of the 52 heads procured in 1894 by H. Meyer from caves in the archipelago.[2] Three distinct types are determined: (1) Guanche, akin to the Cro-Magnon, tall (5 ft. 8 in. to 6 ft. 2 in.), robust, dolicho (78), low, broad face; large eyes, rather short nose; fair, reddish or light chestnut hair; skin and eyes light; ranged throughout the islands, but centred chiefly in Tenerife; (2) "Semitic," short (5 ft. 4 or 5 in.), slim, narrow mesocephalic head (81), narrow, long face, black hair, light brown skin, dark eyes; range, Grand Canary, Palma, and Hierro; (3) *Armenoid*, akin to von Luschan's pre-Semitic of Asia Minor; shorter than 1 and 2; very short, broad, and high skull (hyperbrachy, 84); hair, skin and eyes very probably of the West Asiatic brunette type; range, mainly in Gomera, but met everywhere. Many of the skulls had been trepanned, and these are brought into

---

[1] "Les Chaouias," etc., in *L'Anthropologie*, 1897, p. 1 sq.

[2] *Ueber eine Schädelsammlung von den Kanarischen Inseln*, with F. von Luschan's appendix; also "Ueber die Urbewohner der Kanarischen Inseln," in *Bastian-Festschrift*, 1896, p. 63. The inferences here drawn are in substantial agreement with those of Henry Wallack, in his paper on "The Guanches," in *Journ. Anthr. Inst.* June, 1887, p. 158 sq.; and also with J. C. Shrubsall, who, however, distinguishes four pre-Spanish types from a study of numerous skulls and other remains from Tenerife in *Proc. Cambridge Phil. Soc.* IX. 154–78. The 152 cave skulls measured by Von Detloff von Behr, *Metrische Studien an 152 Guanchen-schädeln*, 1908, agree in the main with earlier results.

direct association with the full-blood Berbers of the Aures
Mts. in Algeria, who still practise trepanning for wounds,
headaches, and other reasons. This type is scarcely to
be distinguished from Lapouge's short brown *Homo alpinus*,
which dates from the Stone Ages, and is found in densest
masses in the Central Alpine regions, but the true Armenoids
are differentiated by their taller stature.[1]

How numerous were the inhabitants of France at that
time may be inferred from the long list of no less than 4000
neolithic stations given for that region by Ph. Salmon. Of
the 688 skulls from those stations measured by him, 57.7 per
cent. are classed as dolicho, 21.2 as brachycephalic, and 21.1
as intermediate. This distinguished palethnologist regards
the intermediates as the result of crossings Origin of the
between the two others, and of these he thinks European
the first arrivals were the round-heads, who Brachycephals.
ranged over a vast area between Brittany, the Channel, the
Pyrenees, and the Mediterranean, 60 per cent. of the graves
hitherto studied containing skulls of this type.[2] Belgium also,
where a mixture of long- and round-heads is found amongst
the men of Furfooz, must be included in this neolithic brachy
domain, which can be traced as far westward as the British
Isles.[3] Attempts have been made, as indicated above, to
derive these brachycephals, as well as the dolichocephals, from
North Africa, in accordance with the view that the latter
region was the true centre of evolution and of dispersion for
all the main branches of the Caucasic family, but this theory
has few supporters at the present time. Sergi recognised the
Asiatic origin of the neolithic round-heads and regarded them
as " peaceful infiltrations," [4] forerunners of the great invasions
of the later Metal Ages. Verneau points out [5] that when all
the neolithic stations in which brachycephalic skulls have been
discovered are plotted out on a map of Europe it is easy to
recognise a current running almost directly from east to west.
Moreover towards the west this current divides, being clearly
separated by zones of dolichocephaly.

[1] For an interpretation of the significance of Armenoid skulls in the Canary Is.
see G. Elliot Smith, *The Ancient Egyptians*, 1911, pp. 156–7.
[2] " Dénombrement et Types des Crânes Néolithiques de la Gaule," in *Rev.
Mens. de l'École d'Anthrop.* 1896.
[3] T. Rice Holmes, *Ancient Britain*, 1907, p. 424.
[4] " Infiltrazioni pacifiche." (*Arii e Italici*, p. 124.)
[5] *L'Anthr.* XII. 1901, pp. 547–8.

Evidence of the presence in early times of tall blond
peoples in Africa, side by side with a short dark population,
and of brachycephals together with dolichocephals, proves that
even in the Stone Age ethnic mixtures had already taken
place, and racial purity—if indeed it ever existed—must be
sought for in still remoter periods.

With Sergi's view which traces the neolithic inhabitants
of the northern shores of the Mediterranean (Iberians, Ligurians, Messapians, Siculi and other Itali, Pelasgians), to North
Africa, most anthropologists agree.[1]   Also that all or most of
these were primarily of a dark (brown), short, dolicho type,
which still persists both in South Europe and North Africa,
and in fact is the race which Ripley properly calls " Mediterranean," although in the west they almost certainly ranged
into Brittany and the British Isles.   But there are some who
hold that the migration was in the opposite direction, and
derive the North African branch from Europe, rather than the
European branches from Africa.   " Anthropologists who have
specially studied the question of the Berbers or Kabyles have
concluded that they are descendants of prehistoric European
invaders who occupied the tracts that suited them best." [2]   In
France the neolithic " Mediterranean type " has been regarded
as lineally descended from palaeolithic predecessors *in situ*.[3]
Some would even go further still, and claim Europe as the
place of origin not only of the Mediterranean but also of the
Alpine and Northern branches.   " The so-called three races
of Europe are in the main the result of variation from a common European stock, a variation due to isolation and natural
selection." [4]

Without making any claim to finality the following perhaps
best represents orthodox opinion at the present time.   It may
be assumed that man evolved somewhere in
Southern Asia in pliocene times, and that the
early groups possessed a tendency to variability
which was directed to some extent by geographical conditions
and became fixed by isolation.   The tall fair blue-eyed dolichocephals (Northern Race) and the short dark dolichocephals

Summary of
Orthodox View.

[1] Cf. G. Elliot Smith, *The Ancient Egyptians*, 1911, p. 58 ff.
[2] T. Rice Holmes, *Caesar's Conquest of Gaul*, 1911, p. 266, with list of authorities.
See also Sigmund Feist, *Kultur, Ausbreitung und Herkunft der Indogermanen*,
1913, p.364, and H. H. Johnston, " A Survey of the Ethnography of Africa," *Journ.*
Roy. Anthr. Inst. XLIII. 1913, pp. 386 and 387.
[3] T. Rice Holmes, *loc. cit.* p. 272.
[4] W. Wright, *Middlesex Hospital Journal*, XII. 1908, p. 44.

(Mediterranean Race) may be regarded as two varieties of a common stock, the former having their area of characterisation in the steppes north of the plateaus of Eur-Asia, and migrating eastwards and westwards as the country dried after the last glacial phase.   The southern branch, entering East Africa from Southern Asia, spread all over North Africa ; those in the east were the archaic Egyptians ; to the west were the Libyans whose descendants are the Berbers ; those who crossed the Mediterranean formed the European branches of the Mediterranean race.   With regard to the third type, while the central plateaus of Asia were the centre of dispersal for the true Mongols the western plateaus were the area of characterisation of a non-Mongolian brachycephalic race, which includes short and tall varieties.   This is the Alpine race, which extends from the Hindu Kush to Brittany, and formerly spread further westwards into the British Isles.[1]

The problem of European origins has often in the past been obscured rather than enlightened by an appeal to linguistics, but linguistic factors cannot altogether be ignored.   No doubt the earliest populations **Linguistic Evidence.** of the Mediterranean shores during the Stone Age spoke non-Aryan languages, but it is only here and there that traces—mostly indecipherable—can be discovered.   On the African side we have the Berber language still in its full vigour ; and apparently little changed for thousands of years. But in Europe the primitive tongues have everywhere been swept away by the Aryan (Hellenic, Italic, Keltic) except in the region of the Pyrenees.   In Italy Etruscan is the only language which can with safety be called non-Aryan,[2] though the place of Ligurian is still under dispute.[3]   Of Pelasgian, nothing survives except the statement of Herodotus, a dangerous guide in this matter, that it was a barbaric tongue like the peoples themselves,[4] but Ridgeway considers it Indo-European.[5] Further east, in Asia Minor, neither Karian inscriptions and glosses nor occasional Lydian [6] and Mysian glosses afford any

---

[1] See A. C. Haddon, *The Wanderings of Peoples*, 1911, pp. 16, 17, 55.
[2] R. S. Conway, *The Italic Dialects*, 1897, and Art. " Etruria : Language," *Ency. Brit.* 1911.
[3] Cf. T. Rice Holmes, *Caesar's Conquest of Gaul*, 1911, p. 283.   " The truth is that linguistic data are insufficient."
[4] I. 57.   [5] See p. 465.
[6] For Lydian see E. Littmann, *Sardis*, " Lydian Inscriptions," 1916, briefly summarised by P. Giles, " Some Notes on the New Lydian Inscriptions," *Camb. Univ. Rep.* 1917, p. 587.

safe basis for establishing relationships ; [1] the fuller evidence of Lycian leaves its position indeterminate [2] and the Cretan script is still undeciphered.[3]

But in Iberia besides the Iberian inscriptions, which, so far, remain indecipherable,[4] there survives the Basque of the western Pyrenees, which beyond question represents a form of speech which was current in the peninsula in pre-Aryan times, and on the assumption of a common origin of the populations on both sides of the Strait of Gibraltar might be expected to show traces of kinship with Berber.

The Basques. In a posthumous work on this subject,[5] the eminent philologist G. von der Gabelenz goes much further than mere traces, and claims to establish not only phonetic and verbal resemblances, but structural correspondences, so that his editor Graf von der Schulenberg was satisfied as to the relationship of the two languages.[6] This conclusion has not, however, met with general acceptance [7] and the affinities of Basque with Finno-Ugrian cannot be overlooked.[8] A study of the physical features of the modern Basques adds complexity to the problem. Most observers are agreed that a distinct Basque type exists, and this physical and linguistic singularity has led to various more or less fanciful theories " connecting the Basques with every outlandish language and bankrupt people under the sun," [9] while G. Hervé [10] would regard them as forming by themselves a separate ethnic group, " a fourth European race." On the other hand Feist [11] has grounds for

---

[1] S. Feist, *Kultur, Ausbreitung und Herkunft der Indogermanen*, 1913, p. 385.

[2] " The attempts to connect the language with the Indo-European family have been unsuccessful," A. H. Sayce, Art. " Lycia," *Ency. Brit.* 1911. But cf. also S. Feist, *loc. cit.* pp. 385–7 ; and Th. Kluge, *Die Lykier, ihre Geschichte und ihre Inschriften*, 1910.

[3] A. J. Evans, *Scripta Minoa*, 1909.

[4] T. Rice Holmes, *Caesar's Conquest of Gaul*, 1911, p. 289 n. 4.

[5] *Die Verwandtschaft des Baskischen mit den Berbersprachen Nord-Afrikas nachgewiesen*, 1894.

[6] " Die Sprachen waren mit einander verwandt, das stand ausser Zweifel." (Pref. IV.)

[7] J. Vinson (*Rev. de linguistique*, XXXVIII. 1905, p. 111) says, " no more absurd book on Basque has appeared of late years." See T. Rice Holmes, *Caesar's Conquest of Gaul*, 1911, p. 299 n. 3.

[8] " In the general series of organised linguistic families it [Basque] would take an intermediate place between the American on the one side and the Ugro-Altaic or Ugrian on the other." Wentworth Webster and Julien Vinson, *Ency. Brit.* 1910, " Basques."

[9] See W. Z. Ripley, *The Races of Europe*, 1900, Chap. VIII. " The Basques," pp. 180–204.

[10] *Rev. mensuelle de l'École d'Anthr.* X. 1900, pp. 225–7.

[11] S. Feist, *Kultur, Ausbreitung und Herkunft der Indogermanen*, 1913.

claiming that the Basques are not, in anthropological respects, essentially different from their Spanish or French neighbours (p. 357) and Jullian [1] denies them more than a superficial unity. These apparently conflicting opinions are reconciled by the conclusions of R. Collignon,[2] himself one of the best authorities on the subject. " The physical traits characteristic of the Basques attach them unquestionably (' indiscutablement ') to the great Hamitic branch of the white races, that is to say, to the ancient Egyptians and to the various groups commonly comprised under the collective name of Berbers. Their brachycephaly, slight as it is, cannot outweigh the aggregate of the other characters which they present. . . . It is therefore in this direction and not amongst Finns or Esthonians that is to be sought the parent stem of this paradoxical race. It is North African or European, assuredly not Asiatic." Collignon's explanation of the Basque type is that it is a sub-species of the Mediterranean stock evolved by long-continued and complete isolation, and in-and-in breeding, primarily engendered by peculiarity of language. The effects of heredity, aided perhaps by artificial selection, have generated local peculiarities and have developed them to an extreme.[3]

" The Iberian question," says Rice Holmes, " is the most complicated and difficult of all the problems of Gallic ethnology." [4] From the testimony of Greek and Roman authors, he draws the following conclusions. The Iberians. " The name Iberian was probably applied, in the first instance, only to the people who dwelt between the Ebro and the Pyrenees. The Iberians once occupied the seaboard of Gaul between the Rhône and the Pyrenees ; but Ligurians encroached upon this part of their territory. They also probably occupied the whole eastern region of the Spanish peninsula. But," he adds, " we must bear in mind that the data are both insufficient and uncertain " (p. 288). Later (p. 301), reviewing the evidence collected by philologists and

[1] *Hist. de la Gaule*, I. 1908, p. 271.
[2] " La Race Basque," *L'Anthrop.* 1894.
[3] W. Z. Ripley, *loc. cit.* p. 200.
[4] *Caesar's Conquest of Gaul*, 1911, p. 287. Cf. J. Déchelette (*Manuel d'Archéologie préhistorique*, II. 1910, p. 27), " As a rule it is wise to attach to this expression (Iberian) merely a geographical value." Reviewing the problems of Iberian origins (which he considers remain unsolved), he quotes as an example of their range, the opinion of C. Jullian (*Revue des Études Anciennes*, 1903, p. 383), " There is no Iberian race. The Iberians were a state constituted at latest towards the 6th century, in the valley of the Ebro, which received, either from strangers or from the indigenous peoples, the name of the river as *nom de guerre*."

by craniologists, he continues, " it seems to me probable that the Iberians comprised both people who spoke, or whose ancestors had spoken, Basque, and people who spoke the language or languages [1] of the ' Iberian ' inscriptions ; that to observers who had not learned to measure skulls and knew nothing of scientific methods, they appeared to be homogeneous ; that the prevailing type was that which is now called Iberian and is seen at its purest in Sardinia, Corsica and Sicily ; but that a certain proportion of the whole population may have been characterised by physical features more or less closely resembling those which the modern Basques—French and Spanish—possess in common, and which, as MM. Broca and Collignon tell us, distinguish them from all other European peoples. Finally it seems probable that the true Iberians were the people who spoke the languages of the inscriptions, and that Basque was spoken by a people who occupied Spain and Southern Gaul before the Iberians arrived. But unless and until the key to those appalling inscriptions is found, the problem will never be solved."

The Ligurian question is still more complex than the Iberian. For while no facts can be brought forward in direct

The Ligurians. contradiction of the assumption that the Iberians were a short dark dolichocephalic population occupying the Iberian peninsula in the Stone Age, and speaking a non-Indo-European language, no such generalisations with regard to race, physical type, culture, geographical distribution or language are accepted for the Ligurians. Some, with Sergi,[2] consider the Ligurians merely as another branch of the Mediterranean race. Others, with Zaborowski,[3] tracing their presence among the modern inhabitants of Liguria, regard them as representing the small, dark, brachycephalic race at its purest. While many who recognise the Ligurians as belonging to the Mediterranean physical type deny their affinity with the Iberians. Meyer [4] considers such a relationship " not improbable," but Déchelette [5] shows that it is absolutely untenable on archaeological grounds. The geo-

---

[1] J. Vinson (*Rev. de linguistique*, XL. 1907, pp. 5, 211) divides the Iberian inscriptions into three groups, each of which, he believes, represents a different language.

[2] *The Mediterranean Race*, 1901.

[3] *Dict. des sc. anthr.* p. 247, and *Rev. de l'École d'Anthr.* XVII. 1907, p. 365.

[4] *Geschichte des Altertums*, I. 2, 1909, p. 723.

[5] *Manuel d'Archéologie préhistorique*, II. 1910, p. 27 *n.*, see also p. 22 for archaeological proofs of " ethnographic distinctions."

graphical range is equally uncertain. C. Jullian[1] distributes Ligurians not only over the whole of Gaul, but also throughout Western Europe, and attributes to them all the glories of neolithic civilisation ; A. Bertrand[2] thinks that they played even in Gaul merely a secondary rôle ; Déchelette,[3] on archaeological evidence, proves that the Ligurian period was *par excellence* the Age of Bronze, and Ridgeway[4] identifies it with the Terramare civilisation. Finally, if we follow Sergi, the Ligurians must have spoken a non-Indo-European language ; but the most eminent authorities are in the main agreed that such traces of Ligurian as remain show affinities with Indo-European.[5] With regard to their physical type Sergi puts forward the view that the true Ligurians were like the Iberians, a section of the long-headed Mediterranean (Afro-European) stock. From prehistoric stations in the valley of the Po he collected 59 skulls, all of this type, and all Ligurian ; history and tradition being of accord that before the arrival of the Kelts this region belonged to the Ligurian domain. " If it be true that prehistoric Italy was occupied by the Mediterranean race and by two branches—Ligurian and Pelasgian—of that race, the ancient inhabitants of the Po valley, now exhumed in those 59 skulls, were Ligurian."[6]

These Ligurians have been traced from their homes on the Mediterranean into Central Europe. From a study of the neolithic finds made in Germany, in the district between Neustadt and Worms, C. Mehlis[7] infers that here the first settlers were Ligurians, who had penetrated up the Rhone and Saône into Rhineland. In the Kircherian Museum in Rome he was surprised to find a marked analogy between objects from the Riviera and from

Ligurians in Rhineland and Italy.

---

[1] *Hist. de la Gaule*, I. Chap. IV. The author makes it clear, however, that his " Ligurians " are not necessarily an ethnic unit, " De l'unité de nom, ne concluons pas à l'unité de race " (119), and later (p. 120), " Ne considérons donc pas les Ligures comme les représentants uniformes d'une race déterminée. Ils sont la population qui habitait l'Europe occidentale avant les invasions connues des Celtes ou des Étrusques, avant la naissance des peuples latin ou ibère. Ils ne sont pas autre chose."

[2] *Gaule av. Gaulois*, p. 248.

[3] *Loc. cit.* p. 23 *n.* 1.

[4] *Early Age of Greece*, 1901, p. 237 ff., and " Who were the Romans ? " *Proc. Brit. Acad.* III. 19, 1908, p. 3.

[5] See R. S. Conway, Art. " Liguria," *Ency. Brit.* 1911. It may be noted, however, as Feist points out (*Ausbreitung und Herkunft des Indogermanen*, 1913, p. 368), this hypothesis rests on slight foundations (" ruht auf schwachen Füßen ").

[6] *Arii e Italici*, p. 60.

[7] *Corresbl. d. d. Ges. f. Anthrop.*, Feb. 1898, p. 12.

the Rhine ; skulls (both dolicho), vases, stone implements, mill-stones, etc., all alike. Such Ligurian objects, found everywhere in North Italy, occur in the Rhine lands chiefly along the left bank of the main stream between Basel and Mainz, and farther north in the Rheingau at Wiesbaden, and in the Lahn valley.

The Ligurians may of course have reached the Riviera round the coast from Illiberis and Iberia ; but the same race is found as the aboriginal element also at the " heel of the boot," and in fact throughout the whole of Italy and all the adjacent islands. This point is now firmly established, and not only Sergi, but several other leading Italian authorities hold that the early inhabitants of the peninsula and islands were Ligurians and Pelasgians, whom they look upon as of the same stock, all of whom came from North Africa, and that, despite subsequent invasions and crossings, this Mediterranean stock still persists, especially in the southern provinces and in the islands—Sicily, Sardinia, and Corsica. Hence it seems more reasonable to bring this aboriginal element straight from Africa by the stepping stones of Pantellaria, Malta, and Gozzo (formerly more extensive than at present, and still strewn with megalithic remains comparable to those of both continents); than by the roundabout route of Iberia and Southern Gaul.[1] This is a simple solution of the problem, but it is a question if it is justifiable to extend the name Ligurian to all that branch of the Mediterranean race which undoubtedly forms the substratum of population in Italy and parts of Gaul, ignoring the presence or absence of " Ligurian " culture or traces of Ligurian language. Déchelette,[2] relying chiefly upon archaeological and cultural evidence, sums up as follows : we must consider the Ligurians as Indo-European tribes, whose area of domination had its centre, during the Bronze Age, in North Italy, and the left bank of the Rhone. They were enterprising and energetic in agriculture and in commerce. Together with neighbouring peoples of Illyrian stock they engaged in an indirect but nevertheless regular trade with the northern regions where amber was collected. Among the Ligurians, as among the Illyrians and Hyperboreans, a form of heliolatry was prevalent, popularising the old solar myths in which the

---

[1] Yet Ligurians are actually planted on the North Atlantic coast of Spain by S. Sempere y Miguel (*Revista de Ciencias Historicas*, I. v. 1887).

[2] *Manuel d'Archéologie préhistorique*, II. 1910, p. 22.

swan appears to have played an important rôle.   Rice Holmes [1] defines more closely their geographical range.   "Ligurians undoubtedly lived in South-eastern Gaul, where they were found at least as far north as Bellegarde in the department of the Ain; and, mingled more or less with Iberians, in the departments of the Gard, Hérault, Aude and Pyrénées-Oriéntales.   Most probably they had once occupied the whole eastern region as far north as the Marne, but had been submerged by Celts: and perhaps they had also pushed westward as far as Aquitania."   He continues, "Were it possible to regard the theory of MM. d'Arbois de Jubainville and Jullian as more than an interesting hypothesis, we should have to conclude that the Ligurians were simply the long-headed and short-headed peoples who, reinforced perhaps from time to time by hordes of immigrants, had inhabited the whole of Gaul since the Neolithic Age, and of whom the former, or many of them, were descended from palaeolithic hunters; in other words that they were the same people who, after they had been conquered by, or had coalesced with, the Celtic invaders, called themselves *Celtae*: but to say which of them were first known as Ligurians or introduced the Ligurian language would be utterly hopeless.   Finally the little evidence we possess tends to show that the people called Ligurians, when they became known to the Greek writers who described them, were a medley of different races."

For Sicily, with which may practically be included the south of Italy, we have the conclusions of G. Patroni based on years of intelligent and patient labours.[2]   To Africa this archaeologist traces the palaeolithic men of the west coast of Sicily and of the caves near Syracuse explored by Von Adrian.[3]   "We are forced to conclude that man arrived in Sicily from Africa at a time when the isthmus connecting the island with that Continent still stood above sea-level.   He made his appearance about the same time as the elephant, whose remains are associated with human bones especially in the west.   He followed the sea coasts, the shells of which offered him sufficient food."[4] He was followed by the neolithic man, whose presence has

Sicilian Origins —Sicani; Siculi.

---

[1] *Caesar's Conquest of Gaul*, 1911, p. 287.

[2] "La Civilisation Primitive dans la Sicilie Orientale," in *L'Anthropologie*, 1897, p. 130 sq.; and p. 295 sq.

[3] *Præhistorische Studien aus Sicilien*, quoted by Patroni.	[4] p. 130.

been revealed by the researches of Paolo Orsi at the station of Stentinello on the coast north of Syracuse.

To Orsi is also due the discovery of what he calls the "Aeneolithic Epoch,"[1] represented by the bronzes of the Girgenti district. Orsi assigns this culture to the *Siculi*, and divides it into three periods, while regarding the neolithic men of Stentinello as *pre-Siculi*. But Patroni holds that the aeneolithic peoples have a right to the historic name of *Sicani*, and that the true Siculi were those that arrived from Italy in Orsi's second period. It seems no longer possible to determine the true relations of these two peoples, who stand out as distinct throughout early historic times. They are by many[2] regarded as of óne race, although both (Σικανός, Σικελός) are already mentioned in the Odyssey. But the evidence tends to show that the Sicani represent the oldest element which came direct from Africa in the Stone Age, while the Siculi were a branch of the Ligurians driven in the Metal Age from Italy to the island, which was already occupied by the Sicani, as related by Dionysius Halicarnassus.[3] In fact this migration of the Siculi may be regarded as almost an historical event, which according to Thucydides took place "about 300 years before the Hellenes came to Sicily."[4] The Siculi bore this national name on the mainland, so that the modern expression "Kingdom of the Two Sicilies" (the late Kingdom of Naples) has its justification in the earliest traditions of the people. Later, both races were merged in one, and the present Sicilian nation was gradually constituted by further accessions of Phoenician (Carthaginian), Greek, Roman, Vandal, Arab, Norman, French and Spanish elements.

Very remarkable is the contrast presented by the conditions prevailing in this ethnical microcosm and those of Sardinia, inhabited since the Stone Ages by one of the most homogeneous groups in the world. From the statistics embodied in R. Livi's

---

[1] See p. 21.

[2] It may be mentioned that while Penka makes the Siculi Illyrians from Upper Italy ("Zur Paläoethnologie Mittel- u. Südeuropas," in *Wiener Anthrop. Ges.* 1897, p. 18), E. A. Freeman holds that they were not only Aryans, but closely akin to the Romans, speaking "an undeveloped Latin," or "something which did not differ more widely from Latin than one dialect of Greek differed from another" (*The History of Sicily*, etc., I. p. 488). On the Siculi and Sicani, see E. Meyer, *Geschichte des Altertums*, 1909, I. 2, p. 723, also Art. "Sicily, History," *Ency. Brit.* 1911. Déchelette (*Manuel d'Archéologie préhistorique*, II. 1910, p. 17) suggests that Sikelos or Siculus, the eponymous hero of Sicily, may have been merely the personification of the typical Ligurian implement, the bronze *sickle* (Lat. secula, sicula).

[3] I. 22.   [4] VI. 2.

Antropologia Militare[1] the Sards would almost seem to be
cast all in one mould, the great bulk of the
natives having the shortest stature, the brownest   Sards and
eyes and hair, the longest heads, the swarthiest   Corsicans.
complexion of all the Italian populations. "They consequently form quite a distinct variety amongst the Italian
races, which is natural enough when we remember the seclusion
in which this island has remained for so many ages."[2]   They
seem to have been preserved as if in some natural museum to
show us what the Ligurian branch of the Mediterranean stock
may have been in neolithic times. Yet they were probably
preceded by the microcephalous dwarfish race described by
Sergi as one of the early Mediterranean stocks. Their presence in Sardinia has now been determined by A. Niceforo
and E. A. Onnis, who find that of about 130 skulls from old
graves thirty have a capacity of only 1150 c.c. or under, while
several living persons range in height from 4 ft. 2 in. to 4 ft. 11 in.
Niceforo agrees with Sergi in bringing this dwarfish race also
from North Africa.[3]

With remarkable cranial uniformity, similar phenomena
are presented by the Corsicans who show "the same exaggerated length of face and narrowness of the forehead. The
cephalic index drops from 87 and above in the Alps to about
75 all along the line. Coincidently the colour of hair and eyes
becomes very dark, almost black. The figure is less amply
proportioned, the people become light and rather agile. It is
certain that the stature at the same time falls to an exceedingly
low level: fully 9 inches below the average for Teutonic
Europe," although "the people of Northern Africa, pure
Mediterranean Europeans, are of medium size."[4]

In the Italian peninsula Sergi holds not only that the
aborigines were exclusively of Ligurian, *i.e.* Mediterranean
stock, but that this stock still persists in the whole of the
region south of the Tiber, although here and there mixed with
"Aryan" elements. North of that river these elements increase gradually up to the Italian Alps, and at present are
dominant in the valley of the Po.[5]   In this way he would

---

[1] *Parte I. Dati Antropologici ed Etnologici*, Rome, 1896.
[2] p. 182.   [3] *Atti Soc. Rom. d' Antrop.* 1896, pp. 179 and 201.
[4] Cf. W. Z. Ripley, "Racial Geography of Europe," *Pop. Sci. Monthly*, New
York, 1897–9, and *The Races of Europe*, 1900, pp. 54, 175.
[5] *Arii e Italici*, p. 188.   Hence for these Italian Ligurians he claims the name
of "Italici," which he refuses to extend to the Aryan intruders in the peninsula.
"A questi primi abitatori spetta legittimamente il nome di Italici, non a popolazioni

explain the rising percentage of round-heads in that direction, the Ligurians being for him, as stated, long-headed, the " Aryans " round-headed.

Similarly Beddoe, commenting on Livi's statistics, showing predominance of tall stature, round heads, and fair complexion in North Italy, infers " that a type, the one we usually call the Mediterranean, does really predominate in the south, and exists in a state of comparative purity in Sardinia and Calabria ; while in the north the broad-headed Alpine type is powerful, but is almost everywhere more or less modified by, or interspersed with other types—Germanic, Slavic, or of doubtful origin—to which the variations of stature and complexion may probably be, at least in part, attributed." [1]

Similar relations prevail in the Balkan peninsula, where the Mediterranean stock is represented by the " Pelasgic " [2]

The Pelasgians.   substratum.   Invented, as has been said, for the purpose of confounding future ethnologists, these Pelasgians certainly present an extremely difficult racial problem, the solution of which has hitherto resisted the combined attacks of ancient and modern students.   When Dionysius tells us bluntly that they were Greeks,[3] we fancy the question is settled off-hand, until we find Herodotus describing them a few hundred years earlier as aliens, rude in speech and usages, distinctly not Greeks, and in his time here and there (Thrace, Hellespont) still speaking apparently non-Hellenic dialects.[4] Then Homer several centuries still earlier, with his epithet of

successive [Aryan Umbrians], che avrebbero sloggiato i primi abitanti " (p. 60). The result is a little confusing, " Italic " being now the accepted name of the Italian branch of the Aryan linguistic family, and also commonly applied to the Aryans of this Italic speech, although the word *Italia* itself may have been indigenous (Ligurian) and not introduced by the Aryans.   It would perhaps be better to regard " Italia " as a " geographical expression " applicable to all its inhabitants, whatever their origin or speech.

[1] *Science Progress*, July, 1894.   It will be noticed that the facts, accepted by all, are differently interpreted by Beddoe and Sergi, the latter taking the long-headed element in North Italy as the aboriginal (Ligurian), modified by the later intrusion of round-headed Aryan Slavs, Teutons, and especially Kelts, while Beddoe seems to regard the broad-headed Alpine as the original, afterwards modified by intrusive long-headed types " Germanic, Slavic, or of doubtful origin."   Either view would no doubt account for the present relations ; but Sergi's study of the prehistoric remains (see above) seems to compel acceptance of his explanation.   From the statistics an average height of not more than 5 ft. 4 in. results for the whole of Italy.

[2] For the identification of the Mediterranean race in Greece with the Pelasgians, see W. Ridgeway, *Early Age of Greece*, I. 1901, though Ripley contends (*The Races of Europe*, 1900, p. 407), " Positively no anthropological data on the matter exist.'

[3] Τὸ τῶν Πελασγῶν γένος Ἑλληνικόν.

[4] I. 57.

δῖοι, occurring both in the *Iliad* and the *Odyssey*,[1] exalts them almost above the level of the Greeks themselves. It would seem, therefore, almost impossible to discover a key to the puzzle, one which will also fit in both with Sergi's Mediterranean theory, and with the results of recent archaeological researches in the Aegean lands. The following hypothesis is supported by a certain amount of evidence. If the pre-Mykenaean culture revealed by Schliemann and others in the Troad, Mykenae, Argos, Tiryns, by Evans and others in Crete, by Cesnola in Cyprus, be ascribed to a pre-Hellenic rather than to a proto-Hellenic people, then the classical references will explain themselves, while this pre-Hellenic race will be readily identified with the Pelasgians, as this term is understood by Sergi.

It is, I suppose, universally allowed that Greece really was peopled before the arrival of the Hellenes, which term is here to be taken as comprising all the invading tribes from the north, of which the Achaeans were perhaps the earliest. On their arrival the Hellenes therefore found the land not only inhabited, but inhabited by a cultured people more civilised than themselves, who could thus be identified with Sergi's Pelasgian branch of the Mediterranean or Afro-European stock, whom the proto-Hellenes naturally regarded as their superiors, and whom their first singers also naturally called δῖοι Πελασγοί.[2] But in the course of a few centuries[3] these Pelasgians became Hellenised, all but a few scattered groups, which lagging behind in the general social progress are now also looked upon as barbarians, speaking barbaric tongues, and are so described by contemporary historians. Then these few remnants of a glorious but forgotten past are also merged in the Hellenic

Theory of pre-Hellenic Pelasgians.

---

[1] *Il.* x. 429 ; *Od.* xix. 177.

[2] " We recognise in the Pelasgi an ancient and honourable race, ante-Hellenic, it is true, but distinguished from the Hellenes only in the political and social development of their age. . . . Herodotus and others take a prejudiced view when, reasoning back from the subsequent Tyrrhenian Pelasgi, they call the ancient Pelasgians a rude and worthless race, their language barbarous, and their deities nameless. Numerous traditionary accounts, of undoubted authenticity, describe them as a brave, moral, and honourable people, which was less a distinct stock and tribe, than a race united by a resemblance in manners and the forms of life " (W. Wachsmuth, *The Historical Antiquities of the Greeks*, etc., Engl. ed. 1837, I. p. 39). Remarkable words to have been written before the recent revelations of archaeology in Hellas.

[3] That the two cultures went on for a long time side by side is evident from the different social institutions and religious ideas prevailing in different parts of Hellas during the strictly historic period.

stream, and can no longer be distinguished from other Greeks by contemporary writers. Hence for Dionysius the Pelasgians are simply Greeks, which in a sense may be true enough. All the heterogeneous elements have been fused in a single Hellenic nationality, built upon a rough Pelasgic substratum, and adorned with all the graces of Hellenic culture.

Now to make good this hypothesis, it is necessary to show, first, that the Pelasgians were not an obscure tribe, a small people confined to some remote corner of Hellas, but a wide-spread nation diffused over all the land ; secondly, that this nation, as far as can now be determined, presented mental and other characters answering to those of Sergi's Mediterraneans, and also such as might be looked for in a race capable of developing the splendid Aegean culture of pre-Hellenic times.

On the first point it has been claimed that the Pelasgians were so widely distributed [1] that the difficulty rather is to discover a district where their presence was un-

Pelasgians and Mykenaean civilisation.

known. They fill the background of Hellenic origins, and even spread beyond the Hellenic horizon, to such an extent that there seems little room for any other people between the Adriatic and the Hellespont. Thus Ridgeway [2] has brought together a good many passages which clearly establish their universal range, as well as their occupation especially of those places where have been found objects of Mykenaean and pre-Mykenaean culture, such as engraved gems, pottery, implements, buildings, inscriptions in picto-graphic and syllabic scripts. In Crete they had the "great city of Knossos " in Homer's time ; [3] not only was Mykenae theirs, but the whole of Peloponnesus took the name of Pelasgia ; the kings of Tiryns were Pelasgians, and Aeschylus calls Argos a Pelasgian city ; an old wall at Athens was attributed to them, and the people of Attica had from all time been Pelasgians.[4] Orchomenus in Boeotia was founded by a colony from Pelasgiotis in Thessaly ; Lesbos also was called Pelasgia, and Homer knew of Pelasgians in the Troad. Their settlements are further traced to Egypt, to Rhodes, Cyprus, Epirus—where Dodona was their ancient shrine—and lastly to various parts of Italy.

---

[1] κατὰ τὴν Ἑλλάδα πᾶσαν ἐπεπόλασε (Strabo, v. 220). This might almost be translated, " they flooded the whole of Greece."

[2] *Early Age of Greece*, 1901, Chaps. I. and II.

[3] *Od.* XIX.   [4] Thuc. I. 3.

Moreover, the Pelasgians were traditionally the civilising element, who taught people to make bread, to yoke the ox to the plough, and to measure land. It would ap- **Aegean** pear from these and other allusions that there **Culture.** were memories of still earlier aborigines, amongst whom the Pelasgians appear as a cultured people, introducing perhaps the arts and industries of the pre-Mykenaean Age. But the assumption, based on no known data, is unnecessary, and it seems more reasonable to look on this culture as locally developed, to some extent under eastern (Egyptian, Babylonian, Hittite ?) influences.[1] Here it is important to note that the Pelasgians were credited with a knowledge of letters,[2] and all this has been advanced as sufficient confirmation of our second postulate. Nevertheless it must be acknowledged that the difficulties are not all overcome by this hypothesis, and the further question of language divides even its stanchest supporters into opposing groups, for while Sergi's Mediterraneans necessarily speak a non-Indo-European language,[3] Ridgeway's Pelasgians speak Aeolic Greek.[4]

The range and importance of the Pelasgians are most strictly limited by J. L. Myres,[5] who thinks that the Alpine type may even be primitive in the Morea, Medi- **Other Views.** terranean man being an intruder from the south merely fringing the coast and never penetrating inland. The researches of von Luschan in Lycia support this view,[6] and Ripley's map of the present inhabitants of the Balkan peninsula shows the "Greek contingent closely confined to the sea-coast."[7] Ripley, however, though carefully avoiding any

---

[1] This idea of an independent evolution of western (European) culture is steadily gaining ground, and is strenuously advocated, amongst others, by M. Salomon Reinach, who has made a vigorous attack on what he calls the "oriental mirage," *i.e.* the delusion which sees nothing but Asiatic or Egyptian influences everywhere. Sergi of course goes further, regarding the Mediterranean (Iberian, Ligurian, Pelasgian) cultures not only as local growths, but as independent both of Asiatics and of the rude Aryan hordes, who came rather as destroyers than civilisers. This is one of the fundamental ideas pervading the whole of his *Arii e Italici*, and some earlier writings. [2] Pausanias, III. 20. 5.

[3] G. Sergi, *The Mediterranean Race*, 1901. In the main he is supported by philologists. "The languages of the indigenous peoples throughout Asia Minor and the Aegean area are commonly believed to have been non-Indo-European." H. M. Chadwick, *The Heroic Age*, 1912, p. 179 *n*.

[4] W Ridgeway, *The Early Age of Greece*, 1901, p. 681 ff.

[5] *The Dawn of History*, 1911, p. 40. For his views on Pelasgians, see *Journ. Hell. St.* 1907, p. 170, and the Art. "Pelasgians" in *Ency. Brit.* 1911.

[6] E. Petersen and F. von Luschan, *Reisen in Lykien*, 1889.

[7] W. Z. Ripley, *The Races of Europe*, p. 404 ff. The map (facing p. 402) does not include Greece, and the grouping is based on language, not race.

dragging of "Pelasgians" into the question, assumes a primitive substratum of Mediterranean type all over Greece. "The testimony of these ancient Greek crania is perfectly harmonious. All authorities agree that the ancient Hellenes were decidedly long-headed, betraying in this respect their affinity to the Mediterranean Race. . . . Whether from Attica, from Schliemann's successive cities excavated upon the site of Troy, or from the coast of Asia Minor ; [1] at all times from 400 B.C. to the third century of our era, it would seem proved that the Greeks were of this dolichocephalic type. . . . Every characteristic of their modern descendants and every analogy with the neighbouring populations, leads us to the conclusion that the classical Hellenes were distinctly of the Mediterranean racial type, little different from the Phoenicians, the Romans or the Iberians." [2] Nevertheless Dörpfeld [3] claims that there were, from the first, two races in Greece, a Southern, or Aegean, and a Northern, who were the Aryan Achaeans of history, and recent archaeological discoveries certainly support this view.

Another attempt to solve the Pelasgian problem is that of E. Meyer.[4] After enumerating the various areas said to have been occupied by the Pelasgians " *ein grosses Urvolk* " who ranged from Asia Minor to Italy, he pricks the bubble by saying that in reality there were no Pelasgians save in Thessaly, in the fruitful plain of Peneus, hence called " Pelasgic Argos," [5] and later Pelasgiotis. They, like the Dorians, invaded Crete from Thessaly and at the beginning of the first millennium were defeated and enslaved by the incoming Thessalians. These are the only true Pelasgians. The other so-called Pelasgians are the descendants of an eponymous Pelasgos who in genealogical poetry becomes the ancestor of mankind. Since the Arcadians were regarded as the earliest of the indigenous peoples, Pelasgos was made the ancestor of the Arcadians. The name " Pelasgic Argos " was transferred

[1] The Mykenaean skull found by Bent at Antiparos is described as " abnormally dolichocephalic." W. Ridgeway, *Early Age of Greece*, I. 1901, p. 78.

[2] But in Ridgeway's view the " classical Hellenes " were descendants of tall, fair-haired invaders from the North, and in this he has the concurrence of J. L. Myres, *The Dawn of History*, 1911, p. 209.

[3] *Mitt. d. K. d. Inst. Athen.* xxx. See H. R. Hall, *Ancient History of the Near East*, 1913, pp. 61–4.

[4] *Geschichte des Altertums*, I. 2, 1909, § 507.

[5] For a discussion of the meaning of " Pelasgic Argos " see H. M. Chadwick, *The Heroic Age*, 1912, pp. 274 ff. and 278–9, and for his criticism of Meyer, p. 285.

from Thessaly to the Peloponnesian city. Attic Pelasgians were derived from a mistake of Hecataeus.[1] So the legend grew. The only real Pelasgian problem, concludes Meyer, is whether the Thessalian Pelasgians were a Greek or pre-Greek people, and he is inclined to favour the latter view. The identity of "the most mysterious people of antiquity" is further obscured by philology, for, as P. Giles points out, their name appears merely to mean "the people of the sea," so that "they do not seem to be in all cases the same stock."[2]

Whether we call them Pelasgians or no, there would seem to be little doubt that the splendours of Aegean civilisation which have been and still are being gradually revealed by the researches of British, Italian, American and German archaeologists are to be attributed to an indigenous people of Mediterranean type, occupying an area of which Crete was the centre, from the Stone Age, right through the Bronze Age, down to the Northern invasions of the second millennium and the introduction of iron. In range this culture included Greece with its islands, Cyprus, and Western Anatolia, and its influence extended westwards to Sicily, Italy, Sardinia and Spain, and eastwards to Syria and Egypt. Its chief characteristics are (1) an indigenous script both pictographic and linear, with possible affinities in Hittite, Cypriote and South-west Anatolian scripts, but hitherto indecipherable ; (2) a characteristic art attempting " to express an ideal in forms more and more closely approaching to realities,"[3] exhibited in frescoes, pottery, reliefs, sculptures, jewelry, etc. ; (3) a distinctive architectural style, and (4) type of tomb, which have no parallels elsewhere. Excavations at Cnossos go far towards establishing a chronology for the Aegean area. At the base is an immensely thick neolithic deposit, above which come pottery and other objects of Minoan Period I. 1, which are correlated by Petrie with objects found at Abydos, referred by him to the First Dynasty (4000 B.C.). Minoan Period II. 2 corresponds with the Egyptian XII Dynasty (2500 B.C.), characteristic Cretan pottery of this period being found in the Fayum. Minoan

---

[1] But see W. Ridgeway, *Early Age of Greece*, I. 1901, p. 138 ff.

[2] Art. " Indo-European Languages," *Ency. Brit.* 1911.

[3] R. S. Conway, Art. " Aegean Civilisation," in *Ency. Brit.* 1911, whence this summary is derived, including the chronology, which is not in all respects universally adopted (see p. 27). For a full discussion of the chronology see J. Déchelette, *Manuel d'Archéologie préhistorique*, Vol. II. 1910, *Archéologie celtique ou protohistorique*, Ch. II. § v. Chronologie égéenne, p. 54 ff.

Period III. 1 and 2 synchronises with Dynasty XVIII (1600 to 1400 B.C.). Iron begins to be used for weapons after Period III. 3, and is commonly attributed to incursions from the north, the Dorian invasion of the Greek authors, about 1000 B.C. which led to the destruction of the palace of Cnossos and the substitution of " Geometric " for " Mykenaean " art.

Turning to the African branch of the Mediterranean type, we find it forming not merely the substratum, but the great bulk of the inhabitants throughout all recorded time from the Atlantic to the Red Sea, and from the Mediterranean to Sudan, although since Muhammadan times largely intermingled with the kindred Semitic stock (mainly Arabs) in the north and west, and in the east (Abyssinia) with the same stock since prehistoric times.   All are comprised by Sergi [1] on two main divisions :—

Range of the Hamites in Africa.

1. EASTERN HAMITES, answering to the *Ethiopic Branch* of some writers, of somewhat variable type, comprising the *Old* and *Modern Egyptians* now mixed with Semitic (Arab) elements ; the *Nubians*, the *Bejas*, the *Abyssinians*, collective name of all the peoples between Khor Barka and Shoa (with, in some places, a considerable infusion of Himyaritic or early Semitic blood from South Arabia) ; the *Gallas* (Gallas proper, Somals, and Afars or Danákils) ; the *Masai* and *Ba-Hima.*

2. NORTHERN HAMITES, the *Libyan Race* or *Berber (Western) Branch* of some writers, comprising the *Mediterranean Berbers* of Algeria, Tunis, and Tripoli ; the *Atlantic Berbers* (*Shluhs* and others) of Morocco ; the *West Saharan Berbers* commonly called *Tuaregs* ; the *Tibus* of the East Sahara ; the *Fulahs*, dispersed amongst the Sudanese Negroes ; the *Guanches* of the Canary Islands.

Of the Eastern Hamites he remarks generally that they do not form a homogeneous division, but rather a number of different peoples either crowded together in separate areas, or dispersed in the territories of other peoples.   They agree

---

[1] In his valuable and comprehensive work, *Africa : Antropologia della Stirpe Camitica*, Turin, 1897. It must not be supposed that this classification is un-challenged. T. A. Joyce, " Hamitic Races and Languages," *Ency. Brit.* 1911, points out that it is impossible to prove the connection between the Eastern and Northern Hamites. The former have a brown skin, with frizzy hair, and are nomadic or semi-nomadic pastors ; the latter, whom he would call not Hamites at all, but the Libyan variety of the Mediterranean race, are a white people, with curly hair, and their purest representatives, the Berbers, are agriculturalists. For the fullest and most recent treatment of the subject see the monumental work of Oric Bates, *The Eastern Libyans : An Essay*, 1913, with bibliography.

more in their inner than in their outer characters, without constituting a single ethnical type. The cranial forms are variable, though converging, and evidently to be regarded as very old varieties of an original stock. The features are also variable, converging and characteristic, with straight or arched (aquiloid) nose quite different from the Negro ; lips rather thick, but never everted as in the Negro ; hair usually frizzled, not wavy ; beard thin ; skin very variable, brown, red-brown, black brown, ruddy black, chocolate and coffee-brown, reddish or yellowish, these variations being due to crossings and the outward physical conditions.

The Eastern Hamites.

In this assumption Sergi is supported by the analogous case of the western Berbers between the Senegal and Morocco, to whom Collignon and Deniker [1] restrict the term " Moor," as an ethnical name. The chief groups, which range from the Atlantic coast east to the camping grounds of the true Tuaregs,[2] are the Trarsas and Braknas of the Senegal river, and farther north the Dwaïsh (Idoesh), Uled-Bella, Uled-Embark, and Uled-en-Nasúr. From a study of four of these Moors, who visited Paris in 1895, it appears that they are not an Arabo-Berber cross, as commonly supposed, but true Hamites, with a distinct Negro strain, shown especially in their frizzly hair, bronze colour, short broad nose, and thickish lips, their general appearance showing an astonishing likeness to the Bejas, Afars, Somals, Abyssinians, and other Eastern Hamites. This is not due to direct descent, and it is more reasonable to suppose " that at the two extremities of the continent the same causes have produced the same effects, and that from the infusion of a certain proportion of black blood in the Egyptian [eastern] and Berber branches of the Hamites, there have sprung closely analogous mixed groups." [3] From the true Negro they are also distinguished by their grave and dignified bearing, and still more by their far greater intelligence.

The Western " Moors."

Both divisions of the Hamites, continues Sergi, agree substantially in their bony structure, and thus form a single

---

[1] " Les Maures du Sénégal," *L'Anthropologie*, 1896, p. 258 sq.

[2] That is, the *Sanhaja-an Litham*, those who wear the *litham* or veil, which is needed to protect them from the sand, but has now acquired religious significance, and is never worn by the " Moors."

[3] p. 269.

anthropological group with variable skull—pentagonoid,
ovoid, ellipsoid, sphenoid, etc., as expressed in
his terminology—but constant, that is, each
variety recurring in all the branches ; face also
variable (tetragonal, ellipsoid, etc.), but similarly identical in
all the branches ; profile non-prognathous ; eyes dark, straight,
not prominent ; nose straight or arched ; hair smooth, curly,
long, black or chestnut ; beard full, also scant ; lips thin or
slightly tumid, never protruding ; skin of various brown shades ;
stature medium or tall.

General Hamitic Type.

Such is the great anthropological division, which was
diffused continually over the greater part of Africa, and
round the northern shores of the Mediterranean. According
to Stuhlmann[1] it had its origin in south Arabia, if not further
east, and entered Africa in the region of Erythrea. He regards the Red Sea as offering no obstacle to migrations, but
suggests a possible land connection between the opposite
shores.

Nothing is more astonishing than the strange persistence
not merely of the Berber type, but of the Berber temperament
and nationality since the Stone Ages, despite the successive
invasions of foreign peoples during the historic period. First
came the Sidonian Phoenicians, founders of Carthage and Utica
probably about 1500 B.C. The Greek occupation of Cyrenaica
(628 B.C.) was followed by the advent of the Romans on the
ruins of the Carthaginian empire. The Romans
have certainly left distinct traces of their presence,
and some of the Aures highlanders still proudly
call themselves *Rumaníya*. These *Shawías* ("Pastors") form
a numerous group, all claiming Roman descent, and even still
keeping certain Roman and Christian feasts, such as *Bu Ini*,
i.e. Christmas ; *Innar* or *January* (New Year's Day) ; Spring
(Easter), etc. A few Latin words also survive such as *urtho*
=hortus ; *kerrúsh*=quercus (evergreen oak) ; *milli*=milliarium
(milestone).

Foreign Elements in Mauretania.

After the temporary Vandal occupation came the great
Arab invasions of the seventh and later centuries, and even
these had been preceded by the kindred *Ruadites*, who had in
pre-Moslem times already reached Mauretania from Arabia.

[1] See F. Stuhlmann's invaluable work on African culture and race distribution, *Handwerk und Industrie in Ostafrika*, 1910, especially the map showing the distribution of the Hamites, Pl. II. B.

With the Jews, some of whom had also reached Tripolitana before the New Era, a steady infiltration of Negroes from Sudan, and the recent French, Spanish, Italian, and Maltese settlers, we have all the elements that go to make up the cosmopolitan population of Mauretania.

But amid them all the Berbers and the Arabs stand out as the immensely predominant factors, still distinct despite a probably common origin in the far distant past and later interminglings. The Arab remains above all a nomad herdsman, dwelling in tents, without house or hamlet, a good stock-breeder, but a bad husbandman, and that only on compulsion. "The ploughshare and shame enter hand in hand into the family," says the national proverb. To find space for his flocks and herds he continues the destructive work of Carthaginian and Roman, who ages ago cleared vast wooded tracts for their fleets and commercial navies, and thus rendered large areas barren and desolate.

The Berber on the contrary loves the sheltering wood-lands ; he is essentially a highlander who carefully tills the forest glades, settles in permanent homes, and often develops flourishing industries. Arab society is feudal and theocratic, ruled by a despotic Sheikh, while the Berber with his *Jemaa*, or "Witenagemot," and his *Kanun* or unwritten code, feels himself a freeman ; and it may well have been this democratic spirit, inherited by his European descendants, that enabled the western nations to take the lead in the onward movement of humanity. The Arab again is a fanatic, ever to be feared, because he blindly obeys the will of Allah proclaimed by his prophets, marabouts, and mahdis.[1] But the Berber, a born sceptic, looks askance at theological dogmas ; an unconscious philosopher, he is far less of a fatalist than his Semitic neighbour, who associates with Allah countless demons and jins in the government of the world.

In their physical characters the two races also present some striking contrasts, the Arab having the regular oval brain-cap and face of the true Semite, whereas the Berber head is more angular, less finely moulded, with more prominent cheek-bones, shorter and less aquiline nose, which combined with a

---

[1] The Kababish and Baggara tribes, chief mainstays of former Sudanese revolts, claim to be of unsullied Arab descent with long fictitious pedigrees going back to early Muhammadan times (see p. 74).

slight degree of sub-nasal prognathism, imparts to the features coarser and less harmonious outlines.   He is at the same time distinctly taller and more muscular, with less uniformity in the colour of the eye and the hair, as might be expected from the numerous elements entering into the constitution of present Berber populations.

In the social conflict between the Arab and Berber races, the curious spectacle is presented of two nearly equal elements (same origin, same religion, same government, same or analogous tribal groupings, at about the same cultural development) refusing to amalgamate to any great extent, although living in the closest proximity for over a thousand years.   In this struggle the Arab seems so far to have had the advantage. Instances of Berberised Arabs occur, but are extremely rare, whereas the Berbers have not only everywhere accepted the Koran, but whole tribes have become assimilated in speech, costume, and usages to the Semitic intruders.   It might therefore seem as if the Arab must ultimately prevail.   But we are assured by the French observers that in Algeria and Tunisia appearances are fallacious, however the case may stand in Morocco and the Sahara.   " The Arab," writes Malbot, to whom I am indebted for some of these details, " an alien in Mauretania, transported to a soil which does not always suit him, so far from thriving tends to disappear, whereas the Berber, especially under the shield of France, becomes more and more aggressive, and yearly increases in numbers.   At present he forms at least three-fifths of the population in Algeria, and in Morocco the proportion is greater.   He is the race of the future as of the past." [1]

This however would seem to apply only to the races, not to their languages, for we are elsewhere told that Arabic is encroaching steadily on the somewhat ruder Berber dialects.[2] Considering the enormous space over which they are diffused, and the thousands of years that some of the groups have ceased to be in contact, these dialects show remarkably slight divergence from the long extinct speech from which all have sprung. Whatever it be called—Kabyle, Zenatia, Shawia, Tamashek, Shluh—the Berber language is still essentially one, and the likeness between the forms current in Morocco, Algeria, the Sahara, and the remote Siwah Oasis on the confines of Egypt,

[1] " Les Chaouias," *L'Anthropologie*, 1897, p. 14.
[2] p. 17.

is much closer, for instance, than between Norse and English in the sub-Aryan Teutonic group.[1]

But when we cross the conventional frontier between the contiguous Tuareg and Tibu domains in the central Sahara the divergence is so great that philologists are still doubtful whether the two languages are even remotely or are at all connected. Ever since the abandonment of the generalisation of Lepsius that Hamitic and Negro were the sole stock languages, the complexity of African linguistic problems has been growing more and more apparent, and Tibu is only one among many puzzles, concerning which there is great discordance of opinion even among the most recent and competent authorities.[2]

The Tibu themselves, apparently direct descendants of the ancient Garamantes, have their primeval home in the Tibesti range, *i.e.* the " Rocky Mountains," whence they take their name.[3] There are two distinct sections, the Northern *Tedas*, a name recalling the *Tedamansii*, a branch of the Garamantes located by Ptolemy somewhere between Tripolitana and Phazania (Fezzan), and the Southern *Dazas*, through whom the Tibu merge gradually in the negroid populations of central Sudan. This intermingling with the blacks dates from remote times, whence Ptolemy's remark that the Garamantes seemed rather more " Ethiopians " than Libyans.[4] But there can be no doubt that the full-blood Tibu, as represented by the northern section, are mainly Mediterranean, and although the type of the men is somewhat coarser than that of their Tuareg neighbours, that of the women is almost the finest in Africa. " Their women are charming while still in the bloom of youth, unrivalled amongst their sisters of North Africa for their physical beauty, pliant and graceful figures." [5]

The Tibus.

[1] The words collected by Sir H. H. Johnston at Dwirat in Tunis show a great resemblance with the language of the Saharan Tuaregs, and the sheikh of that place " admitted that his people could understand and make themselves understood by those fierce nomads, who range between the southern frontier of Algeria and Tunis and the Sudan " (*Geogr. Journ.*, June, 1898, p. 590).

[2] Cf. Meinhof, *Die Moderne Sprachforschung in Africa*, 1910.

[3] *Ti-bu*=" Rock People " ; cf. *Kanem-bu*=" Kanem People," southernmost branch of the family on north side of Lake Chad.

[4] Ὄντων δὲ καὶ αὐτῶν ἤδη μᾶλλον Αἰθιόπων (I. 8). I take ἤδη, which has caused some trouble to commentators, here to mean that, as you advance southwards from the Mediterranean seaboard, you find yourself on entering Garamantian territory already rather amongst Ethiopians than Libyans.

[5] Reclus, Eng. ed. Vol. XI. p. 429. For the complicated ancestral mixture producing the Tibu see Sir H. H. Johnston, " A Survey of the Ethnography of Africa," *Journ. Roy. Anthr. Inst.* XLIII. 1913, p. 386.

It is interesting to notice amongst these somewhat secluded Saharan nomads the slow growth of culture, and the curious survival of usages which have their explanation in primitive social conditions. " The Tibu is always distrustful ; hence, meeting a fellow-countryman in the desert he is careful not to draw near without due precaution. At sight of each other both generally stop suddenly ; then crouching and throwing the litham over the lower part of the face in Tuareg fashion, they grasp the inseparable spear in their right and the shanger-mangor, or bill-hook, in their left. After these preliminaries they begin to interchange compliments, inquiring after each other's health and family connections, receiving every answer with expressions of thanksgiving to Allah These formalities usually last some minutes." [1] Obviously all this means nothing more than a doffing of the hat or a shake-hands amongst more advanced peoples ; but it points to times when every stranger was a *hostis*, who later became the *hospes* (host, guest).

It will be noticed that the Tibu domain, with the now absolutely impassable Libyan desert,[2] almost completely separates the Mediterranean branch from the Hamites

The Egyptian Hamites. proper. Continuity, however, is accorded, both on the north along the shores of the Mediterranean to the Nile Delta (Lower Egypt), and on the south through Darfur and Kordofan to the White Nile, and thence down the main stream to Upper Egypt, and through Abyssinia, Galla and Somali lands to the Indian Ocean. Between the Nile and the east coast the domain of the Hamites stretches from the equator northwards to Egypt and the Mediterranean.

It appears therefore that Egypt, occupied for many thousands of years by an admittedly Hamitic people, might have been reached either from the west by the Mediterranean route, or down the Nile, or, lastly, it may be suggested that the Hamites were specialised in the Nile valley itself. The point is not easy to decide, because, when appeal is made to the evidence of the Stone Ages, we find nothing to choose between such widely separated regions as Somaliland, Upper Egypt, and Mauretania, all of which have yielded superabundant proofs of the presence of man for incalculable ages, estimated by

---

[1] Reclus, Eng. ed. Vol. XI. p. 430.

[2] From the enormous sheets of tuffs near the Kharga Oasis Zettel, geologist of G. Rohlf's expedition in 1876, considered that even this sandy waste might have supported a rich vegetation in Quaternary times.

some palethnologists at several hundred thousand years. In Egypt the palaeoliths indicate not only extreme antiquity, but also that the course of civilisation was uninterrupted by any such crises as have afforded means of chronological classification in Western Europe   The differences in technique are local and geographical, not historic.   The Neolithic period tells the same tale, and the use of copper at the beginning of the historic period only slowly replaced the flint industry, which continued during the earlier dynasties down to the period of the Middle Empire and attained a degree of perfection nowhere surpassed. Prehistoric pottery strengthens the evidence of a slow, gradual development, the newer forms nowhere jostling out the old, but co-existing side by side.[1]

It might seem therefore that the question of Eygptian origins was settled by the mere statement of the case, and that there could be no hesitation in saying that   Origins. the Egyptian Hamites were evolved on Egyptian soil, consequently are the true autochthones in the Nile valley. Yet there is no ethnological question more hotly discussed than this of Egyptian origins and culture, for the two seem inseparable.   There are broadly speaking two schools : the African, whose fundamental views are thus briefly set forth, and the Asiatic, which brings the Egyptians with all their works from the neighbouring continent. But, seeing that the Egyptians are now admitted to be Hamites, that there are no Hamites to speak of (let it be frankly said, none at all) in Asia, and that they have for untold ages occupied large tracts of Africa, there are several members of the Asiatic school who allow that, not the people themselves, but their culture only came from Western Asia (Mesopotamia). If so, this culture would presumably have its roots in the delta, which is first reached by the Isthmus of Suez from Asia, and spread thence, say, from Memphis up the Nile to Thebes and Upper Egypt, and here arises a difficulty.   For at that time there was no delta,[2] or at least it

---

[1] See *Histoire de la Civilisation Égyptienne*, G. Jéquier, 1913, p. 53 ff.   Also, concerning pottery, E. Naville, " The Origin of Egyptian Civilisation," *Journ. Roy. Anthr. Inst.* XXXVII. 1907, p. 203.

[2] The Egyptians themselves had a tradition that when Menes moved north he found the delta still under water.   The sea reached almost as far as the Fayum, and the whole valley, except the Thebais, was a malarious swamp (Herod. II. 4). Thus late into historic times memories still survived that the delta was of relatively recent formation, and that the *Retu* (*Romitu* of the Pyramid texts, later *Rotu, Romi,* etc.) had already developed their social system before the Lower Nile valley was inhabitable.   Hence whether the Nile took 20,000 years (Schweinfurth) or over 70,000, as others hold, to fill in its estuary, the beginning of the Egyptian

was only in process of formation, a kind of debatable region between land and water, inhabitable mainly by crocodiles, and utterly unsuited to become the seat of a culture whose character-istic features are huge stone monuments, amongst the largest ever erected by man, and consequently needing solid founda-tions on *terra firma*. It further appears that although Memphis is very old, Thebes is much older, in other words, that Egyptian culture began in Upper Egypt, and spread not up but down the Nile. On the other hand the Egyptians themselves looked upon the delta as the cradle of their civili-sation, although no traces of material culture have survived, or could be expected to survive, in such a soil.[1] Moreover it is not necessary to introduce Asiatic invaders by way of Lower Egypt. F. Stuhlmann postulates a land connection between Africa and Arabia, but even without this assumption he regards the Red Sea as affording no hindrance to early infiltrations.[2] Flinders Petrie, while rejecting any considerable water trans-port for the uncultured prehistoric Egyptians (whom he derives from Libya), detects a succession of subsequent invasions from Asia, the dynastic race crossing the Red Sea to the neighbour-hood of Koptos, and Syrian invasions leading to the civilisation of the Twelfth Dynasty, besides the later Hyksos invasions of Semito-Babylonian stock.[3]

The theory of Asiatic origins is clearly summed up by H. H. Johnston.[4] He regards the earliest inhabitants of Egypt as a dwarfish Negro-like race, not unlike the Congo pygmies of to-day (p. 375), with possibly some trace of Bushman (p. 378), but this popu-lation was displaced more than 15,000 years ago by Medi-terranean man, who may have penetrated as far as Abyssinia, and may have been linguistically parent of the Fulah.[5] The Fulah type was displaced by the invasions of the Hamites and the Libyans or Berbers. " The Hamites were

Theory of Asiatic Origins.

prehistoric period must still be set back many millenniums before the new era. " Ce que nous savons du Sahara, lui-même alors sillonné de rivières, atteste qu'il [the delta] ne devait pas être habitable, pas être constitué à l'époque quaternaire " (M. Zaborowski, *Bul. Soc. d'Anthrop.* 1896, p. 655).

[1] G. Jéquier, *Histoire de la Civilisation Égyptienne*, 1913, p. 95, but see E. Naville, " The Origin of Egyptian Civilisation," *Journ. Roy. Anthr. Inst.* XXXVII. 1907, p. 209.

[2] *Handwerk und Industrie in Ostafrika*, 1910, p. 143.

[3] " Migrations," *Journ. Anthr. Inst.* XXXVI. 1906.

[4] " A Survey of the Ethnography of Africa," *Journ. Roy. Anthr. Inst.* XLIII. 1913.

[5] See p. 482 below.

no doubt of common origin, linguistically and racially, with the
Semites, and perhaps originated in that great breeding ground
of conquering peoples, South-west Asia.   They preceded the
Semites, and (we may suppose) after a long stay and concentration in Mesopotamia invaded and colonised Arabia,
Southern Palestine, Egypt, Abyssinia, Somaliland and North
Africa to its Altantic shores.   The Dynastic Egyptians were
also Hamites in a sense, both linguistically and physically ; but
they seem to have attained to a high civilisation in Western
Arabia, to have crossed the Red Sea in vessels, and to have
made their first base on the Egyptian coast near Berenice in
the natural harbour formed by Ras Benas.   From here a long,
broad wadi or valley—then no doubt fertile—led them to the
Nile in the Thebaid, the first seat of their kingly power.[1]   The
ancestors of the Dynastic Egyptians may have originated the
great dams and irrigation works in Western Arabia ; and such
long struggles with increasing drought may have first broken
them in to the arts of quarrying stone blocks and building with
stone.   Over population and increasing drought may have
caused them to migrate across the Red Sea in search of another
home ; or their migration may have been partly impelled by the
Semitic hordes from the north, whom we can imagine at this
period—some 9000 to 10,000 years ago—pressing southwards
into Arabia and conquering or fusing with the preceding
Hamites ; just as these latter, no doubt, at an earlier day, had
wrested Arabia from the domain of the Negroid and Dravidian"
(p. 382).

That the founding of the First Dynasty was coincident
with a physical change in the population, is proved by the
thousands of skeletons and mummies examined
by Elliot Smith,[2] who regards the pre-Dynastic   Proto-Egyptian
Egyptians as " probably the nearest approxima-   Type.
tion to that anthropological abstraction, a pure race, that we
know of (p. 83).   He describes the type as follows (Chap. IV.).

The Proto-Egyptian (*i.e.* pre-Dynastic) was a man of small
stature, his mean height, estimated at a little under 5 ft. 5 in.,
in the flesh for men, and almost 5 ft. in the case of women,

---

[1] For an alternative route see E. Naville, " The Origin of Egyptian Civilisation," *Journ. Roy. Anthr. Inst.* XXXVII. 1907, p. 209 ; J. L. Myres, *The Dawn of
History*, 1911, pp. 56-7, also p. 65, and the criticism of Elliot Smith, *The Ancient
Egyptians*, 1911, pp. 88-9.
[2] *The Ancient Egyptians*, 1911.

being just about the average for mankind in general, whereas the modern Egyptian *fellah* averages about 5 ft. 6 in. He was of very slender build with indications of poor muscular development. In fact there is a suggestion of effeminate grace and frailty about his bones, which is lacking in the more rugged outlines of the skeletons of his more virile successors. The hair of the Proto-Egyptian was precisely similar to that of the brunet South European or Iberian people of the present day. It was a very dark brown or black colour, wavy or almost straight and sometimes curly, never "woolly." There can be no doubt whatever that this dark hair was associated with dark eyes and a bronzed complexion. Elliot Smith emphatically endorses Sergi's identification of the ancient Egyptian as belonging to his Mediterranean Race. "So striking is the family likeness between the Early Neolithic peoples of the British Isles and the Mediterranean and the bulk of the population, both ancient and modern, of Egypt and East Africa, that a description of the bones of an early Briton might apply in all essential details to an inhabitant of Somaliland." But he points out also that there is an equally close relationship linking the Proto-Egyptians with the populations to the east, from the Red Sea as far as India, including Semites as well as Hamites. Rejecting the terms "Mediterranean" or "Hamite" as inadequate he would classify his Mediterranean-Hamite-Semite group as the "Brown Race."[1]

A most fortunate combination of circumstances afforded Elliot Smith an opportunity for determining the ethnic affinities of the Egyptian people.

The Hearst Expedition of the University of California, under the direction of G. A. Reisner, was occupied from 1901 onwards with excavations at Naga-ed-Dêr in the Thebaid, where a cemetery, excavated by A. M. Lythgoe, contained well-preserved bodies and skeletons of the earliest known pre-Dynastic period. Close by was a series of graves of the First and Second Dynasties; a few hundred yards away tombs of the Second to the Fifth Dynasties (examined by A. C. Mace), with a large number of tombs ranging from the time of the Sixth Dynasty to the Twelfth. "Thus there was provided a chronologically unbroken series of human remains representing every epoch in the history of Upper Egypt from prehistoric times, roughly estimated at 4000 B.C., up till the close of the

[1] *The Ancient Egyptians*, 1911, pp. 56, 58, 62.

Middle Empire, more than two thousand years later." To
complete the story Coptic (Christian Egyptian) graves of the
fifth and sixth centuries were discovered on the same site.

" The study of this extraordinarily complete series of
human remains, providing in a manner such as no other site
has ever done the materials for the reconstruction of the racial
history of one spot during more than forty-five centuries, made
it abundantly clear that the people whose remains were buried
just before the introduction of Islam into Egypt were of the
same flesh and blood as their forerunners in the same locality
before the dawn of history. And nine years' experience in
the Anatomical Department of the School of Medicine in
Cairo," continues Elliot Smith, " has left me in no doubt that
the bulk of the present population in Egypt conforms to
precisely the same racial type, which has thus been dominant
in the northern portion of the Valley of the Nile for sixty
centuries." [1]

As early as the Second Dynasty certain alien traits began
to appear, which became comparatively common in the Sixth
or Twelfth series. The non-Egyptian characters
are observable in remains from numerous sites *Armenoid Type.*
excavated by Flinders Petrie in Lower and Middle Egypt, and
are particularly marked in the cemetery round the Giza
Pyramids (excavated by the Hearst Expedition, 1903), containing remains of more than five hundred individuals, who
had lived at the time of the Pyramid-builders ; they are therefore referred to by Elliot Smith as " Giza traits," and attributed
to Armenoid influence. Soon after the amalgamation of the
Egyptian kingdoms of Upper and Lower Egypt by Menes
(Mena), consequent perhaps upon the discovery of copper and
the invention of metal implements,[2] expeditions were sent
beyond the frontiers of the United Kingdom to obtain copper
ore, wood and other objects. Even in the times of the First
Dynasty the Egyptians began the exploitation of the mines
in the Sinai Peninsula for copper ore. It is claimed by Meyer [3]
that Palestine and the Phoenician coast were Egyptian dependencies, and there is ample evidence that there was intimate
intercourse between Egypt and Palestine as far north as the
Lebanons before the end of the Third Dynasty. From this

[1] *The Ancient Egyptians*, 1911, pp. 104–5.
[2] G. Elliot Smith, *loc. cit.* pp. 97 and 147.
[3] E. Meyer, *Geschichte des Altertums*, I. 2, 1909, §§ 229, 232, 253.

time forward the physical characters of the people of Lower Egypt show the results of foreign admixture, and present marked features of contrast to the pure type of Upper Egypt. The curious blending of characters suggests that the process of racial admixture took place in Syria rather than in Egypt itself.[1]   The alien type is best shown in the Giza necropolis, and its representatives may be regarded as the builders and guardians of the Pyramids.   The stature is about the same as that of the Proto-Egyptians, possibly rather lower, but they were built on far sturdier lines, their bones being more massive, with well-developed muscular ridges and impressions, and none of the effeminacy or infantilism of the prehistoric skeletons. The brain-case has greater capacity with no trace of the meagre ill-filled character exhibited by the latter.   Characteristic peculiarities were the " Grecian profile " and a jaw closely resembling those of the round-headed Alpine races.

These " Giza traits " were not a local development, for they have been noted in all parts of Palestine and Asia Minor, and abundantly in Persia and Afghanistan.   They occur in the Punjab but are absent from India, having an area of greatest concentration in the neighbourhood of the Pamirs ; while in a westerly direction, besides being sporadically scattered over North Africa, they are recognised again in the extinct Guanches of the Canary Islands.   From these considerations Elliot Smith shapes the following " working hypothesis."

" The Egyptians, Arabs and Sumerians may have been kinsmen of the Brown Race, each diversely specialised by long residence in its own domain ; and in pre-Dynastic times, before the wider usefulness of copper as a military instrument of tremendous power was realised, the Middle pre-Dynastic phase of culture became diffused far and wide throughout Arabia and Sumer.   Then came the awakening to the knowledge of the supremacy which the possession of metal weapons conferred upon those who wielded them in combat against those not so armed.   Upper Egypt vanquished Lower Egypt in virtue of this knowledge and the possession of such weapons. The United Kingdom pushed its way into Syria to obtain wood and ore, and incidentally taught the Arabs the value of metal weapons.   The Arabs thereby obtained the supremacy

---

[1] G. Elliot Smith, *The Ancient Egyptians*, 1911, p. 108, but for a different interpretation see J. L. Myres, *The Dawn of History*, 1911, pp. 51 and 65.

over the Armenoids of Northern Syria, and the hybrid race
of Semites formed from this blend were able to descend the
Euphrates and vanquish the more cultured Sumerians, because
the latter were without metal implements of war. The non-
Semitic Armenoids of Asia Minor carried the new knowledge
into Europe." [1]

This hypothesis might explain some of the difficult problems connecting Egypt and Babylonia.[2] The non-Asiatic
origin of the Egyptian people appears to be Asiatic Influence
indicated by recent excavations, but, as men- on Egyptian
tioned above, there are still many who hold that Culture.
Egyptian culture and civilisation were derived mainly, if not
wholly, from Asiatic (probably Sumerian) sources. The Semitic
elements existing in the ancient Egyptian language, certain
resemblances between names of Sumerian and Egyptian gods,
and the similarity of hieroglyphic characters to the Sumerian
system of writing have been cited as proofs of the dependence
of the one culture upon the other ; while the introduction of
the knowledge of metals, metal-working and the crafts of
brick-making and tomb construction have, together with the
bulbous mace-head, cylinder-seal and domesticated animals
and plants,[3] been traced to Babylonia.

But the excavations of Reisner at Naga-ed-Dêr and those
of Naville at Abydos (1909–10) appear to place the indigenous
development of Egyptian culture beyond question. Reisner's
conclusions [4] are that there was no sudden break of continuity
between the neolithic and early dynastic cultures of Egypt.
No essential change took place in the Egyptian conception
of life after death, or in the rites and practices accompanying
interment. The most noticeable changes, in the character of
the pottery and household vessels, in the materials for tools
and weapons and the introduction of writing, were all gradually
introduced, and one period fades into another without any

---

[1] *Loc. cit.* p. 147.

[2] H. R. Hall (*The Ancient History of the Near East*, 1913, p. 87 *n.* 3) sees " no
resemblance whatever between the facial traits of the Memphite grandees of the
Old Kingdom and those of Hittites, Syrians, or modern Anatolians, Armenians
or Kurds. They were much more like South Europeans, like modern Italians
or Cretans."

[3] Cf. H. H. Johnston, " A Survey of the Ethnography of Africa," *Journ. Roy.
Anthr. Soc.* XLIII. 1913, p. 383, and also E. Naville, "The Origin of Egyptian
Civilisation," *Journ. Roy. Anthr. Inst.* XXXVII. 1907, p. 210.

[4] G. A. Reisner, " The Early Dynastic Cemeteries of Naga-ed-Dêr," Part I.
Vol. II. of *University of California Publications*, 1908, summarised by L. W. King,
History of Sumer and Akkad, 1910, pp. 326, 334.

strongly marked line of division between them. Egypt no doubt had trading relations with surrounding countries. Egyptians and Babylonians must have met in the markets of Syria, and in the tents of Bedouin chiefs. Still, as Meyer points out, far from Egypt taking over a ready-made civilisation from Babylonia, Egypt, as regards cultural influence, was the giver not the receiver.[1]

One more alien element in Egypt remains to be discussed. Most writers on Egyptian ethnology detect a Negro or at least Negroid element in the Caucasoid popula-
Negroid Mixture. tion, and although usually assigning priority to the Negro, assume the co-existence of the two races from time immemorial to the present day. Measurements on more than 1000 individuals were made by C. S. Myers, and these are his conclusions. " There is no anthropometric (despite the historic) evidence that the population of Egypt, past or present, is composed of several different races. Our new anthropometric data favour the view which regards the Egyptians always as a homogeneous people, who have varied now towards Caucasian, now towards negroid characters (according to environment), showing such close anthropometric affinity to Libyan, Arabian and like neighbouring peoples, showing such variability and possibly such power of absorption, that from the anthropometric standpoint no evidence is obtainable that the modern Egyptians have been appreciably affected by other than sporadic Sudanese admixture."[2]

It was seen above (Chap. III.) that non-Negro elements are found throughout the Sudan from Senegal nearly to Darfur,
The Fulah. nowhere forming the whole of the population, but nearly always the dominant native race. These are the Fulah (Fula, Fulbe or Fulani), whose ethnic affinities have given rise to an enormous amount of speculation. Their linguistic peculiarity had led many ethnologists to regard them as the descendants of the first white colonists of North Africa, " Caucasoid invaders," 15,000 years ago, prior to Hamitic intrusions from the east.[3]   Thus would be explained the fact that their language betrays absolutely no structural affinity with Semitic or Libyo-Hamitic groups, or with any other

---

[1] *Geschichte des Altertums*, I. 2, 1909, p. 156.
[2] *Journ. Anthr. Inst.* XXXIII. 1903, XXXV. 1905, XXXVI. 1906, and *Journ. Roy. Anthr. Inst.* XXXVIII. 1908.
[3] Cf. H. H. Johnston, " A Survey of the Ethnography of Africa," *Journ. Roy. Anthr. Inst.* XLIII. 1913, p. 382.

speech families outside Africa, though offering faint resemblances in structure with the Lesghian [1] speech of the Caucasus and the Dravidian tongues of Baluchistan and India. Physically there seems to be nothing to differentiate them from other blends [2] of Hamite-Negro. The physical type of the pure-bred Fulah H. H. Johnston describes as follows : " Tall of stature (but not gigantic, like the Nilote and South-east Sudanese), olive-skinned or even a pale yellow ; well-proportioned, with delicate hands and feet, without steatopygy, with long, oval face, big nose (in men), straight nose in women (nose finely cut, like that of the Caucasian), eyes large and " melting," with an Egyptian look about them, head-hair long, black, kinky or ringlety, never quite straight." [3] They were at first a quiet people, herdsmen and shepherds with a high and intricate type of pagan religion which still survives in parts of Nigeria. But large numbers of them became converted to Islam from the twelfth century onwards and gained some knowledge of the world outside Africa by their pilgrimages to Mecca. At the end of the eighteenth and the beginning of the nineteenth centuries an uprise of Muhammadan fanaticism and a proud consciousness of their racial superiority to the mere Negro armed them as an aristocracy to wrest political control of all Nigeria from the hands of Negro rulers or the decaying power of Tuareg and Songhai. This race was all unconsciously carrying on the Caucasian invasion and penetration of Africa.

A less controversial problem is presented by the Eastern Hamites, who form a continuous chain of dark Caucasic peoples from the Mediterranean to the equator, Other Eastern and whose ethnical unity is now established Hamites—Bejas by Sergi on anatomical grounds. [4] Bordering —Somals. on Upper Egypt, and extending thence to the foot of the Abyssinian plateau, is the Beja section, whose chief divisions —Ababdeh, Hadendoa, Bisharin, Beni Amer—have from the earliest times occupied the whole region between the Nile and the Red Sea.

[1] No physical affinity is suggested. The Lesghian tribes " betray an accentuated brachycephaly equal to that of the pure Mongols about the Caspians." W. Z. Ripley, *The Races of Europe*, p. 440.
[2] J. Deniker, *The Races of Man*, 1900, p. 439, places the Fulahs in a separate group, the Fulah-Zandeh group. Cf. also A. C. Haddon, *The Wanderings of Peoples*, 1911, p. 59.
[3] *Loc. cit.* p. 401 *n.*
[4] *Africa*, 1897, *passim.*

C. G. Seligman has analysed the physical and cultural characters of the Beja tribes (*Bisharin, Hadendoa* and *Beni Amer*), the *Barabra*, nomad Arabs (such as the *Kababish* and *Kawahla*), Nilotes (*Shilluk, Dinka, Nuer*) and half-Hamites (*Ba-Hima, Masai*), in an attempt by eliminating the Negro and Semitic elements to deduce the main features which may be held to indicate Hamitic influence. He regards the *Beni Amer* as approximating most closely to the original *Beja* type which he thus describes. " Summarising their physical characteristics it may be said that they are moderately short, slightly built men, with reddish-brown or brown skins in which a greater or less tinge of black is present, while in some cases the skin is definitely darker and presents some shade of brown-black. The hair is usually curly, in some instances it certainly might be described as wavy, but the method of hair dressing adopted tends to make difficult an exact description of its condition. Often, as is everywhere common amongst wearers of turbans, the head is shaved. . . . The face is usually long and oval, or approaching the oval in shape, the jaw is often lightly built, which with the presence of a rather pointed chin may tend to make the upper part of the face appear disproportionately broad. The nose is well shaped and thoroughly Caucasian in type and form." [1] Among the Hadendoa the " Armenoid " or so-called " Jewish " nose is not uncommon. Seligman draws attention to the close resemblance between the *Beja* type and that of the ancient Egyptians.

Through the Afars (Danákil) of the arid coastlands between Abyssinia and the sea, the Bejas are connected with the numerous Hamitic populations of the Somali and Galla lands. For the term " Somal," which is quite recent and of course unknown to the natives, H. M. Abud [2] suggests an interesting and plausible explanation. Being a hospitable people, and milk their staple food, " the first word a stranger would hear on visiting their kraals would be ' Só mál,' *i.e.* ' Go and bring milk.' " Strangers may have named them from this circumstance, and other tribal names may certainly be traced to more improbable sources.

Somal Genealogies.

---

[1] " Some Aspects of the Hamitic Problem in the Anglo-Egyptian Sudan," *Journ. Roy. Anthr. Inst.* XLIII. 1913, p. 604. See also C. Crossland, *Desert and Water Gardens of the Red Sea*, 1913.
[2] *Genealogies of the Somal*, 1896.

The natives hold that two races inhabit the land : (1) Asha, true Somals, of whom there are two great divisions, *Dáród* and *Ishák*, both claiming descent from certain noble Arab families, though no longer of Arab speech ; (2) Háwíya, who are not counted by the others as true Somals, but only "pagans," and also comprise two main branches, *Aysa* and *Gadabursi*. In the national genealogies collected by Abud and Cox, many of the mythical heroes are buried at or near Meit, which may thus be termed the cradle of the Somal race. From this point they spread in all directions, the Dáróds pushing south and driving the Galla beyond the Webbe Shebel, and till lately raiding them as far as the Tana river. It should be noticed that these genealogical tables are far from complete, for they exclude most of the southern sections, notably the *Rahanwín* who have a very wide range on both sides of the Jub.

In the statements made by the natives about true Somals and "pagans," race and religion are confused, and the distinction between Asha and Háwíya is merely one between Moslem and infidel. The latter are probably of much purer stock than the former, whose very genealogies testify to interminglings of the Moslem Arab intruders with the heathen aborigines.

Despite their dark colour C. Keller [1] has no difficulty in regarding the Somali as members of the "Caucasic Race." The Semitic type crops out decidedly in several groups, and they are generally speaking of fine physique, well grown, with proud bearing and often with classic profile, though the type is very variable owing to Arab and Negro grafts on the Hamitic stock. The hair is never woolly, but, like that of the Beja, ringlety and less thick than the Abyssinian and Galla, sometimes even quite straight. The forehead is finely rounded and prominent, eye moderately large and rather deep-set, nose straight, but also snub and aquiline, mouth regular, lips not too thick, head sub-dolichocephalic.

Great attention has been paid to all these Eastern Hamitic peoples by Ph. Paulitschke,[2] who regards the Galla as both intellectually and morally superior to the Somals and Afars, the chief reason being that the baneful influences exercised by the Arabs and Abyssinians affect to a far greater extent the two latter than the former group.

---

[1] " Reisestudien in den Somaliländern," *Globus*, LXX. p. 33 sq.
[2] *Ethnographie Nord-Ost-Afrikas : Die geistige Kultur der Danàkil, Galla u. Somàl*, 1896, 2 vols.

The Galla appear to have reached the African coast before the Danákil and Somali, but were driven south-east by pressure from the latter, leaving Galla remnants as serfs among the southern Somali, while the presence of servile negroid tribes among the Galla gives proof of an earlier population which they partially displaced. Subsequent pressure from the Masai on the south forced the Galla into contact with the Danákil, and a branch penetrating inland established themselves on the north and east of Victoria Nyanza, where they are known to-day as the Ba-Hima, Wa-Tusi, Wa-Ruanda and kindred tribes, which have been described on p. 91.

The Galla.

The Masai, the terror of their neighbours, are a mixture of Galla and Nilotic Negro, producing what has been described as the finest type in Africa. The build is slender and the height often over six feet, the face is well formed, with straight nose and finely cut nostrils, the hair is usually frizzly, and the skin dark or reddish brown. They are purely pastoral, possessing enormous herds of cattle in which they take great pride, but they are chiefly remarkable for their military organisation which was hardly surpassed by that of the Zulu. They have everywhere found in the agricultural peoples an easy prey, and until the reduction of their wealth by rinderpest (since 1891) and the restraining influence of the white man, the Masai were regarded as an ever-dreaded scourge by all the less warlike inhabitants of Eastern Africa.[1]

The Masai.

Amongst the Abyssinian Hamites we find the strangest interminglings of primitive and more advanced religious ideas. On a seething mass of African heathendom, already in pre-historic times affected by early Semitic ideas introduced by the Himyarites from South Arabia, was somewhat suddenly imposed an undeveloped form of Christianity by the preaching of Frumentius in the fourth century, with results that cannot be called satisfactory. While the heterogeneous ethnical elements have been merged in a composite Abyssinian nationality, the discordant religious ideas

Abyssinian Hamites : Religion.

---

[1] M. Merker, *Die Masai*, 1904 ; A. C. Hollis, *The Masai, their Language and Folklore*, 1905.   C. Dundas, " The Organisation and Laws of some Bantu Tribes in East Africa," *Journ. Roy. Anthr. Inst.* XLV. 1915, pp. 236–7, thinks that the power of the Masai was over-rated, and that the Galla were really a fiercer race. He quotes Krapf, " Give me the Galla and I have Central Africa."   The *Nandi* (an allied tribe) are described by A. C. Hollis, 1909, and *The Suk* by M. W. H. Beech, 1911.

have never yet been fused in a consistent uniform system. Hence " Abyssinian Christianity " is a sort of by-word even amongst the Eastern Churches, while the social institutions are marked by elementary notions of justice and paradoxical " shamanistic" practices, interspersed with a few sublime moral precepts.   Many things came as a surprise to the members of the Rennell Rodd Mission,[1] who could not understand such a strange mixture of savagery and lofty notions in a Christian community which, for instance, accounted accidental death as wilful murder.   The case is mentioned of a man falling from a tree on a friend below and killing him.   " He was adjudged to perish at the hands of the bereaved family, in the same manner as the corpse.   But the family refused to sacrifice a second member, so the culprit escaped."   Dreams also are resorted to, as in the days of the Pharaohs, for detecting crime.   A priest is sent for, and if his prayers and curses fail, a small boy is drugged and told to dream.   " Whatever person he dreams of is fixed on as the criminal ; no further proof is needed. . . . If the boy does not dream of the person whom the priest has determined on as the criminal, he is kept under drugs until he does what is required of him."

To outsiders society seems to be a strange jumble of an iron despotism, which forbids the selling of a horse for over £10 under severe penalties, and a personal freedom or licence, which allows the labourer to claim his wages after a week's work and forthwith decamp to spend them, returning next day or next month as the humour takes him.   Yet somehow things hold together, and a few Semitic immigrants from South Arabia have for over 2000 years contrived to maintain some kind of control over the Hamitic aborigines who have always formed the bulk of the population in Abyssinia.[2]

---

[1] A. E. W. Gleichen, *Rennell Rodd's Mission to Menelik*, 1897.

[2] Among recent works on Abyssinia may be mentioned A. B. Wylde, *Modern Abyssinia*, 1901 ; H. Weld Blundell, " A Journey through Abyssinia," *Geog. Journ.* xv. 1900, and " Exploration in the Abai Basin," *ib.* xxvii. 1906 ; the *Anthropological Survey of Abyssinia* published by the French Government in 1911 ; and various publications of the Princeton University Expedition to Abyssinia, edited by E. Littmann.

CHAPTER XIV

THE CAUCASIC PEOPLES (*continued*)

THE SEMITES—Cradle, Origins, and Migrations—Divisions: Semitic Migrations—Babylonia, People and Civilisation—Assyria, People and Civilisation—Syria and Palestine—*Canaanites: Amorites: Phoenicians—The Jews*—Origins—Early and Later Dispersions—Diverse Physical Types—Present Range and Population—THE HITTITES—Conflicting Theories—*The Arabs*—Spread of the Arab Race and Language—Semitic Monotheism—Its Evolution.

THE Himyaritic immigrants, who still hold sway in a foreign land, have long ceased to exist as a distinct nationality in their own country, where they had nevertheless ages ago founded flourishing empires, centres of one of the very oldest civilisations of which there is any record. Should future research confirm the now generally received view that Hamites and Semites are fundamentally of one stock, a view based both on

The Semites— Cradle, Origins, and Migrations. physical and linguistic data,[1] the cradle of the Semitic branch will also probably be traced to South Arabia, and more particularly to that south-western region known to the ancients as Arabia Felix, *i.e.* the Yemen of the Arabs. While Asia and Africa were still partly separated in the north by a broad marine inlet before the formation of the Nile delta, easy communication was afforded between the two continents farther south at the head of the Gulf of Aden, where they are still almost contiguous. By this route the primitive Hamito-Semitic populations may have moved either westwards into Africa, or, as has also been suggested, eastwards into Asia, where in the course of ages the Semitic type became specialised.

On this assumption South Arabia would necessarily be the first home of the Semites, who in later times spread thence

Divisions. north and east. They appear as *Babylonians* and *Assyrians* in Mesopotamia ; as *Phoenicians* on the Syrian coast ; as *Arabs* on the Nejd steppe ; as

[1] The divergent views of orientalists concerning Semitic (linguistic) origins are summarised by W. Z. Ripley, *The Races of Europe*, 1900, p. 375.

Canaanites, Moabites and others in and about Palestine ; as *Amorites (Aramaens, Syrians)* in Syria and Asia Minor.

This is the common view of Semitic origins and early migrations, but as practically no systematic excavations have been possible in Arabia, owing to political conditions and the attitude of the inhabitants, definite archaeological or anthropological proofs are still lacking. The hypothesis would, however, seem to harmonise well with all the known conditions. In the first place is to be considered the very narrow area occupied by the Semites, both absolutely and relatively to the domains of the other fundamental ethnical groups. While the Mongols are found in possession of the greater part of Asia, and the Hamites with the Mediterraneans are diffused over the whole of North Africa, South and West Europe since the Stone Ages, the Semites, excluding later expansions—Himyarites to Abyssinia, Phoenicians to the shores of the Mediterranean, Moslem Arabs to Africa, Irania, and Transoxiana—have always been confined to the south-west corner of Asia, comprising very little more than the Arabian Peninsula, Mesopotamia, Syria, and (doubtfully) parts of Asia Minor. Moreover the whole mental outlook of the Semites, their mode of thought, their religion and organisation, indicate their derivation from a desert people ; while in Arabia are found at the present time the purest examples not only of Semitic type, but also of Semitic speech.[1] Their early history, however, as pointed out above, still awaits the spade of the archaeologist, and the earliest migrations that can be definitely traced are in the form of invasions of already established states.[2]

The first great wave of Semitic migration from Arabia is placed in the fourth millennium B.C., 3500 to 2500 or earlier ; it affected Babylonia and probably Syria and Palestine, judging from the Palestinian place-names belonging to this " Babylonian-Semitic " period, and the close connection between Palestine and Babylonia in

Semitic Migrations.

---

[1] E. Meyer, *Geschichte des Altertums*, I. 2, 1909, § 336. O. Procksch, however, while regarding the origin of the Semites as an unsolved problem, considers Arabia as their centre of dispersal rather than their original home. As far as early Semitic migrations can be traced he thinks they indicate a north to south direction, and he sees no cause for disputing the Biblical account (*Gen.* ii. 10 ff.) deriving the descendants of Shem " from the neighbourhood of Ararat, i.e. Armenia, across the Taurus to the North Syrian plain." " Die Völker Altpalästinas," *Das Land der Bibel*, I. 2, 1914, p. 11. Cf. also J. L. Myres, *The Dawn of History*, 1911, p. 115.

[2] For the discussion as to whether Semites or Sumerians were the earlier occupants of Babylonia see p. 263 above.

culture and in religious ideas, indicating prehistoric relationship.[1] A second wave, Winckler's Canaanitic or Amoritic migration, followed in the third millennium, covering Babylonia, laying the foundations of the Assyrian Empire, invading Syria and Palestine (Phoenicians, Amorites) and possibly later Egypt (*Hyksos*). A third wave, the Aramaean, which spread over Babylonia, Mesopotamia and Syria in the second millennium, was preceded by the swarming into Syria from the desert of the Khabiri (Habiru) or Hebrews (Edomites, Moabites, Ammonites and Israelites among others). From the same area the Suti pressed into Babylonia about 1100, followed by another branch, the Chaldeans from Eastern Arabia.

These are but a few of the earlier waves of migration from the south of which traces can be detected in Western Asia. Of all invasions from the north, that of the Hittites is the most important and the most confusing. The Hittites appear to have moved south from Cappadocia about 2000 B.C., and they are found warring against Babylonia in the eighteenth century. A Hittite dynasty flourished at Mittanni 1420–1411 and in the fourteenth and thirteenth centuries they conquered and largely occupied Syria.[2] Invasions of Phrygians and Philistines from the west followed the breaking up of the Hittite Empire. The last great Semitic migration was the most widespread of all. "It issued, like its predecessors, along the whole margin of the desert, and in the course of a century had flooded not only Syria and Egypt, but all North Africa and Spain; it had occupied Sicily, raided Constance, and in France was only checked at Poitiers in 732. Eastward it flooded Persia, founded an empire in India, and carried war and commerce by sea past Singapore."[3]

"Thus Western Asia has been swept times and again, almost without number, by conquering hordes and the no less severe ethnical disturbances of peaceful infiltrations converging from every point of the compass in turn. . . . How, then, is it possible to learn anything to-day from the contents of this cauldron, filled with such an assortment of ingredients and still

---

[1] Hugo Winckler, "Die Völker Vorderasiens," *Der Alte Orient*, I. 1900, pp. 14–15 and *Auszug aus der Vorderasiatische Geschichte*, 1905, p. 2.

[2] Cf. A. C. Haddon, *Wanderings of Peoples*, 1911, p. 21.

[3] J. L. Myres, *The Dawn of History*, 1911, pp. 118–9. For an admirable description of the Semitic migrations see pp. 104–5, and for the geographical aspect, see E. C. Semple, *Influences of Geographic Environment : on the basis of Ratzel's System of Anthropo-Geography*, 1911, pp. 6–7 and under "Nomads" in the Index.

seething from the effects of the disturbance incidental to the harsh mixing of such incompatible elements ? " [1] Some of the problems must for the present be regarded as insoluble, but with the evidence provided by archaeologists and anthropologists an attempt may be made to read the ethnological history of these obscure regions.

The earliest Semitic wave was traceable in Babylonia, but, as seen above, opinions differ as to its origin and date. " At what period the Semites first invaded Baby-   Babylonia, lonia, when and where they first attained supre-   People and macy, are not yet matters of history. We find   Civilisation. Semites in the land and in possession of considerable power almost as early as we can go back." [2] The characteristic Semitic features are clearly marked, and the language is closely connected with Canaanitic and Assyrian.[3] From the monuments we learn that the Babylonian Semites had full beards and wore their hair long, contrasting sharply with the shaven Sumerians, and thus gaining the epithet " the black-headed ones." In nose and lips, as in dress, they are clearly distinct from the Sumerian type.[4]

When history commences, the inhabitants of Babylonia were already highly civilised. They lived in towns, containing great temples, and were organised in distinct classes or occupations, and possessed much wealth in sheep and cattle, manufactured goods, gold, silver and copper. Engraving on metals and precious stones, statuary, architecture, pottery, weaving and embroidery, all show a high level of workmanship. They possessed an elaborate and efficient system of writing, extensively used and widely understood, consisting of a number of signs, obviously descended from a form of picture writing, but conventionalised to an extent that usually precludes the recognition of the original pictures. This writing was made by the impression of a stylus on blocks or cakes of fine clay while still quite soft. These " tablets " were sun-dried, but occasionally baked hard. This cuneiform writing was adopted by, or was common to, many neighbouring nations, being freely used in

---

[1] G. Elliot Smith, *The Ancient Egyptians*, 1911, p. 133.

[2] C. H. W. Johns, *Ancient Babylonia*, 1913, pp. 18–19. For culture see pp. 16–17.

[3] O. Procksch, " Die Völker Altpalästinas," *Das Land der Bibel*, I. 2, 1914.

[4] Cf. E. Meyer, " Sumerier und Semiten in Babylonien," *Abh. der Königl. Preuss. Akad. des Wissenschaft.* 1906 ; L. W. King, *History of Sumer and Akkad*, 1910, p. 40 ff.

Elam, Armenia and Northern Mesopotamia as far as Cappadocia.

Assyrian culture was founded upon that of Babylonia, but the Assyrians appear to have differed from the Babylonians in character, though not in physical type,[1] while they were closely related in speech. "The Assyrians differed markedly from the Babylonians in national character. They were more robust, warlike, fierce, than the mild industrial people of the south. It is doubtful if they were much devoted to agriculture or distinguished for manufactures, arts and crafts. They were essentially a military folk. The king was a despot at home, but the general of the army abroad. The whole organisation of the state was for war. The agriculture was left to serfs or slaves. The manufactures, weaving at any rate, were done by women. The guilds of workmen were probably foreigners, as the merchants mostly were. The great temples and palaces, walls and moats, were constructed by captives. . . . For the greater part of its existence Assyria was the scourge of the nations and sucked the blood of other races. It lived on the tribute of subject states, and conquest ever meant added tribute in all necessaries and luxuries of life, beside an annual demand for men and horses, cattle and sheep, grain and wool to supply the needs of the army and the city."[2]

Assyria, People and Civilisation.

The early history of Syria and Palestine is by no means clear, although much light has been shed in recent years by the excavations of R. A. S. Macalister at Gezer,[3] where remains were found of a pre-Semitic race, of Ernst Sellin at Tell Ta'anek and Jericho,[4] and the labours of the *Deutscher Palästina-Verein* and especially G. Schumacher at Megiddo.[5] Caves apparently occupied by man in the Neolithic period were discovered at Gezer, and are dated at about 3500 to 3000 B.C.

Syria and Palestine. Canaanites : Amorites : Phoenicians : Jews.

[1] In the Assyrians von Luschan detects traces of the hyperbrachycephalic people of Asia Minor and Armenia, for they appear to differ from the pure Semites especially in the shape of the nose. Meyer regards this variation as possibly due to a prehistoric population, but, he adds, studies of physical types both historically and anthropologically are in their infancy. E. Meyer, *Geschichte des Altertums*, I. 2, 1909, § 330 A.

[2] C. H. W. Johns, *Ancient Assyria*, 1912, p. 8.

[3] *Palestine Exploration Fund Quarterly Statements*, 1902 onwards. See also L. B. Paton, Art. "Canaanites," in Hastings' *Encyclopaedia of Religion and Ethics*.

[4] Tell Ta'anek, 1904, *Denkschriften*, Vienna Academy, and "The German Excavations at Jericho," *Pal. Expl. Fund Quart. St.* 1910.

[5] *Tell el-Mutesellim*, 1908.

from their position below layers in which Egyptian scarabs appear. Fragments of bones give indications of the physical type. None of the individuals exceeded 5 ft. 7 inches (1.702 m.) in height, and most were under 5 ft. 4 inches (1.626 m.). They were muscular, with elongated crania and thick heavy skull-bones. From their physical characters it could be clearly seen that they did not belong to the Semitic race. They burned their dead, a non-Semitic custom, a cave being fitted up as a crematorium, with a chimney cut up through the solid rock to secure a good draught.[1]

The first great influx of Semitic nomads is conjectured to have reached Babylonia, not from the south, but from the north-west, after traversing the Syrian coast lands. They left colonists behind them in this region, who afterwards as the Amurru (Amorites) pressed on in their turn into Babylonia and established the earliest independent dynasty in Babylon.[2]

The second great wave of Semitic migration appears to have included the Phoenicians,[3] so called by the Greeks, though they called themselves Canaanites and their land Canaan,[4] and are referred to in the Old Testament, as in inscriptions at Tyre, as " Sidonians." They themselves had a tradition that their early home was on the Persian Gulf, a view held by Theodore Bent and others,[5] and recent discoveries emphasise the close cultural (not necessarily racial) connection between Palestine and Babylonia.[6]

The weakening of Egyptian hold upon Palestine about the fourteenth century B.C. encouraged incursions of restless Habiru (Habiri) from the Syrian deserts, commonly identified with the Hebrews, and invasions of Hittites from the north. In the thirteenth century Egypt recovered Palestine, leaving the Hittites in possession of Syria. About this time the coast was

---

[1] *Palestine Exploration Fund Quarterly Statements*, 1902, p. 347 ff.

[2] L. W. King, *History of Sumer and Akkad*, 1910, p. 55 ; C. H. W. Johns, *Ancient Babylonia*, 1913, pp. 61–2; L. B. Paton, Art. "Canaanites," Hastings' *Ency. of Religion and Ethics*, 1910 ; E. Meyer, *Geschichte des Altertums*, I. 2, 1909, §§ 396, 436; O. Procksch, " Die Völker Altpalästinas," *Das Land der Bibel*, I. 2, 1914, p. 25 ff. ; G. Maspero, *The Struggle of the Nations, Egypt, Syria, and Assyria*, 1910.

[3] Φοίνικες, probably meaning red, either on account of their sun-burnt skin, or from the dye for which they were famous. For the Phoenician physical type cf. W. Z. Ripley, *Races of Europe*, 1900, pp. 287, 444.

[4] In the Old Testament " Canaanite " and " Amorite " are usually synonymous.

[5] A. C. Haddon, *Wanderings of Peoples*, 1911, p. 22. For a general account of Phoenician history see J. P. Mahaffy, in Hutchinson's *History of the Nations*, 1914, p. 303 ff.

[6] Cf. Morris Jastrow, *Hebrew and Babylonian Traditions* (Haskell Lectures), 1913.

invaded by Levantines, including the Purasati, in whom may perhaps be recognised the Philistines, who gave their name to Palestine.[1]

With the Hebrew or Israelitish inhabitants of south Syria (Canaan, Palestine, " Land of Promise") we are here concerned only in so far as they form a distinct branch of the Semitic family.

The Jews. The term "Jews,"[2] properly indicating the children of Judah, fourth son of Jacob, has long been applied generally to the whole people, who since the disappearance of the ten northern tribes have been mainly represented by the tribe of Judah, a remnant of Benjamin and a few Levites, *i.e.* the section of the nation which to the number of some 50,000 returned to south Palestine (kingdom of Judaea) after the Babylonian captivity. These were doubtless later joined by some of the dispersed northern tribes, who from Jacob's alternative name were commonly called the " ten tribes of Israel." But all such Israelites had lost their separate nationality, and were consequently absorbed in the royal tribe of Judah. Since the suppression of the various revolts under the Empire, the Judaei themselves have been a dispersed nationality, and even before those events numerous settlements had been made in different parts of the Greek and Roman worlds, as far west as Tripolitana, and also in Arabia and Abyssinia.

But most of the present communities probably descend from those of the great dispersion after the fall of Jerusalem (70 A.D.), increased by considerable accessions of converted " Gentiles," for the assumption that they have made few or no converts is no longer tenable. In exile they have been far more a religious body than a broken nation, and as such they could not fail under favourable conditions to spread their teachings, not only amongst their Christian slaves, but also amongst peoples, such as the Abyssinian Falashas, of lower culture than themselves. In pre-Muhammadan times many Arabs of Yemen and other districts had conformed, and some of their Jewish kings (Asad Abu-Karib, Dhu Nowas, and others) are still remembered. About the seventh century all the Khazars—a renowned Turki people of the Volga, the Crimea, and the

---

[1] See S. A. Cook, Art. " Jews," *Ency. Brit.* 1911 ; O. Procksch, " Die Völker Altpalästinas," *Das Land der Bibel*, i. 2, 1914, p. 28 ff.

[2] From Old French *Juis*, Lat. *Judaei*, *i.e.* Sons of Jehúdah (Judah). See my article, " Jews," in Cassell's *Storehouse of General Information*, 1893, from which I take many of the following particulars.

Caspian—accepted Judaism, though they later conformed to Russian orthodoxy.   The Visigoth persecution of the Spanish Jews (fifth and sixth centuries) was largely due to their prose-lytising zeal, against which, as well as against Jewish and Christian mixed marriages, numerous papal decrees were issued in medieval times.

To this process of miscegenation is attributed the great variety of physical features observed amongst the Jews of different countries,[1] while the distinctly red type cropping out almost everywhere has been traced by Sayce and Diverse others to primordial interminglings with the Physical Amorites (" Red People "). " Uniformity only Types. exists in the books and not in reality.   There are Jews with light and with dark eyes, Jews with straight and with curly hair, Jews with high and narrow and Jews with short and broad noses ; their cephalic index oscillates between 65 and 98—as far as this index ever oscillates in the *genus homo* ! " [2]   Never-theless certain marked characteristics—large hooked nose, prominent watery eyes, thick pendulous and almost everted underlip, rough frizzly lustreless hair—are sufficiently general to be regarded as racial traits.

The race is richly endowed with the most varied qualities, as shown by the whole tenour of their history.   Originally pure nomads, they became excellent agriculturists after the settlement in Canaan, and since then they have given proof of the highest capacity for science, letters, erudition of all kinds, finance, music, and diplomacy.   The reputation of the medieval Arabs as restorers of learning is largely due to their wise tolerance of the enlightened Jewish communities in their midst, and on the other hand Spain and Portugal have never recovered from the national loss sustained by the expulsion of the Jews in the fourteenth and fifteenth centuries.   In late years the persecutions, especially in Russia, have caused a fresh exodus from the east of Europe, and by the aid of philanthro-pic capitalists flourishing agricultural settlements have been

[1] W. M. Flinders Petrie attributes the variation to environment, not miscegena-tion.   " History and common observation lead us to the equally legitimate con-clusion that the country and not the race determines the cranium."   " Migra-tions," *Journ. Anthr. Inst.* XXXVI. 1906, p. 218.   He is here criticising the excellent discussion of the whole question in W. Z. Ripley's *The Races of Europe*, 1900, Chap. XIV. " The Jews and Semites," pp. 368–400, with bibliography.   Cf. also R. N. Salaman, " Heredity and the Jews," *Journ. of Genetics*, I. p. 274.

[2] F. von Luschan, " The Early Inhabitants of Western Asia," *Journ. Roy. Anthr. Inst.* XLI. 1911, p. 226.

founded in Palestine and Argentina. From statistics taken in various places up to 1911 the Jewish communities are at present estimated at about 12,000,000, of whom three-fourths are in Europe, 380,000 in Africa, 500,000 in Asia, the rest in America and Australia.[1]

Intimately associated with all these Aramaic Canaanitic Semites were a mysterious people who had been identified

The Hittites. with the *Hittites* [2] of Scripture, and to whom this name has been extended by common consent. They are also identified with the *Kheta* of the Egyptian monuments,[3] as well as with the *Khatti* of the Assyrian cuneiform texts. Indeed all these are, without any clear proof, assumed to be the same people, and to them are ascribed a considerable number of stones, cylinders, and gems from time to time picked up at various points between the Middle Euphrates and the Mediterranean, engraved in a kind of hieroglyphic or rather pictorial script, which has been variously deciphered according to the bias or fancy of epigraphists. This simply means that the " Hittite texts " have not yet been interpreted, and are likely to remain unexplained, until a clue is found in some bilingual document, such as the Rosetta Stone, which surrendered the secret of the Egyptian hieroglyphs. L. Messerschmidt, editor of a number of Hittite texts,[4] declared (in 1902) that only one sign in two hundred had been interpreted with any certainty,[5] and although the system of A. H. Sayce [6] is based on a scientific plan, his decipherments must for the present remain uncertain. The important tablets found by H. Winckler in 1907 [7] at Boghaz Keui in Cappadocia, identified with Khatti, the Hittite capital, have thrown much light on Hittite history, and support many of Sayce's conjectures. The records

---

[1] M. Fishberg, *The Jews*, 1911, p. 10.

[2] As Heth, settled in Hebron (*Gen.* xxiii. 3) and the central uplands (*Num.* xiii. 29) but also as a confederacy of tribes to the north (1 *Kings* x. 29, 2 *Kings* vii. 6).

[3] This identification is based on " the casts of Hittite profiles made by Petrie from the Egyptian monuments. The profiles are peculiar, unlike those of any other people represented by the Egyptian artists, but they are identical with the profiles which occur among the Hittite hieroglyphs " (A. H. Sayce, *Acad.*, Sept. 1894, p. 259).

[4] " Corpus insc. Hetticarum," *Zeitschr. d. d. morgenländ. Gesellsch.* 1900, 1902, 1906, etc.

[5] " Die Hettiter," *Der Alte Orient*, i. 4, 1902, p. 14 *n.* The sign in question, a bisected oval, is interpreted " god."

[6] " Decipherment of the Hittite Inscriptions," *Soc. of Bibl. Archaeology*, 1903, and " Hittite Inscriptions," *ib.* 1905, 1907.

[7] *Orient. Literaturzeitung*, 1907, and *Orient-Gesellsch.* 1907. See D. G. Hogarth, " Recent Hittite Research," *Journ. Roy. Anthr. Inst.* xxxvi. 1909, p. 408.

show that the Hittites were one of the great nations of antiquity, with a power extending at its prime from the Asiatic coast of the Aegean to Mesopotamia, and from the Black Sea to Kadesh on the Orontes, a power which neither Egypt nor Assyria could withstand. " It is still not certain to which of the great families of nations they belonged. The suggestion has been made that their language has certain Indo-European characteristics ; but for the present it is safer to regard them as an indigenous race of Asia Minor. Their strongly-marked facial type, with long, straight nose and receding forehead and chin, is strikingly reproduced on all their monuments, and suggests no comparison with Aryan or Semitic stocks." [1]

F. von Luschan, however, is able to throw some light on the ethnological history of the Hittites. When investigating the early inhabitants of Western Asia he was constantly struck by the appearance of a markedly non-Semitic type, which he called " Armenoid." The most typical were the Tahtadji or woodcutters of Western Lycia living up in the mountains and totally distinct in every way from their Mohammedan neighbours. " Their somatic characters are remarkably homogeneous ; they have a tawny white skin, much hair on the face, straight hair, dark brown eyes, a narrow, generally aquiline nose, and a very short and high head. The cephalic index varies only from 82 to 91, with a maximum frequency of 86." [2] Similar types were found in the Bektash, who are town-dwellers in Lycia, and in the Ansariyeh in Northern Syria. In Upper Mesopotamia these features occur again among the Kyzylbash, and in Western Kurdistan among the Yezidi. " We find a small minority of groups possessing a similarity of creed and a remarkable uniformity of type, scattered over a vast part of Western Asia. I see no other way to account for this fact than to assume that the members of all these sects are the remains of an old homogeneous population, which have preserved their religion and have therefore refrained from intermarriage with strangers and so preserved their old physical characteristics." [3] They all speak the languages of their ortho-

---

[1] L. W. King, " The Hittites," Hutchinson's *History of the Nations*, 1914, p. 263. For this type see the illustration of Hittite divinities, Pl. XXXI. of F. von Luschan's paper referred to below. For language see now C. J. S. Marstrander, " Caractère Indo-Européen de la langue Hittite," *Videnskapsselskapets Skrifter* II *Hist. filos. Klasse*, 1918, No. 2.

[2] " The Early Inhabitants of Western Asia," *Journ. Roy. Anthr. Inst.* XLI. 1911, p. 230. For this region see D. G. Hogarth, *The Nearer East*, 1902, with ethnological map.   [3] *Loc. cit.* p. 232.

K.   32

dox neighbours, Turkish, Arabic and Kurdish, but are absolutely homogeneous as to their somatic characters.   Two other groups with the same physical type are the Druses of the Lebanon and Antilebanos country, who speak Arabic and pass officially as Mohammedans, though their secret creed contains many Christian, Jewish and pantheistic elements.   To the north of the Druses are the Christian Maronites, said to be the descendants of a Monophysite sect, separated from the common Christian Church after the Council of Chalcedon in 451 A.D.   " Partly through their isolation in the mountains, partly through their not intermarrying with their Mahometan or Druse neighbours, the Maronites of to-day have preserved an old type in almost marvellous purity.   In no other Oriental group is there a greater number of men with extreme height of the skull and excessive flattening of the occipital region than among the Maronites. . . . Very often their occiput is so steep that one is again and again inclined to think of artificial deformation."   But " no such possibility is found." [1]

These hypsibrachycephalic groups with high narrow noses, found also in Persia, among Turks, Greeks, and still more commonly among Armenians, were first (1892) called by von Luschan " Armenoid," but " there can be no doubt that they are all descended from tribes belonging to the great Hittite Empire.   So it is the type of the Hittites that has been preserved in all these groups for more than 3000 years." [2]   As to their primordial home von Luschan connects them with the " Alpine Race " of Central Europe, but leaves it an open question whether the Hittites came from Central Europe, or the Alpine Race from Western Asia, though inclining to the latter view.   The high narrow nose (the essential somatic difference between the Hittites and the other brachycephalic Arabs) " originated as a merely accidental mutation and was then locally fixed, either by a certain tendency of taste and fashion or by long, perhaps millennial in-breeding.   The ' Hittite nose ' has finally become a dominant characteristic in the Mendelian sense, and we see it, not only in the actual geographical province of the Alpine Race, but often enough also here in England." [2]

In Arabia itself inscriptions point to the early existence of civilised kingdoms, among which those of the Sabaeans [3] and

---

[1] F. von Luschan, *loc. cit.* p. 233.   [2] *Loc. cit.* pp. 242–3.
[3] Saba', Sheba of the Old Testament, where there are various allusions to its wealth and trading importance from the time of Solomon to that of Cyrus.

the Minaeans [1] stand out most clearly, though their dates and even their chronological order are much disputed. Possibly both lasted until the rise of the Himyar- Arabia and the ites at the beginning of the Christian era.   All are Arabs. agreed however that Arabian civilisation reached a very high level in the centuries preceding the birth of the Prophet, before the increase in shipping led to the abandonment of the caravan trade.

The modern inhabitants are divided into the Southern Arabians, mainly settled agriculturalists of Yemen, Hadramaut and Oman, who trace their descent from Shem, and the Northern Arabians (Bedouin), [2] pastoral tribes, who trace their descent from Ishmael.   The two groups have even been considered ethnologically distinct, but, as von Luschan points out, "peninsular Arabia is the least-known land in the world, and large regions of it are even now absolutely *terrae incognitae*, so great caution is necessary in forming conclusions, from the measurements of a few dozens of men, concerning the anthropology of a land more than five times as great as France." [3] His measurements of "the only real Semites, the Bedawy," gave a cephalic index ranging from 68 to 78, while the nose was short and fairly broad, very seldom of a "Jewish type." Recently Seligman [4] has shown that whereas the Semites of Northern Arabia conform more or less to the type just mentioned those of Southern Arabia are of low or median stature (1.62–1.65 m., $63\frac{3}{4}$–65 in.), and are predominantly brachycephalic, the cephalic index ranging from 71 to 92, with an average of about 82.

Elsewhere—Iberia, Sicily, Malta, [5] Irania, Central Asia, Malaysia—the Arab invaders have failed to preserve either their speech or their racial individuality.   In some places (Spain, Portugal, Sicily) they have disappeared altogether, leaving nothing behind them beyond some slight linguistic traces, and the monuments of their wonderful architecture, crumbling Alhambras or stupendous mosques re-consecrated as Christian temples.   But in the eastern lands their influence is still felt by

---

[1] Ma'īn of the inscriptions.

[2] Arabic *badawīy*, a dweller in the desert.

[3] *Loc. cit.* p. 235.

[4] C. G. Seligman, "The physical characters of the Arabs," *Journ. Roy. Anthr. Inst.* XLVII. 1917, p. 214 ff.

[5] The rude Semitic dialect still current in this island appears to be fundamentally Phoenician (Carthaginian), later affected by Arabic and Italian influences.   (M. Mizzi, *A Voice from Malta*, 1896, *passim*.)

multitudes, who profess Islám and use the Arabic script in writing their Persian, Turki, or Malay languages, because some centuries ago those regions were swept by a tornado of rude Bedouin fanatics, or else visited by peaceful traders and missionaries from the Arabian peninsula.

The monotheism proclaimed by these zealous preachers is often spoken of as a special inheritance of the Semitic peoples, or at least already possessed by them at such an early period in their life-history as to seem inseparable from their very being. But it was not so. Before the time of Allah or of Jahveh every hill-top had its tutelar deity ; the caves and rocks and the very atmosphere swarmed with " jins " ; Assyrian and Phoenician pantheons, with their Baals, and Molochs, and Astartes and Adonais, were as thickly peopled as those of the Hellenes and Hindus, and in this, as in all other natural systems of belief, the monotheistic concept was gradually evolved by a slow process of elimination. Nor was the process perfected by all the Semitic peoples— Canaanites, Assyrians, Amorites, Phoenicians, and others having always remained at the polytheistic stage—but only by the Hebrews and the Arabs, the two more richly endowed members of the Semitic family. Even here a reservation has to be made, for we now know that there was really but one evolution, that of Jahveh, the adoption of the idea embodied in Allah being historically traceable to the Jewish and Christian systems. As Jastrow points out, the higher religious and ethical movement began with Moses, who invested the national Jahveh with ethical traits, thus paving the way for the wider conceptions of the Prophets. " The point of departure in the Hebrew religion from that of the Semitic in general did not come until the rise of a body of men who set up a new ideal of divine government of the universe, and with it as a necessary corollary a new standard of religious conduct. Throwing aside the barriers of tribal limitations to the jurisdiction of a deity, it was the Hebrew Prophets who first prominently and emphatically brought forth the view of a divine power conceived in spiritual terms, who, in presiding over the universe and in controlling the fates of nations and individuals, acts from self-imposed laws of righteousness tempered with mercy." [1]

Semitic Monotheism.

[1] M. Jastrow, *Hebrew and Babylonian Traditions*, 1910.

CHAPTER XV

THE CAUCASIC PEOPLES (*continued*)

THE PEOPLES OF ARYAN SPEECH—European Trade Routes—" Aryan " Migrations—Indo-European Cradle—Indo-European Type—Date of Indo-European Expansion—Origin of Nordic Peoples—The *Cimbri* and *Teutoni—The Bastarnae—The Moeso-Goths*—Scandinavia—Modification of the Nordic Type—THE CELTO-SLAVS : Their Ethnical Position defined—Aberrant *Tyrolese* Type—*Rhaetians* and *Etruscans*—Etruscan Origins—The Celts—Definitions—Celts in Britain—The Picts—Brachycephals in Britain—Round Barrow Type—Alpine Type—Ethnic Relations—Formation of the English Nation—Ethnic Relations in Ireland—Scotland—and in Wales—Present Constitution of the British Peoples—The English Language—*The French Nation*—Constituent Elements—Mental Traits—*The Spaniards and Portuguese*—Ethnic Relations in Italy—*Ligurian, Illyrian,* and *Aryan Elements*—The Present *Italians*—Art and Ethics—*The Rumanians*—Ethnic Relations in Greece—*The Hellenes*—Origins and Migrations—The *Lithuanian* Factor—*Aeolians ; Dorians ; Ionians*—The Hellenic Legend—The Greek Language—THE SLAVS—Origins and Migrations—*Sarmatians* and *Budini*—*Wends, Chekhs,* and *Poles*—The Southern Slavs—Migrations—*Serbs, Croats, Bosnians—The Albanians—The Russians*—Panslavism—Russian Origins—*Alans* and *Ossets*—Aborigines of the Caucasus—THE IRANIANS—Ethnic and Linguistic Relations—*Persians, Tajiks* and *Galcha*—*Afghans*—Lowland and Hill Tajiks—The Galchic Linguistic Family—Galcha and Tajik Types—*Homo Europaeus* and *H. Alpinus* in Central Asia—THE HINDUS—Ethnic Relations in India—Classification of Types—*The Kóls—The Dravidians*—Dravidian and Aryan Languages—The Hindu Castes—OCEANIA—*Indonesians—Micronesians—Eastern Polynesians*—Origins, Types, and Divisions—Migrations—Polynesian Culture.

As the result of recent researches there is an end of the theory that bronze came in with the " Aryans," and it is from this standpoint that the revelation of an independent Aegean culture in touch with Babylonia and Egypt some four millenniums before the new era is of such momentous import in determining the ethnical relations of the historical, *i.e.* the present European populations.

Some idea of cultured relations in prehistoric times may be obtained from a review of the trade communications as indicated by archaeology during the Bronze Age, which lasted through the whole of the third millennium down to the middle of the second. As we have seen, in the Nile valley, in Mesopotamia and in the Aegean area, remains characteristic of Bronze Age culture rest on a neolithic substratum, and a transitional stage, when

European Trade Routes.

gold and copper were the only metals known, often connects the two. From the time of this dawning of the Age of Metals, the inhabitants of the Nile Valley, of Crete, of Cyprus and of the mainland of Greece freely exchanged their products. Navigation was already flourishing, and the sea united rather than divided the insular and coastal populations. Gradually Egeo-Mykenaean civilisation extended from Crete and the Greek lands to the west, influencing Sicily directly, and leaving distinct traces in Southern Italy, Sardinia and the Iberian peninsula, while Iberia in its turn contributed to the development of Western Gaul and the British Isles. The knowledge of copper, and, soon after, that of bronze, spread by the Atlantic route to Ireland, while Central Europe was reached directly from the south. Thanks to the trade in amber, always in demand by the Mediterranean populations, there was a continuous trade route to Scandinavia, which thus had direct communication with Southern Europe. As civilisation developed, the lands of the north and west became exporters as well as importers, each developing a distinct industry not always inferior to the more precocious culture of the south.[1]

With trade communications thus stretching across Europe from south to north, and from east to extreme west, it would

"Aryan" Migrations.

seem not improbable that movements of peoples were equally unrestricted, and this would account for the appearance on the threshold of history of various peoples formerly grouped together on account of their language, as "Aryan." J. L. Myres, however, is inclined to attribute "the coming of the North" to the same type of climatic impulse which induced the Semitic swarms described above (p. 489). After referring to the earliest occurrence of Indo-European names,[2] he continues, "Before the time of the Eighteenth Dynasty of Egypt there had been a very extensive raid of Indo-European-speaking folk by way of the Persian plateau, as far as the Syrian coastland and the interior of Asia Minor." These raids coincide with a new cultural feature of great significance. " It is of the first importance to find that it is in the dark period which immediately precedes the Eigh-

---

[1] Cf. J. Déchelette, *Manuel d'archéologie préhistorique*, Vol. II. 1910, p. 2, and for neolithic trade routes, *ib.* Vol. I. p. 626.

[2] The Tell-el-Amarna correspondence contains names of chieftains in Syria and Palestine about 1400 B.C., including the name of Tushratta, king of Mitanni; the Boghaz Keui document with Iranian divine names, and Babylonian records of Iranian names from the Persian highlands, are a little later in date.

teenth Dynasty revival—when Egypt was prostrate under mysterious ' Shepherd Kings,' and Babylon under Kassite invaders equally mysterious—that the civilised world first became acquainted with one of the greatest blessings of civilisation, the domesticated horse. The period of Arabian drought, which drove forth the ' Canaanite ' emigrants, may have had its counterpart on the northern steppe, to provoke the migration of these horsemen." He adds, however, " our knowledge both of the extent of these droughts and of the chronology of both these migrations, is too vague for this to be taken as more than a provisional basis for more exact enquiry." [1]

The attempt has often been made to locate the original home of the Indo-European people by an appeal to philology, and idyllic pictures have been drawn up of the " Aryan family " consisting of the father the protector, the mother the producer, and the children " whose name implied that they kept everything clean and neat." [2]   They were regarded as originally pastoral and later agricultural, ranging over a wide area with Bactria for its centre.   With advancing knowledge of what is primitive in Indo-European this circumstantial picture crumbled to pieces, and Feist [3] reduces all inferences deducible from linguistic palaeontology to the sole " argumentum ex silencio " (which he regards as distinctly untrustworthy in itself), that the " Urheimat " was a country in which in the middle of the third millennium B.C. such southern animals as lion, elephant, and tiger, were unknown.   It was commonly assumed that the " Aryan cradle " was in Asia, and the suggestion of R. G. Latham in 1851 that the original home was in Europe was scouted by one of the most eminent writers on the subject— Victor Hehn—as lunacy possible only to one who lived in a country of cranks.[2]   But since this date, there has been a shifting of the " Urheimat " further and further west. O. Schrader [4] places it in south Russia, G. Kossinna [5] and H. Hirt [6] support the claims of Germany, while K. Penka and

Indo-European Cradle.

---

[1] J. L. Myres, *The Dawn of History*, 1911, p. 200.

[2] Cf. P. Giles, Art. " Indo-European Languages " in *Ency. Brit.* 1911.

[3] S. Feist, *Kultur, Ausbreitung und Herkunft der Indogermanen*, 1913, pp. 40 and 486–528.

[4] O. Schrader, *Sprachvergleichung und Urgeschichte*, 3rd ed. 1906–7.

[5] G. Kossinna, *Die Herkunft der Germanen*, 1911.

[6] H. Hirt, *Die Indogermanen, ihre Verbreitung, ihre Urheimat und ihre Kultur* 1905–7.

many others go still further north, deriving both language and tall fair dolichocephalic speakers (proto-Teutons) from Scandinavia.[1]

F. Kauffmann,[2] noting the contrast between the cultures associated with pre-neolithic and with neolithic kitchen-middens, is prepared to attribute the former to aboriginal inhabitants, Ligurians, and, further north, Kvaens (Finns, Lapps), and the neolithic civilisation of Europe to Indo-Europeans. "Thus the neolithic Indo-Europeans would already have advanced as far as South Sweden in the Litorina period of the Baltic, during the oak period."

On the other hand the discovery of Tocharish has inclined E. Meyer [3] to reconsider an Asiatic origin, but the information as to this language is too fragmentary to be conclusive on this point. After reviewing the various theories Giles [4] concludes "in the great plain which extends across Europe north of the Alps and Carpathians and across Asia north of the Hindu Kush there are few geographical obstacles to prevent the rapid spread of peoples from any part of its area to any other, and, as we have seen, the Celts and the Hungarians etc. have in the historical period demonstrated the rapidity with which such migrations could be made. Such migrations may possibly account for the appearance of a people using a *centum* language so far east as Turkestan." [5]

More acrimonious than the discussion of the original home is the dispute as to the original physical type of the Indo-European-speaking people. It was almost a matter of **Indo-European Type.** faith with Germans that the language was introduced by tall fair dolichocephals of Nordic type. On the other hand the Gallic school sought to identify the Alpine race as the only and original Aryans. The futility of the whole discussion is ably demonstrated by W. Z. Ripley in his protest against the confusion of language and race.[6] Feist [7] summarises our information as follows. All that we can

---

[1] S. Feist, *Kultur, Ausbreitung und Herkunft der Indogermanen,* 1913, pp. 40 and 486–528.

[2] *Deutsche Altertumskunde,* I. 1913, p. 49.   [3] See Note 3, p. 441 above.

[4] Art. "Indo-European Languages," *Ency. Brit.* 1911, p. 500.

[5] Centum (hard guttural) group is the name applied to the Western and entirely European branches of the Indo-European family, as opposed to the satem (sibilant) group, situated mainly in Asia.

[6] *The Races of Europe,* 1900, p. 17 and chap. XVII. European origins : Race and Language : The Aryan Question.

[7] S. Feist, *Kultur, Ausbreitung und Herkunft der Indogermanen,* 1913, pp. 497, 501 ff.

say about the physical type of the " Urvolk " is that since the Indo-Europeans came from a northerly region [1] (not yet identified) it is surmised that they belonged to the light-skinned people. The observation that mountain folk of Indo-Germanic speech in southern areas, such as the Ossets of the Caucasus, the Kurds of the Uplands of Armenia and Irania, and the Tajiks of the western Pamirs not infrequently exhibit fair hair or blue eyes supports this view. Nevertheless, as he points out, brachycephals are not hereby excluded. His own conclusion, which naturally results from a review of the whole evidence, is that the " Urvolk " was not a pure race, but a mixture of different types. Already in neolithic times races in Europe were no longer pure, and in France " formed an almost inextricable medley " and Feist assumes with E. de Michelis [2] that the Indo-Europeans were a conglomerate of peoples of different origins who in prehistoric times were welded together into an ethnic unity, as the present English have been formed from pre-Indo-European Caledonians (Picts and Scots), Celts, Roman traders and soldiers and later Teutonic settlers. [3]

The evidence that Indo-Europeans were already in existence in Mesopotamia, Syria and Irania about the middle of the second millennium B.C. has already been mentioned. About the same time the Vedic hymns bear witness to the appearance of the Aryans of Western India. The formation of an Aryan group with a common language, religion and culture is a process necessarily requiring considerable length of time, so that their swarming off from the Indo-European parent group must be pushed back to far into the third millennium. At this period there are indications of the settling of the Greeks in the southern promontories of the Balkan peninsula at latest about 2000 B.C., while Thracian and Illyrian peoples may have filled the mainland, though the Dorians occupied Epirus, Macedonia, and perhaps southern Illyria. Indo-European stocks were already in occupation of Central Italy. It would appear therefore that the period of the Indo-European community, before the migrations, must be placed at the end of the Stone Ages, at the time when copper was first introduced. Thus it seems

Date of Indo-European Expansion.

[1] Cf. T. Rice Holmes, *Caesar's Conquest of Gaul*, 1911, p. 273.
[2] E. de Michelis, *L'origine degli Indo-Europei*, 1905.
[3] Even Sweden, regarded as the home of the purest Nordic type, already had a brachycephalic mixture in the Stone Age. See G. Retzius, " The So-called North European Race of Mankind," *Journ. Roy. Anthrop. Inst.* XXXIX. 1909, p. 304.

legitimate to infer that the expansion of the Indo-Europeans began about 2500 B.C. and the furthest advanced branches entered into the regions of the older populations and cultures at latest after the beginning of the second millennium.[1]   About 1000 B.C. we find three areas occupied by Indo-European-speaking peoples, all widely separated from each other and apparently independent.   These are (1) the Aryan groups in Asia ; (2) the Balkan peninsula together with Central and Lower Italy, and the Mysians and Phrygians of Asia Minor possibly the Thracians had already advanced across the Danube) ; and (3) Teutons, Celts and Letto-Slavs over the greater part of Germany and Scandinavia, perhaps also already in Eastern France and in Poland.   The following centuries saw the advance of Iranians to South Russia and further west, the pressing of the Phrygians into Armenia, and lastly the Celtic migrations in Western Europe.

From the linguistic and botanical evidence brought forward by the Polish botanist Rostafínski [2] the ancestors of the Celts, Germans and Balto-Slavs must have occupied a region north of the Carpathians, and west of a line between Königsberg and Odessa (the beech and yew zone).   The Balto-Slavs subsequently lost the word for beech and transferred the word for yew to the sallow and black alder (both with red wood) but their possession of a word for hornbeam locates their original home in Polesie—the marsh-land traversed by the Pripet but not south or east of Kiev.

Origin of the Nordic Peoples.

Although, owing to the absence of Teutonic inscriptions before the third or fourth century A.D. it is difficult to trace the Nordic peoples with any certainty during the Bronze or Early Iron Ages, yet the fairly well-defined group of Bronze Age antiquities, covering the basin of the Elbe, Mecklenburg, Holstein, Jutland, Southern Sweden and the islands of the Belt have been conjectured with much probability to represent early Teutonic civilisation.   " Whether we are justified in speaking of a Teutonic race in the anthropological sense is at least doubtful, for the most striking characteristics of these peoples [as deduced from prehistoric skeletons, descriptions of ancient writers and present day statistics] occur also to a con-siderable extent among their eastern and western neighbours,

---

[1] Cf. E. Meyer, *Geschichte des Altertums*, 1909, l. 2, § 551.
[2] For the working out of this hypothesis see T. Peisker, " The Expansion of the Slavs," *Cambridge Medieval History*, Vol. II. 1913.

where they can hardly be ascribed altogether to Teutonic admixture. The only result of anthropological investigation which so far can be regarded as definitely established is that the old Teutonic lands in Northern Germany, Denmark and Southern Sweden have been inhabited by people of the same type since the neolithic age if not earlier."[1] This type is characterised by tall stature, long narrow skull, light complexion with light hair and eyes.[2]

During the age of national migrations, from the fourth to the sixth century, the territories of the Nordic peoples were vastly extended, partly by conquest, and partly by arrangement with the Romans. But these movements had begun before the new era, for we hear of the *Cimbri* invading Illyricum, Gaul and Italy in the second century B.C. probably from Jutland,[3] where they were apparently associated with the *Teutoni*. Still earlier, in the third century B.C., the *Bastarnae*, said by many ancient writers to have been Teutonic in origin, invaded and settled between the Carpathians and the Black Sea. Already mentioned doubtfully by Strabo as separating the Germani from the Scythians (Tyragetes) about the Dniester and Dnieper, their movements may now be followed by authentic documents from the Baltic to the Euxine. Furtwängler [4] shows that the earliest known German figures are those of the Adamklissi monument, in the Dobruja, commemorating the victory of Crassus over the Bastarnae, Getae, and Thracians in 28 B.C. The Bastarnae migrated before the Cimbri and Teutons through the Vistula valley to the Lower Danube about 200 B.C. They had relations with the Macedonians, and the successes of Mithridates over the Romans were due to their aid. The account of their overthrow by Crassus in Dio Cassius is in striking accord with the scenes on the Adamklissi monument. Here they appear dressed only

The Cimbri and Teutoni.

The Bastarnae.

---

[1] H. M. Chadwick, Art. "Teutonic Peoples" in *Ency. Brit.* 1911. Cf. S. Feist, *Kultur, Ausbreitung und Herkunft der Indogermanen*, 1913, p. 480.

[2] See R. Much, Art. "Germanen," J. Hoops' *Reallexikon d. Germ. Altertumskunde*, 1914.

[3] H. M. Chadwick, *The Origin of the English Nation*, 1907, pp. 210-215. For a full account of the affinities of the *Cimbri* and *Teutoni* see T. Rice Holmes, *Caesar's Conquest of Gaul*, 1911, pp. 546-553.

[4] Paper read at the Meeting of the Ger. Anthrop. Soc., Spiers, 1896. Figures of Bastarnae from the Adamklissi monument and elsewhere are reproduced in H. Hahne's *Das Vorgeschichtliche Europa : Kulturen und Völker*, 1910, figs. 144, 149. Cf. T. Peisker, "The Expansion of the Slavs," *Camb. Med. Hist.* Vol. II. 1913, p. 430.

in a kind of trowsers, with long pointed beards, and defiant but noble features. The same type recurs both on the column of Trajan, who engaged them as auxiliaries in his Dacian wars, and on the Arch of Marcus Aurelius, here however wearing a tunic, a sign perhaps of later Roman influences. And thus after 2000 years are answered Strabo's doubts by modern archaeology.

Much later there followed along the same beaten track between the Baltic and Black Sea a section of the Goths, whom we find first settled in the Baltic lands in proximity to the Finns. The exodus from this region can scarcely have taken place before the second century of the new era, for they are still unknown to Strabo, while Tacitus locates them on the Baltic between the Elbe and the Vistula. Later Cassiodorus and others bring them from Scandinavia to the Vistula, and up that river to the Euxine and Lower Danube. Although often regarded as legendary,[1] this migration is supported by archaeological evidence. In 1837 a gold torque with a Gothic inscription was found at Petroassa in Wallachia, and in 1858 an iron spear-head with a Gothic name in the same script, which dates from the first Iron Age, turned up near Kovel in Volhynia. The spear-head is identical with one found in 1865 at Münchenberg in Brandenburg, on which Wimmer remarks that " of 15 Runic inscriptions in Germany the two earliest occur on iron pikes. There is no doubt that the runes of the Kovel spear-head and of the ring came from Gothic tribes."[2] These Southern Goths, later called Moeso-Goths, because they settled in Moesia (Bulgaria and Servia), had certain physical and even moral characters of the Old Teutons, as seen in the Emperor Maximinus, born in Thrace of a Goth·by an Alan woman—very tall, strong, handsome, with light hair and milk-white skin,[3] temperate in all things and of great mental energy.

Before their absorption in the surrounding Bulgar and Slav populations the Moeso-Goths were evangelised in the fourth century by their bishop Ulfilas (" Wolf "), whose fragmentary translation of Scripture, preserved in the *Codex Argenteus* of Upsala, is the most precious monument of early Teutonic speech extant.

The Moeso-Goths.

---

[1] Cf. H. M. Chadwick, *The Origin of the English Nation*, 1907, pp. 174 and 219.
[2] *Monuments runiques* in *Mém. Soc. R. Ant. du Nord.* 1893.
[3] " Lactea cutis " (Sidonius Apollinaris).

To find the pure Nordic type at the present day we must seek for it in Scandinavia, which possesses one of the most highly individualised populations in Europe. The   Scandinavia. Osterdal, and the neighbourhood of Vaage in Upper Gudbrandsdal in Norway, and the Dalarna district in Sweden contain perhaps the purest Teutonic type in all Europe, the cephalic index falling well below 78.   But along the Norwegian coasts there is a strong tendency to brachycephaly (the index rising to 82–3), combined with a darkening of the hair and eye colour (the type occurs also in Denmark), indicating an outlying lodgement of the Alpine race from Central Europe.   The anthropological history of Scandinavia, according to Ripley, is as follows : " Norway has . . . probably been peopled from two directions, one element coming from Sweden and another from the south by way of Denmark. The latter type, now found on the sea coast and especially along the least attractive portion of it, has been closely hemmed in by the Teutonic immigration from Sweden." [1] Brachycephalic people already occupied parts of Denmark in the Stone Age,[2] and, according to the scanty information available, the present population is extremely mixed.   One-third of the children have light hair and light eyes, and tall stature coincides in the main with fair colouring, but in Bornholm where the cephalic index is 80 there is a taller dark type and a shorter light type, the latter perhaps akin to the Eastern variety of the Alpine race.[3]

The original Nordic type is by no means universally represented among the present Germanic peoples.   From the examination made some years ago of 6,758,000   Modification school children,[4] it would appear that about 31 per   of the Nor- cent. of living Germans may be classed as blonds,   dic Type. 14 as brunettes, and 55 as mixed ; and further that of the blonds about 43 per cent. are centred in North, 33 in Central and 24 in South Germany.   The brunettes increase, generally

---

[1] W. Z. Ripley, *The Races of Europe*, 1900, p. 205 ff.   See also O. Montelius, *Kulturgeschichte Schwedens*, 1906 ; G. Retzius and C. M. Fürst, *Anthropologica Suecica*, 1902.

[2] Commonly called the Borreby type from skulls found at Borreby in the island of Falstar, which resemble Round Barrow skulls in Britain.

[3] For Denmark consult *Meddelelser om Danmarks Antropologi* udgivne af den Antropologiske Komité, with English summaries, Bd. I. 1907–1911, Bd. II. 1913.

[4] The results were tabulated by Virchow and may be seen, without going to German sources, in W. Z. Ripley's map, p, 222, of *The Races of Europe*, 1900, where the whole question is fully dealt with.

speaking, southwards, South Bavaria showing only about 14 per cent. of blonds, and the same law holds good of the long-heads and the round-heads respectively. To what cause is to be attributed this profound modification of this branch of the Nordic type in the direction of the south ?

That the Teutons ranged in considerable numbers far beyond their northern seats is proved by the spread of the German language to the central highlands, and beyond them down the southern slopes, where a rude High German dialect lingered on in the so-called " Seven Communes " of the Veronese district far into the nineteenth century. But after passing the Main, which appears to have long formed the ethnical divide for Central Europe, they entered the zone of the brown Alpine round-heads,[1] to whom they communicated their speech, but by whom they were largely modified in physical appearance. The process has for long ages been much the same everywhere—perennial streams of Teutonism setting steadily from the north, all successively submerged in the great ocean of dark round-headed humanity, which under many names has occupied the central uplands and eastern plains since the Neolithic Age, overflowing also in later times into the Balkan Peninsula.

This absorption of what is assumed to be the superior in the inferior type, may be due to the conditions of the general movement—warlike bands, accompanied by few women, appearing as conquerors in the midst of the Alpines and merging with them in the great mass of brachycephalic peoples. Or is the transformation to be explained by de Lapouge's doctrine, that cranial forms are not so much a question of race as of social conditions, and that, owing to the increasingly unfavourable nature of these conditions, there is a general tendency for the superior long-heads to be absorbed in the inferior round-heads.[2]

The fact that dolichocephaly is more prevalent in cities and brachycephaly in rural areas has been interpreted in various ways. De Lapouge [3] contended that in France the restless and

---

[1] See Ripley's Craniological chart in " Une carte de l'Indice Céphalique en Europe," *L'Anthropologie*, VII. 1896, p. 513.

[2] The case is stated in uncompromising language by Alfred Fouillée : " Une autre loi, plus généralement admise, c'est que depuis les temps préhistoriques, les brachycéphales tendent à éliminer les dolichocéphales par l'invasion progressive des couches inférieures et l'absorption des aristocraties dans les démocraties, où elles viennent se noyer " (*Rev. des Deux Mondes*, March 15, 1895).

[3] *Recherches Anthrop. sur le Problème de la Dépopulation*, in *Rev. d'Économie politique*, IX. p. 1002 ; x. p. 132 (1895–6).

more enterprising long-heads migrated from the rural districts
in disproportionate numbers to the towns, where they died out.
For the department of Aveyron he gives a table showing a
steady rise of the cephalic index from 71.4 in prehistoric times
to 86.5 in 1899, and attributes this to the dolichos gravitating
chiefly to the large towns, as O. Ammon has also shown for
Baden.   L. Laloy summed up the results thus : France is being
depopulated, and, what is worse, it is precisely the best section
of the inhabitants that disappears, the section most productive
in eminent men in all departments of learning, while the
ignorant and rude *pecus* alone increase.

These views have met with favour even across the Atlantic,
but are by no means universally accepted.   The ground seems
cut from the whole theory by A. Macalister, who read a paper at
the Toronto Meeting of the British Association, 1897, on
" The Causes of Brachycephaly," showing that the infantile
and primitive skull is relatively long, and that there is a gradual
change, phylogenetic (racial) as well as ontogenetic (individual)
toward brachycephaly, which is certainly correlated with, and
is apparently produced by, cerebral activity and growth ; in the
process of development in the individual and the race the
frontal lobes of the brain grow the more rapidly and tend to
fill out and broaden the skull.[1]   The tendency would thus
have nothing to do with rustic and urban life, nor would the
round be necessarily, if at all, inferior to the long head.   Some
of de Lapouge's generalisations are also traversed by Livi,[2]
Deniker,[3] Sergi [4] and others, and the whole question is admirably summarised by W. Z. Ripley.[5]

But whatever be the cause, the fact must be accepted that

[1] *Nature*, 1897, p. 487.   Cf. also A. Thomson, " Consideration of . . . factors
concerned in production of Man's Cranial Form," *Journ. Anthr. Inst.* XXXIII.
1903, and A. Keith, " The Bronze Age Invaders of Britain," *Journ. Roy. Anthr.
Inst.* XLV. 1915.

[2] Livi's results for Italy (*Antropometria Militare*) differ in some respects from
those of de Lapouge and Ammon for France and Baden.   Thus he finds that in
the brachy districts the urban population is less brachy than the rural, while in
the dolicho districts the towns are more brachy than the plains.

[3] Dealing with some studies of the Lithuanian race, Deniker writes : " Ainsi
donc, contrairement aux idées de MM. de Lapouge et Ammon, en Pologne, comme
d'ailleurs en Italie, les classes les plus instruites, dirigeantes, urbaines, sont plus
brachy que les paysans " (*L'Anthropologie*, 1896, p. 351).   Similar contradictions
occur in connection with light and dark hair, eyes, etc.

[4] " E qui non posso tralasciare di avvertire un errore assai diffuso fra gli antropologi . . . i quali vorrebbero ammettere una trasformazione del cranio da
dolicocefalo in brachicefalo " (*Arii e Italici*, p. 155).

[5] W. Z. Ripley's *The Races of Europe*, 1900, p. 544 ff.

Homo Europaeus (the Nordics) becomes merged southwards in *Homo Alpinus* whose names, as stated, are many. Broca and many continental writers use the name *Kelt* or *Slavo-Kelt*, which has led to much confusion. But it merely means for them the great mass of brachycephalic peoples in Central Europe, where, at various times, Celtic and Slavonic languages have prevailed.

The Celto-Slavs.

It is remarkable that in the Alpine region, especially Tyrol, where the brachy element comes to a focus, there is a peculiar form of round-head which has greatly puzzled de Lapouge, but may perhaps be accounted for on the hypothesis of two brachy types here fused in one. To explain the exceedingly round Tyrolese head, which shows affinities on the one hand with the Swiss, on the other with the Illyrian and Albanian, that is, with the normal Alpine, a Mongol strain has been suggested, but is rightly rejected by Franz Tappeiner as inadmissible on many grounds.[1] De Ujfalvy,[2] a follower of de Lapouge, looks on the hyperbrachy Tyrolese as descendants of the ancient Rhaetians or Rasenes, whom so many regard as the parent stock of the Etruscans.

Aberrant Tyrolese Type.

Rhaetians and Etruscans.

But Montelius (with most other modern ethnologists) rejects the land route from the north, and brings the Etruscans by the sea route direct from the Aegean and Lydia (Asia Minor). They are the Thessalian Pelasgians whom Hellanikos of Lesbos brings to Campania, or the Tyrrhenian Pelasgians transported by Antiklides from Asia Minor to Etruria, and he is " quite sure that the archæological facts in Central and North Italy . . . prove the truth of this tradition." [3] Of course, until the affinities of the Etruscan language are determined, from

[1] This specialist insists " dass von einer mongolischen Einwanderung in Europakeine Rede mehr sein könne " (*Der europäische Mensch. u. die Tiroler*, 1896). He is of course speaking of prehistoric times, not of the late (historical) Mongol irruptions. Cf. T. Peisker, " The Expansion of the Slavs," *Camb. Med. Hist.* Vol. II. 1913, p. 452, with reference to mongoloid traits in Bavaria.

[2] " Malgré les nombreuses invasions des populations germaniques, le Tyrolien est resté, quant à sa conformation cranienne, le Rasène ou Rhætien des temps antiques—hyperbrachycéphale " (*Les Aryens*, p. 7). The mean index of the so-called Disentis type of Rhaetian skulls is about 86 (His and Rütimeyer, *Crania Helvetica*, p. 29 and Plate E. 1).

[3] " The Tyrrhenians in Greece and Italy," in *Journ. Anthrop. Inst.* 1897, p. 258. In this splendidly illustrated paper the date of the immigration is referred to the 11th century B.C. on the ground that the first Etruscan saeculum was considered as beginning about 1050 B.C., presumably the date of their arrival in Italy (p. 259). But Sergi thinks they did not arrive till about the end of the 8th century (*Arii e Italici*, p. 149).

which we are still as far off as ever,[1] Etruscan origins must remain chiefly an archaeological question.   Even the help afforded by the crania from the Etruscan   **Etruscan Origins.** tombs is but slight, both long and round heads being here found in the closest association.   Sergi, who also brings the Etruscans from the east, explains this by supposing that, being Pelasgians, they were of the same dolicho Mediterranean stock as the Italians (Ligurians) themselves, and differed only from the brachy Umbrians of Aryan speech. Hence the skulls from the tombs are of two types, the intruding Aryan, and the Mediterranean, the latter, whether representing native Ligurians or intruding Etruscans, being indistinguishable.   " I can show," he says, " Etruscan crania, which differ in no respect from the Italian [Ligurian], from the oldest graves, as I can also show heads from the Etruscan graves which do not differ from those still found in Aryan lands, whether Slav, Keltic, or Germanic." [2]   Perhaps the difficulty is best explained by Feist's suggestion that the Etruscans were merely a highly civilised warlike aristocracy, spreading thinly over the conquered population by which they were ultimately absorbed.[3]

The migrations of the Celts preceded those of the Teutonic peoples to whom they were probably closely related in race as in language.[4]   At the beginning of the   **The Celts.** historical period Celts are found in the west of Germany in the region of the Rhine and the Weser.   Possibly about 600 B.C. they occupied Gaul and parts of the Iberian peninsula, subsequently crossing over into the British Isles. In Italy they came into conflict with the rising power of Rome, and, after the battle of the Allia (390 B.C.) occupied Rome itself.   Descents were also made into the Danube valley and the Balkans, and later (280 B.C.) into Thessaly.   At the height of their power they extended from the north of Scotland to the southern shores of Spain and Portugal, and from the northern coasts of Germany to a little south of Senegaglia.   To the

---

[1] See R. S. Conway, Art. Etruria : Language, *Ency. Brit.* 1911.
[2] *Op. cit.* p. 151.   By German he means the round-headed South German.
[3] S. Feist, *Kultur, Ausbreitung und Herkunft der Indogermanen*, 1913, p. 370.
[4] S. Feist, *loc. cit.* p. 65.   For cultural and linguistic influence of Celts on Germans see pp. 480 ff.   Evidence of Celtic names in Germany is discussed by H. M. Chadwick, " Some German River names," *Essays and Studies presented to William Ridgeway*, 1913.

west their boundary was the Atlantic, to the east, the Black Sea.[1]

Unfortunately the indiscriminate use of the term Celt has led to much confusion. For historians and geographers the Celts are the people in the centre and west of Europe referred to by writers of antiquity under the names of *Keltoi, Celtae, Galli* and *Galatae*. But many anthropologists, especially on the continent, regard Celts and Gauls as representing two well-determined physical types, the former brachycephalic, with short sturdy build and chestnut coloured hair (Alpine type), and the latter dolichocephalic with tall stature, fair complexion and light hair (Nordic type). Linguists, ignoring physical characters, class as Celts those people who speak an Indo-European language characterised in particular by the loss of p and by the modifications undergone by mutation of initial consonants, while for many archaeologists the Celts were the people responsible for the spread of the civilisation of the Hallstatt and La Tène periods, that is of the earlier and later Iron Age.[2]

Definition of " Celt."

It is not surprising therefore that it has been proposed to drop the word Celt out of anthropological momenclature, as having no ethnical significance. But this, says Rice Holmes,[3] " is because writers on ethnology have not kept their heads clear." And in particular one point has been overlooked. " Just as the French are called after one conquering people, the Franks ; just as the English are called after one conquering people, the Angles ; so the heterogeneous Celtae of Transalpine Gaul were called after one conquering people ; and that people were the Celts, or rather a branch of the Celts in the true sense of the word. The Celts, in short, were the people who introduced the Celtic language into Gaul, into Asia Minor, and into Britain ; the people who included the victors of the Allia, the conquerors of Gallia Celtica, and the conquerors of

---

[1] H. d'Arbois de Jubainville, *Les Celtes depuis les Temps les plus anciens jusqu'en l'an* 100 *avant notre ère*, 1904, p. 1.

[2] G. Dottin, *Manuel pour servir à l'étude de l'Antiquité Celtique*, 1915, p. 1.

[3] T. Rice Holmes, *Caesar's Conquest of Gaul*, 1911, p. 321. W. Z. Ripley, *The Races of Europe*, 1900, reviewing the " *Celtic Question*, than which no greater stumbling-block in the way of our clear thinking exists " (p. 124) comes to a different conclusion. He states that " the term *Celt*, if used at all, belongs to the . . . brachycephalic, darkish population of the Alpine highlands," and he claims for this view " complete unanimity of opinion among physical anthropologists " (p. 126). His own view however is that " the linguists are best entitled to the name *Celt* " while the broad-headed type commonly called Celtic by continental writers " we shall . . . everywhere . . . call . . . Alpine " (p. 128).

Gallia Belgica ; the people whom Polybius called indifferently Gauls and Celts ; the people who, as Pausanius said, were originally called Celts and afterwards called Gauls. If certain ancient writers confounded the tall fair Celts who spoke Celtic with the tall fair Germans who spoke German the ancient writers who were better informed avoided such a mistake. . . . Let us therefore restore to the word ' Celt ' the ethnical significance which of right belongs to it."

It is not certain at what date the Celtic tribes effected settlements in Great Britain, but it is held by many that the earliest invasions were not prior to the sixth or possibly even the fifth century. At the time of the Roman conquest the Celts were divided into **Celts in Britain.** two linguistic groups, *Goidelic*, represented at the present day by Irish, Manx and Scotch Gaelic, and *Brythonic*, including Welsh, Cornish and Breton. These groups must have been virtually identical save in two particulars. In Brythonic the labial velar q became p (a change which apparently took place before the time of Pytheas), whilst in Goidelic the sound remained unaltered. q is retained in the earlier ogham inscriptions, but by the end of the seventh century it had lost the labial element, appearing in Old Irish as c. Thus O. Irish *cenn*, head, as in Kenmare, Kintyre, Kinsale, equates with Brythonic *pen*, as in Penryn (Cornwall), Penrhyn (Wales), Penkridge (Staffordshire), Penruddock, Penrith and many others. The two groups are therefore distinguished as the Q Celts and the P Celts.[1] From the fact that Goidelic retained the q it has been commonly assumed that the Goidels were separated from the main Celtic stock at a time before the labialisation had taken place, but many scholars maintain that the parent Goidelic was evolved in Ireland, and was carried from that island to Man and Scotland in the early centuries of our era.[2]

From an anthropological point of view, the Picts are if possible more difficult to identify than the Celts. But the question is not between tall fair long-heads **The Picts.** and short dark round-heads, but between short dark long-heads (neolithic aborigines) and Celts. The Pictish

---

[1] Cf. the similar dual treatment in Italic.

[2] " No Gael [*i.e.* Q Celt] ever set his foot on British soil save on a vessel that had put out from Ireland." Kuno Meyer, *Trans. Hon. Soc. Cymmrodorion*, 1895–6, p. 69.

question is summed up by Rice Holmes [1] and the various theories have been more recently reviewed by Windisch [2] giving a valuable summary of earlier writings. On the one hand it is maintained as "the most tenable hypothesis that the Picts were non-Aryans, whom the first Celtic migrations found already settled here . . . descendants of the Aborigines." [3] Windisch, [2] at the other extreme, regards them as late comers into North Britain, when Scotland was already occupied by Brythonic tribes. But the geographical distribution of the Picts in historical times suggests rather a people driven into mountainous regions by successive conquerors, than the settlements of successful invaders. Also it is not improbable that the language of the Bronze Age lingered in these wilder districts, and this would account for the fact that St Columba had to employ an interpreter in his relations with the Picts ; though this is explained by others on the assumption that Pictish was Brythonic. The linguistic evidence is however extremely slight, only a few words presumably Pictish having survived and these through Celtic writers. "The one absolutely certain conclusion to which the student of ethnology can come is that the name of the Picts has not been proved to be of pre-Aryan origin." [4] "For me," continues Rice Holmes (p. 417), "the Picts were a mixed people comprising descendants of the neolithic aborigines, of the Round Barrow Race, and of the Celtic invaders—a mixed people who [or at least whose aristocracy] spoke a Celtic dialect."

Before attempting a survey of the ethnology of Britain it is necessary to ascertain what ethnic elements the area contained before the arrival of the Celts. The **Brachycephals in Britain.** neolithic inhabitants, the short, dark dolichocephals of Mediterranean type have already been described (Ch. XIII.). Their remains are associated with the characteristic forms of sepulchral monuments the dolmens and the long barrows. But towards the end of the Stone Age a brachycephalic race was already penetrating into the islands. This appears to have been a peaceful infiltration, at any rate in certain districts, where remains of the two types are found

[1] *Ancient Britain*, 1907, pp. 409–424.
[2] *Das keltische Britannien*, 1912, pp. 28–37.
[3] J. Rhys, *The Welsh People*, 1902, pp. 13–14.
[4] *Ancient Britain*, 1907, p. 414. The name of the Picts is apparently Indo-European in form, and if the Celts were late comers into Britain (see above) they may well have been preceded by invaders of Indo-European speech.

side by side and there is evidence of racial intermixture. The brachycephals introduced a new form of sepulture, making their burial mounds circular instead of elongated, whence Thurnam's convenient formula, "long barrow, long skull; round barrow, round skull." But the earlier view that there was a definite transition from long heads, neolithic culture and long barrows, to round heads, bronze culture and round barrows can no longer be maintained. "It is often taken for granted that no round barrows were erected in Britain before the close of the Neolithic Age, and that the earliest of the brachy-cephalic invaders whose remains have been found in them landed with bronze weapons in their hands."[1] But there is abundant evidence that the brachycephalic element preceded the knowledge of metals, and a number of round barrows in Yorkshire and further north show no trace of bronze,

Nevertheless the majority of the round barrows belong to the Bronze Age, and the physical type of their builders is sufficiently well marked. The stature is remark-ably tall, attaining a height of 1.763 m. or over 5 ft. 9 ins. The skull is brachycephalic with an average index of about 80. It is also characterised by great strength and ruggedness of outline, with (often) a sloping forehead, prominent supraciliary ridges, and a certain degree of prognathism.

Round Barrow Type.

According to Rolleston's description, "The eyebrows must have given a beetling and probably even formidable appearance to the upper part of the face, whilst the boldly outstanding and heavy cheekbones must have produced an impression of raw and rough strength. Overhung at its root, the nose must have projected boldly forward." And Thurnam adds, "the prominence of the large incisor and canine teeth is so great as to give an almost bestial expression to the skull."[2]

Although this type is conveniently called the Round Barrow type, or even the Round Barrow Race, the round barrows also contain remains of a different racial character. The skull form shows a more extreme brachycephaly, with an index of 84 or 85, and exhibits none of the rugged features associated with the true Round Barrow type. On the contrary, of the two typical groups, one from

Alpine Type.

---

[1] T. Rice Holmes, *Ancient Britain*, 1907, p. 408. Cf. A. Keith, "The Bronze Age Invaders of Britain," *Journ. Roy. Anthr. Inst.* XLV. 1915.
[2] Quoted in T. Rice Holmes, *Ancient Britain*, 1907, pp. 426–427.

round barrows in Glamorganshire, and the other from short cists in Aberdeenshire, not one of the skulls is prognathous, the supraciliary ridges are but slightly developed, the cheek bones are not prominent, the face is both broad and short and the lower jaw is small. But the greatest contrast is in the height, which averages in the two groups, 1.664 m. and 1.6 m. respectively, *i.e.* 5 ft. 5¾ ins. and 5 ft. 3 ins. All these characters connect this type closely with the Alpine type on the continent.

These round-headed peoples have been the subject of much discussion ably summarised and criticised by Rice Holmes, whose conclusion perhaps best represents the view now taken of their affinities and origins.

" The great mistake that has been made in discussing the question is the not uncommon assumption that the brachycephalic immigrants who buried their dead in round barrows arrived in Britain at one time, and came from one place. Some of them certainly appeared before the end of the Neolithic Age : others may have introduced bronze implements or ornaments ; others doubtless came, in successive hordes, during the course of the Bronze Age. Some of those who belonged to the Grenelle race [Alpine type], who certainly came from Eastern Europe and possibly from Asia, and whose centre of dispersion was the Alpine region, may have started from Gaul ; others could have traced their origin to some Rhenish tribe ; and I am inclined to believe that those who belonged to the characteristic rugged Round Barrow type crossed over, for the most part, from Denmark or the out-lying islands." [1]

After the passage of the Romans, who mingled little with the aborigines and made, perhaps, but slight impression on the **Formation of the English Nation.** speech or type of the British populations, a great transformation was effected in these respects by the arrival of the historical Teutonic tribes. Hand in hand with the Teutonic invasions went a lust for expansion on the part of the peoples in Ireland. Settlements were effected by them in South Wales and Anglesey, the Isle of Man and

[1] T. Rice Holmes, *Ancient Britain*, 1907, p. 443. See also John Abercromby, *A Study of the Bronze Age Pottery of Great Britain and Ireland and its associated Grave Goods*, 1912, tracing the distribution and migration of pottery forms : and the following papers of H. J. Fleure, " Archaeological Problems of the West Coast of Britain," *Archaeologia Cambrensis*, Oct. 1915 ; " The Early Distribution of Population in South Britain," *ib.* April, 1916 ; " The Geographical Distribution of Anthropological Types in Wales," *Journ. Roy. Anthr. Inst.* XLVI. 1916, and " A Proposal for Local Surveys of the British People," *Arch. Camb.* Jan. 1917.

Argyll, probably also in North Devon and Cornwall. For many generations the south and east of England were the scenes of fierce struggles, during which the Romano-British civilisation perished. Only in more inaccessible districts, such as the fen country, may a British population have survived, though Celtic languages are not yet dislodged from their mountain strongholds in Wales and Scotland, and lingered for many centuries in Strathclyde and Cornwall. After the strengthening of the Teutonic element by the arrival of the Scandinavians and Normans, all very much of the same physical type, no serious accessions were made to this composite ethnical group, which on the east side ranged uninterruptedly from the Channel to the Grampians. Later the expansion was continued northwards beyond the Grampians, and westwards through Strathclyde to Ireland, while now the spread of education and the development of the industries are already threatening to absorb the last strongholds of Celtic speech in Wales, the Highlands, and Ireland.

Thanks to its isolation in the extreme west, Ireland had been left untouched by some of the above described ethnical movements. It is doubtful whether Palaeolithic man ever reached this region, and but few even of the round-heads ranged so far west during the Bronze Age.[1] The land oscillations during post-Glacial times appear to have been practically identical over an area including northern Ireland, the southern half of Scotland, and northern England. There was a period of depression followed by one of elevation. The Larne beach-deposits prove that Neolithic man was in existence from almost the beginning of the deposition of that series until after its conclusion. The estuarine clays of Belfast Lough correspond to the depression, and the Neolithic period extended from at least near the top of the lower estuarine clay to the beach-deposit of yellow sand which overlies it, or possibly till later. It is to this period of elevation that the Neolithic sites among the sand dunes of North Ireland belong ; those of Whitepark Bay and Portstewart, for example, extend to the maximum elevation. A slight movement of subsidence of about five feet in recent times has left the surface as we now find it. The implements found in the Larne gravels correspond to some extent with those of Danish kitchen-middens ; this

Ethnic Relations in Ireland.

---

[1] W. Z. Ripley, *The Races of Europe*, 1900, p. 310 ; T. Rice Holmes, *Ancient Britain*, 1907, p. 432.

was not a dwelling site but a quarry-shop or roughing-out place, the serviceable flakes being taken away for further manipulation ; it thus belongs to the earliest phase of neolithic times. The sandhill sites were occupied, continuously and occasionally, during neolithic times, through the Bronze Age, and into the Iron and Christian periods.[1] Nina F. Layard has recently studied the Larne raised beach and exposed a new section. She states that, " Taken as a whole the flints certainly do not correspond at all closely either to the Palæoliths or Neoliths so far found in England. . . . Some are strongly reminiscent of well-known drift type. . . . Again, there are shapes that bear a closer resemblance to some of the earliest Neolithic types." [2] She believes that, from their rolled condition, they were derived from another source.

F. J. Bigger [3] described some kitchen-middens at Portnafeadog, near Roundstone, Connemara, which yielded stone hammers but no worked flints, pottery or metal-ware. The chief interest of this paper is due to the fact that it is the first record of the occurrence of vast quantities of the shells of *Purpura lapillus*, all of which were broken in such a manner that the animal could easily be extracted. There can be no doubt that the purple dye was manufactured here in prehistoric times.[4] W. J. Knowles [5] suggests from the close resemblance —in fact identity—of a great number of neolithic objects in Ireland with palaeolithic forms in France (Saint-Acheul, Moustier, Solutré, La Madeleine types), that the Irish objects bridge over the gap between the two ages, and were worked by tribes from the continent following the migration of the reindeer northwards. These peoples may have continued to make tools of palaeolithic types, while at the same time coming under the influence of the neolithic culture gradually arriving from some southern region. The astonishing development of this neolithic culture in the remote island on the confines of the west, as illustrated in W. C. Borlase's sumptuous volumes,[6] is

[1] G. Coffey and R. Lloyd Praeger, " The Antrim Raised Beach : a Contribution to the Neolithic History of the North of Ireland," *Proc. Roy. Irish Acad.* xxv. (c.) 1904. See also the valuable series of " Reports on Prehistoric Remains from the Sandhills of the Coast of Ireland," *P.R.I.A.* xvi.

[2] *Man*, IX. 1909, No. 54.

[3] *Proc. Roy. Irish Acad.* (3), III. 1896, p. 727.

[4] Cf. also J. Wilfred Jackson, " The Geographical Distribution of the Shell-Purple Industry," *Mem. and Proc. Manchester Lit. and Phil. Soc.* LX. No. 7, 1916.

[5] *Survivals from the Palaeolithic Age among Irish Neolithic Implements*, 1897.

[6] *The Dolmens of Ireland*, 1897.

a perpetual wonder, but is rendered less inexplicable if we assume an immense duration of the New Stone Age in the British Isles. The Irish dolmen-builders were presumably of the same long-headed stock as those of Britain,[1] and they were followed by Celtic-speaking Goidels who may have come directly from the continent,[2] and there is evidence in Ptolemy and elsewhere of the presence of Brythonic tribes from Gaul in the east. Since these early historic times the intruders have been almost exclusively of Teutonic race, and Viking invaders from Norway and Denmark founded the earliest towns such as Dublin, Waterford and Limerick. Now all alike, save for an almost insignificant and rapidly dwindling minority, have assumed the speech of the English and Lowland Scotch intruders, who began to arrive late in the 12th century, and are now chiefly massed in Ulster, Leinster, and all the large towns. The rich and highly poetic Irish language has a copious medieval literature of the utmost importance to students of European origins.

In Scotland few ethnical changes or displacements have occurred since the colonisation of portions of the west by Gaelic speaking-Scottic tribes from Ireland, and the English (Angle) occupation of the Lothians. The Grampians have during historic times formed the main ethnical divide between the two elements, and brooklets which can be taken at a leap are shown where the opposite banks have for hundreds of years been respectively held by formerly hostile, but now friendly communities of Gaelic and broad Scotch speech. Here the chief intruders have been Scandinavians, whose descendants may still be recognised in Caithness, the Hebrides, and the Orkney and Shetland groups. Faint echoes of the old Norrena tongue are said still to linger amongst the sturdy Shetlanders, whose assimilation to the dominant race began only after their transfer from Norway to the Crown of Scotland.

Relations in Scotland.

---

[1] They need not, however, have come from Britain, and the allusions in Irish literature to direct immigration from Spain, probable enough in itself, are too numerous to be disregarded. Thus, Geoffrey of Monmouth :—"Hibernia Basclensibus [to the Basques] incolenda datur" (*Hist. Reg. Brit.* III. § 12) ; and Giraldus Cambrensis :—"De Gurguntio Brytonum Rege, qui Rasclenses [read Basclenses] in Hiberniam transmisit et eandem ipsis habitandam concessit." I am indebted to Wentworth Webster for these references (*Academy,* Oct. 19, 1895).

[2] H. Zimmer, "Auf welchen Wege kamen die Goidelen vom Kontinent nach Irland ?" *Abh. d. K. preuss. Akad. d. Wiss.* 1912.

Since 1901 the researches of Gray and Tocher [1] on the pigmentation of some 500,000 school children of Scotland have increased our information as to racial distribution. The average percentage of boys with fair hair is nearly 25 for the whole of the country, and when this is compared with 82 in Schleswig Holstein " we are driven to the conclusion that the pure Norse or Anglo-Saxon element in our population is by no means predominant. There is evidently also a dark or brunette element which is at least equal in amount and probably greater than that of the Norse element " (p. 380). Pure blue eyes for the whole of Scotland average 14.7 per cent., which may be compared with 42.9 in Prussia. The greatest density for fair hair and eyes is to be found in the great river valleys opening on to the German Ocean, and also in the Western Isles. The Tweed, Forth, Tay and Don all show indications of settlements of a blonde race " probably due to Anglo-Saxon invasions," but the maximum is to be found at the mouth of the Spey. The high percentage here and in the Hebrides and opposite coasts, the authors trace to Viking invasions. The percentage of dark hair for boys and girls is 25.2 as compared with 1.3 in Prussian school children, the maximum density as we should expect being in the west. Jet black hair (1.2%) has its maximum density in the central highlands and wild west coast. Beddoe,[2] commenting on Gray and Tocher's results, calculates an even higher percentage of black hair (over 2%), " either within or astride of the Highland frontier. Except Paisley, there is not a single instance south of the Forth, nor one between the Spey and the Firth of Tay. Surely there is something 'racial' here." Beddoe's map, constructed from Gray and Tocher's statistics, clearly indicates the distribution of racial types.

The work carried on in Wales for a number of years by H. J. Fleure and T. C. James [3] has produced some extremely interesting results. The chief types (based on
And in Wales. measurements and observations of head, face, nose, skin, hair and eye colour, stature, etc.) fall into the following groups.

[1] J. Gray, "Memoir on the Pigmentation Survey of Scotland," *Journ. Roy. Anthr. Inst.* XXXVII. 1907.

[2] "A Last Contribution to Scottish Ethnology," *Journ. Roy. Anthr. Inst.* XXXVIII. 1908.

[3] "The Geographical Distribution of Anthropological Types in Wales," *Journ. Roy. Anthr. Inst.* XLVI. 1916.

1. " The fundamental type is certainly the long-headed brunet of the moorlands and their inland valleys. He is universally recognised as belonging to the Mediterranean race of Sergi and as dating back in this country to early Neolithic times." The cephalic index is about 78, with high colouring, dark hair and eyes, and stature rather below the average. A possible mixture of earlier stocks is shown in a longer-headed type (c.i. about 75), with well-marked occiput, very dark hair and eyes, swarthy complexion, and average stature (about 1690 mm. = 5 ft. 6½ ins.). Occasionally in North Wales the occurrence of lank black hair, a sallow complexion and prominent cheekbones suggests a " Mongoloid " type ; and a type with small stature, black, closely curled hair and a rather broad nose has negroid reminiscences. The Plynlymon moorlands contain a " nest " of extreme dolichocephaly and an unusually high percentage of red hair.

2. Nordic-Alpine type, with cephalic index mainly between 76 and 81. This group includes (a) a " local version of the Nordic type " occurring at Newcastle Emlyn and in South and South-West Pembrokeshire with fair hair and eyes, usually tall stature and great strength of brow, jaw and chin ; (b) a heavier variant on the Welsh border, often with cephalic index above 80, and extremely tall stature ; (c) the Borreby or Beaker-Maker type, broad-headed and short-faced with darker pigmentation, probably a cross between Alpine and Nordic, characteristic of the long cleft from Corwen *via* Bala to Tabyllyn and Towyn.

3. Dark bullet-headed short thick-set men of the general type denoted by the term Alpine or more exactly perhaps by the term Cevenole are found, though not commonly, in North Montgomeryshire valleys.

4. Powerfully built, often intensely dark, broad-headed, broad-faced, strong and square jawed men are characteristic of the Ardudwy coast, the South Glamorgan coast, Newquay district (Cardiganshire) and elsewhere.

The authors observe that Type 1 with its variations contributes " considerable numbers to the ministries of the various churches, possibly in part from inherent and racial leanings, but partly also because these are the people of the moorlands. The idealism of such people usually expresses itself in music, poetry, literature and religion rather than in architecture, painting and plastic arts generally. They rarely have a sufficiency of material resources for the latter activities. These types also contribute a number of men to the medical profession. . . . The successful commercial men, who have given the Welsh their extraordinarily prominent place in British trade (shipping firms for example) usually belong to types 2 or 4, rather than to 1, as also do the majority of Welsh members of Parliament, though there are exceptions of the first importance. The Nordic type is marked by ingenuity and enterprise in striking out new lines. Type 2 (*c*) in Wales is remarkable for governmental ability of the administrative kind as well as for independence of thought and critical power " (p. 119).

We have now all the elements needed to unravel the ethnical tangle of the present inhabitants of the British Isles.

Present Constitution of the British Peoples. The astonishing prevalence everywhere of the moderately dolicho heads is at once explained by the absence of brachy immigrants except in the Bronze period, and these could do no more than raise the cephalic index from about 70 or 72 to the present mean of about 78. With the other perhaps less stable characters the case is not always quite so simple. The brunettes, representing the Mediterranean type, certainly increase, as we should expect, form north-east to south-west, though even here there is a considerable dark patch, due to local causes, in the home shires about London.[1] But the stature, almost everywhere a troublesome factor, seems to wander somewhat lawlessly over the land.

Although a short stature more or less coincides with brunetteness in England and Wales, and the observations in Ireland are too few to be relied on, no such parallelism can be traced in Scotland. The west (Inverness and Argyllshire), though as dark as South Wales, shows an average stature of 1.73 m. to 1.74 m. (5 ft. 8 ins. to 5 ft. 8½ ins.), which is higher than the average for the whole of Britain. And South-west Scotland, where the type is fairly dark, contains the tallest population in Europe, if not in the world. Ripley suggests either that " some ethnic element of which no pure trace remains, served to increase the stature of the western Highlanders without at the same time conducing to blondness ; or else some local influences of natural selection or environment are responsible for it " ;[2] and he hints also that the linguistic distinction

---

[1] For the explanation see W. Z. Ripley, *The Races of Europe*, 1900, p. 322 ff.
[2] W. Z. Ripley, *loc. cit.* p. 329.

between Gaels and Brythons may have been associated with physical variation.

The English tongue need not detain us long. Its qualities, illustrated in the noblest of all literatures, are patent to the world,[1] indeed have earned for it from Jacob Grimm the title of *Welt-Sprache*, the " World Speech." It belongs, as might be anticipated **The English Language.** from the northern origin of the Teutonic element in Britain, to the Low German division of the Teutonic branch of the Aryan family. Despite extreme pressure from Norman French, continued for over 200 years (1066—1300), it has remained faithful to this connection in its inner structure, which reveals not a trace of Neo-Latin influences. The phonetic system has undergone profound changes, which can be only indirectly and to a small extent due to French action. What English owes to French and Latin is a very large number, many thousands, of words, some superadded to, some superseding their Saxon equivalents, but altogether immensely increasing its wealth of expression, while giving it a transitional position between the somewhat sharply contrasted Germanic and Romance worlds.

Amongst the Romance peoples, that is, the French, Spaniards, Portuguese, Italians, Rumanians, many Swiss and Belgians, who were entirely assimilated in speech and largely in their civil institutions to their **The French Nation.** Roman masters, the paramount position, a sort of international hegemony, has been taken by the French nation since the decadence of Spain under the feeble successors of Philip II. The constituent elements of these Gallo-Romans, as they may be called, are much the same as those of the British peoples, but differ in their distribution and relative proportions. Thus the Iberians (Aquitani, Pictones, and later Vascones), who may perhaps be identified with the neolithic long-heads,[2] do not appear ever to have ranged much farther north than Brittany, and were Aryanised in pre-Roman times by the P-speaking Celts everywhere north of the Garonne. The prehistoric Teutons again, who had advanced beyond

---

[1] " The Frenchman, the German, the Italian, the Englishman, to each of whom his own literature and the great traditions of his national life are most dear and familiar, cannot help but feel that the vernacular in which these are embodied and expressed is, and must be, superior to the alien and awkward languages of his neighbours." L. Pearsall Smith, *The English Language*, p. 54.

[2] See above, p. 455. T. Rice Holmes points out that the Aquitani were already mixed in type. *Caesar's Conquest of Gaul*, 1911, p. 12.

the Rhine at an early period (Caesar says *antiquitus*) into the present Belgium, were mainly confined to the northern provinces. Even the historic Teutons (chiefly Franks and Burgundians) penetrated little beyond the Seine in the north and the present Burgundy in the east, while the Vandals, Visigoths and a few others passed rapidly through to Iberia beyond the Pyrenees.

Thus the greater part of the land, say from the Seine-Marne basin to the Mediterranean, continued to be held by the Romanised mass of Alpine type throughout all the central and most of the southern provinces, and elsewhere in the south by the Romanised long-headed Mediterranean type. This great preponderance of the Romanised Alpine masses explains the rapid absorption of the Teutonic intruders, who were all, except the Fleming section of the Belgae, completely assimilated to the Gallo-Romans before the close of the tenth century. It also explains the perhaps still more remarkable fact that the Norsemen who settled (912) under Rollo in Normandy were all practically Frenchmen when a few generations later they followed their Duke William to the conquest of Saxon England. Thus the only intractable groups have proved to be the Basques [1] and the Bretons, both of whom to this day retain their speech in isolated corners of the country. With these exceptions the whole of France, save the debateable area of Alsace-Lorraine, presents in its speech a certain homogeneous character, the standard language (*langue d'oïl*) [2] being current throughout all the northern and central provinces, while it is steadily gaining upon the southern form (*langue d'oc*) [2] still surviving in the rural districts of Limousin and Provence.

But pending a more thorough fusion of such tenacious elements as Basques, Bretons, Auvergnats, and Savoyards, we **Mental Traits.** can scarcely yet speak of a common French type, but only of a common nationality. Tall stature, long skulls, fair or light brown colour, grey or blue eyes, still

---

[1] See above, p. 454.

[2] That is, the languages whose affirmatives were the Latin pronouns *hoc illud* (*oil*) and *hoc* (*oc*), the former being more contracted, the latter more expanded, as we see in the very names of the respective Northern and Southern bards : *Trouvères* and *Troubadours*. It was customary in medieval times to name languages in this way, Dante, for instance, calling Italian *la lingua del si*, " the language of *yes* " ; and, strange to say, the same usage prevails largely amongst the Australian aborigines, who, however, use both the affirmative and the negative particles, so that we have here *no*- as well as *yes*-tribes.

prevail, as might be expected, in the north, these being traits common alike to the prehistoric Belgae, the Franks of the Merovingian and Carlovingian empires, and Rollo's Norsemen. With these contrast the southern peoples of short stature, olive-brown skin, round heads, dark brown or black eyes and hair. The tendency towards uniformity has proceeded far more rapidly in the urban than in the rural districts. Hence the citizens of Paris, Lyons, Bordeaux, Marseilles and other large towns, present fewer and less striking contrasts than the natives of the old historical provinces, where are still distinguished the loquacious and mendacious Gascon, the pliant and versatile Basque, the slow and wary Norman, the dreamy and fanatical Breton, the quick and enterprising Burgundian, and the bright, intelligent, more even-tempered native of Touraine, a typical Frenchman occupying the heart of the land, and holding, as it were, the balance between all the surrounding elements.

In Spain and Portugal we have again the same ethnological elements, but also again in different proportions and differently distributed, with others superadded—proto-Phoe- *The* nicians and later Phoenicians (Carthaginians), *Spaniards and* Romans, Visigoths, Vandals, and still later Ber- *Portuguese.* bers and Arabs. Here the Celtic-speaking mixed peoples mingled in prehistoric times with the long-headed Mediterraneans, an ethnical fusion known to the ancients, who labelled it " Keltiberian." [1]   But, as in Britain, the other intruders were mostly long-heads, with the striking result that the Peninsula presents to-day exactly the same uniform cranial type as the British Isles. Even the range (76 to 79) and the mean (78) of the cephalic index are the same, rising in Spain to 80 only in the Basque corner. As Ripley states, "the average cephalic index of 78 occurs nowhere else so uniformly distributed in Europe" except in Norway, and this uniformity "is the concomitant and index of two relatively pure, albeit widely different, ethnic types—Mediterranean in Spain, Teutonic in Norway." [2]

In other respects the social, one might almost say the national, groups are both more numerous and perhaps even more sharply discriminated in the Peninsula *Provincial* than in France.   Besides the Basques and *Groups.*

---

[1] S. Feist points out that two physical types were recognised in antiquity, one dark and one fair, and reference to red hair and fair skin suggests Celtic infusion. *Kultur, Ausbreitung und Herkunft der Indogermanen*, 1913, p. 365.

[2] *Science Progress*, p. 159.

Portuguese, the latter with a considerable strain of negro blood,[1] we have such very distinct populations as the haughty and punctilious Castilians, who under an outward show of pride and honour, are capable of much meanness ; the sprightly and vainglorious Andalusians, who have been called the Gascons of Spain, yet of graceful address and seductive manners ; the morose and impassive Murcians, indolent because fatalists ; the gay Valencians given to much dancing and revelry, but also to sudden fits of murderous rage, holding life so cheap that they will hire themselves out as assassins, and cut their bread with the blood-stained knife of their last victim ; the dull and superstitious Aragonese, also given to bloodshed, and so obdurate that they are said to " drive nails in with their heads " ; lastly the Catalans, noisy and quarrelsome, but brave, industrious, and enterprising, on the whole the best element in this motley aggregate of unbalanced temperaments. The various aspects of Spanish temperament are regarded by Havelock Ellis[2] as manifestations of an aboriginally primitive race, which, under the stress of a peculiarly stimulating and yet hardening environment, has retained through every stage of development an unusual degree of the endowment of fresh youth, of elemental savagery, with which it started. This explains the fine qualities of Spain and her defects, the splendid initiative, and lack of sustained ability to carry it out, the importance of the point of honour and the glorification of the primitive virtue of valour.

In Italy the past and present relations, as elucidated especially by Livi and Sergi, may be thus briefly stated. After the first Stone Age, of which there are fewer indications than might be expected,[3] the whole land was thickly settled by dark long-headed Mediterranean peoples in neolithic times. These were later joined by Pelasgians of like type from Greece, and by Illyrians of doubtful affinity from the Balkan Peninsula. Indeed C.

Ethnic Relations in Italy.

[1] " The Portuguese are much mixed with Negroes more particularly in the south and along the coast. The slave trade existed long before the Negroes of Guinea were exported to the plantations of America. Damião de Goes estimated the number of blacks imported into Lisbon alone during the 16th century at 10,000 or 12,000 per annum. If contemporary eye-witnesses can be trusted, the number of blacks met with in the streets of Lisbon equalled that of the whites. Not a house but had its negro servants, and the wealthy owned entire gangs of them " (Reclus, I. p. 471).
[2] " The Spanish People," *Cont. Rev.* May, 1907, and *The Soul of Spain*, 1908.
[3] T. E. Peet, *Stone and Bronze Ages in Italy and Sicily*, 1909, gives a full account of the archaeology.

Penka,[1] who has so many paradoxical theories, makes the Illyrians the first inhabitants of Italy, as shown by the striking resemblance of the *terramara* culture of Aemilia with that of the Venetian and Laibach pile-dwellings. The recent finds in Bosnia also,[2] besides the historically proved (?) migration of the Siculi from Upper Italy to Sicily, and their Illyrian origin, all point in the same direction. But the facts are differently interpreted by Sergi,[3] who holds that the whole land was occupied by the Mediterraneans, because we find even in Switzerland pile-dwellers of the same type.[4]

Then came the peoples of Aryan speech, Celtic-speaking Alpines from the north-west and Slavs from the north-east, who raised the cephalic index in the north, where the brachy element, as already seen, still greatly predominates but diminishes steadily southwards.[5] They occupied the whole of Umbria, which at first stretched across the peninsula from the Adriatic to the Mediterranean, but was later encroached upon by the intruding Etruscans on the west side. Then also some of these Umbrians, migrating southwards to Latium beyond the Tiber, intermingled, says Sergi, with the Italic (Ligurian) aborigines, and became the founders of the Roman state.[6] With the spread of the Roman arms the Latin language, which Sergi claims to be a kind of Aryanised Ligurian, but must be regarded as a true member of the Aryan family, was

---

[1] " Zur Paläoethnologie Mittel- u. Südeuropas " in *Mitt. Wiener Anthrop. Ges.* 1897, p. 18. It should be noted here that in his *History of the Greek Language* (1896) Kretschmer connects the inscriptions of the Veneti in north Italy and of the Messapians in the south with the Illyrian linguistic family, which he regards as Aryan intermediate between the Greek and the Italic branches, the present Albanian being a surviving member of it. In the same Illyrian family W. M. Lindsay would also include the " Old Sabellian " of Picenum," believed to be the oldest inscriptions on Italian soil. The manifest identity of the name *Aodatos* and the word *meitimon* with the Illyrian names Αὐδάτα and *Meitima* is almost sufficient of itself to prove these inscriptions to be Illyrian. Further the whole character of their language, with its Greek and its Italic features, corresponds with what we know and what we can safely infer about the Illyrian family of languages " (*Academy*, Oct. 24, 1896). Cf. R. S. Conway, *The Italic Dialects*, 1897.

[2] R. Munro, *Bosnia, Herzegovina and Dalmatia*, 1900. See also W. Ridgeway, *The Early Age of Greece*, 1901, ch. v., showing that remains of the Iron Age in Bosnia are closely connected with Hallstatt and La Tène cultures.

[3] *Arii e Italici*, p. 158 sq.

[4] " Liguri e Pelasgi furono i primi abitatori d'Italia ; e Liguri sembra siano stati quelli che occupavano la Valle del Po e costrussero le palafitte, e Liguri forse anche i costruttori delle palafitte svizzere : Mediterranei tutti " (*Ib.* p. 138).

[5] Ripley's chart shows a range of from 87 in Piedmont to 76 and 77 in Calabria, Puglia, and Sardinia, and 75 and under in Corsica. *The Races of Europe*, 1900, p. 251.

[6] But cf. W. Ridgeway, *Who were the Romans?* 1908.

K.

diffused throughout the whole of the peninsula and islands, sweeping away all traces not only of the original Ligurian and other Mediterranean tongues, but also of Etruscan and its own sister languages, such as Umbrian, Oscan, and Sabellian.

At the fall of the empire the land was overrun by Ostrogoths, Heruli, and other Teutons, none of whom formed permanent settlements except the Longobards, who gave their name to the present Lombardy, but were themselves rapidly assimilated in speech and general culture to the surrounding populations, whom we may now call Italians in the modern sense of the term.

When it is remembered that the Aegean culture had spread to Italy at an early date, that it was continued under Hellenic influences by Etruscans and Umbrians, that Greek arts and letters were planted on Italian soil (*Magna Graecia*) before the foundation of Rome, that all these civilisations converged in Rome itself and were thence diffused throughout the West, that the traditions of previous cultural epochs never died out, acquired new life with the Renascence and were thus perpetuated to the present day, it may be claimed for the gifted Italian people that they have been for a longer period than any others under the unbroken sway of general humanising influences.

These "Latin Peoples," as they are called because they all speak languages of the Latin stock, are not confined to the West. To the Italian, French, Spanish, Portuguese, with the less known and ruder Walloon of Belgium and Romansch of Switzerland, Tyrol, and Friuli, must be associated the *Rumanian* current amongst some nine millions of so-called "Daco-Rumanians" in Moldavia and Wallachia, *i.e.* the modern kingdom of Rumania. The same Neo-Latin tongue is also spoken by the *Tsintsars* or *Kutzo-Vlacks* [1] of the Mount Pindus districts in the Balkan Peninsula, and by numerous Rumanians who have in later times migrated into Hungary. They form a compact and vigorous nationality, who claim direct descent from the Roman

Arts and Ethics.

The Rumanians.

---

[1] The true name of these southern or Macedo-Rumanians, as pointed out by Gustav Weigland (*Globus*, LXXI. p. 54), is *Aramáni* or *Armáni*, *i.e.* "Romans," *Tsintsar, Kutzo-Vlack*, etc. are mere nicknames, by which they are known to their Macedonian (Bulgar and Greek) neighbours. See also W. R. Morfill in *Academy*, July 1, 1893. The Vlachs of Macedonia are described by E. Pears, *Turkey and its People*, 1911, and a full account of the Balkan Vlachs is given by A. J. B. Wace and M. S. Thompson, *The Nomads of the Balkans*, 1914.

military colonists settled north of the Lower Danube by Trajan after his conquest of the Dacians (107 A.D.). But great difficulties attach to this theory, which is rejected by many ethnologists, especially on the ground that, after Trajan's time, Dacia was repeatedly swept clean by the Huns, the Finns, the Avars, Magyars and other rude Mongolo-Turki hordes, besides many almost ruder Slavic peoples during the many centuries when the eastern populations were in a state of continual flux after the withdrawal of the Roman legionaries. from the Lower Danube. Besides, it is shown by Roesler [1] and others that under Aurelian (257 A.D.) Trajan's colonists withdrew bodily southwards to and beyond the Hemus to the territory of the old Bessi (Thracians), *i.e.* the district still occupied by the Macedo-Rumanians. But in the 13th century, during the break-up of the Byzantine empire, most of these fugitives were again driven north to their former seats beyond the Danube, where they have ever since held their ground, and constituted themselves a distinct and far from feeble branch of the Neo-Latin community. The Pindus, therefore, rather than the Carpathians, is to be taken as the last area of dispersion of these valiant and intelligent descendants of the Daco-Romans. This seems the most rational solution of what A. D. Xenopol calls " an historic enigma," although he himself rejects Roesler's conclusions in favour of the old view so dear to the national pride of the present Rumanian people. [2] The composite character of the Rumanian language—fundamentally Neo-Latin or rather early Italian, with strong Illyrian (Albanian) and Slav affinities—would almost imply that Dacia had never been Romanised under the empire, and that in fact this region was *for the first time* occupied by its present Romance-speaking inhabitants in the 13th century. [3] The nomadic life of the Rumanians is in itself, as Peisker points out, [4] a refutation of their descent from settled Roman colonists, and indicates a Central Asiatic origin. The mounted nomads grazed during the summer " on most of the mountains of the

---

[1] *Romänische Studien*, Leipzig, 1871.

[2] *Les Roumains au Moyen Age, passim*. Hunfalvy, quoted by A. J. Patterson (*Academy*, Sept. 7, 1895), also shows that "for a thousand years there is no authentic mention of a Latin or Romance-speaking population north of the Danube."

[3] This view is held by L. Réthy, also quoted by Patterson, and the term *Vlack* (*Welsch*, whence Wallachia) applied to the Rumanians by all their Slav and Greek neighbours points in the same direction.

[4] T. Peisker, " The Asiatic Background," *Camb. Med. Hist.* Vol. I, 1911, p. 356, and " The Expansion of the Slavs," *ib.* Vol. II. 1913, p. 440.

Balkan peninsula, and took up their winter quarters on the
sea-coasts among a peasant population speaking a different
language. Thence they gradually spread, unnoticed by the
chroniclers, along all the mountain ranges, over all the
Carpathians of Transylvania, North Hungary, and South
Galicia, to Moravia ; towards the north-west from Montenegro
onwards over Herzegovina, Bosnia, Istria, as far as South
Styria ; towards the south over Albania far into Greece. . . .
And like the peasantry among which they wintered (and
winter) long enough, they became (and become) after a transi-
tory bilingualism, Greeks, Albanians, Servians, Bulgarians,
Ruthenians, Poles, Slovaks, Chekhs, Slovenes, Croatians . . .
a mobile nomad stratum among a strange-tongued and more
numerous peasant element, and not till later did they gradually
take to agriculture and themselves become settled."

The Pelasgians and Minoan civilisation have been briefly discussed above (Ch. XIII.). Later problems in Greek ethnology
are still under dispute. Sergi, who regards the
proto-Aryans as round-headed barbarians of
Celtic, Slav, and Teutonic speech, makes no exception in favour of the Hellenes. These also enter Greece not
as civilisers, but rather as destroyers of the flourishing Mykenaean culture developed here, as in Italy, by the Mediterranean
aborigines. But in course of time the intruders become absorbed
in the Pelasgic or eastern branch of the Mediterraneans, and
what we call Hellenism is really Pelasgianism revived, and to
some extent modified by the Aryan (Hellenic) element.

If it may be allowed that at their advent the Hellenes were
less civilised than the native Aegeans on whom they imposed
their Aryan speech, whence and when came they?
By Penka,[1] for whom the Baltic lands would be
the original home not merely of the Germanic branch but of
all the Aryans, the Hellenic cradle is located in the Oder basin
between the Elbe and the Vistula. As the Doric, doubtless
the last Greek irruption into Hellas, is chronologically fixed
at 1149 B.C., the beginning of the Hellenic migrations may be
dated back to the 13th century. When the Hellenes migrated
from Central Europe to Greece, the period of the general
ethnic dispersion was already closed, and the migratory period
which next followed began with the Hellenes, and was continued by the Itali, Gauls, Germans, etc. The difficulties

[1] *Mitt. Wiener Anthrop. Ges.* 1897, p. 18.

created by this view are insurmountable. Thus we should have to suppose that from this relatively contracted Aryan cradle countless tribes swarmed over Europe since the 13th century B.C., speaking profoundly different languages (Greek, Celtic, Latin, etc.), all differentiated since that time on the shores of the Baltic. The proto-Aryans with their already specialised tongues had reached the shores of the Mediterranean long before that time and, according to Maspero,[1] were known to the Egyptians of the 5th dynasty (3990–3804 B.C.) if not earlier. Allowing that these may have rather been pre-Hellenes (Pelasgians), we still know that the Achaeans had traditionally arrived about 1250 B.C. and they were already speaking the language of Homer.

" The indications of archaeology and of legend agree marvellously well with those of the Egyptian records," says H. R. Hall,[2] " in making the Third Late Minoan period one of incessant disturbance. . . . The whole basin of the Eastern Mediterranean seems to have been a seething turmoil of migrations, expulsions, wars and piracies, started first by the Mycenaean (Achaian) conquest of Crete, and then intensified by the constant impulse of the Northern iron-users into Greece." Herodotus speaks of the great invasion of the Thesprotian tribes from beyond Pindus, which took place probably in the 13th century B.C.[3] As a result " an over-whelming Aryan and iron-using population was first brought into Greece. The earlier Achaian (?) tribes of Aryans in Thessaly, who had perhaps lived there from time immemorial, and had probably already infiltrated southwards to form the mixed Ionian population about the Isthmus, were scattered, only a small portion of the nation remaining in its original home, while of the rest, part conquered the South and another part emigrated across the sea to the Phrygian coast. Of this

---

[1] *Dawn of Civilisation*, p. 391.

[2] *The Ancient History of the Near East*, 1913, p. 69.

[3] Hall notes (p. 73) that " it is to the Thesprotian invasion, which displaced the Achaians, that, in all probability, the general introduction of iron into Greece is to be assigned. The invaders came ultimately from the Danube region, where iron was probably first used in Europe, whereas their kindred, the Achaians, had possibly already lived in Thessaly in the Stone Age, and derived the knowledge of metal from the Aegeans. The speedy victory of the new-comers over the older Aryan inhabitants of Northern Greece may be ascribed to their possession of iron weapons." Ridgeway, however, has little difficulty in proving that the Achaeans themselves were tall fair Celts from Central Europe. *The Early Age of Greece*, 1901, especially chap. iv., " Whence came the Acheans ? " The question is dealt with from a different point of view by J. L. Myres, in *The Dawn of History*, 1911. chap. ix., " The Coming of the North," tracing the invasion from the Eurasian steppes.

emigration to Asia the first event must have been the war of Troy. . . . The Boeotian and Achaian invasion of the South scattered the Minyae, Pelasgians, and Ionians.   The remnant of the Minyae emigrated to Lemnos, the Pelasgi and Ionians were concentrated in Attica and another body of Ionians in the later Achaia, while the Southern Achaeans pressed forward into the Peloponnese." [1]

It is evident from the national traditions that the proto-Greeks did not arrive *en bloc*, but rather at intervals in separate and often hostile bands bearing different names.   But all these groups—Achaeans, Danai, Argians, Dolopes, Myrmidons, Leleges and many others, some of which were also found in Asia Minor—retained a strong sense of their common origin. The sentiment, which may be called racial rather than national, received ultimate expression when to all of them was extended the collective name of Hellenes (Sellenes originally), that is, descendants of Deucalion's son Hellen, whose two sons Aeolus and Dorus, and grandson Ion, were supposed to be the progenitors of the Aeolians, Dorians, and Ionians.   But such traditions are merely reminiscences of times when the tribal groupings still prevailed, and it may be taken for granted that the three main branches of the Hellenic stock did not spring from a particular family that rose to power in comparatively recent times in the Thessalian district of Phthiotis.   Whatever truth may lie behind the Hellenic legend, it is highly probable that, at the time when Hellen is said to have flourished (about 1500 B.C.), the Aeolic-speaking communities of Thessaly, Arcadia, Boeotia, the closely-allied Dorians [2] of Phocaea, Argos, and Laconia, and the Ionians of Attica, had already been clearly specialised, had in fact formed special groups before entering Greece.   Later their dialects, after acquiring a certain polish and leaving some imperishable records of the many-sided Greek genius, were gradually merged in the literary Neo-Ionic or Attic, which thus became the κοινή διάλεκτος, or current speech of the Greek world.

The Greek Language.

Admirable alike for its manifold aptitudes and surprising vitality, the language of Aeschylus, Thucydides, and the other great Athenians outlived all the vicissitudes of the

[1] H. R. Hall, *loc. cit.* p. 68 ; cf. H. Peake, *Journ. Roy. Anth. Inst.* 1916, p. 154.
[2] C. H. Hawes, " Some Dorian Descendants," *Ann. Brit. School Ath.* No. xvi. 1909–10, proves that the Dorian or Illyrian (Alpine) type still persists in South Greece and Crete.

Byzantine empire, during which it was for a time banished from Southern Greece, and even still survives, although in a somewhat degraded form, in the Romaic or Neo-Hellenic tongue of modern Hellas. Romaic, a name which recalls a time when the Byzantines were known as " Romans " throughout the East, differs far less from the classical standard than do any of the Romance tongues from Latin. Since the restoration of Greek independence great efforts have been made to revive the old language in all its purity, and some modern writers now compose in a style differing little from that of the classic period.

Yet the Hellenic race itself has almost perished on the mainland. Traces of the old Greek type have been detected by Lenormant and others, especially amongst the women of Patras and Missolonghi. But within living memory Attica was still an Albanian land, and Fallmerayer has conclusively shown that the Peloponnesus and adjacent districts had become thoroughly Slavonised during the 6th and 7th centuries.[1] " For many centuries," writes the careful Roesler, " the Greek peninsula served as a colonial domain for the Slavs, receiving the overflow of their population from the Sarmatian lowlands."[2] Their presence is betrayed in numerous geographical terms, such as *Varsova* in Arcadia, *Glogova, Tsilikhova*, etc. Nevertheless, since the revival of the Hellenic sentiment there has been a steady flow of Greek immigration from the Archipelago and Anatolia ; and the Albanian, Slav, Italian, Turkish, Rumanian, and Norman elements have in modern Greece already become almost completely Hellenised, at least in speech. Of the old dialects Doric alone appears to have survived in the Tsaconic of the Laconian hills. The Greek language has, however, disappeared from Southern Italy, Sicily, Syria, and the greater part of Egypt and Asia Minor, where it was long dominant.

To understand the appearance of SLAVS in the Peloponnesus we must go back to the Eurasian steppe, the probable cradle of these multitudinous populations. Here they have often been confused with the ancient Sarmatae, *The Slavs.* who already before the dawn of history were in possession of the South Russian plains between the Scythians towards the

---

[1] *Geschichte der Halbinsel Morea*, Stuttgart, 1830. See also G. Finlay's *Mediaeval Greece*, and the *Anthrop. Rev.* 1868, VI. p. 154.

[2] *Romänische Studien*, 1871.

east and the proto-Germanic tribes before their migration to the Baltic lands. But even at that time, before the close of the Neolithic Age, there must have been interminglings, if not with the western Teutons, almost certainly with the eastern Scythians, which helps to explain the generally vague character of the references made by classical writers both to the Sarmatians and the Scythians, who sometimes seem to be indistinguishable from savage Mongol hordes, and at others are represented as semi-cultured peoples, such as the Aryans of the Bronze period might have been round about the district of Olbia and the other early Miletian settlements on the northern shores of the Euxine.

Owing to these early crossings André Lefèvre goes so far as to say that "there is no Slav race," [1] but only nations of divers more or less pure types, more or less crossed, speaking dialects of the same language, who later received the name of Slavs, borne by a prehistoric tribe of *Sarmatians*, and meaning "renowned," "illustrious." [2] Both their language and mythologies, continues Lefèvre, point to the vast region near Irania as the primeval home of the Slav, as of the Celtic and Germanic populations. The Sauromatae or Sarmatae of Herodotus,[3] who had given their name to the mass of Slav or Slavonised peoples, still dwelt north of the Caucasus and south of the *Budini* between the Caspian, the Don and Sea of Azov; "after crossing the Tanais (Don) we are no longer in Scythia; we begin to enter the lands of the Sauromatae, who, starting from the angle of the Palus Moeotis (Sea of Azov), occupy a space of 15 days' march, where are neither trees, fruit-trees, nor savages. Above the tract fallen to them the Budini occupy another district, which is overgrown with all kinds of trees." [4] Then Herodotus seems to identify these Sarmatians with the Scythians, whence all the subsequent doubts and confusion. Both spoke the same language, of which seven distinct dialects are men-

The Sarmatians.

---

[1] *Bul. Soc. d'Anthrop.* 1896, p. 351 sq.

[2] By a sort of grim irony the word has come to mean "slave" in the West, owing to the multitudes of Slavs captured and enslaved during the medieval border warfare. But the term is by many referred to the root *slovo*, word, speech, implying a people of intelligible utterance, and this is supported by the form *Slovene* occurring in Nestor and still borne by a southern Slav group. See T. Peisker, "The Expansion of the Slavs," *Camb. Med. Hist.* Vol. II. 1913, p. 421 *n.* 2.

[3] IV. 21.

[4] These Budini are described as a large nation with "remarkably blue eyes and red hair," on which account Zaborowski thinks they may have been ancestors of the present Finns. But they may also very well have been belated proto-Germani left behind by the body of the nation *en route* for their new Baltic homes.

tioned, yet a number of personal names preserved by the Greeks have a certain Iranic look, so that these Scythian tongues seem to have been really Aryan, forming a transition between the Asiatic and the European branches of the family.

The probable explanation is that the Scythians[1] were a horde which came down from Upper Asia, conquered an Iranian-speaking people, and in time adopted the speech of its subjects. E. H. Minns[2] suggests that the settled Scythians represent the remains of the Iranian population, and the nomads the conquering peoples. These were displaced later by the Sarmatians, and Scythia becomes merely a geographical term. Skulls dug up in Scythic graves throw no light on racial affinities, some being long, and some short, but in customs there is a close analogy with the Mongols, though, as Minns points out, " the natural conditions of steppe-ranging dictated the greater part of them."

Both Slav and Germanic tribes had probably in remote times penetrated up the Danube and the Volga, while some of the former under the name of *Wends* (Venedi),[3] appear to have reached the Carpathians and the Baltic shores down the Vistula. The movement was continued far into medieval times, when great overlappings took place, and when numerous Slav tribes, some still known as Wends, others as *Sorbs, Croats,* or *Chekhs,* ranged over Central Europe to Pomerania and beyond the Upper Elbe to Suabia. Most of these have long been Teutonised, but a few of the *Polabs*[4] survive as Wends in Prussian and Saxon Lausatz, while the Chekhs and *Slovaks* still hold their ground in Bohemia and Moravia, as the *Poles* do in Posen and the Vistula valley, and the *Rusniaks* or *Ruthenes* with the closely allied " Little Russians," in the Carpathians, Galicia, and Ukrainia.

It was from the Carpathian[5] lands that came those *Yugo-Slavs* (" Southern Slavs ") who, under the collective name of

---

[1] Cf. p. 304. [2] *Scythians and Greeks,* 1909.

[3] The meaning of Wend is uncertain. It has led to confusion with the Armorican *Veneti,* the Paphlagonian *Enetae,* and the Adriatic *Enetae-Venetae,* all non-Slav peoples. Shakhmatov regards it as a name inherited by Slavs from their conquerors, the Celtic Venedi, who occupied the Vistula region in the 3rd or 2nd centuries B.C. See T. Peisker, " The Expansion of the Slavs," *Camb. Med. Hist.* Vol. II. 1913, p. 421 n. 2.

[4] That is, the Elbe Slaves, from *po*=by, near, and *Labe*=Elbe ; cf. *Pomor* (Pomeranians), " by the Sea " ; Borussia, Porussia, Prussia, originally peopled by the *Pruczi,* a branch of the Lithuanians Germanised in the 17th century.

[5] *Carpath, Khrobat, Khorvat* are all the same word, meaning highlands, mountains, hence not strictly an ethnic term, although at present so used by the *Crovats* or *Croatians,* a considerable section of the Yugo-Slavs south of the Danube.

Sorbs (Serbs, Servians), moved southwards beyond the Danube, and overran a great part of the Balkan peninsula and nearly the whole of Greece in the 6th and 7th centuries. They were the Khorvats[1] or Khrobats[1] from the upland valleys of the Oder and Vistula, whom, after his Persian wars, Heraclius invited to settle in the wasted provinces south of the Danube, hoping, as Nadir Shah did later with the Kurds in Khorasan, to make them a northern bulwark of the empire against the incursions of the Avars and other Mongolo-Turki hordes. Thus was formed the first permanent settlement of the Yugo-Slavs in Croatia, Istria, Dalmatia, Bosnia, and the Nerenta valley in 680, under the five brothers Klukas, Lobol, Kosentses, Múkl, and Khrobat, with their sisters Tuga and Buga. These were followed by the kindred Srp (Sorb) tribes from the Elbe, who left their homes in Misnia and Lusatia, and received as their patrimony the whole region between Macedonia and Epirus, Dardania, Upper Moesia, the Dacia of Aurelian, and Illyria, *i.e.* Bosnia and Servia. The lower Danube was at the same time occupied by the *Severenses*, "Seven Nations," also Slavs, who reached to the foot of the Hemus beyond the present Varna. Nothing could stem this great Slav inundation, which soon overflowed into Macedonia (Rumelia), Thessaly, and Peloponnesus, so that for a time nearly the whole of the Balkan lands, from the Danube to the Mediterranean, became a Slav domain—parts of Illyria and Epirus (Albania) with the Greek districts about Constantinople alone excepted.

The Southern Slavs.

Hellas, as above seen, has recovered itself, and the *Albanians*,[2] direct descendants of the ancient Illyrians, still hold their ground and keep alive the last echoes of the old Illyrian language, which was almost certainly a proto-Aryan form of speech probably intermediate, as above-mentioned, between the Italic and Hellenic branches. They even retain the old tribal system, so that there are not only two main sections, the northern *Ghegs* and the southern *Toshks*, but each section is divided into a number of minor groups,[3] such as the Malliesors (Klementi, Pulati, Hoti, etc.)

The Albanians.

---

[1] See note 5, p. 537.

[2] That is, "Highlanders" (root *alb, alp*, height, hill). From *Albanites* through the Byzantine *Arvanites* comes the Turkish *Arnaut*, while the national name *Skipetar* has precisely the same meaning (root *skip, scop*, as in σκόπελος, scopulus, cliff, crag).

[3] There are about twenty of these *phis* or *phar* (phratries) amongst the Ghegs, and the practice of exogamous marriage still survives amongst the Mirdites south of the Drin, who, although Catholics, seek their wives amongst the surrounding hostile Turkish and Muhammadan Gheg populations.

and Mirdites (Dibri, Fandi, Matia, etc.) in the north, and the Toxides (whence Toshk) and the Yapides (Lapides) in the south. The southerners are mainly Orthodox Greeks, and in other respects half-Hellenised Epirotes, the northerners partly Moslem and partly Roman Catholics of the Latin rite. From this section came chiefly those Albanians who, after the death (1467) of their valiant champion, George Castriota (*Scanderbeg*, "Alexander the Great"), fled from Turkish oppression and formed numerous settlements, especially in Calabria and Sicily, and still retain their national traditions.

In their original homes, located by some between the Bug and the Dnieper, the Slavs have not only recovered from the fierce Mongolo-Turki and Finn tornadoes, by **The Russians.** which the eastern steppes were repeatedly swept for over 1500 years after the building of the Great Wall, but have in recent historic times displayed a prodigious power of expansion second only to that of the British peoples. The *Russians* (Great, Little, and White Russians), whose political empire now stretches continuously from the Baltic to the Pacific, have already absorbed nearly all the Mongol elements in East Europe, have founded compact settlements in Caucasia and West Siberia, and have thrown off numerous pioneer groups of colonists along all the highways of trade and migration, and down the great fluvial arteries between the Ob and the Amur estuary. They number collectively over 100 millions, with a domain of some nine million square miles. The majority belong to Deniker's Eastern race [1] (a variety of the Alpine type), being blond, sub-brachycephalic and short, 1.64 m. (5 ft. 4½ ins.). The Little Russians in the South on the Black Mould belt are more brachycephalic and have darker colouring and taller stature. The White Russians in the West between Poland and Lithuania are the fairest of all.

We need not be detained by the controversy carried on between Sergi and Zaborowski regarding a prehistoric spread of the Mediterranean race to Russia.[2] The skulls from several of the old Kurgans, identified by **Russian Origins.** Sergi with his Mediterranean type, have not been sufficiently determined as to date or cultural periods to decide the question, while their dolicho shape is common both to the

---

[1] J. Deniker, "Les Six Races composant la Population actuelle de l'Europe," *Journ. Anthr. Inst.* XXXIV. 1904, pp. 182, 202.
[2] *Bul. Soc. d'Anthrop.* VII. 1896.

Mediterraneans and to the proto-Aryans of the North European type.[1] To this stock the proto-Slavs are affiliated by Zaborowski and many others,[2] although the present Slavs are all distinctly round-headed. Ripley asks, almost in despair, what is to be done with the present Slav element, and decides to apply " the term *Homo Alpinus* to this broad-headed group wherever it occurs, whether on mountains or plains, in the west or in the east." [3]

We are beset by the same difficulties as we pass with the *Ossets* of the Caucasus into the Iranian and Indian domains of the proto-Aryan peoples. These Ossets, who are the only aborigines of Aryan speech in Caucasia, are by Zaborowski [4] identified with the Alans, who are already mentioned in the 1st century A.D. and were Scythians of Iranian speech, blonds, mixed with Medes, and perhaps descendants of the Massagetae. We know from history that the Goths and Alans became closely united, and it may be from the Goths that the Osset descendants of the Alans (some still call themselves Alans) learned to brew beer. Elsewhere [5] Zaborowski represents the Ossets as of European origin, till lately for the most part blonds, though now showing many Scythian traits. But they are not physically Iranians " despite the Iranian and Asiatic origin of their language," as shown by Max Kowalewsky.[6] On the whole, therefore, the Ossets may be taken as originally blond Europeans, closely blended with Scythians, and later with the other modern Caucasus peoples, who are mostly brown brachys. But Ernest Chantre [7] allies these groups to their brown and brachy Tatar neighbours, and denies that the Ossets are the last remnants of Germanic immigrants into Caucasia.

The Ossets.

We have therefore in the Caucasus a very curious and puzzling phenomenon—several somewhat distinct groups of aborigines, mainly of de Lapouge's Alpine type, but all except the Ossets speaking

The Caucasus Aborigines.

---

[1] Hence Virchow (Meeting Ger. Anthrop. Soc. 1897) declared that the extent and duration of the Slav encroachments in German territory could not be determined by the old skulls, because it is impossible to say whether a given skull is Slav or not.

[2] Especially Lubor Niederle, for whom the proto-Slavs are unquestionably long-headed blonds like the Teutons, although he admits that round skulls occur even of old date, and practically gives up the attempt to account for the transition to the modern Slav.

[3] " The Racial Geography of Europe," in *Popular Science Monthly*, June, 1897.

[4] *Bul. Soc. d'Anthrop.* 1896, p. 81 sq.   [5] *Bul. Soc. d'Anthrop.* 1894, p. 36.

[6] *Droit Coutumier Osséthien*, 1893.

[7] Quoted by Ujfalvy, *Les Aryens*, etc. p. 11.

an amazing number of non-Aryan stock languages. Philologists have been for some time hard at work in this linguistic wilderness, the "Mountain of Languages" of the early Arabo-Persian writers, without greatly reducing the number of independent groups, while many idioms traceable to a single stem still differ so profoundly from each other that they are practically so many stocks. Of the really distinct families the more important are :—the *Kartweli* of the southern slopes, comprising the historical Georgian, cultivated since the 5th century, the Mingrelian, Imeritian, Laz of Lazistan, and many others; the *Cherkess* (Circassian), the *Abkhasian* and *Kabard* of the Western and Central Caucasus; the *Chechenz* and *Lesghian*, the *Andi*, the *Ude*, the *Kubachi* and *Duodez* of Daghestan, *i.e.* the Eastern Caucasus. Where did this babel of tongues come from? We know that 2500 years ago the relations were much the same as at present, because the Greeks speak of scores of languages current in the port of Dioscurias in their time. If therefore the aborigines are the " sweepings of the plains," they must have been swept up long before the historic period. Did they bring their different languages with them, or were these specialised in their new upland homes? The consideration that an open environment makes for uniformity, secluded upland valleys for diversity, seems greatly to favour the latter assumption, which is further strengthened by the now established fact that, although there are few traces of the Palaeolithic epoch, the Caucasus was somewhat thickly inhabited in the New Stone Age.

Crossing into Irania we are at once confronted with totally different conditions. For the ethnologist this region comprises, besides the tableland between the Tigris and Indus, both slopes of the Hindu-Kush, and the **The Iranians.** Pamir, with the uplands bounded south and north by the upper courses of the Oxus and the Sir-darya. Overlooking later Mongolo-Turki encroachments, a general survey will, I think, show that from the earliest times the whole of this region has formed part of the Caucasic domain; that the bulk of the indigenous populations must have belonged to the dark, round-headed Alpine type; that these, still found in compact masses in many places, were apparently conquered, but certainly Aryanised in speech, in very remote prehistoric times by long-headed blond Aryans of the IRANIC and GALCHIC branches, who arrived in large numbers from the contiguous Eurasian steppe, mingled generally with the brachy aborigines, but also kept aloof in several districts, where they still survive with more or less modified proto-Aryan features. Thus we are at once struck by the remarkable fact that absolute uniformity of speech, always apart from late Mongol intrusions, has prevailed during the historic period throughout Irania, which has been in this respect as completely Aryanised as Europe itself ; and further, that all current Aryan tongues, with perhaps one trifling exception,[1] are members either of the Iranic or the Galchic branch of the family. Both Iranic and Galchic are thus rather linguistic than ethnic terms, and so true is this that a philologist always knows what is meant by an Iranic language, while the anthropologist is unable to define or form any clear conception of an Iranian, who may be either of long-headed Nordic or round-headed Alpine type. Here confusion may be avoided by reserving the historic name of PERSIAN [2] for the former, and comprising all the Alpines under the also time-honoured though less known name of TAJIKS.

Khanikoff has shown that these Tajiks constitute the primitive element in ancient Irán. To the true Persians of

The Tajiks. the west, as well as to the kindred Afghans in the east, both of dolicho type, the term is rarely applied. But almost everywhere the sedentary and agricultural aborigines are called Tajiks, and are spoken of as *Parsiván*, that is, *Parsizabán*,[3] " of Persian speech," or else *Dihkán*,[3] that is, " Peasants," all being mainly husbandmen " of Persian race and tongue." [4] They form endless tribal, or at least social, groups, who keep somewhat aloof from their proto-Aryan conquerors, so that, in the east especially, the

---

[1] The *Yagnobi* of the river of like name, an affluent of the Zerafshan ; yet even this shows lexical affinities with Iranic, while its structure seems to connect it with Leitner's Kajuna and Biddulph's Burish, a non-Aryan tongue current in Ghilghit, Yasin, Hunza and Nagar, whose inhabitants are regarded by Biddulph as descendants of the Yué-chi. The Yagnobi themselves, however, are distinctly Alpines, somewhat short, very hirsute and brown, with broad face, large head, and a Savoyard expression. They have the curious custom of never cutting but always breaking their bread, the use of the knife being sure to raise the price of flour.

[2] F. v. Luschan points out that very little is known of the anthropology of Persia. " In a land inhabited by about ten millions not more than twenty or thirty men have been regularly measured and not one skull has been studied." The old type preserved in the *Parsi* is short-headed and dark. " The Early Inhabitants of Western Asia," *Journ. Roy. Anthr. Inst.* XLI. 1911, p. 233.

[3] *Dih, deh*, village. *Zabán*, tongue, language.

[4] H. Walter, *From Indus to Tigris*, p. 16. Of course this traveller refers only to the Tajiks of the plateau (Persia, Afghanistan). Of the Galchic Tajiks he knew nothing ; nor indeed is the distinction even yet quite understood by European ethnologists.

ethnic fusion is far from complete, the various sections of the
community being still rather juxtaposed than fused in a single
nationality. When to these primeval differences is added the
tribal system still surviving in full vigour amongst
the intruding Afghans themselves, we see how   Afghans.
impossible it is yet to speak of an Afghan nation, but only of
heterogeneous masses loosely held together by the paramount
tribe—at present the *Durani* of Kabul.

The Tajiks are first mentioned by Herodotus, whose
Dadikes [1] are identified by Hammer and Khanikoff with them.[2]
They are now commonly divided into Lowland, and Highland
or Hill Tajiks, of whom the former were always Parsiván,
whereas the Hill Tajiks did not originally speak Persian at
all, but, as many still do, an independent sister language called
Galchic, current in the Pamir, Zerafshan and Sir-darya uplands,
and holding a somewhat intermediate position between the
Iranic and Indic branches.

This term Galcha, although new to science, has long been
applied to the Aryans of the Pamir valleys, being identified
with the *Calcienses populi* of the lay Jesuit
Benedict Goez, who crossed the Pamir in 1603,   The Galcha.
and describes them as "of light hair and beard like the
Belgians." Meyendorff also calls those of Zerafshan "Eastern
Persians, Galchi, Galchas." The word has been explained to
mean "the hungry raven who has withdrawn to the mountains," probably in reference to those Lowland Tajiks who
took refuge in the uplands from the predatory Turki hordes.
But it is no doubt the Persian *galcha*, a peasant or clown, then
a vagabond, etc., whence *galchagi*, rudeness.

As shown by J. Biddulph,[3] the tribes of Galchic speech
range over both slopes of the Hindu-Kush, comprising the
natives of Sarakol, Wakhan, Shignan, Munjan (with the
Yidoks of the Upper Lud-kho or Chitral river), Sanglich, and
Ishkashim. To these he is inclined to add the Pakhpus and
the Shakshus of the Upper Yarkand-darya, as well as those of
the Kocha valley, with whom must now be included the
Zerafshan Galchas (Maghians, Kshtuts, Falghars, Machas and
Fans), but not the Yagnobis. All these form also one ethnic

---

[1] III. 91.
[2] Even Ptolemy's πάσιχαι appear to be the same people, π being an error for τ,
so that τάσικαι would be the nearest possible Greek transcription of *Tajik*.
[3] *Tribes of the Hindoo-Koosh*, 1880, *passim*.

group of Alpine type, with whom on linguistic grounds Biddulph also includes two other groups, the Khos of Chitral with the Siah Posh of Kafiristan, and the Shíns (Dards), Górs, Chilási and other small tribes of the Upper Indus and side valleys, all these apparently being long-heads of the blond Aryan type. Keeping this distinction in view, Biddulph's valuable treatise on the Hindu-Kush populations may be followed with safety. He traces the Galcha idioms generally to the old Baktrian (East Persia, so-called " Zend Avesta "), the Shín however leaning closely to Sanskrit, while Khowar, the speech of the Chitrali (Khos), is intermediate between Baktrian and Sanskrit. But differences prevail on these details, which will give occupation to philologists for some time to come.

Speaking generally, all the Galchas of the northern slopes (most of Biddulph's first group) are physically connected with all the other Lowland and Hill Tajiks, with whom

Galcha and Tajik Types. should also probably be included Elphinstone's[1] southern Tajiks dwelling south of the Hindu-Kush (Kohistani, Berraki, Purmuli or Fermuli, Sirdehi, Sistani, and others scattered over Afghanistan and northern Baluchistan). Their type is pronouncedly Alpine, so much so that they have been spoken of by French anthropologists as " those belated Savoyards of Kohistan."[2] De Ujfalvy, who has studied them carefully, describes them as tall, brown or bronzed and even white, with ruddy cheeks recalling the Englishman, black or chestnut hair, sometimes red and even light, smooth, wavy or curly, full beard, brown, ruddy or blond (he met two brothers near Penjakend with hair " blanc comme du lin ") ; brown, blue, or grey eyes, never oblique, long, shapely nose slightly curved, thin, straight lips, oval face, stout, vigorous frame, and round heads with cephalic index as high as 86.50. This description, which is confirmed by Bonvalot and other recent observers, applies to the Darwazi, Wakhi, Badakhshi, and in fact all the groups, so that we have beyond all doubt an eastern extension of the Alpine brachycephalic zone through Armenia and the Bakhtiari uplands to the Central Asiatic highlands, a conclusion confirmed by the explorations of M. A. Stein in Chinese Turkestan and the

---

[1] *An Account of the Kingdom of Caubul,* 1815.
[2] " Ces Savoyards attardés du Kohistan " (Ujfalvy, *Les Aryens,* etc.).

Pamirs (1900–8).[1] Indeed this Asiatic extension of the Alpine type inclines v. Luschan [2] to regard the European branch as one offshoot, and the high and narrow (" Hittite ") nosed type as another, or rather as a specialised group, of which the Armenians, Persians, Druses, and other sectarian groups of Syria and Asia Minor represent the purest examples. According to his summary of this complicated region " All Western Asia was originally inhabited by a homogeneous melanochroic race, with extreme hypsi-brachycephaly and with a ' Hittite ' nose. About 4000 B.C. began a Semitic invasion from the south-east, probably from Arabia, by people looking like the modern Bedawy. Two thousand years later commenced a second invasion, this time from the north-west, by xanthrochrous and long-headed tribes like the modern Kurds, half-savage, and in some way or other, perhaps, connected with the historic Harri, Amorites, Tamehu and Galatians." [3]

But the eventful drama is not yet closed. Arrested perhaps for a time by the barrier of the Hindu-Kush and Sulimán ranges, proto-Aryan conquerors burst at last, probably through the Kabul river gorges, on to the plains of India, and thereby added another world to the Caucasic domain. Here they were brought face to face with new conditions, which gave rise to fresh changes and adaptations resulting in the present ethnical relations in the peninsula. There is good reason to think that in this region the leavening Aryan element never was numerous, while even on their first arrival the Aryan invaders found the land already somewhat thickly peopled by the aborigines.[4]

Ethnic Relations in India.

The marked linguistic and ethnical differences between Eastern and Western Hindustan have given rise to the theory of two separate streams of immigration, perhaps continued

---

[1] The anthropological data are dealt with by T. A. Joyce, " Notes on the Physical Anthropology of Chinese Turkestan and the Pamirs," *Journ. Roy. Anthr. Inst.* XLII. 1912. " The original inhabitant . . . is that type of man described by Lapouge as *Homo Alpinus*," p. 468.

[2] F. v. Luschan, " The Early Inhabitants of Asia," *Journ. Roy. Anthr. Inst.* XLI. 1911, p. 243.

[3] For the evidence of the extension of this element in East Central Asia see Ch. IX.

[4] R. B. Foote, *Madras Government Museum. The Foote Collection of Indian Prehistoric and Protohistoric Antiquities. Notes on their ages and distribution,* 1916, is the most recent contribution to the prehistoric period, but the conclusions are not universally accepted.

over many centuries.[1] The earlier entered from the north-west, bringing their herds and families with them, whose descendants are the homogeneous and handsome populations of the Punjab and Rajputana. Later swarms entered by way of the difficult passes of Gilgit and Chitral, a route which made it impossible for their women to accompany them. " Here they came in contact with the Dravidians ; here by the stress of that contact caste was evolved ; here the Vedas were composed and the whole fantastic structure of orthodox ritual and usage was built up. . . . The men of the stronger race took to them-selves women of the weaker, and from these unions was evolved the mixed type which we find in Hindustan and Bihar." [2]

An attempt to analyse the complicated ethnic elements contained in the vast area of India was made by H. H. Risley,[3] who recognised seven types, his classification being based on theories of origin.

Classification of Types.

1. The Turko-Iranian type, including the *Baloch, Brahui,* and *Afghans* of Baluchistan and the North-West Frontier Provinces, all Muhammadans, with broad head, long prominent nose, abundant hair, fair complexion and tall stature.

2. Indo-Aryan type in the Punjab, Rajputana and Kashmir, with its most conspicuous members the *Rájputs, Khatri* and *Játs* in all but colour closely resembling the European type and showing little difference between upper and lower social strata. Their characteristics are tall stature, fair complexion, plentiful hair on face, long head, and narrow prominent nose.

3. Aryo-Dravidian or Hindustani type in the United Provinces, parts of Rajputana, Bihar, and Ceylon, with lower stature, variable complexion, longish head, and a nose index exactly corresponding to social station.

4. Scytho-Dravidian of Western India, including the *Maratha Brahmans, Kunbi,* and *Coorgs,* of medium stature, fair complexion, broad head with scanty hair on the face, and a fine nose.

---

[1] A. F. R. Hoernle, *A Grammar of Eastern Hindi compared with the other Gaudian Languages,* 1880, first suggested (p. xxxi. ff.) the distinction between the languages of the Midland and the Outer Band, which has been corroborated by G. A. Grierson, *Languages of India,* 1903, p. 51 ; *Imperial Gazetteer of India,* 1907–8, Vol. I. pp. 357–8.

[2] H. H. Risley, *The People of India,* 1908, p. 54. See also J. D. Anderson, *The Peoples of India,* 1913, p. 27.

[3] *Tribes and Castes of Bengal,* etc. 1892, *Indian Census Report,* 1901, and *Imperial Gazetteer,* Vol. I. ch. VI.

5. DRAVIDIAN, generally regarded as representing the indigenous element. The characteristics are fairly uniform from Ceylon to the Ganges valley throughout Madras, Hyderabad, the Central Provinces, Central India and Chota Nagpur, and the name is now used to include the mass of the population unaffected by foreign (Aryan, Scythian, Mongoloid) immigration. The *Nairs* of Malabar and the *Santal* of Chota Nagpur are typical representatives. The stature is short, complexion very dark, almost black, hair plentiful with a tendency to curl, head long and nose very broad.[1]

6. MONGOLO-DRAVIDIAN or Bengali type of Bengal and Orissa, showing fusion with Tibeto-Burman elements. The stature is medium, complexion dark, and head conspicuously broad, nose variable.

7. MONGOLOID of the Himalayas, Nepal, Assam, and Burma, represented by the *Kanet* of Lahoul and Kulu, the *Lepcha* of Darjiling, the *Limbu*, *Murmi* and *Gurung* of Nepal, the *Bodo* of Assam and the *Burmese*. The stature is short, the complexion dark with a yellowish tinge, the hair on the face scanty. The head is broad with characteristic flat face and frequently oblique eyes.

This classification while more or less generally adopted in outline is not allowed to pass unchallenged, especially with regard to the theories of origin implied. Concerning the brachycephalic element of Western India Risley's belief that it was the result of so-called " Scythian " invasions is not supported by sufficient evidence. " The foreign element is certainly Alpine, not Mongolian, and it may be due to a migration of which the history has not been written." [2] Ramaprasad Chanda [3] goes further and traces the broad-headed elements in both " Scytho-Dravidians " (Gujaratis, Marathas and Coorgs) and " Mongolo-Dravidians " (Bengalis and Oriyas) to one common source, " the *Homo alpinus* of the Pamirs and Chinese Turkestan," and attempts to reconstruct the history of the migration of the Alpine invaders from Central Asia over Gujarat, Deccan, Bihar and Bengal. His conclusions are supported by the reports of Sir Aurel Stein of the *Homo Alpinus* type discovered in the region of Lob Nor,

---

[1] The jungle tribes of this group, such as the *Paniyan, Kurumba* and *Irula* are classed as PRE-DRAVIDIAN. See chap. XII.
[2] A. C. Haddon, *Wanderings of Peoples*, 1911, p. 27.
[3] *The Indo-Aryan Races*, 1916, pp. 65–71 and 75–78.

dating from the first centuries A.D.   This type " still supplies the prevalent element in the racial constitution of the indigenous population of Chinese Turkestan, and is seen in its purest form in the Iranian-speaking tribes near the Pamirs." [1]

But any scheme of classification must be merely tentative, subject to modification as statistics of the vast area are gradually collected.   And W. Crooke,[2] while acknowledging the value of Risley's scheme [3] points out the need of caution in accepting measurements of skull and nose forms applied to the mixed races and half-breeds which form the majority of the people.   " The race migrations are all prehistoric, and the amalgamation of the races has continued for ages among a people to whom moral restraints are irksome and unfamiliar. The existing castes are quite a modern creation, dating only from the later Buddhist age."   " The present population thus represents the flotsam and jetsam collected from many streams of ethnical movement, and any attempt to sort out the existing races into a set of pigeon-holes, each representing a defined type of race, is, in the present state of our knowledge, impossible." [4]

In features, says Dalton, the Kols [5] show " much variety, and I think in a great many families there is a considerable

The Kols.   admixture of Aryan blood.   Many have high noses and oval faces, and young girls are at times

---

[1] "A Third Journey of Exploration in Central Asia 1913–16," *Geog. Journ.* 1916.
[2] *Natives of Northern India,* 1907, pp. 19, 24.   See also his article " Rājputs and Marāthas," *Journ. Roy. Anthr. Inst.* XL. 1910.
[3] " His report, compiled during the inevitable distractions incident to the enumeration of a population of some 300 millions, was a notable performance, and will remain one of the classics of Indian anthropology."   " The Stability of Caste and Tribal Groups in India," *Journ. Roy. Anthr. Inst.* XLIV. 1914, p. 270.
[4] A vast amount of material has been collected in recent years besides *Ethnographical Surveys* of the various provinces, the *Imperial Gazetteer* of 1909, and the magnificent *Census Reports* of 1901 and 1911.   Some of the more important works are as follows :—H. H. Risley, *Ethnography of India,* 1903, *The People of India,* 1908 ; E. Thurston, *Ethnographical Notes on Southern India,* 1906, *Castes and Tribes of Southern India,* 1909 ; H. A. Rose, *Glossary of the Tribes and Castes of the Punjab and N.W. Frontier Province,* 1911 ; E. A. de Brett, *Gazetteer, Chhatisgarh Feudatory States,* 1909 ; C. E. Luard, *Ethnographic Survey, Central India,* 1909 ; L. K. Anantha Krishna Iyer, *The Cochin Tribes and Castes,* 1909, *Tribes and Castes of Cochin,* 1912 ; M. Longworth Dames, *The Baloch Race,* 1904 ; W. H. R. Rivers, *The Todas,* 1906 ; P. R. T. Gurdon, *The Khasis,* 1907 ; T. C. Hodson, *The Meitheis,* 1908, *The Naga Tribes of Manipur,* 1911 ; E. Stack and C. J. Lyall, *The Mikirs,* 1908 ; A. Playfair, *The Garos,* 1909 ; S. Endle, *The Kacharis,* 1911 ; C. G. and B. Z. Seligman, *The Veddas,* 1911 ; J. Shakespear, *The Lushei Kuki Clans,* 1912 ; S. Chandra Roy, *The Mundas and their Country,* 1912, *The Oraons,* 1915 ; and R. V. Russell, *Tribes and Castes of the N.W. Central Provinces,* 1916.
[5] The term *Kol,* which occurs as an element in a great many tribal names, and was first introduced by Campbell in a collective sense (1866), is of unknown origin, but probably connected with a root meaning " Man " (W. Crooke, *Tribes and Castes,* III. p. 294).

met with who have delicate and regular features, finely-chiselled straight noses, and perfectly formed mouths and chins. The eyes, however, are seldom so large, so bright, and gazelle-like as those of pure Hindu maidens, and I have met strongly marked Mongolian features. In colour they vary greatly, the copper tints being about the most common [though the Mirzapur Kols are very dark]. Eyes dark brown, hair black, straight or wavy [as all over India]. Both men and women are noticeable for their fine, erect carriage and long, free stride."[1]

The same variations are found among the Dravidians, where, as should be expected, there are many aberrant groups showing divergences in all directions, as amongst the *Kurumba* and *Toda* of the Nilgiris, the former approximating to the Mongol, the latter to the Aryan standard. W. Sikemeier, who lived amongst them for years, notes that "many of the Kurumbas have decided Mongoloid face and stature, and appear to be the aborigines of that region."[2] The same correspondent adds that much nonsense has been written about the Todas, who have become the trump card of popular ethnographists. "Being ransacked by European visitors they invent all kinds of traditions, which they found out their questioners liked to get, and for which they were paid." Still the type is remarkable and strikingly European, "well proportioned and stalwart, with straight nose, regular features and perfect teeth," the chief characteristic being the development of the hairy system, less however than amongst the Ainu, whom they so closely resemble.[3] From the illustrations given in Thurston's valuable series one might be tempted to infer that a group of proto-Aryans had reached this extreme limit of their Asiatic domain, and although W. H. R. Rivers has cleared away the mystery and established links between the Todas and tribes of Malabar and Travancore, the problem of their origin is not yet entirely solved.[4]

The Dravidians occupy the greater part of the Deccan, where they are constituted in a few great nations—Telugus (Telingas), Tamils (numbers of whom have crossed into Ceylon and occupied the northern and central parts of that island, working in the coffee districts), Kanarese, and the Malayalim

---

[1] *Descriptive Ethnology of Bengal*, p. 190.
[2] In a letter to the author, June 18, 1895.
[3] Edgar Thurston, *Anthropology*, etc., Bul. 4, Madras, 1896, pp. 147-8. For fuller details see his *Castes and Tribes of S. India*, 1909.
[4] *The Todas*, 1906. See chap xxx. " The Origin and History of the Todas."

of the west coast. These with some others were brought at an early date under Aryan (Hindu) influences, but have preserved their highly agglutinating Dravidian speech, which has no known affinities elsewhere, unless perhaps with the language of the Brahuis, who are regarded by many as belated Dravidians left behind in East Baluchistan.

But for this very old, but highly cultivated Dravidian language, which is still spoken by about 54 millions between the Ganges and Ceylon, it would no longer be possible to distinguish these southern Hindus from those of Aryan speech who occupy all the rest of the peninsula together with the southern slopes of the Hindu-Kush and parts of the western Himalayas. Their main divisions are the Kashmiri, many of whom might be called typical Aryans ; the Punjabis with several sub-groups, amongst which are the Sikhs, religious sectaries half Moslem half Hindu, also of magnificent physique ; the Gujaratis, Mahratis, Hindis, Bengalis, Assamis, and Oraons of Orissa, all speaking Neo-Sanskritic idioms, which collectively constitute the Indic branch of the Aryan family. Hindustani or Urdu, a simplified form of Hindi current especially in the Doab, or "Two waters," the region between the Ganges and Jumna above Allahabad, has become a sort of *lingua franca*, the chief medium of intercourse throughout the peninsula, and is understood by certainly over 100 millions, while all the population of Neo-Sanskritic speech numbered in 1898 considerably over 200 millions.

Classification derives little help from the consideration of caste, whatever view be taken of the origin of this institution. The rather obvious theory that it was introduced by the handful of Aryan conquerors to prevent the submergence of the race in the great ocean of black or dark aborigines, is now rejected by many investigators, who hold that its origin is occupational, a question rather of social or industrial pursuits becoming hereditary in family groups than of race distinctions sanctioned by religion. They point out that the commentator's interpretation of the *Pancha Ksitaya*, "Five Classes," as *Bráhmans* (priests), *Kshatriyas* (fighters), *Vaisya* (traders), *Sudra* (peasants and craftsmen of all kinds), and *Nisháda* (savages or outcasts) is recent, and conveys only the current sentiment of the age. It never had any substantial base, and even in the comparatively late Institutes of Manu " the rules of food, connubium and intercourse between the various castes are very different from what we find at present "; also that, far from being eternal and changeless, caste has been subject to endless modifications throughout the whole range of Hindu myth and history. Nor is it an institution peculiar to India, while even here the stereotyped four or five divisions neither accord with existing facts, nor correspond to so many distinct ethnical groups.

All this is perfectly true, and it is also true that for generations the recognised castes, say, social pursuits, have been in a state of constant flux, incessantly undergoing processes of segmentation, so that their number is at present past counting. Nevertheless, the system may have been, and probably was, first inspired by racial motives, an instinctive sense of self-preservation, which expressed itself in an informal way by local class distinctions which were afterwards sanctioned by religion, but eventually broke down or degenerated into the present relations under the outward pressure of imperious social necessities.[1]

Beyond the mainland and Ceylon no Caucasic peoples of Aryan speech are known to have ranged in neolithic or pre-historic times. But we have already followed the migrations of a kindred,[2] though mixed race, here called INDONESIANS, into Malaysia, the Philippines, Formosa, and the Japanese Archipelago, which they must have occupied in the New Stone Age. Here there occurs a great break, for they are not again met till we reach Micronesia and the still more remote insular groups beyond Melanesia. In Micronesia the relations are ex-tremely confused, because, as it seems, this group had already been occupied by the Papuans from New Guinea before the arrival of the Indonesians, while after their arrival they were followed at intervals by Malays perhaps from the Philippines and Formosa, and still later by Japanese, if not also by Chinese from the mainland. Hence the types are here as varied as the colour, which appears, going eastwards, to shade off from the dark brown of the Pelew and Caroline Islanders to the light brown of the Marshall and Gilbert groups,

Oceanic Indonesians.

Micronesians.

---

[1] For the discussion of Caste see E. A. Gait's article in *Ency. of Religion and Ethics*, 1910, with bibliography ; also V. A. Smith, *Caste in India, East and West*, 1913.　　　　[2] See Ch. VII.

where we already touch upon the skirts of the true Indonesian domain.[1]

A line drawn athwart the Pacific from New Zealand through Fiji to Hawaii will roughly cut off this domain from the rest of the Oceanic world, where all to the west is Melanesian, Papuan or mixed, while all to the right—*Maori*, some of the eastern *Fijians, Tongans, Samoans, Tahitians, Marquesans, Hawaiians* and *Easter Islanders*—is grouped under the name POLYNESIAN, a type produced by a mixture of Proto-Malayan and Indonesian. Dolichocephaly and mesaticephaly prevail throughout the region, but there are brachycephalic centres in Tonga, the Marquesas and Hawaiian Islands. The hair is mostly black and straight, but also wavy, though never frizzly or even kinky. The colour also is of a light brown compared to cinnamon or café-au-lait, and sometimes approaching an almost white shade, while the tall stature averages 1.72 m. (5 ft, 7¾ ins.).

Polynesians.

Migrating at an unknown date eastwards from the East Indian archipelago,[2] the first permanent settlements appear to have been formed in Samoa, and more particularly in the island of *Savaii*, originally *Savaiki*, which name under divers forms and still more divers meanings accompanied all their subsequent migrations over the Pacific waters. Thus we have in Tahiti *Havaii*,[3] the "universe," and the old capital of Raiatea ; in Rarotonga *Avaiki*, "the land under the wind " ; in New Zealand *Hawaiki*, "the land whence came the Maori " ; in the Marquesas *Havaiki*, " the lower regions of the dead," as in *to fenua Havaiki*, " return to the land of thy forefathers," the words with which the victims in human sacrifices were speeded to the other world ; lastly in *Hawaii*, the name of the chief island of the Sandwich group.

Migrations.

The Polynesians are cheerful, dignified, polite, imaginative and intelligent, varying in temperament between the wild and energetic and politically capable Maori to his indolent and politically sterile kinsmen to the north, who have been unnerved by the unvarying

Polynesian Culture.

[1] See A. Krämer, *Hawaii, Ostmikronesien und Samoa*, 1906.

[2] For Polynesian wanderings see S. Percy Smith, *Hawaiki : the original home of the Maori*, 1904 ; J. M. Brown, *Maori and Polynesian ; their origin, history and culture*, 1907 ; W. Churchill, *The Polynesian Wanderings*, 1911.

[3] *H* everywhere takes the place of *S*, which is preserved only in the Samoan mother-tongue ; cf. Gr. ἑπτά with Lat. *septem*, Eng. *seven*.

uniformity of temperature. Wherever possible, they are agriculturalists, growing yams, sweet potatoes and taro. Coconuts, bread-fruits and bananas form the staple food in many islands. Scantily endowed with fertile soil and edible plants the Polynesians have gained command over the sea which everywhere surrounds them, and have developed into the best seamen among primitive races. Large sailing double canoes were formerly in use, and single canoes with an outrigger are still made. Native costume for men is made of bark cloth, and for women ample petticoats of split and plaited leaves. Ornaments, with the exception of flowers, are sparingly worn. The bow and arrow are unknown, short spears, clubs and slings are used, but no shields. The arts of writing, pottery making, loom-weaving and the use of metals were, with few exceptions, unknown, but mat-making, basketry and the making of *tapa* were carried to a high pitch, and Polynesian bark-cloth is the finest in the world.

Throughout Polynesia the community is divided into nobles or chiefs, freemen and slaves, which divisions are, by reason of *tabu*, as sharp as those of caste. They fall into those which participate in the divine, and those which are wholly excluded from it. Women have a high position, and men do their fair share of work. Polygyny is universal, being limited only by the wealth of the husband, or the numerical preponderance of the men. Priests have considerable influence, there are numerous gods, sometimes worshipped in the outward form of idols, and ancestors are deified.

Polynesian culture has been analysed by W. H. R. Rivers,[1] and the following briefly summarises his results. At first sight the culture appears very simple, especially as regards language and social structure, while there is a considerable degree of uniformity in religious belief. Everywhere we find the same kind of higher being or god and the resemblance extends even to the name, usually some form of the word *atua*. In material culture also there are striking similarities, though here the variations are more definite and obvious, and the apparent uniformity is probably due to the attention given to the customs of chiefs, overlooking the culture of the ordinary people where more diversity is discoverable.

There is much that points to the twofold nature of Polynesian culture. The evidence from the study of the ritual

[1] *The History of Melanesian Society*, 1914.

indicates the presence of two peoples, an earlier who interred their dead in a sitting posture like the dual people of Melanesia,[1] and a later, who became chiefs and believed in the need for the preservation of the dead among the living. All the evidence available, physical and cultural, points to the conjecture that the early stratum of the population of Polynesia was formed by an immigrant people who also found their way to Melanesia.

The later stream of settlers can be identified with the kava-people.[1] Kava was drunk especially by the chiefs, and the accompanying ceremonial shows its connection with the higher ranks of the people. The close association of the *Areoi* (secret society) of eastern Polynesia with the chiefs is further proof. Thus both in Melanesia and in Polynesia the chiefs who preserved their dead are identified with the founders of secret societies—organisations which came into being through the desire of an immigrant people to practise their religious rites in secret. Burial in the extended position occurs in Tikopia, Tonga and Samoa—perhaps it may have been the custom of some special group of the kava-people. Chiefs were placed in vaults constructed of large stones—a feature unknown elsewhere in Oceania. It is safe also to ascribe the human design which has undergone conventionalisation in Polynesia to the kava-people. The geometric art through which the conventionalisation was produced belonged to the earlier inhabitants who interred their dead in the sitting position.

Money, if it exists at all, occupies a very unimportant place in the culture of the people. There is no evidence of the use of any object in Polynesia with the definite scale of values which is possessed by several kinds of money in Melanesia. The Polynesians are largely communistic, probably more so than the Melanesians, and afford one of the best examples of communism in property with which we are acquainted. This feature may be ascribed to the earlier settlers. The suggestion that the kava-people never formed independent communities in Polynesia, but were accepted at once as chiefs of those among whom they settled would account for the absence of money (for which there was no need), and the failure to disturb in any great measure the communism of the earlier inhabitants. Communism in property was associated with sexual communism. There is evidence that Polynesian chiefs rarely had more than one wife, while

Polynesian Communism.

[1] Cf. p. 139 ff.

the licentiousness which probably stood in a definite relation to the communism of the people is said to have been more pronounced among the lower strata of the community. Both communism and licentiousness appear to have been much less marked in the Samoan and Tongan islands, and here there is no evidence of interment in the sitting position. These and other facts support the view that the influence of the kava-people was greater here than in the more eastern islands : probably it was greatest in Tikopia, which in many respects differs from other parts of Polynesia.

Magic is altogether absent from the culture of Tikopia and it probably took a relatively unimportant place throughout Polynesia. In Tikopia the ghosts of dead ancestors and relatives as well as animals are *atua* and this connotation of the word appears to be general in other parts of Polynesia. These may be regarded as the representatives of the ghosts and spirits of Melanesia. The *vui* of Melanesia may be represented by the *tii* of Tahiti, beings not greatly respected, who had to some extent a local character. This comparison suggests that the ancestral ghosts belong to the culture of the kava-people, and that the local spirits are derived from the culture of the people who interred their dead in the sitting position, from which people the dual people of Melanesia derived their beliefs and practices.

Magic and Religion.

To sum up. Polynesian culture is made up of at least two elements, an earlier, associated with the practice of interring the dead in a sitting position, communism, geometric art, local spirits and magical rites, and a later, which practised preservation of the dead. These latter may be identified with the kava-people while the earlier Polynesian stratum is that which entered into the composition of the dual-people of Melanesia at a still earlier date, and introduced the Austronesian language into Oceania.[1]

[1] Among recent works on Polynesia see H. Mager, *Le Monde polynésien*, 1902 ; B. H. Thomson, *Savage Island*, 1902 ; A. Krämer, *Die Samoa-Inseln*, 1902 ; J. M. Brown, *Maori and Polynesian*, 1907 ; G. Brown, *Melanesians and Polynesians*, 1910 ; F. W. Christian, *Eastern Pacific Islands*, 1910.

APPENDIX A. (p. 5)

SINCE the first few pages of this book were in print an important memoir on the " Phylogeny of Recent and Extinct Anthropoids with Special Reference to the Origin of Man " has been published by W. K. Gregory (*Bull. Am. Mus. Nat. Hist.* Vol. xxxv., Article XIX, pp. 258 ff., New York, 1916). As Gregory's lucid statement of the problems involved is based on a prolonged examination of very varied and abundant material we have considered it advisable to present his summary. The chief conclusions, which appear to be of a conservative character, are as follows (p. 341).

The Origin of Man.

1. Comparative anatomical (including embryological) evidence alone has shown that man and the anthropoids have been derived from a primitive anthropoid stock and that man's existing relatives are the chimpanzee and the gorilla.

2. The chimpanzee and gorilla have retained, with only minor changes, the ancestral habits and habitus in brain, dentition, skull and limbs, while the forerunners of the Hominidæ, through a profound change in function, lost the primitive anthropoid habitus, gave up arboreal frugivorous adaptations and early became terrestrial, bipedal and predatory, using crude flints to cut up and smash the varied food.

3. The ancestral chimpanzee-gorilla-man stock appears to be represented by the Upper Miocene genera *Sivapithecus* and *Dryopithecus*, the former more closely allied to, or directly ancestral to, the Hominidæ, the latter to the chimpanzee and gorilla.

4. Many of the differences that separate man from anthropoids of the *Sivapithecus* type are retrogressive changes, following the profound change in food habits above noted. Here belong the retraction of the face and dental arch, the reduction in size of the canines, the reduction of the jaw muscles, the loss of the prehensile character of the hallux. Many other differences are secondary adjustments in relative proportions, connected with the change from semi-arboreal, semi-erect and semi-quadrupedal progression to fully terrestrial bipedal progression. The earliest anthropoids being of small size doubtless had slender limbs ; later semi-terrestrial semi-erect forms were probably not unlike a very young gorilla, with fairly short legs and not excessively elongate arms. The long legs and short arms of man are due, I believe, to a secondary readjustment of proportions. The very short legs and very long arms of old male gorillas may well be a specialisation.

556

5. At present I know no good evidence for believing that the separation of the Hominidæ from the Simiidæ took place any earlier than the Miocene, and probably the Upper Miocene. The change in structure during this vast interval (two or more million years) is much greater in the Hominidæ than in the conservative anthropoids, but it is not unlikely that during a profound change of life habits evolution sometimes proceeds more rapidly than in the more familiar cases where uninterrupted adaptations proceed in a single direction.

6. *Homo heidelbergensis* appears to be directly ancestral to all the later Hominidæ.

On the evolution of human food habits.

While all the great apes are prevailingly frugivorous, and even their forerunners in the Lower Oligocene have the teeth well adapted for piercing the tough rinds of fruits and for chewing vegetable food, yet they also appear to have at least a latent capacity for a mixed diet. The digestive tract, especially of the chimpanzee and gorilla, is essentially similar to that of man and at least some captive chimpanzees thrive upon a mixed diet including large quantities of fruits, vegetables and bread and small quantities of meat.[1] Mr R. L. Garner, who has spent many years in studying the African anthropoids in their wild state, states[2] that " their foods are mainly vegetable, but that flesh is an essential part of their diet." Other observers state[3] that the gorilla and chimpanzee greedily devour young birds as well as eggs, vermin and small rodents.

Even the existing anthropoids, although highly conservative both in brain development and general habits, show the beginning of the use of the hands, and trained anthropoids can perform quite elaborate acts. At a time when tough-rined tubers and fruits were still the main element of the diet the nascent Hominidæ may have sought out the lairs and nesting places of many animals for the purpose of stealing the young and thus they may have learned to fight with and kill the enraged parents. They had also learned to fight in protecting their own nesting places and young. And possibly they killed both by biting, as in carnivores, and by strangling, or, in the case of a small animal, by dashing it violently down.

We may conceive that the Upper Tertiary ape-men, in the course of their dispersal from a south central Asiatic centre,[4] entered regions where flint-bearing formations were abundant. In some way they learned perhaps that these " Eolith " flints could be used to smash open the head of a small strangled animal, to crack open tough vegetables, or to smash substances into an edible condition. Much later, after the mental association of hand and flint had been well established,

[1] A. Keith, " On the Chimpanzees and their Relationship to the Gorilla," *Proc. Zool. Soc. London*, 1899, I. p. 296.
[2] *Science*, Vol. XLII. Dec. 10, 1915, p. 843.
[3] A. H. Keane, *Ethnology*, 1901, p. 111.
[4] W. D. Matthew, " Climate and Evolution," *Ann. New York Acad. Sci.* XXIV. 1915, pp. 210, 214.

they may have struck at intruders with the flints with which they were preparing their food and in this way they may have learned to use the heavier flints as hand axes and daggers.   At a very early date they learned to throw down heavy stones upon an object to smash it, and this led finally to the hurling of flints at men and small game.   Very early also they had learned to swing a heavy piece of wood or a heavy bone as a weapon.   For all such purposes shorter and stockier arms are more advantageous than the long slender arms of a semi-quad-rupedal ancestral stage and I have argued above (p. 333) that a secondary shortening and thickening of the arms ensued.

One of the first medium-sized animals that the nascent Hominidæ would be successful in killing was the wild boar, which in the Pleistocene had a wide Palæarctic distribution.

From the very first the ape-men were more or less social in habits and learned to hunt in packs.   Whether the art of hunting began in south central Asia or in Europe, perhaps one of the first large animals that men learned to kill after they had invaded the open country was the horse, because, when a pack of men had surrounded a horse, a single good stroke with a coup-de-poing upon the brain-case might be sufficient to kill it.

I have argued above (p. 321) that the retraction of the dental arch and the reduction of the canines is not consistent with the use of meat as food, because men learned to use rough flints, in place of their teeth, to tear the flesh and to puncture the bones, and because the erect incisors, short canines and bicuspids were highly effective in securing a powerful hold upon the tough hide and connective tissue.   It must be remembered that with a given muscular power small teeth are more easily forced into meat than large teeth.

After every feast there would be a residuum of hide and bones which would gradually assume economic value.   The hides of animals were at first rudely stripped off simply to get at the meat.   Small sharp-edged natural flints could be used for this purpose as well as to cut the sinews and flesh.   After a time it was found that the furry sides of these hides were useful to cover the body at night or during a storm. Thus the initial stage in the making of clothes may have been a by-product of the hunting habit.

Dr Matthew (*loc. cit.* pp. 211, 212) has well suggested that man may have learned to cover the body with skins of animals in a cool temperate climate (such as that on the northern slopes of the Hima-layas) and that afterward they were able to invade colder regions.   The use of rough skins to cover the body must have caused exposure to new sources of annoyance and infection, but we cannot affirm that natural selection was the cause of the reduction of hair on the body and of the many correlated modifications of glandular activity.   We can only affirm that a naked race of mammals must surely have had hairy ancestors and that the loss of hair on the body was probably subsequent to the adoption of predatory habits.

The food habits of the early Hominidæ, and thus indirectly the jaws and teeth, were later modified through the use of fire for softening the food. Men had early learned to huddle round the dying embers of forest fires that had been started by lightning, to feed the fire-monster with branches, and to carry about firebrands. They learned eventually that frozen meat could be softened by exposing it to the fire. Thus the broiling and roasting of meat and vegetables might be learned even before the ways of kindling fire through percussion and friction had been discovered. But the full art of cooking and the subsequent stages in the reduction of the jaws and teeth in the higher races probably had to await the development of vessels for holding hot water, perhaps in neolithic times.

This account of the evolution of the food habits of the Hominidæ will probably be condemned by experimentalists, who have adduced strong evidence for the doctrine that " acquired characters " cannot be inherited. But, whatever the explanation may be, it is a fact that progressive changes in food-habits and correlated changes in structure have occurred in thousands of phyla, the history of which is more or less fully known. Nobody with a practical knowledge of the mechanical interactions of the upper and lower teeth of mammals, or of the progressive changes in the evolution of shearing and grinding teeth, can doubt that the dentition has evolved *pari passu* with changes in food habits. Whether, as commonly supposed, the food habits changed before the dentition, or *vice versa*, the evidence appears to show that the Hominidæ passed through the following stages of evolution :

1. A chiefly frugivorous stage, with large canines and parallel rows of cheek teeth (cf. *Sivapithecus*).

2. A predatory, omnivorous stage, with reduced canines and convergent tooth rows (cf. *Homo heidelbergensis*).

3. A stage in which the food is softened by cooking and the dentition is more or less reduced in size and retrograde in character, as in modernized types of *H. sapiens*.

The following is an abbreviation of Gregory's arrangement of the Primates (pp. 266, 267).

Order Primates
    Suborder Lemuroidea
    Suborder Anthropoidea
        Series Platyrrhinæ [New World monkeys]
            Fam. Cebidæ
            Fam. Hapalidæ [Marmosets]
        Series Catarrhinæ [Old World monkeys]
            Fam. Parapithecidæ [extinct]
            Fam. Cercopithecidæ
            Fam. Simiidæ
                Sub-fam. Hylobatinæ [Gibbons]
                Sub-fam. Simiinæ [Simians or Anthropoid apes]

By the courtesy of the author we are permitted to reproduce his provisional diagram of the phylogeny of the Hominidæ and Simiidæ (p. 337).

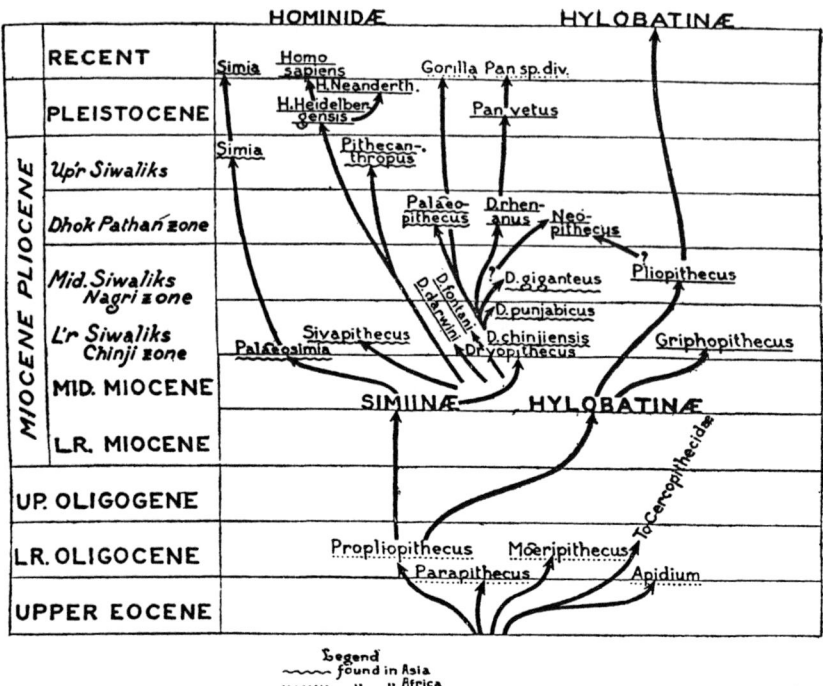

The following explanation is offered for the convenience
of those who may not be familiar with the technical terms
here employed.

Simia, the genus containing the orang-utan.

Pan, a name occasionally employed for the genus containing the chimpanzee. Most authorities place the chimpanzee and the gorilla in
the genus Anthropopithecus.

Hylobatinæ, the sub-family containing the gibbons.

Palæopithecus, Dryopithecus, Palæosimia, and *Sivapithecus* are extinct
simians.

Pan vetus is the name suggested by Miller [1] for the supposed chimpanzee whose jaw was found associated with the Piltdown cranium.
He says "The Piltdown remains include parts of a brain-case
showing fundamental characters not hitherto known except in
members of the genus *Homo*, and a mandible, two molars, and an
upper canine showing equally diagnostic features hitherto unknown, except in members of the genus *Pan* [*Anthropopithecus*].
On the evidence furnished by these characters the fossils must be
supposed to represent either a single individual belonging to an

[1] Gerrit S. Miller, "The Jaw of Piltdown Man," *Smithsonian Misc. Coll.* Vol. 65,
No. 12, 1915.

otherwise unknown extinct genus (*Eoanthropus*) or to two individuals belonging to two now-existing families (*Hominidæ* and *Pon-
gidæ*).'' He argues that the jaw was actually that of a chimpanzee
and that the cranium was that of a true man, whom he terms
Homo Dawsoni. Gregory accepts this hypothesis. W. P. Pycraft [1]
has submitted Miller's data and conclusions to searching criticism
and bases his deductions on far more ample material than that
at the disposal of Miller. He says, '' That the Piltdown jaw does
present many points of striking resemblance to that of the chimpanzee is beyond dispute. Dr Smith Woodward pointed out these
resemblances long ago, in his original description of the jaw. But
Mr Miller contends that because of these resemblances therefore
it *is* the jaw of a chimpanzee '' (*loc. cit.* p. 408). Pycraft points out
that there is more variability in the jaws of chimpanzees than
Miller was aware of, and that most of the features of the Piltdown
jaw are well within the limits of human variation ; in discussing
the conformation of the inner surface of the body of the jaw he
says, '' Between the two extremes seen in the jaws of chimpanzees
every gradation will be found, but in no case would there be any
possibility of confusing the Piltdown fragment, or any similar
fragment of a modern human jaw, with similar fragments of chimpanzee jaws '' (p. 407).

[1] '' The Jaw of the Piltdown Man, a Reply to Mr Gerrit S. Miller,'' *Science Progress*, No. 43, 1917, p. 389.

INDEX

Thanks are due to Hilary and Patrick Quiggin for help in the preparation,
and to Miss L. Whitehouse for help in the revision, of the index.

PLATE 1

1. Hausa, Western Sudanese
Negro

2. Zulu, Bantu Negroid

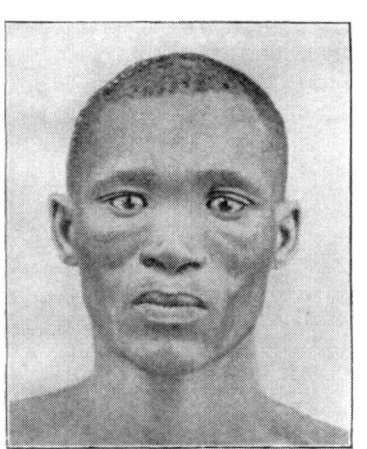

3. Koranna Hottentot

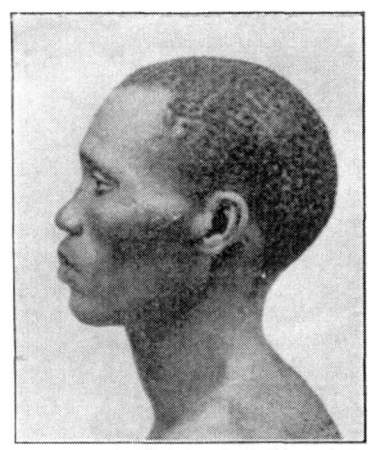

4. Koranna Hottentot

5. Bushman

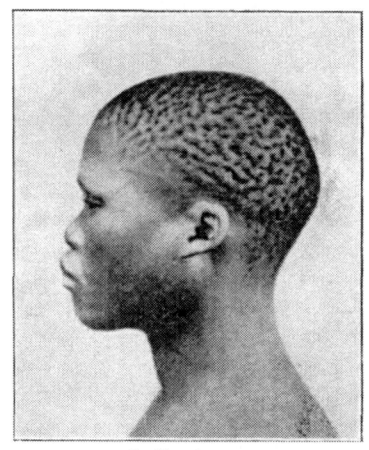

6. Bushman

PLATE II

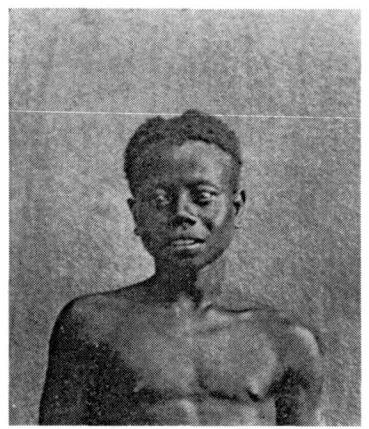

1. Andamanese, Negrito

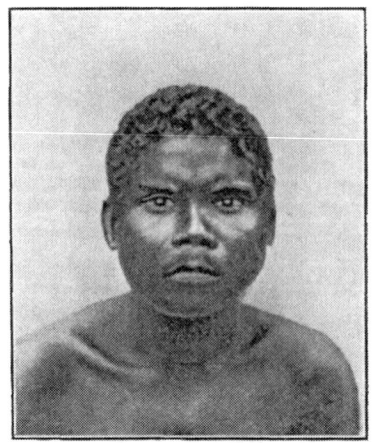

2. Semang, Negrito

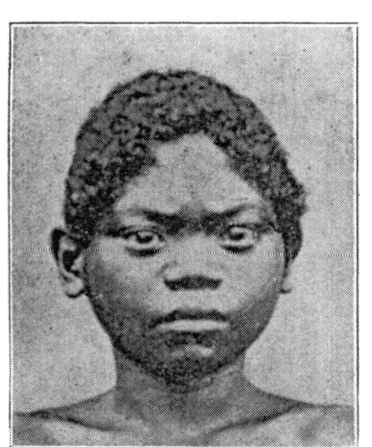

3. Aeta, Negrito

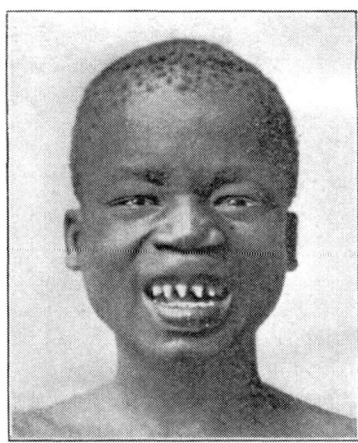

4. Central African, Negrillo

5–7. Tapiro, Negrito

PLATE III

1. Tasmanian

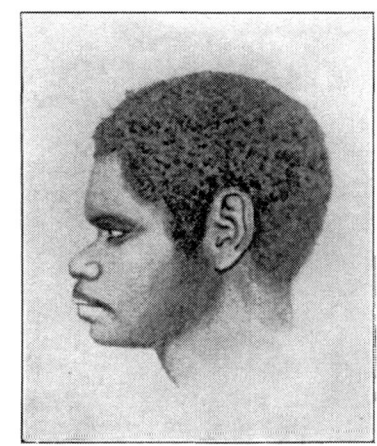

2. Tasmanian

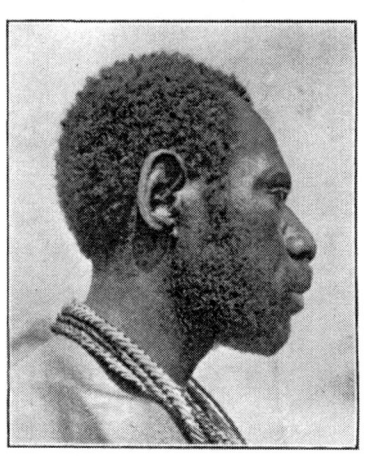

3. Kiwai, Papuan

4. Kiwai, Papuan

5. Hula, Papuo-Melanesian

6. Hula, Papuo-Melanesian

PLATE IV

1. Chinese

2. Chinese

3. Kara-Kirghiz, Mongolo-Turki

4. Kara-Kirghiz, Mongolo-Turki

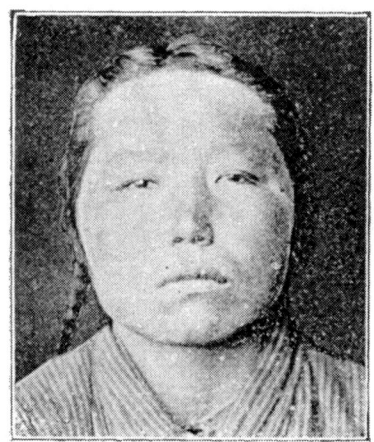

5. Kara-Kirghiz

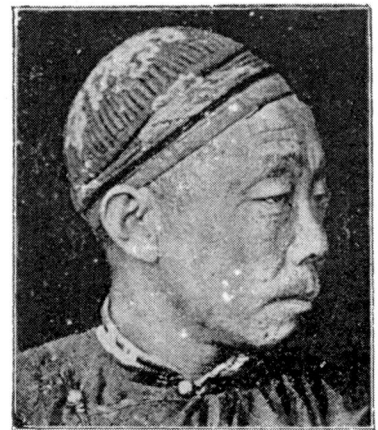

6. Manchu-Tungus

PLATE V

1. Iban, mixed Proto-Malay

2. Buginese, Malayan

3. Bontoc Igorot, Malayan

4. Bagobo, Malayan

5, 6. Kenyah, mixed Proto-Malay

PLATE VI

1. Samoyed

2. Tungus

3. Yenesei Ostiak, Palaeo-Siberian

4. Kalmuk, Western Mongol

5. Gold of Amur River, Tungus

6. Gilyak, N.E. Mongol

PLATE VII

1. Ainu, Palaeo-Siberian

2. Ainu, Palaeo-Siberian

3, 4. Japanese, mixed Manchu-Korean and Southern Mongol

5. Korean

6. Lapp

PLATE VIII

1. Eskimo

2. Indian, North-west coast of
North America

3. Cocopa, Yuman

4. Navaho, Athapascan

5. Dakota, Siouan

6. Dakota, Siouan

PLATE IX

1. Carib

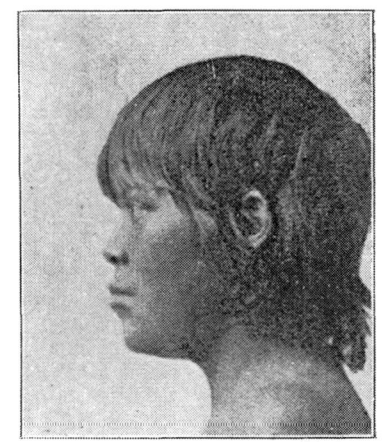

2. Guatuso, Costa Rica

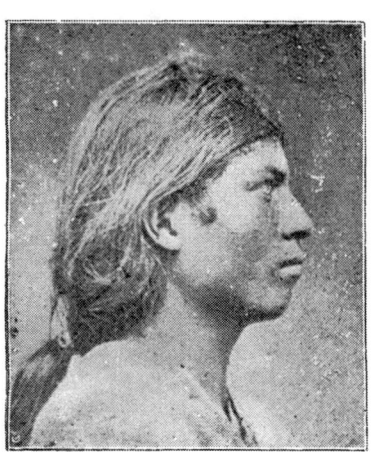

3. Native of Otovalo, Ecuador

4. Native of Zámbisa, Ecuador

5. Tehuel-che, Patagonia

6. Tehuel-che, Patagonia

PLATE X

1. Vedda, Pre-Dravidian

2. Sakai, Pre-Dravidian

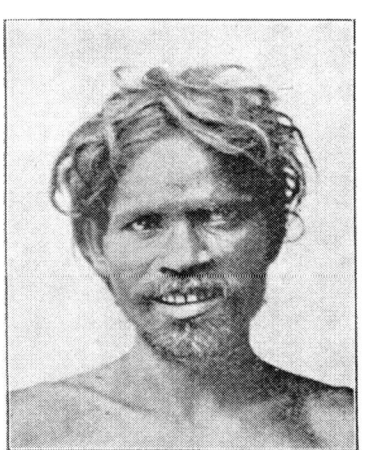

3. Irula, Pre-Dravidian

4. Paniyan, Pre-Dravidian

5. Kaitish, Australian

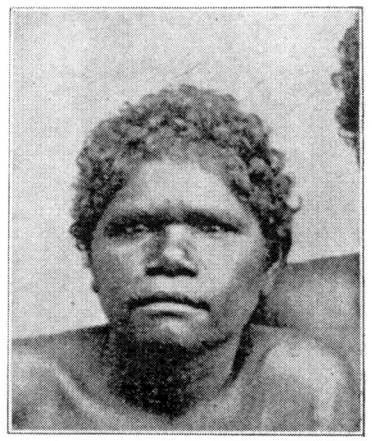

6. Australian

PLATE XI

1. Dane, Nordic

2. Dane, Nordic

3. Dane, mixed Alpine

4. Breton, mixed Alpine

5. Swiss, Nordic

6. Swiss, Alpine

PLATE XII

1. Catalan, Iberian

2. Irishman, Mediterranean

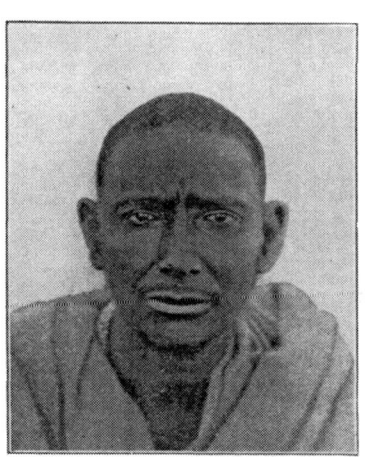

3. Kababish, mixed Semite

4. Kababish, mixed Semite

5. Egyptian Bedouin, mixed
Semite

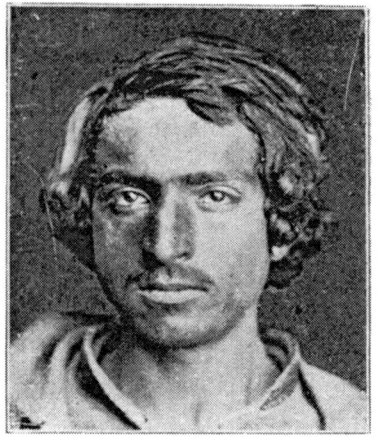

6. Afghán, Iranian

PLATE XIII

1. Bisharin, Hamite

2. Bisharin, Hamite

3. Ben Amer, Hamite

4. Masai, mixed Nilotic Hamite

5. Shilluk, Hamitic Nilote

6. Shilluk, Nilote

PLATE XIV

1. Kurd, Nordic

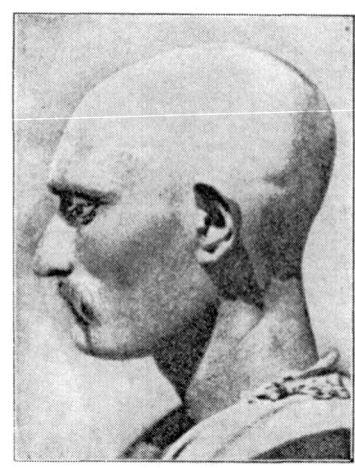

2. Kurd, Nordic

3. Armenian, Armenoid Alpine

4. Armenian, Armenoid Alpine

5. Tajik, Alpine

6. Tajik, mixed Alpine and Turki

PLATE XV

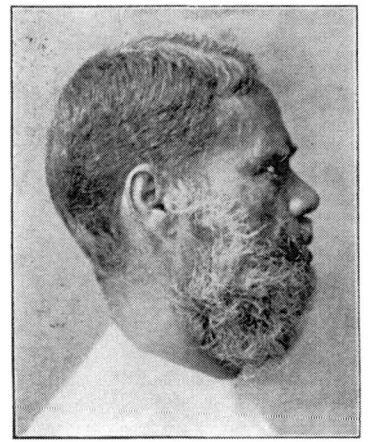

1. Sinhalese, mixed Aryan

2. Sinhalese, mixed Aryan

3. Hindu, mixed Aryan

4. Kling, Dravidian

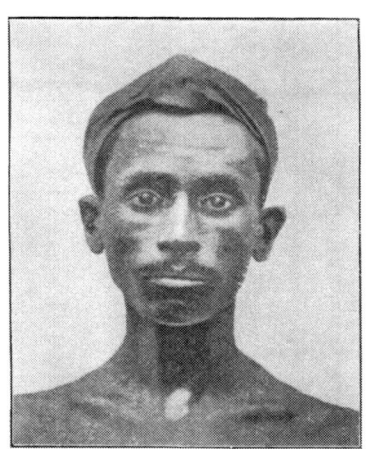

5. Linga, Dravidian

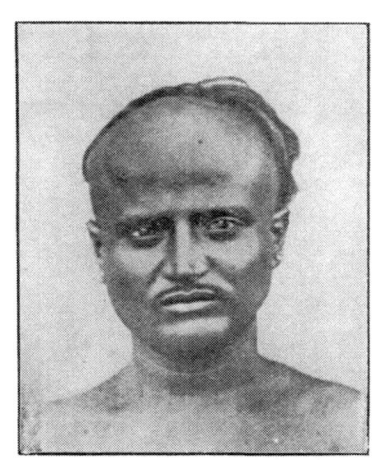

6. Vakkaliga, mixed Alpine

PLATE XVI

1, 2. Raiatea, Polynesian

3. Maori, Polynesian

4. Maori, Polynesian

5, 6. Caroline Islands, Micronesian